NEW DEVELOPMENTS IN BEHAVIORAL RESEARCH

Theory, Method, and Application

In Honor of
SIDNEY W. BIJOU

edited by
BARBARA C. ETZEL
JUDITH M. LeBLANC
DONALD M. BAER

University of Kansas

  LAWRENCE ERLBAUM ASSOCIATES, PUBLISHERS
1977   Hillsdale, New Jersey

DISTRIBUTED BY THE HALSTED PRESS DIVISION OF

JOHN WILEY & SONS

New York   Toronto   London   Sydney

Lawrence Erlbaum Associates, Inc., Publishers
62 Maria Drive
Hillsdale, New Jersey 07642

Distributed solely by Halsted Press Division
John Wiley & Sons, Inc., New York

Library of Congress Cataloging in Publication Data

Main entry under title:

New developments in behavioral research.

    Includes index.
    1. Behaviorism—Addresses, essays, lectures.
2. Psychological research—Addresses, essays, lectures.
3. Bijou, Sidney William, 1908–
I. Bijou, Sidney William, 1908– II. Etzel,
Barbara C. III. LeBlanc, Judith M. IV. Baer,
Donald Merle, 1931–
BF199.N4   150'.19'43   77-4225
ISBN 0-470-99134-8

Printed in the United States of America

Contents

PART IV: BIJOU AS SUBJECT

Introductory Note

On Sunday, September 1, 1974, in New Orleans, a hundred people met for luncheon in the North Ballroom of the Royal Sonesta Hotel, to honor Sidney W. Bijou and to announce the impending publication of this, his *Festschrift*. The group included close colleagues, former students, and many others whom Professor Bijou has known across the years of his very productive career.

This occasion followed Professor Bijou's invited address to the 82nd Annual Meeting of the American Psychological Association. That address, "Development in the Preschool Years: A Functional Analysis," was responded to by a standing ovation from the many hundreds who attended. Professor Lewis P. Lipsitt, who introduced it, then used the tactic of inviting Sid and Janet Bijou to join him and Edna Lipsitt in a "small luncheon." Four blocks later, another standing ovation greeted the very surprised scientist.

Those who spoke for the celebrants assembled that day, and for those sending warm wishes from afar, were Hayne Reese, Donald Pumroy, and Montrose Wolf, who represent different times and orientations in Sid's life. It was on this occasion that most of the original works found in this volume were presented to Professor Bijou by the editors. The preface of this book was read to him then.

A list of those who participated in and/or contributed to this honor (in many different ways) follows this note. But first: The editors are honored by the opportunity to collate this collection of scholarship. We wish to acknowledge the very special editorial advice given by our colleagues, Dean Frances Horowitz, Professors Eli Michaelis, and Marie Z. Cross. Social reinforcers, which are heartfelt, go to: Karen Budd, Jenny Covill, Lois Dixon, Mike Dixon, Elizabeth Goetz, Jacqueline Holman, Phyllis Hunter, Rod Knowles, Helen Lambert, Bonnie Miller, Sandi Plummer, Kathy Schilmoeller, Gary Schilmoeller, Beth Stella, and Russ Tyler for their help in the construction and finishing of this product and at the luncheon in New Orleans. It is not often that the publisher is mentioned in the introductory note of the published volume, but this is a special case. A very good person, Lawrence Erlbaum, agreed to publish this book honoring his good friend, without having seen even one manuscript. That is, at once, a tribute to Larry as a friend, to Sid as a scientist unfailingly associated with important work, and thus, to Larry's acumen as a publisher.

And to you, the reader, we hope this book will show you something of a great person and a science in which he so believes.

B. C. E.
J. M. LeB.
D. M. B.

Celebrants

Eileen Allen
Teodoro Ayllon
Tadasji Azuma
Donald M. Baer
Albert Bandura
Wesley Becker
Janet Bijou
Jay S. Birnbrauer
Yvonne Brackbill
William A. Bricker
Bettye Caldwell
A. Charles Catania
Lawrence Erlbaum
Barbara C. Etzel
Charles Ferster
Jacob Gewirtz
R. Vance Hall
Betty Hart
Robert P. Hawkins
Lloyd Homme
J. McVicker Hunt
Wendell Jeffrey
Fred Keller
Samuel Kirk
Leonard Krasner
Judith M. LeBlanc
Lewis P. Lipsitt
O. Ivar Lovaas
Boyd McCandless
K. Daniel O'Leary
Sue O'Leary
Robert Orlando

Joseph Parsons
G. R. Patterson
Robert F. Peterson
Donald K. Pumroy
Shirley S. Pumroy
Ely Rayek-Zaga
William Redd
Ellen P. Reese
Hayne W. Reese
Harriet L. Rheingold
Emilio Ribes-Iñesta
Todd Risley
Thomas Sajwaj
James Sherman
Murray Sidman
B. F. Skinner
Howard Sloane
Arthur W. Staats
Warren Steinman
Charles Strother
Beth Sulzer-Azaroff
Herbert S. Terrace
Jack Tizard
Leonard P. Ullman
Robert G. Wahler
Ralph J. Wetzel
Grover T. Whitehurst
Montrose Wolf
Kaoru Yamaguchi
David Zeaman
Edward F. Zigler

Preface

These examples of research and scholarly argument are collected in honor of Professor Sidney W. Bijou. In the language of academics, they constitute a Festschrift: a festival of scholarly writing, performed to celebrate the career of a person who produced, and stimulated others to produce, exactly such contributions throughout a long, valuable, and productive professional history. How better to honor Dr. Bijou than to mark the peak of his career with an outpouring of more research and argument, expressly in tribute to him and his work?

These articles are collected in the 65th year of Dr. Bijou's life. They represent work by people who consider themselves much influenced by him, or by his professional work. Some were his students in the formal, academic sense; and all are presently his students in the functional sense — they continue to find his work instructive, and their own work is altered by virtue of their attention to his. Thus, it may seem that this collection has little in common among its separate articles, other than a personal history of learning and encouragement stemming from Dr. Bijou. However, we suggest a further common element: these chapters exemplify good science. They are not perfect, of course; very few examples of science ever are. But they do represent attempts to query the real world, within its frequently severe limitations on what it is possible to do, in a perfect enough manner to allow a firm answer. They need not succeed in this: a good attempt sets the stage, even through its failures, for the next good attempt, which will do better. In our opinion, these chapters all portray exactly that commitment to careful design, accurate measurement, objective evaluation, and logical argument which cumulatively leads to better and better science. Such work often grows out of a dissatisfaction with the status quo of a science; it results from people who consider that current answers are probably seriously incomplete and sometimes thoroughly wrong, and that current practice is pitifully short of both what it could be and what society needs from it. In the personification of this commitment to good science, Dr. Bijou has excelled; it is the major lesson his students, formal and functional, have taken from him.

Since 1955, Dr. Bijou has worked almost exclusively within the approach variously labeled as the functional analysis of behavior, the experimental analysis of behavior, operant conditioning, or Skinnerian psychology. From his point of view, it seems clear, the first of these labels is the correct one. It is the principle of objective, direct, observable analysis that has attracted him. True, this analysis works best when it can be experimental, and so the second label is an appropriate one, too. But there are times when experimental technique is not possible, yet an objective curiosity does not cease at such points. Operant conditioning is a discipline built upon exactly such principles, and so the third label is also appropriate. But it is unlikely that operant conditioning represents a complete analysis of all behavioral development and change, and a perpetually dissatisfied commitment to better science will not readily limit itself to a probably incomplete system (even though it may well choose it as a best starting tactic in any new problem, and will be reluctant to leave it until its full potential has been exhausted and exploited). That Skinner pioneered in this approach is undeniable (and is also a matter of great good fortune to the field and to society); but if our commitment is to science, and if we are always dissatisfied with the current state of science, then we will neither limit ourselves to a given person's approach nor to his findings, nor will we use his name as our label. But as long as a person exemplifies that same values of objective, observable science as we follow, then we will honor that person and study his work with care. So Bijou regards Skinner (and so Skinner regards Bijou).

To a considerable extent, this collection represents work and argument in the manner stereotyped as the functional analysis of behavior; but to some notable extent, it does not. That is perfectly appropriate, in that Dr. Bijou has been committed to the principles just cited, not to any stereotype which may be correlated with them. In the long run, such correlations probably represent historical accidents rather than natural necessities; a scientist with a long view will regard them perhaps fondly but also sceptically. Dr. Bijou's fondness for the operant methods and concepts currently correlated with the fundamental logic of functional analysis (at a level less than +1.00) has not prevented his ability to stimulate workers in other approaches which also value objectivity, observable phenomena, careful measurement, and sound experimental design, but whose theories encompass the possibility of events other than environmental contingencies. Some of those others, understanding exactly that point, have contributed work to this collection, and its presence symbolizes Dr. Bijou's ability and worth better than an exclusive representation only of work performed in his own image would do. That is, we suggest that the most profound essence of Sidney Bijou is good scientist, not functional analyst.

We close with a quotation from the *World-Wide French Dictionary* (p. 35). "Le bijou . . . the jewel, the gem."

B. C. E.
J. M. LeB.
D. M. B.

NEW DEVELOPMENTS
IN BEHAVIORAL RESEARCH
Theory, Method, and Application

In Honor of
SIDNEY W. BIJOU

INTRODUCTION

1

The Force of Coincidence

B. F. Skinner

Harvard University

Editors' Comments: Professor Skinner's argument constitutes an exquisitely appropriate introduction to the collection that follows. The force of coincidence, as he points out, can be considered the essential phenomenon of operant conditioning. Operant conditioners, typically utilizing single-subject designs, impress other scientists (typically utilizing group designs defended against coincidence entirely by statistical techniques) as peculiarly susceptible to being misled by coincidence precisely because of that commitment to single-subject methods. Students of child behavior, especially of child behavior observed in everyday social settings, are specially limited in their ability to defend against coincidence: in the pigeon laboratory, a potential coincidence may be replicated a dozen, or a hundred times, to demolish completely any spectator's belief that the initial pattern observed was a coincidence; by contrast, the environments of children may be manipulated experimentally only infrequently (if at all).

To the extent that the studies that follow have dealt with the possibility of coincidence in wise and convincing ways, despite the limitations inherent in their subjects and settings, the reader may justifiably be impressed, and much of that credit must be referred to the pioneer worker in the area of coincidence-buttressed single-subject child research: Dr. Sidney W. Bijou.

In the grade school that I attended as a child, a single teacher taught two grades in the same room. While one class recited, the other worked on its assignments. One day in third grade, when my teacher was talking with the other class, I raised my hand, waved it wildly to attract her attention, and said "I was *reading* the word "middle" just when you *said* it." Both classes laughed. I had been impressed by the coincidence, but I should have been impressed by the fact that I was impressed.

The current revolt against reason and science has made much of psychic phenomena, such as precognition in dreams and extrasensory perception, and various transcendental states of consciousness. In his book, *The Roots of Coincidence*, Arthur Koestler (1972) has discussed another kind of evidence said to be neglected by the scientific establishment: things happen which cannot be explained "by the laws of chance." After the book was published many people wrote to him to report additional strange coincidences, and a second volume is, I believe, to appear containing further data. The evidence cuts both ways. It shows that there are many coincidences that are hard to explain, but it also shows that coincidences attract an unusual amount of attention and are long remembered.

Coincidence is the heart of operant conditioning. A response is strengthened by certain kinds of consequences, but not necessarily because they are actually produced by it. Indeed, it is quite unlikely that a behavioral process could have evolved which took into account the manner in which a response produces an effect. There are too many reasons why consequences follow behavior, and they depend on features of the environment which are too unstable to play any part in natural selection. But since an event which follows another event is likely enough to have been caused by it, coincidence suffices.

That solution to the problem of causality is not, however, free of trouble. It means that behavior may be strengthened by merely adventitious consequences, and such behavior is not likely to be useful. Vulnerability to coincidence must have increased as the process of operant conditioning accelerated, and when a single instance of response-and-consequence began to work a significant change, various kinds of superstitious behavior were inevitable. The more "intelligent" the organism, the more likely it was to be superstitious. Moreover, superstitious behavior is often self-perpetuating and even self-enhancing. Recovery from a self-limited illness, for example, reinforces any therapeutic action a person may take, and since the action is therefore more likely to be taken again, it is likely to be adventitiously reinforced again and hence further strengthened.

The fact that two basic types of superstitious behavior are commonly observed in such an "unintelligent" organism as a pigeon (Morse, 1957; Skinner, 1948) suggests that superstition must have been very widespread before corrective measures were developed. Such measures are, of course, now common. When a response appears to have had an unlikely consequence, a fairly characteristic move is to repeat it immediately. If the same consequence follows, the response is further strengthened. (Using essentially a synonym for "reinforced," we say it is "confirmed.") If the same response does not follow (as is likely to be the case if the first was adventitious), the acquired strength is lost through extinction and subsequent behavior is then "in better touch with reality."

It is possible that people learn to test the causal efficacy of their behavior simply because they are then more likely to be consistently reinforced, but more complex tests of the significance of consequences are usually acquired from others. Someone must devise each test for the first time, but no one person could devise many of them within a single lifetime. Most people probably learn even the simplest measures from others.

This is all part of the field of self-knowledge and self-management, and it is almost wholly a social product. It is only when other people ask "Why did you do that?" that we begin to examine the contingencies responsible for our behavior. As a simple operant we open a window because we then get fresh air, but it is only when someone asks "Why?" that we describe the relation between our behavior and its consequences, as by saying, "I opened the window because fresh air could then come in." The sequence is taken to be sufficient evidence. Recent power failures turned up a number of stories of people who described adventitious consequences in the same way. A small boy walking along the street striking trees and picket fences with a stick happens to strike an electric light pole, or a housewife happens to plug in an iron, just as all the lights in the city go out, and both may report, and under certain social circumstances may insist, that they have caused the trouble.

To explain *why* fresh air comes in through an open window or *why* plugging in an iron blows a fuse or blacks out a city, it is necessary to describe events which are not related sequentially through personal action. As the history of the idea of causality abundantly demonstrates, one thing has often been said to cause another simply because it precedes it — as the operant paradigm seems to imply. A very simple example, involving spatial features, is seen in the kind of settings studied by Michotte (1946). When one black spot moving on a white field approaches another and the other moves away just as contact is made, the first is said to cause the second to move. The first spot "strikes" the second as one billiard ball strikes another. And if we convert spots into living things a whole new realm of causality seems to open. I once made some small "turtles" for a child by pasting Mexican jumping beans on small squares of paper with the corners bent down as legs. The turtles moved about on a plate of glass as the beans "jumped." When one turtle moved toward another just as the other moved away, the child immediately reported that the second turtle had been frightened.

We gain from analyzing the contingencies which affect our behavior, using scientific and statistical methods, in part because we reduce our vulnerability to merely incidental cases, and our gains lead us to continue to do so when the contingencies are superstitious. Many myths appear to represent this function. Any behavior executed just before it begins to rain is strengthened if rain is reinforcing, as it is at the end of a severe drought. And because the more conspicuous the behavior, the more effective the coincidence, an elaborate ritual such as a rain dance may evolve. In an area in which drought is self-limited, people are likely to begin to dance near the end of a drought — when the probability of "reinforcement" is particularly high — and such a superstition is therefore self-perpetuating and even self-enhancing. People asked why they dance may simply reply that rain soon follows, but if asked why dancing produces rain, may answer by generalizing from instances in which similar consequences are not adventitious. Social contingencies offer the richest sources, and the dance may be interpreted as a form of asking for rain or pleasing and hence appeasing someone who is withholding rain.

We dismiss rain dancing as a form of superstition because the adventitious nature of the consequences can be demonstrated "statistically" but we continue to be fascinated by coincidences "inexplicable according to the laws of chance." This is likely to be the case so long as we forget that the world in which we live is an extremely complex sample space, in which it is doubtful whether there are any "laws of chance" which apply to many of the single events occurring in it. Coincidences are certainly to be expected, and the sheer number may be felt to build up a case for a force or agent which is metaphysical, supernatural, or at least not part of the current corpus of science. But the mere accumulation of instances has less to do with probability than with the striking force of coincidence.

Few people can pick up a hand of thirteen spades at bridge and view it as no less likely to occur than any of the other hands picked up during their experiences as players, or enjoy a run of luck at roulette without calling it their lucky day or acknowledging their debt to Lady Luck, or who when an honest coin has come heads 25 times in a row will not then be more likely to bet on tails. The genetic endowment responsible for our behavioral processes cannot fully protect us from the whims of chance, and the statistical and scientific measures we devise to bring our behavior under the more effective control of nature are not adequate for the extraordinarily complex sample space in which we live. Science has not ignored some underlying order; it has not yet devised ways of protecting us against spurious evidences of order.

REFERENCES

Koestler, Arthur. *The roots of coincidence.* New York: Random House, 1972.

Michotte. *La perception de la causalite.* Paris: 1946.

Morse, W. H., and Skinner, B. F. A second type of "superstition" in the pigeon. *American Journal of Psychology,* 1957, *70,* 308-311.

Skinner, B. F. "Superstition" in the pigeon. *Journal of Experimental Psychology,* 1948, *38,* 168-172.

Part I

CONTRIBUTIONS TO THEORY

Setting Events Due to Sidney W. Bijou

A Bibliography of Bijou's Work in the Area of Theory, with Self-Evident Function for the Papers Published Here

Bijou, S. W. The problem of pseudo-feeblemindedness. *Journal of Educational Psychology,* 1939, *30,* 519-526.

Bijou, S. W. & McCandless, B. R. An approach to a more comprehensive analysis of mentally retarded pre-delinquent boys. *Journal of Genetic Psychology,* 1944, *65,* 147-160.

Bijou, S. W. Motivation in the academic learning of the retarded child. *Exceptional Children,* 1952, *19,* 103.

Bijou, S. W. Learning in children. *Monographs of the Society for Research in Child Development,* 1959, *24,* (5, Whole No. 74).

Bijou, S. W. & Baer, D. M. *Child Development: A systematic and empirical theory* (Vol. 1). New York: Appleton-Century-Crofts, 1961.

Bijou, S. W. Theory and research in mental (developmental) retardation. *Psychological Record,* 1963, *13,* 95-110.

Bijou, S. W. An empirical concept of reinforcement and a functional analysis of child behavior. *Journal of Genetic Psychology,* 1964, *104,* 215-223.

Bijou, S. W. & Baer, D. M. *Child Development: Universal stage of infancy* (Vol. 2). New York: Appleton-Century-Crofts, 1965.

Bijou, S. W. A functional analysis of retarded development. In N. R. Ellis (Ed.), *International review of research in mental retardation* (Vol. 1). Academic Press, 1966.

Bijou, S. W. Implications of behavioral science for counseling and guidance. In J. D. Krumboltz (Ed.), *Revolution in counseling.* New York: Houghton Mifflin, 1966.

Bijou, S. W. Analyse experimentale general de l'apprentissage et du development. *Enfant,* 1967, *2,* 178-192.

Bijou, S. W. Ages, stages, and the naturalization of human development. *American Psychologist,* 1968, *23*(6), 419-427.

Bijou, S. W. Child behavior and development: A behavioral analysis. *International Journal of Psychology,* 1968, *3,* 221-238.

Bijou, S. W. The mentally retarded child. *Psychology Today,* 1968, *2,* 47-51.

Bijou, S. W. Modern meaning of instincts. In R. B. MacLeod (Ed.), *William James: Unfinished business.* Washington, D.C.: American Psychological Association, 1969. Pp. 31-35.

Bijou, S. W. Promoting optimum learning in children. In P. Wolf & R. MacKeith (Eds.), *Planning for better learning.* London: Spastics International Medical Publications, 1969. Pp. 58-67.

Bijou, S. W. Reinforcement history and socialization. In R. A. Hoppe, G. A. Milton, & E. C. Simmel (Eds.), *Early experiences and the processes of socialization.* New York: Academic Press, 1970. Pp. 43-58.

Bijou, S. W. What psychology has to offer education — Now. *Journal of Applied Behavior Analysis,* 1970, *3,* 65-71.

Bijou, S. W. Environment and intelligence: A behavioral analysis. In R. Cancro (Ed.), *Intelligence: Genetic and environmental influences.* New York: Grune & Stratton, 1971. Pp. 211-239.

Bijou, S. W. The critical need for methodological consistency in field and laboratory studies. In F. J. Monks, W. W. Hartup, U. J. de Wit (Eds.), *Determinants of behavioral development.* New York: Academic Press, 1972. Pp. 89-113.

Bijou, S. W. Development in the preschool years: A functional analysis. *American Psychologist,* 1975, *30,* 829-837.

Bijou, S. W. Moral development in the preschool years: A functional analysis. *Mexican Journal of Behavior Analysis,* 1975, *1,* 11-29.

Bijou, S. W., & Redd, W. H. Behavior therapy for children. *Handbook of American Psychiatry.* New York: Basic Books, 1975.

Bijou, S. W. *The basic stage of early childhood development.* Englewood Cliffs, N.J.: Prentice-Hall, 1976.

2

Operant Research in Violation
of the Operant Paradigm?

Margret M. Baltes
Pennsylvania State University

Hayne W. Reese
West Virginia University

This chapter is addressed to the question of whether or not operant research conforms to the basic characteristics of the operant paradigm. First, these characteristics are briefly elaborated, showing that the operant paradigm implies an active organism and a reciprocal relation between behavior and environment. Next, the operant concepts of the active organism and reciprocal relation are analyzed and found to be consistent with the mechanistic world view. Finally, the characteristics of operant research are discussed, and are shown also to be consistent with the mechanistic world view. Consequently, there is no basic conflict between operant research and the operant paradigm. However, neither operant research nor the operant paradigm deals directly with active organisms and reciprocal interactions as conceptualized within the organismic world view. This conceptual dilemma extends to nonoperant mechanistic approaches dealing with dynamic organism-environment interactions, and is not limited to the operant approach.

THE OPERANT PARADIGM

Basic Characteristics

The term "paradigm" is used here to refer to a metatheoretical system or model that represents in symbolic form the interrelations among phenomena in a selected domain. The domain of the operant paradigm is behavior of organisms

11

as it relates to environment. The details of the way in which this paradigm represents the behavior of organisms are important, but for the present purposes only the salient features of the paradigm need to be considered. The operant paradigm is functional, in contrast to structural (Catania, 1973), in that it emphasizes the relations between organism and environment. Environmental conditions do not elicit operant behavior in the all-or-none manner of reflex. Rather, environmental conditions simply make the behavior either more likely or less likely to occur. In this sense, operant behavior is probabilistic in relations to stimuli.

Unlike other S-R paradigms, the operant paradigm depicts the organism as not merely reacting to an environmental setting, but as possibly changing it via his reaction upon this setting. "While we are awake, we act upon the environment constantly" (Skinner, 1965, p. 66); "The characteristic of operant behavior is that it operates on the environment" (Hill, 1963, p. 61). According to the operant paradigm, in an appropriate context (S^D), a response (R) occurs and effects a change in the environment (S^R), which in turn may either change the probability of the response, via reinforcement or punishment, or change the nature of the response by changing the context (S^D). Thus, although the cycle of S^D-R-S^R can be repetitive, the stimuli and responses may change from cycle to cycle. There is, then, an interactive relation between behavior and environment. Each is both a source of change and a result of change, both a cause and an effect. The relation between behavior and environment is therefore a *reciprocal* relation. There is a "reciprocal relationship between the knower and the known" (Skinner, 1961, p. 543), and between the controller and the counter-controller (Skinner, 1971).

In the organismic world view, a reciprocal interaction implies an active organism (Overton & Reese, 1973). It has been explicitly argued that in the operant paradigm the organism is active (Bijou, 1971). Skinner (1971) argued that almost all living beings *act* to free themselves from harmful and aversive contacts (see also Herrnstein, 1969).

The active and dynamic interplay of organism and environment is less obvious and dramatic when one organism is behaving within a physical environmental setting than when two or more organisms are behaving in a social setting. As Skinner (1965) said, "schedules of reinforcement which adjust to rate of the behavior reinforced do not often occur in inorganic nature" (p. 301), but a social "reinforcing system is seldom independent of the behavior reinforced" (p. 300). That is, in a social reinforcing system each organism provides S^Ds and S^Rs for the responses of the other organism(s). Skinner referred to these reciprocal relationships as "social episodes." Reynolds, Catania, and Skinner (1963) referred explicitly to such an episode as an "interaction."

It appears, then, that the operant paradigm involves an active organism and an interactive relation between behavior and environment, each exerting changes in the other. The next task is to analyze the concepts of the active organism and the interactive relationship in the operant paradigm to determine what world view or metatheoretical model they are consistent with.

Reciprocal Interaction

The dictionary meaning of "interaction" is mutual action or reciprocal action. In science, these two meanings are retained, but one should note that the meanings are not synonymous. *Mutual action,* with reference to causes, means "interaction" in the analysis-of-variance sense, a "conjunctive plurality of causes," which is a variety of simple efficient causation (Bunge, 1963). That is, the interaction refers to an interdependency of determinants, not an interaction between cause and effect but between causes. In other words, the determinacy is unidirectional. Unidirectional determinacy means that the direction of determinacy is one-way, from cause to effect. The one variable is active and the other is the recipient of the activity. The effect may, however, function as a cause of a further effect, forming a linear chain of cause-effect sequences. The linear chain may be diagrammed as circular, as in cybernetic feedback models, but linearity is preserved in that each event in the loop can be traced to an immediately preceding event in the loop. Each event is both a cause and an effect, but its character as an effect is not influenced by its character as a cause. Rather, its causal character is predetermined by its effected character. It may be useful to note that the circular diagram is reasonable only if time is ignored. If time is included in the diagram and is represented by a straight line, then the circular array becomes a rectilinear array in which the components are given time subscripts. (This point is apparently not always understood; see Powers' 1973 reply to Reese, 1973.)

The determinacy in a "mutual action" of causes is also summative, because even though interaction means nonadditivity of treatment effects in the analysis of variance (Hays, 1963, pp. 389, 454), the interaction is an additive component of the total effect. Nonadditivity of treatment effects means that the joint effect of treatments is not the sum of their individual effects, but rather it is the sum of the individual effects plus a term reflecting a joint effect. Thus, Herrnstein *adds* an interaction component (mR_i) to the other components of the total frequency of reinforcement (1970, e.g., Equation 20, p. 259).

Reciprocal action means that one variable, the cause, produces an effect on another variable, the effect, which *at the same time* functions as a cause that produces an effect on the initial variable. The cause-effect relation between the variables is confounded by the cause-effect character of each variable. Each variable is "both the cause and the effect of the other. If a candle is lighted, the flame melts the paraffin; the molten paraffin, saturating the wick, aids the burning; and the burning, in turn, melts more paraffin; and so on" (Werkmeister, 1948, p. 635). There is an organismic or dialectic relation between the two variables, and the notions of unidirectional and summative determinacy are inapplicable.

It is a firmly established principle that genes interact with their environments and in some cases interact with each other as in polygenic inheritance. Regarding the interaction among genes, Dobzhansky (1955) has asserted that "Every gene may affect many visible traits; most traits are influenced by several or by many genes" (p. 37). However, Dobzhansky considered genetics to be a mechanistic science (pp. 19-21, 230, 358-363), and therefore the interaction among genes must be a mutual action, not a reciprocal action. With respect to the interaction between genes and environment, "every organism exists in an environment and at the expense of the environment to transform a part of it into their own copies" (p. 74). Thus, organisms must change the form of (part of) the environment in order to survive and reproduce. However, it seems clear that the interaction is again intended to be unidirectional and hence not to refer to reciprocal action.

The issue with respect to the operant paradigm is whether the organism-environment interaction is better represented by the burning candle or by the genetic model — by the interaction between flame and paraffin or by the interaction between genes and environment. If the former, it is a reciprocal interaction, implying a nonmechanistic world view (Overton & Reese, 1973). The problem is complicated, because in strong reciprocal interactions it is "impossible to distinguish in any meaningful way individual components" (Overton, 1973, p. 78), which means that "the action of subsystems within the total event cannot be analyzed in terms of one-way causality" and implies that "the interactions between components would preclude identification of the components themselves." However, "Relatively short-term occurrences, well defined features, and traumatic events ... might be analyzed under the convenient fiction that they are independent, i.e., weak interactions. To the extent this fiction is considered reasonable, the traditional experimental procedures and statistical techniques are appropriate" (Overton, 1973, pp. 86-87).

Reynolds *et al* (1963) used the term "interaction" in referring to the laboratory observation that a second pigeon will react to "conditioned" aggression of a first bird with "unconditioned" aggression. However, this "interaction" is described merely as the effect of conditioned aggression on unconditioned aggression. The conditioned aggression is controlled by an external stimulus (light) and the unconditioned aggression is controlled by the occurrence of conditioned aggression. Thus, this particular kind of interaction is unidirectional rather than truly reciprocal.

Other interactions in the operant paradigm seem to be reciprocal. For example, in social episodes each participant provides S^Ds and S^Rs to the other participant, and therefore each participant is both a cause and an effect. (Or more accurately, each participant's behavior is a source of stimuli that are causally related to the other's behavior, and is itself an effect of causal stimuli produced by the other's behavior.) However, it is clear that these interactions are not conceptualized as *strong* reciprocal interactions, because the components are assumed to be distinguishable meaningfully. Nevertheless, there remains the problem of determining whether the interactions are conceptualized as mechanistic mutual actions or as weak reciprocal interactions. In view of another feature of the operant paradigm it seems reasonable to surmise that in fact the interactions are mechanistic. This other feature is related to the nature of explanation. In mechanistic models, explanation refers to the ability to control and predict; in organismic models, explanation refers to description (Overton & Reese, 1973). The operant approach is intended to yield complete control and predictability — that is, complete causal explanation of behavior — when all antecedents and consequents are known (Krasner, 1965; Skinner, 1966). Whether any paradigm can be entirely successful in this quest is debatable (Catania, 1973), but the quest itself characterizes the operant approach as basically mechanistic. In a mechanistic paradigm, the interactions must be mutual actions.

The Active Organism

According to the dictionary, "active" means: designating the agent or doer; in action, busy; causing change; dynamic, characterized by change; and live. Each of these meanings can give rise to a different (in some cases, more than one) active-organism model.

The organism may be said to be active in the sense that it is the *agent or doer.* However, if this is the only sense of "active" intended, the resulting "active-organism" model is identical to the "reactive-organism" model. The reactive-organism model is associated with the mechanistic world view. It characterizes the organism, like other parts of the universal machine, as inherently at rest and as active only as a result of external forces (efficient causes). The organism is active only in the sense that it is the agent which receives the forces and exhibits the reactions to them.

The organism may be said to be active in the sense that it is *in action; it behaves or responds.* This is essentially the same as the first meaning, and since the reactive-model organism also behaves and responds, this kind of activity does not generate an alternative model.

The organism may be said to be active in the "in action" sense that it emits certain kinds of responses, *namely operant ("active") responses as distinguished from respondent ("reactive") behavior.* In this sense, the active-organism model covers the domain of operant behavior. According to this view, the reactive-organism model covers the antecedent-consequent relation between stimulus and respondent behavior. The operant paradigm seems to deny the antecedent-consequent relation because the response is not elicited by the antecedent stimulus but only is emitted in the presence of the antecedent stimulus. That is, the antecedent (the S^D) "sets the stage for" or "occasions" the response, or "signals the availability of reinforcement" for occurrences of the response. Thus, in the operant paradigm the antecedent-consequent relation is not causal, or productive (Bunge, 1963), as it is in the case of respondent behavior. In this sense, it is not S-R relations that are emphasized, but R-S relations. However, the R-S formulation is misleading, because the direction of determinism is not assumed to be from the contingency back to the present response, which would be a teleological determinacy. Rather, it is assumed to be from the contingency "forward" to subsequent response occasions, which is efficient determinacy. Thus, the statement that an operant response is controlled by its consequents is not a teleological statement, but a statement of the relation between responses and their history of contingencies, or between present contingencies and future occurrences of the responses. Therefore, the response-contingency relation turns out to be an antecedent-consequent relation.

Consequently, operant behaviors are like respondent behaviors in that both are under the control of environmental events, S^D and S^R in the case of operant behaviors, S in the case of unconditioned respondent behaviors, and S and reinforcement history in the case of conditioned respondent behaviors. Given the appropriate circumstances, both kinds of behavior occur inexorably, and the models again have no other essential distinctions.

The organism may be said to be active in the sense that it *causes changes in behavior.* As an agent of change, the organism is a source of causal variables. These variables can be designated as "organismic" variables, to reflect that their source is the organism. However, as used by psychologists, "organismic" has two meanings. In a first sense, the adjective "organismic" is used to distinguish a set of concepts predicated about the organism from a set predicated about the environment in a purely descriptive manner. In this sense, any internal state or process, however defined, is an organismic variable. In a second sense, it is used to identify a particular general model of phenomena, a world view, labeled organismic (Pepper, 1942). Concepts can be characterized as "organismic" when they are meaningful only within this world view (Pepper's adjectives were "organic" and "organistic"). In contrast with the mechanistic world view, which represents the universe as a machine, the organismic world view represents the universe as an organic whole, or organized system (Overton & Reese, 1973; Reese & Overton, 1970). In the mechanistic world view, the properties of a whole are predictable from the properties of its parts; but in organicism the whole has emergent properties, not predictable from decomposition into parts. Thus, in organicism, concepts are not necessarily defined in terms of antecedents, because they can be emergent, and they have no fixed function or consequent independent of the whole that contains them. Any concept that has these characteristics can be identified as an "organismic" concept.

Mental operations as conceived by Piaget are organismic in both senses. However, there are variables that are organismic in the first sense but not in the second sense. Responses that are ordinarily discriminated can become clustered into a sequence that functions as a unit, or new response class. However, such a unit is not organismic in the second sense, because it is not emergent: it is predictable from the laws of reinforcement (Herrnstein, 1970, p. 251), and it seems to be controlled by application of the same laws of reinforcement. In S-R behaviorism, organismic variables are defined in terms of antecedents and are related by theory to consequents (usually through hypothesized relations with other intervening variables). Such variables are often "historical" (Bergmann, 1957, p. 66) in the sense that they are defined in terms of past events, or remote antecedents (Baltes, 1973). An example is "learned laziness" (Engberg *et al.,*

1972). It is related to previous experience with noncontingent delivery of food (not "noncontingent reinforcement," which is a contradiction in that reinforcement is defined as an effect of a contingent stimulus). It is related to a consequent — speed of autoshaping — by an implied theory. In a criticism of this concept, Gamzu, Williams, and Schwartz (1973) noted correctly the need for theoretical analysis (see Reese, 1971), but incorrectly considered the concept to be organismic in the second sense. In a reply, Welker, Hansen, Engberg, and Thomas (1973) argued that the concept is entirely descriptive. In their first paper, however, they referred to it as an "underlying mechanism" (Engberg *et al.,* 1972, p. 1004). Apparently, then, the intended conception fits the behavioristic definition of an organismic variable, or at least will fit once the implicit theory is made explicit. A source of confusion about the status of the concept is that it was also referred to as a learned anticipation that the noncontingency of food and behavior will continue. "Anticipation" sounds like a mentalistic concept unless defined carefully in behavioristic terms, as "expectancy" has been (Brown, 1961, pp. 176ff).

Similarly, in a statement such as "an experiment . . . held the interval component constant at 15 minutes, but varied the ratio component . . ." (Herrnstein, 1970, p. 244), the "experiment" is reified as an active agent or organism. This particular figure of speech, in which the vehicle becomes the agent, is commonplace and not likely to be misleading. However, when the vehicle is literally an organism, reifying it as an agent can be critically misleading. For example, if a writer intends to convey that performance of an act becomes more efficient across a series of trials, it is misleading to state that "animals . . . are likely to improve upon it (the act) until they find something like the optimal performance" (Herrnstein, 1970, p. 243). Is the writer deliberately ascribing cognitive powers to the animals, or is he only using the commonplace figure of speech? It seems unlikely that operant psychologists who refer to active organisms intend the organicist's sense. Rather, the reference seems more likely to reflect an unintended figure of speech. There are, then, first-sense organismic variables that fit the behavioristic paradigm, which is mechanistic (Overton & Reese, 1973; Reese & Overton, 1970).

To return to the meaning of "active" under consideration, the question is how the organism as an agent of change is conceptualized as being active. There are three possibilities:

1. If the organism is conceptualized as causing changes in the behavior of another organism, as in social episodes, then the active organism is functioning as an environmental determinant of the behavior of the other organism, and the other organism can be reactive. Furthermore, in that the behavior of the first organism may be reactive to other environmental determinants, this usage does not require a change from the reactive-organism model. The key point is that from this view the organism is "active" in the same sense that any functional stimulus is "active," and this sense is consistent with the reactive-organism model.

2. If the organism is conceptualized as causing changes in its own behavior, the model might be reactive, as, for example, when the organismic determinants are postulated to be drives, habits, attentional mechanisms, covert mediators, etc., all of which are defined in terms of observable antecedent and consequent conditions.

3. The model might, however, be inconsistent with the reactive-organism model, if the organismic determinants are mental processes, defined independently of antecedents and therefore defined as emergent processes. That is, a model in which performance is influenced by mental acts, such as reflection, comparison, wishing, thinking, and the like, is inconsistent with the reactive-organism model and is therefore a truly alternative model.

The organism may be said to be active *if the causal determinants of the responses are unknown.* This usage implies that if the causes were known, the organism would be said to be reactive. More to the point, the reactive-active dichotomy is usually intended to distinguish between two ontological positions; but in the sense under consideration, the "reactive-active" dichotomy would refer to two epistemological positions. Epistemological uncertainty has nothing to do with the presumed ontological nature of the organism (or more precisely, the nature of the organism as modeled ontologically).

The organism may be said to be active in the sense that it is *dynamic, characterized by change.* However, change can occur in the reactive-organism model, if change is quantitative, as in the strength, frequency, or rate of a behavior. Thus, the critical concept here is the nature of the change. The only basic kind of change possible in the reactive-organism model is quantitative, a requirement to preserve consistency with the mechanistic world view. That is, behavior can change in displacement, duration, force, frequency, or rate. In this model, changes that appear to be qualitative are either actually quantitative or reducible to quantitative changes. The changes that occur in operant shaping, for example, appear to be qualitative, but can be conceptualized — and in the reactive-organism model, *must* be conceptualized — as quantitative changes in the strengths of topographically similar responses rather than as qualitative or topographical changes of a single response. Changes in strength rearrange the response hierarchy, and thereby determine which of the similar responses will occur at any time; but although the rearrangement results from dynamic variability, the variability produced by the rearrangement is static (Millenson, 1967).

1. If the change is quantitative, then the reactive-organism model incorporates it. Furthermore, if it is qualitative but reducible to quantitative change, the reactive-organism model may incorporate it. For example, the changes in behavior resulting from the introduction of extinction, such as the appearance of emotional responses, might be considered qualitative, but are reducible to quantitative changes in the strengths of the preceding behavior controlled by a particular reinforcement schedule. The same analysis holds for superstitious behavior occurring with changes in ratio schedules or DRL (differential reinforcement of low rates).

2. If the change is qualitative and not reducible to quantitative change, then it requires a different model. In the past such models have referred to changes in forms, patterns, or structures, and have been basically contextualistic (e.g., the Gestalt model, generative grammar), organismic (as the Piagetian model), or dialectic (Riegel, 1973). In those models, the changes are not only qualitative, but also emergent. This usage of "active" — and the metaphysical positions it presupposes — implies that a complete causal determinism is impossible. The usage would lead to an abandonment of an analysis of behavior in terms of efficient causes (in substantive or statistical form) and consequently would lead to rejection of the ideal of in-principle complete predictability and control. Here, then, is an active-organism model that is a real alternative to the reactive-organism model.

The organism may be said to be active in the dynamic sense that it is *spontaneously active*. This is not the same as the epistemological usage considered when causal determinants are unknown, in which "spontaneity" would mean "unpredicted" or "at-present unpredictability." Here, spontaneity has an onto-logical status, equivalent to "in-principle unpredictability." The usage is there-fore also different from the usage in the operant-respondent distinction discussed above, in which both kinds of behavior are in principle predictable. As in the case of qualitative change there is a denial of complete predictability.

The organism may be said to be active in the sense that it is a *biological organism interacting with its environment*. This usage, in order to be scientifical-ly fruitful, needs further explication to clarify the meanings of "biological" and "interacting."

1. If "biological" means that the organismic world view is applicable, then "interaction" must mean reciprocal action (Bunge, 1963), or the interaction of environment and mental processes (Taylor, 1964). "Active" in this usage be-comes identical with the "spontaneously active" sense, and the same active-organism model is implied.

2. However, if "biological" means that the organism is alive, or that "or-ganism" is being used in a literal sense as opposed to its figurative sense in referring to groups, such as the "social organism" or "body politic," then either the active-organism model or the reactive-organism model could be used to represent the organism, and the meaning of "interaction" would not be pre-determined but could refer to either interpenetration, as in the "qualitative change" usage of "active," or to (complex) reaction, as in the usage of "active" to mean operant. Whichever meaning is intended, therefore, this usage is sub-sumed under one of the other usages.

Summary

It appears that in the operant paradigm, "interaction" is being used in the mechanistic sense of mutual action. Either this meaning is the one intended, in which case the operant paradigm is mechanistic at least with respect to this basic conceptual category, or the intended meaning is reciprocal interaction and the "convenient fiction" is adopted that the reciprocal interaction is weak and hence adequately represented as a mutual action.

With respect to the alternative senses of "active organism" discussed, the senses that seem to be consistent with other features of the operant paradigm (all except those cases in which the determinants are mental processes; the changes are qualitative; or the changes are spontaneous) do not generate an active-organism model that differs in any essential way from the mechanistic, reactive-organism model. Hence, it appears that the "active organism" in the operant paradigm is actually the mechanistic, reactive organism. Even weak reciprocal interactions are possible only in the active-organism models that are real alternatives to the reactive-organism model, that is, those "exceptions" cited above. Therefore, the interactions in the operant paradigm must be mutual actions. One can conclude, then, that the operant paradigm is mechanistic.

OPERANT RESEARCH

Is operant research consistent with the mechanistic model implied by the operant paradigm? This research will be shown to be mechanistic, and therefore inadequate to deal with strong reciprocal interactions.

Laboratory Research

Operant research in laboratory settings often seems to imply an active organism and the operation of reciprocal interactions. However, these implications have only a superficial basis.

Conditioning process. The S^D-R-S^R interaction is controlled by the experimenter in operant laboratory research in such a way that stability of behavior is achieved by maintaining stability of the environment. That is, S^D and S^R are preprogrammed so that the response determines their occurrence but does not change their nature. Consequently, there is no real reciprocal interaction: The environment is stable in the sense that the changes produced by the response are regular and predictable — a static cycle of action and reaction, not a dynamic interpenetration. There is an interaction, but it is unidirectional.

Operant schedules. It might be argued that the dynamic interchange occurs in compound schedules, in which the antecedent environment (S^D) as well as the consequent environment (S^R) are changed by the response. Again, however, in the long run the cycle is static in its regularity and predictability. Progressive schedules are dynamic, in a sense, but again the changes are preprogrammed and regular. The nature of the changes is determined not by the organism's behavior but rather by the experimenter, as a kind of deus ex machina. The organism's behavior determines only when the changes will occur. By the same argument, a conjugate reinforcement schedule is not truly dynamic because the changes in S^R that are determined by the organism are only quantitative; the qualitative changes are preprogrammed by the experimenter.

Operant shaping and fading. The unidirectional relationship between organism and environment in operant laboratory research becomes most obvious when one looks at two of the major tools in behavior modification: shaping and fading. With the present state of knowledge, effective shaping and fading often require considerable ingenuity and innovativeness from the experimenter. In programmed instruction, for example, the programmer must respond to patterns of errors that frequently are unanticipated and apparently unpredictable. In such situations the experimenter presents material, to which the subject responds in an unexpected way; and the experimenter responds in turn by modifying the material or procedure. Note, however, that it is the experimenter and not the subject who decides what the modifications will be. Thus, from the experimenter's perspective the problem is to manipulate the environment in such a way that the subject will emit certain responses. When the environment functions in the anticipated way, it is modified by the experimenter in accordance with the experimenter's predetermined schedule of modifications. When it does not function in the anticipated way, it is modified by the experimenter in other ways. In either case, qualitative changes in the environment are determined by the experimenter alone; the subject's behavior determines only the timing of the changes.

In the shaping process the experimenter decides upon the differential use of reinforcement contingencies applied to specific responses. The behavior of an organism will generally result in variations between organisms with respect to time of introduction or specific sequence of new reinforcement contingencies, and variations with respect to which specific responses are sequenced. Nevertheless, the end response is determined by the experimenter, who alone decides which response "pieces" to reinforce or not to reinforce. Similarly, in the fading process the experimenter alone is responsible for the sequential changes in discriminative stimuli. The organism's behavior determines only when the changes occur. Although quantitative changes in the shaping and fading processes are determined by the organism, the qualitative changes in both processes are determined by the experimenter.

This exclusive unidirectional analysis of how the environment operates on the behavior cannot be argued away by Skinner's (1971) reference to the scientist in the laboratory or the apparatus as being controlled by the organism studied. The argument is that the behavior of the organism has determined the design of the apparatus and the procedures of its usage. However, this fact is responsible only for success or failure in operant conditioning. Breland and Breland (1961) and Seligman (1970) argued in that direction when they questioned the equal associability for all behavioral events in all species. The fact that, for example, successful avoidance can be achieved only when the avoidance response is chosen from among the natural, species-specific defensive repertoire of the organism does not indicate reciprocal control between organism and experimenter.

Generalization and discrimination.   Generalization and discrimination have long been considered not inadvertent consequences of some learning setting, but necessarily programmed in order to occur (Kazdin & Bootzin, 1972; Terrace, 1966). In both cases, operant laboratory research puts the experimenter in the active role and the organism in a reactive role.

Maximizing and superstitious behavior.   Both maximizing and superstitious behavior seem, at first glance, to be exceptions to the rule developed in the discussion thus far. Here, the organism appears to escape from experimental control and to act upon its environment even in the laboratory setting.

Maximizing behavior was defined by Shimp (1969) as consistently emitting the responses or choices which have the greatest momentary reinforcement probabilities. However, "choice" is a behavior, not a psychological process (Herrnstein, 1970). The "decision making" is merely exhibiting a preference for one of two alternatives provided to the organism by the experimenter. The organism does not make a "free choice," but rather emits a response determined by the momentary reinforcement probability, which was predetermined by the experimenter.

Superstitious behavior is "behavior that occurs as if it influences environmental consequences but in fact does not" (Zeiler, 1972, p. 27). Superstitious behavior in a laboratory setting, and presumably in natural settings as well, is learned without direct programming; the relation between the behavior and the reinforcing event is not necessary, but purely temporal. That is, the occurrence or nonoccurrence of the behavior has no effect upon the occurrence or nonoccurrence of the reinforcing event. Thus, superstitious behavior is operant but is not *instrumental* behavior and cannot involve a reciprocal interaction between organism and environment.

Autoshaping.   "Autoshaping" by its very name appears to suggest an active organism. It refers to the development of responding after response-independent presentations of incentives. The process was first labeled by Brown and Jenkins (1968), who interpreted it as a form of adventitious conditioning of superstitious behavior. In subsequent research greater control was applied, however, in a truly noncontingent reward situation. The findings now seem to support an interpretation of autoshaping as a respondent conditioning process (Gamzu & Williams, 1971). Most recent research (Bilbrey & Winokur, 1973) supports this respondent conditioning interpretation, with specification of additional genetic components (as in the sense of Seligman's preparedness notion). In any case, the term autoshaping is obviously misleading and in contrast to its etymology seems not to refer to the "active" organism as described in those cases treated as exceptions above.

Response classes. Some behavior appears to be controlled by rules rather than by specific training. In language, for example, there are rules for forming plurals; in imitation the rule is "Do as the model does"; and in creativity the rule is "Do something new." Operant researchers have studied such behaviors (Gewirtz, 1971; Goetz & Baer, 1971; Sherman, 1971), but have avoided the mentalistic connotations of "rule learning" by attributing the behaviors to the development of "response classes" (Gewirtz, 1971). However, the development of a response class results from the same kinds of environmental contingencies that control specific behaviors, and the functional relation of a response class to the environment is the same as that of specific behaviors (Baer, 1976). As might be expected, therefore, the operant research on such phenomena as generative grammar, generalized imitation, and creativity takes the same form as research on specific behaviors and consequently, according to the preceding analyses, is mechanistic.

Naturalistic Research

Most operant research conducted within naturalistic settings can be classified as intervention research. No operant research done in naturalistic settings has been aimed at clarification of purely theoretical issues, such as the question of external validity of operant principles. Most applied operant research is concentrated upon a single subject or patient, a single response, a single kind of reinforcement. By definition, intervention places emphasis upon a patient, whose behavior needs to be changed via shaping, fading, or some other procedure. For example, the introduction of token systems, be it in mental wards, classrooms, or other settings, promotes environmental changes which are hoped to spin off behavioral changes intended by the researcher.

The direction of experimental analysis, however, follows a one-way street. Behavioral effect is analyzed only with respect to the target person. Behavioral changes occurring in the environmental setting — for example, mediating agents such as nurses, teachers, and parents — are generally mentioned or referred to only when the experimental picture is cloudy. For instance, in a reversal design, behavioral change in mediating agents is often cited as a possible reason for nonreversal of the target behavior of the target person during second baseline, in which the mediating agents are intended to be functionally inactive (see Tharp & Wetzel, 1969). Instead of being incorporated into the experimental analysis as legitimate phenomena, the behavioral changes of mediating agents are considered as confounding, extraneous variables. For example, in Tharp and Wetzel's (1969) triadic model the effect of the target person on the mediating agent is discussed, but always from the perspective of the way this effect will influence the effect of the mediating agent on the target person. The central concern is the effect of the mediating agent upon the target person. All other concerns in the model are with how to develop and maintain the effectiveness of the mediating agent.

Similarly, in the Reynolds *et al.* (1963) analysis of the interaction between conditioned and unconditioned aggression in pigeons, the interest shifts from one target subject to two target subjects. However, the two target subjects are the objects of unidirectional observation and control, in that the conditioned aggression is under the control of a discriminative stimulus imposed by the experimenter and the unconditioned aggression is under the control of the conditioned aggression, which functions as an eliciting stimulus.

Even in naturalistic settings which are characterized by the presence of "social episodes," operant research is by and large an image of laboratory research. The experimenter decides upon the target behavior, the treatment conditions, the mediators, etc., and then records what is happening with the so-controlled organisms and analyzes the behavioral events with one-way perspective. Thus, the operant label — which implies that the target of research is the behavior as it operates on the environment — has been used almost exclusively in the analysis of how the environment operates on the behavior. This is true of operant research in clinical settings such as mental wards and homes for the retarded (most prominently represented in the work of Ayllon, Azrin, and Holz) and operant research in educational settings (associated mostly with Bijou, Baer, and their coworkers), to name the two areas most heavily studied currently by operant researchers. Bijou (1970) summarized this one-way direction of analysis very explicitly in defining the role of the teacher as a manager of contingencies of reinforcement and as an effective instructional programmer.

In this context the argument could be raised that the active role of the instructional programmer extends into programs of self-control, which therefore require an active organism in constant interaction with his environment. Operant treatment programs based on self-control can be characterized as contingency programs set up on an individual level with the organism as the target person and experimenter at the same time. However, the target person must be trained in self-analysis and self-control: he is trained to observe "the contingencies, the environmental conditions, that govern his behavior" (Goldiamond, 1973, p. 95). Thus, the patient is taught to record environmental conditions as antecedent and consequent determinants of his behavior. The behavioral determinants are clearly defined in terms of observables. The fact that the target person himself plays the role of the experimenter and as such controls the direction of change and the pace of change, does not make him necessarily dynamic or spontaneously active. On the contrary, the examples in Goldfried and Merbaum's book (1973) on self-control — such as aversion therapy and stimulus control — clearly show that the target behavior is controlled by observable antecedents and consequents although recorded and dispensed by the target person himself. Self-control programs require only a reactive organism (as in the case in which organismic determinants are defined behaviorally).

To cite Skinner (1973) on this matter: "He controls himself precisely as he would control the behavior of anyone else — through the manipulation of variables of which behavior is a function" (p. 59), although the behavior of self-control might often relate to private events. Self-control in Skinner's view is mainly a choice between two *alternatives,* that is, in face of a behavior conse-quated by reinforcement (usually immediate) as well as punishment (usually delayed), the subject will alter the variables to make the punished response less probable. Skinner (1973) in a closing remark argues: "This view, of course, is in conflict with traditional treatments of the subject, which are especially likely to cite self-control as an important example of the operation of personal respon-sibility. But an analysis which appeals to external variables makes the assump-tion of issues originating in determining agents unnecessary" (p. 69).

Conclusion

Operant research in both laboratory and naturalistic settings is designed to yield an essentially "reactive" and additive analysis of behavior-environment inter-actions. No attempt is made to provide a dynamic, interactive synthesis. The research is therefore consistent with a mechanistic analysis and inconsistent with an organismic synthesis. Consequently, operant research is consistent with the operant paradigm.

IS THE OPERANT APPROACH ADEQUATE?

Basic operant research has yielded a body of psychologically interesting and important data. In addition, the operant approach has provided educational and clinical technologies of well-documented utility. The operant approach is, in other words, adequate in many areas and for many purposes. Nevertheless, the adequacy of the operant approach to interactions can be questioned.

The operant paradigm seems to have been intended to deal with active organ-isms and reciprocal interactions as conceptualized nonmechanistically. It ap-pears, however, that the operant paradigm is fully consistent with the mechanistic world view (at least with respect to these and related concepts), and that the operant research model is also consistent with this world view. Both can be interpreted as a part of S-R behaviorism, albeit a part dealing with a special do-main of behaviors. The question, then, is whether a mechanistic approach can deal adequately with nonmechanistic concepts. The answer seems to be negative, because of a shortcoming in the available methodological tools. Consider, for example, Skinner's analysis of "social episodes." He proposed an additive, unidirectional analysis, in that the social behaviors are considered one at a time and alternating between the organisms involved. In principle, one can identify and quantify the specific contribution of each component of the situation — the general environmental context, the changed S^D, the changed S^R, and the changed schedules of S^Rs, each with reference to each of the organisms in-volved. Hence, in principle one can fully predict the sequence of behaviors in the social episode. An example of just this approach is the work of Patterson and Cobb (1973).

As Donald M. Baer has put it, the operant approach is to study each member of a dyad in turn, analyzing each "turn" before it is changed by the reaction to it. The components must be studied before their "interactive assembly" can be studied; "to analyze interactions (in the sense of how changing behavior in itself typically changes the conditions which originally changed the behavior . . .) we must first understand what they are made of." This approach, as Baer noted, is based on the article of faith that "the quick sequence characteristic of psychodynamic interaction can be analyzed, turn by turn, by holding time still for each turn while we delve into it" (Baer, personal communication, June 7, 1973).

In this approach the interactions are treated as feedback loops, which are "mutual actions" and not "reciprocal actions" (see section on reciprocal interactions). The problem with the approach is that from a dialectic position (Riegel, 1973) the interaction is a continuous flux in which organisms and environments are active and changing, and in which each is simultaneously both actor and acted upon. This simultaneity of action and reaction, or actor and reactor, is intended in its most literal possible sense, and hence prevents a one-way analysis in terms of the organism and environment as components of a sequential process (Overton, 1973; Overton & Reese, 1973; Reese & Overton, 1970). In fact, the components are not even identifiable in a strong reciprocal interaction, which is conceptualized as a single unit (Overton, 1973). Hence, the operant approach cannot come to grips with reciprocal interactions (at least not with strong ones).

It should be noted that the methodological shortcoming is not limited to the operant approach. No mechanistic approach can deal adequately with strong reciprocal interactions. In the research designs used most frequently in experimental branches of psychology, effects of a treatment are compared with effects of its absence. The treatment and its absence may be varied between groups, or, as in most operant research, in a single subject. Either way, these designs are based on John Stuart Mill's Method of Difference. However, as Werkmeister noted, "Mill's Methods do not enable us to cope with . . . reciprocal relations of cause and effect" (1948, p. 635). Such designs require an additive, unidirectional analysis, and are not suitable for analyzing strong reciprocal interactions.

In experimental psychological research dealing with organism-environment interactions, such as child-parent and child-teacher, it seems that some researchers have become uneasy about the unidirectional outlook of their analysis of dynamic interactions. Bell (1968), for instance, said: "The model of unidirectional effect is overdrawn, a fiction of convenience rather than belief" (p. 82). The awareness of this rigidity in research, however, has led until now to a mere refocusing of the unidirectional control within a dyadic process (Gewirtz, 1968; Osofsky & O'Connell, 1972; Rheingold, 1969). Instead of defining the child's behavior, for instance, as the dependent variable and the environmental agents as independent variables, now the child's behavior is manipulated as the independent variable and its effect upon the environmental agents is studied (Berberich, 1971).

This refocusing is worthwhile, but comes no closer to reciprocal interactions than does the additive analysis of social episodes proposed by Skinner. The experimental design is based on a fixed, preprogrammed strategy; the changes in the child's behavior are completely controlled by the experimenter and are nothing more than changes in reinforcement schedules when the focus is upon the adult's behavior.

How can the interactions be studied? If they are actually mutual actions, there is no problem. Mutual actions are additive and unidirectional, and consequently can be studied with the traditional methods, or with the refinements described by Baer. Furthermore, if they are weak reciprocal interactions, there is again no problem because they can also be understood through the usual methods. The problem is strong reciprocal interactions, which are unitized structures that cannot be analyzed (broken down) into component processes. To deal with them, one must take a different, nonexperimental approach. An example is in Piaget's work on intelligence (for discussion of the relevant issues, see Overton, 1973). Interest shifts from the behavior of individual components to the behavior of the whole. For example, mother-infant attachment can "be regarded as characteristic of neither the mother nor the infant, but as a structural property of mother-child interactions" (Hartup & Lempers, 1973, p. 242; italics deleted).

The question of whether or not there are strong reciprocal interactions in a given domain is a factual matter. The organismic approach is intended to detect them directly, if they exist; but in the operant approach and the other experimental approaches they would appear as anomalies in experimental outcomes and would be unexplainable within the paradigm (Kuhn, 1962). Thus, if there are no strong reciprocal interactions in the domain of interest — in social episodes, for example — the operant approach and the other experimental approaches are, in principle, fully adequate. However, if there are strong reciprocal interactions in the domain of interest, these experimental approaches must fall short of yielding complete understanding.

ACKNOWLEDGMENTS

We are indebted to Dr. Donald M. Baer for an extensive and very useful commentary occasioned by an earlier version of this paper. We are also indebted to Dr. Willis F. Overton, whose discussions with one of us (HWR) were instrumental in the development of many of our analyses, especially in the section on the active organism.

REFERENCES

Baer, D. M. The organism as host. In H. W. Reese (Chair), Conceptions of the 'active organism.' *Human Development*, 1976, *19*, 87-98.

Baltes, P. B. Prototypical paradigms and questions in life-span research on development and aging. *Gerontologist*, 1973, *13*, 458-467.

Bell, R. Q. A reinterpretation of the direction of effects in studies of socialization. *Psychological Review, 1968, 75,* 81-91.

Berberich, J. P. Do the child's responses shape the teaching behavior of adults? *Journal of Experimental Research in Personality, 1971, 5,* 92-97.

Bergmann, G. *Philosophy of science.* Madison, Wis.: University of Wisconsin Press, 1957.

Bijou, S. W. What psychology has to offer education – now. *Journal of Applied Behavior Analysis, 1970, 3,* 65-71.

Bijou, S. W. Informal panel discussion. In P. B. Baltes & L. R. Goulet (Chair), *Strategies for the analysis and explication of age changes.* Symposium presented at the meeting of the Society for Research in Child Development, Minneapolis, April 1971.

Bilbrey, J., & Winokur, S. Control for and constraints on autoshaping. *Journal of the Experimental Analysis of Behavior, 1973, 20,* 323-332.

Breland, K., & Breland, M. The misbehavior of organisms. *American Psychologist, 1961, 16,* 681-684.

Brown, J. S. *The motivation of behavior.* New York: McGraw-Hill, 1961.

Brown, P. L., & Jenkins, H. M. Autoshaping the pigeon's key peck. *Journal of the Experimental Analysis of Behavior, 1968, 11,* 1-8.

Bunge, M. *Causality: The place of the causal principle in modern science.* New York: World Publishing Co., 1963.

Catania, A. C. The psychologies of structure, function, and development. *American Psychologist, 1973, 28,* 434-443.

Dobzhansky, T. *Evolution, genetics, and man.* New York: Wiley, 1955.

Engberg, L. A., Hansen, G., Welker, R. L., & Thomas, D. R. Acquisition of keypecking via autoshaping as a function of prior experience: "Learned laziness"? *Science, 1972, 178,* 1002-1004.

Gamzu, E., & Williams, D. R. Classical conditioning of a complex skeletal response. *Science, 1971, 171,* 923-925.

Gamzu, E. R., Williams, D. R., & Schwartz, B. Pitfalls of organismic concepts: "Learned laziness"? *Science, 1973, 181,* 367-368.

Gewirtz, J. L. On designing the functional environment of the child to facilitate behavioral development. In L. L. Dittman (Ed.), *Early child care: The new perspectives.* New York: Atherton, 1968.

Gewirtz, J. L. Conditional responding as a paradigm for observational, imitative learning and vicarious-reinforcement. In H. W. Reese (Ed.), *Advances in child development and behavior* (Vol. 6). New York: Academic Press, 1971.

Goetz, E. M., & Baer, D. M. Descriptive social reinforcement of "creative" block building by young children. In E. A. Ramp & B. I. Hopkins (Eds.), *A new direction for education: Behavior analysis 1971.* Lawrence, Kansas: The University of Kansas Support and Development Center for Follow Through, 1971.

Goldiamond, J. A diary of self-modification. *Psychology Today, 1973,* November, 95-102.

Goldfried, M. R., & Merbaum, M. (Eds.). *Behavior change through self-control.* New York: Holt, Rinehart & Winston, 1973.

Hays, W. L. *Statistics.* New York: Holt, Rinehart & Winston, 1963.

Hartup, W. W., & Lempers, J. A problem in life-span development: The interactional analysis of family attachments. In P. B. Baltes & K. W. Schaie (Eds.), *Life-span developmental psychology: Personality and socialization.* New York: Academic Press, 1973.

Herrnstein, R. J. Method and theory in the study of avoidance. *Psychological Review, 1969, 76,* 49-69.

Herrnstein, R. J. On the law of effect. *Journal of the Experimental Analysis of Behavior, 1970, 13,* 243-266.

Hill, W. F. *Learning: A survey of psychological interpretations.* San Francisco: Chandler, 1963.

Kazdin, A. E., & Bootzin, R. B. The token economy: An evaluative review. *Journal of Applied Behavior Analysis,* 1972, *5,* 343-372.

Krasner, L. The behavioral scientist and social responsibility. *Journal of Social Issues,* 1965, *21,* 9-30.

Kuhn, T. S. *The structure of scientific revolutions.* Chicago: University of Chicago Press, 1962.

Millenson, J. R. *Principles of behavioral analysis.* New York: MacMillan, 1967.

Osofsky, J., & O'Connell, E. J. Parent-child interaction: Daughters' effects upon mothers' and fathers' behaviors. *Developmental Psychology,* 1972, *7,* 157-168.

Overton, W. F. On the assumptive base of the nature-nurture controversy: Additive versus interactive conceptions. *Human Development,* 1973, *16,* 74-89.

Overton, W. F., & Reese, H. W. Models of development: Methodological implications. In J. R. Nesselroade & H. W. Reese (Eds.), *Life-span developmental psychology: Methodological issues.* New York: Academic Press, 1973.

Patterson, G. R., & Cobb, J. A. Stimulus control for classes of noxious behavior. In J. F. Knutson (Ed.), *The control of aggression: Implications from basic research.* Chicago: Aldine, 1973.

Pepper, S. C. *World hypotheses: A study in evidence.* Berkeley, Cal.: University of California Press, 1942.

Powers, W. T. Behaviorism and feedback control. *Science,* 1973, *181,* 1116-1120. (Letter)

Reese, H. W. The study of covert verbal and nonverbal mediation. In A. Jacobs & L. B. Sachs (Eds.), *The psychology of private events: Perspectives on covert response systems.* New York: Academic Press, 1971.

Reese, H. W. Behaviorism and feedback control. *Science,* 1973, *181,* 1114-1116. (Letter)

Reese, H. W., & Overton, W. F. Models of development and theories of development. In L. R. Goulet & P. B. Baltes (Eds.), *Life-span developmental psychology: Research and theory.* New York: Academic Press, 1970.

Reynolds, G. S., Catania, C. S., & Skinner, B. F. Conditioned and unconditioned aggression in pigeons. *Journal of the Experimental Analysis of Behavior,* 1963, *6,* 73-74.

Rheingold, H. L. The social and socializing infant. In D. Goslin (Ed.), *Handbook of socialization theory and research.* Chicago: Rand McNally, 1969.

Riegel, K. F. Developmental psychology and society: Some historical and ethical considerations. In J. R. Nesselroade & H. W. Reese (Eds.), *Life-span developmental psychology: Methodological issues.* New York: Academic Press, 1973.

Seligman, M. On the generality of laws of learning. *Psychological Review,* 1970, *77,* 406-418.

Sherman, J. A. Imitation and language development. In H. W. Reese (Ed.), *Advances in child development and behavior* (Vol. 6). New York: Academic Press, 1971.

Shimp, C. P. Optimal behavior in free-operant experiments. *Psychological Review,* 1969, *76,* 97-112.

Skinner, B. F. The design of cultures. *Daedalus,* 1961, *90,* 534-546.

Skinner, B. F. *Science and human behavior.* New York: Free Press, 1965.

Skinner, B. F. What is the experimental analysis of behavior? *Journal of the Experimental Analysis of Behavior,* 1966, *9,* 213-218.

Skinner, B. F. *Beyond freedom and dignity.* Westminster, Md.: Knopf, 1971.

Skinner, B. F. Self-control. In M. R. Goldfried & M. Merbaum (Eds.), *Behavior change through self-control.* New York: Holt, Rinehart & Winston, 1973.

Taylor, C. *The explanation of behavior.* New York: Humanities Press, 1964.

Terrace, H. S. Stimulus control. In W. K. Honig (Ed.), *Operant behavior: Areas of research and application.* New York: Appleton-Century-Crofts, 1966.

Tharp, R. G., & Wetzel, R. J. *Behavior modification in the natural environment.* New York: Academic Press, 1969.

Welker, R. L., Hansen, G., Engberg, L. A., & Thomas, D. R. Untitled reply to Gamzu, Williams, and Schwartz. *Science,* 1973, *181,* 368-369.

Werkmeister, W. H. *An introduction to critical thinking.* Lincoln, Nebraska: Johnsen, 1948.

Zeiler, M. D. Superstitious behavior in children: An experimental analysis. In H. W. Reese (Ed.), *Advances in child development and behavior* (Vol. 7). New York: Academic Press, 1972.

3

Maternal Responding and the Conditioning of Infant Crying: Directions of Influence within the Attachment-Acquisition Process

Jacob L. Gewirtz

National Institute of Mental Health
Bethesda, Maryland

INTRODUCTION

In this chapter I discuss attachment, as metaphor and as process. I then survey some behavioral criteria of attachment, in particular cued-infant crying. Following that, I discuss the highly influential but ultimately uninterpretable report by Bell and Ainsworth (1972), showing an inverse relation between maternal responding to infant crying and subsequent infant crying. That report's questionable conclusion (as will become apparent) serves as my point of departure for considering how operant crying can enter the human infant's (interaction) repertory, how it can be maintained, modified, eliminated, or come under discriminative control, and how, in the process of its conditioning, cued crying can come to control diverse concurrent maternal responses to that infant. Finally, I consider how the conditioning of that cued operant crying (or, for that matter, the conditioning of various cued responses) can index the acquisition of a focused attachment.

However, before beginning my analysis, it is best that I share with the reader the dilemma I face, of how to manage the presentation of the topics just listed. My unease stems from the fact that I am attempting to blend concepts and phenomena from two social-development literatures that, for most, have been separate, involving very different foci, analytic levels, and data bases. Thus, the global and abstract "attachment" concept has been used variably, has been denoted by different numbers of diverse criterion response indicators, and indeed to some has implied an "under-the-skin" structural basis. By contrast, the arena of maternal responding to infant crying for the most part has involved considerations at the level of direct stimulus control over responding, where the functional relations may be referred to the operant-conditioning paradigm but not routinely to a superordinate global concept like attachment or mother love. My problem of presentation here is complicated further by the fact that child-rearing values may enter to confound the two conceptual foci of attachment and responding to infant crying. Against this background, those of my points that would be novel for the readers of one literature could be commonplace for the readers of the other literature (and vice versa). Regrettably, all I can do is share this concern with my readers and ask for their patience.

ATTACHMENT: METAPHOR AND PROCESS

In this analysis, the *attachment* metaphor is synonymous with the terms "affectional bond," "tie," and "object relationship." In his evaluation of Freud's theory of object choice, Robert Sears (1943) employed the term "attachment" extensively for children's differential relations ("cathexes") to their parents. However, the attachment term did not come into consensual use until after 1958 when Bowlby used it to characterize the child's tie to the mother. In my own approach, "attachment," as in physical bonding, has stood as a convenient metaphor for aspects of the close reliance (often reciprocal) of one individual upon another, expressed in a variety of cued-response patterns. This reliance may involve such pairs as mother and child, wife and husband, lover and loved one, child and child, person and animal and, on rare occasions, even person and inanimate object or place. Specifically, I have applied the attachment concept to one individual's involvement in what is typically a two-person, sequenced, mutual-influence process in which that individual's responses have come under the control of cue (discriminative) and reinforcing stimuli provided by the appearance and responses of another person (Gewirtz, 1961, 1972c, e).

In the literature of early human social development, the term "attachment" can only be interpreted as a label for a complex of child-response patterns controlled by the discriminative (cue) and reinforcing stimulus characteristics of the behaviors of an adult, usually the mother or main caregiver, termed the primary attachment "figure" or "object." Thus, an attachment can be denoted by the occurrence of child responses under the control of stimuli from the attachment figure, and by the child maintaining proximity to that person. The attachment metaphor has been used also to order concurrent manifestations of that control process. Hence, it has been denoted by the child's differential responding to the attachment figure, or by emotional behaviors, like crying, when separated from the figure or upon that figure's preparations to depart, or even by an increase of the child's explorations of strange objects or places in the figure's presence (Gewirtz, 1972e). In that same social-development literature, the attachment term has also served occasionally to order adult-response patterns under the control of a child's behaviors (e.g., Gewirtz, 1961). The stimulus-response functions ordinarily denoting attachment are pervasive. Upon disruption, for instance by separation or rejection, these functions can become highly disorganized and often may be accompanied by intense emotional responding. Hence, increasingly, the wide ranging attachment term has become the central focus of several approaches to social development in humans and animals (Bowlby, 1969, 1973; see also Gewirtz, 1972b, for a survey of five diverse approaches to attachment).

As discussed here and in my own conditioning account of attachment (Gewirtz, 1961, 1972c, e), a specific attachment may be denoted by any one of a variety of child-response patterns under the control of stimuli from the mother or other attachment figure. In addition, the dyadic functional relations labeled attachment are *not* limited to any developmental segment of life or to any particular interaction partners. Moreover, these dyadic functions may involve *several* attachment figures concurrently, and in *any* given time span. At the same time, the initiations these functions imply need not be reciprocated on each occasion by the attachment figure. Further, when a dyadic attachment pattern involving a parent, child, or mate is broken, such as by death or divorce, this conception would encompass the acquisition of new ("replacement") functions with other partners (Gewirtz, 1961). The conditioning conception of attachment I have outlined is entirely open with regard to such issues as whether or not a positive relation is to be expected between the formation of one of a few primary attachments in early life and the later capacity of the individual to enter close interpersonal relationships, for instance as Bowlby (1969) has proposed. There is little systematic information about the origins and course of attachments, and even less about the reciprocal influences of one partner's (e.g., the child's) characteristic behaviors on the behaviors of the other partner (e.g., an adult); or about the relation between the formation of attachments in early life and the capacity in adulthood for developing close personal relationships (Gewirtz, 1972c).

This overview of attachment may be completed with the note that there has been considerable overlap in the theoretical and research literatures between the concepts "attachment" and "dependence" ("dependency") and the cued-response functions ordered by those terms (Gewirtz, 1972b; Maccoby & Masters, 1970). This overlap has been general, notwithstanding the fact that Bowlby (1969) and Ainsworth (e.g., 1972), giving little consideration to the extensive literature generated under the aegis of dependence (e.g., Beller, 1955, 1959; Gewirtz, 1954, 1956; Sears, Whiting, Nowlis, & Sears et al., 1953), separated that term from attachment because of what they took to be its perjorative connotations. The heuristic distinction I have proposed between the two terms accounts for many of the behavioral phenomena in the literature, including those that have denoted dependence. That distinction is determined by whether an individual's responses are under the control of stimuli from a *particular* person — *attachment* — or stimuli offered by any member of some *class* of persons — *dependence.* The latter term would account for responses under close social-stimulus control, but not under the control of stimuli from a particular person.

Ways in which the attachment concept has been, and can be, used were detailed in the preceding discussion. Moreover, the attachment metaphor has served to demonstrate the utility of the operant-conditioning paradigm in the analysis of mother-infant interchange to which that metaphor occasionally has been applied. In this framework, a note about the use of such metaphoric abstractions is in order. Abstract terms like attachment and dependence may be useful on occasion. Such terms may have preliminary utility:

1. in summarizing classes of stimulus-response functions within a wide range, especially when the relevant receptor and effector capacities of the child will undergo developmental changes;

2. in describing different phenotypic stimulus-response functions (or their sequential changes in time) under the same process model; and/or

3. as a preliminary chapter heading.

However, even when useful, such abstract terms carry a burden of surplus meaning. Moreover, their use may be unnecessary, particularly for descriptions of straightforward demonstrations of acquired social stimulus control over instrumental responses. For these reasons, the approach outlined stresses exploration of the underlying data base through the use of concepts tied closely to observable environmental and behavioral events (Gewirtz, 1972c).

CUED CRYING AND CRITERIA OF ATTACHMENT

There have been few constraints on the use of conceptual metaphor of attachment, and investigators and theorists have often differed on the sets of attachment indices (indicators, criteria) they have emphasized. The level of analysis of such indices has often been so remote from the level characterizing the global attachment term, that the need for even using such global terms at all has occasionally been questioned (e.g., Gewirtz, 1972c). At the same time, there are students of attachment who seem uncritically to hold implicit assumptions such as:

1. The various attachment measures that happen to be in use are interchangeable indices of a unitary process.

2. Therefore, they should be highly intercorrelated (in principle, perfectly).

3. The coefficients comprising a single intercorrelation matrix of these indices should characterize *all* subjects and *all* situations.

By contrast, consider the suggestion that almost *any* response cued by stimuli from another person serves as a direct criterion of attachment to that other, in *any* segment of the life span; and that diverse patterns of disorganization (including withdrawal and avoidance) and/or concomitant emotion brought on by interference with those discriminated-response systems also serve as attachment criteria, albeit as potentially less efficient ones because they are indirect (Gewirtz, 1961, 1969, 1972e).

Attachment theorists have emphasized the infant's behavior with reference to the mother (or other main caregiver), who is assumed typically to be the main attachment figure for the infant. In particular, attention has focused on the infant's behavior when the mother makes preparation to, or actually does, move away ultimately to remain in view or separate ultimately to disappear from view. Thus, Bowlby (1969) has proposed than an infant's attachment may be "activated" when the mother moves away or disappears from view, and Ainsworth (e.g., 1972) has been concerned with conditions (like distance from mother) that serve to "activate" attachment behavior. In this context, infant responses to conditions of departure and separation, particularly cries, have provided the basis for attachment indicators often employed in research.

Crying (including fussing, whimpering, and whining) has been conceived as stimulating a mother to come into closer proximity with her infant; and, like various other behaviors, crying is said to become focused on an attachment figure (Bowlby, 1958, 1969; Bell & Ainsworth, 1972). Hence, crying in particular contexts, for instance upon signs of a mother's departure (Schaffer & Emerson, 1964) or upon a stranger's approach (Ainsworth, 1967, 1972; Yarrow, 1967, 1972), has customarily served as an attachment criterion. Indeed, on occasion crying has been the sole attachment index employed, for instance when cued by separation (Schaffer & Emerson, 1964). Given the consensual emphasis on this attachment index, it becomes important for any theoretical conception to inquire how *any* cues from caregivers could come to control responses such as crying in the human infant's repertory, how they could be maintained, modified, or eliminated, and generally how they are related to the attachment metaphor. (This inquiry is of course axiomatic for a conditioning approach to attachment.) At the same time, crying can serve to exemplify how *any* attachment behavior cued by *any* attachment figure is acquired in *any* segment of the life span (Gewirtz, 1961, 1972a, e).

CRYING AND THE ANOMALOUS BELL AND AINSWORTH (1972) FINDING

In 1972, Bell and Ainsworth reported that maternal responding to infant crying interacted with that crying. Their report bears directly on the determinants of infant crying as well as on attachment, and relates to my own analysis of such crying and its relevance to attachment. From patterns of correlations across the 4 quarters of the first year of life, derived from longitudinal observations of 26 mother-infant pairs, Bell and Ainsworth reported that consistent and prompt maternal responding to infant crying was associated with a reduction in the frequency and duration of infant crying in later time quarters.

Bell and Ainsworth (1972, pp. 1187-1188) referred this finding to the "popular belief" that, under the instrumental-learning paradigm, contingent maternal responding should reinforce (increase) infant crying and maternal failure to respond contingently should extinguish (decrease) that crying (see also Ainsworth, 1972, 1973). Thus Bell and Ainsworth (1972) concluded that their ". . . findings clearly indicated that the processes implicit in a decrease in crying must be more complex than these popular extrapolations from learning theory would suggest" [p. 1188], and accompanied this with the interpretation that contingent maternal responding did not promote those demanding and dependent behaviors that denote the "spoiled child." The Bell and Ainsworth report has often been cited (e.g., Hinde, 1974) or reprinted (e.g., Rebelsky & Dorman, 1973).

It has long been implicitly assumed in the child-care literature that proper caregiving requires that the caregiver respond to alleviate the physical distress apparently underlying the types of crying termed "elicited," "unconditioned," or "expressive." In that same literature it has also been assumed that consistent caregiver responding to nonelicited infant crying could foster that very crying and thus "spoil" the child. Here the implicit emphasis has been on nondistress or operant infant crying and its considerable potential for controlling caregiver behavior. Thus, it is not difficult to see the potential for great practical appeal to parents and other caregivers of a finding like the one highlighted in the Bell and Ainsworth (1972, p. 1171) report, that responding to any infant crying actually reduces its incidence: one simple rule then could govern caregiver responding to *all* infant crying. But that report has also been conceptually provocative, apparently because many have assumed, with Bell and Ainsworth, that its conclusion contradicts standard expectations under the operant-learning paradigm, notwithstanding the fact that Bell and Ainsworth did not distinguish between elicited distress crying and operant crying. Thus, Sutton-Smith (1973) counterposed that finding to a demonstration by Etzel and Gewirtz (1967) that high-rate infant operant crying decreased systematically when caregivers ceased responding to the crying and instead responded contingently to eye contacting and smiling.

The Bell and Ainsworth conclusion has also provided a more general basis for questioning operant-conditioning accounts of infant social learning, beyond those involving crying (e.g., Bijou, 1974; Bijou & Baer, 1965; Gewirtz, 1969, 1971a, b, 1972c, d). And when used in arguments over the differential adequacy of theoretical accounts, it has played a central role in the wider frame of the competition among conceptual and applied approaches to social development, both scientific and popular. Hence, such theorists as Stone and Church (1973), routinely unsympathetic with conditioning accounts of social development, interpreted the Bell and Ainsworth finding as indicating that ". . . responding to a baby's crying does not reinforce and so increase crying, but instead reduces it" [p. 117]. Stone and Church (1973) used this interpretation contentiously to support their conclusion that operant-conditioning principles, ". . . while highly useful and correct for application to a narrow range of conditions, are inadequate and irrelevant for much of the important learning that goes on in life" [p. 117]. Given their sweeping indictment of an operant-conditioning approach, it is remarkable that those critics failed to explain why the Bell and Ainsworth finding they welcomed so warmly should prevail over any other outcome.

Thus, also, the Bell and Ainsworth conclusion, paraphrased as ". . . the babies whose mothers always responded promptly cried less than the infants whose cries were often ignored," was the explicit basis of popularized pediatric advice given by a syndicated physician-columnist (Kapel, 1974) to newspaper-reading parents: "My advice to mothers is to respond to crying even when it's frequent. It is the infant's strongest language, and it expresses needs, not hostility or a demand to be spoiled" [p. 12A]. Based on the reported Bell and Ainsworth finding, Kapel's prescription assumed that there is no such thing as too much attention to a crying baby. He held that "slavish" attention would not spoil a baby (which in this context I take to mean would not increase the baby's crying rate).

Thus far I have discussed the concept of attachment and the relation between the attachment process and cued crying. I have noted that various writers have used the prominent Bell and Ainsworth conclusion that maternal nonresponding fosters later infant crying, not only to impeach conditioning analyses and a conditioning analysis of crying in particular, but also more generally to support nonlearning-based approaches to social development. At the same time, these critics have not articulated a plausible theoretical basis for the expectation that the outcome reported by Bell and Ainsworth that they welcomed should prevail over any other outcome. In this context, it becomes necessary to examine closely the bases for the Bell and Ainsworth conclusion, and to consider constructively how a learning conception accounts for various infant-crying patterns that could emerge from different patterns of caregiver responding to crying.

The importance of this analysis stems not only from the need to understand the determinants of crying, but also from the fact that the arena of crying provides a testing ground for the adequacy of an instrumental-learning approach to human social development, given that caregiver responding constitutes a substantial portion of the environment (actual and potential) impinging upon the infant in early life. My conceptual analysis begins in the next section, in which I examine the published correlation matrices on which Bell and Ainsworth based their interpretation and report that the conclusion those authors drew, that maternal responding to any infant crying reduced the incidence of that crying, was unwarranted.

The Bell and Ainsworth Report was Indeterminate on the Direction of Effects and as an Operant-Conditioning Account and Unwarranted on Maternal Responding Reducing Infant Crying

Between quarters, Bell and Ainsworth (1972, Tables 3 and 4) used rank correlations (rhos) to intercorrelate their frequency and duration measures for the maternal *ignoring* of infant crying and total infant crying. In this endeavor, the measures for later time quarters were conceived to be the dependent variables and those for earlier quarters the independent variables. Thus, the dependent variables were total infant crying (for rhos tabled below the diagonal of their Tables 3 and 4) and maternal ignoring of infant crying (for rhos tabled above that diagonal). (Because their Table 5 involved variables that were not fully described and results that seemed indeterminate, its data are not considered here.)

Some Limitations of Method

At least three independent technical problems limit the interpretability of the Bell and Ainsworth correlations and, therefore, raise questions about the conclusions drawn from those correlations. These are: (1) the problem of intercorrelating measures that are intrinsically contingent; (2) the problem of determining Type-I-error levels for intercorrelations correlated within and between matrices; and (3) the absence of important statistical controls for the effects of relevant antecedent and concurrent determinants of the two sets of outcome variables. A fourth technical problem, considered in the next section, involves the meanings of the variables that entered the correlations on which the main Bell and Ainsworth conclusion depended.

The *first* technical limitation is that there was a special dependence between infant and mother variables that qualified the validity and meaning of the Bell and Ainsworth correlations. A mother could neither respond to, nor ignore, her infant's crying *until* the infant actually cried, making the scoring of both maternal responses a contingent function of infant crying.

A *second* technical limitation is that there was a lack of independence of the correlations within and between Table 3 and Table 4. All rhos were based on the same mother-infant pairs, and thus the within-infant and within-mother frequency and duration measures were likely to be correlated as alternative indices of the same process. Further, each infant or mother frequency or duration measure defining a table row or column was involved in every correlation in that row or column, yielding correlated intercorrelations. Therefore these inherent correlations within and between tables must have inflected in an unknown way the Type-I-error probabilities, generated on the assumption of independence among correlation coefficients, that were used by Bell and Ainsworth for determining the significance of the coefficients of Tables 3 and 4. On this basis, their decisions about significance levels and their interpretations based on them are suspect.

A *third* limitation of the Bell and Ainsworth correlations is due to the absence of control over antecedent and concurrent variables (other than the earlier-quarter independent variables) that could have determined each of their two sets of dependent variables (of their Tables 3 and 4). Because those uncontrolled variables entered some of the reported correlations, their scores were available. Specifically, where total infant crying constitutd the dependent variable and earlier-quarter maternal ignoring of crying the independent variable, it was important to control for the effects of same-quarter maternal ignoring and earlier-quarter total infant crying; and where maternal ignoring of crying constituted the dependent variable and earlier-quarter total infant crying the independent variable, it was important to control for the effects of same-quarter infant crying and earlier-quarter maternal ignoring. (These procedures would likely have required separating the two components of the total infant-crying variable, infant crying that the mother *ignored* and infant crying to which the mother *responded*.) Uncontrolled, those variables determined the behavior outcomes to an unknown extent and thus compromise the interpretability of the rank correlations Bell and Ainsworth presented.

Although the number (26) of mother-infant pairs in the Bell and Ainsworth sample may have been marginal for the efficient use of parametric regression procedures, such partial- or multiple-correlation techniques exist and might have been used to provide a degree of statistical control over at least some of the variables left uncontrolled. However, the use by Bell and Ainsworth of non-parametric rank correlations precluded the use of such statistical-control procedures, leaving compromised the interpretation of their published rhos.

I have noted the problem of intercorrelations between Bell and Ainsworth measures that are intrinsically contingent and the problem of determining Type-I-error levels for intercorrelations correlated within and between matrices. I have noted also the absence of some important controls in their analysis for the effects of relevant antecedent and concurrent determinants of the two outcome variables, total infant crying and maternal ignoring of crying. These reservations about the rank-order correlations under consideration are important, as is the issue of the meaning of those correlations that I raise later in this section when I question the Bell and Ainsworth assumption that maternal responding to crying is the inverse of maternal ignoring of crying. Apart from this last point, I question the correlations no further on technical ground, leaving such issues to the formal critique (Gewirtz & Boyd, in press-a). In the remainder of this chapter, I treat as definitive the conclusion that Bell and Ainsworth drew from the correlational data, to facilitate my didactic analysis.

On the Direction of Effects

From trends in several arrays of nonparametric rank correlations across the four quarters of the first year of life, Bell and Ainsworth (1972) concluded that there was a pattern of positive relation (for frequency and duration measures) between their variables maternal ignoring of infant crying and later infant crying. From this, those authors deduced that a mother's responding to her infant's crying in earlier quarters *reduced* that infant's subsequent crying. With regard specifically to the direction of effects, Bell and Ainsworth (1972, p. 1180) emphasized the hypothesis supported by this result pattern over the hypothesis that infant crying in earlier time quarters *increased* later maternal responding to crying. The latter hypothesis was also supported by patterns of positive correlation. However, Bell and Ainsworth (1972, p. 1181) also have written of an interaction of effects that complicates the directional picture as it implies a pattern of mutual influence between mother and infant.

Boyd and I (Gewirtz & Boyd, in press-a) have addressed ourselves specifically to the direction-of-effects issue in a recent report. We examined the published Bell and Ainsworth between-quarter rank-correlation matrices as a whole, as well as pairs of corresponding coefficients for trends favoring one or the other of these direction-of-effects hypotheses. Routine criteria of statistical inference indicated that the direction of effects could not be determined definitively from the Bell and Ainsworth between-quarter correlations of maternal ignoring and infant crying. The patterns of positive correlation found were compatible with both the mother-influences-infant and the infant-influences-mother hypotheses.

Does Maternal Responding Really Decrease Infant Crying?

A fourth technical problem with the Bell and Ainsworth rank-order correlations involves the meanings of the variables entering the coefficients on which their main conclusion depended. At issue is the Bell and Ainsworth assumption that maternal responding to crying is actually the inverse of maternal ignoring of crying. Bell and Ainsworth have emphasized that their between-quarter correlations for frequency and duration measures indicate a pattern of *positive* relation between the maternal *ignoring* of infant crying and subsequent infant crying. However, from this apparent pattern of relation, those authors concluded that maternal *responding* to infant crying inversely determined subsequent infant crying. It is the validity of this conclusion from their published correlational data that I question in this section.

Bell and Ainsworth neither presented nor discussed the between-quarter correlations of their variables maternal *responding* to infant crying and infant crying. Yet, apparently as a corollary of their main conclusion involving only the maternal *ignoring* of crying, those authors concluded that "consistency and promptness of maternal *response* is associated with decline in frequency and duration of infant crying [Bell & Ainsworth, 1972, p. 1171, my italics]." In effect, they treated the variable maternal responding to crying as the *inverse* of the orthogonally-defined variable, maternal ignoring of crying, as if the two frequency scores involved had been converted to proportions of their sum before the maternal ignoring variable was correlated with infant crying between quarters. However, the Bell and Ainsworth (1972, pp. 1174-1176) description of their data-analysis methods nowhere indicated that such a procedure was implemented. Hence, on the assumption that the quarterly frequency scores of maternal responding to, and maternal ignoring of, crying were free to vary independently, and in the absence in their paper of an empirical between-quarter analysis of the actual relation between maternal responding and infant crying, the question must be raised whether maternal ignoring and maternal responding are inversely related. This question is particularly appropriate in view of the *positive* within-quarter pattern of relation between the maternal-responding and maternal-ignoring variables.

Bell and Ainsworth termed the within-quarter correlations of their Tables 3 and 4 a pattern of *positive* relation between infant crying and maternal ignoring of infant crying, for each of the last three-quarters of the first year. However, to establish the variables infant crying and maternal ignoring of crying as independent in this within-quarter analysis, Bell and Ainsworth defined as infant crying the frequency/duration *only* of those crying episodes to which the mother *responded.* Given this definition, the within-quarter correlation pattern is, operationally, a *positive* relation between mothers' *ignoring* of, and *responding* to, their infants' crying. That is, the more a mother ignores her infant's cries, the more she also responds to her infant's cries. (I have already indicated that both maternal responses were direct functions of the infants' crying.) I noted earlier that, between quarters, there is a pattern of positive relation between mothers' ignoring of crying and total infant crying. Hence, although each correlation accounts for less than one-half of the common variance of the pair of variates involved, their pattern nevertheless suggests other plausible organizations of the Bell and Ainsworth between-quarter data.

As earlier indicated, Bell's and Ainsworth's organization of their published between-quarter data was that there is a *positive* relation between maternal ignoring and total infant crying and a *negative* relation between maternal responding and total infant crying. In the absence of actual between-quarter correlations of maternal responding and total infant crying and of maternal responding to, and ignoring of, infant crying, and given the *positive* within-quarter correlation pattern between the latter two variables, one alternative view is simply that, between-quarters, there may be a *positive* relation between total infant crying and maternal *responding* to infant crying, rather than the negative relation Bell and Ainsworth assumed. In the same vein, another seemingly more complete way of organizing the published Bell and Ainsworth between-quarter correlations is also possible. There is a positive relation between maternal responding to, and ignoring of, infant crying; and there is a positive relation between maternal responding to infant crying and subsequent crying, and also between maternal ignoring of infant crying and subsequent crying.

I have noted that Bell and Ainsworth nowhere presented the actual between-quarter correlations of maternal responding with maternal ignoring or of maternal responding with total infant crying. In this context, my suggested organizations of their correlational data, that diverge so sharply from the one they advanced, are proposed as plausible and parsimonious alternatives for their data as published in 1972. Of course, the empirical relation between earlier maternal responding to crying and infant crying that is at issue here could be determined readily by Bell and Ainsworth from their data. Hopefully, for this determination there would be controls implemented for as many of the following factors as possible: concurrent responding to, and ignoring of, (the dependent variable) infant crying, and earlier infant crying and the ignoring of that crying (factors concurrent with the independent variable, maternal responding to crying). Until then, it is hoped that Bell's and Ainsworth's main conclusion about maternal responding reducing infant crying, impeached by the multiple reservations raised so far in this chapter as well as in the next section and by Gewirtz and Boyd (in press-a), would be overtaken and arrested in the numerous places in which that conclusion has been reported, reprinted, and/or built on.

Bell's and Ainsworth's Data are Remote from the Requirements of an Operant-Learning Account

I have described how Stone and Church (1973) used the Bell and Ainsworth conclusion to impeach operant-learning theory, on the assumption that the procedures on which that conclusion was based could provide data at the level of precision required for an operant analysis. It is recalled also that Bell and Ainsworth (1972) attributed to popular belief the extrapolation from learning theory that maternal responding should be a positive reinforcer for *any* infant crying and therefore that an instrumental-learning model would predict an increase in infant crying due to maternal responding, rather than the decrease those authors thought was apparent in their data. Therefore, it is instructive to sketch how elementary reinforcement-schedule and -latency conditions provided by contingent maternal responding might determine infant-crying patterns. In this process, I can examine the relevance of the summary variables Bell and Ainsworth employed for demonstrating conditioning contingencies between maternal responding and infant crying. Under an operant-conditioning paradigm together with such environmental variables inevitable to that paradigm, as schedule and latency of reinforcement brought about by caregiver responding, various infant-crying patterns would be plausible outcomes, including the pattern emphasized by Bell and Ainsworth. These outcomes would depend entirely on the specific reinforcement-history pattern for the response that occurred in each instance.

In the operant-conditioning frame, numerous definitions are possible for stimuli and responses in a behavior arena. A functional analysis is a method for examining the relationships, if any, between particular sets of definitions of these terms. It requires a systematic change in the rate (or some other measure) of a behavior event (the response) under a set of definitions for that response and the event contingent on it. The conditioning denoted confirms the functional utility of the series of category definitions developed, and leads to the contingent event being termed the reinforcing stimulus (or reinforcer) for the behavioral event that is termed the response. In connection with this last point, it is useful to keep in mind that the reinforcement conception implies nothing more than that there exist events which, when made contingent on behaviors, will change systematically the rates of some of them (that is, of responses). Thus, reinforcing stimuli (reinforcers) need not exist under all (or even many) conditions for every response; a contingent event that can reinforce one response need not serve as a reinforcer for that response under all other contextual-setting conditions, nor for another response; and the fact that an event functions as a reinforcing stimulus in one stimulus context does not preclude its functioning in different stimulus roles in other contexts (Gewirtz, 1971b, 1972f).

I have noted that a response and its reinforcing stimulus are defined functionally by systematic changes in some attribute of the response (for instance, its rate) when the stimulus is presented contingent on it, compared to when the stimulus is not so presented. On this basis, there can be defined a great variety of potential operant classes of infant crying and of stimuli provided by maternal-response contingencies on that crying, including combinations of such crying attributes as latency, duration, and intensity. Thus, crying or short of long duration, or short but consistently intense crying, may comprise the response class on which the reinforcing maternal behavior is consistently contingent. Alternatively, a mother may respond only to precursors of crying or to noncrying responses (as on a DRO schedule), but never to crying itself. At the same time, diverse definitions of maternal responses involving combinations of these same attributes may function to provide discriminative (cue) and/or reinforcing stimuli for diverse classes of infant-crying responses. To simplify the exemplary cases that follow, it is assumed that a particular infant-crying response class constitutes a functional unit, that a mother will respond consistently and contingently to that class, and that the maternal response will, according to some schedule, provide reinforcing stimuli for crying responses in that class.

One responsive mother may shape effectively her infant's loud, lengthy cries by ignoring both short, low-intensity precursors of crying and short, low-intensity cries, and by responding expeditiously only to high-intensity, long-duration cries. A second responsive mother may shape the short low-intensity cries of her infant by ignoring both the precursors of crying and lengthy, loud cries, while she responds rapidly and decisively only to short, low-intensity cries. In yet another contrast, a third responsive mother may foster behavior incompatible with her infant's crying; she may respond with dispatch only to short, low-intensity precursors of her infant's crying and/or to noncrying responses, to rear a child who cries rarely (and then mainly when painful events elicit crying). Each of these three interaction patterns (and various other patterns) could contribute to a *positive* correlation between infant crying and maternal ignoring of crying, much like the pattern Bell and Ainsworth (1972) reported. However, the *process* denoted by the functional relations between infant and mother behaviors would be very different for each case. Additional comments on how variegated reinforcement histories for infant crying might all contribute to a positive correlation between infant crying and maternal ignoring of crying are made in a subsequent section on patterns of maternal responding to crying.

Even in the best of circumstances, the goal of specifying causal relations from correlations is elusive (Gewirtz & Boyd, in press-a). But apart from this generic concern, the preceding examples can illustrate that the correlations between gross behavioral and environmental events that Bell and Ainsworth present summarize configurations that omit the details required for determining the relevance or irrelevance of an operant-learning account. These details include the definition of the class of crying responses; whether that definition was used consistently; whether maternal responding was contingent; the latency distribution and consistency of that responding; and the like. Thus, it is not constructive to use such data as Bell's and Ainsworth's, remote from the level of precision required by an operant-learning account, to test the value of such an account.

This is *not* to agree with the earlier-quoted statement of Stone and Church (1973, p. 117) that the phenomenon *occurs* only under highly restrictive conditions. Indeed, the phenomenon is seen in very commonly achieved conditions. However, it is *understood* for what it is only under highly specified conditions.

The next section details how instrumental-conditioning concepts order the effects of diverse maternal-responsiveness patterns on infant crying in early life and, more specifically, how cued operant crying patterns could be acquired, maintained, eliminated, and/or brought under discriminative control by different maternal-responding patterns.

THE CONDITIONING OF CRYING

Assumptions Underlying an Operant Analysis

A distinction has sometimes been made between *respondent* (reflexive, expressive) crying originally elicited by unconditioned stimuli, and *operant* (instrumental, communicative) crying originally emitted in the absence of identified antecedent stimuli and maintained by its stimulus consequences. Under this paradigm distinction, in the early months of life it might be assumed that contingent caregiver responding to these two types of crying could result in diametrically opposite outcomes. Contingent caregiver responding would not affect elicited crying responses, but could raise the rates of nonelicited, operant crying responses. For my analysis in this chapter, I disregard this distinction between respondent and operant. crying. Instead, I emphasize only the conditioning of infant operant crying, for several reasons:

1. Insofar as they have been distinguished, respondents and operants often appear to occur in the same situations and frequently both can be affected by the same operations (Bijou & Baer, 1965).

2. Recent experimental and theoretical analyses have blurred the meaningfulness of a distinction between the respondent and operant conditioning paradigms (see, for example, Catania, 1971; Gewirtz, 1969, p. 94; Miller, 1969).

3. I note that where behaviors (such as crying) have been scrutinized at all, the definition of a respondent (when employed) has often been a negative one: if a behavior is *not* shown to be under the control of its consequences, or if it cannot be brought readily under that control, then it might be labeled *respondent;* otherwise it would likely be termed *operant*.

While it is easy enough to show consequence control (when it exists), it is indeed difficult to show that there is *no* such, nor can be such, control. Thus, literally, respondents have often been those behaviors not yet shown to be operant. For these reasons, I deal only with operant crying in my analysis. (It is of interest to note that Bell and Ainsworth made a theoretical distinction like ours between "expressive" (respondent) and "communicative" (operant) crying, and similarly did not attempt to maintain that distinction in their empirical analysis.)

In the sections that follow, I consider a variety of possible infant-crying patterns that could be generated by an operant-conditioning paradigm, together with a few of the long-familiar environmental variables that are inevitable to that paradigm, in particular the schedule and the latency of reinforcement. As noted earlier, several theorists have conceived mistakenly that the kind of research procedures Bell and Ainsworth used could yield data relevant to a functional-conditioning analysis. It is therefore instructive to sketch how the elementary (reinforcement) schedule and latency conditions provided by maternal responding might determine infant-crying patterns. I sketch also how conditions provided by infant crying might, at the very same time, determine patterns of maternal responding. Highlighting a few routine variables that can affect the conditioning of infant-crying attributes in life settings may illustrate how to conduct a behavioral analysis, the range of outcomes for which that analysis might account, and its potential utility and power.

To simplify this survey, for each case I assume that a particular class of infant-crying responses constitutes a functional unit, that there is present a reinforcing agent who responds consistently and contingently to that class (e.g., a parent), and that the parent's responses, according to some schedule, will provide reinforcing stimuli for the crying responses. Again, a variety of potential definitions of response classes of infant crying and of caregiver-response contingencies can come to mind. These could include combinations of such crying attributes as latency, duration, intensity, and topography or pattern. Precursors to crying, as well as crying itself, may comprise the response class on which the parental reaction that constitutes effective reinforcement is made contingent.

Similarly, various classes of parental responses could be defined by combinations of these same dimensional attributes of latency, duration, intensity, and topography, together with content, and could provide discriminative or reinforcing stimuli to control infant-crying response classes. It is also conceivable that only certain kinds of contingent parental responding would provide reinforcing stimuli. Thus, a parent picking up or briefly holding and rocking the infant, but not the parent speaking quietly to the infant, might reinforce some combination of attributes comprising a crying response class. In the sections that follow, emphasis is placed on contingent maternal responding to units of her infant's crying and on the timing of those maternal responses, rather than on their definitions or definitions of the infant crying-response units involved.[1]

---

[1] After this chapter was written, it was brought to the author's attention that an analysis by Parsley and Rabinowitz (1975) considered the finding reported by Bell and Ainsworth in ways compatible with several of the exemplary cases of this paper.

Patterns of Maternal Responding to Infant Crying

Intermittent schedules of contingent stimulation can produce higher and more stable rates of operant responding than can continuous schedules (Ferster & Skinner, 1957; Schoenfeld, 1970). For the Bell and Ainsworth case, it is conceivable that mothers who often ignored episodes of crying were maintaining certain classes of their infants' crying through intermittent schedules of reinforcement. Under a variety of fixed and variable ratio-based and time-based schedules of contingent maternal responding, an infant would be expected to show relatively high rates of these crying responses. If, in addition to the intermittent basis of their contingent responding, some mothers tended to delay their responding until crying episodes were intense and/or lengthy, stable crying patterns of high frequency and long duration might develop. Such training histories could produce operant crying that was relatively resistant to change. Hence, efforts to ignore those responses (extinction) might not be readily successful, and the mothers involved might continue to respond intermittently to these crying responses.

The thesis is practical because it is readily possible to produce much behavior with little reinforcement or little behavior with much reinforcement, as long as some (relatively short) period of time is allowed for the environmental agency to move from the initial continuous reinforcement (CRF) schedule (probably typical of the original pattern of maternal responding to neonate crying) to the schedule chosen. Some simple exemplary schedules include variable interval (VI), variable ratio (VR), differential reinforcement of high or low rates of responding (DRH or DRL), and differential reinforcement of other (than crying) responses (DRO). In particular, the DRO schedule may have special relevance to the Bell and Ainsworth case, for it is a well-known technique for accomplishing the outcome they reported.

Latency of Contingent Maternal Responding to Infant Crying

Immediacy of stimulus presentation contingent on a response is ordinarily critical in determining the reinforcing efficacy of the stimulus for that response. Thus, a social stimulus that followed immediately a vocal response of 3-month-old infants was an effective reinforcer of that response (Ramey & Ourth, 1971); and a nonsocial visual and auditory event contingent upon a hand-pull of 4- to 7-month-old infants was an effective reinforcer if it followed that response within 2 sec (Millar, 1972). But, in both instances, if the event was delayed 3 or more sec, it did not reinforce the response. As a response becomes established (stabilized) in a setting, the delay between it and its contingent consequence may be increased systematically without a change in its rate. As noted earlier, a mother who usually responds expeditiously to her infant's loud but short-lived crying, and who responds rarely to precrying, to lengthy crying, or to low-intensity crying, would be expected to produce an infant who characteristically emits short, loud crying responses. By the same token, the rapidity of mothers' contingent responding to their infants' protest-fuss precrying responses at 1 month of age would be expected to be correlated with the infants' fussing at 3 months of age, as reported by Moss (1974).

Given the latency criterion in initial conditioning, a maternal response that follows the offset of a crying episode by more than 2 sec may be nonfunctional for the infant's crying, but functional for infant responses other than crying that either follow a crying episode or occur during episodic pauses in crying. Hence, delayed responding to an infant's crying may effectively place that response on a DRO schedule. The DRO schedule calls for reinforcement of behavior — any behavior — other than the target behavior. To apply a DRO schedule to crying, a caregiver would respond contingently on (reinforce) any response other than crying only after a specific interval of noncrying (for example, 30 sec). If crying ever occurred, caregiver responding would cease until there had been a 30-sec noncrying interval, whereupon it would resume at regular 30-sec intervals until crying again occurred. This schedule is often thought of as reinforcement of nontarget behaviors (in this instance, reinforcement of noncrying). If it were used by a mother, observation would show *much* attention to baby and *little* crying by baby. It is the failure to observe the contingency which the DRO (or *any* other) schedule represents that could lead the observer astray. This sketched possibility would represent a triumph of operant-conditioning logic rather than the reverse, and yet would produce the reported Bell and Ainsworth pattern that has been used to impeach the operant-learning conception.

To flesh out this case further, it is conceivable that some mothers credited with frequent responding to crying episodes actually respond often, or only, to such responses as thumbsucking or orienting, evoked by unidentified stimuli or by the distal stimuli of maternal approach. Further, maternal-approach stimuli might acquire discriminative functions for attentive, noncrying infant responses that occasion the appearance of the smiling, soft-spoken mother. These maternal-approach responses in turn may be reinforced by the appearance of the quiet, attentive infant and also serve to cue further infant responses, thus maintaining an interchange of mutual discriminative and reinforcing stimuli for both mother and infant.

Let us put aside for the moment the main Bell and Ainsworth finding, and my technical (rather than theoretical) questioning of it. It is interesting to note that the Bell and Ainsworth way of looking at infant crying occasionally appears compatible with essentials of the learning conception advanced in this chapter. For instance, Bell and Ainsworth had the impression that mothers who responded promptly to their infants' cries tended as well to be sensitively responsive to other infant signals; and that infants of the more responsive mothers were likely to cry less and to acquire more varied modes of communication (Bell & Ainsworth, 1972, pp. 1184-1185). Taking "signals" and "modes of communication" to be responses, this statement may be read as implying that the noncrying responses of those infants were likely to be reinforced differentially. If such an assumption is made, this Bell and Ainsworth conception of infant crying in mother-infant interaction would be compatible also with the Etzel and Gewirtz (1967) finding that infant operant crying decreased systematically when caregivers ceased to respond to this crying and instead responded contingently upon eye contacting and smiling. Even so, my purpose in this chapter is to use the main Bell and Ainsworth finding as the occasion for considering constructively how an instrumental-learning conception might account for the various infant-crying patterns, including the pattern those authors detected, that could emerge from different patterns of caregiver responding to crying. Hence, I note here only that, at a number of points, the Bell and Ainsworth conceptualization may be compatible with the assumptions of a learning approach, and leave it to the interested reader to check out the details of congruence or incongruence.

On An Anomalous Infant-Crying and Maternal-Responding Pattern

In the conditioning context sketched, it is conceivable that some of an infant's characteristic crying patterns would not be affected readily by contingent caregiver responding. In a reciprocal vein, a caregiver's contingent response patterns might not be readily modifiable by contingencies provided by diminutions of her infant's crying. Consider the crying pattern of the baby labeled "colicky." From the mother's perspective, this infant cries inexplicably and is difficult to quiet. The mother initially may be highly responsive to crying, but her interventions are rarely successful (they are not reinforced by the infant's cessation of crying). Given this fairly consistent aversive feedback from an inconsolable infant, the rate of maternal responding would be expected to decrease, unless social intervention (say, by a concerned grandparent) should externally maintain the mother's response to the crying.

Dyads involving a colicky infant typically contain an initially responsive mother whose frequent interventions are unreinforced (even punished) by an infant whose crying is difficult to terminate. In the early months of life, therefore, such dyads also could contribute to the correlational pattern emphasized by Bell and Ainsworth (1972) showing that unresponsive mothers have infants with high crying rates. (In this discussion, I ignore the earlier-cited reservations questioning the meaning of Bell's and Ainsworth's maternal nonresponding variable.) However, it is likely that the direction-of-influence hypothesis emphasized by those authors was not intended to apply to such a dyad. At the same time, these examples of variables that may interact to produce similar mother-infant response patterns as outcomes can serve to caution against drawing conclusions from relationships between response measures summed over an extended period of time (as were Bell's and Ainsworth's), in the absence of a focus upon the functional contingencies operating between response and stimulus units.

Some Likely Mutual-Conditioning Features of Infant
Crying and Maternal Responding to that Crying

Parents the world over will give priority to their attempts to terminate the crying of their infants (Bowlby, 1958; Gewirtz, 1961). In the natural course of events, a mother may respond conscientiously to her infant's cries. When contingent, this responding will often reinforce features of her infant's crying, as noted in the preceding section. At the same time, these maternal interventions may come under the control of the very infant crying they were intended to terminate — whose causes they were to alleviate. Thus, a mother's specific intervention response to her infant's crying may be reinforced by the crying's termination, the intended consequence (Gewirtz, 1968, 1969). Concomitantly, a mother's unsuccessful interventions, being unreinforced, could well cease occurring (unless closely accompanied by the successful techniques).

As a function of this differential reinforcement of her responding, that mother's interventions should come under the control of discriminative-stimulus cues from her infant's appearance or behavior, whereas others of the mother's responses would likely come under the control of other cues from her baby's appearance and behavior (Gewirtz & Boyd, in press-b). If one employs the criteria used earlier to denote an infant's attachment to the mother, all or part of this pattern wherein a mother's responses come under the control of cues from her infant could denote that she had acquired an attachment to her infant.

If a mother is initially unresponsive to her infant's cries, she may not acquire readily a pattern of discriminative responding. A mother who fails to intervene effectively to quiet her infant inadvertently may shape lengthy or intense operant-crying episodes. This outcome could result also if a lengthy process is involved before a mother's responding to the infant's crying comes under the control of cues from its behavior. In addition, this process could involve increasingly lengthy unsuccessful interventions aversive to her. But if a mother learns to respond discriminatively to her infant's physical pain-induced distress cries while ignoring (not reinforcing) other operant cries, the overall crying rate should decrease. Indiscriminate interventions also may constitute a time-independent intermittent schedule of reinforcement of operant-crying episodes. As indicated earlier, such reinforcement schedules are expected to generate relatively high crying-response rates, with the response pattern involved relatively resistant to modification or reversal.

In this frame, a mother who responded expeditiously to short, low-intensity precursors of her baby's crying could be fostering behaviors incompatible with all but pain-induced crying. (In effect, Moss, 1974, appears to have detected such a pattern across a two-month time gap between antecedent conditions and outcome.) In turn, such precrying responses may provide positive reinforcers for a mother's approach and attentive responses to her infant. Hence, in such cases a mother would be expected to continue responding to these short, low-intensity precrying vocalizations of her infant. By contrast, a mother may ignore the fussy precursors of her infant's crying and shape loud and long cries. Her interventions would not be reinforced, nor in turn could they reinforce those of her infant's responses (like eye contact, vocalization) that are incompatible with crying. This mother's dutiful intervention responses under conditions aversive to her might become locked in to maintain a pattern of long and loud crying episodes in her infant.

ATTACHMENT AND THE CONDITIONING OF CUED CRYING

In this section, I describe how various infant responses cued by their mothers' departure might be understood as plausible outcomes of routine operant-conditioning procedures. Following that, I consider how one might conceptualize a discriminated-responding system, like one denoting attachment, in a context where some (e.g., Ainsworth, 1969) have found it necessary to postulate an inner structure that endures in the absence of an attachment figure. Finally, I question the use, in a research approach, of a single attachment indicator like crying cued by separation, or of very few such indices.

The Conditioning of Crying to Departure or Separation Cues

The increasingly differentiated data base of operant conditioning in human infants (see, for example, Hulsebus, 1973) has attested to the plausibility of conceiving that, through conditioning, infant-behavior units within a wide range might come under the direct control of cues from the behavior or appearance of a particular other (attachment figure), given that some response from environmental agents has been presented effectively contingent on that behavior unit. In the preceding discussion of the conditioning of crying, it was seen that, like any instrumental response, crying could come under the direct control of its consequences. In this section, emphasis is placed on how crying could come under the control of the cues (discriminative stimuli) that precede it.

Insofar as contingent maternal responding provides positive-reinforcing stimuli for infant protests and cries, it may be assumed that those responses will come readily under the discriminative control of cues denoting the physical distance, departure, or absence of a parent. There is no reason to expect that discriminative stimuli associated with parental distance, departure, or absence would function differently from discriminative stimuli associated with the presence of such attachment figures. Hence, like cues from the presence of parents that ordinarily control such infant responses as orienting or smiling, cues from parental distance, departure, or absence that control such responses as protesting or crying also can denote attachment in a conditioning account (Gewirtz, 1972c, e). It is important to note that such cued crying would no more need to connote affective states like those termed unhappiness, distress, or despair than would such cued responses as smiles, orientating, approaching, or vocalizing need to connote joy, satisfaction, or pleasure.

Exemplars of conditions for the acquisition of positive stimulus control by cues denoting a mother's departure or absence may be sketched. On the assumption that contingent maternal responding provides effective reinforcers for various infant responses, an infant's protests or other cries (that may denote distress, e.g., Ainsworth & Wittig, 1969) may become conditioned to cues from the mother's preparations for departure (and to the short- or long-term separations that would ensue) if the mother (perhaps influenced by her knowledge that she is leaving) softens and responds, thereby delaying her departure, or otherwise hesitates or vacillates prior to departing. Further, particular types of cries may be shaped differentially under the control of cues denoting departure or absence, for instance by a mother who responds only to her infant's plaintive cries, for similar reasons.

Likewise, an infant's cries may be conditioned to cues from the mother's actual absence, when those cries result in her return to the infant's vicinity (on some schedule). In this case, the infant's cries very likely would have to overcome physical and distance barriers in addition to the absent parent's need to be away, to evoke a response from her. Therefore, those reinforced cries that come to be cued by that attachment figure's absence should often be lengthy or intense. (To be sure, these examples of the straightforward discriminative-stimulus control of cries are not necessarily the only bases underlying the infant's responding to the departure, or in the absence, of the attachment figure.)

Discriminated Crying and the Enduring Features of an Attachment

This process of acquisition of stimulus control can account for much infant responding in separations and reunions, and during absences. Hence, the marked decrease in crying or in other cued responses that are taken to denote attachment in the absence of the attachment figure is explained simply as due to the removal of the cue and reinforcing stimuli that had been supporting those responses. When the controlling stimuli for orienting, smiling, and similar responses are again presented after reunion, those cued responses should again be displayed to the attachment figure (Gewirtz, 1961).

This discriminative-control axiom of a conditioning analysis bears directly on the reciprocal issue of the locus of an attachment during a separation, as well as on whether or not a concept of inner structure is required as the basis for an attachment. Differences between response patterns prior to, and during, separation from an attachment figure, and differences between patterns during separation and at subsequent reunion with that figure, have constituted evidence for attachments having an inner structure in Ainsworth's 1969 analysis. Ainsworth conceived that this concept of inner structure was required to permit accounting for the enduring nature of attachments, specifically for their surviving periods of the attachment figure's absence, undiminished in strength, despite a diminution in the incidence of attachment behaviors during that separation period.

When Cued Crying Is the Sole Attachment Index

The molar conditioned-stimulus control conception discussed in the preceding section accounts routinely for responses under close discriminative control not occurring in the absence of their controlling stimuli, but reoccurring when those controlling stimuli reappear. This conditioning conception also provides bases for understanding some types of delays occasionally noted at reunion after separation, before attachment responses are again exhibited to the reunited attachment figure: it may take some time before the controlling discriminative stimuli are presented effectively so as to be functional. A response under close discriminative-stimulus control (like that denoting an attachment) will routinely diminish markedly in incidence, in the absence of the discriminative stimulus (like that from the attachment figure); just as routinely, it will increase markedly in incidence, when the attachment figure providing the controlling stimulus reappears. Hence, it is axiomatic in a conditioning framework that discriminated operants denoting an attachment will endure undiminished in strength in the absence of an attachment figure, precluding the requirement to postulate an inner structure. Indeed, absence of the stimulus cue means that its function is unavailable for modification; thus its absence insulates its function, preserving its value for controlling responding undiminished in strength.

An index based on a single cued response (or a small set of such responses) might serve efficiently and usefully, under any attachment conception, when that index would be prescribed uniquely by the theory or when it would be representative of the broader set of stimulus-control functions that characterize the individual's responses directed toward the attachment figure (Gewirtz, 1961, 1972e). But an attachment index based on a single response (or on a small number of such responses) may reflect only the conditioning history of an isolated response system that is unrepresentative of the social stimulus control implied by the attachment conception used. Where this is the case, or where, because that index was under conditioned control it might be problematic for a researcher operating outside of a conditioning approach, reliance on a single attachment index would be artifact prone (Gewirtz, 1972e).

For infants in the early weeks of life, Etzel and Gewirtz (1967) demonstrated the modifiability of crying by caretaker attention (such as is provided by hovering over, talking, and/or picking up the child). Various investigators have demonstrated similarly how diverse operant responses, that also have served occasionally as bases for attachment indices, can be conditioned by actual or simulated behavior contingencies in the first three months of life (well before the time some would expect that an attachment could have been acquired). The responses conditioned include eye contact, smiles, vocalizations, and cries (e.g., Brackbill, 1958; Etzel & Gewirtz, 1967; Ramey & Ourth, 1971; Rheingold, Gewirtz, & Ross, 1959; Weisberg, 1963; see also the summary in Hulsebus, 1973). Therefore, if a single attachment index is used, a researcher working outside of a conditioning approach would do well to take account of the possibility that the attributes of the discriminated response on which it is based might reflect only a history in which the child's display of that behavior had been routinely reinforced in the same situation, for instance crying cued by the mother's preparations to leave the child's vicinity.

I have indicated that a response like cued crying could serve as an index of attachment in a conditioning analysis. But that response index might not be satisfactory under theoretical conceptions that do not emphasize a conditioning model, for which a conditioned cued-response index of attachment might imply an artifact that would impeach the results of an attachment investigation. Alternatively, such a conditioning basis might imply only a confounded rather than a direct attachment index under a researcher's model. Therefore, a nonlearning approach often would find it necessary to address directly the issue of possibly-conditioned behavior systems serving as its criterion indices.

An argument for this position can be made with a report by Schaffer and Emerson (1964). Widely reprinted and highly influential in the attachment literature, that report can serve as a useful vehicle for considering the types and the number of indices to use. Schaffer and Emerson employed several measures derived from what was essentially a single cued-response-based index of attachment. Those measures summarized the occurrence, intensity, and direction of infant protests (comprised of whimpers, fusses, and cries) after 7 different types of separations from their mothers and others. On the basis of mothers' reports, Schaffer and Emerson (1964, p. 50) reported that the "intensity of attachment-to-mother at 18 months" (measured in terms of the characteristic intensity of protests at separation) was a positive function of the frequency and speed with which a mother responded to her infant's crying (initiations).

As was proposed earlier, under an operant-learning paradigm one possible basis for these results is that the infants who protested/cried most intensely at separation were largely those whose mothers attended immediately to their protests/cries, directly or by hesitating or vacillating prior to departing. In this way, those mothers might have positively reinforced protests/cries, such that cues provided by a mother's preparations for departure became discriminative for positive reinforcement of those responses. Schaffer and Emerson (1964, p. 51) raised this very possibility in their discussion of the relationship between attachment intensity and the frequency and speed of maternal responding to infant crying. However, they discounted this conditioning explanation of their results, stating that cause and effect could not be disentangled in the context studied. At the same time, they suggested that the result could just as likely have reflected a mother's having learned to give in to her infant's persistent crying. However, this explanation appears simply to be another way of saying the very same thing; that contingent maternal responding can provide reinforcement for infant crying. Even so, there may still remain an issue for resolution. The composite of the various measures of protests-in-separation situations used in their investigation to index the child's attachment to the mother might have reflected only what the Schaffer and Emerson theory would take to be a limited fact: that, for the sample of children that happened to be studied, mothers had systematically reinforced the protests/cries of their babies on some schedule, particularly when making preparations to leave them.

The Schaffer and Emerson findings have implications for another facet of this conditioning issue. Those authors found pronounced individual differences in the age of onset of a specific attachment. Differences in specific protest-training conditions, particularly in the discriminability of the unique cues provided by the mother when they prepared their departures, might have accounted for this result. Whether single or multiple criteria of attachment are used, an analysis of the stimulus conditions that have acquired discriminative control over relevant responses of the individual could help a researcher to hold constant these conditioning factors when they may confound the indices selected under a particular theoretical conception. Of course, such phenomena are the primary focus of a conditioning account (Gewirtz, 1972c).

SUMMARY

In this chapter, there was a discussion of attachment as metaphor and as process. A survey was made of some behavioral indicators of attachments of infants to others, particularly their mothers, with emphasis on their crying cued by separation from their mothers. The influential but flawed Bell and Ainsworth report, that maternal responding to infant crying reduced subsequent infant crying in the first year of life was examined. It was concluded that the main finding Bell and Ainsworth reported: (1) was unwarranted on technical grounds; and (2) did not involve the detailed facts concerning crying-maternal responding contingencies required for an operant-conditioning account, to which several theorists had referred them. At the same time, it was noted that various infant-crying outcomes are plausible under that operant-learning paradigm (including the outcome emphasized by Bell and Ainsworth), depending on the specific crying-maternal-responding contingency histories involved. Also considered was the impact in the wider conceptual context of the main finding of the Bell and Ainsworth report that was impeached in this chapter.

The questioned conclusion of the Bell and Ainsworth report provided the impetus for a didactic sketch of how various infant operant-crying patterns and, in particular, patterns of crying cued by a mother's departures or absences (separations), might be understood as plausible outcomes of routine discriminated-operant-conditioning procedures effected by the pattern of that mother's responding to her infant's crying. Such cued crying has been a frequently used index of a baby's attachment to the mother and, occasionally (and riskily), has been the only index employed.

ACKNOWLEDGMENTS

For helpful editorial suggestions at various points in the preparation of this paper, the author is grateful to his colleagues, the Doctors Elizabeth Boyd, Gail Browne, Rose Caron, Claire Poulson, and particularly Donald Baer. This work was sponsored by the Intramural Research Program of the National Institute of Mental Health and is therefore not subject to copyright.

REFERENCES

Ainsworth, M. D. S. *Infancy in Uganda: Infant care and the growth of love.* Baltimore: John Hopkins Press, 1967.

Ainsworth, M. D. S. Object relations, dependency, and attachment: A theoretical review of the infant-mother relationship. *Child Development,* 1969, *40,* 969-1025.

Ainsworth, M. D. S. Attachment and dependency: A comparison. In J. L. Gewirtz (Ed.), *Attachment and dependency.* Washington, D.C.: Winston, 1972. Pp. 97-137.

Ainsworth, M. D. S. The development of infant-mother attachment. In B. M. Caldwell & H. N. Ricciuti (Eds.), *Review of child development research* (Vol. 3). Chicago: University of Chicago Press, 1973. Pp. 1-94.

Ainsworth, M. D. S., & Wittig, B. A. Attachment and exploratory behavior of one-year-olds in a strange situation. In. B. M. Foss (Ed.), *Determinants of infant behaviour IV.* London: Methuen, 1969. Pp. 111-136.

Bell, S. M., & Ainsworth, M. D. S. Infant crying and maternal responsiveness. *Child Development,* 1972, *43,* 1171-1190.

Beller, E. K. Dependency and independence in young children. *Journal of Genetic Psychology,* 1955, *87,* 25-35.

Beller, E. K. Exploratory studies of dependency. *Transactions of the New York Academy of Sciences,* 1959, *21,* 114-426.

Bijou, S. W. *Development in the preschool years: A functional analysis.* Paper presented at the meeting of the American Psychological Association, New Orleans, September, 1974.

Bijou, S. W., & Baer, D. M. *Child development. Vol. 2. Universal stage of infancy.* New York: Appleton-Century-Crofts, 1965.

Bowlby, J. The nature of the child's tie to his mother. *International Journal of Psycho-Analysis,* 1958, *39,* 350-373.

Bowlby, J. *Attachment and loss. Vol. 1. Attachment.* London: Hogarth, 1969.

Bowlby, J. *Attachment and loss. Vol. 2. Separation: Anxiety and anger.* New York: Basic Books, 1973.

Brackbill, Y. Extinction of the smiling response in infants as a function of reinforcement schedule. *Child Development,* 1958, *29,* 115-124.

Catania, A. C. Elicitation, reinforcement, and stimulus control. In R. Glaser (Ed.), *The nature of reinforcement.* New York: Academic Press, 1971. Pp. 196-220.

Etzel, B. C., & Gewirtz, J. L. Experimental modification of caretaker-maintained high-rate operant crying in a 6- and a 20-week-old infant *(Infans tyrannotearus):* Extinction of crying with reinforcement of eye contact and smiling. *Journal of Experimental Child Psychology,* 1967, *5,* 303-317.

Ferster, C. B., & Skinner, B. F. *Schedules of reinforcement.* New York: Appleton-Century-Crofts, 1957.

Gewirtz, J. L. Three determinants of attention-seeking in young children. *Monographs of the Society for Research in Child Development,* 1954, *19* (2, Serial No. 59).

Gewirtz, J. L. A program of research on the dimensions and antecedents of emotional dependence. *Child Development,* 1956, *27,* 205-221.

Gewirtz, J. L. A learning analysis of the effects of normal stimulation, privation and deprivation on the acquisition of social motivation and attachment. In B. M. Foss (Ed.),
Determinants of infant behaviour. London: Methuen, 1961. Pp. 213-299.

Gewirtz, J. L. On designing the functional environment of the child to facilitate behavioral
development. In L. L. Dittmann (Ed.) *Early child care: The new perspectives.* New
York: Atherton, 1968. Pp. 169-213.

Gewirtz, J. L. Mechanisms of social learning: Some roles of stimulation and behavior in
early human development. In D. A. Goslin (Ed.), *Handbook of socialization theory and
research.* Chicago: Rand McNally, 1969. Pp. 57-212.

Gewirtz, J. L. Conditional responding as a paradigm for observational, imitative learning
and vicarious reinforcement. In H. W. Reese (Ed.), *Advances in child development and
behavior* (Vol. 6). New York: Academic Press, 1971. Pp. 273-304. (a)

Gewirtz, J. L. The roles of overt responding and extrinsic reinforcement in "self-" and
"vicarious-reinforcement" phenomena and in "observational learning" and imitation. In
R. Glaser (Ed.), *The nature of reinforcement.* New York: Academic Press, 1971. Pp.
279-309. (b)

Gewirtz, J. L. Attachment and dependence: Some strategies and tactics in the selection and
use of indices for those concepts. In T. Alloway, L. Krames, & P. Pliner (Eds.), *Communication and affect.* New York: Academic Press, 1972. Pp. 19-49. (a)

Gewirtz, J. L. (Ed.) *Attachment and dependency.* Washington, D.C.: Winston, 1972. (b)

Gewirtz, J. L. Attachment, dependence, and a distinction in terms of stimulus control. In
J. L. Gewirtz (Ed.), *Attachment and dependency.* Washington, D.C.: Winston, 1972.
Pp. 139-177. (c)

Gewirtz, J. L. Deficiency conditions of stimulation and the reversal of their effects via en-
richment. In F. J. Mönks, W. W. Hartup, & J. de Wit (Eds.), *Determinants of behavioral
development.* New York: Academic Press, 1972. Pp. 349-375. (d)

Gewirtz, J. L. On the selection and use of attachment and dependence indices. In J. L.
Gewirtz (Ed.), *Attachment and dependency.* Washington, D.C.: Winston, 1972. Pp. 179-
215. (e)

Gewirtz, J. L. Some contextual determinants of stimulus potency. In R. D. Parke (Ed.),
Recent trends in social learning theory. New York: Academic Press, 1972. Pp. 7-33. (f)

Gewirtz, J. L., & Boyd, E. F. Does maternal responding imply reduced infant crying?: A
critique of the 1972 Bell and Ainsworth Report. *Child Development,* in press. (a)

Gewirtz, J. L., & Boyd, E. F. Experiments on mother-infant interaction underlying mutual
attachment acquisition: The infant conditions the mother. In T. Alloway, P. Pliner, &
L. Krames (Eds.), *Attachment behavior. Advances in the study of communication and
affect* (Vol. 3). New York & London: Plenum Press, 1977. Pp. 109-143. (b)

Hinde, R. A. *Biological bases of human social behaviour.* New York: McGraw-Hill, 1974.

Hulsebus, R. C. Operant conditioning of infant behavior: A review. In H. W. Reese (Ed.),
Advances in child development and behavior (Vol. 8). New York: Academic Press, 1973.
Pp. 111-158.

Kapel, S. Baby's cries denote needs. *The Kansas City Star,* June 13, 1974, p. 12A.

Maccoby, E. E., & Masters, J. C. Attachment and dependency. In P. H. Mussen (Ed.),
Carmichael's manual of child psychology (Vol. 2, 3rd ed.). New York: Wiley, 1970.
Pp. 73-158.

Millar, W. S. A study of operant conditioning under delayed reinforcement in early infancy. *Monographs of the Society for Research in Child Development,* 1972, *37* (2,
Serial No. 147).

Miller, N. E. Learning of visceral and glandular responses. *Science,* 1969, *163,* 434-445.

Moss, H. A. Communication in mother-infant interaction. In L. Krames, P. Pliner, & T.
Alloway (Eds.), *Nonverbal communication: Comparative aspects.* New York: Plenum,
1974, Pp. 171-191.

Parsley, N. J., & Rabinowitz, F. M. Crying in the first year: An operant interpretation of the Bell and Ainsworth (1972) findings. *Child Study Journal,* 1975, *5,* 83-89.

Ramey, C. T., & Ourth, L. L. Delayed reinforcement and vocalization rates of infants. *Child Development,* 1971, *42,* 291-297.

Rebelsky, F., & Dorman, L. (Eds.). *Child development and behavior* (2nd ed.). New York: Knopf, 1973.

Rheingold, H. L., Gewirtz, J. L., & Ross, H. W. Social conditioning of vocalizations in the infant. *Journal of Comparative and Physiological Psychology,* 1959, *52,* 68-73.

Schaffer, H. R., & Emerson, P. E. The development of social attachments in infancy. *Monographs of the Society for Research in Child Development,* 1964, *29* (3, Serial No. 94).

Schoenfeld, W. N. *The theory of reinforcement schedules.* New York: Appleton-Century-Crofts, 1970.

Sears, R. R. *Survey of objective studies of psychoanalytic concepts.* New York: Social Science Research Council, 1943.

Sears, R. R., Whiting, J. W. M., Nowlis, V., & Sears, P. S., in collaboration with E. K. Beller, J. C. Cohen, E. H. Chasdi, H. Faigin, J. L. Gewirtz, M. S. Lawrence, & J. P. McKee. Some child-rearing antecedents of aggression and dependency in young children. *Genetic Psychology Monographs,* 1953, *47,* 135-234.

Stone, L. J., & Church, J. *Childhood and adolescence* (3rd ed.). New York: Random House, 1973.

Sutton-Smith, B. *Child psychology.* New York: Appleton-Century-Crofts, 1973.

Weisberg, P. Social and non-social conditioning of infant vocalizations. *Child Development,* 1963, *34,* 377-388.

Yarrow, L. J. The development of focused relationships during infancy. In J. Hellmuth (Ed.), *Exceptional infant: The normal infant* (Vol. 1). Seattle, Wash.: Special Child Publications, 1967. Pp. 429-442.

Yarrow, L. J. Attachment and dependency: A developmental perspective. In J. L. Gewirtz (Ed.), *Attachment and dependency.* Washington, D.C.: Winston, 1972. Pp. 81-95.

4

A Three-Stage Functional Analysis
for Children's Coercive Behaviors:
A Tactic for Developing a
Performance Theory [1]

G. R. Patterson

Department of Special Education, University of Oregon
   and
Oregon Research Institute

Early personality theorists, such as Baldwin (1946) and Fiske and Rice (1955), advocated investigation of the functional relations which characterize intra-individual variations in behavior across time and/or settings. A similar emphasis upon intraindividual studies is found in the work of some writers who espouse a functional analysis viewpoint (Bijou & Baer, 1961; Sidman, 1960). However, most of these investigators have focused upon only a narrow range of variables. For example, within the functional analysis paradigm, the emphasis has been limited to manipulations of reinforcing contingencies as determinants for intra-individual variations in performance. This writer hypothesizes that in natural settings, variations in reinforcing contingencies account *directly* for only a small proportion of the variance which characterizes intraindividual variations in rate over time and settings: Rather, the assumption is that rates of many social behaviors vary primarily as a function of covariations in the densities of the stimuli which control the initiations and maintenance of children's social behaviors. Presumably, these controlling stimuli are in turn determined by reinforcing contingencies.

[1] This chapter is a revision of an earlier report, "Dyadic Aggression: A Six-Second Performance Theory About Children," prepared for the 1973 American Psychological Association in Montreal, Quebec, Canada.

In this chapter, field observations provide the basis for measuring the intra-individual variations in rate across time. Alternate sampling of the child and social environment provides a sequential description of these molecular inter-changes. This, in turn, provides the basis for functional analyses of the environmental events which initiate and maintain the child's ongoing social behavior. Such data constitute the first phase in the construction of a theory which might account for intraindividual variations in performance. The second phase requires experimental manipulation to establish the causal status of the controlling stimuli identified in the prior functional analyses of field observation data.

The position taken here is that a proper theory should be able to account for the variations in the behavior of a child in the natural environment. The greater the amount of variance accounted for, the better the theory. Thus, testing for predictability constitutes a necessary third phase in constructing a performance theory.

This sequence of phases constituted the guidelines for analyses which focused upon understanding children's coercive behavior. Available data are summarized as they relate to each of the phases.

COERCIVE BEHAVIORS

Field observations in homes of aggressive children suggested that the boys employed a wide spectrum of aversive behaviors in shaping and controlling family members. This general process of control-by-pain was labeled "coercion" (Patterson & Reid, 1970). The network of coercion hypotheses described by Patterson and Cobb (1971, 1973) detailed the means by which aversive behaviors serve as stimulus events in punishment and/or negative reinforcement arrangements. As shown in the laboratory study by Devine (1971), normal pre-school children, under negative reinforcement arrangements, showed significant changes in behaviors in as few as three $S \rightarrow R \rightarrow C$ (aversive stimulus-child response-removal of aversive stimulus) repetitions. Presumably, this arrangement is particularly powerful in many social interchanges because the contingency can simultaneously involve both positive and negative reinforcement. Shaping occurs as these aversive stimuli are applied contingently and repeatedly to accelerate or decelerate behaviors exhibited by the other person.

The coercion hypothesis further suggests that with training there are significant increases in both rate and intensities of coercive behaviors. In extended interchanges, where one or both persons employ aversive stimuli, when one member suddenly increases the intensity of his aversive behavior, the other person is likely to terminate his attack. In this manner, high-amplitude aggression is more likely to be reinforced. During such training, one member may adopt a consistently submissive stance, for example, terminating such inter-actions by "complying." If not, then it is hypothesized that both members are likely to escalate in the rate and intensity of their coercive behaviors. Cairns

(1973) and J. Knutson (personal communication) have noted similar escalations in their laboratory investigations of pain induced aggression. Although formal analysis of escalating processes is badly needed, such studies are difficult to execute. The difficulty lies in the problem of defining "increasing intensity of aversive stimuli."

At the inception of the Social Learning Project at ORI, it seemed reasonable to select children labeled as highly aggressive and to study only a limited set of responses such as "hit." However, actual field observations in families (Reid, 1967) suggested that a large number of additional behaviors had functional characteristics similar to those noted for hit. Eventually 14 "noxious" behaviors were identified which occurred with rather high frequency for boys labeled as "aggressive": command negative, cry, dependency, destructive, disapproval, high rate, humiliate, ignore, negativism, noncomply, physical negative, tease, whine, and yell.

It was hypothesized that identified aggressive children would display higher rates for all 14 categories. Data were collected in the homes for 6 to 10 sessions using a 29-category code system described in Patterson, Ray, Shaw, and Cobb (1969). Studies of its psychometric properties were reviewed by Jones, Reid, and Patterson (1975). The demographic characteristics of the samples were detailed in Patterson and Cobb (1973, pp. 165-168). The comparisons between the samples of 27 problem and 27 matched nonproblem boys showed the expected differences were significant for 11 of the categories (Patterson, 1976a).

Acquisition

Three different "mechanisms" are assumed to be involved in the acquisition of coercive behaviors: (1) instinctual patterns; (2) modeling; and (3) reinforcement.

Ethological studies of children and primates reviewed by Eibl-Ebesfeldt (1975) showed that the complex pattern of noxious behaviors labeled "temper tantrum" may be unlearned. For example, he cited a study which showed that a deaf and blind girl displayed the same pattern of facial grimace, muscle tension, and accompanying behaviors found in normal children. He also referred to studies which demonstrated that young primates displayed similar patterns of behaviors.

The newborn's repertoire of screaming and crying behaviors may have survival value in that they can be used to quickly train most mothers in the skills necessary to adequate feeding and temperature control. The infant presents these stimuli to the mother until she makes the correct response, at which point the infant terminates the aversive stimulation. Conceivably, grandmothers, Dr. Spock, and infants all share in the teaching of mothering skills.

The young child may also learn additional coercive skills by *observing* these behaviors in siblings and parents (Bandura, 1973). Behaviors modeled by the family teach him various refinements in application which are well beyond the repertoire of an infant. For example, data from 6 to 10 observation sessions in each of 27 homes of normal families showed that yelling, teasing, and hitting by young children occurred at the rate of .025, .021, and .014 responses per min (Jones *et al.*, 1975). Certainly these findings suggest rich modeling schedules for the other siblings in these homes. Similarly, observations in two nursery schools (Patterson, Littman, & Bricker, 1967) showed a range of from 11 to 40 verbal and nonverbal attacks per session. The latter·constitutes a rich presentation of peer modeling for both verbal and nonverbal modes of attack. There are, in addition, a vast range of potential models available on TV and in comic books. Taken together, these situations provide a rich basis for children acquiring coercive skills through modeling.

In this early stage in the development of coercive skills, reinforcement from interchanges with peers, siblings, and adults supplements modeling. As shown in one field study, the reactions of the "victims" train the attacker as to which response, and which victim, to select (Patterson *et al.*, 1967). In the initial try-out of these complex coercive skills, which may have been modeled for him, the reinforcement by the first victims determine whether the performance of coercive behaviors will remain at near-zero rate or gradually accelerate. This process of accelerating performance can be very subtle. In the nursery school study cited above, 21 children were identified, each of whom had displayed 2 or less coercive behaviors in the first 5 nursery-school sessions. During the next 5 sessions 12 of this group were observed to interact at high rates with their peers and were victimized an average of 70 times. For these 12, their counter aggression was reinforced on the average 69% of the time by the withdrawal of the attacker. The data showed that this "reinforcement" was followed, in turn, by an increase in the rate with which these children *initiated* coercive interchanges with other children. Children who were seldom victimized, or were not successful in their counter attacks, showed little or no change in the rate with which they initiated coercive interchanges. Presumably, this drama is repeated in the home, the neighborhood, and the school. These multiple training programs produce children who differ markedly in their performance rates for coercive behaviors.

In summary, it is assumed that for most children in our society, the "learning" of coercive skills is a given. The problem for a theory of aggression is to identify these variables which determine inter- and intraindividual variations in performance.

As a tactic in constructing a "performance" theory relating to coercion, it was assumed that many, but not all, children's coercive behaviors are under control of *observable* stimuli. The first step involved is simply defining the dependent variables (Jones *et al.*, 1975; Patterson *et al.*, 1969) and then applying the definitions in collecting data in field settings. As these data became available, it became clear that coercive behaviors collected in homes had one very interesting characteristic. Given intraindividual data samples from time intervals ranging from 6 sec to 6 days, then behaviors seemed extraordinarily variable. As an example, Figure 1 summarizes a segment from 2 days of observation data for

VARIATIONS IN RATE FOR DENNY'S HOSTILE BEHAVIOR

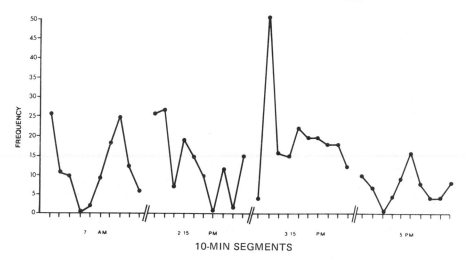

Figure 1   Two days of observation data for 10 consecutive 10-min intervals for Denny's hostile behavior. First 200 min on first day and second 200 min on second day.

the *same child* (Denny). On the first day 200 min of data were collected and 200 on the second day. The dependent variable was a composite score labeled "hostile" comprised of the coercive responses, whine, yell, and disapproval.

This segment was fairly representative of Denny's behavior and also it characterized the variability found for other coercive behaviors and subjects, in different settings. Within this context, such intraindividual variations in rate of performance were not thought of as "error of measurement;" rather, *they constitute that which is to be explained.* Second, it was hypothesized that a functional analysis of the sequential dependencies found within family interactions could provide a data base for an empirical analysis of the variables which determine such intraindividual variations.

THREE STAGES OF FUNCTIONAL ANALYSES

Stage 1:   The Search for Functional Relations in Observation Data

The family observations systematically sampled the sequential interchanges between the child and parents or siblings. Both child and social environment were coded each 6 sec. Such data lend themselves to an empirically based search for "controlling variables," those events which are associated with alterations in the probability of occurrence of ongoing social behaviors. The collection and analyses of these data constituted Phase 1.

In conceptualizing these analyses, it was assumed that variations in the frequency with which the "controlling stimuli" were presented would produce corresponding variations in intraindividual performance.

The current Zeitgeist is such that the assumption seemed at first glance to be almost counterintuitive. The landmark contribution by Ferster and Skinner (1957), *Schedules of Reinforcement,* and by the publications in *JABA,* naturally leads one to consider an operant analysis when searching for determinants of performance variations. Certainly, there is ample evidence that changes in reinforcing contingencies *can* produce corresponding changes in rate for a wide spectrum of social behaviors. There are also a number of observation studies which show that both peers and parents provide impressive schedules of positive consequences for children's coercive behaviors. For example, verbal statements about delinquent behavior were observed to be positively consequated 88% of the time by delinquent peers in several different institutional settings (Buehler, Patterson, & Furniss, 1966). Peers in 2 nursery schools were observed to positively consequate 54% to 97% of the occurrences for 3 different classes of coercive behaviors (Patterson *et al.,* 1967). Similarly data from the ORI clinical sample showed that parents of aggressive boys positively consequated 27% of aggressive behaviors in the study by Shaw (1971), and 19% and 31% in the studies by Sallows (1972), and Taplin (1974).

It is hypothesized that schedules of both positive *and* negative reinforcement partially determine the *level,* or *average rate,* at which a child performs coercive behaviors. It should be noted however, that the major determinants for level of performance consist of variables which relate to extended chains of coercive interactions Patterson (1976b). These variables in turn are only distantly related to reinforcement schedules. It is hypothesized that variations about these average rates are determined by concomitant variations in the density of controlling stimuli provided by the social environment.

As yet, there are only preliminary data which suggest that reinforcement schedules may not account for intraindividual variability. For example, Taplin (1974) carried out an intensive analysis of the impact of parental consequences provided by parents for the deviant behaviors of 27 aggressive boys. The analysis showed a modest stability (correlation of .56; $df = 26$; $p < .01$) over a period of several months in the proportion of parental positive consequences supplied for these behaviors. The across-subjects correlation between rates of parental positive consequences and deviant child behaviors was .34 (N.S.) at baseline and .06 (N.S.) at termination of treatment. However, a careful analysis of treatment process showed the deviant child behaviors were reduced in rate at a time when there was an overall *increase* in positive consequences provided by parents for these behaviors. A cross-lag correlation analysis of these data showed that changes in these two variables were independent of each other. In the nursery school study, intraindividual analyses were carried out for high rate aggressive boys to determine possible covariations, over sessions, between rates of their aggressive behavior and the proportion of positive consequences provided by peers (Patterson *et al.,* 1967). Most of the covariations obtained were of low magnitude; fewer significant correlations were obtained than would be expected by chance. Ebner (1967) studied 4 retarded children in a special day care school.

The median intraindividual correlation between daily rates of positive consequences and deviant child behaviors was −.19 (N.S.).

These findings suggest reinforcement schedules, as defined in the rather primitive fashion which characterized these studies, may not be a promising variable for the task of identifying intraindividual variability.[2] These findings led to a search for other variables which might relate to variability. The series of empirical findings have led us to emphasize variations in rates of controlling stimuli as the major determinants for intraindividual variability.

Examination of the sequential dependencies characterizing family interactions suggest *two kinds* of stimulus events which affect the probability of occurrence in children's ongoing social behavior (Patterson & Cobb, 1971). The events differ only in terms of their ordering on a time line, vis-a-vis the "target response" (R_j). Events which precede the R_j by a 6-sec interval *and* are associated with significant increases in the conditional probability for its occurrence, $p(R_j/A_i)$ are labeled "facilitating stimuli" (F^S). Those associated with significant decreases in probability for the R_j are labeled "inhibiting stimuli" (I^S). A second class of events consists of consequences (C_i) which follow the R_j on the time line. However, their occurrence is associated with altered probabilities for the response's immediate recurrence (or persistence) $p(R_{j_2}/R_{j_1} \cdot C_i)$. Those events which significantly increase the probability of R_{j_2} are labeled "accelerating stimuli" (Acc^S); those associated with decreases are termed "decelerating stimuli" (Dc^S). The format for data analyses and the decision rules for identifying these events are detailed in a report by Patterson (1974).

Each of these stimuli has several dimensions other than just its position in the sequence.

1. Its "power" which can be expressed as the conditional probability that the target response (R_j) will occur given that stimulus has occurred [$p(R_{j_1}/A_i)$ or $p(R_{j_2}/R_{j_1} \cdot Acc)$]. However, the day-by-day variations in rate of R_j are probably not determined by fluctuations in the *power* of this stimulus.

2. It is more likely that they are related to the *frequency* with which the child is presented with the stimulus [$p(A_i)$ or $p(R_{j_1} \cdot Acc)$]. On days when many of the stimuli are presented to him, his rates of R_j would presumably be high. On days when only a few are presented, his rates would be correspondingly low.

3. "Efficiency," will vary jointly as some function of the base rate with which the stimulus event occurs and its power. For example, a given stimulus may have a very large conditional probability value but itself occur only a few times per day. The "predictive efficiency" would be low. Or the stimulus may be

---

[2] For all three studies, the *a priori* classification of consequences as "positive" may have been in error. At yet another level, the more appropriate conceptualization of the problem might be in terms of concurrent operants. That perspective would require simultaneous information for the reinforcement schedules for the target response and the other behaviors which are also controlled in that setting. However, these more precise assessments of the potential contribution of reinforcement schedules to this problem must await conceptual and methodological refinements.

"powerful" and occur at a high rate, but constitute only a small part of the spectrum of stimuli which control a given R_j. In either instance, knowledge of this variable adds but little to our ability to predict behavior even though the variable may be "significant" in the traditional sense.

In the final analysis, it is an empirical question as to what kind of variables will be useful in predicting ongoing social behaviors.

Studies by Patterson & Maerov (in preparation) demonstrated that settings differ in terms of the *kinds* and densities of stimuli which are available. To the extent that this is so, one would, for example, expect little across-subject correlation in rates of aggressive responses for data collected in the school and the home. Studies from two different laboratories showed that the controlling stimuli for deviant behaviors were quite different in the home and the school, Wahler (1975), Patterson & Maerov (in preparation). As would be expected, for a given R_j, there seemed to be little covariation in rate in the two settings.

Some tactical problems

The first problem encountered is that of the scope or breadth of the dependent variable. On the one hand, the most reasonable tactic is to select a very specific response such as "smile" or "hit with the fist" as a dependent variable. Generally speaking, using such readily definable responses, one should be able to collect reliable data. However, generally the more specific its definition, the *lower its rate of occurrence*. To deal with this problem, it was assumed that each coercive response would have a network of facilitating (and inhibiting) stimuli. Furthermore, it was assumed (hoped) that *some* responses would have overlapping networks and could thus be combined into classes. These classes might, in turn, constitute dependent variables comprised of reliably coded categories, and with base rates sufficiently high to facilitate intensive analyses.

The nexus of the second problem lies in the question of generalization across subjects. If the coercive behaviors for each subject were under control of different stimuli, then a performance theory would be idiosyncratic to each child. Such a situation would constitute a very limited intraindividual theory, a state of affairs less than satisfying to the present author and to most psychologists as well.

These two considerations led to some preliminary analyses of family interaction data to determine whether classes of coercive behaviors, defined by overlapping networks, existed; and the extent to which across-subject generalizability might hold. The study by Patterson and Cobb (1973) used data from 6 to 10 observation sessions in the homes of 32 clinical and 26 matched "normal" families. This served as a base from which to identify networks of stimuli which initiated each of 14 coercive behaviors. Two classes were identified: hostile and social aggression. Members of each class differed in topography, but shared common networks of initiating stimuli. Different family members controlled the initiation of different classes of noxious behaviors. The mother and older sister provided the majority of the antecedents (A_i) which effectively initiate hostile behaviors. Siblings, particularly younger ones, provided most of the A_i for social aggression.

In the next stage, the classes, hostile and social aggression, served as dependent variables in the search for networks of maintaining stimuli Patterson (1977). That analysis showed that such networks of accelerators did indeed exist for both response classes. For example, when a hostile response occurred, if the family members reacted with "disapproval" there was a reliable increase in the probability that another hostile response was immediately forthcoming. Family members of problem children were five times as likely to supply such consequences for hostile behaviors as were their nonproblem counterparts.

Further analyses showed that the problem child's reactions to aversive consequences for his coercive behaviors reliably differentiated him from his "normal" compatriot Patterson (1976a). For the clinical sample, behavioral "bursts" followed parental attempts to punish hostile responses. Punishment had no impact upon social aggression responses. Comparable attempts by parents of normal children produced suppression of both classes of ongoing coercive behaviors.

These analyses emphasized the functional utility for these classes of coercive behaviors. The fact that they seemed to hold across subjects was an encouraging step toward dealing with the problem of generalizability of findings. Presumably, more intensive N_1 studies would identify these and perhaps a finite number of additional classes of coercive behaviors. This being the case, then it seemed that dependent variables were available which were both reliable and of moderately high base rates. It seemed reasonable to assume that 40 to 50 hrs of observation data might be sufficient for fine grain functional analyses on an individual subject basis. The details of such an analysis are presented in a later section of this chapter.

Stage 2: The Testing of Functional Relations in the Laboratory

To determine the meaning of these functional relations, it is necessary to follow the lead of the ethologists such as Eibl-Ebesfeldt (1970, 1975) and Hinde (1975), and subject functional relations identified from field observations to experimental manipulation. This second stage is, in fact, a necessary step in establishing the causal status of F^S or Acc^s events as determinants for R_js. To date, three studies have been completed which explore this problem.

In the first study, Atkinson (1971) investigated the question of the specificity of "mother's presence but nonavailability" as a stimulus controlling the coercive behaviors of nine preschool boys. Presumably, if a child's behavior were under "stimulus control," it might be demonstrated using this powerful, albeit complex, "stimulus." Observation data were collected in a laboratory setting. In the reversal design (ABAB), the first phase was a baseline period during which the mother was available to the child. During the experimental session, she made no response to his initiations. This was followed by a second baseline period and another experimental period. Seven child behaviors demonstrated to be under stimulus control showed the expected increases when the "stimulus" was present and decreases when the stimulus was absent. The ANOVA for repeated measures showed the control to be significant for four of the coercive behaviors. The data in Table 1 summarize these findings.

The study by Devine (1971) replicated and extended the effect.

The results from these analogue studies were encouraging. They suggested that presenting an obviously "powerful" F^S could produce a wide range of coercive initiations from a young child. This finding was not, of course, a surprise; most people can list a variety of social stimuli which will "make" a child whine, cry, or yell. The fact that removing the F^S produced abrupt cessation of the coercive behaviors came as a surprise even to some of the mothers involved. They had not thought the child's behavior was under such tight stimulus control.

The studies, however, left unanswered the question of most concern. Do co-variations identified in sequential field observation data imply a causal status for F^S or Acc^S? An unpublished study by Patterson, Arnold, Whalen, and Ishaq investigated this question.

Ten preschool children interacted with their mothers in a laboratory setting during 2 different trials. A half hour's semistructured interaction between mother and child produced the data necessary to identify the F^S which was most likely to lead to the child's initiating a whine (WH). A few days later they returned for a second session. Trial 2 followed an ABA design in which each baseline condition (A) lasted for 10 min. During that time, the mother and child

TABLE 1

Means and *F* Values for "Coercive" Child Behaviors

Coercive Child Behaviors	Mean Rate Per Minute				
	Baseline 1	Experimental 1	Baseline 2	Experimental 2	*F* Values
Command	0.014	0.029	0.007	0.021	1.224
Cry	0.003	0.211	0.030	0.183	7.980[a]
Destructiveness	0.014	0.125	0.002	0.069	19.528[a]
High rate noise	0.004	0.022	0.001	0.017	1.028
Negativism	0.000	0.011	0.009	0.028	1.321
Whine	0.007	0.049	0.038	0.043	3.220[b]
Yell	0.003	0.074	0.001	0.074	4.109[b]
Mean	0.014	0.053	0.021	0.046	

[a] $p < .001$
[b] $p < .05$

interacted freely. During the experimental period (B), the mother was told to employ that behavior previously identified as an F^S for WH. The mean p(WH) values during the conditions (ABA) were .007, .317, and .043, respectively. The F value of 4.21 (df = 1:8; $p <$ .05) was significant. This study established a correspondence between 2 or 3 kinds of F^Ss for whine identified by observation data and their later impact as causal agents in eliciting whine.

Taken together, the three studies have explored a limited aspect of the problem. However, the most that one can say is that field observations *may* identify stimuli that do indeed control behavior. The studies which followed employed data from intensive case studies done in the field. Observation data from extended baseline studies identified controlling stimuli for the individual child (Patterson & Whalen, in preparation; Patterson & Maerov, in preparation). Cueing the parent, in situ, to present these behaviors was carried out following an ABA design. The resulting data clearly demonstrated the controlling status of these parental behaviors. The findings thus far suggest that the approach seems to be a feasible enterprise, a conclusion reached earlier by ethologists (Eibl-Ebesfeldt, 1970, 1975; Hinde, 1975).

Stage 3:   Tests for Predictive Efficiency

Even if events embedded in family interaction survived the first two phases, there would be no way of knowing how well one "understood" any given coercive behavior. For instance, any given set of antecedents or consequences might account for only a trivial amount of the information needed to make useful in vivo predictions about the child. Aside from a clinician's interest in utilities, there is a more important reason for testing for predictive efficiency.

To this writer, the prediction test seems an empirical means for deciding whether one has a good theory of aggression. The feedback to the experimenter from information about predictive utilities could tell him when to stop adding variables, the hypothetical but happy state of affairs when the data show he is already accounting for most of the variance in intraindividual variability. At current stages of development, such data are almost certain to tell him, "Refine your existing measures and/or add new variables." In this sense, theory building is seen as a continuous but empirically oriented boot-strapping operation.

There is obviously no single means by which one checks for predictive efficiency. Thus far, three different means have been employed in analyzing predictions from the stimulus control framework. Each of these has employed different time units.

1.   Conditional probability statements $p(R_j/\text{Sum of several } F^S\text{s})$. Given all this information about F^Ss for an R_j for one child, what is the increment over the base rate value $p(R_j)$? How well does it stand up in a replication sample of data for that child? The same questions could be asked of $p(R_{j_2}/R_{j_1} \rightarrow C_i)$.

2. Conditional probability statements expressed as probability trees describing the outcome of extended (18 sec) chains. Presumably, the context of interaction may itself set constraints upon the child's behavior such that he becomes *more* predictable. For example, the analysis by Karpowitz (1971) showed that the analysis of patterns occuring 18 sec prior to the R_j provided modest increases in the number of F^Ss, as contrasted to the number of those found occurring only immediately prior to R_j. In the present context, it is assumed that there are bilateral effects occurring in child-family member coercive interactions. In these sequences, *both* members become more predictable.

3. One might also calculate the $p(R_j)$ for a given child for each successive 5-, 10-, or 20-min chunk of interaction. Given the estimates for $p(F^S)$, $p(I^S)$, $p(Acc)$ and (Dc), for that R_j, it should be possible to calculate a (Cattell-type P) correlation between each independent variable and the R_j. In each instance, the N is defined by the number of time intervals sued in the calculation of the correlation.

Each definition of predictive efficiency has its own unique set of liabilities and assets. They will be discussed in the section which follows, where data are presented which describe the first in a series of N_1 studies. The data are illustrative of Phase 1 and 3 analyses.

An Intraindividual Analysis of Phases 1 and 3

Thus far, only the data for one subject have been analyzed in a manner corresponding to the sequence of steps outlined above. These analyses were done over a period of three years. The components were analyzed separately. The ordering of the analyses corresponded to our understanding of what the questions were at that time. The "model" described above emerged only slowly and obviously was completely post hoc. For this reason, the illustrative case is not as tight and clean an exemplar as future N_1 studies might be. The analyses might be thought of as illustrative rather than as making a substantive contribution. The discrepancies between data and requirements of the model will be noted as the discussion proceeds.

Fifty observation sessions were carried out in the home of one extremely high rate aggressive, 6-year-old boy (Patterson, 1973). Later an additional 22 observations were made over a 3-month period. In the first analysis, a search was made for noxious classes of responses for this child. The analysis of 742 coercive initiations by Denny during the baseline study showed that 10 noxious responses (R_js) occurred at a rate sufficient for analysis (Patterson, 1974). There were 8 different F^Ss, provided by family members, which controlled these R_js. It is interesting to note that all 8 A_js controlling his R_js had been previously identified in the across-subjects analysis (Patterson & Cobb, 1973) as being under the control of the same noxious behaviors. Because of the small Ns, it was necessary to use all of the A_i data from all family agents. The fact that some agents contributed disproportionately to one R_j or another introduced the possibility of a serious confound in identifying F^Ss and I^Ss. For this reason, it was necessary to carry out an iterative analysis, in which the identification of the class "hostile," was only the first step. The data from the mother, father, and younger sister were then analyzed separately as A_is with Denny's hostile behavior as a dependent variable. The findings from this second analysis are summarized in Figure 2. The data showed "talk" for all family members and father's "disapproval" functioned as initiators for F^Ss for Denny's hostile behaviors. This class constituted about 38% of Denny's total initiations. For his general interactions, the base rate p(hostile) was .1196. This constituted a dependent variable with an acceptably high base-rate value.

The same report described the decision rules used to determine whether A_is were significant and the rules for determining the comparability of stimulus networks necessary in constructing response classes. For Denny, two classes of responses were identified. The first was labeled "immaturity" and consisted of "destructive," "tease," and "cry." A second class was comprised of "whine," "disapproval," and "yell," and to a lesser extent, "negativism." With the exception of yell, all of these responses were previously found in the across-subjects analysis to comprise the hostile class. It constituted the dependent variable for all the analyses which followed.

The third set of analyses searched for consequences which altered the recurrence or persistence of Denny's hostile behaviors. There were 468 new (or first) initiations of Denny's hostile behavior. For each agent behavior, the conditional probability value $p(Ho_2/Ho_1 - C_i)$ was compared to the corrected value for the recurrence of a hostile response, given that the preceding one had been consequated by a non-C_i $[p(Ho_2/Ho_1 \cap C_i)]$ (Patterson, 1974).

As shown in Figure 2, all family members provided consequences which affected the duration or recurrence of hostile behaviors. The mother seemed to be caught in a peculiar trap. If the consequence she gave was "talk," the probability was .446 that he would continue being hostile in the next time frame. If, on the other hand, she chose to follow the typical advice of some child management experts and ignored it, the probability was .56 that he would repeat. Either reaction exceeded the value $p(Ho_2/Ho_1)$ of .3657.

Predictive Utility: Phase 3

Prediction to Adjacent Time Intervals (6 sec).

Only a small subsample of Denny's 18,900 behaviors consisted of "initiations." Thus, about 4% of his total output served as the basis for identifying the F^S and I^S which controlled hostile. For his total interactions, including initiations, the p(Ho) was .1196. The combined contribution of Mother/, Father/,

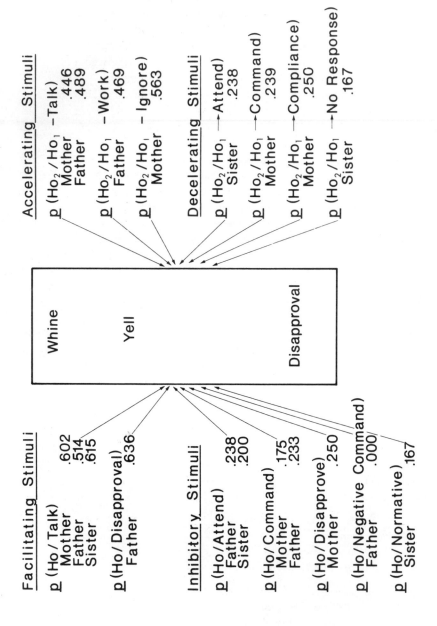

Figure 2   Summary of an analysis of Denny's hostile behavior as the dependent variable.

and Sister/talk as the F^Ss was .2007 [p(hostile/Family talk as A_i)] (Patterson, 1974). Clearly, information about this one set of F^Ss provided a substantial increment in the ability to predict the occurrence or nonoccurrence of his hostile behaviors.

The fact that data from the derivation sample supported the notion of predictive efficiency would be expected. The more crucial test would be provided by an analysis of a replication sample. For this, there were available 9,867 of Denny's interactions.[3] Of these, .0073 were hostile behaviors. The fact that the base-rate values for the 2 Ho values differed presumably reflected the result of family intervention program which had taken place during this interval. The conditional probability of Ho, given talk (for all 3 agents), was .1308.

In summary, the combined information from all three agents about a single F^S doubled our ability to predict his hostile behavior during the general interaction.

Prediction from Larger Time Units (18 sec).

It was assumed that several constraints operated in extended interactions such that both members of a dyad would become more predictable. To test this notion, only one Acc (talk) for Denny's hostile behavior was analyzed. The analysis required many extended interchanges of at least 12 to 18 sec in which the same child and the same family agent interacted throughout. A "probability tree" was a convenient means for describing such extended interchanges.

Such an analysis was carried out using the 50 hrs of baseline data for Denny with hostile as the dependent variable (Patterson, 1974). Each bifurcation in the probability tree specified the probability of hostile or $\sim$hostile and accelerate or $\sim$accelerate. The data were sufficient only for the specification of 3 consecutive episodes.

As the parents supplied the first, then second, and third Acc^s, the effect was to produce very rapid acceleration from the baseline value of .1196 for his hostile behaviors to values around .50. Within the context of these interactions, Denny's Ho behavior also altered the probability that the parents would go on providing him with Acc^s. In effect, the context of interaction set constraints upon the future behavior for both child and family members. In terms of predictive utility, the conditional probability value $p(Ho_3/Ho_1 - Acc_1 - Ho_2 - Acc_2)$ was .471. Denny's behavior did seem to be under the control of external events. The magnitude of this conditional probability value suggests that for one class of responses for this one boy, the analyses of extended units produced substantial reductions in our uncertainty about predicting occurrence or nonoccurrence for the target behavior. This mode of testing predictive utilities was more expensive than the simple two-step analysis, in terms of the amount of data required

---

[3]This second set of data was collected during treatment. For this reason, the data will not really constitute a proper "replication sample" for this boy.

for adequate analyses. However, it also seemed to be more powerful in terms of the magnitude of the increment in predictability.

Prediction from Yet Larger Time Units (5, 10, 20 min).

When one considers intraindividual variations in behavior, they are usually expressed in terms of rate and for time intervals of a magnitude considerably larger than 6 or 18 sec; e.g., intervals of an hour, a day, or a week. Because of the general state of ignorance in these matters, it was decided to begin by analyzing smaller time intervals, 5, 10, and 20 min of data. There is a trade-off for any of these decisions; the larger the time interval, the more reliable the estimate of $p(\text{Ho})$ or $p(F^S)$, $p(\text{Acc})$, etc. On the other hand, the larger the time interval, the smaller the N used to calculate the correlations. It should also be kept in mind that as one moves into time units of this size, the estimate of the frequency of a controlling stimulus does *not* specify whether the event was contingent. The data describe only the number of times a given family agent presented a given stimulus to the child during that time interval.

Denny's rate of hostile behaviors again served as the dependent variable in a series of multiple regression analyses. The corresponding rates for only 4 events were the independent variables. These events were Mother/, Father/talk (both F^Ss and Acc^s), and Sister/talk (F^S), Mother/command (I^S and Dc), Mother/ Play,[4] Father/Command Negative (I^S). To provide replication, the analysis was carried out separately for the baseline (50 sessions) and the intervention data (22 sessions). Only those data were used in which both parents were present. The results for the analysis of the 3 different time intervals for baseline and treatment are summarized in Table 2.

Prior estimates of the amount of data required for stable estimates of code categories (Jones, Reid, & Patterson, 1975) suggested 60 to 100 min of sampling as necessary to provide a minimally reliable estimate for any given code category. Given this finding, then the magnitude of R^2 should increase as a function of increases in the time interval. The data in Table 2 are generally in keeping with this hypothesis. For the largest time interval, the data showed stimulus control variables accounted for 20% to 36% of the variance.[5] While the Rs were of the same relative magnitude at each time interval for both samples, they were at best of only borderline significance.

---

[4] The correlational analysis was run following the first search for networks of controlling stimuli (F^S); thus, it preceded our understanding of the need for iterative analyses. This is another respect in which the "illustrative case" does *not* provide an exact fit to the model.

[5] Even at this early, rather primitive level of analysis, it is of interest to raise the question of which variables contributed the most in accounting for the intraindividual variance. During baseline conditions, the independent variables fulfilling the function in the order of their magnitude were: Sister/talk, Father/command negative and talk. During the second block they were: Father/command negative, Mother/command, and Sister/talk.

TABLE 2

Multiple Regression Analysis of Variations
In Performance of Hostile Behavior for Two Samples of Behavior

Time Interval (min)	Derivation sample				Replication Sample			
	R	F value	df	p value	R	F value	df	p value
5	.295	2.01	6:127 ⟨	.08	.359	1.98	6:80 ⟨	.10
10	.393	1.83	6:60 ⟨	.20	.382	1.02	6:36	n.s.
20	.606	2.51	6:26 ⟨	.05	.461	.63	6:14	n.s.

In general, the findings are viewed as supportive in that for both samples covariations in controlling stimuli seem significantly related to covariations in this one class of noxious behaviors. How well does a stimulus control "theory" account for Denny's hostile behavior? As the most optimistic "best guess," we can account for only a fourth of the variance (information?).

Unfortunately, there is a facet of interaction data which violates an assumption which is crucial to multiple-regression analyses. Parametric statistics require independence of the events which sample any given variable. Given that estimates for the rate of Sister/talk for adjacent time intervals are serially dependent, then correlations between this variable and some criterion such as Denny's hostile may be inflated.

To test for this, an autocorrelational analysis was run for each of the 6 independent variables separately for each of the 3 time intervals for both blocks of data. Only the standard sessions were used in which the target subject shifted every 5 min. The data strongly support the notion of serial dependencies for the behaviors of these family members for the 4 behavioral events examined here. As pointed out by Hoffman (1967), autocorrelations of this magnitude mean that the degrees of freedom used to estimate the significance of the correlations must be drastically reduced. In effect, none of the Rs in Table 2 would even approach statistical significance. The problem is of such a magnitude that even doubling the number of observation sessions would not provide sufficient data

The inescapable conclusion is that to summarize the covariations among variables which are themselves serially dependent, one must seek new models other than multiple regression. In the meantime, my colleague, Richard Jones, suggests that we use only lag 4 data to estimate the correlation across variables. While not shown here, the autocorrelations in Table 1 were actually extended to lag 10. It demonstrated that for most of the variables, the serial dependency seemed to drop out at about lag 4. We plan to follow through on this problem by examining this and alternative modes of analysis.

TABLE 3

Lag$_1$ Autocorrelations for Six Behavioral Events

Interval (min)	N	Mother	Talk Father	Sister	Play Sister	Command Mother	Command Negative Father
Block 1							
5	77	.359	.323	.411	−.027	.136	.286
10	38	.568	.498	.554	−.057	.120	.080
20	19	.719	.418	.584	−.125	.294	.075
Block 2							
5	84	.228	.200	.233	−.046	.154	.025
10	42	.471	.428	.436	−.088	.438	.169
20	21	.295	.466	.465	.225	.274	.135

SUMMARY AND DISCUSSION

An argument was made for developing a "performance" theory of children's noxious behaviors. It was assumed that most children in our society had been exposed to modeling and reinforcing contingencies by age three. Given that most children had learned most of the techniques in applying coercive behaviors, the question is why they vary over time and settings in the rates with which the behaviors are performed.

It was assumed that immediately impinging social stimuli would be associated with altered probabilities of children's ongoing noxious behaviors. A means was described for identifying some of these stimuli as they occur in various dyadic interchanges between the child and other family members. Two kinds of stimuli were found: those associated with the initiation of noxious behaviors; and those which correlate with the immediate recurrence or maintenance of these behaviors. There is every reason to believe that variables other than these particular external social events might function as "determinants." For example, the F^Ss and I^Ss and Accs listed in this chapter very likely interact with such state variables as hunger and fatigue. Others would claim that the cognitions of the participants function as prime determinants. Such variables can, and should, be examined in the present format. The limitation lies only in what can be measured and not within the dictates of one theory or another.

The primary data consisted of two blocks of observation sessions in which one boy and his family provided the data. These were used to construct response classes in which the noxious behaviors were under the control of comparable networks of initiating stimuli. The analyses were extended to include a search for maintaining stimuli for one of these response classes.

These findings, in turn, were used to determine the magnitude of predictions which could be made for different time intervals. The analyses showed that information about initiating stimuli could almost double that which obtains when using only base rate information to predict behavior in the adjacent (6-sec) time frames. This increment held for both the derivation and the replication sample. The third predictive model explored larger interaction units as a basis for prediction. The probability tree was constructed for one class of Acc^S and for one class of the boy's noxious behaviors. Some features of the analyses showed that in extended interaction, the behavior of both the child and parent seem to become more predictable. Some of the transactional chains produced 4-fold increments in the conditional probability values for the boy's behavior. The next prediction model employed a multiple regression analysis to determine the contribution of both initiating and maintaining variables in determing one class of behavior for 5-, 10-, and 20-min time segments. The magnitude of the multiple correlation showed that up to 20-30% of the variance was accounted for. However, the serially dependent nature of the data violated the assumptions underlying the correlational model, so it is not possible to estimate the significance of these findings. Additional means must be found to study this problem.

Upon reading an earlier draft of this chapter, one critic commented, "So stimuli control behaviors, so what else is new?" Is the function of this approach indeed no more than reaffirmation of the obvious? I think not. It is the knowledge of *which* stimuli control behavior that will give the psychologist a key to making predictions about ongoing behavior in natural settings. Until we can make such predictions, all of our "theories" about children's social behavior are probably of little moment.

In examining the data presented here and elsewhere, to say that there exists no performance theory of children's coercive behaviors is no exaggeration. The most that can be asserted is that it may be possible. If it is indeed to be done, then we must search for more powerful data and more complex statistical models which will be adequate to the task of describing complex functional relations.

ACKNOWLEDGMENTS

It is a pleasure to acknowledge the contributions of Dr. Sidney Bijou. Aside from his many papers and books which stimulated much of our own work with children, he also made a much more personal contribution. Early in the 1960s, the "Eugene contingent" was earnestly trying to carry out functional analyses. Even though we were complete novices, Sid was able to identify something in our enthusiasm and high-rate lever pressing which could be reinforced.

This study was supported by MH 25227-01 and MH 25548-01. Computing assistance was obtained from the Health Sciences Computing Facility, UCLA, sponsored by NIH Grant FR-3. The author wished to thank R. Dawes and P. Hoffman for their critiques of earlier drafts of this report.

REFERENCES

Atkinson, J. A. Nonavailability of mother-attention as an antecedent event for coercive mands in the preschool child. Unpublished master's dissertation, University of Oregon, 1971.

Baldwin, A. L. The study of individual personality by means of intra-individual correlations. *Journal of Personality,* 1946, *14,* 151-168.

Bandura, A. *Aggression: A social learning analysis.* Englewood Cliffs, N.J.: Prentice-Hall, Inc., 1973.

Bijou, S. W., & Baer, D. M. *Child development: A systematic and empirical theory.* New York: Appleton-Century-Crofts, Inc., 1961.

Buehler, R. E., Patterson, G. R., & Furniss, J. M. The reinforcement of behavior in institutional settings. *Behavior Research and Therapy,* 1966, *4,* 157-167.

Cairns, R. B. Fighting and punishment from a developmental perspective. *Nebraska Symposium,* University of Nebraska Press, 1972.

Devine, V. T. The coercion process: A laboratory analogue. Unpublished doctoral dissertation, State University of New York at Stony Brook, 1971.

Ebner, M. J. An investigation of the role of the social environment in the generalization and persistence of the effect of a behavior modification program. Unpublished doctoral dissertation, University of Oregon, 1967.

Eibl-Ebesfeldt, I. *Ethology, the biology of behavior.* New York: Holt, Rinehart, & Winston, 1970.

Eibl-Ebesfeldt, I. Ethological approaches to violence. In J. DeWit & W. Hartup (Eds.), *Determinants and origins of aggressive behavior.* The Hague, Netherlands: Mouton Press, 1975.

Ferster, C., & Skinner, B. F. *Schedules of reinforcement.* New York: Appleton-Century-Crofts, 1957.

Fiske, D., & Rice, L. Intra-individual response variability. *Psychological Bulletin,* 1955, *52,* 217-250.

Hinde, R. An overview of ethologic approaches. In J. DeWit & W. Hartup (Eds.), *Determinants and origins of aggressive behavior.* The Hague, Netherlands: Mouton Press, 1975.

Hoffman, W. H. Statistical models for the study of change in the single case. In C. Harris (Ed.), *Problems in measuring change.* University of Wisconsin Press, 1967.

Jones, R. R., Reid, J. B., & Patterson, G. R. Naturalistic observations in clinical assessment. In P. McReynolds (Ed.), *Advances in psychological assessment* (Vol. 3). San Francisco: Jossey-Bass, 1975.

Karpowitz, D. H. Stimulus control in family interaction sequences as observed in the naturalistic setting of the home. Unpublished doctoral dissertation, University of Oregon, 1971.

Patterson, G. R. Changes in status of family members as controlling stimuli: A basis for describing treatment process. In L. A. Hamerlynck, L. C. Handy, & E. J. Mash (Eds.), *Behavior change: Methodology concepts and practice.* Champaign, Ill.: Research Press, 1973.

Patterson, G. R. A basis for identifying stimuli which control behaviors in natural settings. *Child Development,* 1974, *45,* 900-911.

Patterson, G. R. The aggressive child: Victim and architect of a coercive system. In L. A. Hamerlynck, E. J. Mash, & L. C. Handy (Eds.), *Behavior modification and families: I. Theory and research. II. Applications and developments.* New York: Brunner/Mazell, 1976. (a)

Patterson, G. R. A performance theory for coercive behavior in family interaction. In R. Cairns (Ed.), *Social interaction: Methods, analysis and illustration.* Society for Research in Child Development Monograph, in press 1976. (b)

Patterson, G. R. Accelerating stimuli for two classes of coercive behaviors. *Journal Abnormal Child Psychology,* in press 1977.

Patterson, G. R., & Cobb, J. A. A dyadic analysis of "aggressive" behaviors. In J. P. Hill (Ed.), *Minnesota Symposia on Child Psychology* (Vol. 5). Minneapolis: University of Minnesota, 1971.

Patterson, G. R., & Cobb, J. A. Stimulus control for classes of noxious behaviors. In J. F. Knutson (Ed.), *The control of aggression: Implications from basic research.* Chicago: Aldine, 1973.

Patterson, G. R., Littman, R. A., & Bricker, W. Assertive behavior in children: A step toward a theory of aggression. *Monographs of the Society for Research in Child Development,* 1967, *32,* (5, Serial No. 113).

Patterson, G. R., Ray, R. S., Shaw, D. A., & Cobb, J. A. Manual for coding of family interactions, 1968, revision. Document #01234. New York: Microfiche Publications [1969].

Patterson, G. R., & Reid, J. B. Reciprocity and coercion: Two facets of social systems. In C. Neuringer & J. D. Michael (Eds.), *Behavior modification in clinical psychology.* New York: Appleton-Century-Crofts, 1970.

Reid, J. B. Reciprocity in family interaction. Unpublished doctoral dissertation, University of Oregon, 1967.

Sallows, G. O. Responsiveness of deviant and normal children to naturally occurring consequences. Unpublished doctoral dissertation, University of Oregon, 1972.

Shaw, D. Family maintenance schedules for deviant behavior. Unpublished doctoral dissertation, University of Oregon, 1971.

Sidman, M. *Tactics of scientific research.* New York: Basic Books, 1960.

Taplin, P. Changes in parent consequating behavior as an outcome measure in the evaluation of a social reprogramming approach to the treatment of aggressive boys. Unpublished doctoral dissertation, University of Wisconsin, 1974.

Wahler, R. G. Some structural aspects of deviant child behavior. *Journal Applied Behavior Analysis,* 1975, *8,* 27-42.

5

The Development and Maintenance
of Language: An Operant Model

Todd R. Risley

The University of Kansas

Recent years have heralded increased activity in the disciplines concerned with human speech. The most notable impact has been made by the linguists and psycholinquists (see Berko, 1958; Chomsky, 1957; Fraser, Bellugi & Brown, 1963; Ervin, 1964). In psychology, human speech has been investigated by steadily increasing numbers of workers since the turn of the century. The psychologist's activities have evolved into several discrete categories that are delineated by methodology. These categories can be identified with the labels of *verbal learning, language development,* and, more recently, *verbal conditioning.*

Verbal learning, a branch of traditional experimental psychology, focuses on the processes by which individuals link two verbal items together, learn the sequence in which verbal items occur, differentiate between verbal items, and recall a set of items in the laboratory (Cofer, 1971). Certain aspects of verbal behavior are used as the dependent variable in studies of human learning or in the investigation of specific intrarelations of verbal behavior.

Language development encompasses a large portion of the literature of developmental psychology. Descriptions of verbal behavior or the effects of experimental manipulations on verbal behavior are correlated with chronological age (Irwin, 1960; Templin, 1957).

Verbal conditioning is identified closely with clinical psychology and is oriented toward experimentally analyzing psychotherapeutic procedures. The investigation of the effects of contingent social stimuli on various categories of verbal behavior (such as affect statements, self-references) is a standard paradigm (Hersen, 1970; Holz & Azrin, 1966; Kanfer, 1968).

These three categories do not subsume all psychological work in verbal behavior; rather, they represent discrete areas in which the investigative procedures are relatively formalized. Although there has been extensive activity in these areas, no comprehensive and empirical statements of the development and maintenance of verbal behavior have been derived. Upon examination, it does not appear the the methodologies of any of these areas are designed to produce such a statement.

Those approaches that present a comprehensive account of verbal behavior can be characterized as rational formulations, drawing upon informal experiments, observations, and anecdotes. Several authors have presented formulations that emphasize the instrumental or functional nature of verbal behavior. In these presentations verbal behavior is analyzed as a special class of instrumental or operant behavior. The causes of verbal behavior are sought in the environmental events associated with verbal behavior. The principles that describe the interrelation of environmental events and verbal behavior are conceived of as special cases of general principles of operant or instrumental conditioning. The presentations of Lewis (1936, 1948, 1959, 1963), Mowrer (1960), Osgood (1953), and Skinner (1957) are, to varying degrees, oriented toward this position. This chapter discusses the development of verbal behavior in terms of the principles derived from operant or instrumental conditioning.

In operant conditioning the most important consideration is the function of behavior. In this analysis the causes of the verbal behavior of an individual are sought in the functions of the behavior, and the causes of the similarities of behavior between individuals are sought in similarities of functions of behaviors across individuals.

This analysis indicates that given culturally determined functions for verbal behaviors, appropriate approximation procedures, and an initial vocal repertoire, an individual's verbal behavior inevitably will come to conform to the specifications of the culture.

Culturally determined functions for verbal behaviors are simply the arrangement of contingencies in a culture that maintain the verbal behavior of any adult member. The schedule of these contingencies can probably be conceived of as a constant. In general, members of a culture respond similarly to a verbal behavior of an individual. In the instances in which members of a culture respond differently to a behavior, the proportion of people who respond in a particular manner is fairly constant. It might be said, then, that the society into which a young adult enters is programed to provide certain contingencies on his verbal (and other) behavior. The schedule of these contingencies, although intermittent, is relatively constant over a long period of time and tends to stabilize an individual's behavior around certain criteria.

The appropriate approximation procedures are the steps necessary to establish the behaviors of an individual to the level that will enable the society's program to take over and maintain or modify them. If an individual does not exhibit the verbal behaviors to which society is programed to respond, there will be no contact with the contingencies that would strengthen or maintain those behaviors. An equally important approximation procedure is the steps necessary to make the society's contingencies functional for an individual. If an individual has an appropriate verbal repertoire but the responses of other members of society to these behaviors are functionally netural for the individual, those behaviors will not be maintained.

The initial vocal repertoire is the initial characteristics or operant level of an individual's vocal behavior, before the contingencies of the environment are applied.

CULTURALLY DETERMINED FUNCTIONS

The Nature of the Reinforcers

Verbal behavior, as is the case with other operant behavior, is ultimately maintained by a finite number of empirically demonstrable primary reinforcers. These primary reinforcers are by no means limited to the food, water, and shock termination commonly manipulated in the laboratory. The diversity of possible primary reinforcers can be shown by a partial list of those demonstrated in animal studies: temperature change (Carlton & Marks, 1958), sexual stimulation (Beach, 1951), the opportunity to exercise (Premack, Schaeffer, & Hunt, 1964), tactual stimulation (Falk, 1958; Wenzel, 1959), illumination change (Davis, 1958; Keller, 1941), sound intensity change (Azrin, 1958; Harrison & Tracy, 1955), vibration (Schaefer, 1960), and physical pressure (Brodie & Boren, 1958). There are undoubtedly many other primary reinforcers that have not been investigated systematically.

In addition to the classes of primary reinforcers that are general across species, species-specific reinforcers have been demonstrated. For example, the sight of a combatant peer is a reinforcer for a fighting cock (Thompson, 1964). The possibility exists that there are primary reinforcers for humans that differ in kind from those of other species. This awaits an adequate demonstration.

It may be that certain activities are self-reinforcing in that proprioceptive stimuli from the activity is a primary reinforcer. The twirling, rocking, and headbumping of children may be an example of this. Similarly, the sounds resulting from a person's own vocal behavior may be a primary reinforcer for humans. If this is the case, the reinforcer, of course, would be difficult to manipulate and therefore to demonstrate empirically.

At this point it appears that very little adult verbal behavior in a civilized society is maintained by the direct contingencies of primary reinforcers. However, stimuli can acquire or gain effectiveness as reinforcers by being associated with already effective reinforcers. Once a stimulus becomes a conditioned reinforcer it can then enhance the reinforcing effectiveness of other stimuli with which it is associated (Kelleher & Gollub, 1962).

If a stimulus acquires reinforcing effectiveness by being associated with a single primary reinforcer, its effectiveness will vary as deprivation, aversive stimulation, or other motivational states alter the effectiveness of that primary reinforcer. If, however, that stimulus has been associated with many primary reinforcers, variance in motivational states relevant to any one of the primary reinforcers will not alter its reinforcing effectiveness as markedly.

If association with a primary reinforcer is not maintained, the reinforcing effectiveness of a conditioned reinforcer will decrease. If the association with a primary reinforcer is intermittent, the reinforcing effectiveness of a conditioned reinforcer will be less, but the effectiveness will tend to remain more stable with variation in, or termination of, the association with the primary reinforcer.

A stimulus may be established and maintained as a conditioned reinforcer by being associated with a primary reinforcer in one of two ways. It may function as a discriminative stimulus for a behavior that produces a primary reinforcer, or it may simply signal the increased probability of a noncontingent reinforcer (Kelleher, 1966). In the latter case it would be a stimulus present over an interval of time, during which the probability of other reinforcers is increased (not necessarily contingent on any behavior). Many of the social reinforcers, such as attention, smiling, and approval, probably fit into this category.

As one conditioned reinforcer can, in turn, establish or enhance the reinforcing effectiveness of other stimuli, any conditioned reinforcer can be many steps removed from the primary reinforcers that ultimately maintain its reinforcing properties. It is presumably this fact that makes it difficult to identify the primary reinforcers maintaining the verbal behavior of adults. This difficulty also has given rise to the question of a conditioned reinforcer becoming autonomous. That is, the reinforcing properties of a conditioned reinforcer might come to exist independently of its association with primary reinforcers. However, such an autonomous conditioned reinforcer has never been demonstrated experimentally.

It has repeatedly been demonstrated that verbal behavior can be established, maintained, and modified by primary reinforcers. Food has been the most extensively used primary positive reinforcer, probably because it is the most convenient and manipulable. Verbal behavior has been established or reinstated in mute psychotics by the contingent delivery of gum, candy, and portions of meals (Issacs, Thomas, & Goldiamond, 1960; Sherman, 1965a), and in autistic and retarded children with candy, fruits, and portions of meals (Barton, 1970; Risley & Wolf, 1967; Wolf, Risley, & Mees, 1964). Stuttering was decreased in a child by delivering ice cream contingent upon fluent speech (Rickard & Munday, 1965). Vocalizations were increased in a mute, retarded child by the contingent delivery of joggling and singing (Kerr, Meyerson, & Michael, 1965) and in normal infants by the contingent delivery of tickling and clucking (Rheingold, Gewirtz, & Ross, 1959).

The contingent presentation and removal of primary aversive stimuli (negative reinforcers) has been shown to be effective in eliminating and strengthening verbal behavior. The application and termination of shock contingent on silence and speech eliminated hysterical mutism (Kircher, Pear, & Martin, 1971; Yealland, 1918). A contingent increase and decrease in rest periods was effective in modifying functional aphonia (Walton & Black, 1960). Stuttering has been somewhat reduced and increased by the presentation and termination of a loud tone contingent on disfluencies (Felty, 1959; Flanagan, Goldiamond, & Azrin, 1959).

While it is assumed that most of the verbal behavior of adults in our society is maintained by generalized conditioned reinforcers and, therefore, is not under the control of any one primary reinforcer, several studies suggest an interesting approach to investigating this question experimentally. Those aspects of verbal behavior that are primarily under the control of a single primary reinforcer should vary according to variations in deprivation of that reinforcer. Chronic food deprivation has been reported to produce systematic changes in verbal behavior (Atkinson & McLelland, 1948; Levine, Chein, & Murphy, 1942; Sanford, 1936). The most informative study was done by Keys (1950): adults were reduced to 80% of their ad libitum body weights over 6 months, and extensive records were made of the subsequent changes in their verbal and nonverbal behaviors. Although not quantified, verbal behavior concerning food was reported to increase with a related decrease in other verbal behaviors. The verbal behavior that was grossly decreased, general "conversation," is probably maintained by generalized conditioned reinforcers of attention and subtle social contingencies.

A series of studies by Gewirtz and Baer (1958a, b) and Gewirtz, Baer and Roth (1958) demonstrated that deprivation and satiation of social interaction have effects, albeit small, on the effectiveness of attention and approval as reinforcers. This suggests that there may be some primary reinforcing components in attention and approval, because, at least in animal studies, the effectiveness of a conditioned reinforcer seems to be a function of deprivation and satiation of the primary reinforcer with which it has been associated (rather than its own frequency of presentation).

Observations of verbal behavior that is primarily under the control of deprivation conditions frequently emphasize the expressive nature of speech (Brown, 1958). Here, speech is analyzed as if it were respondent behavior (that is, under the control of eliciting stimuli). Probably only a few types of vocal behavior and no verbal behaviors are respondent in nature. The rapid intake or expulsion of breath, accompanied by gasps or grunts, and some components of crying are probably the extent of respondent vocal behavior. Under states of primary deprivation, primary aversive stimulation, and other high-drive conditions, human speech is generally disrupted. The verbal behavior that expresses or comments on the state of affairs is primarily that which would tend to result in the alleviation of that state through mediation by another person. Even the vocalizations associated with crying have a large operant component in that the frequency, intensity, and topography of this behavior appear to be determined largely by the consequences it has produced in the person's past (Etzel & Gewirtz, 1967; Hart, Allen, Buell, Harris, & Wolf, 1964; Williams, 1959).

In attempting to delineate the events that maintain and modify established verbal behavior in our society, we are not limited to a theoretical or speculative analysis. Fortunately, experimental work has been done which demonstrated that at least some of the events occurring in verbal interaction between members of our society are reinforcers that do affect verbal behavior.

The verbal-conditioning literature is replete with instances in which the contingent application of statements such as "yes," "uh huh," "good," and "I agree," and gestures such as head nods and smiles have increased a class of verbal behavior. Similarly, statements such as "no," "wrong," "uh uh," headshakes, and disagreement, have been shown to decrease classes of verbal behavior. Articles by Greenspoon (1962), Holz & Azrin (1966), Krasner (1962), and Salzinger (1959) review much of the work in this area. Many studies have demonstrated that the contingent delivery of attention — which includes many of the above reinforcers accompanying the approach and interaction of another person — markedly affects the verbal and other behaviors of children and adults (Allen, Hart, Buell, Harris, & Wolf, 1964; Bennett & Ling, 1972; Harris, Johnston, Kelley, & Wolf, 1964; Hart, Allen, Buell, Harris, & Wolf, 1964; Liberman, Teigen, Patterson, & Baker, 1973; Zimmerman & Zimmerman, 1962).

Reinforcers of this type are most likely conditioned reinforcers; and, as such, their reinforcing properties depend on their association with primary reinforcers. Very few studies have investigated the dependence of these reinforcers on primary reinforcers. Lovaas, Freitag, Kinder, Rubenstein, Schaeffer, and Simmons (1966) established "good" as an effective reinforcer for autistic children by making it discriminative for a response that resulted in a primary reinforcer (food). Then they demonstrated its reinforcing effectiveness as dependent upon its continued association with the primary reinforcer. In the process, however, they found that "good" could be maintained as a very effective reinforcer even with extremely infrequent association with the primary reinforcer.

The demonstrations that verbal behavior can be established and that already established verbal behavior can be modified by the systematic use of various reinforcers support the conclusion that such reinforcers are operative in establishing, maintaining, and modifying verbal behavior in the natural environment.

The Nature of the Verbal Behavior Maintained by Culturally Determined Functions

A social interaction involving verbal behavior can be described both in terms of physical events and in terms of the function of these events. For example:

1. A speaker emits verbal behavior (physical description).
2. Some components of this verbal behavior affect the listener (functional description).

3. The listener responds (physical description).
4. Some components of this response affect the speaker (functional description).

There is universal agreement that a purely physical description of verbal behavior is inadequate. All approaches emphasize a functional classification of physical events.

Linguists analyze and classify the verbal utterances of a speaker or writer in terms of their effect on a listener (Step 2 in the previous example). For example, a phoneme is the smallest class of the elements of verbal behavior that, in a particular context, have the same effect on a listener of a particular culture. Similarly, morphemes, syntax, and grammar are different and apparently orthogonal classifications based on the various aspects of a listener's behavior that they affect. Linguistic analysis has produced general statements about some aspects of verbal utterances. These higher-order descriptions, or "laws of language" for a given culture, are fertile ground for psychological work on the stimulus function of verbal utterances. For example, a generalization gradient of a particular form generated when two different responses are conditioned to two points on a continuous stimulus dimension (Cross & Lane, 1962; Honig & Day, 1962; Lane & Curran, 1963; Risley, 1964) can account for the linguistic principle of phonemic contrast or opposition (Lane, 1965). Similarly, Mowrer (1954) speculates that the principles of respondent conditioning account for the subject-predicate form of most grammars.

However, in classifying verbal behaviors, most psychologists have not differentiated clearly between the function of verbal behavior in terms of consequences to the speaker and the functions of verbal utterances as stimuli for a listener. Mowrer (1960), Osgood (1953), and Morris (1946), centering their discussion around "meaning," which refers to the discriminative function of language, analyze verbal behavior on the basis of words or, more recently, morphemes, which are described by Lotz (1961), as the "smallest elements with which meaning can be associated" [p. 7]. Thus, these authors dwell on an analysis of verbal discriminative stimuli rather than an analysis of verbal behavior.

While Skinner (1957) also uses this criterion in discussing verbal behavior, he uses it simply to distinguish verbal and nonverbal behavior. He defines verbal behavior in terms of its effect on a listener, but emphasizes that the important effect is that the behavior of the listener, in turn, affects the speaker. His subsequent categorizing of verbal behavior is not based on its discriminative function for a listener, but on the consequences of the behavior for the speaker.

If the effects of verbal behavior on a listener, in terms of the observable responses of a listener (Steps 2 and 3 in the example above), can be assumed to be a culturally determined constant, then the important determinants in establishing, maintaining, and modifying the verbal behavior of an individual can be sought in the consequences of that behavior for the speaker (Steps 1 and 4 in the example). Linguists and others who emphasize the stimulus functions of verbal utterances universally support this assumption. In fact, their classifications and principles, which they strongly assert to be inclusive of all aspects of verbal behavior, can be operationally defined to be based on the constant effects that verbal behavior has on a listener and the generality of those effects across most members of a culture. For example, a phoneme is defined as all those sound patterns that are responded to as being the "same" sound by most listeners of a culture. When viewed in this fashion, the work of some of the most ardent dissenters to Skinner's emphasis on the function of verbal behavior for the speaker (e.g., Chomsky, 1959) in fact support the importance of that emphasis.

Verbal behavior can be classified according to its function for the speaker in two ways: (1) by the nature of the reinforcers that maintain it; and (2) by the characteristics of the verbal behavior that vary together with manipulations of reinforcers. Skinner (1957) distinguishes between verbal behavior that is maintained by reinforcers, usually primary, whose strength varies with deprivation and satiation ("mands"), and that maintained by conditioned, generalized reinforcers. This latter category is further divided into echoic and textual behaviors, intraverbals, tacts, and autoclitics, according to the types of discriminative stimuli controlling them.

A more recent emphasis in operant language analysis has been a focus on response classes. A response class is a set of topographically distinguishable responses whose probabilities of occurrence vary together. A response class is identified by altering the probability of occurrence of some members through manipulation of their consequences and observing a concomitant change in the probabilities of other responses. The simplest case is response induction (Skinner, 1938), in which changes in the probability of one response result in similar, although usually weaker, changes in the probability of other responses of similar topography. However, more arbitrary response classes can be established. The verbal-conditioning literature is replete with studies in which "response classes" have been established. Unfortunately, most reports of verbal conditioning do not provide sufficient information to determine whether a response class had been established, rather than each response having been increased independently by being directly reinforced during training. The increase in some responses as a function of the reinforcement of other responses has been explicitly reported in only a few studies. Fahmy (1953) reported that the reinforcement of references to humans in responses to ink-blot cards increased the frequency of other references to humans on subsequent cards. Weide (1959) increased the proportion of using malevolent adjectives and nouns by reinforcing sentences containing malevolent verbs in another situation. Sarason (1957) reinforced sentences containing verbally active or bodily active verbs under one condition and obtained a higher proportion of other verbs of the same class under another condition. Greenspoon (1955), and Salzinger, Portney, Zletegura, and Keisner (1963) reported that reinforcement of plural nouns increased the frequency of new plural nouns emitted. Many other verbal conditioning studies appear to have established response classes of other aspects of verbal behavior such as verbs (Kanfer, 1958; Patterson, Helper, & Wilcott, 1960), plural responses (Sidowski, 1954), family and nonfamily reminiscences (Quay, 1959), hostile verbs (Ferguson & Buss, 1960), aggressive responses (Zedek, 1959), positive and negative self-referent statements (Rogers, 1960), emotional words (Weiss, Krasner, & Ullmann, 1960), and statements about food (Simkins, 1962); but the classes can only be inferred from the procedures and results presented.

Imitation generally has been recognized as extremely important in the acquisition of verbal and nonverbal behaviors (e.g., Bandura & Walters, 1963; Miller & Dollard, 1941; Mowrer, 1960). It has been demonstrated that a response class of imitation can be established through reinforcement procedures. Baer and Sherman (1964) systematically increased and decreased the frequency of three imitative responses of nursery-school children in successive periods of reinforcement and extinction. A fourth imitative response, which was never reinforced, increased and decreased along with the imitative responses for which the reinforcers were manipulated. In other words, reinforcing three topographically dissimilar responses (nodding head, mouthing, and strange vocalizations), all of which were imitative, increased the probability of a fourth topographically dissimilar but imitative response (bar pressing). Sherman (1965a) established some imitative verbal behavior in a completely mute psychotic by reinforcing nonverbal imitative responses. Metz (1965) found that after slowly shaping several simple imitative responses in autistic children they began to emit approximate imitative responses to novel behaviors presented by a model. Thus, it has been demonstrated that a response class of imitation can be established, and, once established, intermittent reinforcement of some imitative behaviors will maintain a high probability of all established imitative behaviors and a tendency to emit new imitative behaviors.

The establishment of a response class of imitation would be a sufficient condition for the acquisition of verbal behavior of the complexity demonstrated by a linguistic analysis. The linguistic units of verbal behavior are not necessarily the building blocks, which are learned independently and then simply combined to form complex speech units. It is more probable that many large speech units are acquired in toto through imitation, and that the linguistic units have been discriminated from these larger units as the individual acquires more large units that have these individual properties in common, as these linguistic units themselves become response classes. Many of the formal educational practices of our culture are designed to insure that response classes of semilinguistic units (grammar, words, syllables, sounds) are established.

Several investigators have extended the procedures used to establish a response class of imitation in retarded children (Baer, Peterson, & Sherman, 1967) to produce generative grammar. Briefly, when retarded children were taught by imitation and reinforcement procedures to respond with an appropriate grammatical form (past- or present-tense verbs, for example) to a set of stimuli, they were able to generalize or "apply the rule" to untrained stimuli.

That operant procedures can result, at least in a laboratory with retarded children, in more behavior than was actually trained, helps to clarify a crucial objection to an operant view of language development; that people produce more language than they have been taught directly (Baer, Guess, & Sherman, 1972; Guess, Sailor, Rutherford, & Baer, 1968; Schumaker & Sherman, 1970; Wheeler & Sulzer, 1970). Recently, Lutzker and Sherman (1974) demonstrated that normal toddlers could be taught the generative use of sentences with correct subject-verb agreement, lending greater support to the view that similar procedures may be operating in the natural environment.

In general, the work with response classes of verbal behavior indicates that a response class can be produced across almost any aspect of verbal behavior. Probably an emitted verbal response is a member of many response classes, each determined by the history of reinforcement of each individual. However, the likelihood that in any given culture the reinforcement histories of most individuals will be similar enables many response classes to be identified by their formal characteristics. Aggressive responses or plural nouns are probably already-existing response classes in most members of our culture. In the verbal conditioning studies, differentially reinforcing aggressive or plural responses simply increased the strength of all members of these already-established classes (Salzinger, 1959).

The culturally determined functions of language are the aggregate of conditions that maintain the verbal behavior of mature members of a society. If these conditions are in part the differential reinforcement for that verbal behavior that matches the characteristics of the society's verbal behavior (be it phonemes, morphemes, grammar, inflections, rhythm, vocabulary, or whatever), then the individual's verbal behavior will stabilize in correspondence to these characteristics.

THE INITIAL VOCAL REPERTOIRE

The initial sounds of a child are under the control of antecedent conditions. Some crying of the neonate is an unconditioned response to immediate eliciting stimuli; blows, pricks, or restraint (Pratt, Nelson, & Kuo, 1930). Most crying, although under the control of antecedent events, does not fit precisely the conditions that usually define respondent behavior. An example is the crying that is correlated with the passage of time since the ingestion of food. This crying is not controlled (elicited) by any measurable immediately preceding event, but rather appears to be controlled by what are usually called motivational variables or setting events. Other instances of crying in the neonate occur without any known antecedent events.

In actuality, crying in the neonate is not usually categorized by the events that cause the behavior, but more often by the events that terminate it. Thus, in some cases crying is terminated by food, and the neonate is then said to have been crying because of hunger. In other cases it is interminable, as when a neonate is said to be crying because of colic. There has been some contention that after the first month, various types of discomfort elicit different patterns of crying (Vetter, 1971), but spectrographic analyses of infant cries showed that judgments of the cause of crying are more likely due to prior knowledge of the state of the infant (Brackbill, 1971). All of the crying of the neonate is usually classified as an unconditioned response, and eliciting stimuli are inferred when they are not apparent, such as hunger pangs or colic pains (Darwin, 1896; Osgood, 1953). But a distinction between the types of controlling conditions may be important in investigations of this behavior.

However, the initial crying of a neonate is probably of little importance to the development of speech. It does not appear to be related to the behavior that is most probably the first step in the sequence of speech development. This behavior, the so-called "comfort sounds" (Lewis, 1959; McCarthy, 1930), is under the control of a different set of conditions than those which control crying. These sounds, at first merely undifferentiated soft noises, are most probable in the absence of the conditions that produce crying; they do not appear to be evoked or elicited by any immediately antecedent event. These sounds may initially occur solely as a function of a relaxed vocal apparatus with the tongue dropped toward the soft palate and an excess of saliva in the mouth, as they are most probable when neonates are placed on their backs in the period between feeding and sleep (Lewis, 1959).

APPROXIMATION PROCEDURES

The constant contingencies that a culture provides for verbal behavior are based on the consistent manner in which that verbal behavior affects the members of that culture. This would indicate that the verbal behavior in question would have to be a fair approximation to the normal verbal behavior of the culture in order for it to have a consistent effect on, and, consequently, receive a consistent response from the members of the culture. Because the contingencies that a culture is programed to deliver are relevant only to already established verbal behavior, how, then, does the verbal behavior of an individual reach the point at which it comes into contact with, and is maintained by, the culture's contingencies?

Although taken as a whole, the contingencies that a culture programs for verbal behavior are a constant, the contingencies that parents program for their children's verbal behavior are not. The verbal behavior of young children that would not affect the behavior of a stranger does affect the behavior of their parents. In other words, parents respond to their children's verbalizations when other members of the culture do not. This is probably a function of the parents being under the control of past situational stimuli in addition to the verbal stimuli of the child. A stranger would respond appropriately to the child's verbalization "boo" if the child was holding a book ("Yes, that's a book. Do you want to read a story?") but not in the absence of the book. A parent who has responded appropriately to "boo" in the presence of a book would probably respond appropriately to "boo" in the absence of a book ("Oh, you want me to read you a story.").

Although baby talk initially produces reinforcers in the presence of parents, they increasingly respond with corrective prompts ("Can you say book?") before responding to the content of the verbalization. Furthermore, the child is progressively apt to be in the presence of more and more people who have less and less experience with her baby talk, and thereby receive more frequent prompts for comprehensible speech. In this manner, the contingencies gradually change until, at the age of five or six, the child begins to spend extended periods of time at school in the presence of an adult who responds differentially to verbal behavior more closely approximating that of the culture. Subsequently, the contingencies for verbal behavior change systematically in the education curriculum. Thus, it is not difficult to delineate in a general fashion the approximation procedures that can bring about the change from initial approximation (baby talk) to adult verbal behavior.

The probable approximation procedures that bring about the change from the initial operant level vocalizations of a neonate to the baby-talk approximations of society's verbal behavior are more complicated. Just prior to the first instance of recognizable speech, infants exhibit vocalizations that approximate the language of their culture. On the average, by the age of eight months the level of vocalizations that approximate the language of the culture is quite high. These vocalizations differ considerably from those exhibited at birth and shortly thereafter. Infants repeat heard sounds and syllables and imitate their own vocal productions. These syllables may have intonations resembling questions or exclamations (Lenneberg, 1967). At first there is an expansion of the range of sounds emitted, probably to the point at which all possible sounds that could be produced by the infant's vocal apparatus are emitted. This development is apparently similar for infants born in every culture (Gregoire, 1937; Jakobson, 1941; Osgood, 1953). Subsequently, there is a marked decrease in the emission of some sounds and a change in several aspects of those sounds that continue to be emitted. This change is specific to the culture in which the child lives. The sounds that decrease in frequency are generally those sounds that do not appear in the language of the culture, and those sounds that continue to be emitted begin to conform in length, inflection, and combination to the language of the culture (Lewis, 1936; McCarthy, 1930; Osgood, 1953; Watts, 1948).

We probably cannot appeal to differential reinforcement by the parents to account for this change in behavior from the undifferentiated gurgling after feeding of the neonate to the babbling of the eight-month-old. It does not appear that the primary and secondary reinforcers provided by the parents are made contingent on the verbal behavior of infants with the requisite frequency and precision to shape babbling. For example, Hursh and Sherman (1973) showed that combined modeling and praise produced greater increases in vocalizations than either component alone, when parents were instructed to apply these techniques. However, when other parents were merely instructed to increase vocalizations they used only modeling, which was less effective.

Parents do provide contingencies for the vocal behavior of infants, and these contingencies include most of the probable reinforcers for infants. However, these reinforcers are differentially contingent on the presence or absence of noise of any sort, and are not specific to any characteristics of the noise except, perhaps, intensity or volume. In addition to the obvious contingencies for crying (such as feeding, changing, or rocking), other vocal noises of infants increase the probability of parents speaking to, picking up, and playing with them. These latter contingencies, when precisely applied, have been demonstrated to affect the quantity and quality of infants' vocalizations (Rheingold, Gewirtz, & Ross, 1959; Routh, 1969; Todd & Palmer, 1968; Wahler, 1969; Weisberg, 1961). It seems unlikely that in normal parenting, these contingencies would be applied precisely enough to change the characteristics of the infants' vocal noises. They are probably sufficient only to maintain a higher frequency of making vocal noise in general.

However, the maintenance of a rate of making undifferentiated noises creates the conditions under which other weaker or more subtle reinforcers, which would not be sufficient in and of themselves to maintain much vocal behavior, can serve to modify the ongoing behavior. In other words, if vocal behavior of any characteristic results in the same amount of reinforcers from the parent, but vocal behavior of certain characteristics results in slight additional reinforcers from another source, behavior of these characteristics will tend to predominate to the exclusion of other vocal behaviors. The additional reinforcers for certain vocal behaviors are considered to be the conditioned reinforcers intrinsic to some of the sounds produced by the infants themselves. These "autistic" reinforcers are the sounds that resemble the language of the parents.

Early infancy is a unique period in an individual's life in which all primary reinforcers are provided directly by other people (the parents). The parents provide the food, liquids, tactual stimulation, temperature regulation, and most of the auditory and visual stimulation for an infant. They remove the aversive stimuli of wet diapers, pin pricks, cramped limbs, and tangled bedclothes. Immediately preceding and during these occasions, parents usually talk to the infant. Their verbal stimuli are therefore closely associated with all the infant's reinforcers; and consequently should become generalized conditioned reinforcers.

At this point, it is necessary to separate what is called "verbal behavior" into the actual behaviors of the mouth, throat, and respiratory movements, and the resulting sounds this behavior produces. This distinction has been irrelevant in analyzing the effects of verbal behavior that are mediated through the behavior of another person, for which it is sufficient to consider as behavior the sounds that result from the behavior. It is necessary to make this distinction here because the analysis at this point is that some of the mouth, throat, and larynx responses are differentially reinforced by the sounds they produce. Those responses that result in sounds that approximate the verbal stimuli of the parents (which have become conditioned reinforcers) will be differentially reinforced. And further, the closer the resulting sounds are to the parents' verbal stimuli, the more reinforcing they are (Mowrer, 1954).

This analysis of the development of imitation of the parents' speech raises several questions about the establishment of conditioned reinforcers.

1. Simply pairing a neutral stimulus with a reinforcer usually does not make that stimulus a strong conditioned reinforcer (Kelleher & Gollub, 1962). In general, to be a strong conditioned reinforcer, a stimulus must become a discriminative stimulus for some response that produces a reinforcer (Zimmerman, 1957; 1959). As most of the primary reinforcers of an infant are not immediately contingent on any specific response, it appears unlikely that the parents' vocalizations would become discriminative stimuli for any specific response.

2. Even if the parents' vocalizations do become conditioned reinforcers by being paired with primary reinforcers, they should serve as conditioned reinforcers only when the infant has been deprived of these primary reinforcers. Therefore, the infant would emit the behaviors that produced "parent-like" sounds more frequently when deprived than when satiated. This is contrary to the observations of infant babbling, which agree that babbling is more frequent in the absence of any identifiable deprivation or aversive stimulation (Lewis, 1959; McCarthy, 1930; Watts, 1948).

3. Sound spectrographs reveal that sounds produced by an infant differ greatly in most aspects from sounds produced by the parent (Lenneberg, 1964). When one considers that the stimuli reaching the child's ears through tissue conduction would actually increase the differences between the stimuli from the parents' vocalizations and the stimuli produced by the infant's own vocal apparatus, it is apparent that whatever reinforcing properties the parents' vocalizations have attained would be considerably less for the sounds that are produced by the infant.

These points cast doubts on the possible magnitude of conditioned-reinforcing properties of the infant's own sounds, and consequently on the explanatory power of the autistic imitation paradigm.

However, infants' vocal behavior does come gradually to approximate the sounds, inflections, and length of their parents' verbal utterances, as if this paradigm were operating. Deviant children exhibit echolalia; and normal children in solitary play reproduce some of their parents' comments, complete with inflections and gestures. We can identify (manipulate) no extrinsic consequences that could serve to maintain this behavior. Furthermore, we can easily construct an analogue of this paradigm with a laboratory animal, where the animal's behavior will produce a stimulus that will serve at least temporarily as a weak reinforcer by the fact of its previous association with a primary reinforcer under other conditions. And finally, the conditioned reinforcers provided by the infant's sounds do not have to be strong to account for the observed change in characteristics of the infant's vocal behavior if other reinforcers are maintaining a high rate of vocalizations and the "autistic" reinforcers serve only to modify the proportions of the different sounds that occur. This paradigm can be illustrated by an observation of another behavior.

Between music lessons, reluctant students are required by parents to practice. During such practice there is often no differential reinforcement for producing melodic sequences of sounds; parental contingencies serve merely to maintain a high rate of striking the keys. Under these conditions, the students gradually begin to approximate recognizable tunes and random notes ("errors") gradually decrease. Tunes, which are conditioned reinforcers, are not strong enough to maintain "practice" on the piano. However, when a high rate of striking the piano keys is maintained by other reinforcers, the weak conditioned reinforcers of melodic sequences of notes are effective in differentially increasing the behavior that produced them. Thus, while the overall rate of striking the keys does not greatly change, the proportion of sequences of responses that produce melodies increase.

This observation not only illustrates the autistic-imitation paradigm, but also suggests that this paradigm may be important in the development of behaviors other than early vocal behaviors. It also suggests a technique for investigating experimentally the conditions necessary for autistic imitation with a dependent variable more easily recorded and analyzed than verbal behavior.

Most writers who have emphasized its importance have defined imitation in terms of the physical similarity between the behavior of a model and the behavior of a subject. An analysis in terms of the consequences of the behavior indicates at least three distinct subclasses:

1. "autistic" imitation, for which the reinforcers are the stimuli produced directly by the behavior;

2. discriminated imitation, for which reinforcers are produced by the effect of the behavior on persons or objects only in the presence of certain stimuli ("Say_____," or "Do it this way."); and

3. generalized imitation, which is a higher order response class of imitating the behavior of other persons maintained by an increased probability of reinforcement (produced by the effects of the behavior on persons or objects) for this behavior.

This last class may be somewhat under the control of the discriminative stimuli of the observed success of another person's behavior. Several authors have labeled this discriminative control "vicarious reinforcement" (Bandura, Ross, & Ross, 1963; Bandura & Walters, 1963), an unfortunate term that tends to obscure the function of this class of discriminative stimuli.

Thus, the sequence of conditions that can account for the development of verbal behavior from the initial vocal repertoire of the neonate to a close approximation of the adult verbal behavior of the culture includes:

1. the establishment of verbal stimuli as conditioned reinforcers;
2. the establishment of response classes of discriminated and generalized imitation; and
3. reinforcers given by all members of a culture that maintain the rate of verbal behavior and gradually differentially strengthen imitative and nonimitative verbal behavior approximating that of the culture.

While there is little experimental evidence to support many of the statements in this chapter, and this account is therefore largely theoretical, its theory is an extension of the general statements about the control of behavior that have evolved from experimentation. It is an attempt to analyze verbal behavior in terms of demonstrated principles of behavior rather than in terms of "new" principles of behavior that may, in fact, not exist. While there are unique problems posed for the investigation of verbal behavior, this chapter advances the position that there are no unique principles of verbal behavior.

REFERENCES

Allen, K. E., Hart, B. M., Buell, J. S., Harris, F. R., & Wolf, M. M. Effects of social reinforcement on isolate behavior of a nursery school child. *Child Development,* 1964, *35,* 511-518.

Atkinson, J. W., & McLelland, D. C. Projective expression of needs II. *Journal of Experimental Psychology,* 1948, *38,* 643-658.

Azrin, N. H. Some effects of noise on human behavior. *Journal of the Experimental Analysis of Behavior,* 1958, *1,* 183-200.

Baer, D. M., Guess, D. & Sherman, J. A. Adventures in simplistic grammar. In R. L. Schiefelbusch (Ed.), *Language of the mentally retarded.* Baltimore: University Park Press, 1972. Pp. 93-105.

Baer, D. M., Peterson, R. F., & Sherman, J. A. The development of imitation of reinforcing behavioral similarity to a model. *Journal of the Experimental Analysis of Behavior,* 1967, *10,* 405-416.

Baer, D. M., & Sherman, J. A. Reinforcement control of generalized imitation in young children. *Journal of Experimental Psychology,* 1964, *1,* 37-49.

Bandura, A., Ross, D. & Ross, S. A. Vicarious reinforcement and imitative learning. *Journal of Abnormal and Social Psychology,* 1963, *67,* 601-607.

Bandura, A., & Walters, R. H. *Social learning and personality development.* New York: Holt, Rinehart, & Winston, 1963.

Barton, E. S. Inappropriate speech in a severely retarded child: A case study in language conditioning and generalization. *Journal of Applied Behavior Analysis,* 1970, *3,* 299-307.

Bennett, C. W. & Ling, D. Teaching a complex verbal response to a hearing-impaired girl. *Journal of Applied Beahvior Analysis,* 1972, *5,* 321-327.

Berko, J. The child's learning of English morphology. *Word,* 1958, *14,* 150-177.

Brackbill, Y. (Ed.). *Infancy and early childhood: A handbook and guide to human development.* New York: The Free Press, 1967.

Brodie, D. A., & Boren, J. J. The use of pinch as an aversive stimulus. *Journal of the Experimental Analysis of Behavior,* 1958, *1,* 301-302.

Brown, R. (Ed.). *Words and Things.* Glencoe, Illinois: Free Press, 1958.

Carlton, P. L., & Marks, R. A. Cold exposure and heat reinforced operant behavior. *Science,* 1958, *128,* 1344.

Chomsky, N. *Syntactic Structure.* The Hague: Mouton, 1957.

Chomsky, N. Review of B. F. Skinner, Verbal behavior. *Language,* 1959, *35,* 26-58.

Cofer, C. N. Properties of verbal materials and verbal learning. In J. W. Kling & L. A. Riggs (Eds.), *Woodworth and Schlosberg's experimental psychology.* New York: Holt, Rinehart, & Winston, 1971. Pp. 847-904.

Cross, D. V., & Lane, H. L. On the discriminative control of concurrent responses; the relations among response frequency, latency, and topography in auditory generalization. *Journal of the Experimental Analysis of Behavior,* 1962, *5,* 487-496.

Darwin, C. R. *The expression of the emotion in man and animals.* New York: Appleton, 1896.

Davis, J. D. The reinforcing effect of weak-light onset as a function of amount of food deprivation. *Journal of Comparative and Physiological Psychology,* 1958, *51,* 496-498.

Ervin, S. M. Imitation and structural change in children's language. In E. Lenneberg (Ed.), *New directions in the study of language.* Cambridge, Mass.: MIT Press, 1964. Pp. 163-189.

Etzel, B. C., & Gewirtz, J. L. Experimental modification of caretaker-maintained high-rate operant crying in a 6- and a 20-week old infant *(Infans tyrannotearus):* Extinction of crying with reinforcement of eye contact and smiling. *Journal of Experimental Child Psychology,* 1967, *5,* 303-317.

Fahmy, S. A. Conditioning and extinction of a referential verbal response class in a situation resembling a clinical diagnostic interview (doctoral dissertation). *Dissertation Abstracts,* 1953, *13,* 873-874. (University Microfilms No.)

Falk, J. L. The grooming behavior of the chimpanzee as a reinforcer. *Journal of the Experimental Analysis of Behavior,* 1958, *1,* 83-86.

Felty, J. E. An investigation into the operant nature of the stuttering behavior of adolescent boys. Unpublished master's dissertation, University of Washington, 1959.

Ferguson, D. C., & Buss, A. H. Operant conditioning of hostile verbs in relation to experimenter and subject characteristics. *Journal of Consulting Psychology,* 1960, *24,* 324-327.

Flanagan, B., Goldiamond, I., & Azrin, N. H. Instatement of stuttering in normally fluent individuals through operant procedures. *Science,* 1959, *130,* 979-981.

Fraser, C., Bellugi, U., & Brown, R. Control of grammar in imitation, comprehension and production. *Journal of Verbal Learning and Verbal Behavior,* 1963, *2,* 121-135.

Gewirtz, J. L., & Baer, D. M. The effect of brief social deprivation on behaviors for a social reinforcer. *Journal of Abnormal and Social Psychology,* 1958, *56,* 49-56. (a)

Gewirtz, J. L., & Baer, D. M. Deprivation and satiation of social reinforcers as drive conditions. *Journal of Abnormal and Social Psychology,* 1958, *57,* 165-172. (b)

Gewirtz, J. L., Baer, D. M., & Roth, C. H. A note on the similar effects of low social availability of an adult and brief social deprivation on young children's behavior. *Child Development,* 1958, *29,* 149-152.

Greenspoon, J. The reinforcing effect of two spoken sounds on the frequency of two responses. *American Journal of Psychology,* 1955, *68,* 409-416.

Greenspoon, J. Verbal conditioning and clinical psychology. In A. J. Bachrach (Ed.), *Experimental foundations of clinical psychology.* New York: Basic Books, 1962, 512-553.

Gregoire, A. *L'apprentissage du Langage: les deux premieres annees.* Paris: Droz, 1937.

Guess, D., Sailor, W., Rutherford, G., & Baer, D. M. An experimental analysis of linguistic development: The productive use of the plural morpheme. *Journal of Applied Behavior Analysis,* 1968, *1,* 297-306.

Harris, F. R., Johnston, M. K., Kelley, C. S., & Wolf, M. M. Effects of positive social rein-forcement on regressed crawling of a nursery school child. *Journal of Educational Psychology,* 1964, *55,* 35-41.

Harrison, J. M., & Tracy, W. H. The use of auditory stimuli to maintain lever pressing be-havior. *Science,* 1955, *121,* 273-274.

Hart, B. M., Allen, K. E., Buell, J. S., Harris, F. R., & Wolf, M. M. Effects of social rein-forcement on oeprant crying. *Journal of Experimental Child Psychology,* 1964, *1,* 145-153.

Hersen, M. Controlling verbal behavior via classical and operant conditioning. *The Journal of General Psychology,* 1970, *83,* 3-22.

Holz, W. C., & Azrin, N. H. Conditioning human verbal behavior. In W. K. Honig (Ed.), *Operant behavior: Areas of research and application.* New York: Appleton-Century-Crofts, 1966. Pp. 790-826.

Honig, W. K., & Day, R. W. Discrimination and generalization on a dimension of stimulus difference. *Science,* 1962, *183,* 29-31.

Hursh, D. E., & Sherman, J. A. The effects of parent-presented models and praise on the vocal behavior of their children. *Journal of Experimental Child Psychology,* 1973, *15,* 328-339.

Irwin, O. C. Language and communication. In P. H. Mussen (Ed.), *Handbook of research methods in child development.* New York: Wiley, 1960. Pp. 487-516.

Isaacs, W., Thomas, J., & Goldiamond, I. Application of operant conditioning to reinstate verbal behavior in psychotics. *Journal of Speech and Hearing Disorders,* 1960, *25,* 8-15.

Jakobson, R. *Kindersprache. Aphasie, und allgemeine Lautgesetze.* Uppsala: Almqvist & Wiksell, 1941.

Kanfer, F. H. Verbal conditioning: Reinforcement schedules and experimenter influence. *Psychological Reports,* 1958, *4,* 443-452.

Kanfer, F. H. Verbal conditioning: A review of its current status. In T. R. Dixon & L. P. Horton (Eds.), *Verbal behavior and general behavior theory.* Englewood Cliffs, N.J.: Prentice-Hall, 1968. Pp. 254-290.

Kelleher, T. R. Chaining and conditioned reinforcement. In W. K. Honig (Ed.), *Operant behavior: Areas of research and application.* New York: Appleton-Century-Crofts, 1966. Pp. 160-212.

Kelleher, T. R., & Gollub, L. R. A review of positive conditioned reinforcement. *Journal of the Experimental Analysis of Behavior,* 1962, *5,* 543-597.

Keller, F. S. Light averson in the white rat. *The Psychological Record,* 1941, *4,* 235-250.

Kerr, N., Myerson, L., & Michael, J. A procedure for shaping vocalizations in a mute child In L. P. Ullman & L. Krasner (Eds.), *Case studies in behavior modification.* New York: Holt, Rinehart, & Winston, 1965.

Keys, A. B. *The biology of human starvation.* Minneapolis: University of Minnesota Press, 1950.

Kircher, A. S., Pear, J. J., & Martin, G. L. Shock as punishment in a picture-naming task with retarded children. *Journal of Applied Behavior Analysis,* 1971, *4,* 227-233.

Krasner, L. The therapist as a social reinforcement machine. In H. H. Strupp & L. Luborsky (Eds.), *Research in psychotherapy* (Vol. 2), Washington, D.C.: American Psychological Association, 1962. Pp. 61-94.

Lane, H. Personal communication, 1965.

Lane, H., & Curran, C. Auditory generalization gradients of blind, retarded children. *Journal of the Experimental Analysis of Behavior,* 1963, *6,* 585-588.

Lenneberg, E. H. Speech as a motor skill with special reference to nonaphasic disorders. In U. Bellugi & R. Brown (Eds.). The acquisition of language. *Monographs of the Society for Research in Child Development,* 1964, *29,* (92).

Lenneberg, E. H. *Biological foundations of language.* New York: Wiley, 1967.

Levine, R., Chein, I., & Murphy, G. The relation of intensity of a need to the amount of perceptual distortion. *Journal of Psychology*, 1942, *13*, 283-293.

Lewis, M. M. *Infant speech*. New York: Harcourt, Brace, 1936.

Lewis, M. M. *Language in society*. New York: Social Sciences Publishers, 1948.

Lewis, M. M. *How children learn to speak*. New York: Basic Books, 1959.

Lewis, M. M. *Language thought and personality in infancy and childhood*. London: Harrap, 1963.

Liberman, R. P., Teigen, J., Patterson, R., & Baker, V. Reducing delusional speech in chronic, paranoid schizophrenics. *Journal of Applied Behavior Analysis*, 1973, *6*, 57-64.

Lotz, J. Linguistics: Symbols make man. In S. Saporta (Ed.), *Psycholinguistics*. New York: Holt, Rinehart, & Winston, 1961. P. 7.

Lovaas, O. I., Freitag, G., Kinder, M. I., Rubenstein, B. D., Schaeffer, B., & Simmons, J. Q. Establishment of social reinforcers in two schizophrenic children on the basis of food. *Journal of Experimental Child Psychology*, 1966, *4*, 109-125.

Lutzker, J. R., & Sherman, J. A. Producing generative sentence usage by imitation and reinforcement procedures. *Journal of Applied Behavior Analysis*, 1974, *7*, 447-460.

McCarthy, D. A. *The language development of the preschool child*. Minneapolis: University of Minnesota Press, 1930.

Metz, J. R. Conditioning generalized imitation in autistic children. *Journal of Experimental Child Psychology*, 1965, *2*, 389-399.

Miller, N. E., & Dollard, J. *Social learning and imitation*. New Haven: Yale University Press, 1941.

Morris, C. W. *Signs, language and behavior*. New York: Prentice-Hall, 1946.

Mowrer, O. H. The psychologist looks at language. *American Psychologist*, 1954, *9*, 660-694.

Mowrer, O. H. *Learning theory and the symbolic processes*. New York: Wiley, 1960.

Osgood, C. E. *Method and theory in experimental psychology*. New York: Oxford University Press, 1953.

Patterson, G. R., Helper, M. E. & Wilcott, R. C. Anxiety and verbal conditioning in children. *Child Development*, 1960, *31*, 100-108.

Pratt, K. E., Nelson, A. K., & Kuo, H. S. *The behavior of the newborn infant*. Columbus: Ohio State University Press, 1930.

Premack, D., Schaeffer, R. W., & Hunt, A. Reinforcement of drinking by running: Effect of fixed ratio and reinforcement time. *Journal of the Experimental Analysis of Behavior*, 1964, *7*, 91-96.

Quay, H. C. The effect of verbal reinforcement on the recall of early memories. *Journal of Abnormal and Social Psychology*, 1959, *59*, 254-257.

Rheingold, H. L., Gewirtz, J. L., & Ross, H. W. Social conditioning of vocalizations in the infant. *Journal of Comparative and Physiological Psychology*, 1959, *52*, 68-73.

Rickard, H. C., & Mundy, M. B. Direct manipulation of stuttering behavior: An experimental-clinical approach. In L. P. Ullman & L. Krasner (Eds.), *Case studies in behavior modification*. New York: Holt, Rinehart, & Winston, 1965.

Risley, T. R. Generalization gradients following two-response discrimination training. *Journal of the Experimental Analysis of Behavior*, 1964, *7*, 199-204.

Risley, T. R., & Wolf, M. M. Establishing functional speech in echolalic children. *Behavior Research and Therapy*, 1967, *5*, 73-88.

Rogers, J. M. Operant conditioning in a quasi-therapy setting. *Journal of Abnormal and Social Psychology*, 1960, *60*, 247-252.

Routh, D. K. Conditioning of vocal response differentiation in infants. *Developmental Psychology*, 1969, *1*, 219-226.

Salzinger, K. Experimental manipulation of verbal behavior: A review. *Journal of General Psychology*, 1959, *61*, 65-94.

Salzinger, K., Portney, S., Zletegura, P., & Keisner, R. The effect of reinforcement on continuous speech and on plural nouns in grammatical context. *Journal of Verbal Learning and Verbal Behavior,* 1963, *1,* 477-485.

Sanford, R. N. The effects of abstinence from food upon imaginal processes. *Journal of Psychology,* 1936, *2,* 129-136.

Sarason, B. R. The effects of verbally conditioned response classes on post-conditioning tasks. *Dissertation Abstracts,* 1957, *17,* 679.

Schaefer, H. H. Vibration as a reinforcer for infant children. *Journal of the Experimental Analysis of Behavior,* 1960, *3,* 160.

Schumaker, J. & Sherman, J. A. Training generative verb usage by imitation and reinforcement procedures. *Journal of Applied Behavior Analysis,* 1970, *3,* 273-287.

Sherman, J. A. Use of reinforcement and imitation to reinstate verbal behavior in mute psychotics. *Journal of Abnormal Psychology,* 1965, *70,* 155-164.

Sidowski, J. B. Influence of awareness of reinforcement on verbal conditioning. *Journal of Experimental Psychology,* 1954, *48,* 355-360.

Simkins, L. Scheduling effects of punishment and non-reinforcement on verbal conditioning and extinction. *Journal of Verbal Learning and Verbal Behavior,* 1962, *1,* 208-213.

Skinner, B. F. *The behavior of organisms.* New York: Appleton-Century-Crofts, 1938.

Skinner, B. F. *Verbal behavior.* New York: Appleton-Century-Crofts, 1957.

Templin, M. C. *Certain language skills in children.* Minneapolis: University of Minnesota Press, 1957.

Thompson, T. I. Visual reinforcement in fighting cocks. *Journal of the Experimental Analysis of Behavior,* 1964, *7,* 45-49.

Todd, G. A., & Palmer, B. Social reinforcement of infant babbling. *Child Development,* 1968, *39,* 591-596.

Vetter, H. J. The ontogenesis of language. In S. Cohen (Ed.), *Child development: A study of growth processes.* Chicago: Peacock, 1971.

Wahler, R. G. Infant social development: Some experimental analyses of an infant-mother interaction during the first year of life. *Journal of Experimental Child Psychology,* 1969, *7,* 101-113.

Walton, D., & Black, D. A. The application of modern learning theory to the treatment of chronic hysterical aphonia. In H. J. Eysenck (Ed.), *Behaviour therapy and the neuroses.* London: Pergamon Press, 1960. Pp. 256-271.

Watts, A. F. *The language and mental development of children.* Boston: Health, 1948.

Weide, T. N. Conditioning and generalization of the use of affect-relevant words. Unpublished doctoral dissertation, Stanford University, 1959.

Weisberg, P. Social and nonsocial conditioning of infant vocalizations. *Child Development,* 1961, *34,* 377-388.

Weiss, R. L., Krasner, L., & Ullmann, L. P. Responsivity to verbal conditioning as a function of emotional atmosphere and pattern of reinforcement. *Psychological Reports,* 1960, *6,* 415-426.

Wenzel, B. M. Tactile stimulation as reinforcement for cats and its relation to early feeding experience. *Psychological Reports,* 1959, *5,* 297-300.

Wheeler, A. J., & Sulzer, B. Operant training and generalization of a verbal response form in a speech-deficient child. *Journal of Applied Behavior Analysis,* 1970, *3,* 139-147.

Williams, C. D. The elimination of tantrum behavior by extinction procedures. *Journal of Abnormal and Social Psychology,* 1959, *59,* 269.

Wolf, M., Risley, T., & Mees, H. Application of operant conditioning procedures to the behaviour problems of an autistic child. *Behavior Research and Therapy,* 1964, *1,* 305-312.

Yealland, L. R. *Hysterical disorders of warfare.* London: Macmillan, 1918.

Zedek, M. E. The conditioning of verbal behavior with negative cultural connotations. *Journal of Personality,* 1959, *27,* 477-486.

Zimmerman, D. W. Durable secondary reinforcement: Method and theory. *Psychological Review,* 1957, *64,* 373-383.

Zimmerman, D. W. Sustained performance in rats based on secondary reinforcement. *Journal of Comparative and Physiological Psychology,* 1959, *52,* 353-358.

Zimmerman, E. H., & Zimmerman, J. The alteration of behavior in a special classroom situation. *Journal of the Experimental Analysis of Behavior,* 1962, *5,* 59-60.

6
Generalized Imitation and the Setting Event Concept

Warren M. Steinman

University of Rhode Island

A functional analysis of behavior is predicated on the assumption that operant behavior is controlled by its consequences. Through the manipulation of differential consequences, behavioral frequencies can readily and predictably be increased or decreased and responses can be shaped into increasingly precise and complex topographies. Similarly, by differentially correlating specific stimuli with particular behavioral consequences, the stimuli can acquire antecedent control over the occurrence or nonoccurrence of the behavior, thereby restricting and refining the occasions on which the behavior is likely to be emitted in the future. Thus, a thorough analysis of behavior requires that the functional properties of specific stimuli that are antecedent and consequent to a given behavior be delineated, manipulated, and assessed.

Most of the concepts and procedures involved in the analysis of behavior are straightforward and exceedingly well documented. However, the analysis of interactions involving multiple sources of control has been less well developed. Behavioral control frequently is far more complex than the mere presence or absence of a specific antecedent or consequent stimulus. Indeed, organisms amass long, subtle, and complex histories of stimulus control and a given situation may simultaneously contain a host of stimuli that have acquired functional properties in the past. Thus, the resulting behavior may be a function not only of the specific stimuli being manipulated at the time, but may also be a function of the combined influence of several interacting past and present stimuli. If the experimenter has been attending to only one or a few of these controlling variables, the behavior observed may differ markedly from that expected.

J. R. Kantor (1958) has acknowledged this complexity by suggesting two categories of environmental control: the control exerted by specific stimulus events, that is, eliciting, occasioning, and consequating functions; and the control exerted by "setting events." Using Kantor's analysis, Bijou and Baer (1961) have described setting events as follows:

> Setting events, like stimulus events, are environmental changes which affect behavior. But, in contrast to stimulus events, setting events are more complicated than the simple presence, absence, or change of a stimulus . . . Instead, a setting event is a stimulus-response interaction, which, simply because it has occurred, will affect other stimulus-response relationships which follow it . . . one stimulus-response interaction may be changed because a preceding stimulus-response interaction related to it also has been changed . . . In fact, a child's history of past interactions with his environment may be looked upon as a collection of setting events influencing current behavior [pp.21-22].

Thus, through the development of the setting event concept, Bijou and Baer have proposed a broadened historical context for the functional analysis of behavior. It is in interaction with this context that the effects of specific stimulus manipulations must be assessed. Of course, as Bijou and Baer note, "a setting event can indeed be analyzed into component stimulus events," [p. 22] and no new stimulus functions are being proposed by the concept. But, by separating environmental influences into two categories of stimulus control, Bijou and Baer have highlighted the conditional and interactive nature of behavioral control and therefore have drawn attention to the potential functional properties of variables beyond those being manipulated in the immediate environment.

An example of the subtle interactive effects that setting events can have on behavioral control can be found in the literature on "generalized imitation."

While investigating the role of reinforcement in the development and maintenance of imitative behavior, Baer and Sherman (1964) found that the precise and consistent use of differential reinforcement failed to establish antecedent discriminative control over the imitative behaviors being differentially reinforced. The children in their study imitated, and continued to imitate, responses that they were never reinforced for imitating, as long as the imitation of other responses was reinforced. Baer and Sherman assumed from their results that the reinforcement of imitative behavior was sufficient to develop a general response class, imitating, and therefore the imitation of the unreinforced responses was considered a generalization of the newly acquired response class. Hence the term, "generalized imitation," was used when describing the occurrence and persistence of the unreinforced imitative behavior (Baer & Sherman, 1964; Baer, Peterson, & Sherman, 1967; Peterson, 1968a, b).

Since the Baer and Sherman study, many experiments have been conducted which replicate and extend their initial findings. A major interest in this research has been the curious ineffectiveness of differential reinforcement in these findings. Indeed, repeatedly in generalized imitation research, well-conceived and

properly implemented differential reinforcement procedures have failed to establish the antecedent stimulus control that such procedures should create. The
discriminative behavior that one might reasonably expect to result, simply does
not develop. Thus, several experiments have been conducted in recent years to
determine what is controlling behavior in generalized imitation research and why
differential reinforcement is not.

Within these studies, there is now ample evidence to indicate that the differential reinforcement procedures do in fact establish the specific antecedent
stimuli, that is, the particular responses modeled, as discriminated occasions for
reinforcement or nonreinforcement. The contingencies in operation are discriminated by the children, even though the children continue to imitate indiscriminately as if the contingencies had not been learned. The lack of stimulus
control is evidenced only in the children's imitative behavior. Indeed, research
manipulating discrimination procedures (Peterson, 1968; Steinman, 1970a,b,
1971; Steinman & Boyce, 1971), the number of modeled responses to be discriminated (Bufford, 1971; Steinman, 1971, 1973; Wilcox, Meddock, & Steinman, 1973), the topographical similarity of the responses modeled (Steinman,
1970a; Bandura & Barab, 1971; Steinman & Boyce, 1971; Garcia, Baer &
Firestone, 1971); the social context of the experimental situation (Waxler &
Yarrow, 1970; Peterson, Merwin, Moyer, & Whitehurst, 1971; Peterson &
Whitehurst, 1971), the instructions under which the imitative behavior is
assessed (Burgess, Burgess, & Esveldt, 1970; Steinman, 1970a, b, 1971, 1973;
Bufford, 1971; Martin, 1971, 1972; Wilcox, Meddock, & Steinman, 1973), and
various recognition tasks (Steinman, 1970a, b, 1971, 1973; Bufford, 1971), all
show that a child may be able to identify and clearly state which modeled responses result in reinforcement if imitated and which do not, even though the
child may continue to imitate indiscriminately. The imitative behavior fails to
come under stimulus control, but the stimuli do acquire differential properties as
a result of the differential reinforcement operations.

A number of studies have found that generalized imitation is a function of
the particular discrimination procedures used in such research (Peterson, 1968;
Steinman, 1970a, b, 1971, 1973; Bandura & Barab, 1971; Bufford, 1971; Steinman & Boyce, 1971). In generalized imitation research, responses typically are
modeled successively by an experimenter or a peer, with the modeling of each
response constituting a trial. Following the modeling of a response, an interval
is provided, during which the child may or may not perform by imitating the
response just modeled. Imitations of some responses result in reinforcement,
whereas imitations of other responses are unreinforced (extinction). Thus, the
child performs in a "go-no go" successive discrimination task where discriminative control can be demonstrated only by imitating on some (reinforced) trials
and failing to imitate on the other (unreinforced) trials.

When these successive-discrimination procedures are used, generalized imitation typically results — the child imitates almost every response modeled regardless of whether the particular response has occasioned reinforced imitation or

not. However, if other discrimination procedures are used, such as providing two responses on each trial and having the child choose which response to imitate, discriminative imitation is obtained. That is, under choice conditions the child will consistently imitate responses which result in reinforcement rather than imitating responses indiscriminately. Indeed, if the same set of responses that a child imitates indiscriminately under successive-discrimination procedures is presented under choice or concurrent-discrimination procedures, the child will imitate these responses discriminately.

When successive-discrimination procedures are used, generalized imitation has been shown to be dependent upon the social context under which the imitative behavior is examined (Waxler & Yarrow, 1970; Peterson, Merwin, Moyer, & Whitehurst, 1971; Peterson & Whitehurst, 1971; Steinman, 1971, 1973). Peterson and his colleagues, for example, have shown that generalized imitation continues only if the experimenter (or an equivalent) remains present during the postmodeling interval, that is, the interval provided for the child's response. If the experimenter leaves the room immediately after modeling a response, thereby leaving the child alone to either imitate or not do so during the experimenter's absence, the child will imitate responses resulting in reinforcement and stop imitating responses that are not correlated with reinforcement. In other words, the differential reinforcement procedures are functional in producing discriminative imitation when the child is alone, but not when in the presence of the experimenter.

Another parameter that controls the development and maintenance of generalized imitation involves the nature of the instructions used to initiate the imitative behavior (Burgess, Burgess, & Esveldt, 1970; Steinman, 1970a, b, 1971, 1973; Bufford, 1971; Martin, 1971, 1972; Wilcox, Meddock, & Steinman, 1973). In every generalized-imitation study, some form of instructional prime has been used to begin the imitative behavior. These primes may be quite explicit, such as the use of verbal instructions ("Do this") or the use of physical help (like moving the child's body through the response just modeled). However, in other instances, primes may be more subtle, as having the child watch another child behaving imitatively. If no steps are taken to inform the child that nonresponding is an acceptable alternative, generalized imitation will result. However, if the child is told that there is no need to imitate on every trial, or if the child is permitted to observe someone imitating discriminately before beginning the study, discriminative imitation is likely to develop.

Recently, evidence has been accumulating indicating that results comparable to generalized imitation are not limited to imitative behavior (Martin, 1971, 1972; Theobald, 1971; Wilcox, Meddock, & Steinman, 1973; Saunders & Sherman, 1974). In these studies, successive-discrimination procedures like those used in generalized imitation research have been applied to stimuli and responses other than those involved in imitation. For example, Wilcox et al. differentially reinforced children for pressing a panel upon which a triangle or circle was projected. The stimuli were presented successively using procedures comparable to those used in generalized imitation research. It was found that unless the children were instructed at the beginning of the experiment to behave differentially, they pressed the panel indiscriminately whenever either stimulus appeared. Thus, the results of the Wilcox *et al.* study closely resemble the results found in generalized imitation research.

Taken together, the above studies indicate that:

1. continued indiscriminative responding under conditions of consistent and repeated differential reinforcement may not be unique to imitative behavior;

2. having learned the contingencies associated with the various stimuli being presented may not be sufficient to produce discriminative behavior;

3. generalized imitation may be uniquely related to the specific discrimination procedures used in such research;

4. instructions and social setting conditions can strongly influence the probability of obtaining generalized or discriminative behavior under the procedures used in generalized imitation research.

Thus, it would appear that generalized imitation and its extensions to non-imitative behavior are a joint function of the instructions, social setting conditions, and discrimination procedures used in the research. If the discrimination procedures require that the child withhold responding or respond incorrectly on unreinforced trials in order to demonstrate discriminative behavior, the child is not likely to behave discriminately, expecially if there have been explicit or implicit instructions to respond and the experimenter continues to monitor the child's behavior. Depending upon the child's history of consequences for complying or failing to comply with an adult's instructions, it simply may be more aversive for the child to withhold responding under these circumstances than to respond. In generalized imitation, the modeled response may be discriminative for an unreinforced imitation, but failing to imitate the response in the experimenter's presence may also be discriminative for the possible presentation of aversive consequences. Thus, two sources of control, the differential reinforcement manipulated in the experiment and the child's history of consequences for disobeying an instruction, suggest opposite results. And, in generalized imitation and related research, the latter — the setting event — has been found to determine the behavior.

Clearly, research is needed investigating the interaction between specific social-learning histories and the social and instructional context in which a given behavior is assessed, as well as between the specific contingencies being manipulated for that behavior. Disregarding these historical and contextual variables can lead to mistaken or needlessly complex analyses of behavioral control. However, by investigating these subtle but often very powerful sources of behavioral control and the means by which they interact with the contingencies being manipulated, a more complete and perhaps more useful explanation of behavioral control can be attained.

REFERENCES

Baer, D. M., Peterson, R. F., & Sherman, J. A. The development of imitation by reinforcing behavioral similarity to a model. *Journal of the Experimental Analysis of Behavior,* 1967, *10,* 405-516.

Baer, D. M., & Sherman, J. A. Reinforcement control of generalized imitation in young children. *Journal of Experimental Child Psychology,* 1964, *1,* 37-49.

Bandura, A., & Barab, P. G. Conditions governing nonreinforced imitation. *Developmental Psychology,* 1971, *5,* 244-255.

Bijou, S. W., & Baer, D. M. *Child development* (Vol. 1). New York: Appleton-Century-Crofts, 1961.

Bufford, R. K. Discrimination and instructions as factors in the control of non-reinforced imitation. *Journal of Experimental Child Psychology,* 1971, *12,* 35-50.

Burgess, R. L., Burgess, J. M., & Esveldt, K. C. An analysis of generalized imitation. *Journal of Applied Behavior Analysis,* 1970, *3,* 39-46.

Garcia, E., Baer, D. M., & Firestone, I. The development of generalized imitation within topographically determined boundaries. *Journal of Applied Behavior Analysis,* 1971, *4,* 101-112.

Kantor, J. R. *Interbehavioral psychology.* Bloomington: Principia Press, 1958.

Martin, J. A. The control of imitative and non-imitative behaviors in severely retarded children through "generalized instruction-following." *Journal of Experimental Child Psychology,* 1971, *11,* 390-400.

Martin, J. A. The effect of incongruent instructions and consequences on imitation in retarded children. *Journal of Applied Behavior Analysis,* 1972, *5,* 467-475.

Peterson, R. F. Imitation: A basic behavioral mechanism. In H. N. Sloane, Jr., and B. Mac Aulay (Eds.), *Operant procedures in remedial speech and language training.* Boston: Houghton Mifflin, 1968. (a)

Peterson, R. F. Some experiments on the organization of a class of imitative behaviors. *Journal of Applied Behavior Analysis,* 1968, *1.* (b)

Peterson, R. F., Merwin, M. R., Moyer, T. J., & Whitehurst, G. J. Generalized imitation: The effects of experimenter absence, differential reinforcement, and stimulus complexity. *Journal of Experimental Child Psychology,* 1971, *12,* 114-128.

Peterson, R. F., & Whitehurst, G. J. A variable influencing the performance of non-reinforced imitative behaviors. *Journal of Applied Behavior Analysis,* 1971, *4,* 1-9.

Saunders, R. R., & Sherman, J. A. Analysis of the "discrimination-failure hypothesis" in generalized matching and mismatching behavior. Paper presented at the meeting of the American Psychological Association, New Orleans, La., 1974.

Steinman, W. M. Generalized imitation and the discrimination hypothesis. *Journal of Experimental Child Psychology,* 1970, *10,* 79-99. (a)

Steinman, W. M. The social control of generalized imitation. *Journal of Applied Behavior Analysis,* 1970, *3,* 159-167. (b)

Steinman, W. M. The effect of instructions, discrimination, difficulty, and methods of assessment on generalized imitation. A symposium paper presented at the biennial meetings of the Society for Research in Child Development, Minneapolis, Minn., 1971.

Steinman, W. M. Implicit instructions and social influence in "generalized imitation" and other "Go-No Go" situations. Symposium paper presented at the biennial meetings of the Society for Research in Child Development, Philadelphia, Pa., March 31, 1973.

Steinman, W. M., & Boyce, K. D. Generalized imitation as a function of discrimination difficulty and choice. *Journal of Experimental Child Psychology,* 1971, *11,* 251-265.

Theobald, D. E. Social interactions and experimentally determined reinforcement histories in generalized imitation. Unpublished master's dissertation, University of Illinois, 1971.

Waxler, C. Z., & Yarrow, M. R. Factors influencing imitative learning in preschool children. *Journal of Experimental Child Psychology*, 1970, *9*, 115-130.

Wilcox, B., Meddock, T. D., & Steinman, W. M. "Generalized imitation" on a nonimitative task: Effects of modeling and task history. *Journal of Experimental Child Psychology*, 1973, *15*, 381-393.

7
Nutrition and Human Development[1]

Jack Tizard

University of London Institute of Education

In all mammalian species the brain growth spurt occurs early in life. We know that the brain, like all organs, is "vulnerable" to insult, stress, and nutritional deficiency during the period of maximum growth. We also know that deficits in growth — that is, in the number of brain cells which are produced during the brain growth spurt — cannot be made good later on in life. Furthermore we know that even moderate malnutrition during the vulnerable period will affect brain weight, cell number, and the chemical composition of brain cells (Dobbing & Smart, 1973).

In humans the brain growth spurt occurs during the last trimester of prenatal life and the first 18 months to 2 years of postnatal life. We would therefore expect that children malnourished during this period would show long-term effects in brain size and composition, but that such effects would not be seen as a consequence of malnourishment in later life. There is convincing evidence from animal studies that supports both of these propositions.

Much less is known about the *functional* consequences of brain stunting. Animal research indicates that organisms malnourished during the period in which the brain is growing most rapidly do exhibit some cognitive and motor defects In general the effects so far demonstrated have not been great; however the amount of comparative research by behavioral scientists is still limited, and species differences in behavior make generalizations difficult.

Research on malnutrition in humans is concentrated on two main types of problem: (1) the effects upon later growth and behavior of an episode of *severe*

---

[1]This chapter is based on a paper presented in a symposium, Undernutrition and the Developing Brain, given at the Third International Congress of the International Association for Scientific Study of Mental Deficiency, I.A.S.S.M.D., 4-12th September, 1973, The Hague, The Netherlands.

clinical malnutrition in infancy or early childhood; and (2) the effects of *chronic undernutrition* upon growth and behavior.

Let us start by considering the effects of undernutrition upon *growth,* since growth is easier to measure unambiguously than is behavioral competence. It is well known that children in poor countries are shorter in stature than those in rich ones. And even in industrial countries there has been a secular increase, which is still continuing, in the height of the adult population, of something like 2.4 cm per generation (25 years) over the last 100 years, owing to changes in diet (Khosla & Lowe, 1968). Of course there are still social class and ethnic differences – the mean weights and heights of Japanese children growing up in the United States, though greater than those of Japanese children growing up in Japan, are still below the Harvard growth standards means. This does not mean that Japanese children living in the United States are malnourished, or that the differences are due to genetic factors. Indeed we know that between 1950 and 1960 the mean heights of Japanese children in Japan showed an increase as great as that observed in other countries in three or four decades (Mitchell, cited Birch & Gussow, 1970). In view of how little is known about intergenerational increments in growth following changes in nutrition no very definitive statements about genetic differences, which would hold over all environments, can be made.

It is also well established that in any single community children of poor people are shorter in stature than children of rich people; and in poor communities the height of a child may depend more on whether the crops have been good or bad over the last few years than on whether his parents are tall or short. Indeed Habicht *et al.* (1974) have shown that, as compared with differences between well fed and poorly fed children of the same stock, differences between children of different races are quite small. Clearly, physical growth in childhood is more a function of diet than of genetic differences between races.

What about mental growth? Here the situation is greatly complicated by the nature of the intellectual diet which a child gets and by uncertainties about the intellectual potential of different social classes in a racially homogeneous population. Speculations are also made, on dubious evidence, about supposed genetic differences between ethnic subgroups. Because of the importance of non-nutritional factors, studies which have attempted to investigate the specific effects of malnutrition, or of food supplementation, in undernourished populations, and which have ignored environmental factors, have produced somewhat conflicting results and have been for the most part, not very informative. Rather than present an overview of such studies I propose to describe three investigations which largely summarize our present state of knowledge and from which one can make suggestions about useful directions for future research.

The Studies

The first study is a major longitudinal investigation carried out by Cravioto and his colleagues (Cravioto & DeLicardie, 1972) in Mexico. This indicates that, in a poor Mexican village community, in which most children are physically and intellectually stunted, certain children are more likely to suffer from *severe* clinical malnutrition than are other children in the village. That is, malnutrition is, to a considerable extent, predictable. The second study, in Jamaica, planned by Birch and Richardson, and with which I was associated (Hertzig *et al.*, 1972), shows that children who are hospitalized for severe clinical malnutrition during the first two years of life and who make a clinical recovery, are still retarded as compared with their siblings or classmates, when they are 6-11 years of age. However the extent of their retardation depends upon the nature of the environment in which they live. The third study, also from Mexico, and carried out by Chavez, Martinez, and Yaschine (1973), shows that feeding undernourished mothers *and* children results in marked changes not only in the physical growth of the children and in their intellectual development, but also in the stimulus value they have for their parents and in the nature of parent-child interactions.

Cravioto and his colleagues have made an intensive longitudinal study of all children born in a rural village in South West Mexico during 1966. The method of study is ecological. The children and their families were studied over time in their social environment, and the investigators attempted to analyze three sets of factors: (1) the influence of social, economic, and family conditions on the incidence of malnutrition; (2) the effect of malnutrition on physical growth, mental development and learning; and (3) the interaction of nutritional factors with infectious disease, family circumstances, and social circumstances, on processes of growth and development.

Of the 300 children born in this village during 1966 there were 22 who developed severe clinical malnutrition before they were 5 years of age, despite the fact that they were offered advice and medical treatment — which they did not take. Only one of these children became clinically malnourished before his first birthday, and only 4 after the age of 3. The remaining 17 became severely malnourished during the second or third year of life.

Because the study was a longitudinal one of a total birth cohort, data being collected at frequent intervals on all children in the cohort and their families, it was possible to make serial comparisons over time between the children who became malnourished and their families (the index cases), and the rest of the children born in the village during the same year. To give greater precision to the analyses, a "control" group of (nonmalnourished) children who could be matched with the (malnourished) index cases from records obtained at the time of the children's birth — gestational age, body length and body size — were selected for comparison with the index cases. The records of the two groups were subjected to detailed study to see which social and biological factors differentiated index children from matched controls prior to the time that the index cases themselves became malnourished. It was, of course, also possible to examine the subsequent development of these and all other children in the village, in order to study relationships between early growth and development, and later progress.

How did the index cases differ from matched controls? The results can be summarized very briefly. The two sets of families, index cases, and controls matched according to characteristics of the children at birth, did not differ in family structure, family economic status, or sociocultural characteristics as measured by personal cleanliness, literacy, or educational level. Nor did they differ in the biological characteristics of the parents: height, weight, age, number of pregnancies, size of families. However, they did differ very significantly indeed in characteristics of the microenvironment as assessed by the Caldwell inventory. This measures frequency and stability of adult contacts, vocal stimulation, gratification of needs, emotional climate, avoidance of restriction, breadth of experience, aspects of the physical environment, and available play materials. Even at 6 months, when only one of the index cases was already beginning to show signs of clinical malnutrition, the control families were providing a much better home environment. A quarter of the homes of the children who later became malnourished scored below the level of *any* of the homes of the control group, and nearly half had scores on the Caldwell inventory lower than that of all but one of the families in the control group. These differences persisted over time.

The significance of this finding is that it draws attention to the profound importance of factors in the family environment in influencing the course of a child's development, even within a social group in which the living conditions appear from the outside to be very homogeneous.

What about the development of the children themselves, both prior to and following severe malnutrition? Cravioto's findings showed first that susceptible infants cannot be identified in early infancy since they do not differ from the rest of their birth cohort somatically or behaviorally. However, delays in language development were already becoming strikingly manifest before the index children became ill. And the children who recovered from severe clinical malnutrition continued to lag behind control children in language development; their retardation could not, however, be fully accounted for statistically by poor environmental conditions, but was also related to their subsequent physical growth.

The above study leaves unanswered as yet the question whether differences between index cases and controls will persist over time. Some light is shed on this by the study which Birch, Richardson, Hertzig and I carried out in Jamaica in 1970 (Birch & Richardson, 1972; Hertzig et al., 1972; Richardson, 1972).

Our subjects were 74 boys aged between 6 and 11 years who had been admitted to Professor Waterlow's ward in the Tropical Metabolism Research Unit within the first 2 years of life because of clinical malnutrition. They had all made a clinical recovery and we saw them several years later when they were of primary-school age. Male siblings of the index cases within the same age range were also studied; and for each index case and sibling, the boy attending the same class at school and who was nearest in age was also examined. Home interviews with mothers and with teachers were carried out. I wish only to mention some of the principal findings which bear directly upon the issues already raised.

Index cases were different from those in the comparison groups on almost all the measures we took. They were on average shorter in stature, lighter in weight, and had smaller heads. More of them were intellectually dull and educationally backward when tested on the Wide Range Achievement Test (Bijou, Jastak, & Jastak, 1965). They had fewer friends at school, were more often rated by their teachers as being dull and timid, and by mothers as being docile and un-aggressive. Their siblings shared some of these characteristics although to a much less marked degree, that is, they tended to be intermediate between the index and comparison cases.

Like Cravioto and his colleagues we looked at home stimulation, and Richard-son drew up an index of intellectual stimulation which covered many of the areas explored in the Caldwell inventory. Table 1 presents the findings which relate home stimulation and nutritional history to intelligence. The control children who scored above the median on our scale of intellectual stimulation had mean intelligence test scores of 71.4; those below the median had scores of 60.5. The index children who scored above the median on our scale of intellec-tual stimulation had scores of 62.7; those who were below the median had scores of only 52.9. There was no significant difference between the mean scores of malnourished children living in homes which provided good intellectual stimula-tion and those of the comparison group given poor intellectual stimulation. Both of these groups were, however, significantly duller than the control group with good intellectual stimulation; and significantly brighter than the index cases with poor intellectual stimulation (see also Richardson, 1976).

These data are in agreement with Cravioto's, indicating that both home stimu-lation and good nutrition are important for intellectual growth and that both continue to exert a powerful influence on the development of children through-out childhood. Relatively good home circumstances can do something to repair the damage caused by malnutrition in infancy but, at least within the somewhat

TABLE 1

Relations Between Nutritional Status, Home Stimulation
and Scores on IQ Tests[2]

	Stimulation	
	+	−
Controls	71.4	60.5
Index cases	62.7	52.9

[2]From Richardson (1972).

narrow limits set by the Jamaican environment we studied, the effect of malnutrition is still very evident.

The Chavez *et al.* (1974) study is a different sort. He obtained detailed normative data about the development of a small group of Mexican village children, and then, in the same village, provided supplementary feeding; first for pregnant women, and then for these mothers and their babies. The results were very dramatic. The supplemented children grew faster and developed more quickly than did the control group. They slept less, spent more time out of their cots, talked and walked at a younger age, and were more vigorous in play and more likely to take the lead in games with their siblings and age mates. And because they were precocious, healthy and lively, they became more interesting to their parents and more highly regarded by them. Hence they received much more attention than did other children in the village, and this in turn increased their behavioral competence. In other words, the children themselves brought about changes in the social environment which in turn contributed to their own development. The results were certainly very impressive.

Conclusions

What are we to conclude from all this? The studies above as well as others, leave little doubt that there is an association between protein/calorie malnutrition in infancy and early childhood and reduction in physical growth, retardation in I.Q., immature social behavior, backwardness in school, and poor physical health in later childhood. The mechanisms underlying these associations are not entirely clear. Nonetheless we can say that for children of school age (and most probably for adults also, though the evidence here is indirect), the current level of functioning is a product of an interaction between biological characteristics and the environment in which the child lives.

It should be noted that all these studies were carried out in poorly fed communities. The factors which distinguish malnourished children from controls in these communities are "precipitating" variables, that result in clinical malnutrition only in undernourished communities. They would not be associated with malnutrition in Holland or Britain since, for practical purposes, clinical malnutrition does not exist in these countries; nor would they distinguish families in famine areas in which the whole population was starving. Malnutrition is a manmade condition which is totally preventable. And it has many adverse consequences quite apart from those which directly affect growth and development.

I do not believe myself that it is any longer very profitable to attempt to determine whether malnutrition makes a specific and unique contribution to later retardation in social and emotional development irrespective of the environmental conditions within which the child lives. We know enough now to say that early nutritional status is a significant factor influencing later development, and we require no further research to justify projects designed to improve the health and nutritional status of children. I hope that when further studies are planned they will concern themselves with the problem of how to improve nutrition — and the cultural milieu within which undernourished families usually live — rather than with the academic, and indeed unanswerable, question of whether nutrition or the social environment makes the more important contribution to a child's development.

The most promising lines for further research on the behavioral side are through studies which aim to cause mothers to change child upbringing practices — not only as they affect the children's diet but also the cognitive and social stimulation they receive. And we require educational studies concerned with the child himself. There is abundant evidence that even in severely damaged organisms behavior is remarkably modifiable. Both comparative studies of malnourished animals (Frankova, 1974) and the human studies summarized in this chapter show how important the circumstances of the child's environment are in determining his behavioral recovery and development.

REFERENCES

Bijou, S., Jastak, J. F., & Jastak, S. R. Wide Range Achievement Test. Guidance Associates, 1965.

Birch, H. G., & Gusson, J. D. *Disadvantaged children: Health nutrition and school failure.* New York and London: Grune and Stratton, 1970.

Birch, H. G., & Richardson, S. A. The functioning of Jamaican school children severely malnourished during the first two years of life. In *Nutrition, the nervous system and behavior.* Pan American Health Organization (World Health Organization) Scientific Publication No. 251, 1972.

Chavez, A., Martinez, C., & Yaschine, T. The importance of nutrition and stimuli on child mental and social development. In J. Cravioto, L. Hambraeus, & B. Vahlquist (Eds.), *Early malnutrition and mental development.* (Symposia of the Swedish Nutrition Foundation No. 12). Stockholm: Almquist & Wiksell, 1974.

Cravioto, J., & Delicardie, E. Environmental correlates of severe clinical malnutrition and language development in survivors from kwashiorkor or marasmus. In *Nutrition, the nervous system and behavior.* Pan American Health Organization (World Health Organization) Scientific Publication No. 251, 1972.

Dobbing, J. Prenatal development and neurological development. In J. Cravioto, L. Hambraeus, & B. Vahlquist (Eds.), *Early malnutrition and mental development.* (Symposia of the Swedish Nutrition Foundation, No. 12). Stockholm: Almquist & Wiksell, 1974.

Dobbing, J., & Smart, J. L. Early under-nutrition, brain development and behaviour in ethology and development. In S. A. Barnett (Ed.), *Clinics in Developmental Medicine No. 47.* London: Wm. Heinemann, 1973.

Frankova, S. Interaction between early malnutrition and stimulation in animals. In J. Cravioto, L. Hambraeus, & B. Vahlquist (Eds.), *Early malnutrition and mental development.* (Symposia of the Swedish Nutrition Foundation No. 12). Stockholm: Almquist & Wiksell, 1974.

Habicht, J. P., Martorell, R., Yarbrough, C., Malina, R. M., & Klein, R. E. Height and weight standards for preschool children: how relevant are ethnic differences in growth potential? *The Lancet,* 1974, *1,* 611-614.

Hertzig, M., Birch, H. G., Richardson, S. A., & Tizard, J. Intellectual levels of school children severely malnourished during the first two years of life. *Pediatrics,* 1972, *49,* No. 6.

Khosla, T., & Lowe, C. R. Height and weight of British men. *The Lancet,* 1968, *1,* 742-45.

Richardson, S. A. Ecology of malnutrition: nonnutritional factors influencing intellectual and behavioral development. In *Nutrition, the nervous system and behavior.* Pan American Health Organization (World Health Organization) Scientific Publication No. 251, 1972.

Richardson, S. A. The relation of severe malnutrition in infancy to the intelligence of school children with differing life histories. *Pediat. Res.,* 1976, *10,* 57-61.

8

Imitation, Response Novelty, and Language Acquisition

Grover J. Whitehurst

State University of New York at Stony Brook

"The most important thing psychology is likely to get from linguistics is the reminder that human behavior includes the response that is novel but appropriate." [Brown, 1958, p. viii]

Brown's assertion has proved remarkably prescient, for the notion of the novel but appropriate ("rule-governed") response has been at the core of the "new linguistics" (Chomsky, 1965). In particular, the observation that children produce sentences that display regularities but that are not word for word replicas of adult sentences has been used to argue against the role of imitation in the process of language acquisition. As Slobin (1968) has phrased it: "If a child were to spend a lifetime imitating the sentences he heard, we could never account for the outstanding ability of every human being to speak and understand sentences he has clearly never heard before but which are nevertheless acceptable as sentences of his language." [p. 437]

The observation that many sentences produced by children are not direct copies of adult models is undeniably correct. That this fact undercuts a role for imitation in language acquisition is not at all evident. One reason that novel but appropriate utterances may have seemed devastating to the role of imitative processes in language acquisition is that there has been no well developed statement of the relationship between imitation and language. Early investigators of language acquisition were preoccupied with developmental norms as is evidenced by McCarthy's (1954) review. Occasionally, prominent learning theorists have commented on imitation and language acquisition but the comments have been brief or have ignored the "creative" aspect of language that seems to require special attention (Mowrer, 1960; Skinner, 1957; Staats, 1971). The theorist who has been most concerned with the topic of imitation has dealt with language acquisition in the most cursory manner (Bandura, 1971). A recent theoretical note on the relationship of imitation and language development took a very limiting view of what imitation is and failed to place imitation in a larger context of learning theory (Slobin, 1968). Applied behavior analysts have been more concerned with training conditions which utilize imitation to teach language than with the processes involved (Sherman, 1971). This lack of theoretical comment has made it necessary for those investigators who are interested in the learning context of language acquisition to draw their own inferences from existing learning theories. This is a difficult task even for those who are sympathetic and conversant with learning approaches and research. It is too much to ask of those many developmental psycholinguists who are not.

Therefore, it would seem to be useful to articulate a preliminary statement on the relationship between imitation processes and language acquisition. Such a statement could serve as a guide to research and as a base for evaluation of much previous work. Also, since all learning or conditioning theories of language acquisition include imitation processes, a theoretical statement such as is being suggested would serve as an extension of basic learning conceptions such as those suggested by Skinner (1957) as they have been applied to the language development of children (Bijou & Baer, 1965).

WHAT IS IMITATION?

A discussion of how imitation relates to language acquisitions necessarily involves some specification of what exactly imitation is. Though this may seem a simple task, current observational learning theories (Bandura, 1971; Gewirtz, 1971) ignore many of the characteristics of the imitation process that appear critical for language acquisition as well as the acquisition of other complex skills. In lieu of an extended treatment of this topic, which appears elsewhere (Whitehurst, in press), some consideration will be given the most important concerns.

Nontopographical Imitation

In addition to being controlled by the topography of a model's response, an observer may come under the control of the stimuli which set the occasion for the model's response. Such an occurrence might be called the imitation of stimulus control or an *observational discrimination.*

The formation of an observational discrimination would be demonstrated by an observer who prior to modeling uses "cup" in the presence of both cups and glasses. A model holds up a cup and says "cup," then holds up a glass and says "glass." The observer's overall probability of saying "cup" does not change, but the circumstance in which it is said does. The response is subsequently controlled by the object, cup, rather than by both cups and glasses.

Others have chosen to focus on the matching of topography to the exclusion of the matching of stimulus control. For example, Bandura (1971) speaks of place learning (imitation of a discrimination) as being much less frequent than response learning (imitation of topography). Baer and Sherman (1964) note that a child may be able to learn which of two cranks to turn in order to produce reinforcement by observation of a model who turns one crank and receives nothing while turning the other crank and obtaining a payoff. They suggest that phenomena such as this (imitation of a discrimination) are of limited concern as compared with situations in which similarity between the model's behavior and the observer's behavior is an important dimension (imitation of topography).

The approach favored here is to treat the acquisition of control by stimuli preceding the model's behavior as of equal status with acquisition of control by the model's behavior itself. Observational discrimination is particularly relevant for language acquisition. The difference between a sophisticated three-year-old mynah bird and a normal three-year-old child is not in the response topographies that have been differentiated through imitation but in the discriminative control of those response elements. The child comes to talk about things while the mynah bird merely comes to talk. Operant programs for developing language in speech deficient children (Sloane & MacAuley, 1968) have relied heavily on the child's imitative responses coming under the control of those objects that are paired with the model's verbal prompts. Similarly, recent experimental analyses of generative grammatical repertoires (Premack, 1970; Sherman, 1971; Whitehurst & Vasta, 1975) have depended on the observer's responses coming under control of stimulus relationships which are contained within the materials described by a model. It is, therefore, important that this phenomenon be viewed in the context of an imitation process.

"Partial" Imitation

Several attempts to confront the issue of the relationship between imitation and language acquisition have proceeded with an implicit definition of imitation that must be rejected. This definition includes as imitative only those behaviors that are more or less exact copies of a modeled sentence or phrase. The fault of this definition is the requirement of a more or less exact match between what is defined as the modeled stimulus and what is measured as the response. The problem is that the modeled stimulus that is functional in controlling responding by the subject may be a subset of the total stimulus array defined as *the* modeled stimulus by the investigator. This is a problem that is not unique to the process of imitation. Numerous difficulties have arisen in the psychology of learning because key terms such as reinforcer or discrimination have been defined on the basis of experimental procedures instead of functional relationships (Millenson, 1967).

An excellent example of an "exact copy definition" of imitation leading to perhaps erroneous conclusions is provided by Ervin (1964). Ervin collected samples of the spontaneous speech of five children. Sentences were classified as imitative if they were overt immediate repetitions of adult utterances. Sentences not meeting the criterion for imitation were placed in a nonimitative category. A grammar written for the nonimitative sentences was applied to the imitative sentences to determine whether the imitated sentences were grammatically different from the nonimitated sentences. The results of the study were that the grammar written for the nonimitative sentences could account for the utterances in the imitative category. According to Ervin, if the process of imitation exercised a progressive influence on grammatical development, then the imitated sentences would not have been grammatically consistent with the nonimitated sentences. Ervin (1964) concluded that, "We cannot look to overt imitation as a source for the rapid progress children make in grammatical skill in these early years." [p. 172] We will return to this study after examining the alternative to viewing imitation as exact copying.

Selective Imitation

A corollary of the notion that an imitative response need not be an exact copy of the totality of a model's response is that an observer may respond to a selected subset or relationship within the behavioral interaction that is labeled as the modeling stimulus. This phenomenon, *selective imitation,* is to be differentiated on the basis of its systematic quality from a simple lack of fidelity between the model's and the observer's behavior.

For example, consider the following study by Whitehurst and Novak (1973). Four preschool children were exposed to modeling of participial, prepositional, appositive, and infinitive phrases within a multiple-baseline design. A given phrase type was modeled for a number of sessions while measures of the occurrence of that as well as the three other phrase types were taken. Subsequently, the second phrase type was modeled and so forth until the subject had sequentially been exposed to all four types of phrases. The phrases were modeled for the child in the context of describing one set of pictures, called the training set. Interspersed among the training pictures were probe pictures which were similar in form to the training set but different in the content items portrayed. The subjects were asked to describe these probe pictures without benefit of direct modeling or feedback. The general nature of the results was that each subject produced descriptions of probe pictures that included the phrase type modeled by the adult on the training trials, but with content words appropriate to the probe pictures. For example, on trial 77, the model would hold up a picture and say, "The boy, the big one, is chasing the girl." On trial 78, in response to a probe picture, the child would say, "The dog, the small one, is jumping." As the model would change, for example, from appositive to infinitive phrases the child's grammatical usage would concomitantly change. Thus, the subjects were matching a systematic subset of the total language samples presented to them by the model; they were *selectively imitating* language structure.

It should be evident that this result is highly pertinent to the conclusions of studies such as those by Ervin (1964) in which more or less exact copying has been the basis for the definition of imitation. If selective imitation is indeed a frequent phenomenon, as evidence from a variety of studies would seem to suggest (Whitehurst & Vasta, 1975), then conclusions about the frequency and importance of imitation in the acquisition of language which have been based solely on the observation of exact copying are obviously open to question.

Four characteristics of imitation processes have been suggested in the previous discussion. These are: (1) observers may imitate the topography of a model's behavior; (2) observers may form an observational discrimination by coming under the control of those stimuli which set the occasion for the model's response; (3) imitation is not limited to an attempt to copy all of the behavior which is involved in a modeling episode; and (4) that it is possible for observers to selectively imitate abstracted features of the behavior of a model (such as grammatical features). Each of these characteristics will be important in the discussion which follows of the relationship of imitation to language acquisition.

IMITATION AND VOCABULARY ACQUISITION

There seems little doubt that the first wordlike utterances produced by a normally developing child involve topographical imitation. Consider the following evidence.

Kaye (1971) has used a procedure with 7- to 10-month-old infants in which an adult repeats a pattern of phonemes (like "ba-ba-ba-ba") for numerous trials followed by five-second opportunities for the infant to respond. To quote from Kaye: "In the first few pauses the infant typically does no more than look at us; gradually, however, he smiles, vocalizes, repeats different phonemes with similar intonation ("ga-ga-ga"), and finally says "ba-ba-ba-ba." This may take as many as 70 repetitions by the model, followed by pauses." [p. 4]

Whitehurst, Bouzas, and Barrett-Goldfarb (described in Whitehurst, in press) exposed a 16-month-old English speaking child to a model who described objects in Spanish sentences. There were 27 daily sessions, each session lasting 20 minutes. The child would be brought to the laboratory and placed in a playpen. Periodically, the adult would hold up a toy and label it in Spanish (for example, "Este es el caballo"). The toy would then be placed in the playpen for a fixed period of time. At intervals during this period, the model would pick up the toy and describe it further ("Tu puedes doblar el caballo") while pointing to or acting out the characteristic described. The same sequence of 42 Spanish sentences was repeated during each session. An observer recorded vocalizations made by the child which were later scored as Spanish, English, or mixed. There never were any consequences associated with any of the child's behaviors.

Two results of the study are relevant for the present discussion. First, a substantial amount of Spanish was produced by the subject in the absence of any contingency for such productions. Second, of these Spanish productions, 76% were immediately imitative of topography in that they were taken wholly from the preceding modeled utterance and occurred within 20 sec of the modeling. The remaining Spanish utterances virtually always occurred in the context in which they had been modeled but were more than 20 sec removed from the matching word or phrase of the model.

Whitehurst, Novak, and Zorn (1972) conducted a study of the influence of parental modeling on the development of speech by an otherwise normal child with severely delayed language development. The study occurred in the home of the child and the independent variable consisted of the frequency with which the child's mother engaged in a number of categories of verbalization including imitative prompts, which implied that the child should respond imitatively, and conversation, which was speech directed towards the child which did not require a verbal reply. The frequency with which the child was exposed to these categories of stimulation, both of which may be viewed as modeling, had powerful positive effects on the frequency of his production of new words and phrases. Reinforcement for speech was held constant across all conditions. Of particular interest is the fact that in conditions of the study in which the child was using over four new words per session, approximately one-half of these words were immediately imitative in that they followed an imitative prompt by the mother which included the new word produced by the child.

These studies and others not cited suggest the critical role played by imitation in the differentiation of new vocal responses. However, as previously noted, there is a tremendous leap between the differentiation of a vocal repertoire and the acquisition of words, as witness the difference between mynah bird and child speech. The usual response to this observation would be that the mynah bird is limited to imitative speech while the child's responses are spontaneous, novel, and nonimitative. However, in the context that both observational discrimination and topographical matching are processes of imitation, the generative, "spontaneous" quality of the child's speech is also seen to be a function of imitation, albeit a more complicated process of imitation than the simple topographical matching which characterizes the mynah bird's productions.

To give a concrete frame to this phenomenon, consider a classic study performed by Church (1957). In his procedure, rats were trained to follow leader rats in an elevated T maze to secure a reward of water. An incidental cue of 2 lights was then introduced such that leaders responded consistently with respect to it. After 100 trials of following leaders who were responding to the incidental cue, subjects were given 20 trials alone. On 77% of these test trials, subjects went to the arm marked by the cue to which the leader had been going. Thus a running response that was originally under the control of the topography of the model's behavior was brought under the control of discriminative stimuli that were functional for the model but not initially functional for the observers. The Church demonstration has a parallel in ordinary discrimination learning in which existing responses are brought under the control of new stimuli. What is involved is a transfer of control from one set of stimuli to another. What is unique to imitation of language is that the stimuli from which response control is transferred are topographical stimuli and the stimuli to which control is transferred are "semantic" stimuli (objects, actions, and relationships).

Another example of this process is provided by Miller and Dollard (1941): "A little boy, aged four and a half, is with his mother in a department store. While she is busy with other merchandise, he becomes fascinated by the BB guns on the adjoining counter. As soon as his mother is free, he drags her there, points to one of the guns, and asks, What's that? His mother answers, a BB gun. . . He then repeats the word BB several times while looking at guns." [p. 205]

The prior stimulus in the preceding example is the BB gun which sets the occasion for the mother's labeling and the child's subsequent response. This situation is an example of both topographical imitation (the child had never said "BB" before) and the observational acquisition of a discrimination (the child's response, "BB", came under the stimulus control of the BB gun).

In the two examples above, there is an obvious interplay between the formation of an observational discrimination and the imitation of topography. One of the many important questions that arises regarding these two processes is whether there is a usual or necessary sequence in their development. In research with retarded or autistic children (e.g., Sloane & MacAuley, 1968) matching of topography seems to precede and perhaps set the stage for the acquisition of control by the semantic stimuli which accompany a model's response. For these exceptional children as well as normal children, a learning-to-learn process (Harlow, 1959) might be postulated. That is, over many trials, the child learns that in almost every situation he must discriminate the appropriate semantic stimuli for the verbalizations that are heard. Thus the two-year-old child may have to imitate the topography of a model's response many times before control is acquired by the appropriate discriminative stimuli. This process could continue to the point at which observational discrimination was immediate.

It is obvious that this is the final point in development for normal adults as may be quickly demonstrated. Cut a nonsense form out of paper and make up a nonsense word to go with it, like, "COS." Tell a friend that you wish to demonstrate a phenomenon and that silence is necessary during the demonstration. Hold up the paper cut out and say "COS." Tell your friend that that is all you wish to do for the moment. Five minutes later, a day later, or a week later ask "What is this?" while holding up the paper form. Most people will say "COS."

Whether a learning-to-learn history, in which immediate topographical imitations set the stage for the later occurrence of observationally acquired discriminations, is the route of development for normal children cannot now be determined. Children might well be sensitive to the correlations between what models say and the events which cue the model's verbalizations from the very beginning of the language acquisition process. This is a question for future research.

The most important point of the previous discussion is that the acquisition of vocabulary for children is critically tied to two imitative processes; the first is topographical matching and the second is observational discrimination of the circumstances in which a response of a given topography is uttered by the model. We know a reasonable amount about the variables which encourage the imitation of verbal topographies by children, but much less is understood about how a child comes not only to reproduce the form of a word modeled but also to reproduce that word in its appropriate semantic context.

The important variables in the formation of observational discriminations probably will have to do with the nature of the pairings between particular words as uttered by a model and particular semantic events which are presented with those words. For example, the variations in the consistency of given word-event pairings might be important. Modeling of many different words for the same or similar events might influence a child's fluency while modeling of the same word for many different but abstractly similar events might influence a child's conceptual skills. Another important pairing variable might be the simple frequency of occurrence of a given word-event relationship in a parent's speech. More frequently occurring word-events might be acquired more frequently. The timing or delay of pairing might also be important. A model who typically talks about events in the past or the future might be less effective in producing early acquisition of vocabulary by a child than a model who talks about events in the immediate present.

IMITATION AND COMMUNICATION

The above discussion might be attacked because it seems to tie the acquisition and use of vocabulary items to a reference theory of word meaning. Presumably a child is learning new response forms and the referents for those responses at least as they are modeled in parental speech. However, we know that a specification of the referents for various words does not explain a child's use of words to communicate with others in a social exchange. For example, if a marble is placed under a red striped cup and a six-year-old is asked to explain where the marble is to a peer who has not observed the hiding process, the child might say, "its under the red thing," "its under the cup," "its under the striped thing," "its under that," etc. In each case the referent is the same but the verbalization differs. Such differences might be studied under the rubric of communication style.

What accounts for the variation between and within children in communication style and what, if anything, does imitation have to do with this variation? There is little doubt that much of the explanation for the style of communication has to do with the larger context in which a particular verbalization is produced (Olson, 1970) and the contingencies which are applied by the social community (Skinner, 1957). Both of these classes of variables lie outside the survey of the current presentation.

However, it is clear that imitation is one process which can contribute to determining the format of a communication. Whitehurst (1976) examined the performance of school children of different ages on a communication task similar to the cup and marble example above. Children had to describe to a peer which of two or three cups a marble was placed under. The cups varied in size (big or small), color (red or blue), and design (striped or spotted). As compared with older children, first graders were found to produce a high frequency (27%) of descriptions which were ambiguous, for example, with the marble under the big red cup and with a small red cup as the second option, the child would tell a listener that the marble was under the red cup.

In an attempt to isolate some of the variables responsible for these age differences, comparable groups of first graders were exposed to a good modeling or poor modeling procedure and then tested on the same task. In good modeling, each subject was exposed to a model who produced highly accurate and efficient communications on problems similar but not identical to those that the child would eventually be asked to describe. In poor modeling, the child was exposed to a series of ambiguous communications similar to the example previously given in which a cup is described as the red cup even though more than one red cup is present. The poor modeling group subsequently produced 76% ambiguous communications on the reference test while the good modeling group dropped to 8% ambiguous communications.

Thus, imitation is seen as one process that determines the actual verbal behavior produced by a child as well as the acquisition of individual vocabulary items. Of interest is the fact that the imitative responses of the children were selective. That is, instead of producing the same verbalizations as those used by the poor model, the children simply imitated the ambiguous or efficient character of those communications.

IMITATION AND SYNTAX

Questions involving the development of language structure, or syntax, have been at the core of the resurgence of interest in language acquisition that has marked the field of psychology in the last ten years. Chomsky's (1965) theory of transformational grammar is in no small part responsible for this emphasis. As mentioned earlier, it has seemed to some that the fact of a generative-abstract linguistic structure as evidenced in novel utterances is incompatible with a theory of language acquisition which places any stress on imitation processes.

However, it should be evident that the fact of selective imitation, that is, the reproduction of abstracted elements of the speech of models, was not considered when the presumed incompatibility between imitation and novelty was argued. If a child imitates the grammar of an adult's vocalization, like the passive construction, but not the content of the modeled utterance, then verbal behavior is produced which is simultaneously imitative and novel. To date, selective imitation has been demonstrated with the following structural relationships: grammatical complexity (Harris & Hassemer, 1972), question-asking style (Rosenthal, Zimmerman & Durning, 1970), sentence phrase types (Whitehurst & Novak, 1973), the passive construction (Whitehurst, Ironsmith & Goldfein, 1974), and verb tense (Carroll, Rosenthal & Brysh, 1969; Rosenthal & Whitebrook, 1970).

While the occurrence of selective imitation answers some questions, it raises still others. Primary among these is why and how the child comes to be controlled by particular structural relationships within the speech of the parents. Why are these relationships abstracted? One answer to this question might appeal to contingencies of reinforcement. If a child attempts to produce a sentence which is grammatically inappropriate as compared with the structure of the utterances that have been modeled by parents in similar settings, the child might be corrected by the parents. This differential reinforcement of particular grammatical structures might develop and refine the control over the child's speech exercised by the structure of the parents' speech.

Certainly this process has been demonstrated to be effective in applied research with exceptional children (Sherman, 1971). Unfortunately there are many difficulties with the notion of differential reinforcement of good grammatical imitations as an account of how normal children acquire syntax, not the least of which is the demonstrated infrequency with which parents do explicitly reinforce the grammar of their children's speech (Brown, Cazden & Bellugi, 1969; Brown & Hanlon, 1970).

Whitehurst and Vasta (1975) have constructed the *CIP* (comprehension-imitation-production) hypothesis as a possible model of the role and determinants of selective imitation in the acquisition of grammar. In brief, a three-stage process is hypothesized. In the *comprehension* stage, a child will come under the control of the relationship between a syntactic structure as produced in the speech of adults and the stimuli in the environment which are correlated with the usage of that structure. Responses by the child will be simple verbal and nonverbal actions which will be explicitly reinforced as discriminated operants because the social environment is replete with natural contingencies for comprehending the speech of parents.

In the second stage, the child will begin to use the structure in his own utterances. These initial productions will fit the model of *selective imitation* in that they will match and be controlled by the grammatical structure of a previously occurring utterance of a model but they will not include identical content words since the semantic events being described by the child will typically differ from those described by the model. Explicit contingencies of reinforcement would not be necessary for these productions. In the relationship between comprehension and selective imitation, neither a unidirectional effect nor a model in which comprehension reaches asymptote prior to the initiation of production is implied. Rather, it is suggested that the structure as used by adults need only to have acquired some discriminative control over the responses of the child as a listener prior to the selective imitation of it. Comprehension can continue to develop and be aided by the selective imitation process. Finally, in the third stage *spontaneous production* of the structure would occur in the absence of an imitative component.

A variety of evidence supportive of the CIP hypothesis is presented by Whitehurst and Vasta (1975). Of particular relevance is a demonstration that the form of direct-indirect object sentences produced by normal preschool children in the production mode can be manipulated by the application of contingencies to the pointing responses of the children as they respond in the comprehension mode to direct-indirect object sentences used by models. The demonstration that comprehension training can directly influence the emergence of a form in the productive mode even in the absence of contingencies for production is certainly supportive of the CIP hypothesis.

SUMMARY

Several relationships between imitation and language acquisition have been discussed. The basic response units of language, words, are seen to be acquired through the joint occurrence of topographical imitation and observational discrimination. These two processes of observational learning allow a child to produce new response forms under the appropriate discriminative control. Evidence from several sources supports the assertion that the child's first wordlike utterances clearly involve imitation of topography and that eventually, if not from the very beginning of development, normal humans are able to simultaneously imitate new vocal topographies and come under the control of the semantic events which were correlated with the modeling of those response forms.

A vocabulary, acquired through imitation, is a prerequisite for but not an explanation of the production of verbal behavior to communicate with others. A given object or action may be described in many different ways by a speaker. This phenomenon has been studied under the topic of communication style or effectiveness. Data were presented to show that imitation can be a powerful process in producing differences among children in their effectiveness of communication.

Imitation was seen as a critical process in the acquisition of syntax in opposition to the logical and empirical arguments that have previously been raised against its role in this area. Selective imitation as a process of matching the structure but not the content of a model's utterance results in productions which are simultaneously imitative and novel. Selective imitation of new syntactic forms can occur in the absence of direct contingencies of reinforcement for the grammar of new productions as long as comprehension training on the new syntactic form has previously occurred.

The facts of language creativity or novelty, which often have been viewed as the nemesis of imitation theory, are instead seen as the logical outcome of imitation. A child who learns word forms as well as their semantic referents through the observation of others can produce those words in the presence of the appropriate referents long after the relevant modeling episode has passed. Such "spontaneous verbalization" is often viewed as creative or novel. A child can selectively imitate the style, for example, ambiguity or efficiency, of the communications that are modeled by caretakers, even though the exact form of the child's verbal behavior might differ. Thus, "novel and generative" communications are not incompatible with imitation of communication style. In a like manner, a child can selectively imitate the syntax of utterances modeled while using content words appropriately under the control of semantic characteristics of the scene being described. Resulting language productions would be simultaneously novel and imitative. In each of the areas of vocabulary, communication effectiveness, and language structure, imitation lies at the core of the acquisition process.

ACKNOWLEDGMENTS

This chapter is dedicated to Sidney W. Bijou. My debt to him is too large to be repaid.

REFERENCES

Baer, D. M., & Sherman, J. A. Reinforcement control of generalized imitation in young children. *Journal of Experimental Child Psychology,* 1964, *1,* 37-49.

Bandura, A. Analysis of modeling processes. In A. Bandura (Ed.), *Psychological modeling: Conflicting theories.* Chicago: Aldine-Atherton, 1971.

Bijou, S. W., & Baer, D. M. *Child Development* (Vol. 2). New York: Appleton-Century-Crofts, 1965.

Brown, R. W. *Words and things.* New York: Free Press, 1958.

Brown, R. W., Cazden, C., & Bellugi, U. The child's grammar from I to III. In J. P. Hill (Ed.), *Minnesota symposium on child psychology* (Vol. 3). Minneapolis: University of Minnesota Press, 1969.

Brown, R. W., & Hanlon, C. Derivational complexity and order of acquisition in child speech. In J. R. Hayes (Ed.), *Cognition and the development of language.* New York: Wiley, 1970.

Carroll, W. R., Rosenthal, T. L., & Brysh, C. Socially induced imitation of grammatical structures. Paper presented at the meeting of the Society for Research in Child Development, Santa Monica, March, 1969.

Chomsky, N. *Aspects of the theory of syntax.* Cambridge, Massachusetts: M.I.T. Press, 1965.

Church, R. M. Transmission of learned behavior between rats. *Journal of Abnormal and Social Psychology,* 1957, *54,* 163-165.

Ervin, S. M. Imitation and structural change in children's language. In E. H. Lenneberg (Ed.), *New directions in the study of language.* Cambridge, Mass.: M.I.T. Press, 1964.

Gewirtz, J. L. Conditional responding as a paradigm for observational imitative learning and vicarious reinforcement. In H. W. Reese (Ed.), *Advances in child development and behavior* (Vol. 6). New York: Academic Press, 1971.

Harlow, H. F. Learning set and error factor theory. In S. Koch (Ed.), *Psychology: A study of a science* (Vol. 2). New York: McGraw-Hill, 1959.

Harris, M. B., & Hassemer, W. G. Some factors affecting the complexity of children's sentences: The effects of modeling, age, sex, and bilingualism. *Journal of Experimental Child Psychology,* 1972, *13,* 447-455.

Kaye, K. Learning by imitation in infants and young children. Paper presented at the meeting of the Society for Research in Child Development, Minneapolis, April, 1971.

McCarthy, D. Language development in children. In L. Carmichael (Ed.), *Manual of child psychology* (2nd ed.). New York: Wiley, 1954.

Millenson, J. R. *Principles of behavioral analysis.* New York: Macmillan, 1967.

Miller, N. E., & Dollard, J. *Social learning and imitation.* New Haven: Yale University Press, 1941.

Mowrer, O. H. *Learning theory and behavior.* New York: Wiley, 1960.

Olson, D. R. Language and thought: Aspects of a cognitive theory of semantics. *Psychological Review,* 1970, *77,* 257-273.

Premack, D. A functional analysis of language. *Journal of the Experimental Analysis of Behavior,* 1970, *14,* 107-125.

Rosenthal, T. L., & Whitebook, J. S. Incentive versus instructions in transmitting grammatical parameters with experimenter as model. *Behavior Research and Therapy,* 1970, *8,* 189-196.

Rosenthal, T. L., Zimmerman, B. J., & Durning, K. Observationally induced changes in children's interrogative classes. *Journal of Personality and Social Psychology,* 1970, *16,* 681-688.

Sherman, J. A. Imitation and language development. In H. W. Reese (Ed.), *Advances in child development and behavior* (Vol. 6). New York: Academic Press, 1971.

Skinner, B. F. *Verbal behavior.* New York: Appleton-Century-Crofts, 1957.

Sloane, H. N., & MacAulay, B. D. *Operant procedures in remedial speech and language training.* Boston: Houghton Mifflin, 1968.

Slobin, D. I. Imitation and grammatical development in children. In N. S. Endler, L. R. Boulter & H. Osser (Eds.), *Contemporary issues in developmental psychology,* New York: Holt, Rinehart, & Winston, 1968.

Staats, A. W. Linguistic-mentalistic theory versus an explanatory S-R learning theory of language development. In D. I. Slobin (Ed.), *The ontogenesis of grammar.* New York: Academic Press, 1971.

Whitehurst, G. J. The development of communication: Changes with age and modeling. *Child Development,* 1976, *47,* 473-482.

Whitehurst, G. J. Observational learning. In T. A. Brigham & A. C. Catania (Eds.) *Analysis of behavior: Social and educational processes.* New York: Irvington-Wiley, in press.

Whitehurst, G. J., Ironsmith, E. M., & Goldfein, M. R. Selective imitation of the passive construction through modeling. *Journal of Experimental Child Psychology,* 1974, *17,* 288-302.

Whitehurst, G. J., & Novak, G. Modeling, imitation training, and the acquisition of sentence phrases. *Journal of Experimental Child Psychology,* 1973, *16,* 332-345.

Whitehurst, G. J., Novak, G., & Zorn, G. A. Delayed speech studied in the home. *Developmental Psychology,* 1972, *7,*169-177.

Whitehurst, G. J., & Vasta, R. Is language acquired through imitation? *Journal of Psycholinguistic Research,* 1975, *4,* 37-59.

Part II

CONTRIBUTIONS TO METHODOLOGY
AND PRACTICE

Setting Events Due to
Sidney W. Bijou

A Bibliography of Bijou's Work in the Area of Methodology and Practice, with Self-Evident Function for the Papers Published Here

Bijou, S. W. Psychometric similarities between habitual criminals and psychotics. *Delaware State Medical Journal*, 1938, *11*, 126-129.

Bijou, S. W., & Jastak, J. Wide range achievement test. New York: Psychological Corporation, 1941.

Bijou, S. W. The development of conditioning methodology for studying experimental neurosis in the rat. *Journal of Comparative Psychology*, 1942, *44*, 91-106.

Bijou, S. W. An experimental analysis of Arthur Performance quotients. *Journal of Consulting Psychology*, 1942, *6*, 247-252.

Bijou, S. W. A genetic study of the diagnostic significance of psychometric patterns. *American Journal of Mental Deficiency*, 1942, *47*, 171-177.

Bijou, S. W. The measurement of adjustment by psychometric pattern techniques — Its needs in the selective service program. *American Journal of Orthopsychiatry*, 1942, *12*, 435-438.

Bijou, S. W. The psychometric pattern approach as an aid to clinical analysis — A review. *American Journal of Mental Deficiency*, 1942, *46*, 354-362.

Bijou, S. W., & Werner, H. Vocabulary analysis in mentally deficient children. *American Journal of Mental Deficiency*, 1944, *48*, 364-366.

Bijou, S. W., & Werner, H. Language analysis in brain-injured and nonbrain-injured mentally deficient children. *Journal of Genetic Psychology*, 1945, *66*, 239-254.

Bijou, S. W. (Ed. & co-author of 3 chapters). The psychology program in the AAF convalescent hospitals. *Aviation Psychology Reports* (Vol. 15). United States Government Printing Office, 1947.

Bijou, S. W. A conditioned response technique to investigate experimental neurosis in the rat. *Journal of Comparative Physiology*, 1951, *44*, 84-87.

Bijou, S. W., & Kenny, D. T. Ambiguity value of TAT cards. *Journal of Consulting Psychology*, 1951, *15*, 203-209.

Bijou, S. W. Therapeutic techniques with children. In L. A. Pennington, & I. A. Berg (Eds.), *An introduction to clinical psychology* (2nd Ed.). New York: Ronald, 1954. Pp. 608-631.

Bijou, S. W. A systematic approach to an experimental analysis of young children. *Child Development*, 1955, *26*, 161-168.

Bijou, S. W. Methodology for an experimental analysis of child behavior. *Psychological Reports*, 1957, *3*, 243-250.

Bijou, S. W. A child study laboratory on wheels. *Child Development*, 1958, *29*, 425-427.

Bijou, S. W., & Sturges, P. T. Positive reinforcers for experimental studies with children — Consumables and manipulatables. *Child Development*, 1959, *30*, 151-170.

Bijou, S. W., & Baer, D. M. The laboratory-experimental study of child behavior. In P. H. Mussen (Ed.), *Handbook of research methods in child development.* New York: Wiley, 1960.

Bijou, S. W., & Oblinger, B. Responses of normal and retarded children as a function of the experimental situation. *Psychological Reports,* 1960, *6,* 447-454.

Orlando, R., Bijou, S. W., Tyler, R. M., & Marshall, D. A. A laboratory for the experimental analysis of developmentally retarded children. *Psychological Reports,* 1960, *7,* 261-267.

Bijou, S. W. Discrimination performance as a baseline for individual analysis of young children. *Child Development,* 1961, *32,* 163-170.

Bijou, S. W., & Orlando, R. Shaping behavior to multiple schedule performances with retarded children. *Journal of Experimental Analysis of Behavior,* 1961, *4,* 7-16.

Bijou, S. W., & Baer, D. M. Some methodological contribution from a natural science approach to research in child development. In L. P. Lipsitt, & C. C. Spiker (Eds.), *Recent advances in child development and behavior.* New York: Academic Press, 1963.

Bijou, S. W. Experimental studies of child behavior, normal and deviant. In L. Krasner, & L. P. Ullmann (Eds.), *Research in behavior modification: New developments and implications.* New York: Holt, Rinehart, & Winston, 1965.

Birnbrauer, J. S., Bijou, S. W., Wolf, M. M., & Kidder, J. D. Programmed instruction in the classroom. In L. P. Ullmann, & L. Krasner (Eds.), *Case studies in behavior modification.* New York: Holt, Rinehart, & Winston, 1965.

Lovaas, O. I., Baer, D. M., & Bijou, S. W. Experimental procedures for analyzing the interaction of symbolic social stimuli and children's behavior. *Child Development,* 1965, *36,* 237-248.

Bijou, S. W. Application of experimental analysis of behavior principles in teaching academic tool subjects to retarded children. In N. G. Haring, & R. J. Whelan (Eds.), *The learning environment: Relationships to behavior modification and implications for special education.* Lawrence, Kansas: University of Kansas, Publications of the School of Education, *16,* (Whole No. 2), 1966.

Bijou, S. W., & Baer, D. M. Operant methods in child behavior and development. In W. K. Honig (Ed.), *Operant behavior: Areas of research and application.* New York: Appleton-Century-Crofts, 1966.

Bijou, S. W., & Sloane, H. N. Therapeutic techniques with children. In L. A. Pennington, & I. A. Berg (Eds.), *An introduction to clinical psychology* (3rd rev.). New York: Ronald, 1966.

Johnston, M. K., Sloane, H. N., Jr., & Bijou, S. W. A note on the measurement of drooling in free-ranging young children. *Journal of Experimental Child Psychology,* 1966, *4,* 292-295.

Bijou, S. W., & Baer, D. M. *Child development: Readings in experimental analysis.* New York: Appleton-Century-Crofts, 1967.

Orlando, R., & Bijou, S. W. Rapid acquisition of multiple-schedule discrimination performance in a single response free-operant situation with retarded children. In S. W. Bijou, & D. M. Baer (Eds.), *Child development: Readings in experimental analysis.* New York: Appleton-Century-Crofts, 1967. Pp. 81-92.

Bijou, S. W. Behavior modification in the mentally retarded: Application of operant conditioning principles. In J. J. Grossman (Ed.), *Pediatric Clinics of North America,* 1968, *15,* 969-987.

Bijou, S. W., Peterson, R. F., & Ault, M. A method to integrate descriptive and experimental field studies at the level of data and empirical concepts. *Journal of Applied Behavior Analysis,* 1968, *1,* 175-191.

Bijou, S. W., Peterson, R. F., Harris, F. R., Allen, K. E., & Johnston, M. S. Methodology for experimental studies of young children in natural settings. *Psychological Record,* 1969, *19,* 177-210.

Bijou, S. W., & Peterson, R. F. Psychological assessment in children: A functional analysis. In P. McReynolds (Ed.), *Advances in psychological assessment* (Vol. 2). Palo Alto, Cal.: Science & Behavior Books, 1971. Pp. 63-78.

Bijou, S. W. These kids have problems and our job is to do something about them. In J. B. Jordon, & L. S. Robbins (Eds.), *Let's try doing something else kind of thing.* Arlington, Va.: Council of Exceptional Children, 1972. Pp. 66-75.

Bijou, S. W. Tecnologica de la enseñanza de niños impedidos. In S. W. Bijou, & E. Ribes-Inesta (Eds.), *Modificacion de conducta: Problemas y extensiones.* Mexico: Editorial F. Trillas, S. A., 1972. Pp. 57-79.

Bijou, S. W. The technology of teaching young handicapped children. In S. W. Bijou, & E. Ribes-Inesta (Eds.), *Behavior modification: Issues and extensions.* New York: Academic Press, 1972. Pp. 27-42.

Bijou, S. W., & Ribes-Inesta, E. (Eds.), *Behavior modification: Issues and extensions.* New York: Academic Press, 1972.

Bijou, S. W., & Ribes-Inesta, E. *Modificacion de conducta: Problemas y extensiones.* Mexico: Editorial F. Trillas, S. A., 1972. Pp. 57-79.

Bijou, S. W. Behavior modification in teaching the retarded child. In C. E. Thoreson (Ed.), *72nd yearbook of national society for study of education.* Chicago, Ill.: University of Chicago Press, 1973. Pp. 259-290.

Bijou, S. W. Helping children develop their full potential. *The pediatrics clinics of North America,* 1973, *20*(3), 579-585.

Bijou, S. W., & Warren, S. A. Objective observations in field situations for clinical assessment. In R. Eyman, E. Meyers, & G. Tarjan (Eds.), *Memorial volume to Harvey Dingman.* University of California Press, 1973. Pp. 82-86.

Grimm, J. A., & Bijou, S. W. Principles and objectives in an academic program for young handicapped children. In G. Semb (Ed.), *Behavior analysis and education – 1972.* Lawrence, Kansas: University of Kansas, 1975. Pp. 146-154.

Bijou, S. W., & Grimm, J. A. Behavioral diagnosis and assessment in teaching young handicapped children. In T. Thompson, & W. S. Dockens III (Eds.), *Proceedings of the national symposium on behavior modification.* New York: Academic Press, 1975. Pp. 161-180.

Bijou, S. W., & Wilcox-Cole, B. The feasibility of providing effective educational programs for the severely and profoundly retarded. *Educating the 24-hour retarded child.* Arlington, Tex.: National Association for Retarded Citizens, 1975.

Bijou, S. W. Behavior analysis applied to early childhood education. In B. Spodek, & H. L. Walberg (Eds.), *75th yearbook of national society for study of education.* Chicago, Ill.: University of Chicago Press, in press, 1977.

Bijou, S. W., & Rayek-Zaga, E. *Analisis de la conducta aplicado a enseñanza.* Mexico: Editorial Trillas, in press, 1976.

9

Are Experimental Procedures and Service Obligations Compatible in a Preschool Program for Young Handicapped Children?

K. Eileen Allen
University of Kansas

Keith D. Turner[1]
University of Texas

The experimental analysis of young children's behavior with its research emphasis on observable, measurable, and replicable interactions between the child and his environment is often seen as incompatible with good early-childhood programs that emphasize the freedom and spontaneity preschool teachers traditionally prize. In fact, the incompatibility frequently is seen as rooted in divergent philosophical frameworks — researchers viewing themselves as engaged in scientific pursuits, preschool teachers viewing themselves as engaged in more intuitive and artistic pursuits.

There has been some bridging of this gap starting in the early 1960's through the collaborative efforts of psychologists and teachers in the Developmental Psychology Laboratory Preschool classrooms at the University of Washington. These studies became the prototypes for the application of behavioral principles to many other early childhood programs. The time was good for experimentalists and preschool teachers to cooperate, in that, even though they disagreed on many issues, they found they had come to share a few basic things in common. One bond was their mutual resistance to statistics' "indifference" to

---

[1] Eileen Allen was, at the time this study was in progress, the Educational Training Coordinator, Developmental Disabilities Project, for the Experimental Education Unit. Keith D. Turner was a Project Coordinator-Trainer for the Model Preschool at the University of Washington at Seattle.

individual differences in children. Both questioned the usefulness of statistical observations that attributed a child's uniqueness to error variance with concern mainly for the mean performance of the total group.

Both groups were seriously committed to identifying effective teaching procedures. Even though preschool teachers might have expressed the view differently in those days, probably they *and* experimentalists would have agreed in principle with Evans' (1971) statement of a decade later: "In one way or another, all educational strategies are designed to modify behavior in desired ways" and "this is true whether one seeks a gross objective such as 'positive growth and adjustment' or a specific one such as 'the ability to discriminate visually the letters of the alphabet'." [p. 147] They would have agreed, too, that inasmuch as "behavior never occurs in a vacuum, that is, always occurs in an environmental context, an educator obviously must attend to the characteristics of an environment which influences behaviors." [p. 148]

Such statements, of course, are compatible with Bijou's (1970) article, in which he argued that a small minority of psychologists, those engaged in the experimental analysis of behavior, feel that a real contribution can be made to education through their efforts to present: (1) "a set of concepts and principles derived exclusively from experimental research"; (2) "a methodology for applying these concepts and principles directly to teaching practice"; (3) "a research design which deals with changes in the individual child (rather than inferring from group averages)"; and (4) "a philosophy of science which insists on accounts of the observable relationships between individual behavior and its determining condition." [p. 69] Seemingly, these ideas are quite appropriate for preschool educators to consider, and, certainly, many of the foregoing suggestions have been employed in various educational settings. There is still only a relatively small minority of preschool teachers who espouse the behavioral analysis approach to early childhood education, just as there is, according to Bijou, only a small minority of psychologists making behavioral recommendations. However (Evans, 1971), there is a good body of data available to show that a "behavioral analysis framework is a most fruitful alternative to traditional methods for those who value precision teaching." [p. 192]

Further, most teachers set as a major goal that of bringing children to the point where they are developmentally able individuals; this is, of course, another area of agreement between research and education, for according to Baer, Wolf, and Risley (1968), "Applied research is eminently pragmatic; it asks how it is possible to get an individual to do something." [p. 93] When teachers do discover how significant they can be in effecting important, desirable, and developmentally appropriate changes in the behavior of young children, they tend to become more enthusiastic about systematic, research-oriented teaching procedures. In fact, one of the outstanding characteristics of teachers who do base their teaching strategies on the principles of behavior analysis and precision teaching is their commitment to the system. Lovitt (1970) described it well when he suggested that, "As a group and as individuals, they have an energetic and positive outlook. One reason for their optimism is their conviction that any behavior can be changed if the environment can be arranged in an appropriate way. Another factor that may account for their exuberance is that they measure continuously, thus obtaining immediate feedback about a student's progress and the effectiveness of their teaching." [p. 157]

Measurement, of course, is one of the major aspects of the behavioral approach and does necessitate developing skills in data taking. Evans (1971) suggests that this requisite skill may at once be the greatest strength and the greatest provocation to criticism of this educational alternative, and that many teachers, especially teachers of preschool children, who must be here, there, and everywhere at once, will argue (in spite of a fairly extensive literature to the contrary) that it is not practical to expect teachers actively involved in teaching and supervising to take data. However, to demonstrate that priorities of busy preschool teachers can be made compatible with those of the experimental behaviorist, a case study of a young autistic child is presented.

THE EXPERIMENTS

The subject. Ivan was one of nine children enrolled in a classroom for children with severe behavior problems. The class, which met for two hours each morning, was staffed by an experienced head teacher in the beginning stages of learning behavior analysis techniques, and an assistant teacher who had little experience in working with either problem children or behavior modification procedures.

At the beginning of the study Ivan was four years and six months old, and had been attending school less than one month. He was a vigorous, handsome, and physically healthy child but was markedly deficient in social, intellectual, and verbal skills. His verbal repertoire, for example, consisted of only seven words. In addition to the foregoing, he had been labeled hyperactive and had been clinically diagnosed as autistic by the clinical team who referred him to the preschool.

The setting. During the child's first two weeks in the classroom an initial assessment was made in which two behaviors were identified as objectives needing immediate attention: running away from the classroom and nonparticipation in group activities at snack time. A number of other objectives for the present study emerged from the initial assessment of the child:

1. to provide the child immediate and much needed service by modifying both problem behaviors at the same time;

2. to ascertain the efficacy of social reinforcement procedures in altering the hyperactivity of a child who did not have as well developed a repertoire of motor, social, and intellectual skills as did the child in the Allen, Henke, Harris, Baer, & Reynolds study (1967);

3. to assess the feasibility of a teacher's collecting functional and reliable data while fulfilling a teaching and supervising role;

4. to measure the effects on the child's behavior when reinforcers inherent in the environment (hypothesized as effective) were held contingent on the child's responses; and

5. to do a follow-up assessment on the maintenance of the desired behavior changes.

Since the child's departures from the classroom required a disproportionate amount of the teachers' time in retrieving him, it was decided to decrease this behavior as a first phase of the program. During the second phase of the program, efforts were directed toward increasing the amount of time the child sat with the group for snack-time activities, his attending behavior during this activity, and his snack-time verbalizations.

Experiment I

Procedures. The child's high rate of leaving the classroom was postulated as a function of the consequent teacher attention. An ABA reversal design was used to demonstrate empirically that the hypothesized teacher attention was the variable maintaining the maladaptive behavior. The response definitions were classified as:

1. inappropriate behavior: each time Ivan crossed the threshold and was outside of the classroom;
2. appropriate behavior: Ivan's presence in the classroom, regardless of what he was doing;
3. teacher attention: talking to Ivan, touching him, or giving him materials.

Departures from the classroom were recorded by the assistant teacher who made a slash mark on a piece of paper posted beside the door each time Ivan left the classroom. Observer reliability was checked on three separate days, with 100% agreement each day.

A baseline period, in effect for eight days, gave evidence that there was a greater proportion of teacher attention for the inappropriate behavior of running from the room than for the appropriate behavior of remaining in the classroom. For example, when Ivan was just over the threshold, the teacher invariably requested that he return to the classroom and, invariably, these requests were ineffective. The child would continue on his way and the teacher would run down the hall in order to catch him. He was a fleet child and often gained several hundred feet of corridor before the teacher caught up with him. Then, all the way back to the classroom, the teacher gently admonished Ivan and patiently explained why he was to remain in the classroom. The teachers felt that such retrieval and explanatory measures were necessary in view of the physical layout of the building: a long, modern school building with many doors on the front of the building giving access to the busy traffic patterns of a large medical school, and many doors along the rear corridors giving access to a wide and deep ship canal parallel to the building and only several hundred feet away. (Fire protection measures prevented the locking of any doors.)

Phase 1. During the seven days of Phase 1, the teachers differentially reinforced the child; that is, they gave a maximum amount of attention to him while he was in the classroom and a minimum amount of attention when he was outside of the classroom. For example, when Ivan left the classroom, both teachers remained silent; when he was almost out of sight, one teacher moved to an inconspicuous place to observe him and to prevent (if need be) his leaving the building. Immediately apparent was that the child was not going to run far if no one was in hot pursuit. During the first two days of the program he would run 100 feet or so, stop, and look back. The observing teacher was careful to keep out of sight at that moment when he peered about to see if he had a pursuer. During this initial period, the teacher did give attention for successive approximations to returning to the classroom. Thus, when Ivan stopped momentarily he was asked to return. If he ran again after the request to stop, the teacher again withdrew to an inconspicuous vantage point and waited until he stopped to look back the next time. By the third day Ivan was returning to the classroom on request so the teacher was able to withhold any further attention until he was in the classroom. The procedure of reinforcing successive approximations to staying in the classroom was designed to eliminate the game of chase which (retrospectively) the teachers recognized as inadvertently having been a highly reinforcing event for Ivan. Concurrent with this procedure, the teachers attempted to engage Ivan in constructive play with materials or other children whenever he was in the classroom. They did not, however, coerce or wheedle him into these activities.

Phase 2. In a return to baseline conditions it proved to be a simple matter to reinstate the maladaptive running-away behavior, in that Ivan still probed the situation several times during the course of the preschool session by putting one foot over the threshold and looking back at the teacher. On the first day of reversal, when the teacher responded obligingly with "Stay in the room," Ivan was off and running with the teacher hard on his heels, as in the baseline days. The return to baseline condition was in effect for five days.

Phase 3. The desired behavior was reinstated in the final phase of the study by replicating the experimental conditions for four days. For the remainder of the experiment, a maintenance schedule was introduced. The teachers began reducing the amount of overall attention for appropriate behavior until they gave no more attention than they had during baseline conditions. The appropriate behavior of staying in the classroom was maintained under this reduced schedule of social reinforcement. If the inappropriate behavior occurred, the teachers gave only minimal attention, as described above.

Results and discussion. The rate of exits per hour for each of the experimental phases is presented in Figure 1. The range was 13 to 44 with a median rate of 27 in 8 days of baseline observation. There were 2 reasons for instituting a phase change after 8 days even though a stable baseline had not been achieved. First, the behavior was most disruptive to the classroom routine and greatly reduced the amount of teacher attention available for other children. Second, the trend was increasing and would not invalidate the experimental variable introduced to decrease this behavior.

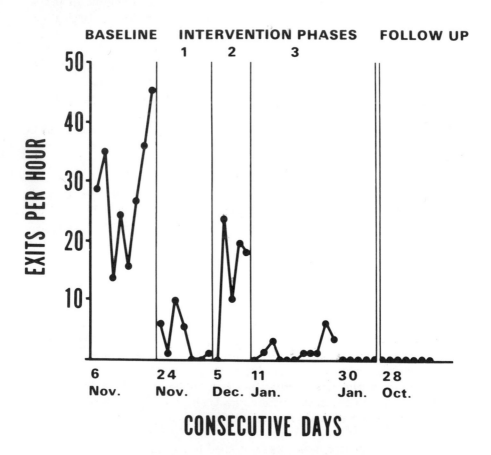

Figure 1   Exits per hour through five conditons of the study and follow-up. During Phase 1, following baseline, teacher attention was provided when the child was in class. In Phase 2 baseline conditions were reinstated. During Phase 3 procedures were similar to those of Phase 1.

During the first experimental phase (differential reinforcement), there was a marked decrease in the rate of exits. In the 7 days of this phase, exits per hour ranged from 0 to 9 with a median rate of 1.

During the 5 days of reversal, the rate of exits per hour ranged from 0 to 25 with a median rate of 18. Although the rate did not return to the original baseline level, it was typical of the baseline rate and demonstrated a marked increase from the rate in the previous experimental phase. Thus it was demonstrated empirically that teacher attention was maintaining the maladaptive behavior.

In the 16 days of the reinstatement and maintenance phase, the rate of exits ranged from 0 to 6 with a median rate of 0. During the last 5 days of this phase the child received an amount of teacher attention typical of that received by other children, in other words, an amount that could be considered an average amount. It appeared, therefore, that the child was generally maintaining his new behavior.

In the follow-up data a year later, there were no occurrences of unwarranted departures from the classroom in 7 randomly selected days of observation. At that time, Ivan was in the same classroom but had moved from the morning session to the more advanced afternoon session.

Experiment 2

Procedure. All of the children in the class were expected to participate in group activities such as snack time (which lasted for approximately 15 minutes). Food was available during the first half of the group experience; the second half was usually given over to a singing or rhythmic activity. The 9 children sat in a semicircle on individual mats with the teacher who was leading the group sitting in front, facing the children, and the other teacher behind, serving as assistant in whatever capacity was needed. Two conditions were in effect for all the children: (1) receiving snack was contingent upon verbal requests or approximations thereof, according to each child's verbal skills; and (2) any children who left the group received no teacher attention until they returned to the group of their own volition. These were the conditions prevailing while baseline data were collected.

The teachers postulated that the reason Ivan did not stay on his mat was that he had never engaged in the activity long enough to experience the reinforcers (food) available during the snack time activities. A multiple-baseline design was used to assess the effects of providing Ivan with a particular type of cracker that his parents reported was a favorite.

A time-sampling observational system similar to that described by Bijou, Peterson, Harris, Allen & Johnston (1969) was used to record the child's behaviors. Data were collected in consecutive 15-second intervals for the total snack time which averaged 15 minutes. Data were recorded on the following responses: verbalization, attending, nonattending, absence from the group, and teacher attention. These responses were defined as follows:

1. verbalization: whenever Ivan said any dictionary word;
2. attending: whenever Ivan's head and body were oriented toward the teacher or teacher-presented materials for more than half the 10-second interval and his body was in contact with his mat for the entire interval;
3. nonattending: when one or more of the attending behaviors as defined in response 2 were not occurring;
4. absence from the group: whenever the child's body was not in contact with his mat;
5. teacher attention: whenever the teacher talked to the child, touched him, or gave him materials or food.

Observer reliability was checked on 4 separate days by having a second observer record Ivan's behavior independently, using the same code the teacher was using. Agreements on each 15-second observation interval were computed for each of the 5 measures. Mean percentages of agreements for the 5 measures were: verbalization, 97%; attending, 92%; nonattending, 96%; absence, 100%; teacher attention, 95%. The lowest daily percentage of agreement for any measure was 87%.

Phase 1. The first experimental condition was an attempt to decrease the amount of time the child spent away from the group. The supporting teacher, who also assumed the role of data collector, dispensed tiny pieces of cracker approximately one-tenth the size of the crackers that Ivan would have received had he made a verbal request for snack. For every 15 seconds that any part of his body was in contact with his mat Ivan received a tiny piece of cracker.

Phase 2. During the second phase, the reinforcer was dispensed on the same schedule not only for sitting with the group but also for attending. The teacher who collected data and dispensed the crackers moved to the front of the group so that the dispensing procedure would not be incompatible with Ivan's attending to the teacher leading the group.

Phase 3. During the last experimental phase, reinforcement was contingent solely on a verbal request for food. The question posed for this experimental phase (maintenance) was: would Ivan's verbal skills increase sufficiently so that he could receive snack through his own efforts and thus maintain his own sitting and attending behavior, independent of any additional contingencies and reinforcers except those inherent in the snack situation itself?

Results and discussion. The percentage of time Ivan was in attendance and absent at snack time in each of the conditions is presented in Figure 2. In the 5 days of baseline, 4 of the days were characterized by his leaving the group immediately. Thus, the hypothesis that he was having little experience with the potential reinforcers inherent in the snack time was verified.

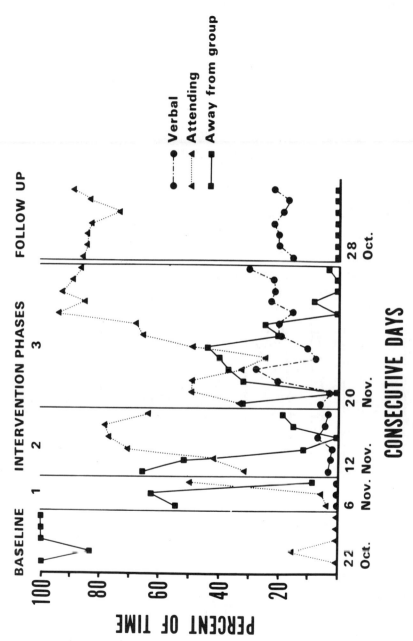

Figure 2 Percentage of time child participated in group activity. During the first intervention phase crackers were contingent on sitting. Throughout the second intervention crackers were contingent on sitting and attending. During the third phase crackers were contingent on requests for food.

When conditions were arranged so that Ivan had experience with food paired with teacher attention for 3 days (sitting phase, i.e., Phase 1), the percentage of time away from the group dropped from 100% to 9%.

The next condition (Phase 2 sitting and attending) was a continuation of the previous phase in that Ivan still had to be with the group but he also had to attend in order to receive reinforcement. At first, time away from the group increased, but then it decreased, and attending behavior increased to 70% for more than 3 days.

At the beginning of the sitting and attending phase, Ivan's first spontaneous verbalization at snack time occurred. He said "cracker" and received, from the teacher leading the group, a cracker approximately 10 times the size of the crackers he had received from the supporting teacher for just sitting and attending. Verbalizations increased from 0% to approximately 4% of the time. It was hypothesized that the increase in verbalizations was minimal because receiving reinforcement was not contingent solely on verbal requests.

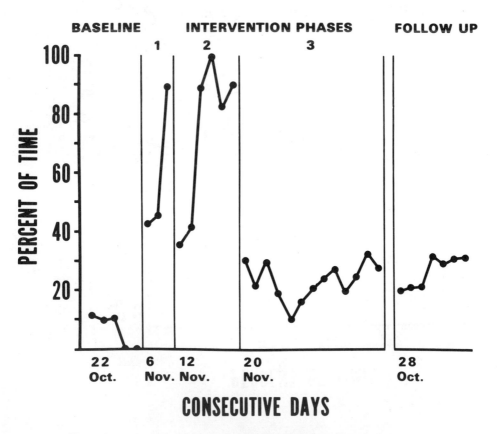

Figure 3   Percentage of teacher attention throughout the experiment.

In Phase 3 (maintenance), primary reinforcement was made solely contingent upon verbal requests. Ivan's verbalizations increased to 27% of the time in 4 days. After this initial increase, there was a decrease and then a continual increase to approximately 20% of the time for the last 4 days of the study. This level of verbalization was sufficient for him to receive pieces of snack the entire time it was being served. Thus, in the multiple-baseline design, three behaviors (sitting, attending, and verbalization) improved when primary reinforcement was held contingent upon occurrence of the successively selected target behaviors.

There was a decrease in attending at the beginning of the maintenance phase, then a recovery trend similar to the verbal recovery trend. By the end of the study Ivan was sitting and attending approximately 90% of the time even after an interim period of 4 weeks of midwinter holiday vacation. The increase in his verbal skills was demonstrably sufficient for him to obtain the reinforcers inherent in the snack situation and thus maintain the other behaviors appropriate to snack time.

In the postcheck made approximately one year later, the appropriate behaviors gave evidence of having been well maintained. Attending occurred at least 80% of the time for 6 of the 7 days, with no time away from the group. Verbalization occurred approximately 20% of the time, but shaping had changed the quality from single words ("cracker") to functional sentences ("I want a cracker," "I want a napkin," etc.).

The amount of teacher attention in each of the phases is displayed in Figure 3, to demonstrate that the teachers' behaviors were still in accord with the experimental design of the study. These data show a combination of reinforcers: any time a teacher talked to or touched the child or gave him materials or food.

SUMMARY

The primary objective of the study was to provide immediate service to the child within the context of an experimental approach. This objective was achieved within the first 2 months that the child was enrolled in the program. Only 22 school days were required to assess and modify both his rate of exits from the classroom and his lack of attending at snack time.

In addition, this study provides an example of the general applicability of social reinforcement procedures in altering hyperactivity in a child clinically diagnosed as autistic. Although in an earlier study, Allen *et al.* (1967) demonstrated that hyperactivity could be altered in a normally developing child, these same techniques had not been systematically studied with children diagnosed as autistic. Among these children there is, of course, fairly general clinical consensus that they are usually less responsive to social reinforcement than their "normal" peers.

This study also gave evidence that teachers, while in a teaching role, can collect reliable data. Experiment 1 employed a simple data-collection procedure which did not interfere with the teachers' activities. Experiment 2 employed a more complex data system which an assisting teacher, while not conducting a group but responsible for being generally supportive, could use to assess the problem behavior of a child in a group activity.

Haring and Phillips (1972) stated that the goal of behavior modification is to provide the skills for self-management. The maintenance of the modified behaviors at a desired level one year later emphasizes the importance of eliminating the artificial experimental reinforcers in the last phase of a behavior modification study. In both experiments this was done to determine whether the child had acquired the necessary experience and skill to maintain his own behavior with the reinforcers inherent in the environment. The terminal behaviors in this study indicate that Ivan was indeed responding to the natural reinforcers available on a variable interval schedule to all children in a well-conducted preschool classroom. This study would appear to support rather conclusively that the priorities of the educator can be made compatible with an experimental analysis of behavior, and that a preschool staff can collect and utilize data in a school setting in which a major commitment is to provide service to children.

ACKNOWLEDGMENTS

This study was conducted in the Model Preschool Center for Handicapped Children at the Experimental Education Unit, Child Development and Mental Retardation Center, University of Washington. Dr. Alice H. Hayden is Director of the Project which is funded in part through P.L. 91-230, Title VI, Part C, Section 623.

REFERENCES

Allen, K. E., Henke, L. B., Harris, F. R., Baer, D. M., & Reynolds, N. J. Control of hyperactivity by social reinforcement of attending behavior. *Journal of Educational Psychology*, 1967, *58*, 231-237.

Baer, D. M., Wolf, M. M., & Risley, T. R. Some current dimensions of applied behavior analysis. *Journal of Applied Behavior Analysis*, 1968, *1*, 91-97.

Bijou, S. W., Peterson, R. F., Harris, F. R., Allen, K. E., & Johnston, M. S. Methodology for experimental studies of young children in natural settings. *Psychological Record*, 1969, *19*, 177-210.

Bijou, S. W. What psychology has to offer education — now. *Journal of Applied Behavior Analysis*, 1970, *3*, 65-71.

Evans, E. D. *Contemporary influences in early childhood education*. New York: Holt, Rinehart, & Winston, 1971.

Haring, N. G., & Phillips, E. L. *Analysis and modification of classroom behavior*. Englewood Cliffs, N.J.: Prentice-Hall, 1972.

Lovitt, T. C. Behavior modification: Where do we go from here? *Exceptional Children*, 1970, *37*(2), 157-167.

10

Changing-Criterion Designs: An Alternate Applied Behavior Analysis Procedure

R. Vance Hall

Richard G. Fox

University of Kansas and
University of Wisconsin, Milwaukee

Any researcher, in the course of investigating the effects of a particular set of independent variables, must demonstrate that the observed changes in behavior are functionally related to the presence of those variables. That is, there must be a correlated change in the level of responding in an experimental subject with the introduction and, if a return to baseline conditions is possible, the withdrawal of experimental procedures. Experimental control is built on at least two concepts. First, baseline logic, as presented by Sidman (1960), suggests that some estimate of the pretreatment level of behavior must be incorporated in the design in order for one to have a benchmark against which to compare subsequent behavioral changes. In other words, what the level of responding would look like if the experimental procedures had not been attempted. The spirit of the second concept is captured by Baer, Wolf, and Risley (1968) in the statement ". . . replication is the essence of believability." [p. 95] This would suggest that it is not merely enough to effect a behavioral change upon a single occasion. The researchers must show that this change may be repeated, again and again, either within subjects or in a number of subjects.

These two concepts can be identified in the two basic designs promoted by the practitioners of applied behavior analysis (see Baer, Wolf, & Risley, 1968). The reversal design represents a procedure that can be used to verify changes within subjects or a group (when considered as a single responding organism). Typically, a pretreatment measure of the behavior of interest is ascertained. This measure or baseline will serve as the standard to determine the relative effectiveness of the experimental procedures. Once a stable level of responding has been recorded, the environment is in some way altered with the intention, if at least some of the critical variables have been built in the procedure, of changing the level of responding in the subject. Depending on whether or not this change occurs, two avenues are open to the researchers. If a change is not effected, the researcher must continue to search for novel arrangements in the environment that will produce a change. However, if a change is recorded then the possibility that it was not an adventitious change (that is, due to an extraneous variable not related to the experimental procedure) must be rejected. This may sometimes be accomplished by discontinuing the experimental treatment. If, in fact, the baseline level of responding is recovered, one's confidence is strengthened that the observed change was responsive to the experimental procedure. Finally, if, on the reinstatement of treatment, the initial effect is replicated, not only has one provided some estimate of how the untreated behavior might have maintained over time but also that the change was not merely fortuitous.

The concerns of baseline logic and replication are also inherent in the multiple baseline design. Here, concurrent baseline measures of behavior are generated either across behaviors, subjects, or settings. Once this has occurred, an experimental treatment is introduced in one of the baselines, the remaining baselines serving as estimates of the behavior had it not been treated. If these estimates remain consistent or do not express a new trend coincidental with the treatment, one can be reasonably sure that the change was a function of the efforts of the experimenter. In addition, as the effect is replicated in the second and subsequent baselines the experimenter can conclude that it is not a novel occurrence.

Baer, Wolf and Risley (1968) did not intend that applied behavior analysis strategies should be limited to those they set forth in their classic article, however, in fact they proposed, "The two general procedures described hardly exhaust the possibilities . . . current experience suggests that many variations are badly needed . . ." [p. 95]

Sidman (1960) has also spoken to this issue:

> But we are now reaching the stage, made possible by our greatly increased technical and systematic sophistication, where subtle and complex phenomena heretofore untouchable in the laboratory are becoming available for experimental examination. Increasing subtlety in the behavioral phenomena under investigation must be matched by increasing subtlety and rigor of experimental control. It is unlikely we can continue to ignore variations in response topography within an operant class, particularly when the phenomena under investigation require quantitative evaluation. If we adhere too rigidly to the assumption that the components of an operant unit are equivalent in all respects, we are not likely to appreciate and subsequently control major sources of variability in studies of subtle behavioral phenomenon.
> . . . It is possible to make reinforcement contingent on a specified value of an aspect of behavior, and to treat that value as a response in its own right. [p. 391]

The designs described above are appropriate for cases in which the behaviors of subjects are of sufficient strength to be well within their behavioral capabilities. But what of the situation in which there are clear indications that a shaping procedure must be used to facilitate behavior acquisition or in which it is difficult to identify another subject, setting, or behavior to provide an esti-mate of how the behavior would look if untreated? Perhaps one might be tempted to implement treatment procedures without a concern for verification and if an acceptable change has been accomplished the change must compensate for the lack of scientific documentation. But what of the development of an empirically based behavioral technology? The fact that an important change in behavior has occurred will do nothing to demonstrate to a scientific audience that these changes are responsible to the environmental manipulations of the experimenter. It should be emphasized that it is only after this has occurred that the procedures can be publicized as having merit for further application.

THE CHANGING-CRITERION DESIGN

How, then, does one build the traditional ideas of baseline logic and repli-cation in a behavior change task where, because of the initial low levels of responding, the experimenter is reluctant to return to baseline conditions? Hall (1971) has proposed that these concerns are embodied in the changing-criterion design and can be used to document the effects of shaping procedures. In the changing-criterion design the experimenter successively changes the criterion for consequation, usually in graduated steps, from baseline level until the desired terminal behavior is achieved. It is proposed that if the behavior change corresponds at or close to the criterion level, experimental control has been demonstrated.

Initially, as with other applied behavior analysis designs, a baseline is generated to determine the pretreatment level of the behavior. Then a criterion for con-sequation is established, usually based on the mean level of responding in the baseline condition. This would suggest that the first criterion is within the behavioral capabilities of the subject.

Then in the treatment condition the reinforcers or punishers are delivered contingent on performing at or beyond criterion levels. It is also advisable that a stability criterion be established, in other words, that the subject should per-form at or close to preestablished levels for a set number of sessions. This would be an indication that responding is stable around this criterion and that ad-vancing to the next criterion level might be indicated. This is continued until a terminal level of responding has been achieved. If the behavior conforms neatly to the established criterion the design can be conceived of as a series of repeated AB designs and that the effect is replicated again and again only when the crite-rion has been changed. In other words, behavior change is associated with crite-rion change.

It is conceivable that the behavior will not conform to the criterion, thereby compromising the verification procedures of this design. If this is the case and a convincing change has been produced, although it does not conform neatly to the criteria, a reversal may be employed to suggest the changes are associated with treatment, that is, consequation and the criterion.

There are also a number of other possibilities to further demonstrate behavioral (or experimental) control. The experimenter may leave the criterion at an established level for a longer period of time than indicated in the stability criterion. Here, if the behavior must conform at or near criterion for three days he may leave it in for five days. If it continues to conform neatly to the criterion it is a convincing demonstration that it is related to the presence of the criterion. Another possibility is that the experimenter may return to a former criterion and if the behavior conforms to this criterion level there is also a cogent argument for a high degree of behavioral control.

As will be seen in the experiments below, experimental control is demonstrated as the behavior changes according to the criterion levels set as a requirement for their associated consequences.

EXPERIMENT 1

Subject and Setting

The subject-experimenter was a 22-year-old female graduate student who had been smoking for five years. She felt that the elimination of the smoking behavior was imperative because she had a history of asthma. She had tried at least three times previously to quit smoking but had been unsuccessful.

Experimental Procedures and Results

The behavior measured was the number of cigarettes smoked by the subject during one day. The number of cigarettes in her pack was counted each morning when she got up and then recounted just before going to bed. Reliability counts made periodically by a friend during baseline and subsequent experimental conditions yielded 100% agreement each time. On reliability check days the subject-experimenter started the day with a fresh cigarette pack and had the friend make an independent count of the number remaining at day's end.

Baseline$_1$. The smoking behavior was measured for a period of 15 days to obtain baseline. During baseline the mean number of cigarettes smoked per day was 14.1 (see Fig. 1).

Punishment procedure. The subject gave a friend $25.99 to hold as bond. This was the price of a new pair of shoes the subject wanted and would buy if the experiment was a success. A descending criterion was set on the number of cigarettes the subject was allowed to smoke per day. If the subject exceeded the criterion amount set for that day $3.00 would be deducted from the $25.99.

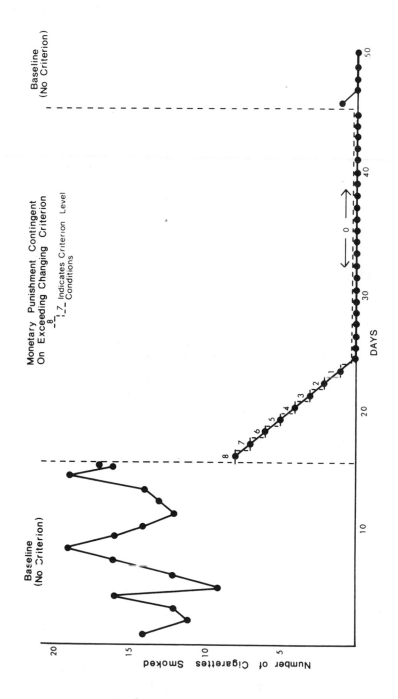

Figure 1   A record of the number of cigarettes smoked by a 22-year-old female under baseline and loss of $3.00 contingent on exceeding a daily decreasing criterion number of cigarettes.

155

The $3.00 would be kept by the friend who was holding the money. The criterion level was set at 8 cigarettes for the 16th day, 7 cigarettes for the 17th day in a descending order to 0 on the 24th day. The punishment procedure was kept in effect for 30 days. Figure 1 shows that the subject met but never exceeded the criterion level throughout the experimental condition.

Baseline₂. Beginning on the 46th day, reversal procedures were put into effect and the friend returned the $25.99 bond. The subject bought her shoes. Subsequently, no reversal effect was noted. The subject smoked one cigarette on the 46th day, the first day of reversal, but smoking behavior returned to the 0 level and remained at 0 until systematic observation was terminated.

EXPERIMENT 2

Subjects and Setting

Dennis and Steve were both elementary students in a classroom for children with behavior disorders. Both had been referred to this program because they were extremely disruptive and refused to complete assignments or completed them at a low rate. When first entering the program, they would not complete their arithmetic assignments. They usually crumpled their papers, threw their texts into their desks, handed in blank paper or otherwise sat idle in their seats during the arithmetic session.

Experimental Procedures

In order to measure the level of his behavior each student was given a worksheet with nine problems (subtraction for Dennis; division for Steve) and one example. These problems were selected from the respective review sections of their arithmetic textbooks representing many levels of difficulty and problem types. Before school each day the teacher selected a number of problems from this problem bank in a restricted, random sequence. This procedure depletes the problem bank before returning previously programmed problems for computation.

Each student was given his prepared worksheet. The teacher worked the example for him and then told him to work as many problems as he could before recess (this amounted to a 45-min work session). If the student threw his worksheet away the teacher ignored the student and retrieved the paper at the end of the session. When the student turned in a worksheet, it was corrected and returned to the student. The number of problems correct at the end of the session was used as the measure of his behavior.

Throughout the study, checks were made to determine the accuracy of the grading by the teacher. Here, an acetate (clear plastic) cover was placed over the worksheet and a grease pencil was used to identify correct and incorrect responses. Then another acetate cover was used by a reliable student to again correct the problems and compare with the teacher's record. This problem by problem check revealed the reliability to be 100% for every worksheet.

During the experimental phases, the student had to correctly compute a specified number of problems each session. He was told that if he worked these problems correctly by the end of the session he could take his recess and play basketball. If he failed to complete these problems by recess, he remained in the room until they were correctly computed.

The criterion for each step was initially determined by computing the mean for the baseline condition and setting the criterion at the next highest whole problem. After three consecutive days of performing at the specified level, the criterion was advanced by one problem. The terminal goal was to shape and maintain enough behavior to complete a textbook assignment.

Results

Dennis. Figure 2 shows that Dennis correctly computed an average of 4.25 subtraction problems per session during the baseline condition.

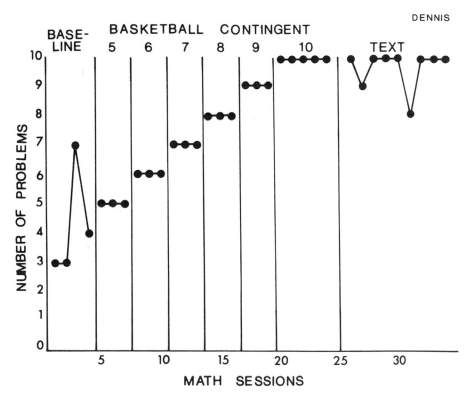

Figure 2   A record of the number of math problems correctly solved by Dennis, a "behavior disordered" boy during baseline, recess, and the opportunity to play basketball contingent on changing levels of performance and return to textbook phases.

The first criterion was set at 5 problems with the opportunity to go to recess and to play basketball contingent on meeting the criterion level of performance. Dennis met the criterion in the minimum number of days as he did for all the remaining criterion steps.

In the sixth criterion-step the criterion was held at 10 problems for 5 days to demonstrate that the behavior was functionally related to the experimental procedure.

The final criterion-step was different from the previous step only in that the subject was returned to the formal textbook. The section on subtraction was the point of reentry making the problems to be computed nearly identical to those in the problem bank. While working in his textbook Dennis met the criterion on 7 of the 9 days.

Steve. Figure 3 shows that during the baseline phase Steve's rate of computing division problems dropped to 0 after three sessions. The mean number of correct problems was 1.5.

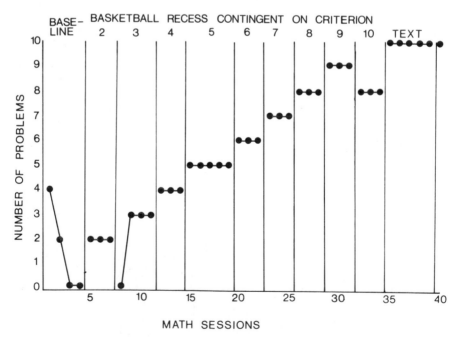

Figure 3   A record of the number of math problems correctly solved by Steve, a "behavior disordered" boy, during baseline, recess, and the opportunity to play basketball contingent on changing levels of performance and return to textbook phases.

In the first criterion-step the criterion was set at 2 since this was the next highest whole problem. Figure 3 shows that Steve met the criterion in the minimum number of sessions. Steve did not correctly compute the problems on his worksheet in the first session when the criterion was raised to 3. He did meet the criterion in the next 3 days, however.

Each criterion was met successfully thereafter. During the fourth criterion-step the criterion was held at 5 problems to demonstrate control of the behavior. In addition another control procedure was instituted during the ninth criterion-step. The subject was returned to a former level of responding. He performed at that level for the minimum number of sessions and was subsequently returned to the advancing criterion sequence.

After the tenth criterion-step, Steve was reintroduced to the textbook programming. He returned to the section on division; he was asked to complete 10 of the exercises from the textbook with the same contingencies operating as in the criterion-steps.

Unfortunately it was possible to maintain Steve in this phase for but one day since he discontinued attending the school due to transportation problems. He did, however, meet the criterion level for the one day he was working in his textbook.

EXPERIMENT 3

Subject and Setting

The subject was John, a 10-year-old boy diagnosed as educable mentally retarded and a victim of spina bifida, a condition which had caused paralysis from the waist down. He was a student in an orthopedically handicapped classroom in the University of Kansas Medical Center Children's Rehabilitation Unit.

Behavior Measured

In John's classroom, the children worked individually at their own levels with a series of ten programmed tasks to be completed daily. These tasks included work in various academic areas, reading, arithmetic, phonics, spelling, etc. John experienced much difficulty in completing the expected amount of work and frequently failed to finish a page of work unless the teacher stood near him as he worked. The measured behavior was completion of the number of assigned pages with no adult supervision nor encouragement to finish. (Consideration was given to John's difficulty in understanding new material. He was given all the help he needed before beginning an assignment.) Each time John completed one page of work, the teacher recorded one point. The teacher observed John all day and marked the number of academic tasks he completed. A student aide using the same procedure as the teacher recorded pages completed during each phase of the experiment. Their reliability checks uniformly yielded 100% agreement.

Experimental Procedure and Results

Baseline₁. Baseline data were recorded for 10 days. The teacher recorded the number of tasks completed daily, out of the first 10 assigned. If John required encouragement to complete his work or failed to finish the page, he did not receive a point. As can be seen in Fig. 4, during baseline the mean of completed tasks was 2.5.

Tokens backed by job opportunity₁. In searching for the most effective reinforcer the teacher noted John's interest in being a classroom helper. Initially, John was told he would receive a token for every page of work he completed. If he received the designated number of tokens, he was allowed to go to cafeteria duty. This phase of the experimental procedure was carried out over 15 days. As can be seen in Fig. 4 the criterion was raised from 4 to 7 completed tasks over the 15 days and John met the changing criterion on 12 of the days.

Criterion-No Tokens. On the 26th day of the study, John was told that the teacher wanted him to stay in the classroom with the other children in the afternoon, so he could not have cafeteria duty. He was instructed to continue working at the level of his last criterion which was 7 tasks. This phase continued for 5 days, with completed tasks ranging from 2 to 4.

Tokens₂. On the 31st day, reinforcement was reinstated under the same conditions as previously described. Because John's study completion had decreased significantly during the Criterion-No Tokens phase the tokens were reinstated with the criterion level at 5 tasks for 2 days. The criterion number of tasks to be completed was then raised to 6 and maintained at that level.

A post check taken on the 40th day showed John continuing to complete 6 of the tasks.

DISCUSSION

The initial realization of the need for, and the possibility of, a changing-criterion strategy for presenting data and demonstrating experimental control came while the senior author was perusing a multitude of behavioral records generated by Marion Panyan, Donald Horner, and their colleagues at Wheatridge, Colorado State Training School. These researchers, using procedures described by Panyan (1972) had generated an impressive number of case studies which showed that using shaping procedures, retarded patients throughout the institution had been systematically taught to use self-help skills. He was struck by the fact that the records were impressive but since neither reversal nor multiple-baseline procedures had been used the work did not seem to qualify as applied behavior

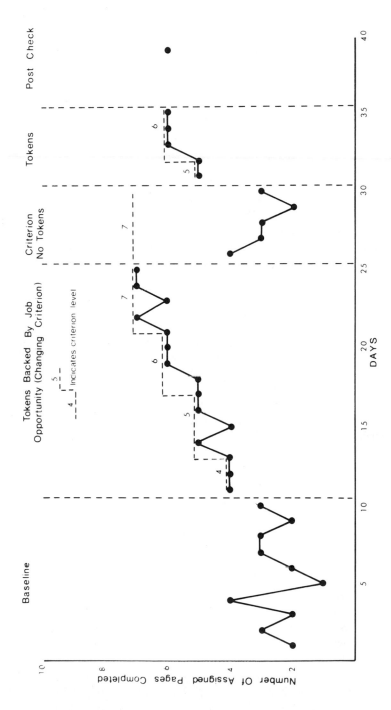

Figure 4   A record of the number of assignments completed by a 10-year-old spina bifida boy during baseline-, tokens-backed-by-job-opportunities upon performing at a set criterion level, criterion-without-token backup and reinstatement-of-tokens-plus-criterion phases.

analysis research. Yet, he was convinced that the subjects of these studies had changed the levels of their behavior from zero baseline levels to a simple first step on to a more complex next step and finally to the desired terminal behavior. Furthermore these changes came only when they had met criterion performance at one level and then were taught the responses necessary for success at the next level.

Hall (1971), in his writing, could find no published data which satisfactorily demonstrated shaping in spite of the fact shaping procedures were widely reported in the applied behavior analysis literature.

These experiences lead up to the first use of the label "changing-criterion design" in reference to a study by Weis and Hall (1971). In this experiment the subject of the study, the senior author, decreased his level of smoking cigarettes by avoiding the consequence of having to tear up a one-dollar bill if he exceeded a maximum criterion of the number of cigarettes he allowed himself to smoke each day. The criterion was set at 15 cigarettes per day for the first 5 days the experimental condition was in effect. During each subsequent 5-day period the criterion number of cigarettes was reduced by one cigarette until the criterion became 0. On 33 occasions out of 50 days between the time the 15-cigarette criterion and the 6-cigarette criterion was in effect the subject exactly matched the maximum criterion line and in no cases did he exceed it. When the criterion reached 6 cigarettes the number of cigarettes smoked decreased to 0 and remained at that level to the end of the study. When a planned reversal was instituted there was no return to smoking behavior. In fact, the experimenter-subject and his colleagues reported that the level of smoking remained at or near 0 for several years subsequent to the removal of experimental conditions.

Since no reversal effect was observed and no multiple baseline analysis had been attempted our first inclination was to surmise that no experimental control over smoking behavior had been demonstrated since neither of the accepted applied behavior analysis single-subject research designs had been successfully employed. On perusing the data, however, it became apparent that at least during the phase when the criterion for avoiding punishment had been in effect, some kind of control had indeed been exerted.

The smoking study presented in Experiment 1, above, in general replicates the Weis and Hall study. An examination of the data indicates that once again some kind of control over smoking was demonstrated. After establishing a baseline in which the number of cigarettes smoked varied over a range from 9 to 18, a maximum criterion beginning at 8 cigarettes and decreasing 1 cigarette per day was instituted. Under the condition that if the criterion was exceeded the subject would lose $3.00 the number of cigarettes smoked exactly matched the criterion through 30 days, including 22 days when the criterion level remained at 0.

When baseline conditions of no criterion or money loss contingency were reinstituted, as in the Weis and Hall study, there was no return to baseline levels of smoking. Once again, however, though no reversal was observed it is obvious on inspection of the data that some kind of control over the behavior has been demonstrated, at least during the experimental phase.

It is not the purpose of this chapter to assert definitively whether the control demonstrated is due entirely to the consequences employed or to the instructional aspects of setting up the criterion. The purpose is rather to suggest that since the behavior of concern conforms so closely to the criteria in effect there is very little possibility that changes in behavior are entirely independent of the criteria.

There may be several ways to look at and interpret changing criteria data. One possibility is that it is a series of AB changes. For instance, in Experiment 3 the first ten days of the Baseline$_1$ phase may be considered a baseline for the first three days of the four-assignments-completed criterion. The three days of the criterion-four phase could be considered as baseline for the four days of the next phase in which the criterion was set at five assignments completed, and so forth throughout the tokens backed by job opportunity phase. Thus a series of replications of effect are shown.

Another possible way to look at the changing-criterion strategy is as if it were an adaptation of the multiple-baseline design. For instance the data presented in Experiment 1 might be presented as shown in Figure 5 in which there is a dichotomy of whether or not the number of cigarettes smoked is at a given level or lower.

As is shown by this analysis, the behavior changes with absolute consistency as a function of the experimental conditions employed. Thus it not only demonstrates a replication of effect but also conforms to the premise of baseline logic that had not the experimental conditions including the changing criterion been in effect the baselines in each case would have continued unchanged.

Experiment 2, in which the number of math problems worked by two boys was systematically increased, the number required for reinforcement demonstrates how the changing criterion can be varied to further indicate that the experimental variables are controlling behavior. In Steve's case (see Figure 3), by leaving the criterion level at five problems for five rather than three days, it was demonstrated rather conclusively that the behavior was changing as a function of the criterion rather than merely progressing regularly every three days due to uncontrolled variables. Further control was demonstrated by lowering the criterion to eight after the behavioral level had been shaped to nine. That the behavior decreased and then increased again to the ten level when this subsequently became the criterion demonstrates very tight control, and amounts to a controlled reversal.

In Experiment 3 the effect of tokens backed by the job was demonstrated to be functional and independent of merely setting a criterion for performance because the criterion without tokens phase did not maintain the behavior at criterion levels.

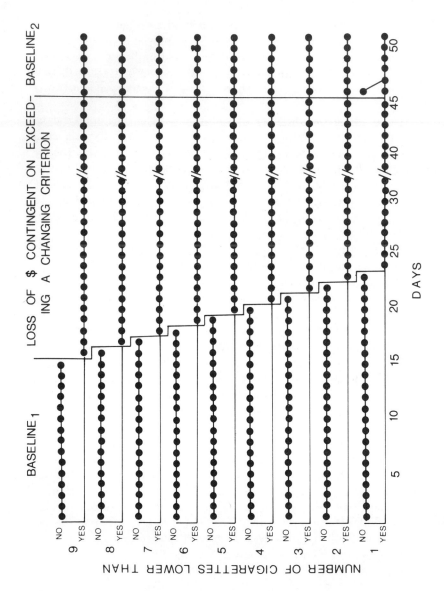

Figure 5   A multiple-baseline record of cigarette smoking in a 22-year-old female, each baseline indicating whether or not the number of cigarettes exceeds the number indicated.

A number of studies have been carried out by teachers and parents at the University of Kansas in which the subject has seldom matched the criterion. Yet, in at least some cases there did seem to be some correlation between the criterion, the associated ocntingencies, and the levels of behavior. For instance, one parent attempted to increase the level of cleaning various living areas in the home by making allowance contingent on the number of areas cleaned. Although cleaning behavior increased as the criterion levels were increased, exact correspondence to the criterion was observed on only 6 of 26 days. However, the criterion level was consistently exceeded and the behavior thus seemed to be affected. In this case the mother carried out a reversal and was thus able to show experimental control since she was not satisfied with criterion correspondence.

Saul Axelrod has suggested that the Pearson correlation (Winer, 1971) might be applied to indicate the degree of correspondence between the criterion and the performance. If this were applied in the case of Experiment 1 the Pearson correlation coefficient would be $r = 1.00$. In Experiment 2 the correlation for Dennis was $r = 0.975$, and for Steve, $r = 0.985$.

It is hoped the changing-criterion concept will prove useful to other researchers, if not as a bona fide applied behavior analysis design then as a novel means of presenting data which will allow them to present the use of shaping procedures more effectively than has usually been possible.

However, the authors feel that the changing-criterion design meets the basic criteria set forth by Baer, Wolf and Risley (1968) along the dimensions of baseline logic and replication and is one answer to the need they have expressed for developing additional applied behavior analysis approaches.

Furthermore, it seems to be a step in the direction toward the need expressed by Sidman (1960) to "... make reinforcement contingent on a specified value of an aspect of behavior, and to treat that value as a response in its own right." [p. 391]

ACKNOWLEDGMENTS

This research was partially supported by the National Institute of Child Health and Human Development HD 03144-06, Bureau of Child Research and Department of Human Development and Family Life and the Bureau of the Educationally Handicapped OEG-0-72-0253 (603) Bureau of Child Research and School of Education.

The authors are indebted to Saul Axelrod, Temple University for his suggestions regarding this chapter, specifically for the suggestion of using a correlation coefficient to show correspondence to criterion.

Experiment 1 was carried out by Darlene Hughes, assisted by Ace Cossairt (from Hall and Fox, 1973).

Experiment 2 was conducted by Richard G. Fox.

Experiment 3 was conducted by Pam Reusser assisted by Barbara Terry, Cynthia Montgomery and Jeane Crowder.

REFERENCES

Baer, D. M., Wolf, M. M., & Risley, T. R. Some current dimensions of applied behavior analysis. *Journal of Applied Behavior Analysis,* 1968, *1,* 91-97.

Hall, R. V. *Behavior management series: Part II, basic principles.* Lawrence, Kansas: H & H Enterprises, Inc., 1971.

Hall, R. V. & Fox, R. G. *Responsive teaching transparency kit manual.* Lawrence, Kansas: H & H Enterprises, Inc., 1972.

Panyan, M. *Behavior management series: Part IV, new ways to teach new skills.* Lawrence, Kansas: H & H Enterprises, Inc., 1972.

Sidman, M. *Tactics of scientific research.* New York: Basic Books, Inc., 1960.

Weis, L. & Hall, R. V. Reduction in smoking behavior through avoidance of punishment. In Hall, R. V., *Behavior management series: Part II, applications in school and home.* Lawrence, Kansas: H & H Enterprises, Inc., 1971.

Winer, B. *Statistical principles in experimental design* (2nd ed.). New York: McGraw-Hill, 1971.

11

Behavioral Definitions in Applied Behavior Analysis: Explicit or Implicit? [1]

Robert P. Hawkins
Robert W. Dobes

Western Michigan University [2]

A basic canon of science is that its methods be replicable. If scientists employ independent variables that they cannot specify (preferably quantitatively), then their findings cannot be related to other findings or principles and thus cannot contribute to the body of scientific knowledge. If scientists use methods to measure the dependent variable that are not generally available to other scientists or are not explicated satisfactorily, judging the validity of the findings they report is difficult.

In many natural sciences the specification of independent and dependent variables is very straightforward. In a laboratory setting these variables often consist of such measures as Ohms, degrees centigrade, millimeters, pounds, or seconds; and scientists simply need to specify certain familiar conditions under which they measure the variables in order to make this measurement replicable in other laboratories. However, in some kinds of research the specification of measurement methods is not so readily accomplished. This is often the case with applied behavior analysis, because in this field we are typically interested in

---

[1] Based on a paper presented at the American Psychological Association Convention, Montreal, August, 1973.

The experimental research reported herein is based upon a thesis submitted by the second author to the Department of Psychology, Western Michigan University, in partial fulfillment of requirements for the MA degree.

[2] Robert P. Hawkins is now at West Virginia University.

socially significant behaviors as they occur in naturalistic settings (Baer, Wolf, & Risley, 1968). It is sometimes possible to automate the recording of a significant behavior in a naturalistic setting, and at other times the behavior analyst can measure a readily defined *product* of the behavior, such as the number of words spelled correctly by a school child (Hall, 1971). But often the varying topography of the response, the absence of a uniform definition of the response in the culture (whether verbal or not), or the complexity of the environmental context for the response is such that only a complex verbal definition can adequately specify the behavior to be recorded.

An example of certain problems and solutions is found in Wahler's (1969) reported definition of oppositional and cooperative child behavior that was to be recorded in home and school settings. The definition was simply that "When a request or command was presented to Steve, observers scored his future behavior as either oppositional or cooperative, depending on whether or not the instruction was followed" [p. 240]. If Wahler's observers were attempting to record these two classes of behavior under free-ranging home and school conditions, the term "instruction" would clearly require definition as well, so that an observer would know what to do if the child's teacher simply said "Steven!" in a warning tone during the independent work time, or if the child's mother told him "Don't forget to put away your toys when you finish playing" (the time for cooperation or opposition being thus left to subjective definition by the observer, since "finished" playing is not a clear event). However, Wahler wisely selected and listed the instructions that the parents and teachers were to give, and assumedly the observers recorded cooperation and oppostition only in regard to these listed instructions. One problem to which Wahler did not describe any solution was that the observer apparently would be required to record the child's behavior as oppositional for every ten-second interval following a command if what the child was doing did not clearly constitute compliance with the instruction, such as the child's leaving the room to get a container when instructed by his mother "Put your puzzle away now." Possibly this problem was prevented from occurring by the careful selection of the specific instructions to include in the list.

Herbert and Baer (1972) also recorded a child's compliance in the home, but their brief definition, which was "following an instruction within 20 seconds" [p. 140], apparently was not accompanied by procedures that made the recording of this response a simple, objective decision process. In fairness to these researchers, however, it should be added that their observation code was long and complex, being designed to include the whole universe of the subject's behavior in a particular setting, and that further written instructions on the recording of this response may have been available to the observers but omitted from the published report to save space.

The defining of such responses as "teacher praise," "handraising," and "laughing" can pose similar problems to those indicated above, making complex definitions necessary (or procedures to simplify the observer's decision making).

On the other hand, there are also responses that may require no definition beyond their name alone, because the culture has a nearly uniform definition that suits the experimenter's purpose. For example, although Hopkins (1968) did define the smiling response he modified in two retarded boys, it is possible that the term "smiling" alone would constitute a highly adequate definition upon which two observers would get nearly identical data without further elaboration, discussion, or collaborative practice.

However, in general it appears that an adequate response definition should have at least three somewhat overlapping characteristics.

1. The definition should be *objective*, referring only to observable characteristics of the behavior (and environment, if needed) or translating any inferential terms (such as "expressing hostile feelings," "intended to help," or "showing interest in") into more objective ones.

2. The definition should be *clear* in that it should be readable and unambiguous so that experienced observers could read it and readily paraphrase it accurately.

3. The definition should be *complete*, delineating the "boundaries" of what is to be included as an instance of the response and what is to be excluded, thereby directing the observers in all situations that are likely to occur and leaving little to their judgement.

Thus "asking a question" may be both a clear and objective response definition in that it is easily repeatable and refers only to observable events, but it is an incomplete definition for use in recording a teacher's behavior because it does not instruct the observer what to do in various likely situations such as when a teacher has asked one child a question, received no answer, and then simply says another child's name (or even nods to the child), or when the teacher asks rhetorical questions like "John, is that the way we walk in the hall?"

In general, to the extent that these three characteristics are present in a response definition, interobserver agreement regarding the occurrence of that response should be high.[3] The ideal response definition would be one that could be handed to a competent observer in printed form and immediately produce data-recording behavior from that observer that closely matched the data-recording behavior of the other competent, independent observers. This ideal appears to be approximated only occasionally in applied behavior analysis today. Instead, the common practice in preparing observers for recording experimental data is to provide extensive guided experience in the recording of the

---

[3] Other factors influence interobserver agreement as well, so that a high correlation between the presence of these characteristics and actual agreement scores cannot be anticipated. Among the other factors that influence agreement scores are the ease with which the response can be detected (due to its amplitude, its duration, the social and other effects it produces, its social significance to the observer, etc.), the observers' motivation, the complexity of the recording method, observer fatigue and the presence of stimuli distracting to the observers.

behaviors in which the experimenter is interested, with a more experienced observer recording the same behaviors as a less experienced observer, and giving the less experienced observer frequent feedback on the accuracy with which his recording matches that of the more experienced observer. The training is usually continued until the data of the novice closely match those of the experienced observer, as indicated by high reliability scores.

The risk involved in this extensive guided experience is that the functional definition involved in the recording of the data may have only a loose correspondence to the definition subsequently reported when the experimenters publish their study.[4] That is, the observers record data by an implicit definition rather than by the explicit one. During training they learn numerous discriminations regarding the behavior that are not in the written definition and that may even contradict the written definition.[5] They may learn to record a school child's "talking out" behavior only when it attracts other children's or the teacher's attention even though there is no mention of such a criterion in the written definition. They may learn to record a child's behavior as "on task" even when the child looks up from work for reasonable periods of time (by the experimenter's or the observer's judgment), despite the fact that the definition says to record "off task" whenever the child is not looking at work. Or they may learn exactly what responses to record as "ritualistic autisms" when there is no written definition of those behaviors aside from the name itself. They may not even be able to verbalize several major discriminations they have learned.

For a science of behavior, the use of such implicit definitions has the general disadvantage that other scientists cannot replicate the measurement employed unless they are directly trained by the first scientist. The published description of the measurement simply misrepresents the actual measurement employed. A more serious potential disadvantage is that data based on implicit definitions may be much more subject to various kinds of error than data based on explicit, written definitions to which an observer can repeatedly return for guidance. When observers have no written definition to refer to, or only an incomplete one, their data may change over the course of an experiment due to such factors as their forgetting some of the discriminations they learned during training or their knowing what results the experimenter (or others involved in the study, such as parents, teachers, attendants, or therapists) would like to see. If this latter effect were a common one, many of the experiments upon which behavior analysts base their daily practice would be in need of replication to verify that

---

[4]In fact, it may not be unusual for experimenters to actually write down their definitions only after the experiment is well under way or even completed. Altering a definition during an experiment may also be common.

[5]The authors recognize that it is often impractical to put every single defining criterion into writing; and it may not even be possible to put some criteria into precise words. The point is that many behavior analysts (and other researchers as well) make little serious effort to put their defining criteria in writing.

the experimental effects were valid and did not represent a change in the observer's behavior rather than the subject's behavior (Baer, Wolf & Risley, 1968; Hawkins & Dotson, 1972).

THE EXPERIMENT

This study was designed to empirically assess the adequacy of a few behavioral definitions selected from the published literature on applied behavior analysis in education. If several published definitions were found to be inadequate, thus forcing observers to make a significant number of decisions regarding definitional criteria, it would suggest that the issues raised here are serious enough to warrant further exploration. It would also suggest that behavior analysts (and other researchers) need to take the task of defining responses more seriously.

The experimental design involved having two pairs of observers simultaneously and independently record the same behavior of the same subjects, each employing the same printed definition. Observers within a pair were allowed to collaborate on alternate, nonexperimental sessions, so that if additional definition were needed they could arrive at joint decisions regarding such definition. That is, they were allowed to develop implicit definitional criteria between them as needed, which appears to be common practice in the training of observers (e.g., Madsen, Becker, & Thomas, 1968). No collaboration was allowed across pairs of observers. By comparing within-pair agreement scores with across-pair agreement scores, an estimate of definition adequacy could be made. With a highly adequate definition, the difference between these scores should be small because all four observers' recording should be determined by the same clear, objective, complete, written definition. With an inadequate written definition, the within-pair agreement should be much greater than the across-pair agreement due to the large number of unwritten decisions a collaborating pair of observers is forced to make. The study was replicated with a second set of two observer pairs employing the same definitions in a second setting.

Subjects

The subjects were three eighth grade and three ninth grade students from two public junior high school classrooms.

Observer Recruitment and Instruction

Eight observers were recruited. Some were from a senior division psychology course in which participating as a research observer was a course requirement for which they received a grade, while others were recruited independently from the psychology department and were given two hours of academic credit for their participation. Prior to any training, each observer signed the following pledge:

> I swear that I will observe and record as accurately as I can and that I will follow all procedures requested by _____
> even though I do not know the purpose. This includes (a) not comparing my data with my partner or any other observer — either visually or orally — when requested, (b) observing independently when requested, (c) not changing my data to make it more like my partner's, or (d) anything else requested.

Then the observers received a minimum of 20 minutes instruction on the use of interval recording (Hall, 1971), including a simple exercise in recording by this technique. All data recording was in blocks of 5 10-sec intervals with a 10-sec rest interval separating each block. If a response appeared to occur on the border of 2 10-sec intervals, the observers recorded it in the latter interval.

Procedure

Recording with unpublished definitions. The observers were then given printed definitions of three behaviors to record: two student behaviors and one teacher behavior. These definitions were written by the experimenters and intended to be relatively clear, objective and complete (see Table 1). This phase of the study was designed to assure that the observers were demonstrably competent, but the data from this phase also provide some basis for evaluation of the data obtained with the definitions from the published literature.

The 8 observers were divided into 2 sets of 4, and each set observed in a different classroom for 50 minutes daily. The 4 observers in a set sat side by side in a row facing the students. They selected 3 children (without informing them) who could be easily viewed to serve as subjects, and these same children were used throughout the experiment, but only 1 was observed on any particular day. The use of 3 children, rather than 1, minimized the probability of wasting a session due to the absence of a child or of obtaining insufficient reliability data due to a child's low response rate. The role of "subject" was rotated among the children, but if a child was absent the observers recorded the behavior of the next child in the sequence. The observers always agreed on the child to be observed prior to each session. The teacher's talking was also observed daily, regardless to whom the talking was directed.

In the first three training sessions each observer recorded independently of the other observers. Then the four observers in each set were divided into pairs and, beginning with session four, each pair alternated daily between dependent and independent recording. During dependent sessions each pair of observers was encouraged to quietly collaborate on any questions encountered while recording

TABLE 1

Training Definitions

Definitions for Child Behaviors

Writing: any time that the subject, holding a writing utensil (pen, pencil, crayon), makes contact between the writing end of the utensil and the writing material (paper, notebook, workbook, etc.).
Exclude writing on the desk and erasing.
Include writing on a book or something of that nature even though you may think it inappropriate.
Talk-out: any audible vocalization directed at the teacher without the child's first raising a hand, or any other audible vocalization directed at other students without permission from the teacher.
Exclude nonsense noises and animal noises, etc.
Include instances when the child raises hand and vocalizes at the same time.

Definition for Teacher Behavior

Talking: any oral sounds involving the vocal cords. It is not necessary to be able to understand the words, merely to hear the sound of the subject's voice.
Exclude coughing, belching, sneezing, and clearing the throat even though they often involve the vocal cords. Whispering is also excluded by the above definition since it does not involve the vocal cords.
Include simple sounds like "oh," "huh?," "uh," and laughing aloud.

---

the three defined behaviors. A cardboard partition separated one pair of observers from the other to assure independence of decision making between observed pairs. At the end of the session each pair of observers was separately given an opportunity to bring unresolved questions to the attention of the experimenter. If questions were raised, the experimenter would ask what each observer in the pair thought regarding the problem, and after both views were expressed the observers were encouraged to quickly agree upon a solution. They were instructed not to discuss their recording at other times or with anyone else involved in the study.

During independent sessions independence of recording was assured by placing cardboard partitions between all observers. Observers were also instructed not to discuss their observations or any questions with any other observer during or after these sessions, and no assistance with definition problems was available from the experimenter. After independent sessions the paired observers tallied their disagreements from their data sheets. The experimenter later computed agreement scores and informed each pair of their score prior to the beginning of the next session (school day).

All four observers in a classroom synchronized their observations by viewing the same timing mechanism, a large General Electric kitchen clock, and by having one observer always designate a common strating point. The clock was placed such that it was in front of the observers when they were facing the child being observed. To further synchronize the time intervals for the observers, one observer audibly tapped the cardboard partition at the beginning of each rest interval.

In order to assure that interobserver agreement scores would reflect the adequacy of the definitions and not the conscientiousness of the observers, a supplementary observer was employed in each classroom on every independent session. This observer recorded the attending behavior of the primary observers by a one-minute time sampling method. At the end of each minute the supplementary observer would look at the four primary observers and determine whether, at that moment, each was attending to the observing task. Attending behavior for the primary observers was defined as looking at the subject, glancing at the clock or writing on the data sheet. Looking away from the subject, looking at the clock for more than 10 sec, or looking at the data sheet without writing were considered nonattending. Behavior during the 10-sec rest intervals was not recorded. Each primary observer was told that the course grade for the observation would be determined by the ratio of attending to nonattending behaviors recorded by the supplementary observer. The primary observers were not told the definition for attending or the recording technique used.

After each session the experimenter computed the percentage of time devoted to attending by each observer. If an observer's overall attending was above 80%, which it was on every session for every observer, the experimenter told the observer the attending score and complimented the observer on this performance.

Reliability assessments. Because interobserver reliability scores were the dependent variable in the study, it was essential that they be a sensitive measure of the agreement between observers. The typical method of calculating agreement scores when interval recording is used does not provide a sensitive measure, as Hawkins and Dotson (1972) have demonstrated. This measure is the interval-by-interval method, and the formula involved (from Bijou, Peterson & Ault, 1968) is

$$\frac{\text{agreements}}{\text{agreements plus disagreements}}$$

where an agreement is counted for every interval in which both observers recorded the behavior as occurring or both recorded it as not occuring, (the latter often being the failure to record the behavior as occurring), while a disagreement is counted when one observer recorded it as not occurring. This ratio is usually converted to a percentage agreement by multiplying by 100. Hawkins and Dotson provide evidence that interval-by-interval reliability scores are almost inevitably high when response rate or duration is either high or low. Therefore, interval-by-interval scores were not employed as the measure of definition adequacy. Instead, a more sensitive measure was used: scored interval reliability (Hawkins & Dotson, 1972).

In calculating scored interval reliability only those intervals in which one or both observers recorded the behavior as occurring are considered. Thus it is also called "occurrence reliability" or "agreement on occurrence" (Bijou *et al*, 1968). All intervals in which both observers recorded the behavior as absent (not occurring) are ignored. An agreement is tallied when both observers recorded the behavior as present and a disagreement when only one observer recorded it as present. The ratio of agreements to the sum of agreements and disagreements provides the reliability score. While scored-interval reliability constituted the primary data, interval-by-interval reliability was also calculated to further assess Hawkins and Dotson's (1972) contention that interval-by-interval scores are insensitive.

To assess the adequacy of any definition the scored-interval agreement between the two observers in a pair was compared with the scored-interval agreement between unpaired observers. That is, agreement between observers who had been collaborating was compared with agreement between observers who had never collaborated, the assumption being that when the former agreement score is considerably higher than the latter it suggests that the explicit definition is greatly deficient in guiding the recording behavior of the observers.

As a criterion of the observers' competence to begin the assessment of definitions from the published literature, the two pairs of observers in an observer set had to both achieve an interval-by-interval agreement of 85% or greater and a scored-interval agreement of 50% or greater for 2 consecutive sessions on all 3 of the unpublished definitions used in training (except talk-out responses in one classroom, which never were observed to occur, thus preventing calculation of a scored-interval reliability).[6] One observer set took 16 sessions (of which 8 were collaboration sessions) to reach criterion and the other set took 6 sessions (of which 3 were collaboration). Observers were not informed of the criterion or even that one existed.

Recording with published definitions. When a set of observers reached criterion on the unpublished definitions they were given a new group of 3 responses to record. These were selected from a well-known (Madsen, Becker & Thomas,

---

[6]The 50% criterion will seem surprisingly low to many readers, but consideration of a specific example may make clear how stringent a test of agreement the scored-interval reliability is. If one observer recorded a response in 2 intervals and the second recorded it in those same 2 intervals plus 2 more, their scored interval agreement would be 50% while their interval-by-interval agreement would be 99.2% (there being 250 intervals per session).

1968), published behavior code consisting of 38 responses. The observers were given the entire code (see Glossary 1) but recorded only 3 responses. For child behavior they recorded what Madsen *et al.* defined as "turning around" and "appropriate behavior." The teacher behavior recorded was "academic recognition."

The same procedures and subjects were used as in the recording of "writing," "talk-out," and "teacher talking." The observers alternated dependent and independent observation sessions, beginning with an independent session that allowed assessment for any chance tendency toward greater agreement within pairs prior to their collaborating in the recording of a response. On independent sessions all observers were separated from all other observers by cardboard partitions, while on dependent or collaboration sessions a partition separated one *pair* of observers from the other pair.

Questions directed to the experimenter about the definitions were treated as before, and observers continued to receive the same feedback regarding their attentiveness to the task and their agreement scores.

After several independent recording sessions with the Madsen *et al.* (1968) definitions (including the one that preceded any collaboration, seven for Observer Set 1, eight for Observer Set 2) the observers were given a second group of three definitions from another published behavior code (Wasik, Senn, Welch & Cooper, 1969). In this case, the definitions used for child behavior were "desirable seeking of support, assistance and information," and "inappropriate sharing and helping." The definition for teacher behavior employed was for "redirection." (The full list is supplied in Glossary II.) As with the previous three definitions, the observers were given the whole code rather than only the three definitions, because the whole code could provide a context that constituted a significant part of the individual definitions. The three selected definitions were simply underlined on the code for the observers.

All procedures continued to be the same as those employed in recording the previous definitions. Observer Set 1 recorded the second group of published definitions until they had completed six independent recording sessions, while Observer Set 2 completed five independent recording sessions (in both cases, including the initial independent recording session that preceded any collaboration).

Results

Only the results from independent recording sessions are reported, as scores from dependent recording would be meaningless. The two within-pair agreement scores obtained from the paired observers within an observer set were averaged to give within-pair reliability for a session. The mean of all within-pair reliability scores obtained with a particular definition by an observer set was then determined. Across-pair reliability for a session was computed by averaging the four agreement scores of the unpaired observer combinations in an observer set. The

TABLE 2

Mean scored interval agreement from Observer Set 1

	$\overline{X}$ Scored- Interval Agreement in Percentages		Difference:
	Within Pairs	Across Pairs	Within-Pair Minus Across-Pair
Unpublished Training Definitions			
Writing	66.6	65.2	1.4
Talking-out	—	—	—
Teacher Talking	87.6	85.0	2.6
Published Definitions, Group 1			
Appropriate on-task	90.3	87.0	3.3
Turning around	42.3	23.1	19.2
Academic recognition	23.2	13.7	9.5
Published Definitions, Group 2			
Appropriate seeking support	35.3	14.3	21.0
Inappropriate sharing and helping	30.6	14.2	16.4
Redirection	51.7	15.4	36.3

mean of the across-pair reliabilities for a particular definition was then calculated. The difference between the mean within-pair agreement and the mean across-pair agreement for a particular definition was considered the datum of prime interest.

Observer Set 1. The mean scored-interval agreement scores obtained by Observer Set 1 for each definition are presented in Table 2 in the typical form of percentages. These means are based on independent recording sessions that followed one or more dependent recording sessions with any particular set of definitions. There were eight such sessions for the training definitions, six for definitions from Madsen *et al.* (1968) and five for definitions from Wasik *et al.* (1969). No scores could be calculated for "talking-out" because none occurred, and scored-interval agreement cannot be computed under such a condition.

In no instance did across-pair mean agreement exceed within-pair agreement, as might be expected by chance. Difference scores were smallest for "writing," "teacher talking," and "appropriate (on-task) behavior." "Redirection," "appropriate seeking support," and "inappropriate sharing and helping" yielded the largest differences.

TABLE 3

Mean scored-interval agreement from Observer Set 2

	$\bar{X}$ Scored-Interval Agreement in %		Difference: Within-Pair Minus Across-Pair
	Within Pairs	Across Pairs	
Unpublished Training Definitions			
Writing	76.5	71.9	4.6
Talking-out	60.3	62.4	−2.1
Teacher talking	88.6	86.3	2.3
Published Definitions, Group 1			
Appropriate on-task	81.6	64.9	16.7
Turning around	47.7	23.9	23.8
Academic recognition	49.8	19.2	30.6
Published Definitions, Group 2			
Appropriate seeking support	19.1	0.9	18.2
Inappropriate sharing and helping	71.9	32.8	39.1
Redirection	41.5	0.9	40.6

Observer Set 2. The mean scored-interval agreements obtained by Observer Set 2 for each definition are presented in Table 3. These means are based on independent recording sessions that followed one or more dependent sessions. There were three such sessions for the training definitions, six for the first set of definitions from the behavior analysis literature, and four for the second set of published definitions.

With this observer set there was one definition for which across-pair agreement was greater, on the average, than within-pair agreement. Among the other definitions, difference scores were smallest for "teacher talking," "writing," and "appropriate (on-task) behavior." Difference scores were greatest for "redirection," "inappropriate sharing and helping," and "academic recognition."

Comparison of Scored-Interval and Interval-by-Interval

All reliabilities were calculated by the interval-by-interval method also, thereby allowing further assessment of Hawkins and Dotson's (1972) contention that interval-by-interval (I-I) scores are insensitive for determining such things as observer competence or definition adequacy. A comparison of the scored-interval (S-I) scores already presented with I-I scores from the same sessions is made in Table 4, with all scores rounded to the nearest 1%.

TABLE 4

Comparison of S-I with I-I mean agreement
scores for each definition and observer set

Definition	Agreement Scores Expressed in Percentages							
	Observer Set 1				Observer Set 2			
	Within Pairs		Across Pairs		Within Pairs		Across Pairs	
	S-I	I-I	S-I	I-I	S-I	I-I	S-I	I-I
Writing	67	93	65	92	77	86	72	82
Talking-out	–	100	–	100	60	90	62	88
Teacher talking	88	94	85	92	89	90	86	87
Approp. on-task	90	92	87	90	82	85	65	73
Turning around	42	92	23	84	48	86	24	78
Acad. recognition	23	90	14	86	50	80	19	65
Approp. seeking supp.	35	96	14	91	19	77	9	48
Inapprop. sharing	31	89	14	81	72	88	33	62
Redirection	52	88	15	85	42	98	9	94

By comparing adjacent scores within any column it is possible to observe the magnitude of the difference between I-I and S-I scores. The largest difference is evident in the across-pair agreement on "redirection," where observers saw the behavior in the same intervals only 9% of the time, on the average, yet because the behavior was infrequent (producing many "agreements" on the absence of the behavior) I-I agreement was 94%.

It may also be noted that the lowest I-I score in Table 4 is 62%; but this should not be interpreted to mean that I-I scores on individual sessions were never below this level. Because most behavior analysts appear to report the range of single session agreement scores as well as the mean of the agreement scores obtained on all reliability checks combined, it would be instructive to compare I-I and S-I agreement scores obtained on a few individual sessions. For this purpose one behavior was arbitrarily selected from each group of three behaviors recorded, and one pair of observers was arbitrarily selected from each observer set; then the first five I-I and S-I agreement scores obtained by these observers on each of these responses were drawn from the data. These scores are comparable to individual reliability scores usually reported in the literature and are presented in Table 5.

The range of I-I scores in Table 5 is from 63 to 100, while the range of S-I scores is from 0 to 100. These scores are typical of those obtained on all responses by observers that constituted a pair (recorded dependently on alternate sessions through most of the study). Of course, both I-I and S-I scores tended to be lower when calculated from unpaired observers, as was evident in Tables 2, 3 and 4; but S-I scores were much lower, while I-I scores were only slightly lower (because I-I scores are largely determined by response rate instead).

Precollaboration Agreement

Too few sessions were conducted prior to collaboration, on the two groups of published definitions, to allow an adequate assessment of the agreement that could be expected on the basis of the printed definitions alone, but a rough estimate might be obtainable from the single precollaboration sessions that were conducted. These data, along with comparable data from the unpublished definitions, are presented in Table 6 in terms of both S-I and I-I agreement scores.

The data from the unpublished definitions are based on the pooled results from seven sessions for Observer Set 1 and three sessions for Observer Set 2, while data from published definitions are from one session for each observer set. Each session produced six agreement scores from each observer set, there being six possible observer pairings among four observers.

Most of the definitions failed in at least one instance (observer pair and session) to produce a single interval of agreement on the presence of a response

TABLE 5

Comparison of individual S-I and I-I agreement scores obtained by
arbitrarily selected observer pairs on three selected responses

Response	Observer Pair from Set 1		Observer Pair from Set 2	
	S-I	I-I	S-I	I-I
Writing	50	93	72	75
	50	94	60	72
	65	92	56	80
	0	98	57*	72*
	69	79	76*	89*
Appropriate on-task	76	76	19	63
	79*	87*	53*	75*
	82*	82*	64*	82*
	100*	100*	87*	88*
	93*	93*	65*	69*
Redirection	0	99	8	95
	0*	89*	55*	96*
	75*	98*	0*	96*
	65*	80*	71*	98*
	60*	82*	50*	98*

These observers constituted a pair during this session, having collaborated at least once prior to this session while recording this behavior.

(S-I), and some of the definitions seldom produced such agreement. On the other hand, of the published definitions "appropriate on-task" achieved a fairly high degree of agreement between most observer pairs considering that this was their first experience at recording with this definition and none of them had yet discussed it with each other. Likewise, two of the training definitions produced fairly high agreement between most observer pairs, especially considering the fact that the observers were then getting their first extended practice at recording behavior.

Discussion

If the six definitions taken from the published literature in applied behavior analysis and employed in this study are at all representative of other definitions in the field, the results of this study appear to indicate a need for much more care in the writing and testing of definitions. Through the kind of collaboration that is commonly a part of observer training, paired observers developed definitions that differed so much from another observer pair's definition as to make within-pair agreement scores on subsequent independent recording sessions as much as 40% higher than across-pair agreement scores. Even paired observers agreed on the presence of a response less than half the time, on the average, as the within-pair agreement scores below 50% attest.

TABLE 6

Precollaboration mean S-I and I-I
agreement scores on all definitions,
based on data from both observer sets

Definition	Mean Agreement		Range of Agreement Scores from Observer Pairs	
	S-I	I-I	S-I	I-I
Writing	55	83	0 - 95	65 - 100
Talking-out	63*	85	42 - 70*	58 - 100
Teacher talking	77	82	33 - 100	54 - 100
Approp. on-task	59	65	10 - 94	13 - 94
Turning around	20**	95**	8 - 40**	91 - 99**
Acad. recognition	19	78	0 - 51	47 - 100
Approp. seeking supp.	2	98	0 - 18	94 - 100
Inapprop. sharing	1	94	0 - 13	85 - 100
Redirection	1	96	0 - 8	90 - 100

*Based on just one observer set, because response did not occur for other observer set, preventing calculation of S-I scores.
**Due to misunderstanding, Observer Set 1 did not record this response on the first session; therefore, these data are from only Observer Set 2.

Some additional support for the conclusion that most of the published definitions tested were insufficient in guiding observers is provided by the data ·from initial, precollaboration sessions. With 5 of the 6 published definitions virtually every pairing of observers produced S-I agreement scores below 50%, and on 3 of the definitions no pairing produced agreement above 20% (see Table 6). Of course, it should also be recognized that these results reflect a combination of inadequacy of definitions and lack of practice, because all 6 of the responses are probably of a nature that requires an observer to practice recording them for a time before maximum proficiency is reached.

The data from precollaboration sessions also provide a means of determining the likelihood that the differences between within-pair and across-pair agreement is due to accidentally pairing observers who already had similar preconceptions as to what a particular behavior was like (preexisting implicit definitions). If paired observers happened to have unusually similar preconceptions regarding a response, within-pair scores on that response would be higher than across-pair scores due to learning that occurred prior to the experiment rather than to the collaboration during the experiment. However the average S-I difference between within-pair and across-pair scores (using the subsequently-created pairs) before collaboration on the 3 training definitions was only 0.1%, the average difference before collaboration on the Madsen *et al.* (1968) definitions was only 6.3%, and the average difference before collaboration on the Wasik *et al.* (1969) definitions was only 1.5%.

The difference between within-pair agreement and across-pair agreement obtained in the present study is similar to results obtained by O'Leary and Kent (1973). They noted that observers divided into separate groups and computing their agreement only within the two groups developed sufficiently unique definitions that on seven of the nine behavioral categories the two groups recorded significantly different frequencies of behavior. They conclude "It seems that the process of computing reliability and discussing differences in recording modifies an observer's interpretation of the behavioral code to more closely match those observers with whom he is working" [p. 89]. The remedies they propose include such practices as rotating observers and videotaping sessions from each experimental condition. While these practices are probably desirable and may prove necessary, one might suggest that the first measure taken is to write definitions that are complete, objective, and clear.

The teacher response, "redirection," which fared among the worst in the present study, may provide a useful example. The definition seems to be objective in that it does not require the observer to draw inferences. It seems to be clear, in that it is easy to understand and readily repeatable by itself. However, its clarity may be considerably reduced by one or more other definitions in the same code. The definition immediately following it in Wasik *et al.* (1969) appears to refer to very similar behavior: "Negative: Any statement that disapproves of a child's behavior. It may be defined by negative content or strong emphasis in speaking, e.g., 'Stop that!' 'Don't do that'" [p. 183]. The definition of "redirection" would appear to include a statement like "Stop that," but it is possible that the experimenters only meant that the statement should be recorded as "redirection" if it included an indication of what behavior the subject *should* engage in. In that case, of course, the statement "Stop that and get back to your seat" might be recordable as both a "negative" and a "redirection," except that it is not clear whether this was considered permissible by the experimenters. In addition to possible problems of clarity, the definition of "redirection" appears to be incomplete. Only one example is given, a response that was to be included as an instance of "redirection;" whereas examples that were to be excluded as noninstances would likely have helped define the boundaries of the response, especially if some of the examples were of a borderline nature and were accompanied by rationale for excluding them. It is not difficult to imagine likely situations that would confront an observer with difficult decisions. For example, the teacher might look at a girl who is whispering to a neighbor during social studies period and say "Is that your social studies?" This could be interpreted as a "negative" or a "redirection" or both. Likewise, the teacher's saying to a daydreaming child "It is math time, Tim" could be recorded as a "redirection," a "negative," or even a "neutral" instruction (see Glossary II). An experimenter testing the definition in a classroom would doubtless discover several other problems requiring supplementing or otherwise altering the definition of "redirection" or other responses in the code.

Upon reading the definition of "appropriate on-task" behavior one might question why agreement scores on that response were generally high. The definition appears to be less complete than any of the others. The answer appears to lie primarily in the amount of time the behavior was occurring. When a behavior occurs in more than half of the intervals of a session, S-I scores, like I-I scores, can no longer range to zero. If both observers record a response in 80% of the intervals, the lowest possible S-I agreement is 30% and much higher agreement is likely by chance alone. Because "appropriate on-task" behavior occurred during much of the time, high agreement may have resulted from this more than from the adequacy of the definition. However, it is also possible that this class of behavior is one which needs little defining; American college students employed as observers may have such similar, preconceived, implicit definitions that little explicit definition is needed.

It is recommended that behavior analysts attempt to develop complete, objective, clear definitions that allow for replication of their measurement methods in other "laboratories" and help prevent possible observer biases that either mask real experimental effects or exaggerate effects that are inconsequential or absent. It is further recommended that experimenters test the adequacy of each definition they employ by having three or more experienced observers who have never used the definition read it and independently record the behavior of the same subject for one or more sessions without any collaboration or experimenter elaboration to determine the agreement produced by the explicit definition *alone,* using a sensitive index of agreement in this determination. Finally, it is recommended that experimenters make available their exact definitions by either publishing them in any reports of their research or, if too long and complex, offering them publicly as available on request.

The comparison between S-I and I-I scores (see Table 5) appears to further substantiate Hawkins and Dotson's (1972) claim that I-I agreement scores are unsatisfactorily insensitive. The difference between the two scores is remarkable in several instances, and rarely do I-I scores fall below commonly accepted levels, even when observers disagree on half of the occurrences of the response or more. Thus, S-I scores appear to be an improvement over I-I scores in providing the kind of information a behavior analyst wants to know about the data recording procedures being used.

However, it should be noted that S-I or "occurrence reliability," scores also have drawbacks, as pointed out by Hawkins and Dotson (1972). First, when response frequency or duration is high, S-I agreement will be high even if the two observers are recording by moderately different definitions; only when the behavior occurs in half of the intervals or fewer are agreement scores of 0% possible. (For this analysis it is necessary to assume that both observers recorded the behavior as occurring in the same total number of intervals.) Second, S-I agreement becomes more variable as response frequency or duration declines, the ultimate case being where each observer records the behavior as occurring in only one interval but their S-I agreement can only be one of two scores, 100% or 0%. Third, while it is very useful as a test of the adequacy of a definition, it does not as adequately reflect the degree to which the observers agreed on how much of the behavior occurred in total. For example, two observers might agree perfectly that a behavior occurred in one-fourth of the intervals, yet the S-I agreement between them could be as low as 0%. Since data are normally reported in terms of *total* percentage of intervals, it can be argued that the reliability of that datum is the most important reliability to assess (e.g., by dividing smaller total by larger total and multiplying by 100), not whether the observers saw the behavior at the same precise moments. Finally, whenever the behavior is seen by neither observer during the session, no S-I agreement score can be calculated. Clearly, the appropriate assessment of interobserver agreement with interval data remains an issue for behavior analysts to resolve.

GLOSSARY I[7]

Behavioral Coding Categories for Children

 I. Inappropriate Behaviors
  A. Gross Motor. Getting out of seat, standing up, running, hopping, skipping, jumping, walking around, moving chair, etc.

[7]Behavior Code From Madsen, Becker and Thomas, 1969, pp. 142-143.

B. Object Noise. Tapping pencil or other objects, clapping, tapping feet, rattling or tearing paper, throwing book on desk, slamming desk. Be conservative, only rate if you can hear the noise when eyes are closed. Do not include accidental dropping of objects.

C. Disturbance of Other's Property. Grabbing objects or work, knocking neighbor's books off desk, destroying another's property, pushing with desk (only rate if someone is there). Throwing objects at another person without hitting them.

D. Contact (high and low intensity). Hitting, kicking, shoving, pinching, slapping, striking with object, throwing object which hits another person, poking with objects, biting, pulling hair, touching, patting, etc. Any physical contact is rated.

E. Verbalization. Carrying on conversations with other children when it is not permitted. Answers teacher without being called on; making comments or calling out remarks when no questions have been asked; calling teacher's name to get her attention; crying, screaming, singing, whistling, laughing, coughing, or blowing loudly. These responses may be directed to teacher or children.

F. Turning Around. Turning head or head and body to look at another person, showing objects to another child, attending to another child. Must be of 4-sec duration, or more than 90 degrees using desk as a reference. Not rated unless seated. If this response overlaps two time intervals and cannot be rated in the first because it is less than 4-sec duration, then rate in the interval in which the end of the response occurs.

G. Other Inappropriate Behavior. Ignores teacher's question or command. Does something different from that directed to do including minor motor behavior such as playing with pencil or eraser when supposed to be writing, coloring while the record is on, doing spelling during the arithmetic lesson, playing with objects. The child involves himself in a task that is not appropriate. Not rated when other inappropriate behaviors are rated. Must be time of task.

H. Mouthing Objects. Bringing thumb, fingers, pencils, or any object in contact with the mouth.

I. Isolate Play. Limited to kindergarten free-play period. Child must be farther than 3 ft. from any person, neither initiates or responds to verbalizations with other people, engages in no interaction of a non-verbal nature with other children for the entire 10-sec period.

II. Appropriate Behavior. Time on task; e.g., answers questions, listens, raises hand, works on assignment. Must include whole 10-sec interval except for Turning Around responses of less than 4-sec duration.

Coding Definitions for Teacher Behaviors

I. Teacher Approval following Appropriate Child Behavior
   A. Contact. Positive physical contact such as embracing, patting, holding arm or hand, sitting on lap.
   B. Praise. Verbal comments indicating approval, commendation or achievement. Examples: that's good, you are doing right, you are studying well, I like you, thank you, you make me happy.
   C. Facial attention. Smiling at child.

II. Teacher Approval following Inappropriate Child Beahvior
   Same codes as under I

III. Teacher Disapproval following Appropriate Child Behavior
   A. Holding the child. Forcibly holding the child, putting child out in the hall, grabbing, hitting, spanking, slapping, shaking the child.
   B. Criticism. Critical comments of high or low intensity, yelling, scolding, raising voice. Examples: that's wrong, don't do that, stop talking, did I call on you, you are wasting your time, don't laugh, you know what you are supposed to do.
   C. Threats. Consequences mentioned by the teacher to be used at a later time. If _____ then _____ comments.
   D. Facial attention. Frowning or grimacing at a child.

IV. Teacher Disapproval following Inappropriate Child Behavior
   Same codes as under III.

V. "Timeout" Procedures
   A. The teacher turns out the lights and says nothing.
   B. The teacher turns her back and waits for silence.
   C. The teacher stops talking and waits for quiet.
   D. Keeping in for recess.
   E. Sending child to office.
   F. Depriving child in the classroom of some privilege.

VI. Academic Recognition
   Calling on a child for an answer. Giving "feedback" for academic correctness.

GLOSSARY II[8]

Child Coding System

Desirable
1. Manipulating and Directing Others: Manipulating, commanding or directing others appropriately; enforcing rules.
2. Self-Directed Activity: Working independently, such as reading, writing, or constructing; continuing to work in the absence of immediate supervision.
3. Sharing and Helping: Contributing ideas, interests, materials; helping others; initiating conversation.
4. Social Interaction: Cooperative behavior, such as talking, studying or playing with a peer.
5. *Seeking Support, Assistance, and Information:* Asking teachers or peers for help, support, direction or explanation.
6. Following Directions Passively and Submissively: Following requests, answering direct questions, working only with teacher supervision.

Inappropriate
7. Resisting Authority: More than a 10-sec delay in carrying out teacher's directions.
8. Observing Passively: Watching others work, "Checking on" activities of adults or peers.
9. *3, 4* and *5:* These categories have the same definitions as those with corresponding numbers under the "Desirable" heading, but are coded as inappropriate when they occur at other than the appropriate time or place.

Unacceptable
10. Aggressive Behavior: Direct attack on a child or teacher — grabbing, pushing, hitting, pulling, kicking, name-calling, destroying property.

11. Inappropriate Behavior — Getting Behavior: Activities which seem to result in attention from others such as annoying, bothering, belittling, or criticizing others; noise-making or loud talking.

12. Resisting Authority: Physically resisting instructions or directions, for example — saying "I won't do it" and leaving the room.

Teacher Coding System

13. Positive — Any verbalization which encourages or approves of the behavior of a child, e.g., "That's good." "You are doing fine."

[8]Behavior Code adapted from Wasik, Senn, Welch, and Cooper (1969), pp. 181-194.

14. Neutral — Any statement related to academic work which explains, describes, directs, instructs, or sets limits for a child, e.g., "Complete pages 6 and 7 in your reading book." "You may go to the library for thirty minutes."
15. Question — Any interrogative sentence in which the teacher asks for academic information only, e.g., "What is the answer to this problem?"
16. *Redirection* — Any statement with which the teacher attempts to redirect a child from an inappropriate behavior to an appropriate behavior, e.g., "You are supposed to be reading instead of coloring."
17. Negative — Any statement that disapproves of a child's behavior. It may be defined by negative content or strong emphasis in speaking, e.g., "Stop that!" "Don't do that."

REFERENCES

Baer, D. M., Wolf, M. M., & Risley, T. R. Some current dimensions of applied behavior analysis. *Journal of Applied Behavior Analysis*, 1968, *1*, 91-97.

Bijou, S. W., Peterson, R. F., & Ault, M. H. A method to integrate descriptive and experimental field studies at the level of data and empirical concepts. *Journal of Applied Behavior Analysis*, 1968, *1*, 175-191.

Hall, R. V. *Behavior modification, vol. I: The measurement of behavior.* Lawrence, Kansas: H & H Enterprises, 1971.

Hawkins, R. P., & Dotson, V. A. Reliability scores that delude: An Alice in Wonderland trip through the misleading characteristics of inter-observer agreement scores in interval recording. Paper presented at the Third Annual Symposium on Behavior Analysis in Education, Lawrence, Kansas, May, 1972.

Herbert, E. W., & Baer, D. M. Training parents as behavior modifiers: Self-recording of contingent attention. *Journal of Applied Behavior Analysis*, 1972, *5*, 139-149.

Hopkins, B. L. The effect of candy and social reinforcement, instruction, reinforcement and schedule learning on the modification and maintenance of smiling. *Journal of Applied Behavior Analysis*, 1968, *1*, 121-129.

Madsen, C. H., Becker, W. C., & Thomas, D. R. Rules, praise and ignoring: Elements of elementary classroom control. *Journal of Applied Behavior Analysis*, 1968, *1*, 139-151.

O'Leary, K. D., & Kent, R. Behavior modification for social action: Research tactics and problems. In L. A. Hamerlynck, L. C. Handy & E. J. Mash (Eds.), *Behavior change: Methodology, concepts, and practice.* Champaign, Ill.: Research Press, 1973.

Wasik, B. H., Senn, K., Welch, R. H., & Cooper, B. R. Behavior modification with culturally deprived school children: Two case studies. *Journal of Applied Behavior Analysis*, 1969, *2*, 181-194.

Wahler, R. G. Setting generality: Some specific and general effects of child behavior therapy. *Journal of Applied Behavior Analysis*, 1969, *2*, 239-246.

12

Laboratory Investigations of Applied Behavior Analysis Techniques: Procedures Designed to Decrease or Eliminate Responding [1]

Judith M. LeBlanc
Katherine E. Reuter
Donald N. Miller
Gary L. Schilmoeller[2]

University of Kansas

Applied behavior analysis research has demonstrated that behavior can be changed through gross reinforcement and extinction manipulations in the natural environment. This is clearly evidenced by the research represented in the Journal of Applied Behavior Analysis since 1968. In this type of research, it is not

[1] This research was in part supported by: General Research Grant #37615038 from the University of Kansas to Judith M. LeBlanc; PHS Research Grant #HD02528/05 from National Institute of Child Health and Human Development to the Bureau of Child Research, the University of Kansas; Office of Equal Opportunity Evaluation and Research Grant 4125 from the Executive Office of the President to the Department of Human Development, the University of Kansas; National Institute of Child Health and Human Development Training Grant HD00247 to the Department of Human Development at the University of Kansas by the U.S. Department of Health, Education and Welfare. This chapter is based in part on theses submitted to the Department of Human Development, University of Kansas in partial fulfillment for Master of Arts Degrees or Doctor of Philosophy Degrees by the first authors of each section.

[2] Dr. Donald N. Miller is currently at the Department of Psychology, Southbury Training Center, Southbury, Connecticut. Dr. Katherine Reuter is currently at The Division of Pediatric Psychology, University of Maryland School of Medicine, Baltimore, Maryland. Gary L. Schilmoeller is currently at the College of Human Development, The Pennsylvania State University, University Park, Pennsylvania.

usually necessary to know the schedules of reinforcement which have maintained the behavior that is to be changed. Knowing a contingency exists between the behavior and the stimulus event (predicted to be the maintaining reinforcer) is, in most instances, enough for prescribing modification procedures.

However, for purposes of increasing the effectiveness of modification techniques, more emphasis should be placed upon information which must come from experimental analysis laboratory research involving reinforcement schedules. Research in applied or clinical settings provides evidence that collections of procedures are effective for changing specified problem behaviors. However, these settings frequently preclude analyzing the specifics of the combined procedures. Investigation of the specific details of functional relationships (leading to the advancement of the technology of applied science of human behavior) frequently can only be obtained in laboratory experimentation, because in applied research the most important concern is the client(s) for whom the procedures are prescribed rather than specific analyses of the effectiveness of those procedures. Thus, the thrust in applied research is, of necessity, one of rapid implementation of procedures that will successfully change behavior rather than the analysis of how those procedures can be made optimally effective.

Bijou (1970) described the behaviors involved in the development of a child's social repertoire as being a function of the concurrent application of many different schedules of reinforcement for the many and varied responses emitted by the child. He described research which indicated some generality of results between applied and laboratory settings. He warned, however, that even though the concepts and principles derived from laboratory research would certainly be expected to apply to applied settings, it is not enough to expect laboratory findings to pertain in these settings. Consequently, there is a need to advance the technology from basic research findings, at a level that is not always possible in applied settings. This calls for an alternate research program in the laboratory, oriented toward laboratory analogues of applied procedures.

Such a research orientation would enhance the potential of generality between results derived from the laboratory and their application in applied environments. This would involve designing laboratory research which is more analogous to procedures which are functionally possible in natural settings.

Because of the infinite variety of possible schedule combinations concurrently available to a child in applied settings, such laboratory analogues (either human or infrahuman) are difficult to design and implement. However, even though implementation of exact analogues of applied settings might not be feasible in the laboratory, analyzing the effects and side effects of certain schedules which are, or could be, useful behavioral change mechanisms in applied settings would provide valuable developmental information. When procedures are implemented in applied settings to change behaviors, the goal of the prescribed procedures may be reached, but all too often little information is added to our knowledge of what other behavioral effects may be occurring. Such information can and should come from the laboratory. Only with this information can our applied behavior analysis procedures be examined in sufficient detail to add to our everdeveloping knowledge of the principles involved in human behavior.

The experiments presented below evolved from just such an orientation. They are laboratory studies involving both human and infrahuman organisms, but examine procedures which have been or could potentially be used as modification procedures in applied settings. All involve procedures designed to decrease behavior, specifically extinction and differential reinforcement of other behavior (DRO). Procedures designed to decrease undesirable behavior are the hallmark of the current technology involved in behavior modification. However, questions and issues surrounding the use of these procedures continue to arise with respect to why their implementation is sometimes effective and other times not for changing behavior. Through the intensive behavioral analysis obtained in the laboratory one can closely examine the variables involved in these procedures. Such research does not have to concern itself with the immediate solving of a specific behavioral problem and thus, it can afford the luxury of investigating the specifics of the procedural content as related to response outcome, rather than concentrating primarily on response outcome only.

The studies presented examine either the effects of prior reinforcement schedules upon DRO and extinction or compare the effects of different methods of implementing these procedures. There are five studies included in this chapter and each is presented separately as a single complete work with credit given to the authors responsible for each. Study 1 was designed to examine the applied potential of the partial reinforcement effect. It was a between- and within-subject analysis of the effects of interpolating continuous reinforcement (CRF) subsequent to variable interval reinforcement (VI) on responding during extinction. A similar question was posed in Study 2 with responses during differential reinforcement of other behavior (DRO) being the dependent variable. Because it was hypothesized that differential reinforcement of other behavior (DRO), as used in basic research, was difficult to precisely implement in applied environments, Study 3 compared response decrement during fixed interval DRO and variable interval DRO. Likewise, it was thought that extinction alone was seldom implemented in applied settings. That is, procedures designed to decrease behavior usually involved some form of DRO. Thus, Study 4 was designed to compare response decrement during DRO and extinction and response resumption during a concurrent schedule of reinforcement after exposure to DRO and extinction. Some of the previous research indicated that there might be a difference in responding during variable interval DRO for high- and low-rate responders. Thus, Study 5 was designed to look at this problem because it is possible that one might wish to prescribe different response decrement procedures based on the rate of the behavior to be decreased.

STUDY 1
Continuous Reinforcement:
A Modification Procedure Prior to Extinction?
Judith M. LeBlanc

One behavioral principle utilized in modification procedures is extinction (Sherman & Baer, 1969). The effectiveness of extinction as an experimental manipulation is demonstrated by results from infrahuman and human laboratories (Ferster & Skinner, 1957; Bijou, 1957, 1958; Etzel & Gewirtz, 1967). Furthermore, its effectiveness as a modification procedure has been demonstrated through behavioral analyses conducted in the natural environment (Hart, Reynolds, Baer, Brawley & Harris, 1968; Pinkston, Reese, LeBlanc, & Baer, 1973; Williams, 1959).

Evidence further indicates that partial or intermittent reinforcement produces greater resistance to extinction than continuous reinforcement. This phenomenon, referred to as the partial reinforcement effect, has been observed in restricted as well as free-operant experimentation (Brackbill, 1958; Carment & Miles, 1962; Jenkins & Stanley, 1950; Kass, 1962; Kass & Wilson, 1966; Lewis & Duncan, 1958; Myers, 1960; Siqueland, 1968; Skinner, 1938). It would, therefore, seem at least plausible, from several points of view, for example discrimination theory, that a problem behavior might be made less resistant to extinction (in terms of rate, number of responses emitted during extinction, and/or length of the extinction period) if it were shifted from a maintenance schedule of partial reinforcement to one of continuous reinforcement just prior to the implementation of extinction.

Most basic laboratory studies which focused upon this question have produced nonsignificant results. Four used free-operant (Likely, 1958; Quartermain & Vaughan, 1961; Quartermain, Vaughan, & Mangan, 1961; Spradlin, 1962), and three, restricted-operant paradigms (Jenkins, 1962; Sutherland, Mackintosh, & Wolfe, 1965; Theois, 1962). Restricted-operant experimental results may not be relevant to behavior modification because most problem behaviors in the natural environment appear to be free-operant, that is, there are few restrictions upon their occurrence. The free-operant studies also may have little relevance because they did not include experimental procedures comparable to modification procedures used in the natural environment. For example, in the free-operant laboratory studies only one to four sessions of intermittent and/or intermittent-followed-by-continuous-reinforcement conditioning were programmed prior to one or four sessions of extinction. In behavior modification procedures, several days or weeks of baseline are usually recorded prior to implementing a manipulation such as extinction. This manipulation and the subsequent reversal control procedures also require several days or weeks. Additionally, extinction conditions should consist of several sessions to observe behavioral trends over time; the reason being, that initial behavioral patterns during extinction might not be indicative of eventual behavioral patterns. For example, if spontaneous recovery of responding occurs during extinction, it is a variable important for practical behavior modification considerations. If one procedure produced more efficient initial results but less efficient eventual results, it might not be considered a practical procedure for behavior modification where the long-term durability of results is of prime importance.

Rather than a natural environment examination of continuous reinforcement as a possible modification procedure for decreasing resistance to extinction of intermittently reinforced behaviors, it seemed more practical to examine the effects of these procedures first with infrahuman organisms in the more precisely controlled laboratory setting. In the first experiment (A) two possible modification procedures were compared between groups. One group had extinction programmed after establishing baseline responding with variable-interval reinforcement and the second had continuous reinforcement interpolated between variable-interval reinforcement and extinction. The second experiment (B) compared these same manipulations using a within-subjects experimental design.

Experiment A Procedure

In the first experiment, 12, 3-month-old, naive albino rats were maintained at 85% of their free-feeding body weight. Prior to shaping, the 12 rats were randomly assigned to 1 of 2 groups of 6. Most were hand-shaped, during a 1-hour session, to press the bar in an experimental rat chamber. During all experimental conditions, a white light, directly over the response bar, was momentarily illuminated to signal the delivery of a pellet. Subsequent to shaping, all subjects had 1, 30-min experimental session per day for 52 days.

The group programmed for variable-interval reinforcement just prior to extinction (the VI-EXT Group) received 20 sessions of continuous reinforcement prior to the introduction of 14 sessions of variable-interval 1-min conditioning. The group programmed for continuous reinforcement just prior to extinction (the VI-CRF-EXT Group) received 10 continuous reinforcement sessions prior to and 10 subsequent to 14 sessions of variable-interval 1-min conditioning. Therefore, the number of continuous reinforcement sessions (20) and the number of variable-interval reinforcement conditioning sessions (20) was equated for all subjects in both groups (see Table 1).

Experiment A Results

In Figure 1 the line graph compares the mean rate per minute across extinction sessions for each of the two groups of six subjects. The mean response rate of the group programmed for VI-EXT was initially higher and descended faster across sessions to its eventual extinction level than those of the group programmed for VI-CRF-EXT. Additionally, the eventual extinction rate was lower and showed less variability after the initial response decrement for the VI-EXT

TABLE 1

Study 1

Group VI-EXT N = 6		Group VI-CRF-EXT N = 6	
Sequence of Conditions	Number of Sessions	Sequence of Conditions	Number of Sessions
CRF	20	CRF	10
VI	14	VI	14
		CRF	10
EXT	18	EXT	10

Group than the mean rate for the VI-CRF-EXT Group. These differences are more apparent in the bar graph also shown in this figure. The bars represent the differences across sessions in mean rate per minute between the two groups. For example, when the mean extinction response rate was higher for the group which had VI-EXT (as the first bar) the bar appeared above the zero line. If the mean extinction response rate was higher for the group programmed for VI-

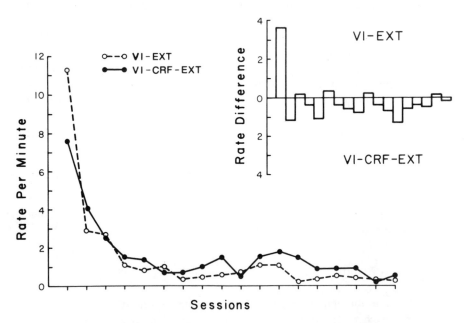

Figure 1   Mean response rate per minute during extinction for Group 1 (VI-EXT) and Group 2 (VI-CRF-EXT) in Study 1, Experiment A. The points on the line graph represent the mean rate for each group for all sessions of extinction. The bar graph depicts the mean rate difference between groups across sessions (higher minus lower rate per session).

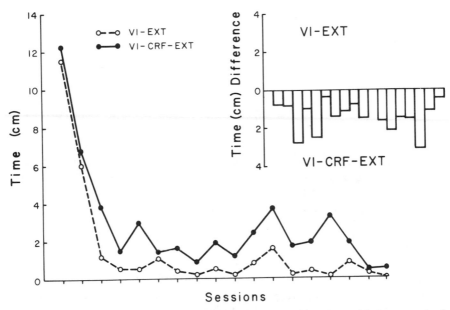

Figure 2   Elapsed time (as measured in cm from cumulative records) from onset of extinction session to onset of the first 1-min interresponse time for Group 1 (VI-EXT) and Group 2 (VI-CRF-EXT) in Study 1, Experiment A. The points on the line graph represent the mean elapsed time for each group for each session. The bar graph depicts the mean time difference between groups across sessions (longer minus shorter time per session).

CRF-EXT (like the second bar), the bar appears below the zero line. Therefore, the bars show an initial higher resistance to extinction for the VI-EXT Group but greater overall resistance to extinction for the VI-CRF-EXT Group.

Because the amount of time required to extinguish a response is an important consideration in behavior modification, time was also used as a dependent measure in the present study. Time was recorded as the number of minutes (measured in centimeters from cumulative records) that elapsed from the onset of each extinction session to the onset of the first occurrence of a 60-sec interresponse time. In Figure 2 it can be seen in the line graph that mean time to this extinction criterion demonstrated small initial differences in extinction resistance between groups. However, as with the dependent measure of rate, the group programmed for VI-EXT again demonstrated a faster descent to its eventual extinction level. This group had a shorter and less variable duration during extinction after the initial response decrement than did the VI-CRF-EXT Group. The bar graph indicates that the VI-CRF-EXT Group had longer session response times during extinction than the VI-EXT Group. In fact, during every session the VI-EXT Group always reached the 60-sec interresponse time faster than the other group.

Experiment B Procedure

In the second experiment, 4 albino rats, all 3-months old, were maintained at 85% free-feeding body weight. The apparatus and shaping procedures were essentially the same as for the first experiment. In this within-subjects design, each subject was programmed for 4 different extinction conditions and 4 conditioning and reconditioning experimental conditions. Subjects 1 and 2 (see Table 2) were programmed for 12 sessions of VI 1-min reinforcement prior to 12 EXT sessions for the first experimental condition and 6 sessions of VI 1-min reinforcement followed by 6 of CRF prior to 12 EXT sessions for the second experimental condition. This entire sequence was then replicated for these 2 subjects. Subjects 3 and 4 were programmed for opposite conditioning and reconditioning sequences, that is, VI followed by CRF preceded the first EXT sessions and VI only preceded the second EXT condition. Subjects 3 and 4 also had the sequence of experimental conditions replicated.

Experiment B Results

The response rates per minute for each session of each of the extinction conditions can be seen in Figure 3. The data across extinction sessions for the different conditions can be read from left to right, with Subject 1 appearing at the top of the graph and Subject 4 appearing at the bottom. During the first extinction condition, Subjects 1 and 2 (VI-EXT) had a higher initial rate, a faster descent to their eventual extinction level, and less variability after this decrease than

TABLE 2

Study 2

Subjects 1 and 2		Subjects 3 and 4	
Sequence of Conditions	Number of Sessions	Sequence of Conditions	Number of Sessions
VI	12	VI	6
		CRF	6
EXT	12	EXT	12
VI	6	VI	12
CRF	6		
EXT	12	EXT	12
VI	12	VI	6
		CRF	6
EXT	12	EXT	12
VI	6	VI	12
CRF	6		
EXT	12	EXT	12

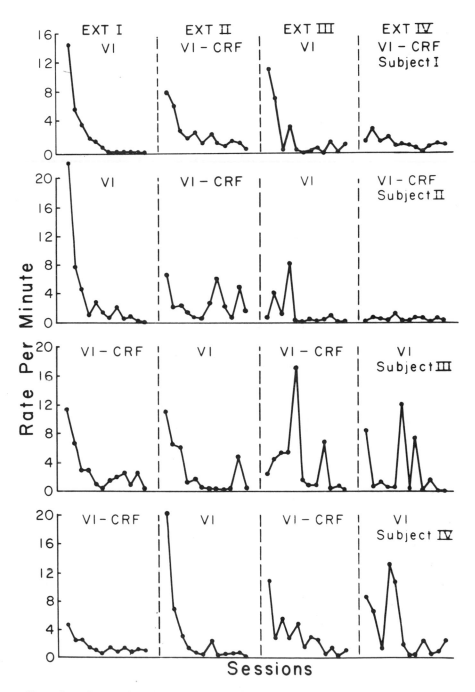

Figure 3   Repeated extinction response rates for Subjects 1 through 4 in Study 1, Experiment B.

subjects 3 and 4 (VI-CRF-EXT). These patterns are also seen when the first extinction condition for Subjects 1 and 2 (VI-EXT) is compared with the second extinction condition (VI-CRF-EXT) for these same subjects. A comparison between the first (VI-CRF-EXT) and second (VI-EXT) extinction conditions for Subjects 3 and 4 somewhat supports the results of Subjects 1 and 2, even though the first extinction for 3 and 4 followed VI and the second followed VI-CRF conditioning. (The exception is Subject 3 whose initial extinction rate after VI reinforcement was not higher, nor did that rate descend faster to its eventual extinction level than after VI followed by CRF. However, the eventual extinction level was lower and less variable after VI-EXT than after CRF-EXT).

Comparisons of the third and fourth extinction conditions, both between and within subjects, did not yield these same results with the possible exception of Subjects 1 and 2. However, the differences between the two conditions for these two subjects in these latter extinction sessions were not as pronounced as between the first and second extinction conditions for all subjects.

Discussion

The results of the two studies demonstrated that extinction responding subsequent to VI-CRF-EXT had a lower initial resistance to extinction, but then a slower descent to the eventual extinction level, and a higher and more variable resistance to extinction (after reaching this extinction level) resulted as compared to the VI-EXT condition. Therefore, there appears to be more overall resistance to extinction subsequent to the interpolation of CRF after intermittent reinforcement than after only intermittent reinforcement.

These results do not at first appear to agree with prior research involving the partial reinforcement effect. In fact, the results are in direct opposition to that body of literature. There are essentially two major differences between this and earlier research. One is the difference in amount of time during which each subject is programmed for each experimental manipulation and the second is in the number of different schedules programmed prior to extinction. As was indicated above none of the previous research utilized conditions involving several days. Therefore, substantiation or refutation of the present results cannot be obtained. However, there are some data which can be considered with reference to the second possible reason for the differences.

If the number of different schedules prior to extinction is a variable for consideration, the present data agree with those of Wertheim and Singer (1964). The experimental conditions in their study had a sequence of two reinforcement schedules prior to extinction. Two schedules preceding extinction produced higher initial extinction resistance, a faster descent to the eventual extinction level, with less extinction resistance and variability of rate after this decrement than only one reinforcement schedule preceding extinction. In the present study the two schedule sequence was VI followed by CRF. In contrast, the schedule combination used by Wertheim and Singer was CRF followed by VI reinforcement. The single schedule condition used by Wertheim and Singer was CRF; for the present studies it was VI. Therefore, perhaps the schedule or sequence of schedules of reinforcement are not as important a variable for affecting resistance to extinction as is the prior experience of the subjects with more than one reinforcement schedule.

From the two experiments presented here, it is possible to say that group and individual analysis experimental designs produced similar results and conclusions. Perhaps this kind of comparison should be pursued more frequently to expand a body of knowledge which could be quite profitable in experimental psychology. There are some experimental questions which are more easily pursued using one or the other design. Therefore, it would be advantageous to know the generality of data resulting from the two different experimental approaches as applied to the same basic question.

Examination of the procedures used in the present studies led to the consideration that a closer laboratory analogue of behavior modification procedures might be accomplished with different reinforcement schedules. Schedules which maintain a "natural" baseline of behavior are probably not a simple variable-interval or any other single reinforcement schedule. The schedule which probably most closely approximates baseline conditions is a random schedule, that is, the behavior in question is sometimes reinforced but other behaviors are also reinforced in the same setting (this schedule is also referred to as a noncontingent reinforcement schedule). Secondly, the modification procedures used to decrease a problem behavior usually include both extinction of the problem behavior and reinforcement of specific other, more desirable behaviors. Therefore, rather than extinction, differential reinforcement of other behavior (DRO) would probably more closely approximate a typical modification procedure. It was not known whether these changes in experimental conditions would produce results different from those of the present study. Therefore, before concluding that programming continuous reinforcement of a problem behavior prior to implementing procedures to decrease that behavior is not an effective behavior modification practice, the next question was examined in the laboratory with closer approximations to the contingencies in the natural environment, that is, Study 1 was systematically replicated in Study 2.

However, on the basis of the above data, it was tentatively concluded that the use of continuous reinforcement as a modification procedure to decrease the resistance to extinction of a problem behavior would not be a recommended procedure for modifying behavior in applied settings.

STUDY 2
Response Elimination by Reinforcement:
Continuous and Differential Reinforcement of Other Behavior
Judith M. LeBlanc and Katherine E. Reuter

Differential reinforcement of other behavior (DRO) is a procedure frequently used in applied behavioral analysis as either a modification procedure for decreasing an undesirable behavior or as a reversal procedure for demonstrating reinforcer control over behaviors previously manipulated. Unlike most procedures used in applied behavioral analysis, minimal animal or human laboratory data are available which closely examine the functional and/or programmatic parameters of DRO. For example, the durability of effect and the efficiency (measured in time) of DRO as compared with other modification procedures is not known. Potential side effects of DRO when used as a reversal procedure have not been examined. It is possible that reinforcing an undesirable behavior (using DRO for experimental reversals) may produce results contrary to the ultimate experimental goal of increasing a desirable behavior. It could, for example, make reacquisition of the desired behavior, after a reversal, difficult to achieve.

Applied behavioral analysis research, especially that conducted in applied environments, cannot, in reality, avoid the use of DRO in typical ABA reversals. Because of the complexities of interactions between an organism and the available reinforcers in the environment, extinction (as produced in the laboratory) is almost nonexistent. For example, extinction or nonreinforcement of one behavior does not preclude, for other behaviors, the availability of that reinforcer which is no longer available for the behavior-on-extinction. Nor does it preclude the availability of other reinforcers for either the behavior-on-extinction or other behaviors. An example of this might be the teacher who no longer attends to a child when the child is out of seat. The teacher does not withdraw all attention from the child, but only during those out-of-seat times. It is also plausible that the child will be reinforced by peers while out of seat, as well as while seated. Therefore, extinction, in its purest form, is almost impossible to employ in the natural environment. More likely, the procedures used to increase and/or decrease behavior in the natural environment are in some way related to the procedure which has become known as DRO. That is, it is more probable that desirable or incompatible behaviors are reinforced simultaneously with the application of extinction for a specified response.

To encompass all the definitional and usage variations of DRO in experimental literature, one must accept a global definition of the term. For example, it might be best described as reinforcement of something other than a behavior which had been previously reinforced. Reynolds (1961) introduced the term DRO as reinforcement for not emitting a previously reinforced response for x period of time. He further specified that if that response were emitted the time interval between reinforcers would reset. Uhl and Garcia (1969) suggested Reynold's description should be termed omission training, (reinforcement for omitting a previously reinforced response) and that DRO should be reserved for reinforcement of any response other than that which had been previously reinforced. Considering these differences, along with Schoenfeld and Farmer's (1970) postulation that not responding should be considered a response, it becomes rapidly clear why DRO has been used to encompass a variety of procedures. Nevertheless, whichever definition one accepts, DRO is definitely a widely used procedure in applied behavioral analysis, and, therefore, this study, and those which follow represent some initial examinations of some of the parameters and potential side effects of DRO as a modification procedure.

The two experiments encompassed in this study were originally based upon the assumption that resistance to extinction is greater subsequent to partial than to continuous reinforcement. It would, therefore, seem at least plausible that problem behaviors, currently maintained by some partial reinforcement schedule, might be made less resistant to extinction if they were shifted to continuous reinforcement just prior to the implementation of extinction. However, results of Likely (1958) and LeBlanc (1970; also Study 1 this chapter) indicated, at least with infrahumans, this does not seem to be the case. If a concern is the functionality of these laboratory results for applied usage, the question might better be stated as: can behaviors be made less resistant to response decrement during DRO by the interpolation of continuous reinforcement prior to implementing DRO (rather than extinction)? Thus, it is proposed, because DRO procedures are more analogous to those which pertain in applied environments, that the interpolation of CRF prior to DRO as an experimental procedure is more clinically relevant than its interpolation prior to extinction. Also, it was felt that the use of children as subjects provided a more appropriate analogue for extension to applied environments.

Procedures

In this study, both experiments (A and B) compared preschool children's barpress response decrement during conditions of DRO subsequent to VR 6 only and subsequent to VR 6 followed by CRF. The first experiment (A) interpolated 4 sessions of CRF prior to DRO, the second, 1 session of CRF.

In both experiments, 3- and 4-year-old preschool children were trained to push a telegraph key on a response box which had a blue light over the key during the session and red light over the key prior to the onset and at the termination of each session. The children were instructed to press the key to obtain marbles and a demonstration of marble delivery was provided. If they obtained 50 marbles, enough to fill a small paper cup, they could trade them for a small toy of their choice. All experimental conditions and data recording were electromechanically programmed. After the first training session, the experimenter was not present in the experimental room but watched the children through a one-way mirror from an adjacent room which housed the electromechanical equipment.

Experimental sessions lasted until the child received 50 marbles or until 10 minutes had elapsed. This either/or procedure for concluding the sessions was employed because some children might continue responding for long periods of time during DRO before responding decreased enough to receive 50 marbles. Long experimental sessions had in other studies resulted in decreased response efficiency. Additionally, long sessions with few reinforcers, which initial sessions of DRO might create, previously resulted in refusals to come to the next day's experimental session. Only in the first or second session of DRO did some children not meet the 50-marble criterion before the end of 10 minutes.

Variable ratio 6 (VR 6) sessions were programmed for the children to receive 1 marble on the average of every 6 responses. The ratio ranges were from 2 to 10 responses. During CRF the subjects were to receive 1 marble for every response. However, because most children had extremely high response rates and because the marble dispenser did not operate at these high rates, reinforcement was delivered once for approximately every 1.5 responses. DRO was programmed according to Reynold's (1961) definition, in that every 5 sec of no responding resulted in the delivery of a reinforcer. If the child responded during the 5 sec, the 5-sec interval was reset. Therefore, the reinforcement-reinforcement intervals and the response-reinforcement intervals were the same.

All children initially received four sessions of VR 6. A few children were eliminated from the experiment during these first 4 sessions because they either had extremely low response rates or refused to press the key. Each experiment used 10 children as its population; 5 in each of 2 groups. The groups were matched according to response rate during the first 4 sessions of VR 6.

In the first modification condition (see Table 3) in Experiment A (top), Group 1 was programmed for 10 sessions of DRO 5 sec and Group 2 for 4 sessions of CRF, then 6 sessions of DRO 5 sec. If the number of CRF sessions had to be added to the total number of sessions required to decrease a response in a modification procedure, then the interpolation of CRF, as a procedure to more rapidly decrease responding, would not be functional since it would require more time overall. Therefore, the number of CRF plus DRO sessions for one group equalled the total number of DRO sessions programmed for the other group in the 2 modification conditions. Both groups then resumed responding during 4 sessions of VR 6. Subsequently, the opposite modification condition was programmed for each group. That is, Group 1 had CRF interpolated prior to DRO and Group 2 did not. In this experiment, one of the subjects in Group 1 and two in Group 2 were not available for the last 4 sessions of VR 6. However, the remaining subjects provided a within-groups comparison of response reacquisition subsequent to 6 (with CRF interpolated) versus 10 (with no interpolation) sessions of DRO. This design, therefore, provided both within and between subjects analyses of the data.

Experiment B (see bottom of Table 3) was essentially the same as Experiment A. The only differences were that only one session of CRF was interpolated prior to DRO rather than four as in the previous experiment, and the total number of sessions in each of the DRO modification conditions was seven rather than ten. Again, all subjects were programmed (in reverse order for the two groups) for both interpolation of CRF and no interpolation. That is, Group 1 was programmed first for seven sessions of DRO with no interpolation of CRF and then for one session of CRF followed by six sessions of DRO. Group 2 was programmed for opposite modification conditions.

TABLE 3

Study 2

Group 1 N = 5		Group 2 N = 5	
Sequence of Conditions	Number of Sessions	Sequence of Conditions	Number Sessions
Experiment A			
VR 6	4	VR 6	4
		CRF	4
DRO 5-sec	10	DRO 5-sec	6
VR 6	4	VR 6	4
CRF	4		
DRO 5-sec	6	DRO 5-sec	10
VR 6	4	VR 6	4
Experiment B			
VR 6	4	VR 6	4
		CRF	1
DRO 5-sec	7	DRO 5-sec	6
VR 6	4	VR 6	4
CRF	1		
DRO 5-sec	6	DRO 5-sec	7
VR 6	4	VR 6	4

Results

The interpolation of four sessions of CRF prior to DRO in both the first and second modification condition in Experiment A (see Fig. 4), did not enhance the efficiency of DRO as a procedure for decreasing responding. In fact, the four CRF sessions delayed response decrement to the point that the group not programmed for CRF interpolation in both modification conditions had reached near-zero levels of responding before the group programmed for interpolation began sessions of DRO. This point is important if one is considering the use of these techniques in applied settings. For this reason, Experiment B (see bottom graph, Fig. 4) was executed with only one session of CRF interpolated prior to the implementation of DRO. In the first DRO condition, the interpolation of one session of CRF had little, if any, effect upon the number of sessions required to reach near-zero levels of responding. In the second DRO condition, the effects were similar to those in Experiment A. The interpolation of CRF for Group 1 resulted in a slower response decrement during DRO than for Group 2 who had no interpolation in this condition.

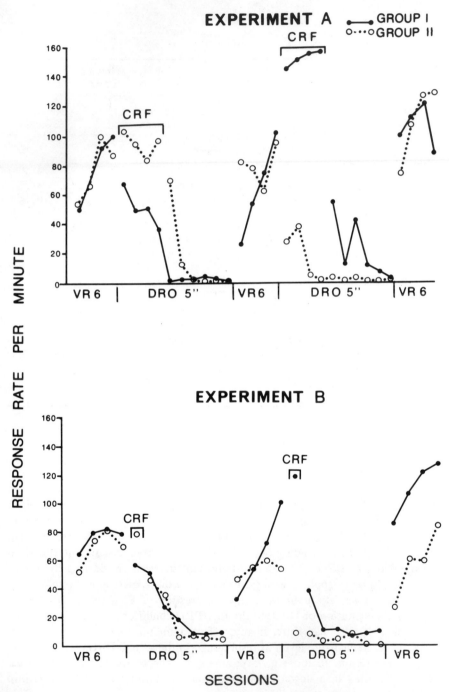

Figure 4   Mean responses per minute for Groups 1 and 2 in Study 2, Experiments A and B.

A comparison of response reacquisition during the second and third VR 6 conditions in Experiment A (see top graph, Fig. 4) indicated that after 10 sessions of DRO and no interpolation of CRF, response levels were initially moderate and ascended rapidly to levels higher than previous VR 6 conditions. However, after interpolation of CRF and only 6 sessions of DRO responding immediately resumed to levels equal to or higher than previous VR 6 conditions. These differences also occurred subsequent to the first DRO condition of Experiment B when only one session of CRF was interpolated, but did not occur subsequent to the second DRO condition.

When comparing the within-group results in Experiments A and B, it was found that the between groups results were substantiated with one exception. Group 1, Experiment B, showed faster response decrement subsequent to the interpolation of CRF. However, for this group CRF interpolation occurred as the second response decrement condition and thus faster response decrement might be expected.

Discussion

In summary, it appears that the interpolation of CRF to enhance the response decrement properties of DRO would not be a recommended behavior modification procedure. If anything, such procedures seem only to delay the business of decreasing undesired behaviors. Further, if DRO is used as a reversal procedure, it appears the number of DRO sessions should be minimized to those needed for adequate reversal demonstration. This is because reacquisition of the desired response may take longer the more DRO sessions are programmed in the reversal. However, the slower reacquisition phenomenon is a plus for the use of DRO as a modification procedure to decrease undesired responses, because in this case the more permanent and stable the change, the better. Since DRO procedures are frequently involved in most reversal designs, perhaps all reversals should attempt to include as few sessions as possible so as to not deter response reacquisition subsequent to the reversal. A two or three data point condition is convincing especially if the demonstrated behavioral differences are great.

A comparison of these results with those obtained in Study 1 leads one to the same conclusion regarding the interpolation of CRF as a modification procedure designed to enhance response decrement in either DRO or extinction. However, the results of this study are not the same as those obtained in Study 1. Interpolation of CRF prior to DRO did not result in lower initial response rates and slower response decrease across sessions to eventual extinction levels as it did when interpolated prior to extinction. The differences in results could be attributed to any number of variables such as differences in populations, in schedules, in response topography, and in reinforcement. Despite this, the important outcome of each study is that programming CRF prior to the implementation of response decrement procedures does not appear to be a viable alternative for purposes of enhancing the effectiveness of those procedures.

STUDY 3
Variable Differential Reinforcement of Other Behavior (VDRO):
Its Effectiveness as a Modification Procedure
Katherine E. Reuter and Judith M. LeBlanc

Differential reinforcement of other behavior (DRO) is an effective procedure for decreasing specified behaviors. This effectiveness has been demonstrated both in the use of DRO as a modification procedure to decrease undesirable behaviors (Bostow & Bailey, 1969; Doubros & Daniels, 1966) and in its use as a reversal procedure for deomonstrating reinforcer control over previously manipulated behaviors (Goetz, Holmberg, & LeBlanc, 1975; Reynolds & Risley, 1968; Sherman, 1965).

Most studies which compared the efficiency of DRO with other response decrement procedures (for example, extinction), were conducted in infrahuman laboratories (Davis & Bitterman, 1971; Uhl & Garcia, 1969; Zeiler, 1971). These studies always employed a fixed time during which no response was to occur as the criterion for reinforcement during DRO. Further, these intervals were usually short (e.g., 10, 20 or 30 sec).

Systematic application of specific timed contingencies is more difficult to obtain in applied research than in the laboratory where intervals can be programmed with electromechanical equipment. Therefore, a time interval during DRO in applied settings might not always be a precisely fixed number of seconds. The time for no responding during DRO in applied research might more adequately be described in terms of variable intervals. These programmed differences imply that the extension of laboratory results to application in the natural environment should be undertaken with some caution since there might be different end results.

To examine differences in potential outcome, the present study compared response decrement during fixed-interval DRO (DRO) and variable-interval DRO (VDRO). This study was a follow-up of Study 2 (first presented by Le Blanc & Reuter, 1972) and the general procedures were essentially the same.

Procedures

Two groups of 5 preschool children, aged 3 to 5 years, were trained to push a telegraph key to obtain a cupful (50) of marbles. If the subject obtained *all* marbles within a 10-min session, they could be traded for a toy chosen before the beginning of the experimental session. In addition, a token, redeemable in the preschool classroom, was earned daily for participating in the research, regardless of the number of marbles obtained.

After a brief demonstration and shaping period (4-5 marbles), the subject was left alone in a small room in front of the response panel while the experimenter observed the sessions through a one-way mirror from an adjacent room

TABLE 4

Study 4

Group 1 N = 5		Group 2 N = 5	
Sequence of Conditions	Number of Sessions	Sequence of Conditions	Number of Sessions
VR 6	4	VR 6	4
DRO 5-sec	10	VDRO approx. 5-sec	10
VR 6	4	VR 6	4
		VDRO[a]	6

[a]Subjects 1 and 2 only

which housed the electromechanical equipment used to program the contingencies and record the data.

As seen in Table 4, all subjects were intially programmed for 4 sessions of variable ratio 6 reinforcement (VR 6). Mean responses per minute revealed an ascending response rate across sessions for both groups, which leveled off at 100 responses per min.

Group 1 was then programmed for 10 sessions of DRO, during which marbles were delivered every 5 sec if the subject did not respond. The interval prescribed for "no responding" reset when either a response was made or when a marble was delivered. Group 2 was programmed for a variable-interval 5-sec DRO. The intervals between reinforcers were systematically randomized to provide an average interval of 5.3 to 5.5 sec, with a range of 2 to 10.

Results

Group 1's response rate during fixed DRO 5 sec decreased to near-zero by the fifth session (see Fig. 5). The group data are representative of all subjects in this group. One subject stopped responding by the second session; two, by the third session; and one each by the fourth and fifth session. In contrast, the mean response rate of Group 2 never decreased to the near-zero level, and the decrease which did occur was gradual and variable. Responding of two subjects in this group did reach the near-zero level by the fifth session of VDRO and one additional subject reached this level by the sixth session. The remaining two subjects in the group never responded at the near-zero response rate.

The individual data for these two subjects, whose resistance to response decrement during VDRO was great, are shown in Fig. 6. The initial VR 6 rate of Subject 1 averaged 122 responses per min, and of Subject 2, 64 responses per min. Despite this difference, their responding during VDRO was very similar.

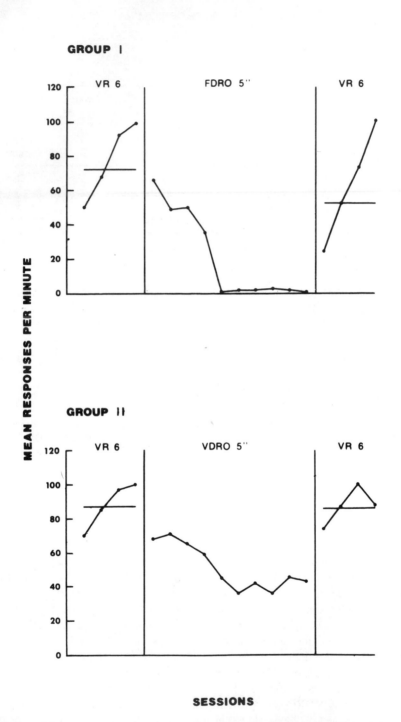

Figure 5   Mean responses per minute across sessions for Group 1 (FDRO) and Group 2 (VDRO) in Study 3.

208

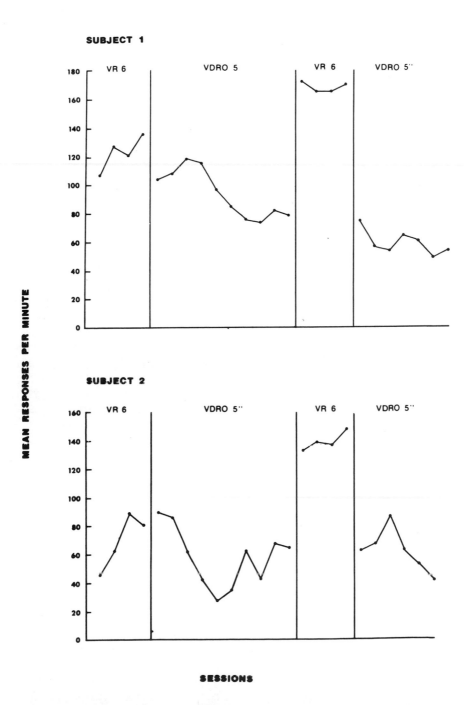

Figure 6　Mean responses per minute across sessions for Subject 1 and Subject 2 in Study 3.

A return to VR 6 resulted in higher response rates for both subjects. Past re-search (LeBlanc & Reuter, 1972; also Study 2) has shown that resistance to re-sponse decrement decreased across subsequent applications of DRO. These results were similar to those obtained for repeated extinction (Bullock & Smith, 1953). To test this finding for variable DRO, both subjects were again program-med for the VDRO contingency. Though their response rates during the first session were lower than during the first session of the first application of VDRO, response rates across sessions were similar to those during the first application.

Response patterns during DRO and VDRO were different as shown by the cumulative records for two Group 1 subjects during the first session of fixed interval DRO (see Fig. 7). These records show that the subjects emitted a burst of responses, paused the required 5 sec, received a marble, emitted another burst of responses, paused, received a marble, etc. Experimenter observations also found that the DRO subjects exhibited rhythmic, "superstitious" behaviors, such as tapping the response panel, rocking, etc.

Two examples of cumulative responding by subjects during VDRO are shown in the bottom records. The cumulative record for Subject B4 was typical of all of the subjects. Despite the fact that they stopped responding long enough to obtain 5-10 marbles, they again emitted long runs of responses before pausing. These long response runs appeared to occur most often during the longer inter-vals of no responding, but not always. The record for one child whose respond-ing was highly resistant to extinction (Subject B1), did show a response pattern similar to that emitted by the fixed interval DRO subjects. This occurred in the 20th session during the second VDRO application. This was the only VDRO subject to demonstrate any response pattern and it occurred only after consider-able exposure to the schedule. However, in this subject's case, this pattern or chain of behavior served to maintain the rate of response rather than to reduce it as in fixed interval DRO.

Group 1, which responded at a minimal rate for the last six DRO sessions, recovered its baseline rate gradually (see Fig. 5). However, Group 2 showed no resistance to reconditioning (responding resumed immediately). This was probably an indirect function of variable DRO — response rates during the previous VDRO, were high and thus response resumption began at a higher rate in the subsequent VR 6 condition.

Discussion

In summary, response decrement occurred more rapidly in conditions of fixed-interval DRO than in variable interval DRO (VDRO) and individual response rate patterns did not appear to be good predictors of successfully decreasing responding during either DRO or VDRO. Responding was totally eliminated for all subjects programmed for DRO but for two of the five subjects programmed for VDRO responding was never totally eliminated. This could be due to the fact

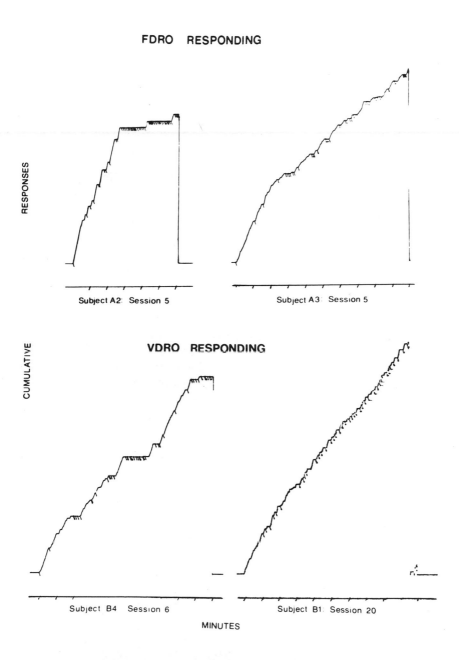

Figure 7 Sample cumulative response records for FDRO responding (Subjects A2 and A3 on top) and VDRO responding (Subjects B4 and B1 on bottom) in Study 3.

that "superstitious" responding developed for all subjects programmed for fixed interval DRO and the accidental reinforcement of this other (superstitious) behavior appeared to facilitate response decrement. Past studies have indicated that the specification of an alternative response to be reinforced increases response decrement during extinction (Holz, Azrin, & Allyon, 1963; Leitenberg, Rawson, & Bath, 1970).

In conclusion, varying 3-5 sec the interval of no responding required to obtain reinforcement within a session substantially decreased the effectiveness of DRO for eliminating the key-press responding of preschool children in a laboratory setting. Therefore, it would appear that the variability of interval length, which frequently occurs in the application of DRO in applied settings, could be detrimental to the effectiveness of using DRO to decrease or eliminate responding. However, as was earlier indicated, in applied behavior analysis, the "other" response to be differentially reinforced is often specified. As indicated here, it appears that even when specific "other" behavior develops superstitiously, response decrement in DRO is facilitated. Thus, it is possible that the success of VDRO, as used in applied settings, can be attributed to the specification of the "other" response to be reinforced which overrides the potentially negative effects of the imprecise timing involved in its application.

STUDY 4

Response Decrement and Resumption:
A Comparison of Responding During and After Differential
Reinforcement of Other Behavior with that
During and After Extinction
Donald N. Miller and Judith M. LeBlanc

In applied environments, a behavior will sometimes result in contingent reinforcement, and sometimes not. Similarly, the same reinforcement might be contingent upon other behaviors. It is in this seemingly chaotic state of affairs that applied behavioral analysis techniques successfully change behavior. Laboratory researchers seldom consider how analogs of the applied environment might be drawn, in spite of the fact that applied experimental analysis procedures draw heavily upon the results from laboratory research. To be analogous to reinforcement as it operates in applied environments, research on schedules of reinforcement should take into consideration the many potential discriminative and reinforcing stimuli that may be associated with a single response or many responses. Of the many single and combined schedules of reinforcement often used in the laboratory, one which seems most analogous to occurrences of reinforcement in the natural environment is the concurrent schedule (Bijou, 1970). Combinations of schedules can simultaneously provide both contingent (response-dependent), as well as uncorrelated (response-independent) reinforcement of a specific response or of many different responses. In the laboratory both schedules could be programmed for the same or different response keys. If they are programmed for the same response key, then the organism can potentially receive reinforcers for responding or while not responding. Thus, in this case not responding takes on characteristics of a response (Schoenfeld & Farmer, 1970).

Although some research with infrahuman organisms has compared response decrement during DRO and EXT after a single schedule of reinforcement (Topping, Pickering, & Jackson, 1971b; Uhl & Garcia, 1969; Uhl & Sherman, 1971), these comparisons have not been examined with concurrent schedules of reinforcement preceding the response decrement procedures. Since it was felt that the use of concurrent schedules in laboratory research was more analogous to the behavioral and consequent situations found in applied settings, and since attempts to decrease behavior in applied settings have utilized both DRO and EXT, it was felt that a systematic replication of the research by Uhl and Garcia would provide results more applicable to the building of a technology of applied behavior analysis.

This experiment used concurrent variable-interval 1-min, uncorrelated variable-time 1-min schedules of reinforcement to establish an initial rate of responding on one lever prior to a comparison of response decrement during differential reinforcement of other behavior (DRO) and extinction (EXT). The concurrent schedules operated simultaneously on one response lever and thus functionally provided an uncorrelated schedule of reinforcement.

TABLE 5

Study 4

Group 1 N = 6		Group 2 N = 6	
Sequence of Conditions	Number of Sessions	Sequence of Conditions	Number of Sessions
Concurrent VI 1 min, uncorrelated VT 1 min	15	Concurrent VI 1 min, uncorrelated VT 1 min	15
DRO 20-sec	5	EXT	5
Concurrent VI 1 min, uncorrelated VT 1 min	15	Concurrent VI 1 min, uncorrelated VT 1 min	15
EXT	5	DRO 20-sec	5
Concurrent VI 1 min, uncorrelated VT 1 min	15	Concurrent VI 1 min, uncorrelated VT 1 min	15

Procedures

Twelve male, hooded rats maintained at 85% of their free-feeding weight were run 5 days a week, 30 min a day. After 15 sessions of concurrent VI 1 min, uncorrelated VT 1 min, the subjects were assigned to 1 of 2 experimental groups, matched in terms of high and low response rates (see Table 5). Group 1 was then programmed for 5 sessions of a 20-sec DRO while Group 2 was programmed for 5 sessions of EXT. During DRO, if no response was made during the 20-sec interval, a pellet of food was delivered at the termination of the interval. If a response was made during this time, the interval for not responding was reset for another 20-sec without delivering a pellet. Therefore, the response-reinforcer interval and the reinforcer-reinforcer interval were the same. The experimental conditions were for Group 1, concurrent, DRO, concurrent, EXT, concurrent; and for Group 2, concurrent, EXT, concurrent, DRO, concurrent. Thus, results could be compared both within and between groups.

Results

Figure 8 compares response decrement during DRO and EXT. These percentages were calculated by dividing each subject's rate for each session during DRO and EXT by the mean rate for that subject's preceding concurrent schedules rate. By taking the mean of the percentages of the subjects in each group, the group percents were obtained. The line graphs indicate these percentages and the bar graphs indicate the difference between the two groups across sessions. The difference between the groups is the absolute difference in mean response rate per session between Group 1 and Group 2. The top graphs show decreased responding during DRO for Group 1 and during EXT for Group 2 in the first response decrement condition. The bottom graphs show decreased responding during the second response decrement condition, that is, during EXT for Group 1 and during DRO for Group 2. These data indicate that a group programmed for EXT always demonstrated somewhat greater resistance to response decrement than a group programmed for DRO. These results occurred in both response decrement conditions. An analysis of variance, based on Edwards (1953) trend analysis of trial means: different treatments, resulted in significant trials effects at the .01 level. Square root transformations of the data resulted in significant Main effects as well as significant Groups X Trials interaction effects at the .05 level for the second response decrement condition, but not the first.

Figure 9 shows the elapsed time to the first minute of no responding for each group for each session of the two-response decrement conditions. The line graphs indicate elapsed time, and the bar graphs indicate the absolute differences between the two groups. In the top graphs, for the first response decrement condition, Group 2, programmed for EXT, had somewhat more resistance to

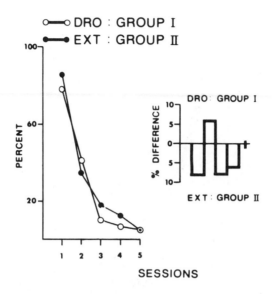

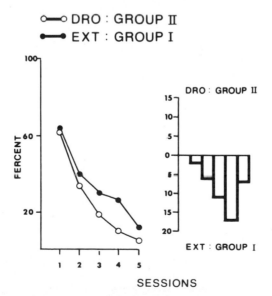

Figure 8   Mean DRO and extinction response rates as a percentage of the mean response rate during the previous concurrent schedule in Study 4.

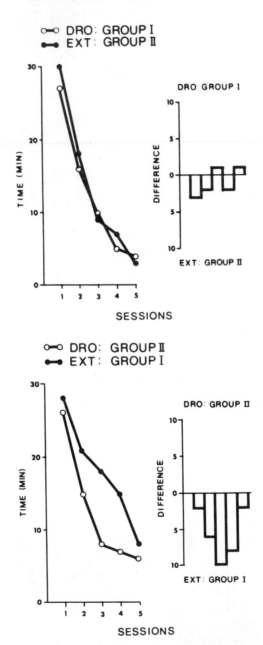

Figure 9   Elapsed time in minutes to the first minute of no responding for Groups 1 and 2 in the two response decrement conditions. The line graphs indicate elapsed time in minutes, and the bar graphs indicate the absolute difference between the two groups in Study 4.

216

response decrement than Group 1, programmed for DRO. The bottom graphs, for the second response decrement condition, show that Group 1, programmed for EXT, had much greater resistance to response decrement than Group 2, programmed for DRO. The main effect of Groups and the interaction effect of Groups X Trials were not significant for the first or second response decrement condition. The trials effect was significant at the .01 level. Log transformations of the data resulted in significant Group X Trials interaction effects at the .05 level for the second response decrement condition.

In Figure 10 the line graphs show the percentages for both groups for the first 5 sessions of each of the 2 response resumption conditions, that is, during the second and third concurrent schedules conditions. The bar graphs show the absolute differences between these percentages for the same 5 sessions. In the first response resumption condition (top graphs), Group 1 previously was programmed for DRO; Group 2 for EXT. In the second response resumption condition (bottom graphs), Group 1 was previously programmed for EXT, Group 2 for DRO. In the second concurrent schedules condition (the first response resumption condition), Group 1 showed the greatest resistance to response resumption (top graphs). In the second response resumption condition, Group 2 showed the greatest resistance to response resumption. Therefore, the group previously programmed for DRO took longer to resume responding during concurrent schedules conditions than the group previously programmed for EXT. An analysis of variance for the first response resumption condition showed significant main effect of Groups and significant Trials effects at the .05 and .01 levels, respectively. For both response resumption conditions, the interaction effect of Groups X trials was not significant and the Trials effects were significant at the .01 level.

Discussion

These results demonstrated that response decrement during EXT was slower than during DRO. They are in agreement with Topping, Pickering, & Jackson (1971b), though they are not in agreement with results of Uhl & Garcia (1969), who found response decrement faster during EXT than during DRO using a time-to-no-responding measure. The differences could be attributed to the use of different training schedules. Uhl and Garcia used a variable-interval 30-sec contingent schedule of reinforcement prior to implementing response decrement conditions instead of the concurrent VI 1-min, VT 1-min schedules of reinforcement used in the present experiment. The uncorrelated component of the concurrent schedules may have facilitated faster response decrement during DRO than EXT. That is, previous response rates were probably lower during the concurrent schedules than during Uhl and Garcia's VI 30-sec schedule. Therefore, delivery of reinforcement during DRO could occur sooner with low rate responding.

Response Resumption as Per Cent of Previous Concurrent Schedules

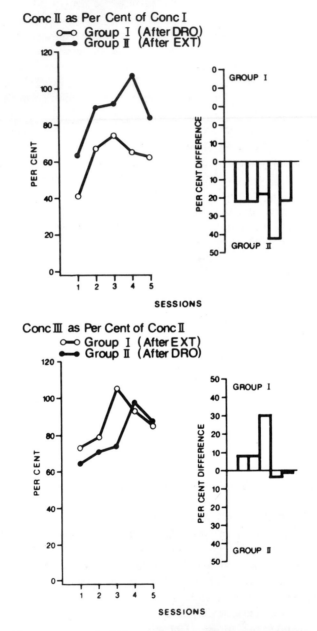

Figure 10   Mean response rate during reacquisition of concurrent schedule responding as a percentage of the mean response rate during the previous exposure to the concurrent schedule in Study 4.

The present results seem to indicate that DRO might be more effective than EXT as a modification procedure for eliminating undesirable behaviors in the natural environment since response decrement occurs more rapidly. Furthermore, DRO probably better represents response decrement procedures used in the natural environment, as it is difficult, if not impossible, to totally remove all reinforcers for all responses from a person's environment. Another problem to be dealt with in the natural environment is that many uncontrolled reinforcers may exercise control over an undesirable behavior when only EXT is used. DRO enables us to reinforce any specified, more appropriate, behavior that may occur other than the target behavior that is to be eliminated.

DRO was also demonstrated to be more resistant to response resumption. These results are similar to those of Uhl and Garcia (1969). This possibly occurred in the present experiment because the concurrent schedules contained an uncorrelated (response-independent) component. Therefore, the reinforcement which occurred during periods of no responding in the concurrent component might have been similar enough to DRO that it maintained a low rate of responding.

DRO would again seem more desirable than EXT as a procedure for decreasing undesirable behaviors because of its more durable effects, as evidenced by the slower response resumption. However, the use of DRO for an experimental reversal, especially in applied environments, could be detrimental to both the subject and to the intentions of the behavior modifier, because it might prevent or delay resumption of the desirable behavior after the reversal has been effected.

STUDY 5
Interaction of Variable-Interval DRO with DRL and VR
Response Decrement and Reacquisition
Gary L. Schilmoeller and Judith M. LeBlanc

Differential reinforcement of other behavior (DRO) involves the reduction of a target behavior by a combination of extinction of the target behavior and reinforcement of any, or some specified other behavior (Zeiler, 1972). DRO has been used in applied studies as an experimental control procedure (Brigham & Sherman, 1968; Goetz, Holmberg, & LeBlanc, 1975; Reynolds & Risley, 1968; Stolz & Wolf, 1969) and as a behavior modification procedure to decrease inappropriate behavior (Bostow & Bailey, 1969; Corte, Wolf, & Locke, 1971; Twardosz, & Sajwaj, 1972). In both of these situations, rapid response decrement is desirable, but rapid reacquisition after DRO would not be equally desirable. In an experimental reversal-control procedure, rapid reacquisition of appropriate behavior after DRO would be advantageous, but more durable suppression of the behavior would be desired if DRO were used as a behavior modification procedure.

A number of laboratory investigations examined parameters of DRO, including the effectiveness of DRO compared with extinction on response decrement (Miller & LeBlanc, 1972; Study 4, this chapter; Topping, Pickering, & Jackson, 1971b; Uhl & Garcia, 1969; Uhl & Sherman, 1971) and the effectiveness of DRO on response decrement after different histories (Davidson & Walker, 1970; LeBlanc & Reuter, 1972; Study 2, this chapter; Topping, Pickering, & Jackson, 1971a). Systematic application of timed reinforcement in applied settings is more difficult than in these laboratory settings. In fact, some applied studies reported differentially reinforcing other than the target behavior on a variable-interval basis (Reynolds & Risley, 1968; Twardosz & Sajwaj, 1972). Therefore, laboratory results based on fixed-interval DRO might not be relevant to applied DRO based on variable intervals. When examining a laboratory analogue of variable-interval DRO, Reuter and LeBlanc (1972; Study 3, this chapter) demonstrated that DRO presented on a variable-interval basis is not always successful in producing response elimination. In the above cited Reuter and LeBlanc study, fixed-interval DRO (DRO) resulted in response elimination for all subjects, while variable-interval DRO (VDRO) did not. Although Reuter and LeBlanc indicated response rate prior to implementation of DRO or VDRO was not a good predictor of successful and rapid response decrement, it should also be noted that very low rate responders were eliminated from the study. To look at one variable of response rate differences prior to the implementation of response decrement procedures, the present study examined response decrement during variable-interval DRO (VDRO) subsequent to histories of high rate and low rate responding. A second purpose of the study was to assess reacquisition of baseline responding subsequent to VDRO conditioning.

TABLE 6

Study 5

Group 1: Initial High Rate History N = 4		Group 2: Initial Low Rate History N = 4	
Sequence of Conditions	Number of Sessions*	Sequence of Conditions	Number of Sessions*
VR 10	*	DRL 5-sec	*
VDRO 10-sec	*	VDRO 10-sec	*
VR 10	*	DRL 5-sec	*
DRL 5-sec (N=2)	*	VR 10	*
VDRO 10-sec (N=2)	*	VDRO 10-sec	*
DRL 5-sec (N=2)	*	VR 10	*

*Number of sessions in any conditions was based on a predetermined criterion of stability for each subject.

Procedures

Eight preschool children were trained to press a telegraph key and were reinforced with marbles. Sessions lasted 6 minutes or until the subject received 25
marbles which, at the end of the session, were required for exchange for a
previously selected toy. All subjects were initially programmed for either a
variable ratio reinforcement or a differential reinforcement of low rate responding schedule (see Table 6). For the variable ratio subjects, a marble was delivered
after an average of 10 responses, with a range of 5 to 15 responses per reinforcer.
Subjects programmed for differential reinforcement of low rate were reinforced
for the first response after 5 sec elapsed from the delivery of the previous reinforcer, if not more than two responses occurred during the 5-sec interval. A third
response within the 5-sec interval reset the interval. (Hereafter, VR 10 will be
referred to as the high rate history and DRL 5-sec will be called the low rate
history.)

Four subjects were intially programmed for VR (high rate history) and four
for DRL (low rate history). After reaching a predetermined stability criterion[3]
on their respective baselines, all subjects were programmed for VDRO in which
they were differentially reinforced for not responding according to variable
intervals averaging 10 sec, with a range of 2.5 sec to 20 sec. Any response within
a particular interval reset the timer for that interval. The variable-interval DRO
(VDRO) condition was continued until the subject had 2 consecutive sessions of
1 or fewer responses per minute, or had continued for at least 10 sessions without reaching the 2 consecutive sessions of 1 or fewer responses per minute
criterion.

When the subjects met the VDRO criterion, or did not stop responding after
at least 10 sessions, they were programmed for their original baseline schedule
to examine reacquisition. Subsequent to the first VDRO and return to baseline
conditions, two of the four subjects, who first were programmed for the high rate
history, were now programmed for the low rate history and then a second
VDRO condition. Two of the subjects initially programmed for VR were discontinued because they were no longer available since it was the end of their
school year. All four subjects intially programmed for DRL were now presented
VR and then VDRO. Therefore, irrespective of sequence of conditions, all eight
subjects received the VR VDRO conditions and the six subjects received the
DRL-VDRO conditions. Thus, an individual analysis design was used, with the
sequence of schedules counterbalanced across subjects to provide a between-
subject control for the effects of different initial histories.

---

[3]Criterion responding was required before changing from DRL 5-sec or VR 10 schedules
to VDRO 10-sec. For subjects on VR 10, after the first four sessions the highest and lowest
point of VR responding were established and stability consisted of four consecutive sessions
within these points and with a mean of at least 75 resp/min. Criterion responding during
DRL 5-sec consisted of four consecutive sessions with a rate of 30 or fewer resp/min.

Results

Of the 6 subjects who received the low rate history follwed by VDRO, 83%, or 5 of 6, successfully met the 2 consecutive sessions of one or fewer responses per minute in fewer than 10 DRO sessions (see Fig. 11). Only 50%, 4 of 8, of the subjects who had the high rate history and then VDRO met the same criterion. For the four subjects who stopped responding during VDRO, when VDRO followed high rate responding, the mean number of sessions to criterion was 7.75, with a range of 7 to 9 (see Fig. 12). In VDRO after low rate responding, the mean number of sessions for the 5 subjects was 6, with a range of 4 to 8. Therefore, the mean sessions to near zero responding during VDRO for subjects who showed response decrement were fewer after low baseline response rates than after high baseline rates.

Subjects Meeting Criterion

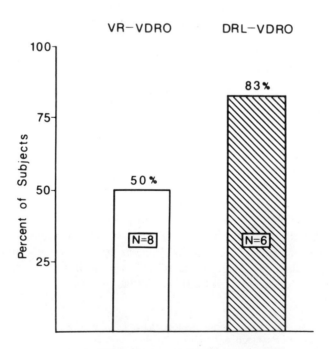

Figure 11   Percentage of subjects meeting VDRO criterion, grouped according to prior history in Study 5.

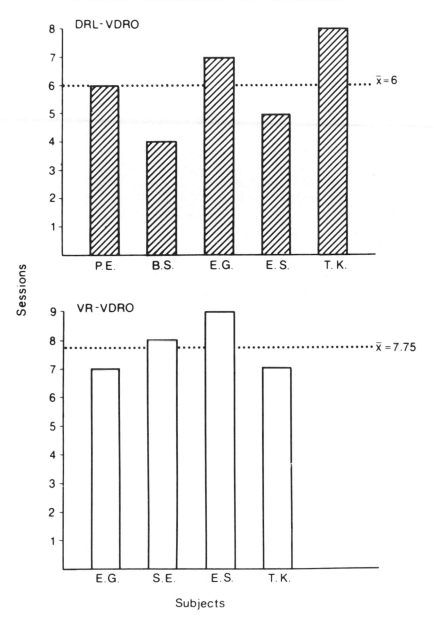

Figure 12   Number of sessions to VDRO criterion for each subject according to prior history in Study 5.

No differential effects on reacquisition of baseline responding were observed regardless of which baseline schedule immediately followed the VDRO conditions. However, of the four subjects who were initially programmed for the low-rate history, three did not acquire high-rate responding after the long history of reinforcement for low rate and then for no responding in VDRO. Sessions of continuous reinforcement or verbal shaping were interspersed to shape the high-rate responding.

These results replicated those of Reuter and LeBlanc in which VDRO was not always successful as a response decrement procedure. However, in this study, baseline histories were found to be good indicators of the probable success of VDRO. Subjects who initially responded at a low rate were more likely to stop responding during VDRO than subjects who responded at a high baseline rate. Therefore, VDRO might be recommended as a response decrement procedure for low rate, but not for high rate behaviors, unless the aim is to show only some decrement, rather than a reduction of the behavior to near zero levels.

Since subjects were returned to either VR or DRL baselines as soon as their responding decreased to near zero levels during VDRO, or when the responding had not stopped after at least ten sessions, no information is available concerning durability of response decrement after a long history of reinforcement for not responding. The difficulty of reacquiring high rate responding after a long history of reinforcement for low rate and no responding suggests that a sequence of differential reinforcement of low rate responding, followed by differential reinforcement of other behavior might be a successful behavior modification procedure for producing durable response decrement. Dietz and Repp (1973) used this procedure to decrease classroom misbehavior. After obtaining a baseline measure, they reinforced high school girls for progressively fewer inappropriate verbal responses during a class period over successive days until they reached a DRL for zero rate of responding which was functionally a DRO procedure. Their results and the results of the present study indicate that perhaps the sequential presentation of DRL and DRO would be a recommended procedure for reducing undesirable behavior in applied settings.

GENERAL SUMMARY

Historically, applied research has taken its beginnings from results obtained from the laboratory. However, with research advancements as represented in the Journal of Applied Behavior Analysis since 1968, applied research has established itself as being able to independently advance our knowledge of procedures designed to change behavior without as much dependence upon laboratory results. If one accepts the premise that laboratory research should have functional relevance to the real world, then perhaps that laboratory research which provides in-depth and more precise analyses of applied procedures and which yields more efficient applied procedures should be considered an important area of contribution to our science of human behavior. The research presented here resulted from such an orientation of observing behavior and procedures used to change behavior in applied settings and then implementing laboratory research analogues to analyze these procedures in a more precisely controlled laboratory environment.

The results of the studies presented here provide some confidence in the potential contribution of such an orientation for increasing the efficiency of applied procedures and for analyzing their effects as well as side effects. As can be seen by comparing the results of the Goetz, *et al.* (1975) research with the research on differential reinforcement of other behavior (DRO) presented here, one can see as Bijou (1970) stated, that generality can be expected to pertain between laboratory and applied settings.

The essential elements of the findings presented in these five studies are simple but begin to add to our knowledge of procedures designed to decrease or eliminate behavior. For example, the interpolation of continuous reinforcement (CRF) prior to the implementation of either extinction or differential reinforcement of other behavior (DRO) might have seemed a plausible procedure for enhancing the efficacy of these two procedures in applied settings. However, the results obtained in Study 1 and 2 indicated that such a procedure did not produce effects which would indicate this as a practical procedure for application in naturalistic settings. Differences were only obtained in the first day of manipulation in the infrahuman research and were not obtained in the human research incorporating DRO (Study 2). The fact that no initial differences occurred in the human research might be confounded by the fact that reinforcement was delivered in DRO and each delivery initially resulted in a momentary increase in responding. This discrimination, based on reinforcement delivery, might have been sufficient to override the small differences that might have been obtained in the first DRO session subsequent to the interpolation of CRF had the discrimination not occurred. Differential reinforcement on a fixed-interval base (DRO) was found in Study 3 to be more efficient for decreasing behavior than that on a variable-interval base (VDRO). Fixed interval DRO is difficult to program in applied settings but initially these results might lead one to conclude that we should attempt to be more precise in our applied procedures and attempt to program fixed-interval DRO. However, Study 3 also indicated that the faster response decrement during FDRO could have been due to the establishment of superstitious responding which facilitated that decrement. In addition, it was found in Study 5 that VDRO was more effective for reducing very low-rate than high-rate behaviors. Thus, it becomes apparent why VDRO is, in fact, effective in applied research. Most behaviors in applied settings do not occur at the very high rates usually obtained in the laboratory and thus VDRO could be expected to be sufficiently effective in such environments. As might be expected, in Study 4, fixed-interval DRO was found to be a more efficient procedure than extinction for reducing responding. However, more important to know, is that these results occurred after the programming of concurrent schedules of reinforcement. As Bijou (1970) indicated, such schedules are the basic components of normal development. Thus, one can infer that laboratory research involving such schedules might lend itself to more direct generality in applied procedures.

Results of these studies provide interesting considerations in the application of differential reinforcement and extinction in naturalistic settings. From the informtion provided one can begin to see the evolution of potential recommendations regarding the use of these procedures in applied settings. For example, the use of DRO to produce response decrement appears to have many advantages over that of extinction, especially if one wishes to produce faster and a potentially more permanent decrement. Since an argument can be made that the only type of extinction which really occurs in applied environments is that which is associated with differential reinforcement, then it is reassuring in one sense to know that DRO can be quite powerful. However, the use of DRO for purposes of control in reversal designs should be approached with some caution in that it appears that prolonged use of DRO might, in fact, lead to difficulties in the reacquisition of the originally treated preferred behavior. The role of "superstitious" behavior with respect to the enhancement of the effectiveness of DRO is also interesting in light of the potential for the occurrence of "superstitious" behaviors in applied settings. Research on the development of "superstitious" behavior is minimal but it is clear that, once developed, these behaviors are strong and appear, as indicated in the research on DRO, to affect other behavior. Such information might not be available from research in applied settings since obtaining measures of all the potential behaviors other than those directly manipulated is at best difficult. Although one study indicated that variable interval DRO might be less efficient than fixed-interval DRO, it was interesting to note, in a subsequent study, that variable-interval DRO could be quite effective for changing low-rate behaviors. This is especially important since most behaviors which occur in applied settings are not at all similar in rate to those high-rate behaviors usually produced in laboratory settings.

Many other implications of these results can be found. However, the important point is that one can begin to see the evolution of what could potentially be an important undertaking in enhancing the effectiveness of applied behavior analysis through research primarily emanating from laboratory sources. The intent is not to suggest that laboratory research should replace applied research, but rather that each should build on the other and thus realize the best potential from both. Through such endeavors laboratory research can begin to suggest better methods for implementation of procedures in applied settings and applied research. Through its very application it can provide indications of areas in which more in-depth research should be executed in the lab. Thus, both types of research essentially reach the same common goals: to provide a greater understanding of behavioral principles and human development and to apply this knowledge, in the most effective manner possible, to the elimination of social and behavior problems.

REFERENCES

Bijou, S. W. Patterns of reinforcement and resistance to extinction in young children. *Child Development,* 1957, *28,* 47-54.

Bijou, S. W. Operant extinction after fixed interval schedules with young children. *Journal of Experimental Analysis of Behavior,* 1958, *1,* 25-29.

Bijou, S. W. Reinforcement history and socialization. In Hoppe, R. A., Milton, G. A., & Simmel, E. C. (Eds.), *Early Experiences and the Process of Socialization.* New York: Academic Press, 1970, 43-58.

Bostow, D. E., & Bailey, J. B. Modification of severe disruptive and aggressive behaviors using brief time-out and reinforcement procedure. *Journal of Applied Behavior Analysis,* 1969, *2,* 31-37.

Brackbill, Y. Extinction of the smiling response in infants as a function of reinforcement schedule. *Child Development,* 1958, *29,* 115-124.

Brigham, T. A., & Sherman, J. A. An experimental analysis of verbal imitation in preschool children. *Journal of Applied Behavior Analysis,* 1968, *1,* 151-158.

Bullock, D. H., & Smith, W. C. An effect of repeated conditioning-extinction upon operant strength. *Journal of Experimental Psychology,* 1953, *46,* 349-352.

Carment, O. W., & Miles, C. G. Resistance to extinction and rate of lever pulling as a function of percentage of reinforcement and number of acquisition trials. *Canadian Journal of Psychology,* 1962, *16,* 145-151.

Corte, H. E., Wolf, M. M., & Locke, B. F. A comparison of procedures for eliminating self-injurious behavior of retarded adolescents. *Journal of Applied Behavior Analysis,* 1971, *4,* 201-213.

Davidson, E. H., & Walker, J. L. Resistance to extinction as a function of acquisition and extinction schedules and type measurement. *Psychonomic Science,* 1970, *19,* 63-64.

Davis, J., & Bitterman, M. E. Differential reinforcement of other behavior (DRO): A yoked-control comparison. *Journal of Experimental Analysis of Behavior,* 1971, *15,* 237-341.

Dietz, S. M., & Repp, A. C. Decreasing classroom misbehavior through the use of DRL schedules of reinforcement. *Journal of Applied Behavior Analysis,* 1973, *6,* 457-463.

Doubros, S. G., & Daniels, G. J. An experimental approach to the reproduction of over-active behavior. *Behavior Research and Therapy,* 1966, *4,* 251-258.

Edwards, A. L. *Experimental design in psychological research* (rev. ed.). New York: Holt, Rinehart, & Winston, 1953.

Etzel, B. C., & Gewirtz, J. L. Experimental modification of caretaker-maintained high-rate operant crying in a 6- and a 20-week-old infant (infans tyrannotearus); extinction of crying with reinforcement of eye contact and smiling. *Journal of Experimental Child Psychology,* 1967, *5,* 303-317.

Goetz, E. M., Holmberg, M. C., & LeBlanc, J. M. The comparison of two different control procedures during the modification of a preschooler's compliance behavior. *Journal of Applied Behavior Analysis,* 1975, *8,* 77-82.

Ferster, C. B., & Skinner, B. F. *Schedules of reinforcement.* New York: Appleton-Century-Crofts, 1957.

Hart, B. M., Reynolds, N., Baer, D. M., Brawley, E. R., & Harris, F. R. Effect of contingent and non-contingent social reinforcement on the cooperative play of a preschool child. *Journal of Applied Behavior Analysis,* 1968, *1,* 73-76.

Holz, W. C., Azrin, N. H., & Ayllon, T. Elimination of behavior of mental patients by response-produced extinction. *Journal of Experimental Analysis of Behavior,* 1963, *6,* 407-412.

Jenkins, H. M. Resistance to extinction when partial reinforcement is followed by regular reinforcement. *Journal of Experimental Psychology,* 1962, *64,* 411-450.

Jenkins, W. O., & Stanley, J. C. Partial reinforcement: A review and critique. *Psychological Bulletin*, 1950, *47*, 193-234.

Kass, N. Resistance to extinction as a function of age and schedules of reinforcement. *Journal of Experimental Psychology*, 1962, *64*, 249-252.

Kass, N., & Wilson, H. Resistance to extinction as a function of percentage of reinforcement, number of training trials and conditioned reinforcement. *Journal of Experimental Psychology*, 1966, *71*, 355-357.

LeBlanc, J. M. Continuous reinforcement: A possible behavior modification procedure for decreasing resistance to extinction. Doctoral dissertation, University of Kansas, 1970.

LeBlanc, J. M., & Reuter, K. E. Response elimination by reinforcement: Continuous and differential reinforcement of other behavior. Paper presented at the American Psychological Association Convention, Honolulu, September, 1972.

Leitenberg, H., Rawson, R. A., & Bath, K. Reinforcement of competing behavior during extinction. *Science*, 1970, *169*, 301-303.

Lewis, D. J., & Duncan, C. P. Expectation and resistance to extinction of a lever pulling response as a function of percentage of reinforcement and number of acquisition trials. *Journal of Experimental Psychology*, 1958, *55*, 121-128.

Likely, F. A. Relative resistance to extinction of aperiodic and continuous reinforcement separately and in combination. *Journal of General Psychology*, 1958, *58*, 165-187.

Miller, D. N., & LeBlanc, J. M. Response decrement and resumption: A comparison of responding during and after differential reinforcement of other behavior and extinction. Paper presented at the annual convention of the American Psychological Association, Honolulu, Hawaii, 1972.

Myers, N. A. Extinction following partial and continuous primary and secondary reinforcement. *Journal of Experimental Psychology*, 1960, 172-179.

Pinkston, E. M., Reese, N. M., LeBlanc, J. M., & Baer, D. M. Independent control of a preschool child's aggression and peer interaction by contingent teacher attention. *Journal of Applied Behavior Analysis*, 1973, *6*, 115-124.

Quartermain, D., & Vaughan, G. Effect of interpolating continuous reinforcement between partial training and extinction. *Psychological Reports*, 1961, *8*, 235-237.

Quartermain, D., Vaughan, G. M., & Mangan, G. L. The effect of continuous following partial reinforcement on resistance to extinction. *Australian Journal of Psychology*, 1961. As cited by Quartermain, D. and Vaughan, G. M. (1961).

Reuter, K. E., & LeBlanc, J. M. Variable differential reinforcement of other behavior (VDRO): Its effectiveness as a modification procedure. Paper presented at the annual convention of the American Psychological Association, Honolulu, Hawaii, 1972.

Reynolds, G. S. Behavioral contrast. *Journal of Experimental Analysis of Behavior*, 1961, *4*, 57-71.

Reynolds, N. J., & Risley, T. R. The role of social and material reinforcers in increasing talking of disadvantaged preschool child. *Journal of Applied Behavior Analysis*, 1968, *1*, 253-262.

Schoenfeld, W. N., & Farmer, J. Reinforcement schedules and the "behavior stream." In W. M. Schoenfeld (Ed.), *The theory of reinforcement schedules*. New York: Appleton-Century-Crofts, 1970.

Sherman, J. A. Use of reinforcement and imitation to reinstate verbal behavior in mute psychotics. *Journal of Abnormal Psychology*, 1965, *70*, 155-164.

Sherman, J. A., & Baer, D. M. Appraisal of operant therapy techniques with children and adults. In C. M. Franks (Ed.), *Behavior therapy: Appraisal and status*. New York: Mc Graw-Hill, 1969.

Siqueland, E. R. Reinforcement patterns and extinction in human newborns. *Journal of Experimental Child Psychology*, 1968, *6*, 323-334.

Skinner, B. F. *The behavior of organisms.* New York: Appleton-Century, 1938.

Spradlin, J. E. Effects of reinforcement schedules on extinction in severely mentally retarded children. *American Journal of Mental Deficiency,* 1962, *66,* 634-640.

Stolz, S. B., & Wolf, M. M. Visually discriminated behavior in a "blind" adolescent retardate. *Journal of Applied Behavior Analysis,* 1969, *2,* 65-77.

Sutherland, N. S., Mackintosh, N. J., & Wolfe, J. B. Extinction as a function of the order of partial and consistent reinforcement. *Journal of Experimental Psychology,* 1965, *69,* 56-59.

Theios, J. The partial reinforcement effect sustained through blocks of continuous reinforcement. *Journal of Experimental Psychology,* 1962, *64,* 1-6.

Topping, J. S., Pickering, J. W., & Jackson, J. A. Omission training effects following VI and FI pretraining. *Psychonomic Science,* 1971, *24,* 113-114. (a)

Topping, J. S., Pickering, J. W., & Jackson, J. A. The differential effects of omission and extinction following DRL pretraining. *Psychonomic Science,* 1971, *24,* 137-138. (b)

Twardosz, S., & Sajwaj, T. Multiple effects of a procedure to increase sitting in a hyperactive retarded boy. *Journal of Applied Behavior Analysis,* 1972, *5,* 73-78.

Uhl, C. N., & Garcia, E. E. Comparison of omission with extinction in response elimination in rats. *Journal of Comparative and Physiological Psychology,* 1969, *69,* 554-562.

Uhl, C. N., & Sherman, W. O. Comparison of combinations of omission, punishment and extinction methods in response elimination in rats. *Journal of Comparative and Physiological Psychology,* 1971, *74,* 59-65.

Wertheim, G. A., & Singer, R. D. Resistance to extinction in the goldfish following schedules of continuous and variable interval reinforcement. *Journal of the Experimental Analysis of Behavior,* 1964, *7,* 357-360.

Williams, C. The elimination of tantrum behaviors by extinction procedures. *Journal of Abnormal and Social Psychology,* 1959, *59,* 269.

Zeiler, M. D. Eliminating behavior with reinforcement. *Journal of Experimental Analysis of Behavior,* 1971, *16,* 401-405.

Zeiler, M. D. Superstitious behavior in children: An experimental analysis. In H. W. Reese (Ed.), *Advances in Child Development and Behavior* (Vol. 7). New York: Academic Press, 1972.

13

Sources of Bias in Observational Recording[1]

K. Daniel O'Leary
Ronald N. Kent

State University of New York Stony Brook

In 1966, Rosenthal's book, *Experimenter Effects in Behavioral Research,* appeared and shortly thereafter a frequently embarrassing question about almost any data presentation reared its head: "How did you control for observer bias?" In 1967 Scott, Burton, and Yarrow reported that recording differences were noted between the senior author and observers who were not informed of the experimental hypotheses. In fact, data recorded by the senior author were more confirming of the experimental hypothesis than were data recorded by naive observers, and these differences were attributed to an expectation effort or observer bias. The study, however, was plagued by insufficient observer training and very poor reliabilities (range, −.09-.91). Nonetheless, the study was important in that it increased awareness of the possibility of observer bias — particularly in naturalistic settings.

About six years ago, Ruth Kass and I (Kass & O'leary, 1970) sought to evaluate the effect of observer bias by manipulating predictions of treatment for three groups of observers. Videotapes of children with behavior problems were prepared which showed a baseline with high rates of disruptive classroom behavior and a sharp decline during what was labeled a "treatment" phase. Three separate groups of observers were given, respectively, the statements below, regarding the effects of baseline and treatment conditions that they were to observe:

1. We expect the rate of disruptive behavior to decrease following baseline.
2. We expect the rate of disruptive behavior to increase following baseline.
3. We cannot predict whether the disruptive behavior will increase or decrease following baseline.

[1]This study was originally presented to the American Psychological Association, August 29, 1973, Montreal, Canada.

All observers watched the same videotapes which showed a substantial *decrease* from baseline to treatment. The dependent measures were nine categories of disruptive classroom behavior, such as being out of chair, aggression, and touching others' property, as well as a composite measure of disruptive behavior (O'Leary, Kaufman, Kass, & Drabman, 1970).

We found significant differences among the observer groups in their recordings of seven of nine behavioral categories as well as on the composite measure of disruptive behavior. In general, the group for which a decrease was predicted recorded a greater decrease from baseline to treatment than did the group for which an increase in the rate of disruptive behavior was predicted (Kass & O'Leary, 1970). Detailed analysis of those data, however, made us suspicious that something other than expectation might be involved in producing the result we observed. For example, significant and unpredicted differences among the groups emerged during the baseline phase. Further, despite an overall effect consistent with our predictions, not all of the significant differences between observer groups in behaviors recorded were in the predicted direction. In fact, following a dissertation by Kent (1972), we realized that the differences in baseline may have resulted from what Patterson (1969) and we have labeled "observer drift," a change in the definition of an observational code across the course of a study. Such drift in definitions may reflect, for example, the influence of group consensus as observers compare and discuss their recordings on repeated occasions. Kent (1972) trained 40 observers simultaneously, divided these observers randomly into 8 groups of 5 members each, and assigned them to view identical videotapes. Although the 40 observers were all trained to observe reliably with one another, after observing and discussing disagreements for only 5 hours, recordings from the different groups were significantly different from one another.

Kent, O'Leary, Diament, and Dietz (1974) again sought to investigate observer bias, but this time we specifically designed the study to avoid the possibility that drift would confound our results. Two groups of high school seniors observed videotapes identical in rate of disruptive behavior from baseline to treatment and recorded the nine categories of disruptive behavior referred to earlier. One group of ten students was told that a token program introduced during the treatment phase would result in a decrease in level of disruptive behavior. The other group was told that following the baseline a control condition would be implemented and no change in level of disruptive behavior was predicted. Within each experimental condition, five pairs of observers computed reliability only with their partner rather than with all members of the same expectation condition. Thus the drift of individual pairs of observers could be separated from the effects of predicted results on behavior recorded.

Feedback of a general and noncontingent nature was given to the observers after each recording session during the treatment phase. Observers in each group were told that a casual examination of their recordings revealed that the predict-ed results were emerging. This feedback was employed to increase the similar-ity to field settings where such casual feedback is often given to observers, and to enhance the likelihood that biases due to predicted results would occur.

After all observational recordings were collected, observers were asked to provide a global evaluation of the treatment effects they had observed by indi-cating whether, overall, they had noted an increase, decrease, or no change in level of disruptive behavior. Nine of 10 observers for whom a decrease was predicted reported witnessing a decrease. Seven of 10 observers for whom no change was predicted reported that they had seen no change. Thus, there was a clear and highly significant relationship between the experimental predictions and global evaluations of behavior change. In contrast, not one of the 9 in-dividual categories of disruptive behavior recorded, nor a composite measure, was significantly affected by predicted results. Further, several of the categories of behavior manifested a significant and occasionally substantial influence of ob-server drift accounting for up to 22% of the variance of the individual cate-gories.

The general results of this study can be stated in slightly different form. We clearly obtained significant drift in the ratings of different pairs of observers. However, the only result of the expectation manipulation was that the subjects told us — in the form of a global rating — that they thought they *saw* a decrease or no change in level of disruptive behavior, depending on the experimental hypothesis they had been given. Thus they told us what we had been telling them all along — *despite the fact that their behavioral recordings were discrepant with this global rating.* We have yet to find that observational recording data (not global evaluations) are influenced by induced expectations alone.

More recently we postulated that experimenter feedback regarding observa-tional recordings was a critical factor in determining the effect of predictions of results. Thus we provided observers not only with predictions of experimental results, but also with contingent feedback from an experimenter designed to shape their recordings toward consistency with our predictions (O'Leary, Kent, & Kanowitz, 1975).

Four observers were told that they were viewing videotape recordings of a study in which children were rewarded, during the treatment phases, for re-duced levels of noise and playing. However, they were told that no contingency was established for levels of vocalization and orienting. Thus, levels of noise and playing were predicted to decrease during treatment, and levels of vocalization and orienting were predicted not to change. In fact, there was no change in the level of any of these four categories of behavior from baseline to treatment.

The basis for feedback in the "treatment" conditions was a comparison of the level of the observers' recordings relative to that of criterion observer recordings during baseline. If observers recorded less noise and playing relative to criterion observations during treatment than they had during baseline, they received positive feedback from the experimenter, such as, "That reduction is a good example of how children will work for a reward." If they recorded more or the same level of noise and playing during treatment as they had during baseline, they received negative feedback from the experimenter, such as, "It's strange that you have recorded so many noises – this treament usually works."

As can be seen in Figures 1 and 2, the behaviors predicted to decrease (manipulated categories) were recorded less frequently by observers during treatment while the behaviors expected to remain the same (nonmanipulated categories) were recorded at approximately the same level as baseline during the treatment phase.

On the basis of these studies we conclude that experimental predictions, per se, have no important influence on observational data. However, when an expectation is given to observers and, in addition, contingent feedback is provided to them, a clear bias is obtained. Given these data, the most conservative stance would be to eliminate all review of incoming data with observers. Unfortunately, such review often serves a clear educational and motivational function in research settings. Furthermore, it is unlikely that noncontingent feedback of a

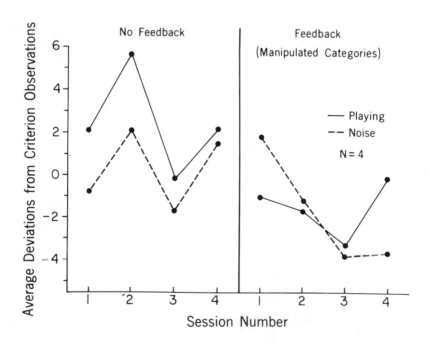

Figure 1   Average deviations from criterion observations for feedback categories.

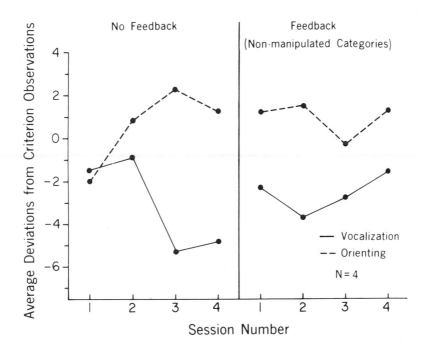

Figure 2   Average deviations from criterion observations for nonfeedback categories.

global nature (like, "the study is progressing well") will bias objective recordings of specific categories of behavior (Kent, O'Leary, Diament, & Dietz, 1974). However, we suggest that all evaluative or contingent feedback must be eliminated if observational data are not to be held suspect.

An equally important yet more subtle problem which we noted is observer drift. In several studies we have documented significant effects of observer drift that have clear implications for any applied research in which observations are made repeatedly across a relatively long period of time (O'Leary & Kent, 1973). Retraining of observers, in which each observer's ratings are matched at periodic intervals against those of the trainer to reinstate group reliability, would be one means of avoiding this problem. Furthermore, withholding of reliability feedback and eliminating discussion of recording procedures between individual observers in research settings would prevent the evolution of idiosyncratic interpretations of the behavioral code within any particular observer group.

ACKNOWLEDGMENTS

This research was supported in part by Office of Education Grant OEG-0-71-2872-607, and NIMH Grant MH 21813-03. The opinions expressed herein, however, do not necessarily reflect the position or policy of either granting agency and no official endorsement should be inferred.

REFERENCES

Kass, R. E., & O'Leary, K. D. The effects of observer bias in field-experimental settings. Paper presented at a Symposium, "Behavior Analysis in Education," University of Kansas, Lawrence, Kansas, April 9, 1970.

Kent, R. N. Expectation bias in behavioral observation. Unpublished doctoral dissertation, State University of New York at Stony Brook, 1972.

Kent, R. N., O'Leary, K. D., Diament, C., & Dietz, A. Expectation biases in observational evaluation of therapeutic change. *Journal of Consulting and Clinical Psychology*, 1974, *42*, 774-780.

O'Leary, K. D., Kaufman, K. F., Kass, R. E., & Drabman, R. S. The effects of loud and soft reprimands on the behavior of disruptive students. *Exceptional Children*, 1970, *37*, 145-155.

O'Leary, K. D., & Kent, R. N. Behavior modification for social action: Research tactics and problems. In L. A. Hamerlynck, L. C. Handy & E. J. Mash (Eds.), *Behavior Change: Methodology, Concepts, and Practice*. Champaign, Illinois: Research Press, 1973.

O'Leary, K. D., Kent, R. N., & Kanowitz, J. Shaping data collection congruent with experimental hypotheses. *Journal of Applied Behavior Analysis*, 1975, *8*, 43-51.

Patterson, G. R. A community mental health program for children. In L. A. Hamerlynk, P. O. Davidson, & L. E. Acker (Eds.), *Behavior Modification and Ideal Mental Health Services*. University of Calgary Press: Calgary, Alberta, Canada, 1969.

Rosenthal, R. *Experimenter Effects in Behavioral Research*. New York: Appleton-Century-Crofts, 1966.

Scott, P. M., Burton, R. V., & Yarrow, M. R. Social reinforcement under natural conditions. *Child Development*, 1967, *38*, 53-63.

14

Complex Interactions:
A Functional Approach

Joseph A. Parsons
Douglas Peter Ferraro

University of New Mexico

Interactions between an organism's behavior and the environment are frequently classified as either simple or complex. Simple interactions are defined by a direct empirical relationship between explicit environmental conditions and overt behavior. By contrast, complex interactions are designated by an indirect or conditional (empirical) relationship between environment and behavior, or by behaviors that involve a heterogeneous sequence of responses. In both instances, the criteria of classification are empirical: observed behavior, and the environmental conditions under which the behavior occurs.

There is another sense in which interactions are complex. In this alternate usage, complex means that the relationship between behavior and its determining conditions is elusive. Thus, complex becomes synonymous with unknown. In this chapter we will discuss complex interactions in which factors not typically observed or manipulated are assumed to contribute to observed behavioral phenomena. Particular emphasis will be given to that class of complex interactions in which children's covert behavior presumably exercises control over their subsequent overt behavior (attending, mediating, problem solving, and self-control).

Even a cursory survey of the literature on complex interactions in humans shows that the relevant data cannot be unified concisely. Despite the limitations of any taxonomy that considers theoretical orientations and experimental methodologies, it still is possible to group the literature into four conceptual approaches, as follows: cognitive (Inhelder & Piaget, 1958; Piaget, 1970), information processing (deGroot, 1966; Paige & Simon, 1966), S-R learning (Gagne, 1964; Kendler & Kendler, 1962), and functional (Bijou, 1976; Skinner, 1969).

In the cognitive approach, complex interactions are viewed as mental activity. Thus, the solution of a problem indicates problem-solving abilities, moral conduct indicates moral reasoning, and selective attention reflects a child's egocentricity. These factors are considered to depend on the level (stage) of development of hypothetical cognitive structures. Quite clearly, this is a reductive approach: children's overt behavior is viewed as a manifestation of inner, unobservable activities. Similarly, the information-processing approach deals with complex interactions metaphorically, that is, in computer language. Children are assumed to encode, process, store, and retrieve information. In turn, these hypothetical processes are assumed to govern overt behavior. As in the cognitive approach, the causes of complex interactions are reduced to hypothetical constructs.

A third approach to complex interactions is based on S-R learning theory. Inferred internal responses and response-produced stimuli are presumed to account for observed relationships between external events and behavior. Although these internal stimulus and response events are assumed to conform to the same principles as do external stimuli and behavior, in fact they remain hypothetical and thus neither directly observable nor manipulable.

An alternative approach, which does not involve inferential or reductive constructs, advocates a functional analysis of behavior (Bijou, 1976; Bijou & Baer, 1965; Goldiamond, 1966; Skinner, 1957, 1969). This functional approach is similar to the S-R learning approach in accepting complex interactions as derived from the conditioning principles established for simpler interactions. However, the functional approach does not invoke hypothetical constructs such as structures, memory stores, or internal stimuli (Skinner, 1953), nor does it analyze complex interactions in terms of their form or location (Kantor, 1959). Complex behaviors, such as attending, mediating, problem solving, and self-control, are analyzed in terms of the independent variables affecting their probability of occurrence. In a functional view, these behaviors are of special interest because they do not have any apparent direct effect on external contingencies of reinforcement, but instead affect subsequent behavior. Behavior having this function is termed precurrent.

Skinner (1968) has suggested that precurrent behaviors are conditioned and maintained by their ultimate effect on subsequent behaviors. For example, we are said to attend to stimuli because in doing so we increase the probability of contacting stimuli that set the occasion for reinforcement. In the case of self-control or moral behavior, we are assumed to act or not act because our subsequent behavior thereby is more likely to be reinforced. So described, precurrent interactions take on the defining characteristics of operant chains. A chain consists of a response sequence in which one response produces the conditions that make the subsequent response more probable. Precurrent responses may be considered as early links in a chain, and the subsequent behaviors they alter as the terminal links that lead to reinforcement. This position has gained some empirical support from studies of attending (Eckerman, Lanson, & Cumming,

1968; Jenkins & Boakes, 1973), problem solving (Grimm, Bijou, & Parsons, 1973), and self-control (Rachlin & Green, 1972).

The literature on response chains presents few analyses of such interactions in children. Perhaps one reason is that those precurrent behaviors that possess topographical import for children often are not easily observed. Even so, such behaviors need not be purged from a functional approach, for the function of a response is considered independently of its form. Furthermore, experimental conditions can be established in which overt precurrent behaviors become manifest. Nevertheless, there have been few attempts to investigate complex human interactions in this manner (Jeffrey, 1953; Flavell, Beach, & Chinsky, 1966; Grimm, et al., 1973). Given the stature that attention, mediation, and self-control have attained in current theories of child development, additional research is merited.

To develop a methodology suitable to the direct study of precurrent interactions in children, we performed two experiments of a preliminary nature. Our research had three objectives: to create a behavioral chain within a complex task assumed to involve covert mediation; to provide overt mediational response opportunities early in the behavioral chain; and, most important, to vary the precurrent efficacy of the overt mediational responses. Arguing from the functional approach advocated here, we predicted that the child's accuracy of performance would reflect the efficacy of the overt precurrent responses. In Experiment 1, children were trained to make a differential overt mediational response that could function precurrently in a delayed conditional discrimination task. In Experiment 2, children were given similar training but with a mediational response in the chain that was precurrently nonfunctional.

RESEARCH

The basic paradigm chosen for study was the match-to-sample task. This task represents a conditional discrimination, in that reliable correct responding can be based only on the relationship between a sample stimulus and two or more comparison stimuli. A response is required to that comparison stimulus which is the same as the sample stimulus. When a delay interval is imposed between the termination of the sample stimulus and the presentation of the comparison stimuli, a short-term memory task is operationally defined. Generally, it has been maintained that implicit verbal responses can mediate between stimuli and overt responses in tasks such as the delayed match-to-sample task (Reese, 1962). In our research, we required that an overt, nonvocal mediation response occur between the termination of the sample stimulus and the presentation of the comparison stimuli. The variable of major experimental interest was not the form but the function of the mediation response. These responses were allowed to function either precurrently or nonprecurrently, either increasing or not increasing the likelihood of a subsequent correct match-to-sample response.

Five normal, experimentally naive boys, from 55 to 59 months of age, served on consecutive weekdays as subjects. Each subject was escorted individually to the experimental room by the experimenter and seated alone in front of the experimental apparatus. This apparatus contained a token dispenser and 5 stimulus-response keys arranged in a Greek cross pattern. The center key was the sample-stimulus key, and the left and right keys were the comparison-stimulus keys. These 3 keys could be illuminated independently with either red or green light. The top and bottom keys served as mediating keys and could be illuminated with white light. Throughout the experiments, reinforcement consisted of the delivery of a token into a receptacle illuminated with white light for 3 sec concurrently with token delivery. At the termination of experimental sessions (10 to 15 min in duration), the experimenter exchanged the subject's earned tokens, regardless of their number, for the opportunity to select one item from an array of inexpensive toys.

PROCEDURE

Experiment 1

The procedures of the first experiment were designed to condition Subjects 1, 2, and 3 to emit differential mediation responses to the top and bottom keys conditional on the color of the sample stimulus.

The 3 subjects were pretrained for 2 48-trial sessions according to the following sequence of events: The sample key was first illuminated either red or green. A response to the sample key darkened it and illuminated the top and bottom keys white. If the sample stimulus had been red (green), a response to the top (bottom) key was reinforced, darkened both mediation keys, and initiated an 8-sec intertrial interval. A response to the inappropriate mediation key (bottom if red sample, top if green sample) darkened both mediation keys and initiated the intertrial interval.

During the third session a 0-sec delayed match-to-sample contingency was added to the pretraining task. Under this contingency, a response to the appropriate mediating key did not terminate the trial, but instead illuminated the left and right comparison keys randomly with red and green stimuli. Inappropriate mediating responses were without consequence, and thus insured that the subject's last mediating response was appropriate. A response to the comparison stimulus that matched the previously presented sample stimulus was reinforced and terminated the trial. A response to the mismatching comparison stimulus simply terminated the trial.

After subjects had achieved a criterion of at least 90% correct matching responses on the 0-sec delay contingency, they were given 6 consecutive variable-delay match-to-sample test sessions. Each of these test sessions consisted of 32 trials at a 0-sec delay and 8 trials each at 5- and 10-sec delays, in a mixed sequence. During Test Sessions 1, 2, 5, and 6, the first appropriate mediation response following the expiration of the delay illuminated the comparison keys. During Test Sessions 3 and 4, subjects were instructed not to respond to the mediation keys. Instead, the comparison stimuli were presented automatically at the termination of the delay interval.

Experiment 2

In this experiment, Subjects 4 and 5 were conditioned to make a positional mediational response to the top or bottom key independently of the color of the sample stimulus.

The procedures used were the same as in Experiment 1, with two exceptions. During the first session of pretraining, the mediation key pressed on the first trial was designated as the appropriate mediation response for the remainder of pretraining. Thus, subjects were reinforced for a position mediation response without regard to the sample stimulus color. During match-to-sample sessions, a response to either mediation key was considered as appropriate if it occurred following the minimal programmed delay.

RESULTS

Experiment 1

At the termination of pretraining, the 3 subjects had learned to respond differentially to the top and bottom mediating keys, conditional on the color of the sample stimulus. This differential behavior was maintained at better than 95% appropriate responding during the subsequent acquisition of the 0-sec delayed match-to-sample task. Achievement of the specified 90%-correct 0-sec delayed matching criterion progressed rapidly. The mean number of sessions to criterion across the three subjects was 2 sessions, and the mean percentage of correct matching at the end of acquisition was 99%.

The data of primary interest in this experiment were the percentage of correct matching and the percentage of appropriate mediation responses obtained during the variable-delay match-to-sample test sessions. To the extent that the mediating responses served a precurrent function, these responses should be maintained and accuracy of matching should not decrease as the length of the match-to-sample delay interval increased. Alternatively, the prohibition of these precurrent responses during Test Sessions 3 and 4 should lead to a decrease in matching accuracy as a function of increased delay length. Figure 1 shows that the expected outcomes with respect to matching accuracy were obtained for the individual subjects. During the first and last 2 of the 6 test sessions, when mediation responses were permitted, accuracy of performance was maintained

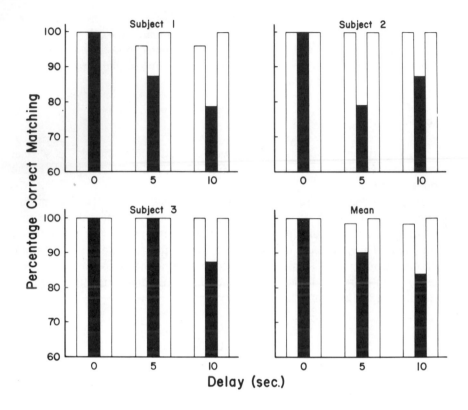

Figure 1   Mean percentages of correct matching responses obtained in Experiment 1 at 0-, 5-, and 10-sec delays during test sessions when precurrent mediating responses were required (unfilled bars) and prohibited (filled bars).

above 90% at all delay values. On the other hand, when mediation responses were prohibited, during the middle 2 test sessions, accuracy of performance decreased as a function of increased delay length.

During variable-delay Test Sessions 1, 2, 5, and 6, only one appropriate mediating response, occurring after the programmed delay had elapsed, was necessary to produce the comparison stimuli. However, if precurrent responses are maintained by the reinforcement contingencies in effect for subsequent behavior, then the precurrent responses should be maintained throughout increasing delay intervals. Again the prediction made from a functional approach was upheld. The mean percentages of appropriate mediating responses across the relevant 4 test sessions for delays of 0, 5, and 10 sec were respectively, 97.5, 97.0, and 94.5%. The corresponding mean frequencies of mediating responses were respectively, 1.2, 5.3, and 9.2 responses.

Experiment 2

In this experiment the subjects were reinforced during pretraining for respond-ing to their preferred mediation key, independent of the color of the sample stimulus. Both subjects emitted 100% appropriate position responses at the termination of pretraining. During the subsequent 0-sec and variable-delay match-to-sample sessions, a response to either mediation key at the termination of the programmed delay was sufficient to produce the comparison stimuli. However, for purposes of data analysis, responses to the subject's preferred posi-tion (as reinforced during pretraining) were considered as appropriate mediation responses. Indeed, during acquisition of the 0-sec delayed-matching task, which required a mean of 4 sessions to meet the 90% matching criterion, the subjects emitted on the average 92% appropriate (preferred position) mediational re-sponses.

Because the mediational responses in this experiment were not related to the color of the sample stimulus, they were not expected to function precurrently. That is, they should not be maintained appropriately across increasing delay lengths, nor should they bridge the longer imposed matching delays, during the variable delay test sessions. Although the frequencies of appropriate mediation responses did increase with increasing delays during the 4 test sessions in which mediation was permitted, the percentage of appropriate mediation responses decreased as a function of delay length. Mean frequencies of all mediation re-sponses for delays of 0, 5, and 10 sec, respectively, were 1.0, 6.4, and 13.2 responses. The corresponding mean percentages of appropriate mediation re-sponses were 91.0, 73.0, and 72.0%.

Figure 2 presents the mean percentage of correct matching as a function of delay length for the first, middle, and last two variable-delay test sessions. When mediational responses were permitted, matching accuracy was impaired as a function of increasing delay length. That the impairment in matching accuracy was actually accentuated by the nonprecurrent mediation responses is suggested by the matching accuracy data obtained during the test sessions when media-tion responses were prohibited. During these test sessions, accuracy of perform-ance was impaired by increasing delay length, but not nearly to the extent that occurred during the mediation sessions.

COMMENTS

Our objective in presenting this research was to demonstrate the function of precurrent responses in a situation that could be considered a complex inter-action. We consider the data to be preliminary, not definitive. More subjects and several control groups are necessary to merit the latter classification. Never-theless, the data suggest that precurrent responses do not affect contingencies of

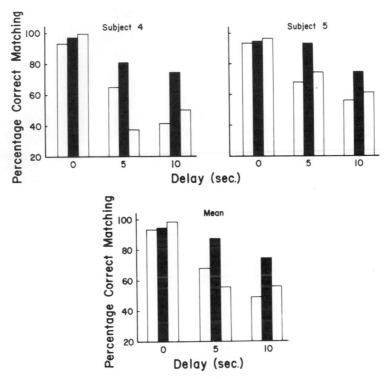

Figure 2   Mean percentages of correct matching responses obtained in Experiment 2 at 0-, 5-, and 10-sec delays during test sessions when nonprecurrent mediating responses were required (unfilled bars) and prohibited (filled bars).

reinforcement directly, but alter subsequent behavior so as to increase the likelihood that the altered behavior will be reinforced.

The separate experiments shared some common elements. In both experiments a response was provided that could mediate delays between the presentation of stimuli. In both experiments the mediation response was a member of an operant chain, in that the mediating response produced the matching comparison stimulus; the discriminative stimulus in the presence of which a response was reinforced. However, the differential outcomes of the two experiments demonstrate that precurrent responses function in a manner beyond mediating or chaining. When the response was permitted to function precurrently, accuracy of responding was enhanced, relative to when precurrent responses were prohibited or when only nonprecurrent responses were permitted.

It is tempting to ask why precurrent responses function as they do. The answer, however, may be an enigma. At least, its pursuit is likely to lead to the use of hypothetico-reductive constructs. It may well be that complex interactions such as attention, problem solving, and moral behavior will be explained more definitively if we determine empirically those conditions affecting the acquisition and maintenance of precurrent behavior.

ACKNOWLEDGMENTS

This research was supported in part by a University of New Mexico Research Grant to J. A. Parsons and by NIDA Grant DA00355 to D. P. Ferraro.

REFERENCES

Bijou, S. W. *The basic stage of early childhood development.* New York: Prentice-Hall, 1976.

Bijou, S. W., & Baer, D. M. *Child development: Universal stage of infancy* (Vol. 2). New York: Appleton-Century-Crofts, 1965.

deGroot, A. D. Perception and memory versus thought: Some old ideas and recent findings. In B. Kleinmuntz (Ed.), *Problem solving: Research, method, and theory.* New York: John Wiley & Sons, 1966.

Eckerman, D. A., Lanson, R. N., & Cumming, W. W. Acquisition and maintenance of matching without a required attending response. *Journal of the Experimental Analysis of Behavior,* 1968, *11,* 435-441.

Flavell, J. H., Beach, D. R., & Chinsky, J. M. Spontaneous verbal rehearsal in a memory task as a function of age. *Child Development,* 1966, *37,* 283-299.

Gagne, R. M. Problem solving. In A. W. Melton (Ed.), *Cateogries of human learning.* New York: Academic Press, 1964.

Goldiamond, I. Perception, language, and conceptualization rules. In B. Kleinmuntz (Ed.), *Problem solving: Research, method, and theory.* New York: John Wiley & Sons, 1966.

Grimm, J. A., Bijou, S. W., & Parsons, J. A. A problem-solving model for teaching remedial arithmetic to handicapped children. *Journal of Abnormal Child Psychology,* 1973, *1,* 26-39.

Inhelder, B., & Piaget, J. *The growth of logical thinking.* New York: Basic Books, 1958.

Jeffrey, W. E. The effect of verbal and nonverbal responses in mediating an instrumental act. *Journal of Experimental Psychology,* 1953, *45,* 327-333.

Jenkins, H. M., & Boakes, R. A. Observing stimulus sources that signal food or no food. *Journal of the Experimental Analysis of Behavior,* 1973, *2,* 197-207.

Kantor, J. R. *Interbehavioral psychology* (Rev. ed.). Bloomington, Indiana: Principia Press, 1959.

Kendler, H. H., & Kendler, T. S. Vertical and horizontal processes in problem solving. *Psychological Review,* 1962, *69,* 1-16.

Paige, J. M., & Simon, H. A. Cognitive processes in solving algebra word problems. In B. Kleinmuntz (Ed.), *Problem solving: Research, method, and theory.* New York: John Wiley & Sons, 1966.

Piaget, J. Piaget's theory. In P. H. Mussen (Ed.), *Carmichael's manual of child psychology* (Vol. 1). New York: John Wiley & Sons, 1970.

Rachlin, H., & Green, L. Commitment, choice, and self-control. *Journal of the Experimental Analysis of Behavior,* 1972, *17,* 15-22.

Reese, H. W. Verbal mediation as a function of age level. *Psychological Bulletin,* 1962, *59,* 502-509.

Skinner, B. F. *Science and human behavior.* New York: Macmillan, 1953.

Skinner, B. F. *Verbal behavior.* New York: Appleton-Century-Crofts, 1957.

Skinner, B. F. *The technology of teaching.* New York: Appleton-Century-Crofts, 1968.

Skinner, B. F. *Contingencies of reinforcement.* New York: Appleton-Century-Crofts, 1969.

15

Hydropsychotherapy: Water as a Punishing Stimulus in the Treatment of a Problem Parent-Child Relationship[1]

Robert F. Peterson
Linda W. Peterson

University of Nevada, Reno

Behaviorally oriented psychologists have relied primarily on two behavioral techniques to alter deviant parent-child relationships. One technique involves increasing social reinforcers and applying them in a contingent manner following the child's appropriate behavior. However, this procedure is often insufficient to reduce deviant responses and is most often coupled with a second technique that involves some form of punishment.

A variety of punishing stimuli have been employed in an attempt to reduce deviant behavior. They include slapping (Lovaas, 1973), contingent electric shock (Backman, 1972; Lovaas & Simmons, 1969; Risley, 1968), periods of brief social isolation (Hawkins, Peterson, Schweid, & Bijou, 1966; Lahey, McNees, & McNees, 1973; Wahler, Winkel, Peterson, & Morrison, 1965; and many others), and restriction of movement (Hamilton, Stephens, & Allen, 1967; Webster & Azrin, 1973).

Punishing stimuli may be evaluated in two ways. One involves measuring the strength of the stimulus by observing its effect on behavior; while the second involves ethical evaluation of physical or psychological discomfort. It is particularly important to be aware of the physical effects of such stimuli on the individual.

[1]This research was undertaken in 1967 when the senior author was at the Child Behavior Laboratory at the University of Illinois, and the junior author was a member of the staff of the Adler Zone Center.

247

Slapping, for example, may cause tissue damage, while electric shock or movement restriction may result in physical discomfort. In contrast the effects of social isolation are not primarily physical but psychological in nature. Typically, investigators have used social isolation with the less severely disturbed and electric shock and movement restriction with individuals whose behaviors are extremely deviant or dangerous to themselves and others.

Nevertheless, the use of punishing stimuli has ethical and social implications. Few therapists or parents enjoy using punishment. Thus it seems important that investigators attempt to assess which stimuli are effective punishers such that when punishment must be employed, it functions effectively and quickly. Given such information, the use of punishing stimuli would not have to be prolonged and discomfort to both parent and child could be minimized.

This chapter attempts to evaluate the effectiveness of water as a punishing stimulus in the treatment of a severely retarded child. In addition, the chapter attempts to elaborate some of the antecedent stimulus conditions which controlled the child's behavior.

METHOD

Subject

Jim E. was three and one-half years old and an only child in a middle-class family. The following, written by his mother, describes some of his problems:

> Jim hits his head on the walls and floor. We haven't found a way to discipline him — he won't pay any attention to us. He seems to be overactive and nervous. [He] can't sit through meals. If he doesn't get our full attention he hits his head and his teeth. [He] will not stay in bed unless tied in. Also he throws things when mad.

Jim attended a nursery school for the mentally retarded and had been diagnosed as suffering from Hurlers Syndrome. Jim was ambulatory but spoke only a half-dozen words. Mrs. E. said she had tried spanking, ignoring, praising, and placing him in his room, but these techniques had no effect on his behavior. He had also been placed on tranquilizing drugs (specific drug unknown) but the drugs were not effective. In his more positive moments Jim liked music, helping with household tasks, and otherwise mimicking his parents. It was obvious that Jim was seriously retarded in behavioral development. However, no psychological tests were given during the course of this study.

Procedure

Jim's mother pointed out that many of his problem behaviors were displayed when she was unable to give him her full attention. Thus, attention withdrawal was used to both observe and treat deviant responses. First, Mrs. E. was instructed to spend a few minutes playing with Jim, and then, on a signal from the authors, to engage in a different activity that excluded Jim. These activities were reading the newspaper, writing letters, or calling friends on the telephone. When the mother was doing so, the authors observed Jim engage in the following behaviors: (1) crying; (2) throwing objects or opening the refrigerator and throwing out food; (3) saying "mama"; (4) pulling mother's clothing; (5) self-hitting; (6) head banging; (7) opening drawers and doors; (8) kicking people or objects; (9) grabbing items his mother was using; and (10) spitting.

A topographical code for each of the above responses was designed. In addition, a code was developed to record the mother's verbalizations and physical contact with Jim. These behaviors and the code appear in Table 1.

Using this code, the authors recorded the frequency of the above behaviors. Responses were scored by dividing the total session into 20-sec intervals. One or more behaviors could be scored in each interval, with the limitation that a particular response (like hitting) would only be counted once within an interval, regardless of how many times it occurred.

Sessions always began with a brief period of contact between mother and child followed by a longer period of no contact. Somewhat later in the study as the frequency of the child's behavior began to change, the authors occasionally instructed the mother to engage in a second period of contact with the child in order to see if termination of the interaction would set the occasion for the occurrence of deviant behavior. All sessions but one included a contact period. The length of the period varied from 2 to 20 min. This variation was introduced in order to explore possible relationships between the length of the period and the frequency of Jim's deviant behavior. No such relationship was found however. All treatment procedures were carried out during the "no contact" periods.

TABLE 1

A. *Jim's deviant behavior*

1.   Cries: 2 sec or more of a loud sound not involving words.
2.   Throws: propels objects horizontally (other than balls or throw toys) more than 6 in without touching the ground.
3.   Says "Mama" or "Mom."
4.   Pulls or grasps mother's clothing.
5.   Hits hand against object or self.
6.   Bangs head against object.
7.   Opens drawers, refrigerator or outside door.
8.   Kicks object, self, or others.
9.   Removes or touches materials or objects mother is using.
10. Spits: propels saliva from mouth.

B. *Mother's reactions*

1.   Verbalizes to Jim
2.   Holds Jim in arms or on her lap.

The study was divided into six phases: a baseline phase, a reinforcement phase, a punishment phase, a reversal phase, a second punishment phase, a time-out phase, and a brief follow-up phase.

Baseline consisted of five sessions of observation. Sessions began with the authors signalling Mrs. E. to play with Jim or read to him. After a few minutes she was signaled to leave him and engage in a solitary activity. Occasionally she would verbalize to Jim, either commenting on his behavior or directing his activities. Her frequency of response was low and not directed to any particular behavior.

During the first reinforcement phase Mrs. E. was instructed to systematically ignore all deviant or undesirable behavior and attend to incompatible responses, such as quiet playing. The authors cued her on many occasions with regard to when she should go to Jim, touch him, and talk or play with him briefly. Cues were given with hand signals and soft verbal commands.

Five sessions later the punishment phase began. Just prior to this phase, Mrs. E. had mentioned that on one occasion she had reduced Jim's tantruming by pouring water on him. Since Mrs. E. and her husband had tried other kinds of punishment (particularly spanking) without success, it was agreed that the use of water should be explored. After some discussion it was decided that the water would be used in the following manner: Before each session Mrs. E. would fill a large pitcher with water. The pitcher, along with an 8-ounce glass would be placed in the living room. Whenever Jim displayed any one of the behaviors listed in Table 1, Mrs. E. would first say "No!," and then splash approximately 4 ounces of water on Jim's face and head. The splashing was carried out with an underhand motion. The water (but not the glass) was released at a distance of 6-12 in from the child. Initially Mrs. E. was verbally cued with regard to when to use the water. These cues were dropped in later sessions. This procedure continued for 15 sessions.

Next, the punishment procedure was discontinued. Throughout, however, a contact and a no-contact period characterized each session. Mrs. E. now verbalized and attended to Jim for both acceptable and unacceptable behavior much as she had during baseline. After four sessions this phase ended and was followed by a second punishment phase.

The second punishment phase was similar to the first. However, Mrs. E. was not cued to respond. Water was used much less frequently than before and discontinued after Session 41. At this time Mrs. E. reported Jim was head banging at other times of the day when the authors were not present. In order to give her an additional technique for controlling this behavior, she was instructed in the use of a time-out procedure. Jim was taken to his room and was told he must remain there for a minimum of 5 min. If no deviant behavior was observed after the minimum time period had elapsed, he was allowed to return to the living room. Formal observations continued for 3 additional sessions. Phone contact was used during the next several weeks to monitor Jim's behavior and advise Mrs. E. on the continued use of time out during the therapist's absence.

RESULTS

On 7 occasions 2 observers also recorded the interaction between Jim and his mother. Observer agreement was calculated by dividing the total number of agreements by agreements plus disagreements. Blank intervals were not counted as instances of agreement. Agreement ranged from 70 to 89%, and averaged 80%.

The tendency for Jim to display his inappropriate behaviors under both contact and no-contact conditions may be seen in Figure 1. The former averaged 5.2 min per session, the latter 26.4 min. Total session time averaged 31.6 min. Figure 1 indicates that whenever Mrs. E. was playing with Jim or attending to him in some way (dark bars) the mean rate of deviant behavior was fairly low — under .5 responses per min. However, when she withdrew her attention (following the author's signal) the mean rate of deviant behavior was higher during all phases. This increase was lowest during the treatment and follow-up phases and highest during baseline reinforcement and reversal phases.

Effects of the treatment procedures employed with Jim may be seen in Figure 2. During baseline the rate of deviant behaviors was high, averaging 4.48 responses per min during the no-contact period. This figure increased during differential reinforcement to 4.88 responses per min. The use of water as a punishing stimulus was employed next. (Numbers above each data point indicate the number of times water was used during a session.) Response rate varied considerably during the first half of this period and then began to show a decreasing trend, averaging 1.5 responses per min over the entire phase. During the

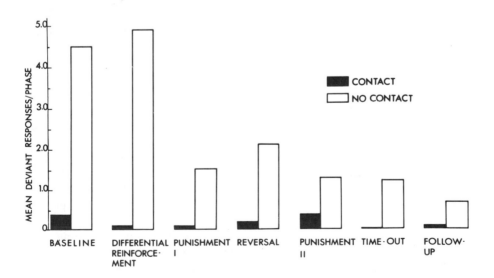

Figure 1   Rate per minute of deviant responses across treatment phases during contact and no-contact periods.

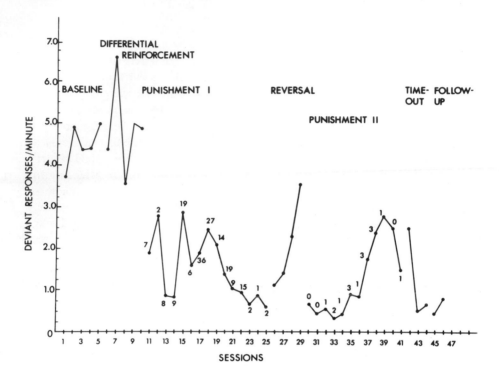

Figure 2   The effects of differential reinforcement, punishment and time out on deviant behavior during no-contact phases.

four-session reversal period, response rate increased and averaged 2.10 responses per min. The second punishment period was marked by a low, relatively stable rate of responding during the first 7 sessions followed by an increase in deviant behavior during Sessions 37-39. This increase in responding was primarily due to a change in the frequency of one response: "Mama." While the rate for all responses (9 behaviors) except "Mama" during this phase was .52 per min, "Mama" alone averaged .74 responses per min. This compares with a baseline rate for "Mama" of .21 responses per min. A more detailed look at this response during Sessions 36-41 reveals "Mama" to be displayed at a frequency of 1.17 responses per min, while the 9 other responses are displayed at a combined rate of .80 per min. The overall rate of deviant behavior during the second punishment period averaged 1.26 responses per min.

In Session 42, Mrs. E. began the use of a brief isolation period (time-out) contingent on deviant behavior. The rate of deviant behavior was 2.47 per min during Session 42 and dropped to .52 per min in Session 43. It was .64 responses per min in Session 44. Time out was employed once in Session 42 and twice in Session 44.

The first follow-up observation was made 49 days after Session 44. During this interval Mrs. E. continued to use time-out (but not water) when necessary. The rate of deviant behavior was .45 responses per min. Eighteen days after this observation the last follow-up visit occurred. The only response observed was "Mama," which occurred at a rate of .83 responses per min.

An analysis of the course of 3 selected responses may be seen in Figure 3, which shows self-hitting, head bangs, and removing mother's materials. Removing materials occurred most often while hitting is least frequent. The introduction of differential reinforcement caused an acceleration in the rate of head banging and hitting (this was also true of crying, and saying "Mama," which are not shown on this graph). Removing materials, however, declined in rate from an average of .90 responses per min per session during baseline to .58 responses per min per session during reinforcement. (Opening doors, spitting, pulling on clothing, and throwing also declined during differential reinforcement but are not shown in Figure 3).

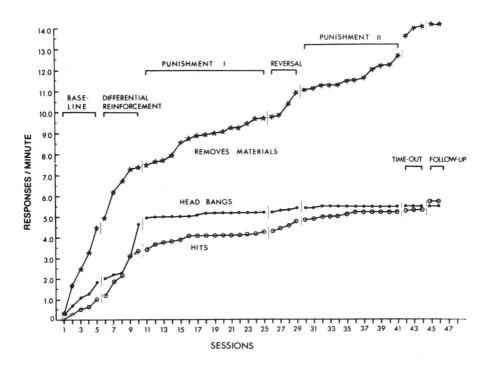

Figure 3   Rate per minute of self-hitting, head bangs, and removing materials.

The introduction of punishment in Session 11 decreased the rate of head banging and hitting markedly. Removing materials also decreased, but not as much. All three responses increased during the reversal phase with removing materials nearly doubling in average rate. During Punishment II, head banging no longer occurred while hitting was only infrequently displayed. Removing materials dropped from its reversal rate of .30 responses per min per session to .14 responses per min per session but showed a tendency to increase somewhat during Sessions 38-40. This increase continued into the first session of time out and then fell to a low rate. Head banging and hitting were rarely seen during time out.

During the follow-up observations, hitting and removing materials increased in Session 45 but were not displayed thereafter. Head banging was not observed.

DISCUSSION

It is interesting to note that while differential reinforcement was not effective in reducing the overall rate of deviant behavior (see Figure 2), this procedure appeared to influence certain individual responses. Head banging, hitting, crying, and saying "Mama" increased during this treatment phase, while kicking, throwing, spitting, removing materials, opening doors, and pulling on the mother's clothing declined. While these increases in rate exceeded decreases, it is not clear why this differential performance was observed. Changes during this phase did not appear to be related to baseline rates — or a particular topography of response.

Although differential reinforcement was not successful in reducing the overall rate of deviant behavior, there were sharp differences in deviant performance (see Figure 1) between the contact and no-contact periods. It may be that a brief mother-child interaction (less than 20 sec), such as that involved in differential reinforcement was an S^D for deviant behavior. In other words, this type of interaction signaled Jim to escalate deviant responses in an attempt to produce a longer period of interaction. Other stimuli ("Look at this pretty picture") may have then set the occasion for behaviors incompatible with deviant responses and the remainder of the period was peaceful, that is, until mother left for a different activity. This analysis is also supported by informal observations. On several occasions the authors observed Jim playing quietly in his room. His mother would then walk down the hall and pass by his door. Deviant behaviors would then be displayed for several minutes. This analysis must be labeled speculative, however. Additional data are needed to firmly establish that those responses which did increase during differential reinforcement were not inadvertently strengthened in some way by their delayed proximity to mother's social consequences.

The control exerted over Jim's deviant behavior during the contact period also suggests that a fading procedure might have been employed to reduce the discriminative effect of brief mother-child interactions. It would be interesting to explore whether one could begin treatment with a contact period and then fade mother's attention in increasing intervals until she could leave him unattended for reasonable periods without occasioning deviant behaviors.

The data in this study suggest that water can function as a punishing stimulus for deviant behavior. It has the advantage of being quantifiable and does not cause physical harm to the individual. For this reason it may be preferable to stimuli (slapping or spanking) that may damage tissue. It may also be preferable to contingent electric shock in cases in which the health of the individual may be of some concern. Shock was not used in this study because Jim was known to have a heart defect which could possibly be aggravated by accidental misuse of the shock device.

While water has certain advantages, it has some liabilities as well. When used frequently, it will wet the area where it is employed. To be effective it must be nearby and ready to use. A trip to the kitchen after each response would limit its value severely.

The rise in deviant behavior during Punishment II, as pointed out earlier, was primarily due to an increase in the response "Mama." (Deviant behaviors except "Mama" averaged 1.04 responses per min during Punishment I and .52 responses per min during Punishment II.) As shown in Figure 1, water was used much less frequently during Punishment II than in Punishment I. The reason for the infrequent use of water was that Mrs. E. was reluctant to punish "Mama" since it was not deviant in topography but only in frequency.

The data presented in this study show a substantial change in the frequency of Jim's deviant behavior during treatment and follow-up. Mr. and Mrs. E. found they could now interrupt their interaction with Jim to answer the telephone, greet a visitor, and read the paper without being subjected to a torrent of Jim's undesirable behavior. Jim had become a greater pleasure in their lives. Nevertheless, in the opinion of the authors, Jim's problems were not totally resolved. He remained considerably behind in intellectual and social skills. Some deviant behaviors were still displayed outside of treatment sessions — particularly at bedtime. Despite these difficulties Mrs. E. had learned to manage Jim more effectively to the extent that both Jim and his mother were now a part of a more normal parent-child relationship.

ACKNOWLEDGMENTS

The authors would like to thank Sidney W. Bijou for his support and encouragement to carry out this study. Publication of this paper was supported in part by Research Advisory Board Grant Number 4-1-228-5115-007 from the University of Nevada, and Research Board Grant 41-32-66-369 from the University of Illinois.

REFERENCES

Backman, J. A. Self-injurious behavior: A behavioral analysis. *Journal of Abnormal Psychology*, 1972, *80*, 211-224.

Hamilton, J., Stephens, L., & Allen, P. Controlling aggressive and destructive behavior in severely retarded institutionalized residents. *American Journal of Mental Deficiency*, 1967, *71*, 852-856.

Hawkins, R. P., Peterson, R. F., Schweid, E., & Bijou, S. W. Behavior therapy in the home: Amelioration of problem parent-child relations with the parent in a therapeutic role. *Journal of Experimental Child Psychology*, 1966, *4*, 99-107.

Lahey, B. B., McNees, M. P., & McNees, M. C. Control of an obscene "verbal tic" through time out in an elementary school classroom. *Journal of Applied Behavior Analysis*, 1973, *6*, 101-104.

Lovaas, O. I. *Behavioral treatment of autistic children*. Morristown, N.J.: General Learning Press, 1973. Pp. 1-17.

Lovaas, O. I., & Simmons, J. Q. Manipulation of self-destruction in three retarded children. *Journal of Applied Behavior Analysis*, 1969, *2*, 143-157.

Risley, T. R. The effects and side effects of punishing the autistic behaviors of a deviant child. *Journal of Applied Behavior Analysis*, 1968, *1*, 21-34.

Wahler, R. G., Winkel, G. H., Peterson, R. F., & Morrison, D. C. Mothers as behavior therapists for their own children. *Behavior Research and Therapy*, 1965, *3*, 113-124.

Webster, D. R., & Azrin, N. H. Required relaxation: A method of inhibiting agitative-disruptive behavior of retardates. *Behavior Research and Therapy*, 1973, *11*, 67-78.

16

A Methodology for Studying Social Stimulus Functions in Children

William H. Redd
Andrew S. Winston
Edward K. Morris

University of Illinois, Urbana-Champaign

Research in children's social behavior has placed great emphasis on the role of adult verbal consequences and, in particular, social reinforcement (Gewirtz & Baer, 1958a; Hartup, 1964). Recent work has focused on the effect of antecedent social stimuli, such as the instructions (Bufford, 1971; Martin, 1972; Steinman, 1970), stated preferences (Redd, 1974) and the presence or absence of an adult (Meddock, Parsons, & Hill, 1971; Peterson & Whitehurst, 1971). Within these three broad categories of events, consequences, antecedents, and prior interaction, there are innumerable variations of the specific verbal stimuli, nonverbal and contextual cues, and past schedules of reinforcement and punishment. The task of assessing and comparing these various social stimuli is a difficult one, involving a number of complex methodological issues. The purpose of this chapter is to discuss a method for studying a variety of social cues with children. Several detailed examples of the use of this methodology will also be presented.

METHODS FOR STUDYING SOCIAL CUES

Assessment of Social Reinforcement Effectiveness

Social reinforcement has been studied almost invariably by assessing its effect on simple motor behavior. The child is typically asked to pick up marbles and drop them one at a time into the apparatus while an adult occasionally praises the child by saying "that's very good," "that's fine," etc. Three different dependent measures of social reinforcement effectiveness have been employed: persistence, change in rate of responding, and change in choice or preference.

The persistence measure (time spent at the task) has been used in a number of studies by Zigler and his colleagues (Berkowitz & Zigler, 1965; Butterfield & Zigler, 1965). In these studies the children were told that they could stop playing a simple marble-drop game any time they wanted to. The game then continued while an adult delivered praise and attention until the child asked to stop or until a predetermined time limit was reached. It was assumed that the time the child chose to spend at the task was a measure of the effectiveness of the social reinforcement the adult provided.

However, it could be argued that persistence is a measure of the time it takes for the reinforcer to satiate. "Resistance to satiation" need not be viewed as identical to other measures of reinforcer effectiveness. For example, persistence might depend on the control exerted by the initial instructions and other social "demand characteristics" (Orne, 1962) of the situation, while rate of responding might depend primarily on the schedule of reinforcement. The problem is further complicated by the fact that the praise is typically presented noncontingently. That is, the occurrence of praise depends only on the passage of time and not on the emission of a particular response class. Thus, the child's responding might be considered an example of "superstition" (Herrnstein, 1966). The use of noncontingent reinforcement may be one reason why some studies have not found that praise affects persistence (Green & Zigler, 1962; Zigler, 1961).

When change in rate of responding is used (Hartup, 1967; Hill & Moely, 1969; Stevenson & Fahel, 1961; Stevenson & Odom, 1962), the subject's base rate under a brief (1 min) nonreinforcement condition is compared with his rate under each minute of a reinforcement period (4 or 5 min). A major disadvantage here is that social reinforcement is being delivered noncontingently. The child is not being specifically reinforced for rate of responding and cannot increase the density of praise by responding faster (Parton & Ross, 1965). Given the use of noncontingent reinforcement, "superstitious" control is again a possibility. If children are told they are "doing a fine job" they might respond to this cue by maintaining rather than increasing their current rate of responding. Many studies of operant conditioning have used noncontingent reinforcement as a control condition for assessing the effect of contingent reinforcement (Hart, Reynolds, Baer, Brawley & Harris, 1968; Weisberg, 1963). In these studies, noncontingent reinforcement has been found to have little or no effect. Therefore, not surprisingly changes in rate of responding obtained in social reinforcement studies are typically quite small (Hartup, 1967 Figs. 2, 4 & 5). In fact, the change is often negative, especially for institutionalized children (Stevenson & Hill, 1966). When rate of responding decreases during social reinforcement, it is likely that there are other unknown, controlling variables in the situation. For example, Parton and Ross (1965) noted that a 1-min baseline may be insufficiently stable to serve as a control for time related changes in responding such as warm-up and fatigue. Another criticism of the response rate measure is that the task imposes a ceiling on rate of responding that may obscure important relationships; if a child's baseline rate is high, little increase is possible. It should be noted that rate change scores have successfully been used to study a wide variety of manipulations (Hartup, 1967; Hill, 1969; Stevenson, 1965). Stevenson and Hill (1966) have also presented data and arguments to counter some of the criticisms of Parton and Ross (1965); however, the use of noncontingent reinforcement remains a major problem. Noncontingent, time-based praise has been used in order to equate the number of praise statements for different groups. Controlling the number of reinforcements could also be accomplished by using a yoked-control technique; thus permitting the use of contingent reinforcement. However, this procedure would not eliminate another problem involved in the use of persistence and rate measures. The child is being told to emit and praised for emitting the same response. It is therefore difficult to determine which variable is controlling performance.

A third measure of social reinforcement effectiveness is choice or preference (Gewirtz & Baer, 1958a, b; Walters & Ray, 1960; Zigler & Kanzer, 1962). This technique allows social reinforcement to be conveniently given contingent upon a specific response class. The studies using persistence or rate change measures have typically used a 6-hole apparatus with the child told to put any marble in any hole. When a choice measure is used, the apparatus generally has two holes and the adult reinforces responses to the hole that was least preferred during baseline. The degree to which the child shifts choices from baseline is used to assess the strength of the reinforcer. The response class being reinforced (least preferred hole) is different than the response class prompted by the initial instructions (put the marbles in either hole), thus avoiding the confound of praise and instructions mentioned above. Parton and Ross (1965) have criticized the preference measure in terms of the assumption that baseline performance is stable. They noted that statistically significant changes away from the response preferred during baseline may be the result of regression to the mean, rather than social reinforcement. Moreover, the variables controlling which response is selected during baseline are unknown. Responding during both baseline and reinforcement periods might be affected by alternation strategies (Craig & Myers, 1963), position preferences (McCullers & Stevenson, 1960), etc. Given current techniques these factors are not within the experimenter's control. Parton and Ross (1965) also noted that in the choice situation the child can increase the density of reinforcement either by increasing the rate of response to both holes, or increasing the proportion of marbles dropped in the "correct" hole. They suggested the use of a discrete trials procedure with a two choice task to avoid this difficulty.

A discrete-trials technique for studying social reinforcement has been used by Cairns and his associates (Paris & Cairns, 1972; Warren & Cairns, 1972). The child is instructed to emit one of two responses whenever a signal or trial light comes on. In this research no baseline period was used because it was assumed that the reinforced choice would be selected 50% of the time by chance; the effect of social reinforcement was therefore assessed against chance level responding. In group designs the absence of a baseline is not likely to be a serious problem since the reinforced choice is counterbalanced. However, this procedure would clearly be unsuitable for experimental analysis with individual subjects. The use of discrete trials also does not resolve the problem of additional sources of control: position preferences, alternation strategies, implicit instructions, etc.

The technique used by Cairns closely resembles the two-choice discrimination tasks often used to compare different types of adult feedback, such as "right" versus "wrong," (Cheyne, 1971; Paris & Cairns, 1972; Spence, 1973). When either the number of trials used is very small or the stimuli are changed from trial to trial (as in Cheyne, 1971; Spence, 1973), an additional problem arises. The measure (percentage correct) may then reflect rates of acquisition of a new response and may not reflect the ability of social reinforcement to maintain or strengthen an already learned response. Which of these processes should be considered the best measure of "reinforcer effectiveness" remains an unanswered question.

Assessment of the Effect of Antecedent Social Stimuli

In contrast to the social reinforcement literature, there is no well-developed set of techniques for assessing antecedent social stimuli. However, some general remarks can be made, particularly regarding the study of individual subjects. Much of the current interest in adult instructions and presence stems from recent studies on generalized imitation (Steinman, 1970; Bufford, 1971; Peterson & Whitehurst, 1971). Results suggest that instructions are an important factor in producing nonreinforced imitation that may persist over many sessions. The powerful control of instructions in such situations creates problems for assessment. Compliant responding may remain at a ceiling despite experimental manipulations and may continue long after the instructions have been eliminated or have become inappropriate (Meddock, 1972). It may therefore be difficult to compare different types of instructions or instruction following under different conditions, such as adult presence or absence. While the effects of experimental manipulations may show up as statistically significant in group designs, individual experimental analysis requires clear shifts in performance that are unlikely to occur if even subtle or temporally distant instructional cues exert strong control.

Greater variability in compliance is more likely to occur when there is some "temptation" not to comply. In traditional methods of studying resistance to temptation, the child violates a prohibition against touching forbidden objects (Walters & Parke, 1964) or breaks the stated rules of a game (Grinder, 1961). These procedures may be viewed as assessments of the strength of instructional control. Research in this area has shown that children's behavior in a temptation situation is sensitive to a variety of manipulations of the instructional stimuli (Biaggio & Rodrigues, 1971; Redd, Amen, Meddock & Winston, 1974).

Assessing social control through the use of resistance-to-temptation procedures has the advantage of providing the child with a clear set of alternative responses. For example, Walters and Demkow (1963) provided the child with the choice of either looking at a book written in an unfamiliar language or playing with attractive, but forbidden toys. Unfortunately, the relative reinforcement value of these alternatives is difficult to define or manipulate. First, it is not always clear that the attractive toy would be chosen if it were not forbidden (Ward & Furchak, 1968). And second, the use of specific, finite objects makes it difficult to vary the reinforcement values of the alternatives in a systematic manner. Thus, it is difficult to control the variables that compete with the social stimuli. This problem is similar to that encountered in assessing social reinforcement effectiveness. In both cases there are additional or competing factors other than the social stimuli: fatigue, boredom, or position preferences in the case of social reinforcement, and attractive toys or outcomes in the case of resistance to temptation.

Since social history is customarily studied by assessing its effect on social reinforcement and instruction following, the problems involved in these two areas of assessment are also problems for the study of interaction history. Thus a greater degree of control over unknown and confounding factors is needed in order to carry out precise, experimental analyses of social cue functions within individual children.

AN ALTERNATIVE METHOD

In order to minimize the problems discussed above we have developed a "variable-consequence choice procedure" for studying the effects of social stimuli on children's behavior. The essential component of this procedure is a two-choice, discrete-trials task in which each response earns varied amounts of tangible (e.g., token) reinforcement. The child's choice behavior is brought under the control of the higher paying of the two alternatives and a stable baseline is established. An adult then provides the child with social cues for emitting the lower paying response. These stimuli, the instructions or praise, compete with the reinforcement contingencies for the higher paying response. The magnitude of token reinforcement for each of the two choices is varied independently and the strength of the adult's particular social cue is assessed against the established reinforcement contingencies.

For example, a child might be instructed to emit the lower paying of the two responses. The difference in material payoff is kept small so that the child's choices are controlled by the instructions. During subsequent sessions the difference between payoffs for the two responses is increased. The point at which control of the child's responding shifts from the instruction to the material reinforcers is determined. That is, the child stops following the instructions and selects the higher paying responses. The strength of the instruction is evaluated by pitting it against known material reinforcers.

The variable-consequence choice procedure has a number of useful features for the study of social stimulus functions. First, it employs a choice rather than a rate measure of responding as the dependent measure. Basic laboratory research with animals has suggested that choice responding is more sensitive to a variety of subsequent manipulations than rate of a single response. For example, the amount and/or duration of reinforcement (Catania, 1963; Neuringer, 1967), force required to execute a response (Chung, 1965), and punishment intensity (Azrin & Holz, 1966) are all more precisely assessed by choice procedures. Thus, choice responding might also be expected to be more sensitive both to subtle manipulations of social stimuli and to changes in reinforcement contingencies. In addition, the choice procedure avoids problems in the use of noncontingent reinforcement conditions associated with rate and persistence measures.

Second, the amounts of token reinforcement can be readily varied for individual children. This feature allows stable responding to be established despite individual differences in strength of token reinforcement or social cues. For example, one child might stop complying with instructions when the difference in payoff is three tokens; for another child the same change in responding might require a difference of ten tokens. If a fixed level of payoffs were used, this difference between the two children might not be detected. Within an individual child two slightly different social stimuli might appear to have the same effect at one level of payoff, but different effects at other levels. Adjusting the payoffs is clearly an advantage when studying individual children; in addition, it is likely to minimize the problems of ceiling effects mentioned previously. Without the competing control of the token reinforcement, social cues may exert control that is too strong to permit its assessment.

Using token reinforcement also has the advantage of allowing the competing factors in the social control situation to be specified and manipulated. In research on the stimulus functions of social cues, the child may be viewed as having a choice between emitting a praised and instructed response or not doing so. As previously pointed out, uncontrolled factors such as position preferences, color preferences, and response strategies may affect baseline performance or compete with the social stimuli. By using a choice procedure there are known sources of control for both responses. The control exerted by the token consequences is likely to override these unknown factors and thus allow the establishment of stable responding.

Finally, the current approach is flexible enough to be used in the study of a variety of possible relationships such as the effects of: (1) different social stimuli from the same adult; (2) social stimuli from different adults; and (3) different adult-child interactional histories on subsequent social control.

Procedural Description

The variable consequence choice procedure has been used with two sets of apparatus. However, the particular response is not critical to the methodology since any two-choice motor discrimination task could be used.

One set of equipment (Redd & Wheeler, 1973) consisted of a two-hole marble-drop apparatus. Above each of the two holes was a lens; the lenses could be illuminated either separately or simultaneously. A second set of equipment (Redd & Winston, 1974) consisted of two-plunger-type manipulanda housed in separate boxes. The visible interior of these boxes could be illuminated, again either separately or simultaneously. For each of these color discriminations tasks, token reinforcer dispensers were located next to apparatuses.

At the start of each session the subjects were escorted to the experimental room and introduced to the experimenter. The experimenter then instructed the subject in the operation of the particular apparatus. The subject was told to make a response (marble drop or lever pull) and that these responses would earn tokens which could be exchanged for prizes later. During each session the subject was presented with single presentation trials (one light) interspersed with choice trials (two lights). This procedure insured that the subject came into contact with the contingencies associated with each response. Presentation order was appropriately balanced for position, color-presentation order, and single-choice trial sequencing. For both single-color and choice trials the appropriate number of tokens was delivered after each response.

EXAMPLES OF THE USE OF THE VARIABLE-CONSEQUENCE CHOICE PROCEDURE

This procedure has been used in a number of studies of adult stimulus functions for young children and mentally retarded adults. In these experiments the effects of social stimuli presented either as antecedent or consequent events were studied within single-subject research designs. What follows is a discussion of the use of the procedures in the investigation of: (1) adult-dispensed social reinforcement; (2) adult instructions and preference statements; and (3) the effects of adult-child interaction histories. These examples are presented in order to show the varied applications of the procedure. Different features of the procedures were included in each of the various experiments.

Social Reinforcement

The first example (Redd, 1974) involved the assessment of the strength of an adult's praise. Using a marble-drop game and the two-choice procedure described earlier, subjects chose between one response that produced monetary reinforcers (tokens) and another response that earned fewer tokens but also resulted in an adult's praise. During successive sessions the relative amounts of monetary reinforcement that each response produced was varied. The purpose was to determine the amount of token reinforcement required for the subject to forego social reinforcement in favor of monetary reinforcement. This procedure is similar to that used by Galloway (1967) in a study of the modification of response bias. He assessed children's bias in a color-form discrimination task under conditions of equal reinforcement for both responses. After the bias was determined the number of tokens delivered for the preferred response was decreased until each subject reversed his response preferences. The present analysis was more extensive than Galloway's in that the amount of token reinforcement for each response was varied and the reversal of the behavior was replicated within each subject.

During daily sessions with two first-grade boys and one institutionalized, mentally-retarded female, the subject and the experimenter sat side-by-side facing the apparatus. After giving initial instructions the adult experimenter remained quietly seated beside the subject while he or she played the game. Each session consisted of 48 trials separated by 5-sec intertrial intervals. On 24 of these trials one colored light was presented (single-color trials) and on the remaining 24 trials one colored light was presented (choice trials). A response to one of the colors was praised by the experimenter ("good," "great," "that's right," etc.) on both single color and choice trials. During baseline phases 2 tokens were dispensed along with experimenter's praise; when the other color was selected 2 tokens and no praise were delivered (2 + praise versus 2). After the subject developed a preference for one of the colors (defined as the same choice for at least 19 out of 24 choice trials for 2 successive sessions) new payoff conditions were introduced. Token reinforcement for the 2 responses was varied from 0 to 8 during 3 assessment phases (separated by 2 + praise versus 2 baseline phases).

Figures 1, 2, and 3 present cumulative records for praised responses on choice trials for two first-grade boys (S-1, S-2) and one mentally-retarded female adult (S-3). Phases are identified by the symbols above the arrows and separated on the records by "plot-reset" at the beginning of each phase. During the initial baseline phase (2 + praise versus 2) all subjects developed a clear preference for the response that the adult praised. When token reinforcement for the non-praised response was increased from 2 to 4 tokens (2 + praise versus 4), S-1 and S-3 switched to nonpraised responding. S-1's percentage of praised responding decreased from 100% to 10%, and S-3's decreased from 100% to 0%. S-2 showed a moderate shift in choice behavior; his praised responding shifted from 100 to 50%. Baseline responding was then reestablished at 2 + praise versus 2. S-1's choice behavior was uneffected when token reinforcement for the nonpraised response was increased to 3 (see Fig 3: 2 + praise versus 3). All subjects consistently emitted the praised response on choice trials during the third baseline (see Fig. 1, 2, and 3: 2 + praise versus 2). During the final phase when token

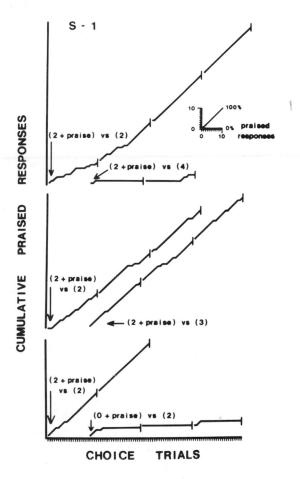

Figure 1   S-1's cumulative choices of the socially reinforced (praised) response on successive choice trials across experimental conditions. A 45-degree line segment indicates a choice of the nonpraised response. Experimental phases are identified by the symbols above the arrows and separated by plot reset at the beginning of each phase.

reinforcement no longer accompanied the experimenter's praise (see Fig. 1, 2, and 3: 0 + praise versus 2), all subjects switched to the nonpraised response. S-1's and S-3's shifts were more rapid than S-2's.

The exact number of tokens required to produce this shift differed among subjects. S-1 and S-2 shifted to nonpraised responding when those responses earned four tokens versus two tokens for the praised response, but these subjects did not shift when nonpraised responses earned only three tokens. S-2 did not show a complete shift to nonpraised responding when such responding earned four tokens, but did shift when it produced eight tokens. When token reinforcement for the praised response was reduced to zero versus two for the nonpraised response all subjects shifted to the nonpraised response.

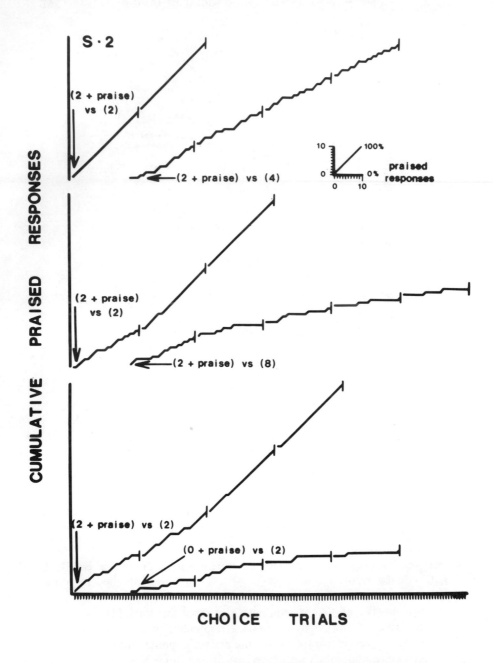

Figure 2   S-2's cumulative choices of the socially reinforced (praised) response on successive choice trials across experimental conditions. A 45-degree line segment indicates a choice of the praised response, and a horizontal line segment indicates a choice of the nonpraised response. Experimental phases are identified by the symbols above the arrows and separated by plot reset at the beginning of each phase.

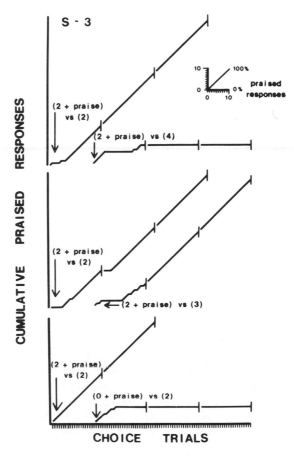

Figure 3   S-3's cumulative choices of the socially reinforced (praised) response on successive choice trials across experimental conditions. A 45-degree line segment indicates a choice of the praised response, and a horizontal line segment indicates a choice of the nonpraised response. Experimental phases are identified by the symbols above the arrows and separated by plot reset at the beginning of each phase.

By varying the amounts of token reinforcement for the two responses, the relative strength of the adult's praise was assessed. When the token payoffs were the same for each response, social reinforcement appeared to be equally effective for all three subjects. However, when the payoffs were systematically changed, differences in the strength of praise did appear. Clear shifts in performance, from 100% to 0% praised responses, occurred for each subject. It is unlikely that such dramatic changes would be obtained using other procedures for assessing social reinforcement effectiveness. As discussed earlier, the payoff for nonpraised responding is unknown and uncontrolled in traditional methods. In the current procedure the payoff for nonpraised responding can be increased to the point where praised responding is completely eliminated.

Instructions and Adult Presence

This method has been used in three studies of instructional control (Redd & Wheeler, 1973; Redd, 1974; Redd & Winston, 1974). In these experiments the adult experimenter either instructed or in some way indicated to the child that he was to choose the lower paying of the two responses. In one study (Redd & Wheeler, 1973), first grade children played the marble-drop game and chose between holes that either earned tokens redeemable for pennies or earned worthless, nonredeemable tokens. After the children developed a preference for the response that earned redeemable tokens, the experimenter instructed the child to try to get as many worthless tokens as possible. All of the subjects switched to the response that earned worthless tokens. During subsequent sessions the experimenter's control was maintained as long as he remained present.

In another study (Redd, 1974), the adult's stated preference for one response exerted similar control. When the experimenter told the child that he liked it better when the child put the marble into a particular hole (the lower-paying choice), six of the eight subjects immediately switched to that response. In both studies the experimenter's instructions overrode the control exerted by explicitly programmed reinforcement contingencies.

While these two studies did not involve manipulation of the amounts of token reinforcement, they do show how explicit material payoffs may be "pitted against" instructions or preference statements. The baseline performance of all subjects was highly stable. That is, they reliably chose the backed-up or high-paying alternative. The token reinforcement provided a strong, known source of control against which social control was assessed.

These procedures have also been used to investigate the effects of different types of instructions. Redd and Winston (1974) compared positively and negatively expressed preference statements. Results for one four-year-old boy are presented here as an example. During daily sessions the subject watched a male assistant play a two-choice discrimination game and then played the game himself. To reduce the evaluative and overt instructional components of the adult's preference statements, the comments were made in reference to another person's behavior prior to the child's actual performance of the task. While the child watched from behind a one-way vision screen an adult commented to the subject about the assistant's behavior. During one phase the adult made positive comments ("I like it; he pulled the red one") when one response was emitted and neutral comments ("He pulled the green one") when the assistant made the other response. During another phase negative comments ("I don't like it, he pulled the yellow one") and neutral comments were made. The assistant chose each color an equal number of times regardless of the adult's preferences. When the assistant finished, he left the room and the experimenter and child sat side by side in front of the apparatus. The adult made no comments while the child played the game. The dependent measure was the degree to which the child complied with the adult's stated preference. Compliance was defined as choosing the color that experimenter liked during positive-comments conditions or not choosing the color that experimenter disliked (choosing the neutral color) during negative-comments conditions.

Figure 4 shows percentage compliance for one of the three subjects during all sessions. In the first phase the subject received one token either for a compliant response or for a noncompliant response. The tokens were exchanged for small toys at the end of the session. Under these conditions positive comments produced a high degree of compliance ($\bar{x}$ = 90.1%). Since compliance was at a "ceiling" a differential reinforcement condition was introduced in order to provide a better comparison of positive and negative comments. Two tokens were given for compliant responses and three tokens for noncompliant responses during all remaining sessions. Under differential reinforcement compliance with positive comments was greatly reduced ($\bar{x}$ = 34.9%). However, a high level of compliance was maintained when experimenter used negative comments ($\bar{x}$ = 86.9%). The greater control exerted by positive ($\bar{x}$ = 2.0%) and negative ($\bar{x}$ = 98.6%) comments was replicated during the last two phases.

The adult's negative comments were strong enough to compete with the greater payoff for noncompliance, but positive comments were not. It is clear

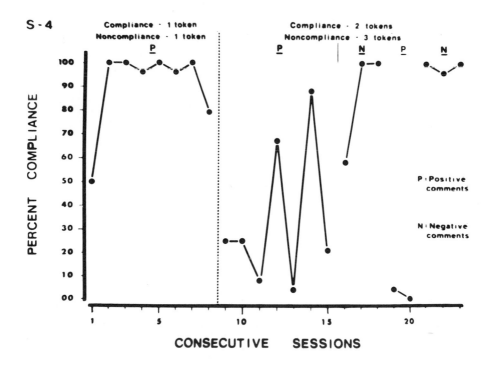

Figure 4   Percentage compliance on choice trials across successive sessions for S-4. Experimental phases and amount of token reinforcement for compliance and noncompliance choices are shown above the graph.

that this assessment would have been difficult without some manipulation of the reinforcement contingencies. If only equal token reinforcement had been used, it is likely that both positive and negative comments would have produced an essentially equal, high degree of compliance. On the other hand, if one token had been given for compliance and ten tokens for noncompliance it is possible that neither type of comment would have been effective and that the child's behavior would be entirely controlled by the reinforcers. For this particular subject, three tokens for noncompliance and two tokens for compliance turned out to be the optimal condition for comparing these two types of social stimuli.

The ability to vary the magnitude of token reinforcement so as to effectively compete with the stimuli being studied has also facilitated the study of the effects of adult presence on children's behavior. In a study with four-year-old boys and with second- and third-grade children, Winston and Redd (1974)

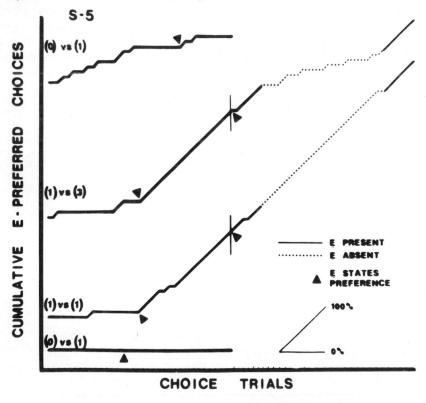

Figure 5   S-5's cumulative choices of the response the experimenter preferred on successive choice trials. A 45-degree line segment indicates choices of the E-preferred response and horizontal line indicates choices of the other (not preferred) response. Experimental phases are identified by the symbols above the records.

compared the effects of adult instructions with and without an adult being present. The first study involved individual analyses with three four-year-old boys.

During daily sessions the subject played the two-choice marble-drop game described previously. At various times the adult experimenter stated a preference for one color by saying "I want you to put the marbles in the _____ -colored hole." No other comments were made to the child except when the experimenter was scheduled to leave the room when he would say, "I have to leave for a while. Go ahead and play the game; I'll be back later."

Data for a typical subject are shown in Figure 5. To insure that token reinforcement was effective in controlling choices, each new reinforcement condition began with a baseline period during which the adult did not state a preference. After stable responding developed under baseline conditions, the experimenter stated a preference for the response which gave fewer tokens. If both responses earned an equal number of tokens the experimenter stated a preference for the color that the subject chose less frequently during baseline.

In the first condition the experimenter-preferred response paid no tokens and the other response one token. The first curve in Figure 5 represents data from one session. During baseline the subject gradually stopped choosing the zero-token color. The experimenter then stated a preference for the zero-token color, but the subject continued to choose the one-token color. That is, the experimenter's preference did not control responding.

The token payoffs were then changed to one token for the experimenter's preferred response and three tokens for the other response. The second curve in Figure 5 represents data from two sessions. During baseline the subject chose the three-token color consistently. As soon as the experimenter stated a preference for the one-token color, the subject shifted to experimenter's preferred response. At the beginning of the next session the experimenter stated the preference again and his statement was still effective. However, when the experimenter was out of the room the subject made only 30% experimenter-preferred choices. When the experimenter returned the subject immediately returned to the experimenter-preferred color.

In the next phase S-5 received one token for each response. During baseline the subject consistently chose one of the colors even though the payoffs were equal. When the experimenter stated a preference for the other color the subject immediately switched to that response. The subject continued to choose the experimenter's preferred color during experimenter's absence as well as presence. That is, the experimenter's absence made no difference in responding under equal payoff.

In the final condition the original payoffs of zero and one tokens were reinstated. The previous effect was replicated; S-5 did not comply with experimenter's preferred response but continued to choose the one-token color.

In summary, with equal payoff the experimenter's preference statements controlled the child's choices with the experimenter present or absent; with one versus three tokens, the experimenter's preference controlled choices only when experimenter remained present; with zero versus one token, experimenter's preference did not control choices even when the experimenter was present. For the other two children in the study, a difference in responding between presence and absence conditions showed up at different payoffs.

This study again illustrates how social control depends upon the competing contingencies. The effect of the presence-absence manipulation was seen only at certain payoff differences. Under equal reinforcement conditions, compliance was at a "ceiling" (100%) and when the adult's preferred response yielded no tokens, compliance was at a "floor" (0%). The procedures thus provide a means of dealing with ceiling and floor effects that might otherwise obscure important relationships.

Social Interaction Histories

Two illustrations are presented here which demonstrate the utility of the procedure in assessing the relative strengths of social cues from different adults. In one case the history was inferred from particular demographic characteristics and, in the other, the history was experimentally manipulated before the assessment. Both of these examples employed the marble-drop task and followed procedures already described.

The first example is taken from the Redd and Wheeler (1973). One of the issues examined in this study was the role of adult personal characteristics in the control of children's instruction-following behavior. Here the child received two different kinds of tokens for choice responses, one type exchanged for pennies, the other thrown away without being backed up. After baseline preference for the backed-up tokens had been established, instructions to earn the worthless tokens were presented by two adult experimenters. E-1, a college-age female dressed in blue jeans, was introduced to subjects by her first name. E-2, an older professional male dressed in tie and jacket, was introduced by title and surname. Instructions from E-1 were ineffective in completely altering the choice behavior of two of the four subjects; those from E-2 were maximally effective for all subjects.

Thus, by comparing the children's choice behavior for valuable and worthless tokens, the relative strengths of the social cue from different adults could be evaluated. The literature on social reinforcement is replete with examples of differential reinforcer effectiveness as a function of variables identical to those manipulated in this study: age, sex, and "status." It therefore seems reasonable to assume that E-2's superior instructional control could be related to one or a combination of these demographic variables.

In a second study a social interaction history was explicitly manipulated and its effect on instructional control was assessed. During daily sessions each of five children was brought to an experimental room to engage in a color-sorting task over a number of sessions. Previously unknown adults then entered the room one at a time for short interactions (3 min). One adult socially and materially reinforced the child for color sorting; a second adult (positively) mildly reprimanded (negatively) any off-task behavior; and a third adult ignored the child (extinction). Each adult followed the same regime of interaction during all sessions. After each daily session a variety of probes assessing the child's adult preferences was conducted until a stable pattern of responding was achieved.

After generating these experimental histories, a probe of instructional control by the positive and negative adult was conducted following procedures previously described. After the child had developed a preference for the response earning one token versus the response earning zero tokens, the adult gave instructions to drop marbles in the no-payoff hole. When the positive adult was present and gave the instructions the child complied on only 20% of the trials; when the experimenter was absent the subject did not comply until enough tokens had been earned to acquire a prize. Baseline preference was then reestablished with the negative adult. When this adult was present and gave instructions the subject complied on 70% of the choice trials; when the experimenter was absent the subject complied 20% of the time. Thus, by pitting instructions against token reinforcement, the adults' instructional control could be compared.

The results of these two analyses are striking; however, it seems unwise to draw definite conclusions regarding relationships between demographic or interactional patterns and adult social control because only a small number of children, adults, and interactional histories have been investigated. In subsequent research the procedure will be used to investigate other differences in children's response to adults' reinforcement and their imitation of adults who differ in experimentally developed interactional histories. We expect that this procedure will also yield clear results in the anlysis of these functions.

DISCUSSION

The data presented above have illustrated how a variety of social stimuli may be studied using a variable-consequence choice procedure. It was demonstrated that the method could be employed both to assess the strength of such social cues as praise, preference, and various forms of instruction. In addition, it can be used in the study of social interaction histories. The procedure avoids many of the problems associated with the rate of responding measures and those associated with ceiling and floor effects in the study of antecedent social stimulus control.

The results clearly demonstrated the advantages of being able to manipulate token reinforcement consequences. Differences in the control of individual children's responding by the different social cues, as well as differences between children, appeared only at certain levels of token payoff. For example, in the assessment of social reinforcement the responses of all three children were equally controlled by praise statements from the adult under unequal amounts of token reinforcement. When the amounts of reinforcement were manipulated the relative strengths of the praise statements could be observed for each child.

The procedure was clearly adequate for the analysis of the behavior of individual children. In single-subject designs performance must be stable and the effects of the manipulations must be clear. Several examples were presented in which the children's choices were completely controlled by the token reinforcement under one set of payoffs and completely controlled by social stimuli under other levels of token consequences.

The use of the choice measure permitted a functional definition of the contingencies that controlled both of the two-choice responses. As a result the procedures yielded 100% shifts in response choice. This control is essential for an individual analysis and would also be valuable for intersubject group designs.

Certain limitations in the methodology might be pointed out. However, these problems are not present in every application of the method and are generally common to most other assessment procedures as well.

When this procedure is used it may be difficult to regain stable baseline performance following certain manipulations. This problem appears to be related to two factors. The effectiveness of antecedent and consequent social cues may deteriorate over sessions because they are never associated with subsequent back-up contingencies. Thus, their strength as cues for additional positive or negative consequences is diminished by repeated, unpaired presentations. Secondly, when the reinforcement for not complying with preferences or instructions is increased the subject will eventually deviate from the demands of the social cues. The subject is reinforced to make the choice response for the high magnitude alternative and, additionally, does not come into contact with any aversive contingencies for not complying with the adult. When smaller reinforcement differences are again presented the probability that the subjects will return to their baseline levels of compliance is decreased. The possible aversive components for deviance may have been eliminated while the other response reinforced. Although this problem cannot be completely resolved within the present paradigm, at least the flexibility to return to baseline conditions permits the evaluation of changes in the strengths of various social stimuli.

Additionally, it is often difficult for the child to detect certain small differences in the amount of tokens delivered for each choice. For example, when both choices are associated with amounts greater than zero some children may be unable to identify the alternative payoffs. This discrimination is much easier when one of the alternatives yields zero tokens.

Some may argue that this procedure evaluates the effect of material reinforcers against social cues rather than the reverse. That is, what is being assessed: the strength of social stimuli or strength of token reinforcers? The strength of the back-up reinforcers is a problem in any assessment technique where tokens or some other reinforcers are used for comparison purposes. This problem points out the importance of using a large variety of back-ups for the tokens or strong generalized reinforcers.

Finally, it is not presumed that all possible sources of social demands (Orne, 1962) within experimental settings have been eliminated through the use of this procedure. Unknown and confounding social cues may still be present. There usually exists more than one set of social-stimulus functions in all research settings and, in studying the relative strengths of social reinforcers or instructions, this method does not necessarily eliminate such unintended factors as facial expression, posture and vocal quality. Nevertheless, as soon as these possible sources are identified the procedures developed here may help facilitate the assessment of their strength of control over behavior.

The research presented here employed individual analysis designs. However, the general procedures can also be used in group studies. For example, in Redd, Amen, Meddock, and Winston (1974) and Winston and Redd (1974), the amount of token reinforcement for noncompliance was varied between rather than within children. While the payoff was not manipulated for each child, this design allowed social stimuli (instructions) to be assessed against a known source of control.

The prcedures are also not limited to the particular social cues described here. The strength of negative verbal consequences ("that's wrong," "bad," etc.), could be assessed by increasing the number of tokens for the punished response. Social cues could be presented non-verbally by having the adult model two-choice responses. Or, various histories of reinforcement for instruction following could be compared. The use of a common procedure to study such diverse cues could prove a distinct advantage.

ACKNOWLEDGMENTS

The research described here was supported in part by Grant 1 RO3 MH24614-01A1 MSM from the National Institute of Mental Health and by Grant G-74-0025 from the National Institute of Education.

REFERENCES

Azrin, N. H., & Holz, W. C. Punishment. In W. K. Honig (Ed.), *Operant behavior: Areas of research and application*. New York: Appleton-Century-Crofts, 1966.

Berkowitz, H., & Zigler, E. Effects of preliminary positive and negative interactions and delay conditions on children's responsiveness to social reinforcement. *Journal of Personality and Social Psychology*, 1965, *2*, 500-505.

Biaggio, A., & Rodrigues, A. Behavioral compliance and devaluation of the forbidden object as a function of probability of detection and severity of threat. *Developmental Psychology*, 1971, *4*, 320-323.

Bufford, R. K. Discrimination and instructions as factors in the control of nonreinforced imitations. *Journal of Experimental Child Psychology*, 1971, *12*, 35-50.

Butterfield, E. C., & Zigler, E. The influence of differing institutional climates on the effectiveness of social reinforcement in the mentally retarded. *American Journal of Mental Deficiency*, 1965, *70*, 48-56.

Catania, A. C. Concurrent performances: A baseline for the study of reinforcement magnitude. *Journal of the Experimental Analysis of Behavior*, 1963, *6*, 299-300.

Cheyne, J. A. Effects of imitation of different response consequences to a model. *Journal of Experimental Child Psychology*, 1971, *12*, 258-269.

Chung, S. H. Effects of effort on response rate. *Journal of the Experimental Analysis of Behavior*, 1965, *8*, 1-7.

Craig, G. J., & Myers, J. L. A developmental study of sequential two-choice decision making. *Child Development*, 1963, *34*, 483-493.

Galloway, C. Modification of a response bias through differential amount of reinforcement. *Journal of Experimental Analysis of Behavior*, 1967, *10*, 357-382.

Gewirtz, J. L., & Baer, D. M. Deprivation and satiation of social reinforcers as drive conditions. *Journal of Abnormal and Social Psychology*, 1958, *57*, 165-172. (a)

Gewirtz, J. L., & Baer, D. M. The effect of brief social deprivation on behaviors for a social reinforcer. *Journal of Abnormal and Social Psychology*, 1958, *56*, 49-56. (b)

Green, C., & Zigler, E. Social deprivation and the performance of retarded and normal children on a satiation type task. *Child Development*, 1962, *33*, 499-508.

Grinder, R. E. New techinques for research in children's temptation behavior. *Child Development*, 1961, *32*, 679-688.

Hart, B. M., Reynolds, N. J., Baer, D. M., Brawley, E. R., & Harris, F. R. Effects of contingent and noncontingent social reinforcement on the cooperative play of a preschool child. *Journal of Applied Behavior Analysis*, 1968, *1*, 73-76.

Hartup, W. W. Friendship status and the effectiveness of peers as reinforcing agents. *Journal of Experimental Child Psychology*, 1964, *1*, 154-162.

Hartup, W. W. Peers as agents of social reinforcement. In W. W. Hartup & N. Smothergill (Eds.), *Young child*. Washington, D.C.: 1967.

Herrnstein, R. J. Superstition: A corollary of the principles of operant conditioning. In W. K. Honig (Ed.), *Operant behavior: Areas of research and application*. New York: Appleton-Century-Crofts, 1966, 33-51.

Hill, K. T., & Moely, B. E. Social reinforcement as a function of task instructions, sex of *S*, age of *S*, and baseline performance. *Journal of Experimental Child Psychology*, 1969, *7*, 153-165.

Martin, J. A. The effect of incongruent instructions and consequences on imitation in retarded children. *Journal of Applied Behavior Analysis*, 1972, *5*, 467-475.

McCullers, J. C., & Stevenson, H. W. Effects of verbal reinforcement in a probability learning situation. *Psychological Reports*, 1960, *7*, 439-445.

Meddock, T. D. Unpublished masters dissertation, University of Illinois, 1972.

Meddock, T. D., Parsons, J. A., & Hill, K. T. Effects of an adult's presence and praise on young children's performance. *Journal of Experimental Child Psychology*, 1971, *12*, 197-211.

Neuringer, A. J. Effects of reinforcement magnitude on choice and rate of responding. *Journal of Experimental Analysis of Behavior*, 1967, *10*, 417-424.

Orne, M. T. On the social psychology of the psychological experiment: With particular reference to demand characteristics and their implications. *American Psychologist*, 1962, *71*, 776-783.

Paris, S. G., & Cairns, R. B. An experimental and ethological analysis of social reinforcement with children. *Child Development*, 1972, *43*, 717-729.

Parton, D. A., & Ross, A. O. Social reinforcement of children's motor behavior: A review. *Psychological Bulletin*, 1965, *64*, 65-73.

Peterson, R. F., & Whitehurst, G. J. A variable influencing the performance of generalized imitation. *Journal of Applied Behavior Analysis*, 1971, *4*, 1-9.

Redd, W. H. Social control by adult preference in operant conditioning with children. *Journal of Experimental Child Psychology*, 1974, *17*, 61-78.

Redd, W. H., Amen, D. L., Meddock, T. D., & Winston, A. S. Instructional control in resistance to temptation: The effect of loss of reinforcement and type of instructions. Unpublished manuscript, University of Illinois, 1974.

Redd, W. H., & Wheeler, A. J. The relative effectiveness of monetary reinforcers and adult instructions in the control of children's choice behavior. *Journal of Experimental Child Psychology*, 1973, *16*, 63-75.

Redd, W. H., & Winston, A. S. The role of antecedent positive and negative comments in the control of children's behavior. *Child Development*, 1974, *45*, 540-546.

Spence, J. T. Factors contributing to the effectiveness of social and nonsocial reinforcers in the discrimination learning of children from two socioeconomic groups. *Journal of Experimental Child Psychology*, 1973, *15*, 367-380.

Steinman, W. M. The social control of generalized imitation. *Journal of Applied Behavior Analysis*, 1970, *3*, 159-167.

Stevenson, H. W. Social reinforcement of children's behavior. In L. P. Lipsitt & C. C. Spiker (Eds.), *Advances in child development and behavior* (Vol. 2). New York: Academic Press, 1965, 97-126.

Stevenson, H. W., & Fahel, L. S. The effect of social reinforcement on the performance of institutionalized and noninstitutionalized normal and feebleminded children. *Journal of Personality*, 1961, *29*, 136-147.

Stevenson, H. W., & Hill, K. T. The use of rate as a measure of response in studies of social reinforcement. *Psychological Bulletin*, 1966, *66*, 321-326.

Stevenson, H. W., & Odom, R. D. The effectiveness of social reinforcement following two conditions of social deprivation. *Journal of Abnormal and Social Psychology*, 1962, *65*, 429-431.

Walters, R. H., & Demkow, L. Timing of punishment as a determinant of response inhibition. *Child Development*, 1963, *34*, 207-214.

Walters, R. H., & Parke, R. D. Influence of the response consequences to a social model on resistance to deviation. *Journal of Experimental Child Psychology*, 1964, *1*, 269-280.

Walters, R. H., & Ray, E. Anxiety, social isolation, and reinforcer effectiveness. *Journal of Personality*, 1960, *28*, 358-367.

Ward, W. D., & Furchak, A. F. Resistance to temptation among boys and girls. *Psychological Reports*, 1968, *23*, 511-514.

Warren, V. L., & Cairns, R. B. Social reinforcement satiation: An outcome of frequency or ambiguity? *Journal of Experimental Child Psychology*, 1972, *13*, 249-260.

Weisberg, P. Social and nonsocial conditioning of infant vocalizations. *Child Development*, 1963, *34*, 377-388.

Winston, A. S., & Redd, W. H. Children's instruction following as a function of surveillance and reinforcement contingencies. Unpublished manuscript, University of Illinois, 1974.

Zigler, E. Social deprivation and rigidity in the performance of feebleminded children. *Journal of Abnormal and Social Psychology*, 1961, *62*, 413-421.

Zigler, E., & Kanzer, P. The effectiveness of two classes of verbal reinforcers on the performance of middle-class and lower-class children. *Journal of Personality*, 1962, *30*, 157-163.

Zigler, E., & Williams, J. Institutionalization and the effectiveness of social reinforcement. *Journal of Abnormal and Social Psychology*, 1963, *66*, 197-205.

17

Behavioral Procedures for Assessing Visual Capacities in Nonverbal Subjects

Ellen P. Reese
Jane S. Howard[1]
Mount Holyoke College

Peter B. Rosenberger
Harvard Medical School; Massachusetts General Hospital

There are now available a number of variations of the traditional reinforcement-extinction procedure which may be used to facilitate teaching and to assess the sensory capacities of individuals so that teaching may be better programmed according to abilities. Effective programming requires a continuing sensitivity and responsiveness to the subject's performance which derive from Skinner's revolutionary proposition, "The rat knows best." This credo, which of course translates "The child knows best" (Lindsley, 1971a), has profound implications for education since it implies that it is procedures, not students, which fail. Given that the only measure of a teacher's success is the student's progress, the teacher is forced to examine the possiblity that errors in performance may be attributable to errors in programming.

The occurrence of errors during discrimination training has been examined by Hively (1962), working with normal children, and by Sidman and Stoddard (1967), Stoddard and Sidman (1967), and Touchette (1968) whose subjects were profoundly retarded. Their analyses reveal three important findings.

[1]Now at Western Michigan University, Kalamazoo

1. Errors derive from accidental reinforcement contingencies inherent in the program and thus reflect "normal" learning. There is no reason to assume that retarded individuals learn differently from other people just because they make more errors.
2. Errors perpetuate errors and thus interfere with the learning of appropriate stimulus-response relations.
3. A history of trial and error training may impair both the retention of a discrimination already learned and the acquisition of subsequent ones.

It has also been shown with "learning-disabled" school children that poor academic development is related to low expectancy of success on academic tasks (Pawluk, 1974) — an attitude likely to hinder future progress.

Given these unattractive features of errors and the evidence that they are not essential for learning (Terrace, 1963a; Storm & Robinson, 1973), a number of procedures have been developed to reduce their occurrence. As Bijou (1970) has noted with respect to education in general, effective discrimination training involves programming *both* the stimulus material and the contingencies of reinforcement. Programming the stimulus material may include: (1) discimination training on a series of related and progressively more difficult tasks (e.g., Hively, 1962); (2) the use of errors as a signal to back up to an earlier, easier task (Holland, 1961); and (3) fading or graduated stimulus change. Fading procedures include the gradual introduction or *fading in* of an incorrect alternative in a discrimination task (Terrace, 1963a) and *fading across* stimulus dimensions, as when Terrace (1963b) transferred control from a relatively easy color discrimination to a more difficult line-tilt discrimination by superimposing vertical or horizontal lines on a colored panel and then gradually fading out the color. The fading out of auxiliary stimuli such as verbal prompts or pictures in a reading task is another example of fading across stimulus dimensions.

The use of fading procedures with human subjects has been found to facilitate the acquisition of a variety of skills including handwriting (Skinner & Krakower, 1968), basic reading skills (Corey & Shamow, 1972; Hewett, 1964; McDowell, 1968; Mosher & Reese, 1976), number concepts (Reese & Werden, 1970; Suppes & Ginsberg, 1962), right-left-position concepts (Jeffrey, 1958; Touchette, 1968), and form discrimination (Macht, 1971; Moore & Goldiamond, 1964; Sidman & Stoddard, 1967). Since effective training procedures need not require language skills, they also provide a means of assessing sensory capacities and psychophysical thresholds in profoundly retarded subjects (Macht, 1971; Stoddard & Sidman, 1967) and in subjects with known brain damage (Rosenberger, 1974) or suspected hearing loss (Bricker & Bricker, 1970; Meyerson & Michael, 1964).

Even when a decision is made to employ some type of fading procedure, there remains the problem of *programming the contingencies of reinforcement.* As Bijou (1970) has suggested, this aspect of discrimination training may be as critical as the arrangement of stimulus material; but it is one that has received relatively limited experimental attention. Discrimination training involves the restriction of specified behavior to specified stimulus contexts: for example, pointing to the word "cat" when presented with a picture of a cat, but not when presented with the picture of another animal. In the laboratory, this is generally accomplished by the reinforcement of correct responding and the extinction of incorrect responding. In other words, the contingencies specified by the traditional reinforcement-extinction prardigm decrease the frequency of errors by providing no consequence for errors. We might, instead, attempt to decrease the frequency of errors by providing a reinforcing consequence for *not* making them. Reinforcement might be made contingent upon the absence of responding for a specified period of time, as in omission training, or upon the emission of another, alternative response. Thus, while a given activity (such as pointing to the word "cat") is extinguished under one stimulus condition (picture of an aardvark), reinforcement could be made contingent upon the absence of this activity (not pointing) or upon another activity (pointing to the word "aardvark").

Usually, the procedure known as omission training (OT) or differential reinforcement of other behavior (DRO)[2] has been used to eliminate behavior that has been well established in the individual's repertoire. Several recent animal studies have established stable responding under various schedules of reinforcement and then compared simple extinction and OT with respect to the immediacy, extent, and durability of response elimination (Miller & LeBlanc, 1972; Topping & Larmi, 1973; Uhl, 1973; and Zeiler, 1971). Omission training has also been used to facilitate the elimination of well-established behavior in human subjects (Johnson, McGlynn, & Topping, 1973; LeBlanc & Reuter, 1972). Few studies, however, have incorporated OT in a discrimination situation. Kolb & Etzel (1973) trained preschool children to wait for reinforcement, and Fuller & Reese (1974) investigated OT and other reinforcement contingencies in a five-component multiple schedule with college students. In neither study was omission training introduced while the primary response was being established.

[2]The term omission training (OT) appears most frequently in studies with animal subjects; the term differential reinforcement of other behavior (DRO) in those with human subjects. Reinforcement is forthcoming when a specified response is not emitted for a specified period of time; each response postpones reinforcement. In DRO, the reinforcement-reinforcement interval (the time between successive reinforcements if no response intervenes) is the same as the response-reinforcement interval (the time which each response postpones the next reinforcement). In OT, these temporal contingencies may differ. For example, reinforcement might be programmed every 20 sec if no responding occurs, but a response will postpone the next reinforcement for 40 sec. (The characteristics of OT are described by Uhl & Garcia (1969).)

Even though omission training refers to the postponement or omission of reinforcement when responding occurs (Uhl, 1973), the term neatly describes the fact that omission of responding is reinforced or trained. DRO refers to the differential reinforcement of other behavior; and the strengthening of this (unspecified) other behavior is assumed to account for the declining strength of the behavior put on DRO. The terms OT and DRO can often be used interchangeably, but OT is adopted here because it seems to describe the experimental operations more explicitly (and more parsimoniously) than does DRO.

The conditioning of alternative, incompatible behavior (Alt R) to replace inappropriate behavior is a procedure widely used in therapy. Problem behavior is extinguished while more adaptive behavior is established in its place. Lovaas, for example, suppressed the self-injurious behavior of an autistic child by reinforcing singing and clapping to music (Lovaas, Freitag, Gold, & Kassorla, 1965). Alt R procedures have also been used in the context of discrimination training when a specified alternative response has been reinforced during the extinction component. In an educational setting, the primary and alternative responses might correspond to "yes-no" or to "A-not A". Both responses are maintained by reinforcement, but only in the presence of specified discriminative stimuli. A third variation of Alt R is a multiple-discrimination task, such as matching to sample, where a student might select from several words the one that matches a given picture. An essential feature of the OT and Alt R training procedures is the opportunity during both stimulus conditions to emit behavior which will be reinforced. Errors may occur, but the situation is so structured that a correct response is always possible.

Like OT, Alt R has generally been introduced after the behavior to be eliminated has long been established. In the context of discrimination training, the animal studies of Leitenberg, Rawson, and Bath (1970) and Girton and Reese (1973) have shown that Alt R eliminates responding during one stimulus component more rapidly than does extinction after equal rates of responding have been established during both stimulus components; and there is some evidence that both Alt R and OT are more effective than extinction in suppressing a simple manual response in human subjects (Fuller & Reese, 1974). However, little use has been made of these procedures in *establishing* a differential response, as opposed to eliminating responding after an extensive history of reinforcement, even though they might provide useful teaching techniques.

THE EXPERIMENT

This study compared three reinforcement procedures for their effectiveness in establishing a differential response and for subsequent determination of a psychophysical threshold. The measurement of thresholds provides a sensitive test of variations in programming because differences may appear during the period when a differential response is established, and they may be assessed throughout the program until the threshold is reached and differential responding becomes impossible. The evaluation of programming procedures which measure thresholds seems important for another reason. Most tests of sensory capacities are terminated when the number of errors reaches a criterion set by the experimenter. The result is that traditional (errorful) procedures will weigh against the subject in that errors ultimately attributable to the program will be confounded with "true" errors, those attributable to sensory limitations. The use of traditional procedures increases the probability that the discriminative potential of an individual will be underestimated.

Stimulus programming, notably fading, has proved useful in assessing visual acuity (Macht, 1971; Stoddard & Sidman, 1967) and auditory thresholds (Bricker & Bricker, 1970; Meyerson & Michael, 1964). The programming of reinforcement contingencies may also affect the sensitivity of threshold measurement. Only with valid tests of individual capacities can teaching programs be designed to develop people's strengths and circumvent their weaknesses.

The threshold investigated in the present study with institutionalized retarded males was the bisection of a horizontal line. (This particular discrimination was selected because comparison data are available from normal subjects and those with brain lesions (Rosenberger, 1974). All procedures incorporated differential reinforcement of a primary response in the presence of a bisected line (S^D) and extinction of this response when the line was transected asymmetrically (S^Δ). They differed with respect to additional contingencies in effect during S^Δ: (1) no reinforcement programmed during S^Δ (EXT); (2) differential reinforcement of not responding (OT); and (3) reinforcement of an alternative response (Alt R). Stimulus programming, including fading, was used in conjunction with all procedures. In addition, an eight-choice procedure for assessing the same threshold was used as a supplementary measure to evaluate the effects of these different contingencies of reinforcement. The results were analysed with respect to the efficiency, in time and errors, of establishing a differential response and the sensitivity of the various procedures in measuring the visual threshold.

Subjects

The subjects were 16 institutionalized, profoundly retarded males, 15 to 21 years old. As members of an ongoing token economy, all subjects were token trained (tokens had been established as generalized reinforcers); and all were familiar with the apparatus. Eight subjects were initially given discrimination training with reinforcement-extinction contingencies. Seven of these subjects were later exposed to the same discrimination task with an OT procedure. Of the 8 remaining subjects, 4 received discrimination training with omission training during one component and 4 were trained with an Alt R procedure.

Apparatus

The apparatus was an adaptation of that described by Sidman and Stoddard (1967) and Rosenberger (1974). The stimulus display was composed of 9 circular, translucent plexiglass windows, each 7.5 cm in diameter, mounted vertically in a panel facing the subject. Eight windows were arranged in a circular matrix, 40 cm in diameter; the ninth window was located in the center of the matrix. The panel was modified according to the requirements of the different procedures to display 2, 3, or 8 windows (See Fig. 1 and 2). Windows not used with a particular procedure were fitted with plugs.

The stimuli were projected onto the rear of the windows by means of a Kodak Carousel 35 mm slide projector. The projected horizontal stimulus lines were 5 cm in length. When the subject indicated his choice on a particular trial by touching a window, a microswitch mounted behind it signaled the electronic programming and recording devices. Photocells located on the other side of the stimulus panel decoded the key that was correct on a given trial. The stimuli displayed on each trial and the pattern of illumination of the photocells were photographed on 35 mm high speed Ectachrome film and mounted in Kindermann frames. A motor-driven shutter located in front of the projector controlled presentation of the stimuli. The programs were arranged so that the projector advanced to the next display if the first response was correct or returned to the previous display if any errors were made during a trial. During the Alt R and 8-choice procedures, the apparatus was programmed so that a correct response had to be emitted before the trial was terminated. In all procedures there was a 2.5 sec intertrial interval, and chimes were sounded automatically following all correct choices.

An Esterline-Angus recorder and a Gerbrands cumulative recorder provided a continuous record of latencies, reinforcements, correct and incorrect choices. Token reinforcement was delivered into a tray in front of the subject. A platform could be placed beneath the subject's chair so that all subjects were at eye level with the display panel.

Procedure

Terminal Performance

The final reinforcement contingencies programmed for the three procedures are illustrated in Figure 1. Trials with the bisected line (S^D) are shown at the left and those with an asymmetrically transected line (S^Δ) are at the right. The line transecting the horizontal appeared equally often to the left and right of center; and until the final stage of the experiment when thresholds were measured, the asymmetry was pronounced: the ratio of the shorter segment of the line to the total horizontal line was .04. For the traditional reinforcement-extinction (EXT) and omission training (OT) procedures, the stimulus window was located above a single response window; for Alt R, the stimulus window was located between two response windows.

Reinforcement-Extinction. Under EXT contingencies, pushing the window beneath a bisected line was reinforced with praise, a token, and the sound of chimes. Tokens were exchanged at the end of a session for a back up reinforcer (coke, candy, coffee) selected by the subject. If the line was transected asymmetrically, pushing the response panel was extinguished. Responses in the

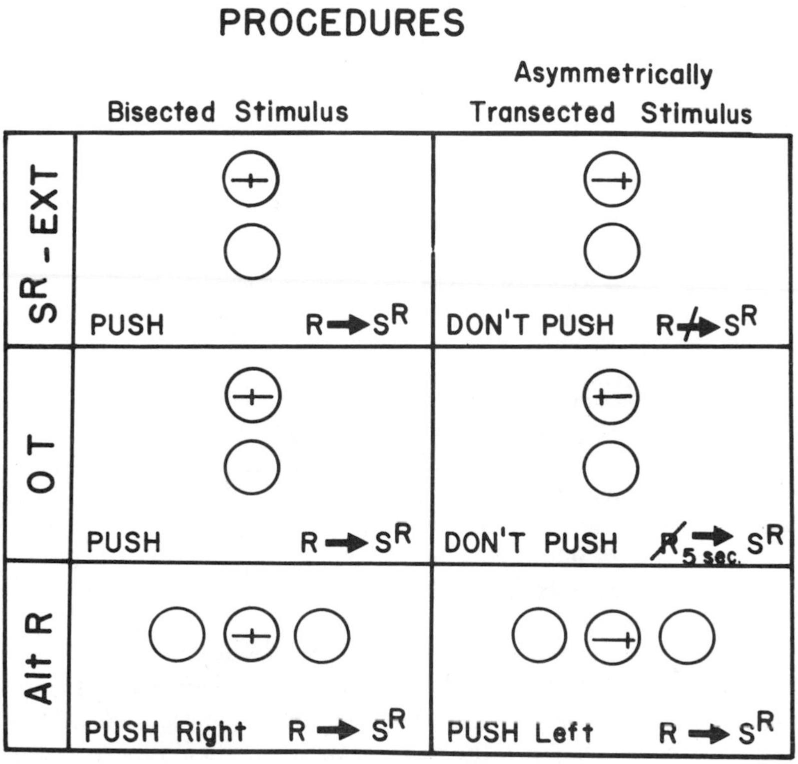

PROCEDURES

Figure 1   Reinforcement contingencies programmed in Alt R, OT, and reinforcement-extinction (EXT) procedures. Lower window is response panel for OT and EXT; peripheral windows are response panels for Alt R.

presence of this stimulus were considered to be errors. The stimuli were presented in random order for 30-sec intervals.

Omission training. Under OT contingencies, pushing the response panel was also reinforced if the stimulus was a bisected line and extinguished if the line was asymmetrically transected, but an additional contingency was programmed during S^Δ. If the subject did not push the response panel beneath an asymmetrically transected line for 5 sec, reinforcement was delivered and the trial was terminated. Temporal contingencies were such that the subject had to respond to the bisected stimulus within 5 sec for it to be a correct response. Failure to respond within that period of time was an error, and the trial was terminated. With an asymmetrically transected stimulus, failure to respond within 5 sec was the correct response, and any responses made within that time period were errors.

Alternative response. The stimulus appeared on the central window of the display between two response windows. When the stimulus was a bisected line, the correct response was pushing the window at the right; for an asymmetrically transected line, the correct response was pushing the window at the left. In either case, pushing the wrong window was considered an error. A correct response that was not preceded by an error produced praise, a token, and chimes, and terminated the trial. When an error occurred, the trial continued until a correct response was made, whereupon the chimes sounded and the trial was terminated, but no token was delivered.

Training Programs

The training programs common to all procedures are summarized in Table 1. No preliminary training was necessary to establish the response of pressing a window as all subjects had previous experience working with the apparatus and were familiar with the response topography required. The subjects had previously been trained on the same apparatus with two eight-choice procedures, one that measured a circle-ellipse discrimination and one using the same discrimination task as the present study. In addition, all subjects were pretested for the ability to match colored cubes.

Throughout all programs and all procedures, there was a correction procedure for errors. At the end of any trial in which an error occurred, the projector automatically reversed and presented the slide from the previous (easier) trial. In all fading programs (but not the assessment of threshold) the program was repeated if the subject made more than 20% errors. This percentage was calculated by dividing the number of errors by the number of slides in the program, not counting correction trials.

Establishing differential responding to color (Program 1). The only differences in *stimulus* programming between procedures occurred during the first program in which a differential response to color was established. These differences were due to the introduction of two response windows in the Alt R procedure.

Initially, for all procedures, only the response window was illuminated (see Table 1, Program 1a). This was the lower window for the EXT and OT procedures and either one of the side windows for Alt R. If the response window was red, pushing it was reinforced. If the window was green, pushing it was not reinforced under EXT or OT, but was reinforced under Alt R. The differential response for EXT and OT was to push red and refrain from pushing green. The differential response for Alt R was to push red on the right and green on the left. In this initial stage, Alt R subjects pushed whichever window was illuminated. (An illuminated window on the left was always green and on the right was always red.)

TABLE 1

Summary of Procedure

Program	Bisected line (S^D)		Asymmetrically transected line (S^Δ)	
Fading Program 1: Establish differential response to color	(a)	Only response window illuminated (red); reinforce pushing	(a)	Only response window illuminated (green); EXT, OT: establish not pushing; Alt R: reinforce pushing green window
	(b)	Red faded in on stimulus window	(b)	Green faded in on stimulus window
	(c)	Alt R only: green faded in on incorrect response window	(c)	Alt R only: red faded in on incorrect response window
Fading Program 2: Establish differential response to transected lines	(a)	Bisected line superimposed on red stimulus window	(a)	Asymmetrically transected line superimposed on green stimulus window
	(b)	Color faded from all windows	(b)	Color faded from all windows
Fading Program 3: Equate length of vertical line		Vertical line gradually reduced to length of vertical on S^Δ		No changes
Program 4: Determine threshold		No changes		Vertical gradually moved closer to center until threshold for bisection reached
Eight-choice program		Bisected line on one of eight windows; pushing reinforced		Asymmetrically transected line on seven windows; pushing not reinforced

It would have been possible with the EXT and OT procedures to have gradually faded in the green window in an attempt to produce errorless discrimination (Terrace, 1963a). It would also have been possible to gradually increase the duration of the green stimulus (Terrace, 1963a; Topping, Larmi, & Johnson, 1972). Neither of these procedures was followed because the experiment was designed to compare traditional reinforcement-extinction with traditional OT and Alt R.

Under EXT conditions, the window was illuminated for 30 sec on each trial. Although the subjects could have earned as many as 30 tokens by repeatedly pushing the window when it was red, they usually received only 6 to 8 tokens during a trial. On the first two trials that green appeared, the subject was instructed not to push the window. (The experimenter pointed to the window and said "Don't push green.") No further instructions were given after these trials. Under OT an S^D trial was terminated when a response was made or when 5 sec elapsed, whichever occurred first. An S^Δ trial was terminated after 5 sec, and reinforcement was delivered if the subject had not pushed the window. As with EXT, at the beginning of the first two S^Δ trials, the subjects were instructed not to push the green window. Under Alt R, a trial was terminated when the subject pushed the illuminated window.

Under all conditions, the stimulus window was gradually faded in after differential responding on the response window(s) was established (see Table 1, Program 1b). At the end of this phase, stimulus and response windows were the same color and brightness. For EXT and OT, both keys were fully illuminated; for Alt R, the center window and one of the side windows were fully illuminated. At this point in the Alt R program, the incorrect response window was gradually faded in (Program 1c); and on two consecutive trials the experimenter pointed to the stimulus window and instructed the subject: "Match." No further instructions were given after these two trials. By the end of this Alt R program, both side windows were fully illuminated. When the center window was red, the subject matched this color by pushing the red window at the right rather than the green one on the left; when the center was green, the subject pushed green on the left.

The first program contained 39 slides in the EXT and OT series and 50 in the Alt R series. The same slides were used for EXT and OT. The Alt R series was longer because a second response window was faded in.

Establishing differential responding to transected lines (Program 2). When differential responding to color was established, line stimuli were abruptly superimposed upon the colored stimulus window. The bisected line was superimposed upon the red stimulus, and the asymmetrically transected line was superimposed upon green. Color was then faded out on all windows, leaving the stimulus pattern on the central window of the display and a white response window beneath it for EXT and OT or a white response window on either side for Alt R (see Figure 1). The EXT and OT programs contained 39 slides; the Alt R program 35 slides.

Throughout this second fading program, the vertical line of the bisected stimulus was longer than the vertical line of the asymmetrically transected stimulus. This was done to call attention to the vertical line, the location of which was the critical feature distinguishing the stimuli.

Equating the length of the vertical line (Program 3). During the third fading program, the length of the vertical line of the bisected stimulus was gradually reduced until it equalled that of the asymmetrically transected stimulus. This program contained 29 slides for all procedures.

Determining the threshold (Program 4). Up to this point, the vertical of the asymmetrically transected line was located close to the right or left end of the horizontal line. To measure the threshold for a bisected line, the vertical was gradually moved toward the center. Initially, the ratio of the shorter segment of the transected line to the total line was .04. This ratio was first increased to .06, and then changed in increments of .05 until the ratio of the shorter segment to the total was .46. Beyond this point, even practiced normal observers respond at chance levels (Rosenberger, 1974). The progression through the ten steps of the program required 59 slides, and the back up correction for errors was maintained. Under all training procedures, the program was continued until the subject completed the program or made five errors at a given ratio.

Eight-choice procedure. The display panel for the eight-choice procedure is shown in Figure 2. Within a trial, the vertical of the seven asymmetrically transected stimuli was displaced from the center by the same distance, but on some stimuli the vertical was displaced to the left and on others to the right. The position of the correct choice, the bisected line, was varied on different trials.

The first 10 slides of the program gradually faded in the incorrect choices. Over the remaining 40 slides, the vertical of the asymmetrically transected line was gradually moved toward the center in the increments described above. In this procedure, as in Alt R, a correct response had to be emitted before the trial was terminated. If the correct response was preceded by an error, the chimes were sounded, but no token was delivered.

All subjects, except one, were tested with this eight-choice procedure 18 months prior to the present study; and, wherever possible, the subjects were also tested before and just after the present study.

Results

Errors

Error data are presented in Table 2, which shows the median number of errors emitted by each group of subjects during each program, and in Figure 3, which shows individual data. The reinforcement-extinction procedure was terminated after 20 min of training on the first program, even before the stimulus window was faded in. Although response rates during S^Δ were lower toward the end of the session for most subjects, only one of the eight subjects stopped pushing the green window. The instructions "Don't push green," given during the first two presentations of S^Δ, did not appear to help the other subjects

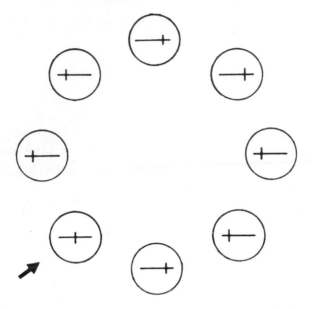

Figure 2　　Arrangement of stimuli in eight-choice procedure.

acquire the differential response. An additional reason for terminating this program was the fact that during the S^Δ several subjects emitted behavior which might be called emotional. Some said "No"; others pounded the table with their fists. There were also many indications of boredom: yawning, fidgeting, fiddling with tokens. Subjects in the other conditions did not emit these classes of behavior, nor did the EXT subjects after they were transferred to the OT program.

The greater number of errors (111) emitted by subjects in the reinforcement-extinction group indicates that it was an inefficient procedure for establishing a differential response, since the median number of errors emitted by subjects trained with either the OT or Alt R contingencies was only 3.5 and 5 respectively. Note that the errors emitted by subjects trained with reinforcement-extinction occurred within 20 min, not after completion of the program, as only one subject was able to complete even the first fading program within that time period.

Seven of the subjects initially trained with reinforcement-extinction were available for training with the first OT program, and 6 were available for all OT programs. They were able to complete all programs under the OT procedure, but with a higher error rate than subjects exposed only to OT contingencies. Four of the 7 had to repeat the first OT program because their error rates exceeded 20%, and 2 of the 6 had to repeat the second program.

The number of errors emitted during OT and Alt R is not directly comparable because the first fading program in the Alt R procedure contained more slides. However, a comparison of "error rate" in terms of errors per stimulus display (see Table 2) reveals that subjects trained with only Alt R or OT made fewer

TABLE 2

Group Median Number of Errors Emitted during each Program
under each Procedure. [Figures in italics show number of
errors divided by number of slides in program. Threshold
figures do not include the five errors which terminated
the program for those subjects who did not complete it.]

Procedure	Establish differential response	Add stimulus, fade color	Fade vertical	Threshold
Reinf-extinction	111*	—	—	—
OT after reinf-ext.	9**	2.5***	0	3.5
(per slide)	*.21*	*.06*	*0*	
OT	3.5	0.5	0	2.5
(per slide)	*.09*	*.01*	*0*	
Alt R	5	4.5	0	5.0
(per slide)	*.08*	*.10*	*0*	

Only one subject completed this program
**Four of the seven subjects repeated program*
***Two of the six subjects repeated program*

errors during the first fading program than did those subjects trained with OT
after exposure to reinforcement-estinction contingencies (Mann Whitney U Test,
$U = 10, p = .025$). These differences between groups decreased during the second
fading program (fade color); and during the third fading program (fade vertical)
the median error for all groups was equal to 0. The fading of the vertical of the
bisected stimulus may have been an important variable affecting a subject's
performance as it probably helped direct the subject's attention to the position
of the vertical with respect to the horizontal line which was the critical feature
of the discrimination.

Figure 3 shows the number of errors emitted by individual subjects. The
order, which is based on the number of errors emitted during the first program,
is the same for all programs. For those subjects initially exposed to reinforcement-extinction contingencies there appears to be a positive relation between
the number of errors emitted during the first fading program with reinforcement-extinction and those emitted during OT contingencies. That is, those
subjects who emitted the greatest number of errors during reinforcement-
extinction training also tended to make the greatest number of errors during the
first fading program with OT contingencies.

The large number of errors emitted during reinforcement-extinction training
seems to have promoted errors in subsequent programs, despite the OT contingencies that were in effect. Subjects initially exposed to reinforcement-extinction training made more errors during the first two OT programs than those

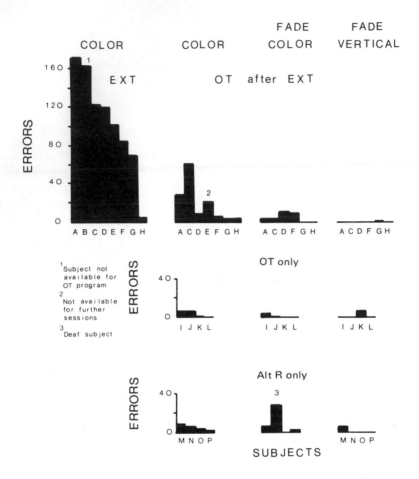

Figure 3   Errors emitted by each subject throughout program. Subjects are presented in the same order across rows. Top: reinforcement-extinction and OT following this program; middle: OT; bottom: Alt R. (First Alt R program contained more slides than comparable OT program.) Numerals over histograms refer to individual subjects: (1) subject unavailable for OT program; (2) subject unavailable for further sessions; (3) deaf subject.

subjects exposed only to OT training. By the third fading program (fade vertical, no color present) subjects in all 3 groups were emitting few errors. The limited effects of errors made during the initial reinforcement-extinction program may be due to the fact that the subjects were exposed to extinction contingencies for such a brief period of time (20 min), or that the OT contingencies minimized those effects, or that the stimuli in the third fading program were sufficiently different from the stimuli to which the errors were emitted, or a combination of these possibilities.

Time

The time required for each group to complete the fading and threshold programs is shown in Table 3 and Figure 4. Although the time to complete the first fading program for the reinforcement-extinction group is recorded as "never" because only one subject ceased responding to the S^Δ in 20 min, it is quite possible that these subjects could have completed all phases of this procedure if given sufficient training. However, this would be inefficient considering that the longest time taken to complete the first OT program was 3.2 min, and for Alt R (which contained more slides) it was 5.6 min. Both programs were completed in significantly less time than the EXT program (Mann Whitney U Test, $U = 0$, $p < .005$ in both cases). In fact, the median time to complete *all* fading programs *and* to measure thresholds was less than 19 min with either the OT or Alt R procedures. Because the OT procedure programmed a 5-sec delay during S^Δ and because the first Alt R program contained more slides than the OT program, it is difficult to compare Alt R and OT. However, subjects with a previous history of reinforcement-extinction required more time to complete the OT fading programs (14.2 min) than those subjects who were exposed only to OT contingencies (10.4 min): Mann Whitney U Test, $U = 3, p = .05$.

Individual time to complete fading programs and reach the threshold are presented in Figure 4. Subjects' data are presented in the same order as the error data in Figure 3. Time data are not shown for the reinforcement-extinction program because that program was terminated after twenty min for all subjects.

Threshold

Thresholds measured with the eight-choice and OT or Alt R procedures are presented in Table 4. Where possible, the eight-choice measure was taken 18 months before, just before, and just after training with either the OT or Alt R procedures. Thresholds are recorded as the ratio of the smaller segment of the horizontal line to the larger segment. Higher numerals thus reflect lower

TABLE 3

Group Median Time (min.) to Complete
Discrimination Programs under each Procedure

Procedure	Establish differential response	Fade color	Fade vertical	Threshold	Total to threshold	Total incl. threshold
Reinf-ext	"Never"	—	—	—	—	—
OT after reinf-ext	8.1	4.5	2.6	5.5	14.2	18.6
OT	3.2	3.6	2.6	6.0	10.4	16.3
Alt R	5.6	4.7	3.2	4.7	13.2	18.7

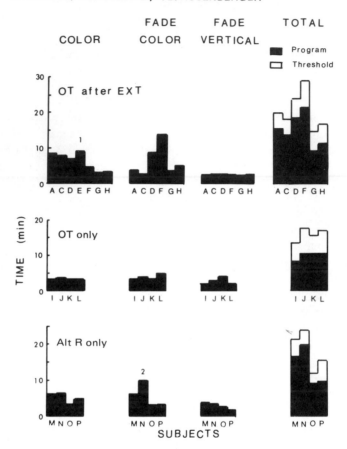

Figure 4   Individual time to complete fading and threshold programs. (1) Subject not available for further sessions; (2) deaf subject.

thresholds: a bisected line would be expressed as .50. (A threshold of .46 indicates that the subject selected a bisected stimulus among ones that were just slightly asymmetrical.) A threshold of .46 is considered appropriate for normal adults (Rosenberger, 1974).

For 12 of the 14 subjects, thresholds measured by either the OT or Alt R procedures were lower than those measured by the eight-choice procedure. The remaining two subjects showed no change. Nine of the 14 thresholds measured by either the OT or Alt R procedures reached the level of normal adults (.46); *none* of the thresholds measured by the eight-choice procedure at any time reached this level.

The eight-choice thresholds for 6 subjects were measured both 18 months before and just before discrimination training with either OT or Alt R. These data should reflect any improvement in threshold that might be a function of maturation, increased ability in other discrimination tasks which could have

TABLE 4

Threshold for Bisection of Horizontal Line Measured
by Eight-Choice and OT or Alt R Procedures
(expressed as the ratio of the smaller segment
to the total length of line)

Disc Training	Eight Choice (baseline)		OT or Alt R		Eight Choice		
	18 Mos. Before	Just Before		Change from Eight-Choice	Just After	Change from OT or Alt R	Change from Baseline
OT after Reinf-ext							
S:A	.41	.41	.46	+.05			
S:C	.06		.46	+.40	.31	−.15	+.25
S:D	.26		.26	0	.26	0	0
S:F	.26	.36	.41	+.05	.36	−.05	0
S:G		.26	.31	+.05			
S:H	.41	.41	.46	+.05	.36	−.10	−.05
OT							
S:I	.36	.36	.46	+.10			
S:J	.36	.41	.46	+.05			
S:K	.21		.36	+.15	.26	−.10	+.05
S:L	0		.46	+.46	.36	−.10	+.36
Alt R							
S:M	.36	.41	.41	0	.41	0	0
S:N	.36		.46	+.10	.41	−.05	+.05
S:O	.21		.46	+.25	.41	−.05	+.20
S:P	0		.46	+.46	.36	−.10	+.36

generalized to this one, or repeated exposure to this one. Three of these 6 subjects showed no change over the 18 month period; 2 improved by 1 step, and 1 by 2 steps. Five of the 6 showed further improvement when thresholds were measured by either the OT or Alt R procedure. The other, who showed no change, was already only 1 step (.41) below the threshold for normal subjects.

Thresholds were measured again with the eight-choice procedure for 10 of the 14 subjects after training with either OT or Alt R. For 8 of these 10 subjects, the scores were lower (meaning that the thresholds were higher or less precise) than those measured by OT or Alt R. The others showed no change. These data indicate that the OT and Alt R procedures provided more sensitive measures of thresholds than did the eight-choice procedure, and that repeated exposure was not the major variable contributing to threshold measurement.

The last column in Table 4 shows the change in eight-choice measures from the eight-choice data collected before our training programs. Even though performance declined in comparison to the OT and Alt R measures, only one subject (H) performed less well than during baseline.

Although one could argue that the lower thresholds (higher scores) measured by the OT and Alt R procedures reflect a lower probability of error — one in two, as compared to a seven in eight probability of error with the eight-choice procedure, there are two reasons which suggest that this is not an adequate explanation. First, there were very few errors emitted during threshold programs until the subject reached his apparent limit. Second, although the subjects were presented with more stimuli with the eight-choice procedure (which increased the probability of errors due to chance), the subject was selecting the one stimulus that was different from all the others, because the other seven stimuli were offset to the same degree. With the eight-choice procedure, the subject is allowed to compare and contrast differences among stimuli. In both the OT and Alt R procedures there is a single stimulus presented within a given trial, and the subject must make an absolute judgment on the basis of that one stimulus. In this particular study, there does not seem to be any reason to assume that responding differentially in the presence of a single stimulus is an easier task than selecting among eight stimuli; it may be more difficult.

Earlier, we suggested that prior experience with the reinforcement-extinction procedure hindered the subjects' subsequent performances during the first program with omission training. These subjects generally made more errors and took more time to complete the first OT program than did the OT and Alt R subjects who were spared the prior experience with errors (see Figs. 3 and 4). There were, however, no reliable differences in time and errors for the remaining fading programs. Although the data are sparse, there is some evidence that the subjects who started with the extinction procedure performed less well on the threshold measures. Only 3 of these 6 subjects reached the "normal" threshold of .46, and most showed only a modest improvement over their eight-choice baselines. In comparison, 6 of the 8 OT and Alt R subjects reached the threshold of normal subjects, and most showed a greater improvement over their eight-choice baselines. The suggestion that the extinction procedure was detrimental is also supported by the last column in Table 4. The eight-choice performance following our training program improved over the eight-choice baseline for only one of the 4 subjects for whom we have data; and for one subject (H), the performance declined. In contrast, of the 6 subjects who were not exposed to the initial extinction procedure, 5 improved over baseline and none declined.

Discussion

Bijou (1963) has described one of the tasks of behavioral research as the investigation of the observable or potentially observable conditions that may produce retarded behavior. This would include an analysis of procedures which program both the stimuli and the contingencies of reinforcement. The use of fading programs to more effectively program the stimuli in discrimination training for the retarded individual has received wide recognition (e.g., Bricker & Bricker, 1970; Sidman & Stoddard, 1967; Touchette, 1968). And ineffective programming of stimuli has been found to adversely affect threshold measurement (Stoddard & Sidman, 1967). The systematic investigation of procedures for programming the contingencies of reinforcement, however, has not received equal attention, even though Barrett (1965) has shown that differential reinforcement per se is not enough.

This study investigated two procedures, Alt R and OT, in which reinforcement could occur in the presence of both of the stimuli associated with the establishment of a differential response. Both OT and Alt R, combined with fading, produced few errors, required little time and revealed thresholds comparable to those of normal subjects, whereas thresholds measured with an eight-choice procedure indicated deficient repertoires. If it is unkind to demand too much of a handicapped child, it is also unkind to demand too little. Only with valid measures of discriminative capacity will it be possible to construct environments which capitalize on the abilities of these individuals and circumvent their deficits.

The OT and Alt R procedures also proved more effective than traditional discrimination training with respect to the acquisition of a differential response. Only one of eight subjects completed the first EXT program, whereas all subjects completed all OT and Alt R programs. Because of the temporal contingencies involved, the superiority of OT over traditional reinforcement-extinction found in this study cannot be attributed solely to the reinforcement of nonresponding during OT. The stimuli were presented for 30-sec intervals in the reinforcement-extinction program and for 5-sec intervals in OT. As noted above (see Procedure), it might have been possible to produce "errorless" learning with both procedures had the intensity and duration of the green window (S^{Δ}) been gradually faded in. The purpose of the study was to compare the effects of different reinforcement contingencies; and, given the parameters employed, both OT and Alt R produced many fewer errors and required far less time than did traditional reinforcement-extinction.

Subjects initially exposed to reinforcement-extinction contingencies were subsequently able to complete all programs with the OT procedure, but with more difficulty than subjects who had been spared this preliminary training. These results support previous work regarding the ill effects of errors (Hively, 1962; Sidman & Stoddard, 1967; Stoddard & Sidman, 1967; Touchette, 1968; Terrace, 1963b). In addition, there is quantitative data from the animal laboratory describing the "emotional" side effects associated with even errorless reinforcement-extinction discrimination training (Rilling & Caplan, 1973). It seems reasonable to suspect that these effects might be present in the human subject as well. During this study, collateral behavior that could be termed "emotional" was observed during the S^{Δ} of reinforcement-extinction training but not with the other procedures. Such behavior has been noted elsewhere in studies with children when the error rate was high (McDowell, 1971).

Another aspect of errors, though not investigated as an independent variable in this study, deserves mention. In many discrimination procedures, the emission of an error schedules a return to an easier, previously mastered step. There is now evidence that these correction procedures may actually reinforce errors (Hawkins & Hayes, 1974; Sajwaj & Knight, 1971), although this does not appear to have happened in the present study. The parameters of this effect of correction procedures require further investigation. The most obvious solution to the ill effects of errors is to reduce the probability of errors occurring. This is not to imply that errors in and of themselves are undesirable, as a certain proportion of errors may be beneficial to a student's progress (Lindsley, 1971b; Duncan, 1971). The opportunity to emit errors might even be programmed into an educational sequence. In this case, one might also want to program the opportunity to discover and to correct the errors — and to learn that there are many problems to which there are, at present, no known solution. If we are to help students discover ways of going about solving problems, the occurrence of errors must become an opportunity for learning, rather than a mark of failure. In any event, we should consider Hively's (1962) warning: "After a bad program has been tested, it can be revised, but the subjects must be thrown away" [p. 297].

A closer analysis of the OT and Alt R procedures reveals advantages other than reduction of errors. Stereotyped errors inherent in programmed contingencies, specifically in the eight-choice procedure, have been described by Sidman & Stoddard (1967). These errors took the form of perseveration on a single key, circling around the key matrix, selecting the key that was correct on the preceding trial, and so forth. Circling around the key matrix is obviated with the OT and Alt R procedures. However, the Alt R procedure is more likely to produce alternation between the two response keys or selection of the response that was correct on the preceding trial. Inspection of the data reveals that this did not occur, presumably because of the errorless introduction of the Alt R task. An advantage of the Alt R and OT procedures, which is not present in a matching task, is the opportunity to measure absolute rather than comparative judgments. Especially with the Alt R procedure, even a nonverbal subject can give a definitive "yes" or "no" response, and might be able to indicate whether a given stimulus pattern were greater than or less than a previously established standard. The Alt R procedure, as contrasted with OT, may have an additional desirable characteristic regarding minimal time required to complete a program. With Alt R, a discrete response can be made immediately rather than waiting for an OT time requirement.

Obviously, the decision to implement any procedure on a broad scale will be based on practical considerations beyond the quantitative data obtained in a laboratory situation. For retarded individuals, the amount of time involved in the acquisition of each new response may prove critical to their overall development. Although their repertoire may be limited at birth, these limitations do not necessarily remain constant throughout life. Unfortunately, the behavioral repertoires of many retarded individuals are further impaired by their interactions with an inadequate environment.

Even if training with reinforcement-extinction contingencies had not resulted in so many errors that the program was abandoned, the time required to acquire the discrimination and then to measure the threshold would have been far greater than the 19 min expended with OT and Alt R. This is partly an artifact of the reinforcement-extinction discrimination paradigm which requires a specified duration of the presentation of the S^D and S^Δ in order for the experimenter to determine if differential responding is present. The emission of an error during the extinction component of discrimination training in a sense costs the subject very little, and so the probability of responding may be high. Although from the subject's point of view, the S^D and S^Δ may be clearly discriminable, the emission of errors may indicate to the experimenter that the subject is unable to make the discrimination. Both Alt R and OT give the subject a "reason" not to make errors. If reinforcement-extinction procedures are to be used, errors can be reduced either by fading in the negative stimulus (Terrace, 1963) or by a "graded choice" procedure which initially introduces the negative stimulus but does not allow the subject to respond and thus make an error (Storm & Robinson, 1973).

In summary, this study supports previous results on the detrimental effects of errors and indicates that both omission training (OT) and the reinforcement of alternative behavior (Alt R) are more effective procedures for the establishment of differential responding in discrimination training than is the traditional reinforcement-extinction procedure. In addition, OT and Alt R proved more sensitive measures of thresholds than an eight-choice procedure testing the same discrimination. It seems likely that these procedures could be employed to teach a variety of discrimination tasks or adapted for the assessment of other sensory capacities. When effective programming procedures are implemented for this purpose we will be better able to program other aspects of an individual's educational environment.

REFERENCES

Barrett, B. H. Acquisition of operant differentiation and discrimination in institutionalized retarded children. *American Journal of Orthopsychiatry*, 1965, *35*, 863-885.

Bijou, S. W. Theory and research in mental (developmental) retardation. *The Psychological Record*, 1963, *13*, 95-110.

Bijou, S. W. What psychology has to offer education – now. *Journal of Applied Behavior Analysis*, 1970, *3*, 65-71.

Bricker, W. A., & Bricker, D. D. A program of language training for the severely language handicapped child. *Exceptional Children*, 1970, *37*, 101-111.

Corey, J. R., & Shamow, J. The effects of fading on the acquisition and retention of oral reading. *Journal of Applied Behavior Analysis*, 1972, *5*, 311-315.

Duncan, A. D. The gifted count and chart. In J. B. Jordan, & L. S. Robbins (Eds.), *Let's try doing something else kind of thing.* Arlington, Va.: Council for Exceptional Children, 1971.

Fuller, E., & Reese, E. P. A comparison of four procedures in suppressing human response rates during a five-component multiple schedule of reinforcement. Paper presented at the Annual Meeting of the American Psychological Association, New Orleans, Louisiana, September, 1974.

Girton, M., & Reese, E. P. Response topography as a variable in the reinforcement of incompatible behavior. Proceedings of the 81st Annual Convention of the American Psychological Association, Montreal, Canada, 1973.

Hawkins, R. P., & Hayes, J. E. The school adjustment program: A model program for treatment of severely maladjusted children in the public schools. In R. Ulrich, T. Stachnik, & J. Mabry (Eds.), *Control of human behavior III: Behavior modification in education.* Glenview, Ill.: Scott, Foresman, 1974.

Hewett, F. M. Teaching reading to an autistic boy through operant conditioning. *Reading Teacher,* 1964, *17,* 613-618.

Hively, W. Programming stimuli in matching to sample. *Journal of the Experimental Analysis of Behavior,* 1962, *5,* 279-298.

Holland, J. G. New directions in teaching machine research. In J. E. Coulson (Ed.), *Programming learning and computer-based instruction.* New York: Wiley, 1961.

Jeffrey, W. E. Variables in early discrimination learning I. Motor responses in the training of a left-right discrimination. *Child Development,* 1958, *29,* 269-275.

Johnson, D. L., McGlynn, F. D., & Topping, J. S. The relative efficiency of four response-elimination techniques following variable-ratio reinforcement training. *The Psychological Record,* 1973, *23,* 203-208.

Kolb, D., & Etzel, B. C. Stimulus control of responding by preschool children during a wait for reinforcement. Paper presented at the Annual Meeting of the American Psychological Association, Montreal, Canada, September, 1973.

LeBlanc, J. M., & Reuter, K. E. Response elimination by reinforcement: Continuous and differential reinforcement of other behavior. Paper presented at the Annual Meeting of the American Psychological Association, Honolulu, Hawaii, September, 1972.

Leitenberg, H., Rawson, R. A., & Bath, K. Reinforcement of competing behavior during extinction. *Science,* 1970, *169,* 301-303.

Lindsley, O. R. Theoretical basis for behavior modification. In C. E. Pitts (Ed.), *Operant conditioning in the classroom.* New York: Crowell, 1971. (a)

Lindsley, O. R. Precision teaching in perspective: An interview with Ogden R. Lindsley. *Teaching Exceptional Children,* 1971, *3,* 114-119. (b)

Lovaas, O. I., Freitag, G., Gold, V. J., & Kassorla, I. C. Experimental studies in childhood schizophrenia: Analysis of self-destructive behavior. *Journal of Experimental Child Psychology,* 1965, *2,* 67-84.

Macht, J. Operant measurement of subjective visual acuity in non-verbal children. *Journal of Applied Behavior Analysis,* 1971, *4,* 23-36.

McDowell, E. E. A programmed method of reading instruction for use with kindergarten children. *The Psychological Record,* 1968, *18,* 233-239.

McDowell, E. E. III A review of learning principles applicable to preschool reading instruction. *Educational Technology,* February 1971, pp. 67-72.

Meyerson, L., & Michael, J. L. Assessment of hearing by operant conditioning. In *Report of the Proceedings of the International Congress on Education of the Deaf.* Washington: United States Government Printing Office, 1964.

Miller, D. N., & LeBlanc, J. M. Response decrement and resumption: A comparison of responding during and after Differential Reinforcement of Other Behavior. Paper presented at the Annual Meeting of the American Psychological Association, Honolulu, Hawaii, September, 1972.

Moore, R., & Goldiamond, I. Errorless establishment of visual discrimination using fading procedures. *Journal of the Experimental Analysis of Behavior,* 1964, *7,* 269-272.

Mosher, P. M., & Reese, E. P. Task difficulty as a variable in teaching word-recognition by fading and nonfading procedures. Paper presented at the Annual Meeting of the Eastern Psychological Association, New York, April, 1976.

Pawluk, M. M. Expectancy of success or failure in the learning disabled child. Unpublished masters dissertation, Mount Holyoke College, 1974.

Reese, E. P., & Werden, D. A fading technique for teaching number concepts to severely retarded children. Paper presented at the Annual Meeting of the Eastern Psychological Association, Atlantic City, New Jersey, April, 1970.

Rilling, M., & Caplan, H. J. Extinction-induced aggression during errorless discrimination learning. *Journal of the Experimental Analysis of Behavior,* 1973, *20,* 85-92.

Rosenberger, P. B. Discriminative aspects of visual hemi-inattention. *Neurology,* January 1974, pp. 17-23.

Sajwaj, T., & Knight, P. The detrimental effects of a correction procedure for errors in a tutoring program for a young retarded boy. In E. A. Ramp & B. L. Hopkins (Eds.), *A new direction for education: Behavior analysis,* 1971. Lawrence, Kansas: Department of Human Development, 1971.

Sidman, M., & Stoddard, L. T. The effectiveness of fading in programming a simultaneous form discrimination for retarded children. *Journal of the Experimental Analysis of Behavior,* 1967, *10,* 3-15.

Skinner, B. F., & Krakower, S. A. *Handwriting with write and see.* Chicago: Lyons and Carnahan, 1968.

Stoddard, L. T., & Sidman, M. The effects of errors on children's performance on a circle-ellipse discrimination. *Journal of the Experimental Analysis of Behavior,* 1967, *10,* 261-270.

Storm, R. H., & Robinson, P. W. Application of a graded choice procedure to obtain errorless learning in children. *Journal of the Experimental Analysis of Behavior,* 1973, *20,* 405-410.

Suppes, P., & Ginsberg, R. Experimental studies of mathematical concept formation in young children. *Science Education,* 1962, *46,* 230-240.

Terrace, H. S. Discrimination learning with and without "errors." *Journal of the Experimental Analysis of Behavior,* 1963, *6,* 1-27. (a)

Terrace, H. S. Errorless transfer of a discrimination across continua. *Journal of the Experimental Analysis of Behavior,* 1963, *6,* 223-232. (b)

Topping, J. S., Larmi, O. K., & Johnson, D. L. Omission training: Effects of gradual introduction. *Psychonomic Science,* 1972, *28,* 279-280.

Topping, J. S., & Larmi, O. K. Response elimination effectiveness of omission and two extinction training procedures. *The Psychological Record,* 1973, *23,* 197-202.

Touchette, P. E. The effects of graduated stimulus change on the acquisition of a simple discrimination in severely retarded boys. *Journal of the Experimental Analysis of Behavior,* 1968, *11,* 39-48.

Uhl, C. N. Eliminating behavior with omission and extinction after varying amounts of training. *Animal Learning and Behavior,* 1973, *1,* 237-240.

Uhl, C. N., & Garcia, E. E. Comparison of omission with extinction in response elimination in rats. *Journal of Comparative and Physiological Psychology,* 1969, *69,* 554-562.

Zeiler, M. D. Eliminating behavior with reinforcement. *Journal of the Experimental Analysis of Behavior,* 1971, *16,* 401-405.

18

Complexities of an "Elementary" Behavior Modification Procedure: Differential Adult Attention Used for Children's Behavior Disorders

Thomas Sajwaj
Anneal Dillon

Lutton Community Mental Health Center
   and
North Mississippi Retardation Center

Within the past 15 years a large number of behavior modification studies have focused on the effects of adult attention on the behavior of children. Experimental analyses have been conducted in a variety of environmental settings with a large number of target behaviors. Most studies have dealt with behavior problems manifested by individual children, although some later research has analyzed the effects of teacher attention on the behavior of entire classrooms. Briefly, the differential attention technique usually involves the application of adult attention following the occurrence of a desired behavior and the removal of the adult's attention after an undesired behavior. The assumption implied in this usage is that adult attention functions as a positive reinforcer for most children and that inappropriate behavior may inadvertently be maintained through the contingent application of adult attention.

This chapter reviews the range of success found with differential attention procedures. However, it is our contention that the great success of differential attention as a behavior-change technique is deceptive and that the procedure is considerably more complex than it appears. Areas of complexity are illustrated by representative case studies.

THE SUCCESSFUL USE OF DIFFERENTIAL ATTENTION

The procedure of differential attention has been utilized with many different types of behavior problems, both deficit and excess aspects of behavioral disturbances. An early application of the procedure was conducted by Zimmerman and Zimmerman (1962) with two 11-year-old boys who frequently engaged in disruptive classroom activities. It was noted that the teachers were spending an excessive amount of time dealing with these inappropriate behaviors. The classroom teachers were instructed to ignore instances of undesirable behavior and to praise, smile, and chat with the students after they performed appropriate classroom behavior. After several weeks of these tactics, rates of disruptive behavior were observed to be at a near-zero level, while appropriate classroom behaviors were occurring most of the time.

Since this pioneering work by Zimmerman & Zimmerman (1962), disruptive classroom behavior has been the target of many studies with the differential-attention procedure. In general, the teachers have been instructed to ignore the inappropriate, disruptive behavior of the children and to attend to the desirable, appropriate classroom behavior that would be incompatible with the behavior to be eliminated or reduced. Many investigative efforts have demonstrated that differential teacher attention is a valuable tool in reducing the inappropriate behavior of children (Becker, Madsen, Arnold, & Thomas, 1967; Hall, Fox, Williard, Goldsmith, Emerson, Owen, Davis, & Porcia, 1971; Hall, Lund, & Jackson, 1968; Holmes, 1966; O'Leary, Becker, Evans, & Saudargas, 1969; Patterson, 1966; Ward & Baker, 1968). Other experiments have attempted to reduce disruptive behavior and to improve classroom productivity by concentrating directly on in-class study behavior (Broden, Bruce, Mitchell, Carter, & Hall, 1970; Cossairt, Hall, & Hopkins, 1973; Madsen, Becker, & Thomas, 1968). Another area of related interest has been the development of reliable instruction following. Becker et al. (1967), Schutte and Hopkins (1970), and Cossairt et al. (1973) instructed the teacher to attend to the children for compliance within a given period. The teachers were to ignore dawdling and failure to follow instructions. While the main focus of these latter studies has been to increase and improve study behavior, there has been a concomitant emphasis on decreasing disruptive, inappropriate behavior.

Investigators have employed differential attention to successfully modify a wide variety of behavior problems other than classroom disruptions. Hart, Allen, Buell, Harris, and Wolf (1964) obtained a significant decrease in crying exhibited by two preschool children as a result of altered teacher attention. Harris, Johnston, Kelley, and Wolf (1964) used a differential attention procedure to eliminate crawling behavior in a nursery school girl. The teacher praised the girl for on-feet behavior and ignored all inappropriate crawling behavior. Harris et al. (1964) summarized an unpublished case by Johnston, Kelley, Harris, and Wolf in which teacher attention decreased excessive passivity in a preschool boy.

Etzel and Gewirtz (1967) reduced excessive crying in two infants by ignoring crying and providing attention for smiling and eye contact. Inappropriate verbalizations ("I can't do it.") were modified in a 10-year-old boy by changing teacher attention (Dietiker, 1970). McQueen (1970) improved the "getting in line" behavior of a 6-year-old girl by praising her for being in line within 50 sec after a command was given. The thumbsucking behavior of 3 8-year-old girls was improved, although not completely eliminated, by having the teacher praise the girls for exhibiting behaviors that were incompatible with thumb-sucking (Skiba, Pettigrew, & Alden, 1971). Hasazi and Hasazi (1972) reported that they were successful in correcting habitual digit reversals in an 8-year-old boy through the use of differential attention. Twardosz and Sajwaj (1972) used teacher attention, together with tokens, to shape sitting in a hyperactive preschool boy.

Differential attention studies have also dealt with several aspects of social functioning in children. Allen, Hart, Buell, Harris, and Wolf (1964) successfully increased peer interaction in a four-year-old nursery-school girl by having the teacher attend to her whenever she approached and played with the other children. Harris, Wolf, and Baer (1964) summarized an unpublished study by Johnston, Kelley, Harris, Wolf, and Baer which demonstrated the successful use of teacher attention in developing the social play of a preschool boy. Foxwell (1966) replicated the Allen et al. study with a three-year-old girl who displayed little interaction with her nursery school peers. Hall and Broden (1967) used differential attention to increase a variety of play skills in three retarded children. Buell, Stoddard, Harris, and Baer (1968) employed differential attention to increase the amount of time a three-year-old nursery school girl spent on outdoor playground equipment; the child, in playing on the equipment, came into more contact with her peers so that the teacher was able to reinforce social interaction. Wahler (1969c) demonstrated differential maternal attention to be a major factor in an infant's social development. Sajwaj, Twardosz, and Burke (1972) systematically reduced the amount of conversation with adults in a six-year-old boy using a differential attention procedure. Increased interaction with children then began to develop without further teacher intervention. Cooper and LeBlanc (1973) used teacher attention together with a structuring of activities and equipment to develop cooperative play in a preschool setting. Pinkston, Reese, LeBlanc, and Baer (1973) used teacher attention to decrease aggression and increase appropriate social behaviors in a preschool boy.

While much research has been conducted in preschool and school environments with the teacher as the prime therapist, several investigators have extended the use of this technique into other areas. The home, where the parents may use differential attention to foster the behavioral development of their children, has been of considerable importance. If it is true that both desirable and undesirable behaviors are maintained by their effects on the natural environment (Bijou & Sloane, 1966), then one of the most efficient ways to alter behavior is to change the reaction of the natural milieu to that behavior. Parents have been counseled to attend to the positive aspects of the behavior of their children and to ignore undesirable aspects (McIntire, 1970; Patterson & Gullion, 1968; Smith & Smith, 1966). Considerable experimental evidence is available to support the contention that parents can be trained to change behavior effectively using a differential attention procedure. Russo (1964) demonstrated that parents can effectively and efficiently act as therapists in home and clinical situations. Another early investigation by Wahler, Winkel, Peterson, and Morrison (1965) concentrated on the uncooperative and aggressive behaviors of three four-to six-year-old boys. The mothers were taught to ignore uncooperative, aggressive behavior and to attend only to cooperative, compliant behavior. The authors report that the mothers were successful in improving the behavior of two of the boys. Hawkins, Peterson, Schweid, and Bijou (1966) used a mother to reduce the incidence of aggressive and disobedient behavior in a four-year-old boy. She was taught to withdraw attention by placing her son in his room whenever such behaviors occurred and to praise him whenever incompatible, appropriate ones were observed. Wahler (1969b) employed a differential attention procedure with an elementary school boy who exhibited a high rate of oppositional behavior. Praise and attention were to follow appropriate, compliant behavior. Success was reported in the home, but no carry-over was observed in the school situation. Although some failures are noted, Wagner and Ora (1970) found differential parental attention to be an effective therapeutic technique for very young oppositional children. Herbert and Baer (1972) reduced destructive, aggressive, and noncompliant behavior in two hyperactive five-year-olds by teaching the mothers to ignore all inappropriate behavior and to attend to all desired responses that were incompatible with the disruptive behaviors. Hall, Axelrod, Tyler, Grief, Jones, and Robertson (1972) were successful in eliminating whining and shouting in a four-year-old boy by instructing the parents to turn away from him or leave the room when one of these behaviors occurred and to praise him for desirable, incompatible responses. Allen and Harris (1966) presented a case of the successful application of differential attention to the scratching behavior of a five-year-old girl. The mother was taught to ignore scratching behavior and to praise the child for other incompatible behaviors that involved the use of her hands. She was also reinforced for not having scratches on herself for a specified period of time. Following treatment, a near-zero incidence of scratching was noted.

The success of differential attention with children is summarized in Table 1. It contains only studies where individual data are presented and where differential attention is used as the prime technique. The authors' evaluations of success and failure were accepted, but were checked against their quantitative data if such were presented. Studies with combined procedures (like differential attention with timeout) are mainly excluded. Group studies (e.g., Thomas, Becker, & Armstrong, 1968) have also been excluded for the sake of simplicity. Also, some relevant studies may have been inadvertently missed.

TABLE 1

Partial Listing of Individual Case Successes and Failures
Where Differential Attention Is Used to Modify Child Behavior Problems

Year of Publication	Authors	Number of Successes	Number of Failures
1962	Zimmerman & Zimmerman	2	0
1964	Allen, Hart, Buell, Harris, & Wolf	1	0
1964	Harris, Johnston, Kelley, & Wolf	1	0
1964	Hart, Allen, Buell, Harris, & Wolf	2	0
1964	Harris, Wolf, & Baer	2	0
1965	Wahler, Winkel, Peterson & Morrison	2	1
1966	Patterson	1	0
1966	Holmes	1	0
1966	Foxwell	1	0
1966	Hawkins, Peterson, Schweid, & Bijou	1	0
1966	Allen & Harris	1	0
1967	Etzel & Gewirtz	2	0
1967	Becker, Madsen, Arnold, & Thomas	8	2
1967	Hall & Broden	3	0
1968	Ward & Baker	3	1
1968	Hall, Lund, & Jackson	6	0
1968	Madsen, Becker, & Thomas	3	0
1968	Buell, Stoddard, Harris, & Baer	1	0
1969	O'Leary, Becker, Evans, & Saudargas	1	6
1969a	Wahler	0	5
1969b	Wahler	1	0
1969c	Wahler	1	0
1970	Broden, Bruce, Mitchell, Carter, & Hall	2	0
1970	Schutte & Hopkins	5	0
1970	Wagner & Ora	4	3
1970	Dietiker	1	0
1970	McQueen	1	0
1970	Hayes & Hawkins	2	0
1971	Skibba, Pettigrew, & Alden	3	0
1971	Sajwaj & Knight	0	1
1971	Sajwaj & Hedges	0	1
1971	Hall, Fox, Williard, Goldsmith, Emerson, Owen, Davis, & Porcia (Exp. I, II, III, & IV)	4	0
1972	Twardosz & Sajwaj	1	0
1972	Sajwaj, Twardosz, & Burke	1	0
1972	Hasazi & Hasazi	1	0
1972	Herbert & Baer	2	0
1972	Hall, Axelrod, Tyler, Brief, Jones, & Robertson (Exp. I & III)	1	1
1973	Cossairt, Hall, & Hopkins	12	0
1973	Pinkston, Reese, LeBlanc, & Baer	1	0
1973	Herbert, Pinkston, Hayden, Sajwaj, Pinkston, Cordua, & Jackson	0	6
1973	Cooper & LeBlanc	2	0
		Successes 87	Failures 27

Even given these exclusions, the reported ratio of successes to failures is impressive: 87 successes with only 27 failures. In addition, success has been obtained by many different therapists with many diverse behaviors (desirable and undesirable) over a wide range of child characteristics in greatly differing situations. This behavior, therapist, child, and setting generality is impressive.

THE DECEPTIVENESS OF SUCCESS

Clearly differential attention has broad generality as a therapeutic tool. The above cited evidence of effectiveness and the apparent simplicity of this procedure have prompted some authors to recommend its usage to a wide range of individuals working with children. In many cases, such a recommendation is appropriate. However, it should be stressed that negative results are usually not published or are noted briefly just before more successful procedures are described. A reluctance to publish negative results seems indicated since the bulk of the failures are reported by only three sets of authors (Herbert, Pinkston, Hayden, Sajwaj, Pinkston, Cordua, & Jackson, 1973; O'Leary et al., 1969; Wahler, 1969a). This bias toward successes has two results. An inflated view of the probability of success using differential attention procedures is presented to the inexperienced practitioner; and, clinically significant information is lost. As Tharp and Wetzel (1969) argue, "A study of those cases and conditions in which difficulty and failure occur can, however, educate the social scientist and social interventionist concerning some of the key elements in that particular environment. Thus, the reporting and analysis of case 'failures' and resistances to change are of an importance at least equal to that of case success" [p. 126].

Recently, a scattering of reports have appeared in which resistances and failures are prominent. These studies strongly suggest that differential attention can be a most complex procedure and that the wide generality implied in the forementioned studies is seriously in need of qualification. Five areas of complexity that have arisen in clinical applications of differential attention are discussed below. Selected case studies are presented to illustrate these complexities.

Parental Attention as Punishing

When parents are taught to attend to their children for socially or academically desirable behavior, they are usually instructed to use some form of praise, like, "That's good. Fine, you're doing a good job." With such positive content, it is assumed that parental attention will function as a positive reinforcer or, at worst, will function as a neutral stimulus. Many of the above mentioned studies validate this assumption. Unfortunately, several recent case studies have shown parental attention, mainly positive in content, to function as a punishing stimulus. Herbert et al. (1973) report four cases where maternal attention, following deviant behavior, resulted in lower rates of deviant behavior than when no attention followed the behavior. Thus, maternal attention fitted Azrin and Holz's (1966) functional definition of punishment. In addition, the quality of the children's behavior worsened. Aggression, self-injury, dangerous climbing, and enuresis appeared during ignoring conditions. These adverse rate and quality changes in behavior did not appear to be transient phenomena. Sajwaj and Hedges (1971) report a case where the father of a six-year-old boy with a severe conduct problem was taught to use differential praise to control disruptive behavior during a bedroom cleanup period. Although the father completely ignored disruptions and praised most instances of compliance, no improvement was observed over a five-month period. The father then suddenly began praising disruptions and ignoring compliance. The rate of disruptions fell to almost zero over a six-day period. Ignoring disruptions brought their rate back to high levels; praise for disruptions again reduced their rate. However, this punishing effect was transient and was lost after four days of the second praise-for-disruptions condition. The authors speculate that praise was discriminative for oppositional behavior; the boy refused to clean his room when praised for that behavior and refused to misbehave when disruptions were praised. The transient effect, then, was due to the boy discovering that he had been tricked into stopping his disruptions.

These cases reported by Herbert et al. (1973) and Sajwaj and Hedges (1971) pose serious implications for clinicians who are teaching parents to use differential attention as a behavior control technique. If parental attention is a positive reinforcer or a neutral stimulus, the worst result will only be one of no effect on behavior. However, if parental praise is functioning as a negative consequence, for whatever reason, then training in the use of differential attention may yield disasterous results: the child's behavior will worsen, as Herbert et al. discovered to their chagrin.

Herbert et al., unfortunately, could cite no compelling reasons or speculations for these adverse effects. It seems safe, though, to assume that the apparent punishing effects of maternal attention were the result of a complex interaction between the setting conditions, historical factors in the parent-child relationship, and discriminative functions of the attention itself. Of course, such an assumption is of little applied value until these conditions, factors, and functions can be reliably described.

Concurrent Punishment

Azrin and Holz (1966) have suggested that the use of punishment procedures may have adverse effects on the socialization of children. That is, if a parent or teacher uses punishment procedures, the adult's attention may become a conditioned punisher itself or the adult's appearance may be a cue for escape or avoidance. Azrin and Holz term this unintended side effect of punishment social disruption. Although these authors drew primarily on research from controlled laboratory settings, such processes may well exist in applied situations. For example, Lovaas, Schaeffer, and Simmons (1965) developed "No!" as a punishing event for autistic children by pairing it with electric shock.

More recently, the reverse finding has begun to appear: the use of concurrent punishment procedures may enhance parental attention as a positive reinforcer. Wahler (1969a) increased the reinforcing function of parental attention on a marble-drop task by the concurrent use of a combined praise and timeout procedure to control oppositional behavior in a command-following situation. Elimination of the concurrent timeout procedure reduced the reinforcing function of the parental attention. Sajwaj and Hedges (1971) replicated this enhancement effect. They report that compliance in a 6-year-old boy could be maintained only when the parents concurrently praised compliance and punished disruptive behavior with a 105 dB blast from a bicycle horn. Parental praise could be demonstrated as a positive reinforcer only under conditions where the horn was used as a punishment. Sajwaj, Hedges, Smith, and Pinkston (unpublished) have further replicated this enhancement effect for parental and teacher attention using concurrent timeout and electric shock procedures. It would appear, then, that the specific manner in which a concurrent punishment is utilized may have marked effects on the functions of adult attention. Attention may be enhanced as a positive reinforcer (Wahler, 1969a) or changed to a punishing event (Azrin & Holz, 1966).

Amount of Attention

Ideally, a differential attention procedure implies much attention for the appropriate behaviors and no attention for the incompatible or undesired behaviors. In most applied situations, it is impractical or impossible to eliminate all attention for the undesired behaviors. In these circumstances, behavior modifiers will have the teachers and parents praise more heavily or emphasize more distinctly the attention given the appropriate behaviors. For example, Hayes and Hawkins (1970) found high error rates for reading assignments with two emotionally disturbed children. The teacher gave much attention following errors by discussing the material but gave relatively less attention following correct answers. Errors were sharply reduced when the teacher reversed this pattern by giving much attention for correct answers and little attention following errors. However, errors were frequent when much attention was given for both correct and erroneous answers. This case study suggests that the critical factor is the *relative* amount of attention following the correct answers and errors and is consistent with most of the research with differential attention.

Unfortunately, a case reported by Sajwaj and Knight (1971) does not validate this simple relationship. They designed a correction procedure for errors in a pre-reading program for a retarded boy that involved a bare minimum of attention following errors. The attention consisted of the tutor pointing to the correct answer while saying, "This is the correct picture." The item was then repeated. To offset this necessary bit of attention following each error, much praise and tokens were given for every correct answer. Despite these procedures, error rate remained high and appeared to be increasing. Successive elimination, reinstatement, and elimination of the correction procedure unequivocally demonstrated that it was functioning as a powerful positive reinforcer for errors. Thus, a modicum of attention served to maintain and increase errors, despite a relatively great amount of praise and tokens for incompatible, correct answers. By way of explanation, the authors only noted that this child was highly oppositional and may have taken the tutor's correction as a cue to do the opposite (make errors) of what the tutor desired (correct answers). However, the authors could not identify any other reinforcers for oppositional behavior inside or outside of the tutorial period.

Discriminative Functions

The operant laboratory suggests that a consequent stimulus may not only have reinforcing or punishing qualities but may also have discriminative functions. For example, Azrin and Holz (1966) explain some of the apparently contradictory results of the punishment research literature by noting concurrent discriminative functions of the punishing stimulus. Certainly, in applied settings the parents' or teachers' "You're doing a good job." not only can denote praise but also can instruct the child to continue that activity.

Sajwaj et al. (1972) postulate a discriminative function of attention and ignoring to account for the multiple behavioral effects that they observed in a six-year-old boy in a remedial preschool. This child engaged in excessively adult-oriented behaviors, the prime manifestation of which was an involved conversation with the teacher. When this behavior was ignored, it declined; behavior relative to children increased, use of "girls' toys" decreased, and compliance in group activities decreased, while disruptions increased. With the teacher again attending to his adult-oriented conversations, these other behaviors returned to their prior rates. Teacher attention for these collateral behaviors was constant. The authors suggest that these behaviors comprised a social role: much behavior relative to adults (conversation, compliance), particularly with women (use of "girls' toys"). When the teacher ignored his conversation, he dropped the entire role and began to behave more "like a little boy" (more child-oriented behavior, less play with "girls' toys"). Thus, how the teacher related to his conversation told the child which role was appropriate.

Attention As Stimulation

In addition to reinforcing, punishing, and discriminative functions, attention may serve as stimulation for the child. That is, the tactual, auditory, and visual stimulation provided the child may, itself, have direct or indirect behavioral effects, independent of any contingent usage. Such effects are clearly suggested in the clinical management of failure-to-thrive infants and ruminating children. Failure-to-thrive is a marked lag of physical development with no evidence of organic etiology. Such infants usually have a narrow range of behavioral skills, typically, with little spontaneous social, play, or speech behaviors (Barbero & Sheehan, 1967). Rumination is the regurgitation and reconsumption of food. Children, who ruminate frequently, exhibit little other activity. They appear to be preoccupied with rumination and show little interest in their environment. Although physical development is retarded, there is little evidence of organic etiology (Kanner, 1972). Both failure-to-thrive and rumination appear to be related to an impoverished environment, neglect, or profound retardation early in infancy.

To date, the most effective treatment for these conditions has been massive, noncontingent attention. Typically, one or more adults are assigned to provide the child with their attention at least for part of the day. This increase of attention is usually accomplished in the context of a pediatrics ward, foster home or daycare program. Elmer (1960), Barbero and Sheehan (1967), and Talbot and Howell (1971), among others, report marked and often dramatic improvements in physical and behavioral development for failure-to-thrive infants coincident with the increase in noncontingent attention. Richmond, Eddy, and Green (1958), Gaddini and Gaddini (1959), Fullerton (1963), and Hollowell and Gardner (1965), among others, report marked reductions in rumination and increases in weight coincident with the start of high levels of noncontingent attention.

Whether attention has any such obvious or indirect effects on the behavior of older or less severely affected children, independent of reinforcing, punishing, and discriminative functions, is a matter for research. However, for young children who are involved in failure-to-thrive or rumination, such stimulation effects of noncontingent attention are fairly clear.

CONCLUSIONS

The positive reinforcing function of adult attention for child behavior is overwhelmingly demonstrated. This great success, together with the superficial simplicity of the technique, may prompt some behavior modifiers to view differential attention as an "elementary" behavior modification tool which has progressed beyond the need for careful and detailed experimental analysis. The few clinical cases cited in the latter sections of the brief review, together with the reminder that failures are usually not reported, should help dispel this faulty belief. The seriously complicated case reports of Herbert et al. (1973) and Sajwaj et al. (1972), the seemingly opposed conclusions of Azrin and Holz (1966) and Wahler (1969a), and the stimulation effects of attention reported in the pediatrics and child psychiatry literature all point in one direction: Differential attention is not a simple behavior modification technique. Not only should clinicians exercise careful scrutiny of the manner in which it is used and the resulting effects, but also more complete experimental analyses are in order.

REFERENCES

Allen, K. E., & Harris, F. R. Elimination of a child's excessive scratching by training the mother in reinforcement procedures. *Behaviour Research and Therapy,* Oxford, England, 1966, *4,* 79-84.

Allen, K. E., Hart, B. M., Buell, J. S., Harris, F. R., & Wolf, M. M. Effects of social reinforcement on isolate behavior of a nursery school child. *Child Development,* 1964, *35,* 511-18.

Azrin, N. H., & Holz, W. C. Punishment. In W. K. Honig (Ed.), *Operant behavior: Areas of research and application.* New York: Appleton-Century-Crofts, 1966.

Barbero, G. J., & Sheehan, E. Environmental failure to thrive: A clinical view. *The Journal of Pediatrics,* 1967, *71,* 639-644.

Becker, W. C., Madsen, C. J., Jr., Arnold, R., & Thomas, D. R. The contingent use of teacher attention and praise in reducing classroom behavior problems. *Journal of Special Education,* 1967, *1,* 287-307.

Bijou, S. W., & Sloane, H. N. Therapeutic techniques with children. In I. A. Berg & L. A. Pennington (Eds.), *An introduction to clinical psychology* (3rd ed.). New York: Ronald Press, 1966.

Broden, M., Bruce, C., Mitchell, M. A., Carter, V., & Hall, R. V. Effects of teacher attention on attending behavior of two boys at adjacent tables. *Journal of Applied Behavior Analysis,* 1970, *3,* 199-203.

Buell, J., Stoddard, P., Harris, F. R., & Baer, D. M. Collateral social development accompanying reinforcement of outdoor play in a preschool child. *Journal of Applied Behavior Analysis,* 1968, *1,* 167-174.

Cooper, A., & LeBlanc, J. An experimental analysis of the effects of contingent related teachers attention and special activities for developing cooperative play. Paper presented at the Biennial Meeting of the Society for Research in Child Development, Philadelphia, Pennsylvania, 1973.

Cossairt, A., Hall, R. V., & Hopkins, B. L. The effects of experimenter's instructions, feedback, and praise on teacher praise and student attending behavior. *Journal of Applied Behavior Analysis,* 1973, *6,* 89-100.

Dietiker, R. Decreasing a fifth grade boy's "I can't do it" responses to written assignments. *School Applications of Learning Theory,* 1970, *1,* 25-32.

Elmer, E. Failure to thrive. *Pediatrics,* 1960, *25,* 717-725.

Etzel, B. C., & Gewirtz, J. L. Experimental modification of caretaker-maintained high-rate operant crying in a 6- and a 20-week old infant (Infans tyrannotearus): Extinction of crying with reinforcement of eye contact and smiling. *Journal of Experimental Child Psychology,* 1967, *5,* 303-317.

Foxwell, H. The development of social responsiveness to other children in a preschool child through experimental use of social reinforcement. Unpublished master's dissertation, University of Kansas, 1966.

Fullerton, D. T. Infantile rumination: A case report. *Archives of General Psychiatry,* 1963, *9,* 593-600.

Gaddini, R., & Gaddini, E. Rumination in infancy. In C. Jessner, & E. Pavenstadt (Eds.), *Dynamic psychopathology in childhood.* New York: Grune & Stratton, 1959.

Hall, R. V., Axelrod, S., Tyler, L., Grief, E., Jones, F. C., & Robertson, R. Modification of behavior problems in the home with a parent as observer and experimenter. *Journal of Applied Behavior Analysis,* 1972, *5,* 53-64.

Hall, R. V., & Broden, M. Behavior changes in brain-injured children through social reinforcement. *Journal of Experimental Child Psychology,* 1967, *5,* 463-479.

Hall, R. V., Fox, R., Willard, D., Goldsmith, L., Emerson, M., Owen, M., Davis, F., & Porcia, E. The teacher as observer and experimenter in the modification of disputing and talking-out behaviors. *Journal of Applied Behavior Analysis,* 1971, *4,* 141-149.

Hall, R. V., Lund, D., & Jackson, D. Effects of teacher attention on study behavior. *Journal of Applied Behavior Analysis,* 1968, *1,* 1-12.

Harris, F. R., Johnston, M. K., Kelley, C. W., & Wolf, M. M. Effects of positive social reinforcement on regressed crawling of a nursery school child. *Journal of Educational Psychology,* 1964, *55,* 35-41.

Harris, F. R., Wolf, M. M., & Baer, D. M. Effects of adult social reinforcement on child behavior. *Young Children,* 1964, *20,* 8-17.

Hart, B. M., Allen, K. E., Buell, J. S., Harris, F. R., & Wolf, M. M. Effects of social reinforcement on operant crying. *Journal of Experimental Child Psychology,* 1964, *1,* 145-53.

Hasazi, J. E., & Hasazi, S. E. Effects of teacher attention on digit reversal behavior in an elementary school child. *Journal of Applied Behavior Analysis,* 1972, *5,* 157-162.

Hawkins, R. P., Peterson, R. F., Schweid, E. L., & Bijou, S. W. Behavior therapy in the home: Amelioration of problem parent-child relations with the parent in a therapeutic role. *Journal of Experimental Child Psychology,* 1966, *4,* 99-107.

Hayes, J. E., & Hawkins, R. P. An analysis of instruction duration as a consequence for correct and incorrect answers. Paper given at the American Psychological Association Convention, Miami, September, 1970.

Herbert, E. W., & Baer, D. M. Training parents as behavior modifiers: Self-recording of contingent attention. *Journal of Applied Behavior Analysis,* 1972, *5,* 139-149.

Herbert, E. W., Pinkston, E. M., Hayden, M. L., Sajwaj, T. E., Pinkston, S., Cordua, G., & Jackson, C. Adverse effects of differential parental attention. *Journal of Applied Behavior Analysis,* 1973, *6,* 15-30.

Hollowell, J. R., & Gardner, L. I. Rumination and growth failure in male fraternal twins: Association with disturbed family environment. *Pediatrics,* 1965, *36,* 565-571.

Holmes, D. S. The application of learning theory to the treatment of a school behavior problem: A case study. *Psychology in the School,* 1966, *3,* 355-359.

Kanner, L. *Child psychiatry* (4th ed.). Springfield, Illinois: Charles C. Thomas, 1972.

Lovaas, O. I., Schaeffer, B., & Simmons, J. Q. Building social behavior in autistic children by use of electric shock. *Journal of Experimental Research in Personality,* 1965, *1,* 99-109.

Madsen, C., Jr., Becker, W., & Thomas, D. Rules, praise, and ignoring: Elements of elementary classroom control. *Journal of Applied Behavior Analysis,* 1968, *1,* 139-150.

McIntire, R. W. *For love of children.* Del Mar, Cal.: CRM Books, 1970.

McQueen, P. The use of positive social reinforcement to help a first grader line up more quickly. *School Applications of Learning Theory,* 1970, *2,* 19-24.

O'Leary, K. D., Becker, W. C., Evans, M. B., & Saudargas, R. A. A token reinforcement program in a public school: A replication and systematic analysis. *Journal of Applied Behavior Analysis,* 1969, *2,* 3-13.

Patterson, G. R. An application of conditioning techniques to the control of a hyperactive child. In L. P. Ullmann & L. Krasner (Eds.), *Case studies in behavior modification.* New York: Holt, Rinehart, & Winston, Inc., 1966.

Patterson, G. R., & Guillion, E. *Living with children: New methods for parents and teachers.* Champaign, Ill.: Research Press, 1968.

Pinkston, E. M., Reese, N., LeBlanc, J. M., & Baer, D. M. Independent control of a preschool child's aggression and peer interaction by contingent teacher attention. *Journal of Applied Behavior Analysis*, 1973, *6*, 115-125.

Richmond, J. B., Eddy, E., & Green, M. Rumination: A psychosomatic syndrome of infancy. *Pediatrics*, 1958, *22*, 49-54.

Russo, S. Adaptations in behavioral therapy with children. *Behaviour Research and Therapy*. Oxford, England, 1964, *2*, 43-47.

Sajwaj, T., & Hedges, D. Functions of parental attention in an oppositional, retarded boy. *Proceedings of the 79th Annual Convention of the American Psychological Association*, 1971, 697-698.

Sajwaj, T., & Knight, P. The detrimental effects of a correction procedure for errors in a tutoring program for a young retarded boy. In E. A. Ramp, & B. L. Hopkins (Eds.), *A new direction for education: Behavior analysis – 1971*. Lawrence, Kansas: University of Kansas, 1971.

Sajwaj, T. E., Hedges, D., Smith, J., & Pinkston, S. The effectiveness of parental and teacher praise as a positive reinforcer as a function of concurrent punishment procedures. Unpublished manuscript, The University of Mississippi Medical Center, 1972.

Sajwaj, T. E., Twardosz, S., & Burke, M. Side effects of extinction procedures in a remedial preschool. *Journal of Applied Behavior Analysis*, 1972, *5*, 163-175.

Schutte, R. C., & Hopkins, B. L. The effects of teacher attention on following instructions in a kindergarten class. *Journal of Applied Behavior Analysis*, 1970, *3*, 117-122.

Skiba, E. A., Pettigrew, E., & Alden, S. E. A behavioral approach to the control of thumbsucking in the classroom. *Journal of Applied Behavior Analysis*, 1971, *4*, 121-125.

Smith, J. M., & Smith, D. E. P. *Child management: A program for parents*. Ann Arbor: Ann Arbor Publishers, 1966.

Talbot, N. B., & Howell, M. C. Social and behavioral causes and consequences of disease among children. In N. B. Talbot, J. Kagan, & L. Eisenberg (Eds.), *Behavioral sciences in pediatric medicine*. Philadelphia: W. B. Saunders, 1971.

Tharp, R. G., & Wetzel, R. J. *Behavior modification in the natural environment*. New York: Academic Press, 1969.

Thomas, D. R., Becker, W. C., & Armstrong, M. Production and elimination of disruptive classroom behavior by systematically varying teacher's behavior. *Journal of Applied Behavior Analysis*, 1968, *1*, 35-45.

Twardosz, S., & Sajwaj, T. E. Multiple effects of a procedure to increase sitting in a hyperactive, retarded boy. *Journal of Applied Behavior Analysis*, 1972, *5*, 73-78.

Wagner, L. I., & Ora, J. P. Parental control of the very young severely oppositional child. Paper given at The Southeastern Psychological Association meetings, Louisville, Kentucky, 1970.

Wahler, R. G. Oppositional children: A quest for parental reinforcement control. *Journal of Applied Behavior Analysis*, 1969, *2*, 159-170. (a)

Wahler, R. G. Setting generality: Some specific and general effects of child behavior therapy. *Journal of Applied Behavior Analysis*, 1969, *2*, 239-246. (b)

Wahler, R. G. Infant social development: Some experimental analyses of an infant-mother interaction during the first year of life. *Journal of Experimental Child Psychology*, 1969, *7*, 101-113. (c)

Wahler, R. G., Winkel, G. H., Peterson, R. F., & Morrison, D. C. Mothers as behavior therapists for their own children. *Behaviour Research and Therapy*, Oxford, England, 1965, *3*, 113-124.

Ward, M. H., & Baker, B. L. Reinforcement therapy in the classroom. *Journal of Applied Behavior Analysis*, 1968, *1*, 323-328.

Zimmerman, E. H., & Zimmerman, J. The alteration of behavior in a special classroom situation. *Journal of the Experimental Analysis of Behavior*, 1962, *5*, 59-60.

19

An Experimental Analysis of Criterion-Related and Noncriterion-Related Cues in "Errorless" Stimulus Control Procedures

Kathryn J. Schilmoeller
Barbara C. Etzel

University of Kansas

Three common and potentially errorless stimulus-control procedures are fading (Terrace, 1963a), superimposition (Terrace, 1963b), and stimulus shaping (Bijou, 1968 and Sidman and Stoddard, 1966). The successful use of these three procedures depends on the programmer's choice of the right element of the stimulus to emphasize at any given time. Various experimenters have suggested effective methods for choosing the correct element. Bijou (1968) has argued that in the absence of research showing which of the many possible fading techniques should be used, the part of the stimulus containing "the cue essential to the discrimination" should be the one manipulated. Newman's study with pigeons, reported by Baron (1965), indicated that one should eliminate any other cue in the stimulus that is *not* critical to the final discrimination, especially if that cue is higher in the organism's attending hierarchy than the critical cue. In other words, there may be some cues in a stimulus complex that are more readily responded to (color as opposed to white lines, with pigeons for example), due to the nature of the organism or its past history. These cues, although readily responded to, nevertheless may not aid a final discrimination. If such a cue is within the initial stimulus complex, then the organism may attend to it and not to the critical cue.

Terrace (1966) has cited two examples of programs developed for pigeons in which the acquisition of a discrimination did not occur after programming procedures were used to transfer control from one stimulus to another. In the first example, in an attempt to shift control from a color (red-green) discrimination to the orientation of a line (vertical-horizontal), the lines were first superimposed on colored backgrounds after the red-green discrimination was acquired. Unless the backgrounds were then faded out in very small steps, the pigeons began to respond to the incorrect stimulus (S−), demonstrating that the final discrimination had not been acquired. Similar results were found when Terrace attempted to establish a vertical-horizontal discrimination by fading the intensity of the stimuli. Again, correct responding was maintained only until the intensity of the S− was within a few increments of the intensity of the correct stimulus (S+). As a result, the criterion discrimination was not acquired.

Studies involving human subjects have contributed to the information concerning cues as well. For example, a study by Touchette (1969) showed that tilted lines could be responded to as complex stimuli. Although the retarded subjects of that study all responded to the criterion-level stimuli with few or no errors, their performance on probes demonstrated that as a result of differences in their experimental histories, they were responding on different bases to the same stimulus. This demonstrated that the potential for correct responding could be based on more than one cue even when the discrimination involved apparently simple stimuli.

In providing detailed descriptions of program development, Sidman and Stoddard (1966) and Dixon, Spradlin, Girardeau, and Etzel (1975) also have provided programs that initially were unsuccessful in shifting stimulus control to the criterion task because their cues were not directed to the solution of the criterion task. However, program revisions were developed that were successful in shifting control. In the initial development of a program to teach the discrimination between a circle and a flat ellipse, Sidman and Stoddard began with the circle and background on the S+ at full brightness. A fading procedure was used in which both the background and the ellipse gradually but simultaneously were faded in on the S− keys. As a result, children could respond correctly throughout most of the program by simply attending to the key that was fully bright: it was not necessary to attend to the shape on that key. When both keys were fully bright, the children (who had previously responded to the brightness cue) were unable to maintain correct responding. To eliminate this problem, Sidman and Stoddard divided the fading procedure into two sections. First, the background of the S− keys was faded to full intensity, and then the shape of the ellipse was gradually intensified. This change in the fading procedure resulted in a more successful shift in stimulus control from the program to the criterion discrimination.

A similar example was described by Dixon et al. (1975) in the development of a program designed to teach an "in-front" spatial relationship. They initially chose object form and color as the dimensions to be faded; however, these fading procedures proved insufficient. In subsequent revisions of the program, the subject was required to respond to the program stimuli by pointing to the front or face of one object (a picture of an animal or person) and then making a moving pointing response to the object in front. This face position and moving response cue was more effective in shifting control from the program to correct responding on the criterion test.

A study by Gollin and Savoy (1968) provides another possible example of failure on a criterion test due to the lack of program cues directed to the criterion solution. An attempt was made to establish a conditional discrimination using programming procedures. During the programs and criterion test, two stimuli, a circle and a triangle, were presented at one time. When the stimuli had multiple-stripe backgrounds, the circle was the S+; however, if the backgrounds consisted of single stripes, the triangle was correct. Again, the fading procedure of increasing the brightness of the S— was used. First the form (circle or triangle) was faded on to the S— key, and then the background was gradually added. Some of the children who received programmed training were unsuccessful on the criterion conditional discrimination. Possibly they were unsuccessful because fading along the dimension of brightness resulted in cues that led to correct responding on the program but were not related to the solution of the criterion task. As with the early form of the circle-ellipse program developed by Sidman and Stoddard, the children could simply choose the key that was fully bright; but once both the correct and incorrect keys were fully bright, they no longer could determine the S+ on that basis. Again, it was not necessary to attend to the specific elements of the forms and backgrounds that composed the complex stimulus in order to respond correctly during the program.

These studies indicate that the determination of cues is essential to the development of an effective program. If a program is to be successful, the cues chosen should fulfill at least two qualifications; the use of the cues should result in: 1) correct responses throughout the program; and 2) a stable shift in stimulus control from those cues to the solution of the criterion task. In most cases, selecting a cue that will meet the first qualification is relatively easy; however, the second (selecting cues that will lead to an effective shift in stimulus control) is more difficult. Programmers often have concluded that they have developed a successful program after subjects have responded with few or no errors on that program, only to find that many errors were made when the criterion task was finally presented to the subjects.

In programming a discrimination in which a child is asked to choose "the different one" from an array of four Cs and one reversed C, a variety of cues might be considered. Baer (1970) has reported that McCleave initially attempted to train this discrimination by first increasing and then gradually reducing the size of the reversed C. The child maintained correct responding until the reversed C was again the same size as the regular Cs, but then reverted to chance-level responding. Size is not related to the criterion discrimination of distinguishing a reversed C from regular Cs. Not surprisingly, correct responding was not maintained once such a noncriterion-related cue was removed. Similar results probably would be obtained if an attempt to emphasize the difference in these stimuli involved filling in the opening of the reversed *C* with red. McCleave was successful in training this discrimination by replacing the reversed *C* with an *O* and then very gradually adding a gap on the left side of the *O*. The child responded correctly to the *O* as the different one and continued to respond correctly as the gap increased to the size of the opening on the standard reversed *C*. The cues in this series of stimulus manipulations were directly related to the criterion discrimination, and thus, would be considered *criterion-related*.

The purpose of the present study was two-fold. The first goal was to design successful programs to teach two fairly complex discrimination tasks. The cues used in these programs and the manipulation of those cues were to be criterion-related. In other words, an attempt was made to design the cues in such a way that would enable the subjects not only to proceed through the programs errorlessly (or nearly so) but also to respond correctly on the criterion tasks, demonstrating that they had, in fact, learned the tasks. The second purpose was to evaluate the effects of adding noncriterion-related cues to the programs that previously had been demonstrated to be successful in teaching two different discrimination tasks.

THE EXPERIMENT

Subjects and Setting

Eight normal children from the Edna A. Hill Child Development Laboratory in the Department of Human Development at the University of Kansas served as subjects. Their ages ranged from 4 years, 4 months to 5 years, 5 months. The children were divided into two groups of two males and two females each, with a mean age of 4 years, 11 months.

All criterion pretests, posttests, retention tests, and programming sessions were conducted in a small experimental room containing a child-sized table and two child-sized chairs (for the experimenter and subject). An adjoining observation room was connected to the experimental room by a one-way mirror.

Stimulus Materials

Two match-to-sample tasks and programs were developed for the present experiment. To minimize extraneous variance, it was important to use tasks that the children would not have experienced and that would be of approximately the same difficulty. Special tasks were developed to fulfill these specifications. These tasks were called the Color Task and the Kanji Task. ("Kanji" is the Japanese word for the characters used in the Japanese writing system.) Although these tasks involved different discriminations, the basic format, number of program trials, and number of criterion-test trials were the same for each. The stimulus materials for these tasks were drawn on unlined 12.8 cm x 20.4 cm (5 in. x 8 in.)

index cards. Each match-to-sample stimulus card was divided in half horizontally, with the sample centered in the top half and four choice positions spread across the bottom half.

Criterion Test

A total of 12 cards made up the criterion test that was used for all pretests, posttests, and retention tests. Six Kanji test cards were alternated with 6 Color cards. The position of the S+ or match was controlled over trials so that it appeared 3 times in each of the 4 choice boxes. Examples of criterion test cards are shown in Figures 1a and 2a. (The notation "S+" appearing under the stimuli in the correct choice was not on the original cards.)

Kanji. The individual stimuli, three pictures and six Japanese characters, that comprised the sample and the choice stimuli on the Kanji Criterion Test cards are illustrated in Figure 3. The sample stimuli consisted of black line drawings of a sun, man, and tree. The six Japanese characters, drawn in black, made up two different groups of characters that were used in the choice positions. The first group, S+ characters, consisted of characters that corresponded in meaning to the pictures found in the sample. The three S— or distractor characters, meaning "turn," "small," and "ground," were visually similar to the sample pictures and S+ characters but did not correspond in meaning.

Figure 4 shows the combinations of individual stimuli that appeared in the sample and four choice positions. Each sample contained the three pictures meaning "sun," "man," and "tree" (see Fig. 4, row a). Three characters were located in each choice position; however, the S+ on each of the six criterion cards was the only choice containing the three S+ characters that corresponded in meaning to the pictures in the sample (see Fig. 4, row b). The three S— choices were made up either of combinations of S+ and S— characters (see Fig. 4, rows c and d) or entirely of S— characters (see Fig. 4, row e). For example, one of the S— choices (see Fig. 4, row d) contained the S+ character "man" and the S— characters meaning "turn" and "ground." The positions of the three different combinations comprising the S— choices were varied systematically across the six Kanji Criterion Test cards. In addition, the order of the pictures within the sample and of the characters within each choice combination also varied from card to card. The characters in the S+ always appeared in an order different from the order of the corresponding sample pictures (see Fig. 1a).

Color. The criterion task of the Color Program involved matching a particular four-color sequence found in the sample and in the correct choice. An example of one of the Color Criterion Test cards is illustrated in Figure 2a. A square-shaped array of 16 small circles appeared in the sample and four-choice positions of each card. The diameters of the circles in the sample were slightly larger (8 mm) than the diameters of those found in each of the choices (7 mm). Of the 16 circles in each of the choice positions and sample, 12 were colored and

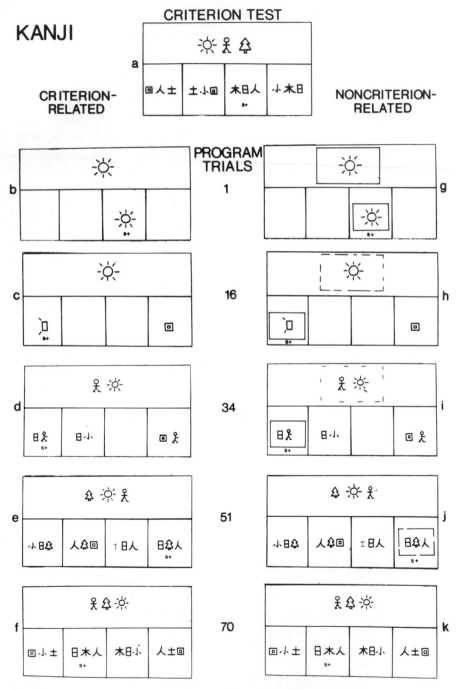

Figure 1. a-k   Examples of Kanji criterion test and criterion- and noncriterion-related program trials.

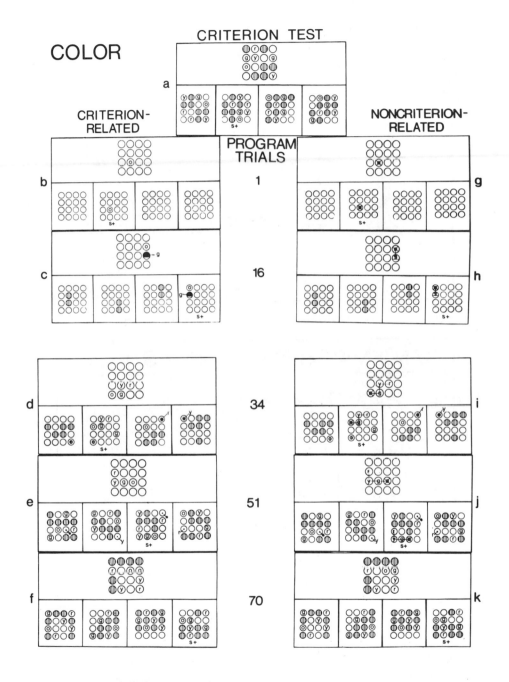

Figure 2. a-k   Examples of Color criterion test and criterion- and noncriterion-related program trials. Orange, green, yellow, and red circles are indicated by *o, g, y,* and *r* respectively. Circles containing vertical parallel lines represent blue, brown, pink, or purple circles. Blank circles indicate the absence of color.

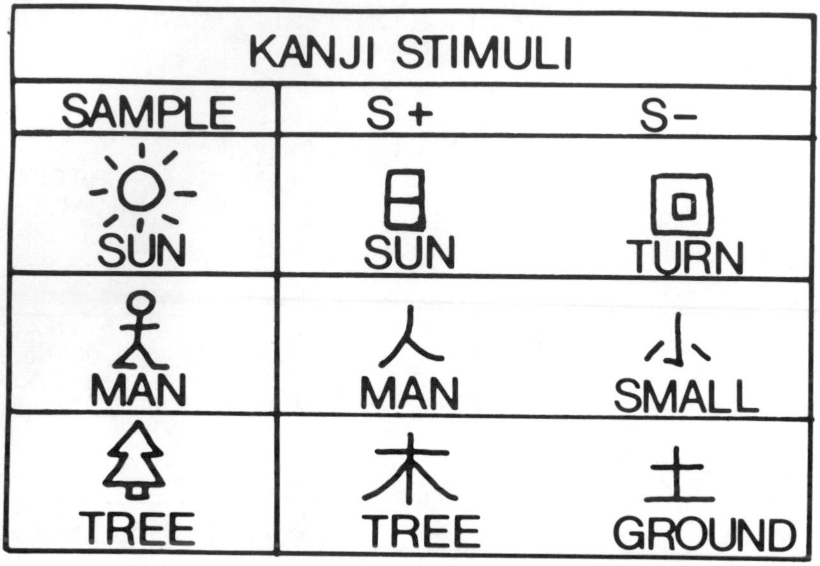

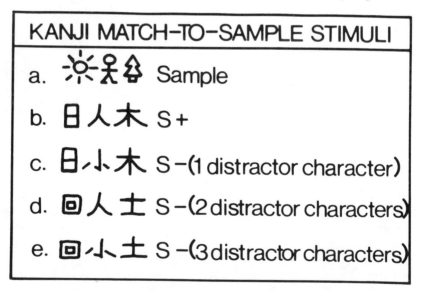

Figure 3   Sample pictures and S+ and S– characters used in Kanji Program.

Figure 4   Combinations of individual Kanji stimuli in the sample, S+, and S– choices.

4 were blank. On the criterion test, each sample contained orange, green, yellow, and red circles adjacent to each other in that order. For example, in Figure 2a, the orange, green, yellow, and red circles in the sample (represented by o, g, y, and r respectively) appear adjacent to each other beginning with the orange circle in the far left column. The S+ also contained orange, green, yellow, and red

circles adjacent to each other and in the same configuration as in the sample, but not in the same location within the array for that particular card.

Each S— also contained these four colors, but they were not adjacent to each other vertically or horizontally. They could not, therefore, appear in the same configuration as the corresponding circles in the sample. Four other colors, blue, brown, pink, and purple were found in all choices, correct and incorrect, as well as in the sample. In Figure 2, the circles filled with parallel vertical lines indicate the position of a blue, brown, pink, or purple circle. These colors served only to make the discrimination more complex. In addition, the four blank circles in the sample and four-choice positions were arranged into configurations which varied across cards. The configuration of the blank circles in one S— matched the configuration in the sample. This S— was purposely arranged so that the pattern of responding by any subject who may have responded to this cue (matching the configuration of the blank circles) in the pretest could be compared with responding during the program, posttest, and retention test conditions.

Programs with Criterion-Related Cues

Kanji Program.   The Kanji Program consisted of 70 cards in the match-to-sample format, progressing from a very simple to the more complex criterion discrimination. Figure 5 summarizes the introduction and manipulation of the stimuli in the sample and choice positions across the 70 program trials. The order of the stimuli within each sample and choice, and the positions of the S+ and 3 S— choices were varied systematically throughout the program. (These variations in order and position are not indicated in Figure 5.) Selected trials of the criterion-related Kanji Program are illustrated in Figure 1b-f.

The program was divided into three stages during each of which the correspondence between one picture and the character with the same meaning was trained. For example, during the first third of the program, the character "sun" was trained. The first trial (see Fig. 1b) of the Kanji Program consisted of the picture for "sun" in the sample and in the S+, but no stimuli appeared in the S— positions. On the second trial (see Fig. 5), the distractor character "turn" was introduced in light pencil in one S—. Over the next five trials (Trials 3-7), the distractor character "turn" gradually faded to black at the same intensity as the picture "sun" in the S+. Throughout the six trials when changes were made in the intensity of the distractor character, the picture for "sun" was maintained as the S+ with no changes. On Trial 8, the *picture* of the "sun" began to change (in the S+ only) to the *character* for "sun" through the process of stimulus shaping. The specific stimulus shaping steps that were used to change the picture "sun" into the character "sun" are shown in Figure 6. At first, the circle for the "sun" gradually became rectangular over three trials (Trials 8-10). Over the next eight trials (Trials 11-18), one by one the rays around the "sun" were removed in random order (see Fig. 6). (One trial from this sequence, Trial 16, is shown in Figure 1c.) Finally, on Trial 19 (see Fig. 6), a dot was added to the center of the

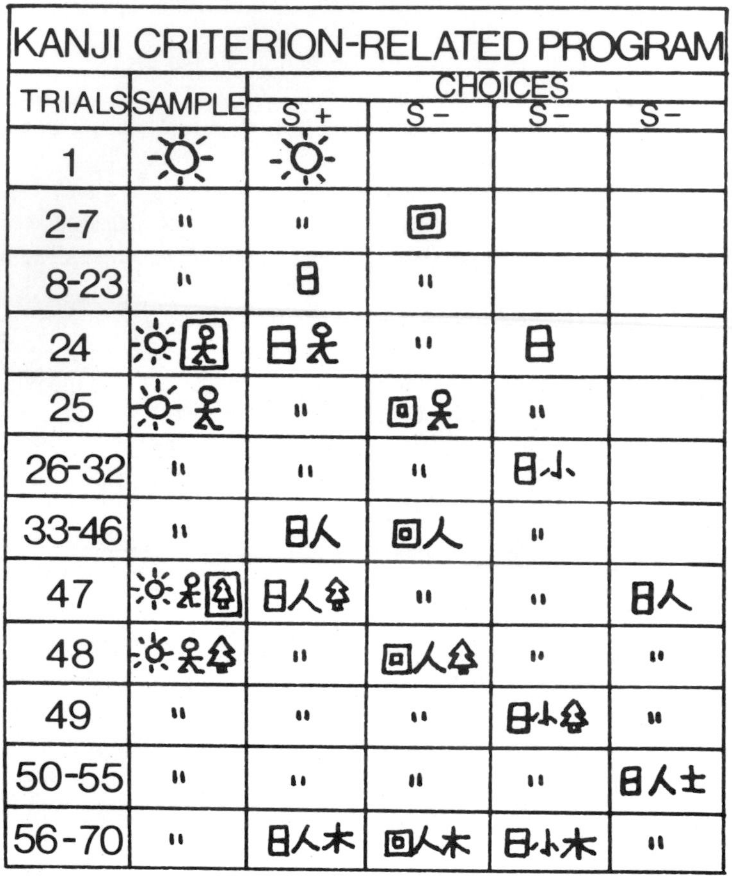

KANJI CRITERION-RELATED PROGRAM

TRIALS	SAMPLE	CHOICES S+	S−	S−	S−
1	☼	☼			
2-7	"	"	回		
8-23	"	日	"		
24	☼[人]	日夂	"	日	
25	☼夂	"	回夂	"	
26-32	"	"	"	日小	
33-46	"	日人	回人	"	
47	☼夂[木]	日人木	"	"	日人
48	☼夂木	"	回人木	"	"
49	"	"	"	日小木	"
50-55	"	"	"	"	日人土
56-70	"	日人木	回人木	日小木	"

Figure 5   Summary of the introduction of the Kanji stimuli in the sample, S+, and S− postions.

rectangle and then was extended to a horizontal line across the rectangle (Trial 20-23). On Trial 23, which completed the first third of the Kanji Program, the S+ contained the character for "sun" and the only S− contained the distractor character "turn" (see Fig. 5).

During the second third of the Kanji Program, the character "man" was trained. On Trial 24 (see Fig. 5), the picture "man" was added to the picture "sun" in the sample and to the character "sun" in the S+. A black rectangle was drawn around the picture "man" in the sample in an attempt to draw attention to the addition in the sample. The character "turn" was maintained as the S−, and a second S−, the single character "sun," was added. The black rectangle around "man" in the sample was eliminated on the next trial (Trial 25), and the

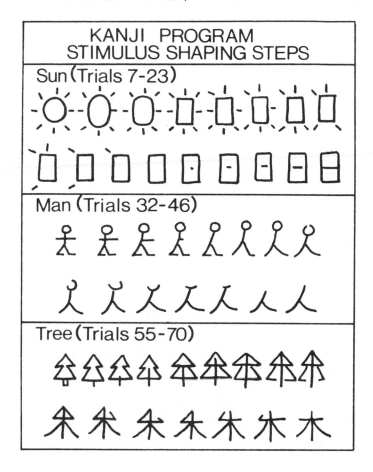

Figure 6   Kanji stimulus-shaping steps for the three S+ stimuli from initial picture to final character.

picture "man" was added to the S— containing the distractor "turn." This was done so that the discrimination could not be made simply by determining which choice contained "man," but instead would have to be made on the basis of which choice contained *both* "man" and "sun." The distractor character "small" was added in light pencil to the S— containing the character "sun" on the next trial (see Fig. 5, Trial 26). Then, on the following 6 trials (Trials 27-32), "small" was faded to black at full intensity. Next, the picture "man" began to change to the character "man" in the S+ and also in one S—. The "man" gradually lost his arms (see Fig. 6, Trials 33-36), feet (Trials 37-38), and head (Trials 39-45). The change to the character "man" was completed on Trial 46 by extending the neck portion of the stick figure upward approximately 3 mm. Trial 34 of this sequence is shown in Figure 1d.

In the final third of the program, the character "tree" was trained (see Fig. 5). On Trial 47, the picture "tree" enclosed in a black rectangle was added to the sample.[1] On the same trial, "tree" was added to the S+ containing the characters "sun" and "man." A third S— was added that contained only the two characters "sun" and "man." On this trial, all three S— choices contained two characters. Then the picture "tree" was added on Trial 48 to the S— containing the character "man" and the distractor "turn," and on Trial 49 to the S— containing the character "sun" and the distractor "small." Trials 50-55 consisted of the gradual introduction of the distractor "ground" to the third S— (containing the characters "sun" and "man") fading again from light pencil to black at full intensity. Trial 51 of this sequence is illustrated in Figure 1e. The gradual shaping of the picture "tree" to the character meaning "tree" in the S+ and two S— choices on Trials 56-70 completed the final section of the program (see Fig. 5). The trunk of the tree changed to a single line on Trial 56 (see Fig. 6) and gradually extended upward over Trials 57-61. The bottom horizontal line was eliminated gradually on Trials 62-64, and the two diagonal lines coming from the top of the tree were eliminated on Trials 65-70. Trial 70 (see Fig. 1f) was essentially the same as a criterion test card, in that the S+ contained the characters "sun," "man," and "tree," and the S— choices contained either a combination of S+ and S— characters or three S— characters.

Color Program.   The Color Program also progressed from a very simple discrimination to the final criterion task in 70 trials. Examples of Color Program Trials with criterion-related cues are shown in Figure 2b-f. As on the criterion-test cards for this program (see Fig. 2a), an array of 16 circles was stamped in the sample and four choice positions for all cards. The S+ appeared in each of the four-choice positions an approximately equal number of times.

The programming sequence for the Color Task can be summarized in stages illustrated in Figure 7. As in Figure 2, the positions of the colors orange, green, yellow, and red are represented by the letters *o, g, y,* and *r* respectively. The distractor colors, blue, brown, pink, and purple, are represented by circles containing parallel vertical lines. The notations in Figure 7 indicate the colors that were found in the sample (second column), S+ (third column), and one S— example (fourth column) on the final trial of each stage. The positions of the orange-green-yellow-red configurations found in the sample and S+ varied systematically throughout the program. Also, the positions of additional colors in the sample and S+ and of all colors in the S— choices were varied within each trial and across trials. Therefore, Column 4 of Figure 7 is only representative of S— choices. On any one trial, the three S— choices were of comparable difficulty, although not identical in terms of the positions of individual colors within each array.

[1] In a revised form of the Kanji Program used in later studies, the black rectangles enclosing the picture "man" (Trial 24) and the picture "tree" (Trial 47) were eliminated because they were found to be nonfunctional.

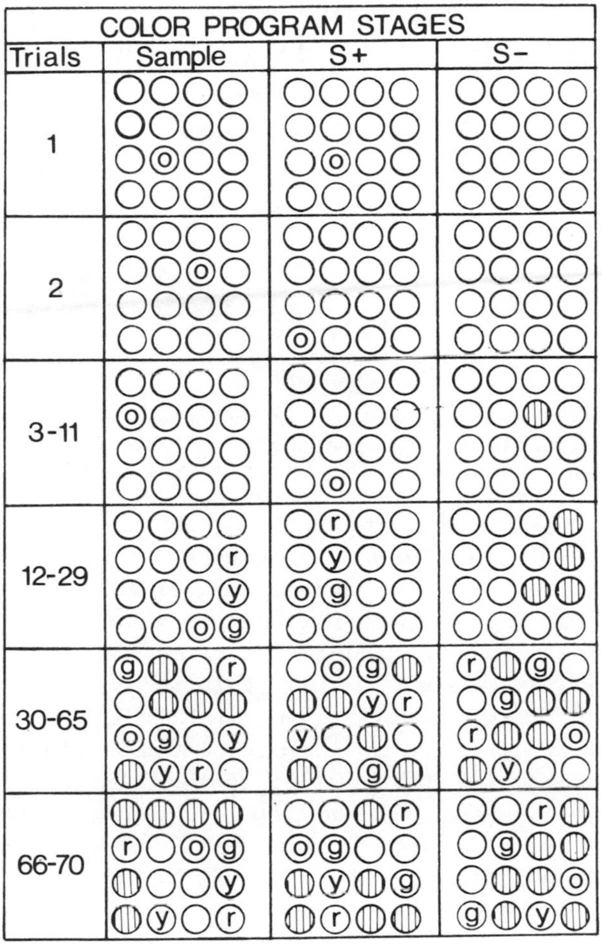

COLOR PROGRAM STAGES			
Trials	Sample	S+	S−
1			
2			
3-11			
12-29			
30-65			
66-70			

Figure 7   Summary of Color Program stages. Orange, green, yellow, and red circles are represented by *o, g, y,* and *r* respectively. Circles containing vertical parallel lines represent blue, brown, pink, or purple circles. Blank circles indicate the absence of color.

The program began with a single orange circle in both the sample and S+ (see Fig. 7, Trial 1). Both orange circles were in the same position within the array of circles (second column, row 3). Again on Trial 2, a single orange circle was found in the sample and S+, but on this trial the positions of the orange circles within the array differed. For these two trials there were no distractor colors for any S−. Trial 1 of this first stage is illustrated in Figure 2b.

Throughout the Color Program, two fading procedures were used (see Fig. 8). After the orange circle was introduced, the Configuration Fading Procedure was used when the colors green, yellow, and red were faded in, in three trials. The introduction of these colors using the Configuration Procedure completed the

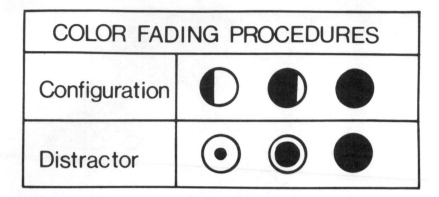

Figure 8   Illustration of the two Color Fading Procedures: top row, orange, green, yellow, and red Configuration Procedure; bottom row, blue, brown, pink, and purple Distractor Procedure (also for orange, green, yellow, and red when used individually as distractors).

four-color configuration that was essential to the final discrimination. For example, green first was faded in as one third of the circle, and then as two thirds, and finally as an entire circle (Fig. 8). Yellow and then red were introduced in the same manner. The Configuration Procedure occurred only in the sample and S+. Colors that were not essential to the final discrimination (blue, brown, pink, and purple as well as orange, green, yellow, and red if they were not part of the four-color configuration) were faded in using the Distractor Procedure (see Fig. 8). This procedure also consisted of three trials. These colors were first introduced as a small dot at the center of the circle, then as a larger dot, and finally as an entire circle. During the first portion of the program, this second type of fading occurred only in the three S— choices. Later it was also used in the S+, and finally in the sample when colors that were not critical to the four-color configuration were faded in. The two fading procedures were never used on the same trials. An example of a configuration-fading trial is shown in Figure 2c, and examples of distractor-fading trials are shown in Figures 2d and 2e.

The second stage of the program consisted of the introduction of one distractor color into each of the S— choices (see Fig. 7, Trials 3-11). The Distractor-Fading Procedure was used to introduce a purple circle into the first S— (Trials 3-5), a blue circle into a second S— (Trials 6-8), and finally a brown circle into the third S— (Trials 9-11).

From Trial 11 to Trial 29 (see Fig. 7), the two fading procedures were alternated. For example, a second distractor color was faded simultaneously into each of the S— choices (Trials 12-14), and then green (Trials 15-17) was introduced in the sample and S+. The two fading procedures continued to alternate throughout the third program stage until the sample, the S+, and the three S— choices each contained four colored circles adjacent to each other (Trial 29). The same configuration of four colored circles appeared across the sample and four choices. The four colors in the sample and S+ comprised the orange-green-yellow-red configuration. The colors found in each S− choice, however, were blue, brown, pink, and purple. These distractor colors appeared in a different order in each of the S− choices.

Eight additional colored circles were added to the S+ and S− arrays (see Fig. 7, Trials 30-53) and to the sample (Trials 54-65) in the fourth program stage. By Trial 65, the sample and all 4 choices each contained 12 colored circles with an approximately equal distribution of the eight colors in the sample and each choice position. These colored circles were added one at a time in the choice arrays (e.g., Figs. 2d and e) and two at a time in the sample using the Distractor-Fading Procedure.

On the final program trials, the remaining blank circles that were randomly dispersed throughout each array on Trial 65 (see Fig. 7) were arranged into configurations in the sample and choices (Trials 66-70). On Trial 70 the configuration of blank circles in the sample and in one S− matched (see Fig. 2f). Each of the blank circle configurations found in the remaining three choices differed. As in the Kanji Program, the final trial of the Color Program was essentially a criterion trial.

Criterion-Related Program Refinement

The final programs used in this study are the result of extended testing and revisions which occurred prior to the study. Approximately 40 subjects were tested during program development. Due to the discovery of several consistent error patterns, major revisions in the programs were made. Those revisions contributed significantly to making the programs criterion-related as well as nearly errorless. A summary of some of the procedures used to refine the programs follows.

Kanji Program. One of the early revisions made in the Kanji Program resulted because all the subjects tested began making errors at a specific point within the program. In the initial form of the program, during the process of using stimulus shaping to change the picture of the sun into the character meaning "sun" (see Fig. 6), the sun's rays were removed before the circle was shaped into a rectangle. The children continued to respond correctly on each trial while the rays were removed one by one and after the last ray was gone, as long as the "corners" were somewhat curved. But when the circle had been changed completely to a rectangle, the children began to point to the S− character "turn" (see Fig. 3). The sequence of stimulus shaping then was altered so that the rays were maintained until the circle was completely shaped into a rectangle, and then were removed one by one. This revision maintained correct responding throughout that specific portion and the remainder of the program.

Another technique used in the Kanji Program to maintain the discrimination between the S+ and S− choices was the manner in which those stimuli were introduced into the stimulus array. The three S+ characters were always introduced initially in the choice positions as pictures. Then stimulus shaping was used to change the pictures into characters. In contrast to the S+ stimulus-shaping procedure, S− characters were always introduced in the form of the final configuration of characters, but were initially drawn in very light pencil. Over several trials, the lines were darkened until the S− characters were at the criterion level of intensity. By always associating a change in *configuration* with the *S+* and a change in *intensity* with S− characters, the distinction between the two types of characters seemed to be heightened.

One revision in the Kanji Program was made on the basis of errors that occurred in the posttest rather than in the program itself. It was observed that children who had responded nearly errorlessly throughout the program were unable to maintain a high level of correct responding on the posttest. At this point, the S+ on program trials was the only choice containing *any* correct characters. The S− choices were made up of various combinations of S− characters. Due to the make-up of S+ and S− choices, it was possible for a child to respond correctly by attending solely to the character that was being trained at a particular point in the program. The posttest, however, required that the discrimination between all three S+ characters and their corresponding S− characters be maintained because two of the S− choices also contained S+ characters. The S+ was the only choice that contained all three S+ characters. When the children were posttested, they responded to one of two choices containing the character for "tree" that had been trained during the final trials of the program, but that choice may or may not have been the S+. The program was changed then to help the children remember *all* of the characters trained, not merely the last one. After the introduction of the pictures for man and tree in the S+, the same pictures were also combined with S− characters in one or two S− choices. As the picture was shaped into the corresponding character in the S+, it was simultaneously shaped in the S− choice(s). An example of how one trial (Trial 34) was changed is illustrated in Figure 9. As a result of this change, it was necessary for the subject to attend not only to the picture that was in the process of changing but to all the stimuli in the S+.

Color Program.   In the Color Program, an effort was made to distinguish clearly between the S+ and S− choices. As in the Kanji Program, two different procedures were used to achieve a contrast between the introduction of those stimuli directly related to the S+ and the introduction of those incorporated in the S− or simply added to increase the complexity of the problem. The colors that in combination with orange were critical to the solution of the discrimination (green, yellow, and red) were faded in as one third of a circle, then two

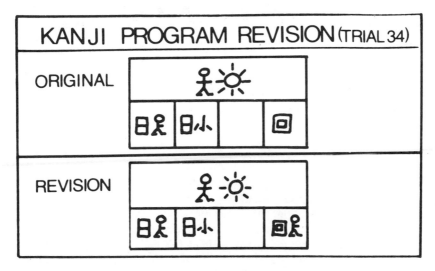

Figure 9   Example of Kanji Program revision to aid memory of all S+ characters.

thirds, and finally as a fully colored circle (see Fig. 8). In contrast, the colors that were not included in the four-color configuration of orange-green-yellow-red were first brought in as a small dot, a larger dot, and then as a full circle. The use of different fading procedures for S+ and S— stimuli proved beneficial in shifting control from the initially simple discrimination to the very complex criterion solution.

During the early portions of the program, it was necessary to emphasize that the S+ consisted of matching a configuration of circles plus a specific sequence of four specific colors. This was accomplished by arranging the distractor colors found in the S— choices in the same configuration as the critical colors in the sample and the S+. Thus, the subject could not respond correctly simply on the basis of a matching configuration of circles that were of different colors.

Since at criterion level the sample and S+ each contained eight colored circles and four blank circles, in addition to the matching orange-green-yellow-red configuration, it was important to incorporate some means of restricting the child's attention to the four colors in the critical configuration. After four colors had been introduced in the sample and each of the four choices, the additional colors began to fade in. This fading was limited initially to the array of circles in the four choice positions. The sample simply contained the orange-green-yellow-red configuration (which varied from trial to trial). This procedure was an attempt to enhance the distinction between those aspects of the sample stimulus array that would lead to a correct solution and stimuli which contributed only to the complexity of the task in all choices.

Programs with Additional Noncriterion-Related Cues

Second sets of both the Color and Kanji Programs were made with the addition of cues designed to be noncriterion-related. The cues chosen for the noncriterion-related programs were considered similar to those often used in children's school workbooks. Examples of trials from the Kanji Program with additional noncriterion-related cues are illustrated in Figure 1g-k and from the Color Program with noncriterion-related cues in Figure 2g-k.

Kanji.   The noncriterion-related cue added to the Kanji Program was a red rectangle enclosing the stimuli found in both the sample and S+. For example, on the first trial of the program, the rectangle enclosed the picture "sun" in the sample and in the S+ (see Fig. 1g). As the pictures "man" and "tree" were added to the sample, they were also enclosed within the area of the rectangle. Similarly, as pictures were added and shaped into characters in the S+, they were included within the red rectangle (see Fig. 1i). Throughout the addition of stimuli to the inside area of the rectangles, the rectangles remained the same size. The proportions remained 4 cm x 7 cm for the sample rectangle and 3 cm x 4 cm for the S+ rectangle. The rectangles were gradually faded out by eliminating 5 mm sections of the rectangles, first in the sample (see Fig. 1h and 1i), and then in the S+ (see Fig. 1j) over the 70 trials of the program. By Trial 70 (see Fig. 1k), the red rectangles were entirely eliminated; therefore, the final card of this program was an exact duplicate of Trial 70 of the Kanji Program with only criterion-related cues (see Fig. 1f). With the exception of the added cue, the Kanji noncriterion-related program stimuli were exactly the same as the criterion-related stimuli.

Color.   The cues added to the Color Program were an X over the orange circle and a line connecting the centers of the orange-green-yellow-red circles, both in the sample and S+ (see Figs. 2g-j). The line was extended each time a new color was introduced to the four-color configuration (see Fig. 2h). For example, when green was introduced in one third of a circle, the line was extended from the center of the orange circle to the center of the circle containing green. The line was extended further with the introduction of yellow (Trial 21) and red (Trial 27). The line was then faded out over Trials 30-60 by replacing segments of the lines with dashes and then dots (see Figs. 2i-j). The dots in the sample and S+ then were gradually eliminated, simultaneously, until the X and a dot at the center of the green, yellow, and red circles remained. Then the lines forming the X were dashed, then dotted, and then partially removed. After the removal of the single dots in the green, yellow, and red circles, one by one, the final portion of the X was removed. By Trial 70 no additional noncriterion-related cues remained. Thus Trial 70 of the noncriterion-related Color Program (see Fig. 2k)

TABLE 1

Individual Analysis Design
(Each subject as own control)

| Group | Program | |
Subjects	Criterion-related	Noncriterion-related
1 A, C, E, G	Kanji	Color
2 B, D, F, H	Color	Kanji

was identical to Trial 70 of the criterion-related Color Program (see Fig. 2f). As with the Kanji Programs, the only difference between the criterion-related and noncriterion-related color stimuli was the addition of the noncriterion-related cues.[2]

Design

In this experiment, an individual analysis design with control groups was implemented (Table 1). Using a within-subject analysis, the effects of the main independent variable (criterion-related versus noncriterion-related cues) were studied. That is, each child had one program with only criterion-related cues and one program with additional noncriterion-related cues. The control for the variable of the different types of cues was within subjects. To avoid any learning-set effects, programs with both types of cues were taught during each session rather than in a successive manner. Another procedure was implemented to control for warm-up effects and attention span: during program administration, a criterion-related program trial was presented first on even-numbered sessions, and a noncriterion-related trial began the session on odd days. In addition, a group design was implemented, in that two groups of subjects (four in each group) were used to control for a possible confounding of the effects of the independent variable with a specific instructional program. That is, the two groups were counterbalanced so that Subjects A, C, E, and G received the Kanji Program with only criterion-related cues and the Color Program with the noncriterion-related cues. The other group had essentially the same instructional programs, but the conditions of the cues were reversed.

[2]Illustrations of the complete Criterion Test, Kanji and Color Criterion- and Noncriterion-related Programs may be obtained at cost from the second author, Department of Human Development, University of Kansas, Lawrence, Kansas 66045.

The primary advantage this individual analysis of the main independent variable has over group designs is the control for individual differences. By using two learning tasks (Kanji and Color), it was possible to have a within-subject comparison. The use of the control group design enabled the experimenter to base discussion on at least two types of conceptual stimuli; therefore, more general conclusions could be made.

Procedure

Throughout the study daily sessions were conducted Monday through Thursday, unless, of course, the subject was absent from the classroom. Before each session, the subject chose a toy from a set of three small toys placed outside the experimental room. When the choice was made, the experimenter and subject entered the experimental room and sat at a table facing a one-way mirror, with the experimenter seated to the right of the subject. A notebook containing the stimulus materials for that session was placed directly in front of the subject. In addition, two paper cups, one containing tokens and one empty, were placed to the right of the notebook with the empty cup closer to the child.

Criterion Tests (Pre-, Post-, and Retention)

At the beginning of each criterion pretest, posttest, and retention test session, the subject was shown the 2 paper cups, one of which contained 12 tokens, and told, "If you point nicely and look carefully today, I'll put a token from my cup into your cup, and if you get all of my tokens, you can trade them for the toy." The experimenter then said, "Today, when we play this game, I won't tell you if your are right or wrong until after we finish playing the game." On the initial criterion-test session, the experimenter demonstrated the pointing response by extending the right index finger, and asked the subject to do likewise.

At this time, the first criterion-test stimulus card was presented. The subject was asked to point to the sample and then to find the one below that was "the most like" the sample. After pointing to one of the four choices on the first card, the subject was praised and given a token for "looking carefully" or "pointing nicely" and reminded that the experimenter would not say whether or not the subject pointed to the right one until after the game. The remaining 11 cards were then presented, one by one, with the instructions gradually faded to "Point" and "Find the one most like it." Throughout the criterion test, the subject received praise and tokens for "pointing nicely" and "looking carefully."

At the end of the session, the tokens earned by the subject were exchanged for the toy. The experimenter said, "You did a pretty good job today. You got some of them right and some of them wrong." On the day of the criterion pretest, the experimenter also added, "This is a pretty hard game to play, but I think I can help you. We'll start tomorrow." This terminated the session.

Program Sessions

There were 14 regular programming sessions. Both groups of subjects went through 5 trials of both of their assigned programs per session. The trials from the two programs were alternated throughout each 10-trial session. On even-numbered program sessions (Sessions 2, 4, 6, etc.) a card from the program with only criterion-related cues was presented first, and on odd-numbered sessions (Sessions 3, 5, 7, etc.), the session began with a trial from the program with the added noncriterion-related cues.

During the first program session after the subject had picked a toy, the experimenter said that the cup containing 9 tokens belonged to the experimenter and that the empty cup was the subject's. The experimenter then explained that the subject would get a token from the experimenter's cup if the "right one" was chosen. The experimenter also said that if the subject earned all of the experimenter's tokens (90% correct criterion), the subject could then trade the tokens for the toy chosen earlier. At the beginning of subsequent program sessions after the subject had chosen a toy, the experimenter simply reminded the subject to try to get all of the tokens by pointing to the "right one" so that the toy could be taken home.

The instructions for each trial were to point to the sample and then to find the one most like the sample and point to it. As on the criterion test, the initial instructions were faded during the first session to "Point" and "Find the one most like it." If the subject then pointed to the S+, praise was given and a token was transferred from the experimenter's cup to the subject's. A correction procedure was used if the subject pointed to an S−. The experimenter said, "That was a good try, but this is the one (pointing to the S+) that is the most like that one (the sample). Now you point to it." If the S+ was then selected, the subject was praised but did not receive a token because the subject "did not point to the right one the first time."

These instructions and correction procedures were slightly modified for both Color Programs. On the first trial, the subject was instructed to "point to this one" while the experimenter demonstrated by pointing to the orange circle in the sample. After the subject had successfully pointed to the orange circle in the sample, the experimenter then instructed the subject to "find the one most like it" and to point to it "just like you did up here [in the sample]." If the subject pointed to the S+, but not to the orange circle in the S+, the subject was praised and given a token, but the experimenter then demonstrated the point to the orange circle and asked the subject to point again. As the green, yellow, and red circles were added to the sample and S+, the experimenter once again demonstrated the pointing response to the sample by pointing to those colors of the four-color configuration which appeared on those particular cards (Trials 15, 21, and 27). If during either (criterion- or noncriterion-related) Color Program (except on the last five trials, 66-70) the subject failed to point to all four colors in the four-color configuration, the experimenter again demonstrated the appropriate pointing response.

The sequence of events for each child consisted of one criterion pretest[3], two programs, a criterion posttest, and either a four-week or seven-week retention test (repeated criterion posttest). The general procedure included the constraint that training and testing never occurred within the same session. It was not possible to assign subjects systematically to either the four-week or seven-week retention test based on their sex, age, or original group membership. This was due to timing difficulties that arose because of the different program completion dates for each child. Three children (one from Group 1 and two from Group 2) were given the retention tests at four weeks, and five subjects were tested at seven weeks (three from Group 1 and two from Group 2).[4]

Measurement

The subject's response was recorded on a data sheet by the experimenter, by marking an X in a box indicating the position of the choice to which the subject pointed. Therefore, the experimenter had a record of not only whether or not the subject had made a correct response on each trial but also the position of the response, correct or incorrect. This procedure allowed an error analysis for all subjects (which is necessary in all programming studies).

Reliability

An observer sitting in the adjoining observation room recorded the position of the subject's choice response on a data sheet. The observer's record was then compared with the experimenter's record for the total of 38 sessions during which reliability was taken. These 38 sessions included at least one session during each of the different phases of the experiment (pretest, program, remedial, posttest, and retention test) and at least 3 sessions for each individual subject. The reliability measure for scoring the position of choice responses was calculated by dividing the number of agreements by the number of agreements plus disagreements.

RESULTS

Reliability

A comparison between the experimenter's and observer's records of the position of the subjects' choice responses showed 100% agreement.

[3]Because their initial pretest percentage correct on one or both tasks was 50% or greater, two subjects were given a second pretest to determine whether or not their initial percentage correct was due to chance. The pretest scores presented for these subjects are the average percentages of both tests.

[4]One subject in the seven-week group was given the retention test both at four and at seven weeks. Only the seven-weeks data are reported.

Pretest, Program, and Posttest

Six of the 8 children completed the 70 trials of each program without interruption. Figure 10 shows the percentage of correct choices by those 6 children during each session of the criterion tests, and throughout the programs with only criterion-related cues and the programs with the additional noncriterion-related cues. The percentage correct on the criterion pretest was 17% for the tasks programmed with criterion-related cues and 5% for the tasks programmed with the additional noncriterion-related cues. The percentage correct during both types of programs ranged from 90% to 100%, showing nearly errorless performance on all programs. On the criterion posttest given at the end of the programs, however, the percentage correct for the tasks programmed with criterion-related cues averaged 97%; whereas, the average was 36% correct for the tasks programmed with the additional noncriterion-related cues.

The two graphs in Figure 11 show the percentage of correct responding by these same 6 children according to the specific programs to which they were exposed. Group 1 (top graph), consisting of Subjects A, C, and G, was given the Kanji Program with only criterion-related cues, and the Color Program with the additional noncriterion-related cues. The bottom graph shows the performance of Group 2, Subjects B, D, and H, who had the opposite programs, that is, Color

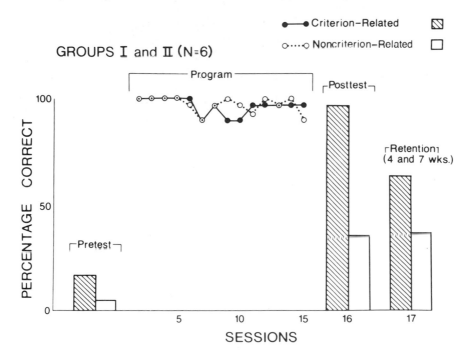

Figure 10   Percentage correct on criterion tests and on criterion-related and noncriterion-related programs for six subjects in Groups 1 and 2.

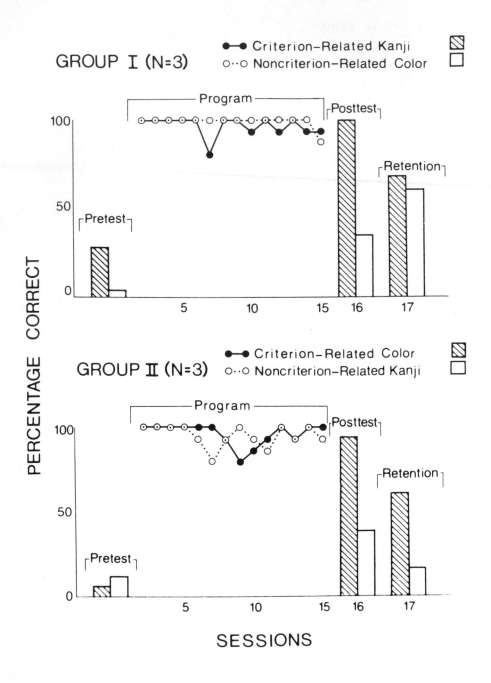

Figure 11   Percentage correct on criterion tests and programs for Groups 1 and 2 according to the specific programs each group received.

with only criterion-related cues, and Kanji with the additional noncriterion-related cues. Both groups, regardless of the type of concept that was being taught, performed above 90% on the criterion posttest when they had been instructed by the program with criterion-related cues. Also, regardless of whether the noncriterion-related cues were added to the Color or Kanji Program, the subjects did not apparently learn the concept being programmed, since both groups were below 40% correct on the criterion posttest.

Two subjects, E and F, were unable to maintain 90% or better correct responding on the programs. Therefore, they were given remedial sessions to help eliminate errors. Subject E began making errors as early as Session 6 (see Fig. 12). This subject tended to improve after Session 7, but by Session 12, was only 40% correct on that day's Kanji trials. An analysis of Subject E's errors showed an apparent failure to respond to one of the criterion-related cues of the Kanji Program. It appeared that this subject was confusing the character "turn," which was visually similar to the picture "sun," with the correct character for "sun." At this point, 10 trials of each program were re-presented to the subject. These trials were selected on the basis of the error analysis for the Kanji and on the basis of what were considered critical trials for the Color Program. The following session (15) resulted in the same number of errors on the Kanji (40% correct)

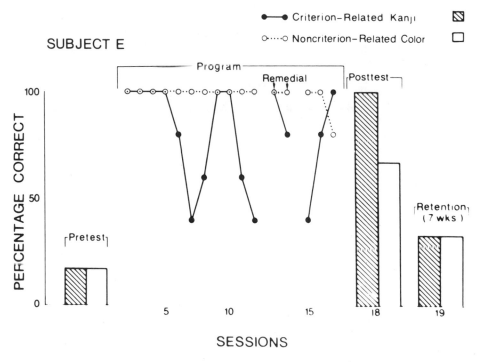

Figure 12   Subject E's percentage of correct responding on criterion tests and on the criterion-related Kanji and noncriterion-related Color Programs.

as had occurred prior to the remedial trials. Over the final two sessions, however, this subject improved on the Kanji Program to 100% correct. In spite of the relatively poor performance on the program, Subject E was able to learn the Kanji Task (with criterion-related cues) demonstrated by 100% correct on the criterion posttest. In addition, this child showed some acquisition on the criterion Color Task (67%) that had been trained with the additional noncriterion-related cues.

Figure 13 shows that Subject F had some difficulty on both the Color Program with only criterion-related cues and the Kanji with the additional noncriterion-related cues. The 10 remedial trials chosen on the basis of the errors on both programs appeared to improve correct responding on the Kanji, but did not necessarily improve correct responding on the Color (Sessions 13, 14, and 15). Pointing-training on 5 trials of the Color Program resulted in an immediate increase in correct responding. Pointing-training was implemented because correct responding always occurred when this subject remembered to point to all 4 critical colors; otherwise, an error was made. Subject F's performance on the criterion posttest was consistent with the rest of the subjects, in that this subject had a fairly low percentage correct (17%) on the test items programmed with the additional noncriterion-related cues and a much higher percentage correct (83%) on the items programmed with only criterion-related cues. The

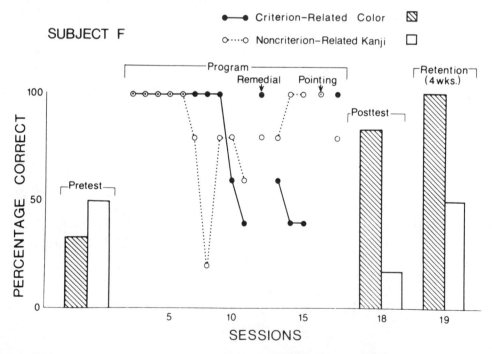

Figure 13   Subject F's percentage of correct responding on criterion tests and on the criterion-related Color and noncriterion-related Kanji Programs.

one error on the Color Task occurred when the subject failed to point to 4 of the critical colors.

Retention Tests

The percentages of correct responses, on both the four-week and the seven-week retention tests, are combined in Figures 10 and 11. Figure 10 shows that the percentage correct on the criterion test for the tasks trained with criterion-related cues decreased from 97% on the criterion posttest to 64% on the retention test, for the 6 subjects from Groups 1 and 2. Performance on the criterion test for the tasks trained with noncriterion-related cues remained essentially the same (36% and 37%). The graphs in Figure 11 show that the decrease in percentage correct from the posttest to the retention test for the Kanji Program trained with criterion-related cues (top graph) was comparable to the decrease on the Color Program trained with the same type of cues (bottom graph). A similar consistent decrease in percentage correct from the posttest to retention test did not occur between the two noncriterion-related programs. The retention test score was higher than the posttest score for the Color Program (top graph, 33% to 59%), but it was lower than the posttest score for the Kanji (bottom graph, 39% to 17%).

Subject E's percentage correct on the seven-week retention test (see Fig. 12) was the same (33% correct) for both the criterion-related Kanji Task and the noncriterion-related Color Task, showing a decrease on both programs from the posttest scores. The four-week retention data for Subject F (Fig. 13), however, showed an increase for both programs, from 83% to 100% correct on the Color trained with only criterion-related cues and from 17% to 50% correct on the Kanji trained with the noncriterion-related cues.

Figure 14 shows comparisons of the percentage correct on the criterion tests for programs with criterion-related cues and for programs with the additional noncriterion-related cues. Although the trend was similar in both criterion-related and noncriterion-related comparisons, the percentage correct was much higher on the posttest and retention tests of the criterion-related programs than on the corresponding tests of the noncriterion-related programs. Specifically, these comparisons show that the percentage correct on the posttest was higher than the pretest scores for both types of programs (20% to 96% for criterion-related pre- and posttests and 15% to 38% for noncriterion-related pre- and posttests). A further increase in percentage correct occurred on the retention test given 4 weeks after the posttest. A decrease occurred on the 7-week retention tests, but the scores of these tests remained above the pretest scores for programs with both types of cues.

Finally, this graph indicates that with the criterion-related programmed training, the children learned and retained (at least through 4 weeks) the task at the above-90% correct response level. In contrast, with the noncriterion-related programmed training, the highest test score ever obtained was only 61%.

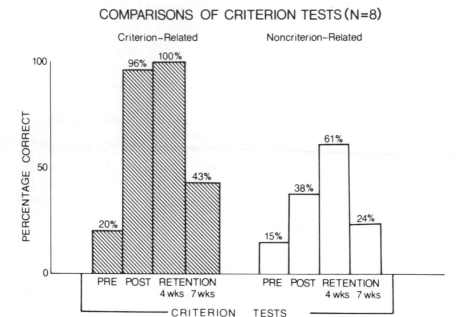

Figure 14   Comparisons of the percentage correct on the criterion tests for programs with criterion-related cues and for programs with additional noncriterion-related cues.

Although it cannot be said that the children learned the tasks on these latter programs, clearly the scores on the 3 tests following the administration of the programs were all higher (38%, 61%, and 24%) than the pretest percentage correct (15%). An error analysis carried out on all of the children's pretests indicated that in addition to a tendency for some children to select a particular position for their choice responses, there was one other identifiable error pattern: on the Color Pretest, this consisted of matching the configuration of the 4 blank circles found in the sample. Of the 4 children who received the noncriterion-related Color Program, 3 responded in this manner on all 6 Color Pretest trials, resulting in a Color Pretest score of 0%. This resulted in a fairly low (below chance) total percentage correct on the pretest for all of the noncriterion-related data. This was shown by the 15% correct pretest score on the noncriterion-related data in Figure 14. An examination of the errors these 3 children made under posttest and retention test conditions indicated that at least one effect of the noncriterion-related program on their responding was the elimination of matching on the basis of the blank circles. Each of these children engaged in this matching response only once on the posttest as opposed to 6 times on the pretest. By not choosing the blank circles, the children may have been demonstrating a partially learned response of pointing to an orange circle as the matching response. Further, one child of 4 who had the noncriterion-related Color

Program scored 100% correct on the 4-week retention test. This child's acquisition elevated the percentage correct on the 4-week retention data on the noncriterion-related portion of Figure 14: without this subject's data, the posttest and 4-week retention test would have been 31% and 41% correct rather than the 38% and 61% shown in the graph.

DISCUSSION

This study is the end product of a series of prior investigations. Those investigations were necessary for the development of two learning tasks and of successful programs to teach those tasks that could then be used in the experimental analysis of errorless stimulus control. In order to contribute to the development of a technology of effective programming or to compare the effects of programmed training with other training procedures, it is essential first to have a program that by some criterion is successful.

The two programs developed prior to the present study, the Kanji and Color Programs, were revised many times before coming to their present form. Thus, part of this study is a replication of the evaluation that these programs were successful, as concluded by the preliminary investigations. Six of the 8 children in the present study consistently maintained errorless behavior (90% or better correct responding) on both of their assigned programs. Further, the 2 children who experienced some difficulty were not lost from the study, in that it was possible to analyze their errors and determine their difficulties. Only programs that allow the experimenter to identify the controlling stimulus at any point in the program, and further, that have had a fairly successful exposure to a wide population, allow effective remedial measures to be developed for their occasional nonlearners. Using remedial measures in this manner with the appropriate controls, the total experimental population can be maintained for further investigations.

The use of two different programmed tasks was an essential part of the design of this experiment. One could then rule out the possible confounding of the manipulation of the main independent variable (establishing criterion-related cues versus adding noncriterion-related cues) with the type of conceptual task being taught. The results indicated that when a noncriterion-related cue is added to a previously and currently successful program, a stable shift in stimulus control does not occur, in either the task that teaches the "meanings" of three Japanese characters or the task that teaches a particular four-color configuration.

Although it might appear that the noncriterion-related cues chosen for the two tasks would have drawn the subject's attention to the correct simulus, they were clearly not related to the final solution of either task. There is nothing about an X with a line extinding from it that is directly related to a four-color configuration, nor does a red rectangle have anything to do with the meanings of pictures and Japanese characters. In contrast, the criterion-related cues were integrated into each program so that a shift from the stimuli in the programs to those in the criterion task would occur. In the Color Program, for example, the two different fading procedures were used to emphasize the differences between colors that were essential for the solution of the problem and those that only added to the complexity of the discrimination. In addition, to show that both the matching configuration and specific colors made up the total correct match, the distractor colors in the S— choices were put into the same configuration as the critical colors in the sample and S+ during the early portions of the program. On the Kanji Program, stimulus-shaping techniques were used to change the pictures into the correct characters. This procedure contrasted with the procedure of fading the intensity of the incorrect characters in the S— choices.

The study shows clearly that the addition of unnecessary stimuli tends to interfere with the subject's observation of the cues critical for the solution of the problem. Such a manipulation is a powerful variable, affecting the child's attention to and subsequent learning of the problem.

A question of the amount of reinforcement as a controlling variable cannot be an issue in this study, in that the children were equally successful (each child receiving essentially the same number of reinforcers) during both criterion-related and noncriterion-related programs.

On the retention tests, even after a break of four weeks with no contact with the stimulus materials, the subjects demonstrated that they had retained the solution of the tasks programmed with criterion-related cues. One subject also demonstrated acquisition of the program taught with noncriterion-related cues. This subject's performance demonstrates that there are children who are able to attend to the critical stimuli and thereby solve the problem in spite of other interfering stimuli. The results of this study indicate, however, that a child with these skills is the exception rather than the rule. The decrease in percentage correct on the seven-week retention test on the tasks programmed with criterion-related cues further indicates that no matter how well-programmed a conceptual task may be, if it is not practiced over a long period of time (in this case, almost two months), it will be forgotten. It is important to point out that teachers, parents, or researchers cannot expect teaching procedures or teaching materials to produce miracles when the laws of learning and, in this case, laws of retention are violated through the nonuse of the conceptual skill.

The results of this study also suggest an extension of the conclusions made by Schreibman (1975) in an article published since the completion of the present study. Schreibman has cautioned teachers of autistic children to restrict the educational environments of these children to stimuli that are relevant to the tasks on which they are being trained. The present study suggests that this should be the concern of *anyone* pursuing the development of effective learning environments. The failure of acquisition to occur when extraneous or noncriterion-related cues are used during training is a phenomenon which is not limited to autistic children.

ACKNOWLEDGMENTS

This study was supported in part by a University of Kansas General Research Award, "A Study of Fading Procedures in the Development of Stimulus Discriminations." In this study, Ronald A. Mann contributed to the development of an early version of the Color Task. Additional support for this study was provided by Grant #HD-02528-07 to the Bureau of Child Research, University of Kansas, by the National Institute of Child Health and Human Development. A portion of the present study was presented in a symposium on errorless learning procedures as a paper, entitled "An Experimental Demonstration of Some Variables Involved in Establishing Functional Cues in 'Errorless' Stimulus Control Procedures" by Kathryn J. Schilmoeller and Barbara C. Etzel, at the Biennial Meeting of the Society for Research in Child Development, Philadephia, Pennsylvania, March, 1973. The research presented in this chapter is a portion of the thesis research submitted by the first author to the Department of Human Development at the University of Kansas, Lawrence, Kansas, in partial fulfillment of the requirements for the degree of M.A.

The authors sincerely appreciate the invaluable assistance given throughout this study by Gary Schilmoeller.

Fellowship support of the first author was received from a University of Kansas Summer Fellowship of the Graduate School, a National Defense Foreign Language Summer Fellowship (Title VI) from the University of Kansas, and PHS Training Grant HD-00183 from the National Institute of Child Health and Human Development.

The authors are indebted to Sidney W. Bijou for his suggestion concerning the labels "criterion- and noncriterion-related" cues.

REFERENCES

Baer, D. M. An age-irrelevant concept of development. *Merrill-Palmer Quarterly of Behavior and Development,* 1970, *16,* 238-245.

Baron, M. R. The stimulus, stimulus control, and stimulus generalization. In D. I. Mostofsky (Ed.), *Stimulus generalization.* Stanford: Stanford University Press, 1965.

Bijou, S. W. Studies in the experimental development of left-right concepts in retarded children using fading techniques. In N. R. Ellis (Ed.), *International review of research in mental retardation* (Vol. 3). New York: Academic Press, 1968.

Dixon, L. S., Spradlin, J. E., Girardeau, F. L., & Etzel, B. C. Development of a programmed stimulus series for training an *in front* discrimination. Parsons Working Paper Number 304. Parsons, Kansas: Parsons State Hospital, 1975.

Gollin, E. S., & Savoy, P. Fading procedures and conditional discrimination in children. *Journal of the Experimental Analysis of Behavior,* 1968, *11,* 443-451.

Schreibman, L. Effects of within-stimulus and extra-stimulus prompting on discrimination learning in autistic children. *Journal of Applied Behavior Analysis,* 1975, *8,* 91-112.

Sidman, M., & Stoddard, L. Programming perception and learning for retarded children. In N. R. Ellis (Ed.), *International review of research in mental retardation* (Vol. 2). New York: Academic Press, 1966.

Terrace, H. S. Discrimination learning with and without "errors." *Journal of the Experimental Analysis of Behavior,* 1963, *6,* 1-27. (a)

Terrace, H. S. Errorless transfer of a discrimination across two continua. *Journal of the Experimental Analysis of Behavior,* 1963, *6,* 223-232. (b)

Terrace, H. S. Stimulus control. In W. K. Honig (Ed.), *Operant behavior: Areas of research and application.* New York: Appleton-Century-Crofts, 1966.

Touchette, P. E. Tilted lines as complex stimuli. *Journal of the Experimental Analysis of Behavior,* 1969, *12,* 211-214.

20

Phenomenological Reports: An Empirical Model [1]

Robert G. Wahler
Robert M. Berland
George Leske

Child Behavior Institute, The University of Tennessee

One of the most commonly voiced objections to applied behavior analysis is its lack of concern with the phenomenological world of the individual. Behaviorists of this ilk, however, have long held the position that their operating strategies dictate this apparent lack of interest: unless the events in question can be made public, there is little utility in pursuing them empirically (Skinner, 1953).

In recent years a few applied behavior analysts (or behavior modifiers) have made conceptual inroads that might permit a tentative examination of such "phenomenological reports" from a behavioristic viewpoint. For example, Tharp (unpublished) has argued that *attitudes* held by adults about deviant children might be usefully conceptualized as observer reports determined by a behavior pattern produced by the child. From this frame of reference, attitudes could be investigated within the operating strategies of applied behavior analysis. That is, the child's behavior pattern is a public event, as is the adult's attitude report. Thus, the attitude report, traditionally held to be an important function of private events (Fishbein, 1963), might be usefully studied as a function of observable events — the referent's recordable behavior.

One might follow the rationale of Wahler and Leske (1973) by considering phenomenological reports as *summary* reports by an observer. These investigators conceptualized a summary report as an observer behavior determined by multiple stimulus events. Such a report might be a discriminative function of a number of stimulus events, some of them private, and some of them public

[1]This study was supported by a research grant from the National Institute of Mental Health, Crime and Delinquency section (MH 18516).

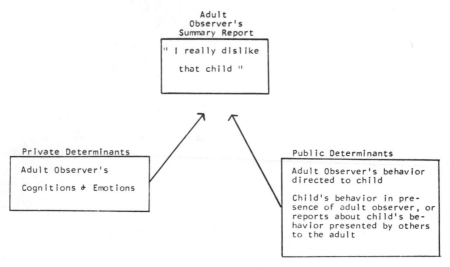

Figure 1   An empirical model of the phenomenological report. The model presumes that public determinants of the report are significant predictors of that report.

(see Fig. 1). For example, an adult's dislike of a child could be determined by that adult's private cognitive and emotional world as well as that adult's, and that child's, observable behaviors. If the adult's phenomenological report about the child can be predicted on the basis of these public behaviors, that report becomes understandable, at least at one level of comprehension.

The utility of this sort of understanding, if it can be achieved, is most readily evident to the clinician concerned with changing child and adult behavior. Phenomenological reports are usually one aspect of the presenting complaints of clinical referrals. Adults may be *worried* about children, they may *dislike* them, they may view them as *bad* or offer other similar reports. The children may feel *inadequate, frightened, angry* or may *hate* or *dislike* the adults. Were these sorts of reports left unchanged following a clinical intervention, the task of behavior modification would be considered incomplete.

Now, there is some evidence that contingency management programs successful in changing a child's problem behaviors also change those adult and child phenomenological reports that were components of the clinical problem (Patterson, 1974; Wahler & Pollio, 1968; Eitzen, unpublished). Despite these successes, however, the functional mechanisms underlying changes in the report remain unknown. Until the determinants of these reports are specified, clinicians must put blind faith in the overall effectiveness of their procedures.

The investigation presented below represents a preliminary effort to explore the utility of the phenomenological report model presented in Figure 1. In essence, we attempted to predict adult attitudes about a problem child — to predict these reports on the basis of *public* events.

METHOD

Subjects

Subjects were two adults (a third grade public school teacher and a mother) and a 9-year-old, male, white child (the pupil and son of these adults, respectively). The boy, Jimmy, and his family lived in a low-income, federally subsidized housing project. The father's and mother's educational levels were tenth and eighth grade, respectively. Included in the family were three other boys and a girl, ranging in age from 6 to 11 years.

Jimmy was referred to the first author's predelinquency research project by his teacher because he frequently disrupted other children and used foul language, all of which typically led to peer punishment of Jimmy. Jimmy was also reported to complete little work unless constantly prodded. Finally, the teacher complained that he regularly came to school with a strong body odor and infected sores.

Jimmy's mother also considered him to be a problem at home. She complained that he disobeyed her, fought with other children, was a chronic whiner, and did no homework. The mother also noted that Jimmy complained of fears and bad dreams at night.

Subject Attitude Reports

Both teacher and mother expressed some degree of dislike for Jimmy. Therefore, it was decided to focus on these attitudes as the summary reports of interest in this study. In the independent interviews, these adults were asked to express their "feelings" about Jimmy with the ultimate purpose of formulating their conceptions of his "problem." The purpose of the interview was two-fold: (1) to have each adult provide a summary term best describing that adult's conception of Jimmy's problem; and (2) to have each adult point to environmental events (Jimmy's behavior, peer behavior, adult behavior) that might elicit this report from these adults.

Jimmy's teacher presented the term *disruptive* as adequately describing her impression of Jimmy. The term was clearly negative in tone for her. She expressed both worry about Jimmy and her dislike of him with *disruptive* as the focal concept. Thus, this term met one set of criteria as a phenomenological report: an observer report, partly related to private events within the observer.

The teacher was then asked to specify public events that might support her disruptive report. She readily identified a number of such events: Jimmy's violation of classroom rules, his lack of schoolwork, peer punishment of Jimmy and her own reprimanding of him contingent upon these occurrences. With these public specifications, *disruptive* met all criteria for our definition of a phenomenological report.

Jimmy's mother offered the term *stubborn-whiney* to describe her conception of Jimmy's problem. The mother expressed clearly negative affect about Jimmy in discussing this conception. While she also expressed worry about his neighborhood fighting and his night fears, her "in house" impressions of him were largely negative, always centering on the term *stubborn-whiney.*

When Jimmy's mother was asked to specify public events that might support her report, she pointed to two features of his behavior: his refusals to obey her instructions; and his whining, nagging, and crying.

Scaling of the Attitude Report

Since the teacher and parent attitude reports supposedly summarized a number of events, it was decided to reflect these summaries through a numerical scaling technique. Each adult was asked to conceptualize their attitude reports on a seven-point scale in which seven represented a maximal impression of the attitude (e.g., very disruptive), and one represented a minimal impression (e.g., calm). The numberical rating thus constituted our attitude data unit.

Procedures for Observations of Subjects

The initial interviews with teacher and mother were also geared to a preparation for the collection of observational data on Jimmy's interactions with adults and peers. There were two features of this preparation. First, time periods were specified when observers were most likely to see Jimmy's problem behaviors in the classroom and home. These settings were to be covered by observer use of a standardized set of behavior categories. (This set will be described below.) Secondly, since some of Jimmy's problem behaviors were infrequent (perhaps once-daily occurrences), it was unlikely that they could be detected through brief time samples of Jimmy's behavior. Therefore, it was necessary to count on the teacher and mother to track these low frequency behaviors. During the interviews these adults were asked to specify concrete definitions of the problem behaviors.

In essence, the interviews set the stage for obtaining observational data through two classes of behavior categories: a class for direct observations of Jimmy and his social environment at school and at home, and a daily set for recording Jimmy's low rate problem behaviors. Data obtained through use of these category systems constituted the *public* events by which teacher and mother attitude reports might hopefully be predicted.

Direct Observational Procedures

A complete description of the standardized category codes used in these procedures will soon be available (Wahler, House, & Stanbaugh, 1976). These codes permit the recording of 19 target child behavior categories and 6 social environment categories of adult and peer behavior. The codes permit an assessment of problem child behaviors, desirable child behaviors, innocuous child behaviors, and social contingencies for all of these behaviors.

(Table 1 provides a brief description of those codes that were relevant to the results of this study. We doubt that the information contained in Table 1 is

TABLE 1

Category Codes[a]

Adult Instruction (Non-Aversive) (IA+). This category is scored for direct commands by an adult.

Adult Instruction (Aversive) (IA−). This category is scored for those direct commands by an adult that are judged to be aversive by an observer.

Adult Social Attention (Aversive) (Sa−). This category is scored for adult noninstructional contacts with the target child. The observer must also consider the contact to be aversive.

Adult Social Attention (Non-Aversive) (Sa+). This category is scored for adult noninstructional contacts with the target child.

Child Social Attention (Aversive) (Sc−). This category is scored for any peer behavior directed to the target child. The observer must also consider this behavior to be aversive.

Child Social Attention (Non-Aversive) (Sc+). This category is defined in the same manner as Sc−. However, in this case the observer does not judge the behavior to be aversive.

Opposition (O). This category is scored for target child behaviors that are rule violations or noncompliances with adult instructions.

Aversive Opposition (O−). This category is identical to opposition (O) but also is judged by the observer to be aversive in content.

Compliance (C). This category is scored for target child compliance with adult instructions.

Self-Stimulation (S). This category is scored for any instance of the target child's manipulation of his body.

Object Play (Op). This category is scored for any instance of the target child's simple manipulation of objects.

Sustained Non-Interaction (NI). This category is scored for a full ten seconds of target child non-interaction with people or objects.

Sustained Schoolwork (Ss). This category is scored for a full ten seconds of schoolwork by the target child.

Sustained Toy Play (St). This category is scored for a full ten seconds of target child play with objects.

Approach Child (Ac). This category is scored for any spontaneous approach to peers by the target child.

Approach Adult (Aa). This category is scored for any spontaneous approach to adults by the target child

Social Interaction Child (SIc). This category is scored for any interaction between peers and the target child.

Social Interaction Adult (SIa). This category is scored for any interaction between adults and the target child.

---

[a]*Brief descriptions of category codes used to record direct observations of subjects and their interaction associates at school and home. With the exception of the three sustained categories (NI, Ss, ST), all can be scored simultaneously in a ten-second interval. These descriptions are not given in enough detail to permit observer scoring. The complete coding system will soon be available (Wahler, House, & Stambaugh, 1976).*

sufficient to permit replication of this aspect of our study; the table is only intended to give a reading knowledge of our procedures.)

Two observers independently covered the school and home settings, making their observations from four to five days weekly. All observations were of a half-hour duration, and always scheduled for that time period designated during the interviews with teacher and mother. Observers coded category occurrences following temporal unit guidelines set by a portable tape recorder. The tape recorder cued observers via earphone to observe Jimmy and his interaction associates for 10-sec intervals; interspersed 5-sec intervals of recording category occurrences were also cued by the tape recorder. On an every other week basis, a third observer made simultaneous, but independent, observations with these regular observers. These paired observations were used to assess the reliability of the overall data collection.

Diary Recording Procedures

As discussed above, an alternative recording procedure was deemed necessary to collect data on Jimmy's low rate problem behaviors. Through discussions with the teacher and mother, the following categories were formulated to enable these adults to track occurrences. To facilitate teacher and mother recall of possible occurrences, these categories were expressed in a simple yes-no format. The observers who conducted the direct observations collected yes-no data on each low rate category at the conclusion of each observational session.

The categories given by the teacher were as follows:

1. Did Jimmy bother or pick on other kids today?
2. Did Jimmy complete an assignment on his own today?
3. Did Jimmy use foul language or gestures today?
4. Did Jimmy smell bad today?
5. Did Jimmy have body sores today?

The categories given by the mother were as follows:

1. Did Jimmy break a rule or disobey you today?
2. Did Jimmy get into a fight today?
3. Did Jimmy cry or whine today?
4. Did Jimmy do any homework last night?
5. Did Jimmy have any night fears or bad dreams last night?

Treatment Conditions

Baseline

For a period of four weeks the preceding three sets of data were collected in Jimmy's school and home settings. Over 18 observational sessions, adult attitude scores, direct observation category scores and low rate diary counts were obtained. These recordings were continued throughout all phases of the study.

Treatment I

This phase constituted the first effort to modify Jimmy's problem behavior. Since Jimmy was considered a more serious problem in school than home, it was decided to initiate intervention in the former setting — leaving the home setting as a control condition to contrast with the school treatment setting.

In line with the teacher's principal concerns, Jimmy's schoolwork and rule violations were designated as the targets for intervention. This was implemented in standard fashion by awarding points for Jimmy's completion of schoolwork units and placing him in time-out following his rule violations. The teacher conducted this program for all of her students. Points could be "spent" near the end of the school day by allowing the child access to a toy play area and, on occasion, field trips outside school. With the beginning of this intervention, the teacher recorded daily counts of each child's completed work units and rule violations. For Jimmy, these data were comparable to the observer-recorded categories, Sustained Schoolwork and Opposition.

Treatment II

After a period of five weeks, it was evident from teacher and observer data that the school intervention had done little to change Jimmy's behavior. In a gamble to strengthen this intervention, it was decided to extend the school point system into Jimmy's home and neighborhood. This was done by providing a "work unit" card for Jimmy. Jimmy's completed work units were recorded daily on the card by the teacher, and Jimmy was instructed to carry this card from school to home and back each day. In the meantime, two interventions were conducted in Jimmy's neighborhood. For one, a consultant met several times weekly with Jimmy's mother teaching her principles of contingency management and encouraging her to arrange a point and time-out system for Jimmy's home behavior. Most importantly, she was encouraged to check Jimmy's school to home work unit card and to arrange rewards for those days when Jimmy had completed all assigned work units. For the second intervention, an "achievement store" was opened in Jimmy's neighborhood. This store was stocked with inexpensive toys that could be purchased once weekly through a teacher completed work unit card. The store served a number of children, including Jimmy, who were considered in need of psychological help in Jimmy's school.

Data Analyses

Observer Reliability Analysis

The direct observational data were the only public events subjected to objective accuracy analyses. Reliability checks by a second observer were anlayzed by comparing each 10-sec time interval for the two observers. Blank intervals were not considered in these comparisons. Matching and nonmatching codes were summarized over the half-hour sessions, and a percentage-agreement measure was computed for each code.

Attitude Predictor Analysis

A scan of all data over the three phases of the study revealed one obvious outcome: the three sets of data in the Treatment II phase showed almost no variance over sessions in either school or home settings. Thus, it was improbable that these data would display covariations of any sort, making it unlikely that we could evaluate the hypothesis of interest in this study. Therefore, only the data from Baseline and Treatment I were used in the attitude prediction analysis.

Measurement units for the three sets of data were as follows: adult attitude units were single numbers, ranging from one to seven. It will be recalled that seven represented a maximal impression of the attitude concept and one a minimal impression. Category instances obtained during direct observations were expressed as percentage scores over all time intervals containing that category. Diary low rate behaviors were given scores from one to five. "Yes" answers were counted as units of one, except for behavior No. 2 in the school and behavior No. 4 in the home. In these cases "No" answers were counted as units of one.

The above data units were taken over 38 Baseline and Treatment I sessions. The 3 sets of 38 scores were then subjected to a Pearson Product-Moment correlational analysis in which all possible intercorrelations were computed for all score distributions. This analysis was conducted separately for the school and home settings.

Two correlational matrices were produced by the above analysis — one for the school and one for the home. Next, correlations between the attitude scores and the other two sets of scores were examined through use of Johnson's hierarchical clustering technique (Johnson, 1967). In essence, this cluster analysis provides some formal decision rules in conducting the search for correlations.

As the results section will show, a number of measures appeared in a cluster with the attitude measures. As a validity check, these covarying categories were inspected for predicted rate changes during the Treatment II condition. During this condition, marked therapeutic changes occurred in Jimmy's behavior and in adult attitude scores. If the behavior cluster obtained in Baseline and Treatment I was in fact a functional class of behaviors, one should be able to predict rate changes in all behaviors given information on rate changes in any of these behaviors.

RESULTS

Reliability analyses were conducted for each category code used in obtaining the direct observational data. Observer agreements and disagreements were tallied for each 10-sec interval and a percentage-agreement figure was computed for each reliability check session. All codes reported in this study met agreement percentages of 80% or better.

Figure 2 describes mean occurrences of the teacher's attitude rating of Jimmy and those public events that were correlates of these ratings. Of immediate interest is the lack of change in Jimmy and teacher impressions of him over the baseline and school intervention phase. Category counts by observers yielded essentially the same behavior profile in both phases. With the initiation of Treatment II, however, marked therapeutic changes are evident. The linking of home-based rewards to Jimmy's school performance appeared to effect some dramatic changes in his sustained schoolwork (Ss), his rule violations (O), and teacher impressions of him (attitude rating and records of his low rate problem behaviors). While the school and home intervention phase cannot be considered an experimentally documented cause of these changes, there is evidence of relationships between teacher summary reports and those public events monitored by observers — the central item of interest in this study.

Figure 3 presents a schematic illustration of these relationships over the 10-week time period of Baseline and Treatment I. It will be recalled that near zero variances prevented the inclusion of Treatment II in this analysis. As Figure 3 shows, two event categories were statistically significant predictors of the teacher's summary report "Disruptive." Increments in Jimmy's spontaneous approaches to peers (Ac) and his teacher-recorded low rate problem behaviors

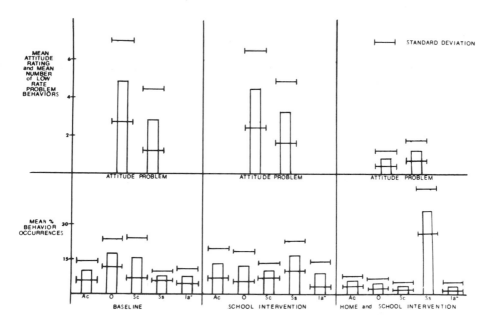

Figure 2   Means and standard deviations of teacher attitude reports, teacher recall of Jimmy's low rate problem behaviors, and observer records of selected category occurrences.

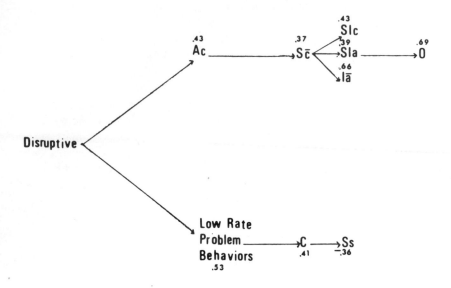

Figure 3   Pearson Product-Moment correlations composing a cluster of categories related to teacher attitude reports.

were clearly associated with her tendency to rate him high on the disruptive dimension.

Only one of these categories (low rate problem behaviors) was considered by the teacher to determine her attitude impression of Jimmy. With reference to the observer-recorded categories, it will be recalled that she pointed to rule violations (O) and Jimmy's lack of schoolwork (Ss) as anchor categories for her subjective impressions. Both categories did display indirect covariations with the teacher attitude rating, but bore no direct relationships to the rating. As mentioned by the teacher, the rule violations and lack of schoolwork usually involved social interactions with her and peers (SIa, SIc), peer aversive reactions to Jimmy (Sc−), her aversive instructions to him (Ia−), and his eventual compliance with these instructions (C).

Further proof of the functional linking of these behaviors is demonstrated in Treatment II (see Fig. 2). The changes in teacher impressions of Jimmy and observer recorded categories of Jimmy's behavior were all predictable on the basis of the Figure 3 correlations among these behaviors. That is, all of the positively correlated behaviors showed a common drop in occurrence and the single negatively correlated behavior (Ss) increased sharply.

Figure 4 describes mean occurrences of the mother's attitude ratings of Jimmy and those public events that were correlates of these ratings. As was true in the school setting, little change is evident in the obtained behavior profiles over Baseline and Treatment I. However, the school and home intervention phase (Treatment II) shows some clear therapeutic changes in mother ratings of Jimmy, as well as her counts of his low rate problem behaviors. Coincident with these shifts in mother's data, observer records of the four child behavior categories also changed. The fact that both teacher and mother behaviors were affected during the same treatment phase lends evidence to the role of the intervention technique in producing such change.

Figure 5 presents a cluster description of those public behaviors that were predictors of the mother's attitude impressions of Jimmy. In common with Jimmy's teacher, mother's counts of Jimmy's low rate problem behaviors were the best predictors of her rating of him on her stubborn-whiney dimension. Strangely enough, the observer-recorded Non-Interaction category (NI) was also a significant predictor of mother ratings, and this category was also correlated with mother counts of Jimmy's low rate problem behaviors. Contrary to the school setting, none of the direct or indirect correlates of the mother's attitude impression were mentioned by her as determinants of the rating. However, neither of the mother mentioned categories (rule violations and complaints) appeared with any appreciable frequency during the observation sessions.

An examination of Figure 4 will show that behavior changes from Treatment I to Treatment II were clearly predictable on the basis of Figure 5. All behaviors positively correlated over Baseline and Treatment I (attitude, low rate problem

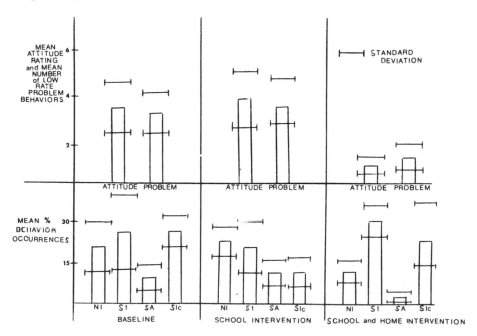

Figure 4   Means and standard deviations of mother attitude reports, mother recall of Jimmy's low rate problem behaviors, and observer records of selected category occurrences.

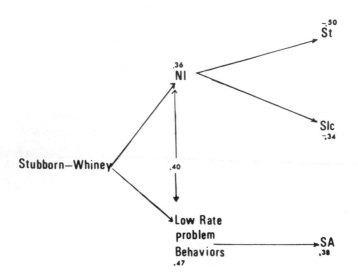

Figure 5   Pearson Product-Moment correlations composing a cluster of categories related to mother attitude reports.

behaviors, NI and SA) showed a common decline during Treatment II. The two negatively correlated behaviors in the cluster (ST, SIc) increased sharply during Treatment II. These predictable changes in all behaviors support a functional interpretation of the Figure 5 cluster.

DISCUSSION

Results of the present study showed reliable covariations between two adults' attitude reports about a child and aspects of that child's behavior, as well as certain peer and adult behavior directed to the child. These covariations continued to be evident during a treatment phase in which major changes occurred in the child's behavior. It therefore seems likely that the predictor events and the adult summary reports were somehow related functionally.

It is of interest to note that the best predictors of adult attitude reports included events not specified by the adults as determining their reports. In both school and home settings, teacher and mother correctly specified one set of predictors of their attitude reports (Jimmy's low rate problem behaviors). However, two other aspects of Jimmy's behavior (the observer-reported categories Ac and NI) were also good predictors of adult attitudes, yet not mentioned by the adults as predictors. This finding, consistent with the laboratory work of

Wahler and Leske (1973), in essence, points to the fact that many caretakers of children cannot specify the complete set of public events that elicit their attitudes about the children.

Our findings add support to already published findings showing that successful contingency management programs do more than change the child behaviors targeted by the program (Wahler & Pollio, 1968; Patterson, 1974). Since the public predictors of these impressions can be specified, the behavior modification consultant would be wise to keep track of these events. While our findings cannot be taken to conclude that these predictors *cause* the adults' impressions, the suggestion that they do so is strong. An obvious next research step would entail direct manipulation of the predictor events in a search for causality.

REFERENCES

Eitzen, D. S. The effects of behavior modification on the attitudes of delinquents. Cited in a grant proposal by Elery Phillips, Bureau of Child Research, University of Kansas, 1974.

Fishbein, M. An investigation of the relationships between beliefs about an object and the attitude toward that object. *Human Relations,* 1963, *16,* 233-239.

Johnson, S. C. Hierarchial clustering schemes. *Psychometrika,* 1967, *32,* 241-245.

Patterson, G. R. Interventions for boys with conduct problems: Multiple settings, treatments, and criteria. *Journal of Consulting and Clinical Psychology,* 1974, *42,* 471-481.

Skinner, B. F. *Science and human behavior.* New York: The MacMillan Company, 1953.

Tharp, R. G. Unpublished symposium report. Western Psychological Association, Seattle, Wash., 1971.

Wahler, R. G., House, A. E., & Stambaugh, E. E. *Ecological assessment of child problem behavior: A clinical package for home, school, and institutional settings.* New York: Pergamon Press, 1976.

Wahler, R. G., & Leske, G. Observer summary reports: A reinforcement interpretation and investigation. *Journal of Nervous and Mental Disease,* 1973, *156,* 386-394.

Wahler, R. G., & Pollio, H. R. Behavior and insight: A case study in child behavior therapy. *Journal of Experimental Research in Personality,* 1968, *3,* 45-56.

21

Technical Developments in Classroom Behavior Analysis

Ralph J. Wetzel
Joseph R. Patterson

University of Arizona

Classroom applications of behavior analysis have been regularly displayed in the *Journal of Applied Behavior Analysis* since its inception in 1968. Subsequently, these applications have been widely examined, discussed, and criticized both within and without the general area of applied behavioral science. This reaction is, of course, a desirable outcome of the publication and attests to the functional utility of the *Journal.* In fact, the original editorial statement (Baer, Wolf, & Risley, 1968) not only hoped for widespread examination of behavioral applications but ". . . their refinement, and eventually their replacement by better applications" [p. 91].

Fundamental in the application of behavioral science to education is the technology for quantifying behavioral and environmental events in the classroom. This technology was reviewed by Sidney Bijou and his colleagues, Robert Peterson and Marion Ault, in the second issue of JABA (1968). Their review summarized various procedures used in classrooms and outlined some provocative suggestions for their application. The classroom observation and recording technology has not been reviewed since. The purposes of this chapter are first, to remedy this situation by summarizing the technology reported in JABA since 1968 and second, to review and discuss the nature of the applications involving the technology. In the words of the inaugural editorial statement, we will discuss the applications, ". . . their refinement, and eventually their replacement by better applications" [p. 91].

REVIEW OF OBSERVATION AND RECORDING TECHNOLOGY

Several procedures have been used by applied researchers to quantify observed behaviors. A representative list of procedures includes: (1) simple frequency counts; (2) 20-pen event recorders (Lovaas, Freitag, Gold, & Kassorla, 1965; Wasik, Senn, Welch, & Cooper, 1969); (3) cumulative clocks (Packard, 1970; Chadwick, & Day, 1971); (4) anecdotal records (Bushnell, Wrobel, & Michaelis, 1968); and (5) paper and pencil recording of time-sampled events. This last procedure is by far the most frequent and apparently the most successful of all the data collection procedures developed for applied research. Thus, this chapter will limit its review of observation techniques to paper and pencil time-sampling procedures.

To illustrate the technology, attempts have been made in this paper to reconstruct recording procedures. With a few exceptions (Bijou, Peterson, & Ault, 1968; Bijou, Peterson, Harris, Allen, & Johnston, 1969; Hall, Lund, & Jackson, 1968; Kubany & Sloggett, 1973) very few articles can be found in which an example of the recording sheet format is illustrated. Brief verbal descriptions suffice for reconstruction as long as the procedure is simple and only a few behaviors are recorded, but as the complexity of the recording procedure increases, so does the difficulty in reconstruction of the format.

There are two major format characteristics involved in reconstruction: (1) the axes on which the target behaviors and time sampling intervals are arranged; and (2) the procedure by which behaviors are recorded. Unless these characteristics are specified in the journal article, two conventions have been followed in the reconstruction of recording sheet formats in this chapter. First, the formats have been arranged with *time sampling intervals in columns* (horizontal axis) and *target behaviors in rows* (vertical axis). Second, target behaviors are recorded by check marks in separate rows rather than by letter codes as is used for studies reporting an exceptionally large number of target behaviors. In these cases some simple codes have been used for ease of illustration (rather than for factors of human engineering).

In earlier articles about recording technology, Bijou and his colleagues (Bijou *et al.,* 1968; Bijou *et al.,* 1969) defined two major classes of observational codes: specific observational codes (records of a fairly limited number of behaviors specific to a certain investigation) and general observational codes (general records of a number of behaviors applicable to a range of field situations). They further subdivided each of these codes into stimulus and response codes. In this chapter samples of the technology are generally arranged in a simple-to-complex order according to a number of criteria. These criteria are: (1) degree of inclusion of both social stimulus and response events; (2) number of behaviors recorded for each subject; (3) number of subjects observed; (4) number of settings studied; and (5) complexity of the time-sampling strategy.

Relatively simple observation instruments have been developed to record attending and disruptive behaviors of whole classrooms (Barrish, Saunders, &

Wolf, 1969; Harris, & Sherman, 1973; McAllister, Stachowiak, Baer, & Conderman, 1969). For example, Harris and Sherman defined classroom disruption in two broad categories. Talking-out included all vocalizations emitted by a child in the absence of the teacher's permission, whistling, laughing, whispering, crying, talking to classmates, talking to the teacher before receiving the teacher's permission, screaming, imitating sounds of cars or animals, etc. Out-of-seat included irregular seating positions such as sitting with knees or feet on the seat of the chair; standing or walking in the room without the teacher's permission; throwing paper airplanes, rubber bands, books, pencils, or other objects at classmates. Target behaviors emitted by any child in the classroom were recorded at one-minute intervals. Figure 1 is a reconstruction of the recording format used in this study. The advantages of this observational system are that the whole class can be watched by a single observer and the recording is simple enough to obtain high observer agreement with relatively untrained observers (the teacher took the data in the Harris and Sherman study).

Of course, simple observation instruments by their very nature will have several limitations. The data are group mean data and do not adequately describe individual behavior. Simple observation instruments which use long sampling intervals are insensitive to high frequencies, as in the above example, frequencies greater than 60 per hour are not differentiated. If the instrument does not record appropriate behavior, no data are available to support inferences made on the basis of decreases in disruptive behavior. Simple instruments do not measure social-stimulus events such as teacher and peer behaviors. In studies using group contingencies such as those in which individual reinforcement depends on group deportment, some measure of peer behavior would seem important. In such cases, group members are likely to prompt or otherwise attempt to control each other.

Subject sampling instruments avoid averaging group behavior. The simplest form of subject sampling observes one subject during the first time interval, another subject during the next interval, and so on. After all of the subjects (sample group or complete population) are observed in this fashion, the series

	1	2	3	4	5	6	7	. . . . .
Out of seat		✓			✓			— — —
Talking-out			✓	✓	✓		✓	— — —

Figure 1   A simple time sampling procedure reconstructed from Harris and Sherman (1973). Minute intervals are denoted across the top of the form and the two categories of target behaviors are listed on the left margin. Checkmarks denote the occurrence of the target behavior during that interval.

of observations is repeated until all the subjects have been observed an equal number of times. Several variations of this procedure are illustrated in the literature.

Wodarski, Hamblin, Buckholdt, & Ferritor (1972) observed two randomly selected subjects in each of five groups (N=10). Cooperative and noncooperative behaviors were recorded as they occurred in 10-sec, fixed order, samples of each child's behavior. Similarly, Kazdin and Klock (1973) sampled and recorded attending behaviors of 12 children in 15-sec intervals. The observations were made in a fixed order until each subject had been observed for 20 intervals, or a total of 5 minutes distributed over 70 minutes of observation. Study and nonstudy behaviors were scored for 30 children by Hall, Panyan, Rabon, and Broden (1968) using a fixed order, 10-sec interval sampling procedure. Study behavior was only scored if observed for the complete interval. In addition, teacher verbal praise or reprimand was also scored as it occurred during each interval. Broden, Bruce, Mitchell, Carter, and Hall (1970) observed and recorded the attending behavior of 2 children in adjacent desks using a 5-sec alternating sampling procedure. Additionally, teacher verbalizations to the subjects and glances between subjects were recorded as they occurred during each interval. Figure 2, a reproduction from Broden *et al.* (1970), is an illustration of a subject sampling instrument.

The advantages of subject-sampling techniques are that data on a number of individual subjects may be obtained, generalization of treatment effects across subjects described, and multiple-baseline designs used. In spite of these advantages there are several limitations which should be considered when using subject-sampling techniques. The confidence that one may have in the data as a valid measure of the individual's behavior is dependent upon the frequency and length of the observation samples. A fixed order of observation samples may lead to an observer bias which Weick (1968) calls "coding relativism." This term refers to

		5	10	15	20	25	30	· · · · ·
Child	Attending	✓	✓		✓	✓		– – –
Child	Non-Attending			✓			✓	– – –
Teacher	Verbal		✓			✓		– – –
Peer	Glances				✓			– – –

Figure 2   A subject sampling procedure using alternating 5-sec intervals reconstructed from Broden, Bruce, Mitchell, Carter and Hall (1970). 5-sec intervals are denoted across the top of the form and the target behaviors listed on the left margin. Child attending or nonattending behaviors were scored at the beginning of the interval (on the signal) and were mutually exclusive categories. Teacher and peer behaviors were scored if either or both occurred at any time during the interval.

the effects of adaptation level on the way that observed events are coded. (For example, if deportment behaviors are being coded and a very "bad" subject is always observed in the same order, then the behaviors of subjects observed immediately afterward may be shifted toward "good" behavior by way of contrast (and the reverse).) A third difficulty lies in the observer's having to rapidly change target subjects every 5 to 10 sec. With large numbers of subjects more restrictions would have to be placed on the order of observations (such as observing from front to back of each row of children) and subjects would have to be stationary. Observer training time required to meet agreement requirements would also be increased. With large classes this type of short-interval, fixed-order observation would seem to be very difficult, although Hall, Lund, and Jackson (1968) report reliabilities above 80% for observations of 30 children.

Discontinuous scoring techniques are one means of avoiding the difficulty involved in rapidly changing targets of observation. Discontinuous scoring involves observing the subject for the sample interval and then not observing for an interval during which the observed behaviors are recorded on the score sheet. This procedure is described by Bijou *et al.* (1969) as a means of increasing reliability and by Weick (1968) as a means of avoiding biased data due to inference from preceding contextual information.

Coleman (1970) used a 10-sec observe/10-sec record procedure to score working, talking, and out-of-seat behaviors in an elementary school classroom. Kazdin (1973) used a 5-sec observe/5-sec record procedure to score attending in retarded children. Herman and Tramontana (1971) and Ringer (1973) used 10-sec observe/5-sec record procedures to score appropriate and inappropriate classroom behaviors.

The advantages of discontinuous scoring are:

1. Observations may be randomized across subjects observed because the observers have time to find each new subject prior to each new observation interval.
2. Reliability is often improved because more time is allowed for scoring.
3. Contextual influence from preceding sample intervals may be diminished by the intervening recording intervals.

These relative advantages of discontinuous scoring are partially offset by the loss of observation time which may be as much as 50% of the total hours (Coleman, 1970; Kazdin, 1973). A second difficulty with the system is the requirement that the observer be able to "turn on" and "turn off" his observations without interference with his judgments. A minimum requirement for use of the technique is an adequate signaling system so that the observers do not become confused. Additionally, the necessity of retaining in memory a number of complex behaviors may cause scoring errors. Errors may be increased during the period as a result of "contamination from associated cues," "assimilation to expected message," or other sources of bias listed by Weick (1968).

The above review has described techniques for scoring specific behaviors within a limited number of categories (attending, notattending, etc.). These techniques have been used to record mean behaviors of a group as well as behaviors of single subjects. Subject sampling techniques were described for recording behaviors of several individual subjects. These procedures are similar to those which Bijou *et al.* (1968) called "specific codes."

Complex observation instruments have been devised to record a greater number of behaviors of subjects as well as record more complex interactions between the subjects, their teacher, their peers, and setting events in their environment. Some of these more complex techniques will now be reviewed.

Buell, Stoddard, Harris, and Baer (1968) recorded 7 behaviors of a preschool child in a study of collateral social development accompanying reinforcement of outdoor play. These 7 child behaviors and the teacher's attention to the child were recorded using a 10-sec interval sampling procedure. Unfortunately, teacher attention was not defined in the report nor were data on teacher behavior reported. Bijou *et al.* (1968) described a 15-sec time-sampling procedure for recording the behaviors of a single hyperactive child (see Fig. 3). The verbal and motor responses of the child were recorded in relation to physical and social events using a 4-track system. Target behaviors coded were: vocalizations by the child, proximity to another person, touching another person, contact with objects or materials, parallel play with other children, shared play with other children, and contact with a specific peer. Additional information noted on the form included changes in activity (shown by vertical line on the recording form), verbal praise to the subject from the teacher, and aggressive verbalizations or contact by the subject.

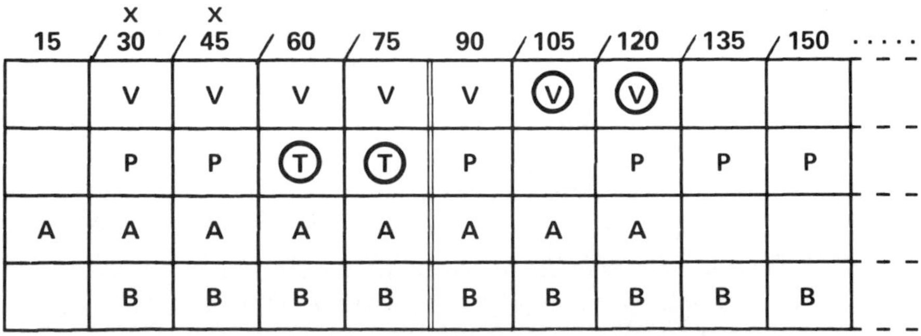

Figure 3   A sample line from a multiple behavior data sheet reproduced from Bijou, Peterson and Ault (1968). Numbers across the top represent consecutive 15-sec intervals. Codes entered are: vocalization (V), proximity to another person (P), touching another person (T), contact with objects (E), parallel play with children (A), shared play (C), interaction with Bill (B), verbal praise from teacher (x), aggressive behavior (O).

Sajwaj, Twardosz, and Burke (1972) recorded 5 behaviors of a retarded child in free play and 2 behaviors in a structured lesson. Teacher attention to those behaviors was also noted in the 10-sec interval time-sampling procedure. Similarly, Pinkston, Reese, LeBlanc, and Baer (1973) recorded 2 classes of aggressive behavior, positive peer interaction, and teacher attention during experimental manipulations of an aggressive preschool child's behavior (see Fig. 4). The child's behavior was observed and recorded 3 times a day for 30 min using a 10-sec time-sampling procedure in which one occurrence of any of the target behaviors in an interval was noted.

A very complex observation instrument was used by Walker and Buckley (1972) in a study of reintegration and maintenance of problem children in regular classrooms with the aid of peer reprogramming (see Fig. 5). Four classes of setting event, 7 classes of child inappropriate behavior, 6 classes of child appropriate behavior, 8 classes of teacher behavior, and 8 classes of peer behavior were observed and recorded. The complexity of the procedure was reflected in the range of observer agreement reported, 12% to 100% with the means for 3 checks being 62%, 84%, and 93%. Problems with reliability may have been instrumental in the failure to report data on peer and teacher behaviors in the article.

There are several advantages to collecting data on multiple behaviors of a subject, teacher interactions, peer interactions, and settings.

1. Recording multiple behaviors of a single subject allows description and functional analysis of collateral behavior changes which may come about through experimental treatment of a single behavior.
2. Collection of data on multiple behaviors allows for use of the within-subjects multiple-baseline design (Sidman, 1960; Baer, Wolf, & Risley, 1968; Kazdin, 1973).

	10	20	30	40	50	60	70	80	90	· · · · ·
Child Aggressive motor	✓						✓			– –
verbal			✓			✓	✓			– –
Peer Interaction	✓	✓	✓		✓	✓	✓			– –
Teacher Attention		•		✓			✓			– –

Figure 4   A multiple-behavior recording instrument reconstructed from Pinkston, Reese, LeBlanc, and Baer (1973). Numbers across the top represent 10-sec time sampling intervals. Checkmarks denote the occurrence of the target behavior listed in the left margin.

Subject

Social Consequent

Set		Inappropriate							Appropriate					Agent			Social Consequent peer (P) teacher (T)						
	NY	AG	NA	IP	MO	IW	NC	NO	WK	RE	VO	IT	C	TI	PI	O	A	P	D	Ph+	Ph−	C	NC
G 15	✓				✓									✓	✓		P		T				
1 30			✓			✓							✓			TP							
45			✓			✓										TP							
60			✓	✓		✓											P		T				
2 15			✓													TP							
30			✓					✓									T	T					
45																							
60																							
15	–	–	–	–	–	–	–	–	–	–	–	–	–	–	–	–	–	–	–	–	–	–	–
30	–	–	–	–	–	–	–	–	–	–	–	–	–	–	–	–	–	–	–	–	–	–	–
. . .																							

Figure 5   A complex multiple behavior recording instrument reconstructed from Walker and Buckley (1972). Inappropriate and appropriate subject behaviors, the agent of social stimuli initiated by others (teacher initiated or peer initiated), and the social consequences of the subject's behavior (contingent teacher or peer behavior) are noted across the top of the form. Codes are: noisy (NY), aggression (AG), not attending (NA), talks to peer (IP), movement around room (MO), inappropriate task involvement (IW), noncompliance with teacher commands (NC), appropriate group behavior (NO), work (WK), recitation (RE), volunteering (VO), initiates interaction with teacher (IT), compliance with teacher (C), teacher initiated interaction (TI), peer initiated interaction (PI), no response to subject (O), attention to subject (A), praise (P), physical approval (Ph+), physical disapproval (Ph−), verbal disapproval (D), compliance with subject (C), and noncompliance with subject (NC). Numbers listed down the left margin of the form indicate minutes broken into 15-sec time-sampling intervals. Setting is noted in the upper left corner for each six min of observation (group, individual, transition, and recess). None of the behavioral categories were exclusive.

370

3. The observation and recording of contiguous or contingent teacher and peer attention to the subject allows for greater specification of treatment effects implicit in the experimental manipulations.
4. Records of peer behavior may also allow measurement of collateral social change brought about through changes in the target subject's behavior.
5. Specification of settings in which target behaviors occur allows for tests of generalization of behaviors.

A disadvantage of these recording procedures is that only a single subject's behavior is recorded. Other methods must be used if similar data are to be collected on more than one subject. Further, the advantage of increased data generated with these procedures is offset to some extent by the increased difficulty of observing and recording multiple behavior. Observers must be trained longer with these instruments and agreements are generally harder to obtain. Finally, the utility of recording the additional categories of behavior, social stimuli, and setting is questionable since most of the studies do not report reliabilities or results on all the target behaviors listed in their methods sections.

Even more complex observational systems allow data collection on multiple behaviors of more than one subject as well as teacher and peer interactions. As noted above, subject sampling techniques are necessary in order to observe and record individual behaviors of several subjects. As the number of target behaviors and related events scored increase, the sampling techniques must be adjusted. Either the time-sample interval must be made longer to accommodate scoring multiple events or the observations of each subject lengthened to include blocks of time-sample intervals. O'Leary *et al.* (1969) observed and recorded 7 categories of disruptive behavior for seven subjects using a discontinuous 20-sec observe/10-sec record procedure. Subjects were observed in random order for 20 min each, 3 times a week. Eight categories of teacher behavior were recorded using the same discontinuous time sampling procedure but the teacher observations were not done at the same time or by the same observer as the child observations. Thus, information about contingent relationships between teacher and child behaviors was limited. Thomas, Becker, and Armstrong (1968) randomized blocks of 5 10-sec interval samples across 10 children in a study of disruptive classroom behavior (see Fig. 6). Each child was observed twice in a 20-min observation period for a total observation of 100 sec per child. The occurrence of any of 5 disruptive behaviors could be recorded in any interval. A single category of appropriate behavior was scored if that behavior included the total interval. "Other task" behavior was scored when no disruptive or appropriate behavior occurred during the interval. Teacher behaviors were recorded simultaneously with child behaviors but a within-interval frequency count was made rather than a time-sampling measure as with child behaviors. This procedural difference was attributed to the greater difficulty in separating child behaviors into discrete response units.

Minutes	1	2	3	4	5	6	7	8	9	10	11	12	13	14	15	16	17	18	19	20
Subject	4	2	1	5	3	7	9	8	6	10	1	5	7	3	6	8	9	10	4	2

Subject sampling procedure: 20-min observation period with 10 Ss randomly observed in blocks of 5 10-sec interval samples (each S observed twice).

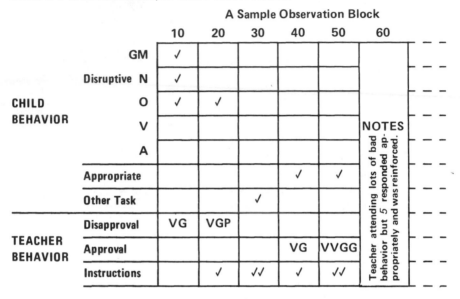

A Sample Observation Block

		10	20	30	40	50	60		
CHILD BEHAVIOR	GM	✓							
Disruptive	N	✓							
	O	✓	✓						
	V							NOTES	
	A							Teacher attending lots of bad behavior but 5 responded appropriately and was reinforced.	
	Appropriate				✓	✓			
	Other Task			✓					
TEACHER BEHAVIOR	Disapproval	VG	VGP						
	Approval				VG	VVGG			
	Instructions		✓	✓✓	✓	✓✓			

Figure 6   A subject sampling multiple behavior recording instrument reconstructed from Thomas, Becker and Armstrong (1968). Subject sampling procedure is illustrated at the top. A sample interval block is illustrated below. Numbers across the top of this sample period indicate 10-sec time-sampling intervals. Target behaviors for the child and teacher are listed down the left margin. Disruptive child behaviors are: gross motor (GM), noise (N), inappropriate orientation (O), verbal (V), and aggression (A). Teacher behaviors are coded as physical (P), verbal (V) and gestural (G). Child behaviors are recorded as occurrences in the 10-sec intervals whereas teacher behaviors are recorded as absolute frequencies. Appropriate child behavior must be uninterrupted for the complete 10-sec interval before recording. Teacher approval and disapproval are only recorded if contingent on one of the child behaviors. Teacher instruction may be noncontingent.

Solomon and Wahler (1973) randomized 6-min blocks of observations across 5 subjects in a 30-min observational period (see Fig. 7). Each block of observations was divided into 10-sec intervals in which the occurrence of child problem or desirable behaviors was noted. These two categories of behavior were further divided into talking, action, and out-of-seat behavior. Additionally, teacher attention, "control peer," and "other peer" attention to the subject was scored. The 6 possible target child behaviors were mutually exclusive and the first occurring behavior was scored for that interval. Teacher, "control peer," and "other peer" attention were not exclusive and all could be scored as occurring in any one interval.

Minutes	6	12	18	24	30
Subject	3	1	4	5	2

Subject sampling procedure: 30-min observation period with 5 *S*s randomly observed for 6-min blocks of 10-sec interval time samples (each *S* observed once in 30 min).

		A Sample Observation Block							
		10	20	30	40	50	60	10	· · ·
CHILD BEHAVIOR	Problem	T	OT	T					
	Desirable				A	AT	A	A	
TEACHER ATTENTION					✓	✓		✓	
CONTROL PEER ATTENTION						✓			
OTHER PEER ATTENTION			✓	✓		✓			

Figure 7   A subject sampling multiple-behavior recording instrument reconstructed from Solomon and Wahler (1973). The subject sampling procedure is illustrated at the top. A sample observation block is illustrated below. Numbers across the top of this sample block indicate 10-sec time-sampling intervals. Target behaviors for the child, teacher, control peer and other peer are listed down the left margin. Problem and desirable child behaviors are further coded as talking (T), action (A), and out-of-seat (O). Problem and desirable child behaviors are mutually exclusive in any one 10-sec interval. Teacher, control peer, and other peer behaviors are nonexclusive.

Observation and recording of multiple behaviors of multiple subjects has many advantages.

1. Measurement of multiple behaviors of a single subject allows description and functional analysis of collateral behavior changes within that subject's repertoire when one behavior is experimentally treated (generalization across behaviors).

2. Multiple-behavior measures permit the use of within-subjects multiple baseline design if those behaviors are relatively independent of each other (Sidman, 1960; Baer, Wolf, & Risley, 1968; Kazdin, 1973).

3. Data on more than one subject permit examination of collateral behavior changes across subjects when one subject is treated (generalization across subjects).

4. Data on more than one subject permit use of across-subjects multiple-baseline designs (Sidman, 1960; Baer, Wolf, & Risley, 1968; Kazdin, 1973).

5. The simultaneous measurement of teacher and peer behavior improves specification of treatment variables.

There are several disadvantages in using a complex coding system required for measurement of multiple behaviors of multiple subjects. The major disadvantage is the increased difficulty in data collection. The increased number of behavior categories scored and the requirement for subject sampling procedures each add to the difficulty of observation and recording. Highly trained observers are needed to obtain acceptable agreement requirements. The classroom teacher will probably be unable to collect data with these procedures. Thus, the researcher should weigh the utility of each bit of additional data against the additional difficulties encountered in data collection.

The advantages and disadvantages of complex recording procedures and some additional considerations in instrument design are illustrated in the description of a multiple behavior recording instrument designed by Patterson (Patterson & Wetzel, 1974). The problem called for measures to assess the effects of group-contingent reinforcement in a special education classroom with high frequencies of disruptive behavior and low frequencies of lesson participation. The effects of group contingent reinforcement for increased participation and for decreased disruption were compared with each other and with individually contingent token reinforcement baselines across two classroom settings. Four subjects were selected by the teacher as representing the two "worst" behaved and two "best" behaved students. Four major categories of behavior were observed and recorded: (1) appropriate student behavior; (2) inappropriate student behavior; (3) teacher verbal behavior directed at target students; and (4) peer verbal behavior directed at target students. Student appropriate behavior was further subdivided into attending (on-task behaviors) and participation behaviors. Inappropriate behavior was subdivided into out-of-area, off-task (but in-area), and disruption. Teacher and peer verbal input to the child were divided into unspecified verbal (instruction, conversation, etc.), verbal praise, and verbal reprimand.

The target behaviors were scored for 4 subjects during 2 20-min periods each day. The 4 children were observed in random order for 30 sec each using a 10-sec time-sampling procedure. Each child was observed for 3 10-sec intervals on an average of every 2 min yielding 10 observations per child per session. The observer used a 10-sec interval timer with an ear phone and the scoring sheet, as shown in Figure 8. Inappropriate behaviors were scored in the top row, appropriate behaviors in the second row, adult verbal attention in the third row, and peer verbal attention in the fourth row. The dark vertical lines divide the sheet into blocks of 3 10-sec intervals and the large numbers in those blocks represent the subject's number which is randomized across observations. At the beginning of any interval (at the signal) one of the mutually exclusive behavior classes, on-task, off-task, or out-of-area was scored. The occurrence of participation, disruption, teacher verbal, or peer verbal behavior at any time during the interval could then be coded.

There are several distinctions to be made between the way behaviors were defined and recorded in this procedure and similar procedures found in the literature. 1. Appropriate behavior was subdivided into passive attending and active participation. These categories are usually lumped together in the studies reviewed. Packard (1970) argued that it is often necessary to shape attention so that the discriminative stimuli for other desired responses may become functional.

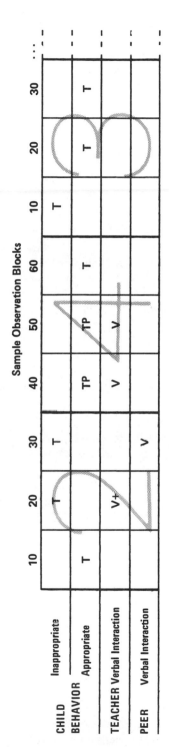

Subject sampling procedure: 20-min observation period with 4 Ss randomly observed in blocks of 3 10-sec interval time samples (each S observed 10 times).

Figure 8   A subject-sampling multiple-behavior recording instrument reproduced from Patterson and Wetzel (1974). The subject sampling procedure is illustrated at the top. Three sample observation blocks are illustrated below. Numbers across the top of the samples indicate 10-sec time-sampling intervals. Target behaviors for the child, teacher, and peers are listed down the left margin. Inappropriate child behavior is further coded as: off-task (T), out-of-area (O), and disruptive (D). Appropriate child behavior is coded as: on-task (T) and participation (P). Teacher and peer verbal interaction with child are coded as: unspecified verbal (V), praise (V+), and reprimand (V−). On-task, off-task, and out-of-area behavioral categories are mutually exclusive, all others are nonexclusive. Dark vertical lines denote change of subject and large numbers denote subject number.

375

However, most recording procedures do not differentiate attention from other behaviors which attention makes possible (as distinguishing looking at the teacher from answering a question). 2. Certain inappropriate behaviors were not considered totally incompatible with attending. Blurting out an answer without permission from the teacher is often placed in the same class of disruption as yelling at another child or banging a ruler on the desk. Many studies may fail to shape approximations to appropriate responses because such approximations are categorized as inappropriate. With this procedure, recording of a disruptive behavior within an interval does not preclude recording of an attending behavior in the same interval. The same is true for nonattending and participation. For example, a child may be resting his head on his desk at the beginning of an interval but before the interval ends, raise his hand to ask a question. In this case, both off-task and participation would be scored. In the same way, a child might be scored on on-task at the beginning of an interval because he is doing his reading, but in the middle of the interval makes a disruptive mouth noise. In this case both on-task and disruption would be scored.

Teacher and peer verbalizations to the target child do not have to be clearly contingent upon target-child behavior, that is, they may be either antecedent, simultaneous, or subsequent events. The observer does not judge contingencies; contingencies are inferences based on contiguity. Only contiguity need be recorded. Behaviors are categorized according to their relative durations. Relatively continuous behaviors are those whose parameter of greatest concern is duration, attention, orientation, location, and other "state" behaviors which are setting events for other behaviors. These behaviors are most commonly reported as percentage of intervals which, in actuality, is a duration measure, (Wolf, 1973). By recording such behaviors at a signal (beginning of the interval) the vigilance and duration judgment problems for the observer are eliminated. Until an empirical comparison is made between this and other procedures, we assume that continuous behaviors can be reliably scored at a signal, as have other researchers (Kubany & Sloggett, 1973; Broden et al., 1970). When the observers note the continuous behaviors at a signal, their entire attention may be then focused on the usual *relatively discrete behaviors* which are scored if they occur at any time during the rest of the interval.

CURRENT APPLICATIONS OF THE TECHNOLOGY

We reviewed the behaviors and settings of 48 classroom studies appearing in *JABA* from 1968 to 1974. Three additional relevant studies were included in the review (Bijou et al., 1969; Hamblin, Hathaway, & Wodarski, 1971; Wodarski et al., 1972). The 48 studies included in the review are cited in the bibliography. In some cases it was necessary to be somewhat arbitrary in the categorization of the behaviors but most often they met the criteria described below.

One behavior commonly analyzed by behavior technology in the classroom is *inappropriate child behavior.* These behaviors are either so labeled in the studies or otherwise defined as undesirable. In most studies an attempt is made to decrease the rate (or occasionally, the duration) of these behaviors. About 75% (36 of the total 48) of the studies in *JABA* observe, record, and manipulate inappropriate behavior. Most of these studies distinguish one or more sub-categories of inappropriate behavior; *disruption* which typically includes speaking out of turn, loud noises, inappropriate materials use, moving furniture, swearing, and fighting; *out-of-area* which is generally limited to out-of-desk but also includes reading circle, rug time, etc.; *off-task* which is sometimes the absence of task behaviors such as not looking at the teacher, not looking at materials with which one is supposed to be working, not looking at a peer who is reciting, or the presence of incompatible behaviors such as playing with inappropriate materials, scribbling, doodling, gazing out the window, and turning around in the desk.

Seventy-seven percent of the studies measured *appropriate child behaviors*. These behaviors are either so labeled in the reports or otherwise represented as desirable. Usually, attempts were made to increase the rate or duration of such behaviors. Most of these reports distinguish one or more subcategories of appropriate behavior. *Participation* includes hand raising, asking questions, making relevant comments (with permission), helping peers, recitation, and working at the chalkboard. *On-task* is looking at the teacher, looking at materials, reading appropriate materials, attending to a reciting peer, working on workbooks, math problems, etc. *Social* behavior most often includes appropriate peer interactions, verbalizing to peers, cooperative play, sharing, peer tutoring, etc. *Academic output* usually includes number of problems solved or pages finished. *Language* frequently includes grammatical units and verbal utterances.

Teacher attention is the next most commonly studied classroom behavior (52% or 25 of the 48 studies). About a fifth of these studies make no further distinction between types of teacher attention. The remainder of the studies scoring teacher attention look at teacher verbal attention and distinguish one or more subcategories: *approval,* generally limited to praising comments of the teacher directed toward the child; *disapproval,* scolding or reprimands; *instruction,* directions, directives, lecture and feedback on task performance. In 10 of the 48 studies teacher attention was scored only if considered contingent on a child's behavior. Teacher *physical contact* was recorded in 9 of the 48 studies. Six differentiate approval (hugs, kisses, pats on the head, etc.) and disapproval (restraint, slaps, pushes, drags, etc).

Peer behavior was recorded in nine studies. Undifferentiated peer attention (other than physical contact) was recorded in six studies and differentiated into verbal approval and disapproval by three. *Approval* is verbal behavior of the peer directed toward the target subject which could be construed as having a positively reinforcing function for the target child's behavior. *Disapproval* is behavior of the peers having a potential punishing function. (The above description of the literature is summarized in Table 1 and Figure 9.)

TABLE 1

Responses Assessed in Applied Classroom Behavior Analysis
(References reviewed for Table 1 but not cited in text are indicated in reference list by asterisk)

Child Behaviors	Number*	Percent**	Teacher Behaviors	Number	Percent	Peer Behaviors	Number	Percent
Total	47	98	Total	26	52	Total	9	19
Inappropriate	36	75	Unspecified attention	5	10	Unspecified attention	6	13
Unspecified	8	17	Verbal attention	21	44	Verbal attention	3	6
Specified	28	58	Unspecified	5	10	Unspecified	0	0
Disruption	24	50	Specified	21	44	Specified	3	6
Out-of-area	14	29	Approval	15	31	Approval	3	6
Off-task	16	33	Disapproval	14	29	Disapproval	3	6
Appropriate	37	77	Instruction	6	13	Contingent	1	2
Unspecified	9	19	Contingent	10	21	Physical contact	3	6
Specified	28	58	Physical contact	9	19	Unspecified	0	0
Participation	6	13	Unspecified	3	6	Specified	3	6
On-task	18	36	Specified	6	13	Approval	3	6
Social	12	25	Approval	5	10	Disapproval	3	6
Academic	10	21	Disapproval	5	10	Contingent	1	2
Language	2	5	Contingent	5	10			

*Number of studies which recorded target behavior (Total number reviewed = 48).

**Percent of the total studies which recorded target behavior.

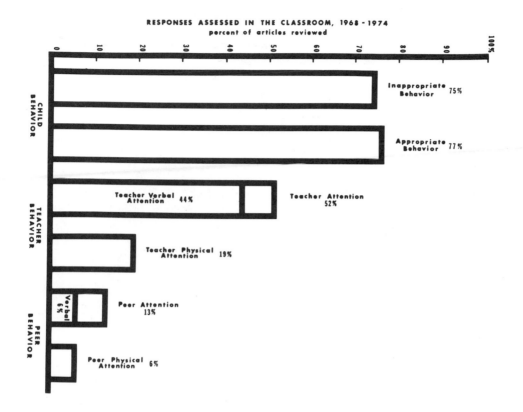

Figure 9   Classroom behaviors analyzed by behavior technology as reported in 48 journal articles, 1968-1974.

The settings in which classroom behaviors have been observed can be similarly described. Ten of the 48 studies record across undifferentiated settings in what appear to be traditional classrooms. The most commonly distinguished setting is independent seat or *desk work* — 29 of the 48 studies. Twenty-one studies observed behaviors in *structured lessons* in which the teacher instructs a group or the whole class. The remaining settings include *free play* (5 studies or 10%), *small group independent* work (2 studies or 4.5%), and *individual lessons* (one study or 2%) (See Fig. 10).

The classroom applications reported in *JABA* have been previously reviewed and criticized on various fronts (Chadwick & Day, 1971; Kazdin, 1973; Winett & Winkler, 1972). Behavioral researchers are being taken to task for using the apparently effective techniques of behavior modification to support those questionable procedures and aims of traditional education, the teacher dominated, fixed-desk, workbook-oriented, everyone-learn-the-same-thing-at-the-same-time-in-the-same-way, education establishment which has been under fire by Charles Silberman (1970) and countless others for at least a decade.

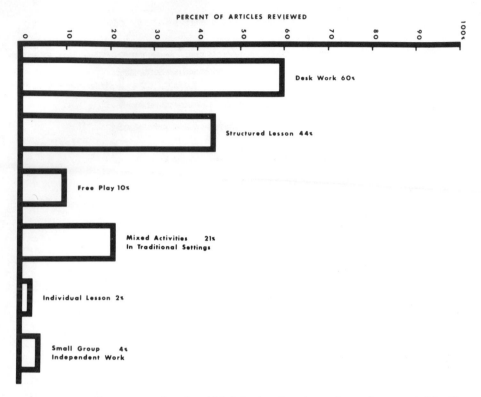

Figure 10   Classroom settings in which behaviors have been observed as reported in 48 journal articles, 1968-1974.

It seems rather clear from the above tabulations that the "traditional" class-room procedures and behavioral goals *are* overly represented in the applied be-havior analysis literature and that within the traditional domain, application has been limited to a few categories of so-called inappropriate and appropriate be-havior. Although there are obviously many possible explanations, the tendency to restrict research focus to the experimental manipulation of a relatively few categories of traditional classroom behavior might be traced to certain theoreti-cal concerns, aspects of research convenience, and technological limitations.

Theoretical Concerns

From the standpoint of education, the theoretical interests of applied behavioral researchers would appear particularly narrow. Although theoretically committed to the principles underlying the learning process, classroom researchers are exces-sively concerned with one aspect of that process — the sensitivity of operant be-havior to reinforcing stimulus events. Thus, classroom research tends, in one form or another, to be a demonstration of reinforcement control. Variation occurs mostly in the nature of the reinforcement and the type of behavior. The social importance of the manipulated behavior does not appear to be of particular concern. Task analysis and development of complex academic and social behaviors, which have obvious theoretical bases and importance, are relatively ignored in the literature. Education as a socially significant enterprise is very much in need of data based, empirical theories. Continued narrow theoretical concern of classroom researchers can do little to meet that need.

Research Convenience

Traditional classrooms are conveniently arranged to study teacher attention and disruption: 25 to 35 children confined to one room in desks in rows aimed at one adult who controls most of the available reinforcement in the environment (peer reinforcement is eliminated as much as possible). Such situations are easily disrupted and the list of potentially inappropriate behaviors very long. Since the teacher is the central and dominant figure, teacher attention can be readily demonstrated to have some connection with almost any student behavior which can be identified (appropriate or inappropriate). With the cards stacked against them by the traditional arrangement, teachers usually need help and both they and the institution are likely to cooperate with anyone who holds out the promise of behavior control (and by intimation, peace and quiet).

It is relatively easy for the researcher to work in a classroom which aims mostly at student inaction and workbook fixations. Inactive subjects are easier to track and record. Simple behaviors can be simply managed; complex behaviors are more difficult to specify, quantify, and control. In the traditionally organized classroom, the researcher can use fewer and less sophisticated or untrained staff.

In the literature, appropriate behaviors tend to be defined as the mirror images of the inappropriate: on-task; in-desk; in-area; not talking to peers; not pinching, hitting, or poking. Really appropriate, educationally significant behaviors which a student needs in order to become an active, curious, independent learner, are seldom considered. Frequently the researcher begs off on the basis that these behaviors are too difficult to identify and quantify. They *are* difficult to identify and quantify in the traditional classroom because they are not occurring. The development of "really appropriate" learning behaviors would require physical rearrangement of the classroom, new materials, retraining of the teacher and students, and a tremendous, imaginative research effort. Amongst other consequent events, researchers who suggest such a course are likely to lose what institutional cooperation they have enjoyed. Thus, researchers are prey to a host of reinforcers which shape them into participating in the maintenance of traditional educational forms and the control of "inappropriate" classroom behavior.

Technological Limitations

Just as readily as any other scientist, the behavioral scientist can fall into a common trap: dominance by the technology. Presumably, we design instruments for observing and recording behavior in the classroom because we have important questions to ask about behavioral processes in the educational system. Our research questions determine the design and development of the technology. However, once a technology begins to develop it is easy for researchers to be lead by it, formulating only those questions which the technology permits them to answer. The scientist becomes enslaved by tools, technical and linguistic.

Behavioral researchers may study traditional classrooms because such study is more readily permitted by their technology. Simple behavior and stimulus events can be more readily specified and quantified; highly trained observers are not necessary; observer agreements are more respectable. But the gains are at the expense of technological advance and sophisticated experimental designs.

SUGGESTIONS FOR BETTER APPLICATION

Improving the applications of a science is a behavior emitted by the scientists. All scientists may not agree with this, but the statement has validity if one is speaking of applied scientists. Some psychologists (Bijou's (1970) "small minority,") are concerned with improvement of behavioral applications in classrooms. Applied behavioral scientists are constrained to evaluate variables which can be effective in improving behaviors which are socially important (rather than convenient), and to communicate the techniques making up a particular behavioral application. This review suggests some dimensions for improvement.

Evaluation

Applied researchers seldom have the option of choosing a response easily and reliably quantified and, as a result, must try harder to evaluate the effects of their efforts. Assessment methods for the evaluation of reinforcement programs in educational settings have been recently reviewed and criticized by Kazdin (1973). He points out that in spite of the apparent success of behavioral research in educational settings, the evaluations of many programs are poorly designed.

Adequate specification of functional treatment variables is required for tracing the results of an experiment to the experimental manipulations. Wolf (1973) suggests that important variables are often omitted from reports of research in applied settings because the researcher is only interested in the impact of the complete "package" of variables. According to Sidman (1960) such descriptions may be ". . . omitted from published reports simply because their relevance is not recognized at the time, or because fine details of a technique may be too lengthy and confusing to describe in print" [p. 108]. The complete specification of treatment variables requires the quantification of many events. For example, to better specify the variables involved in the application of a token economy, measures of the teacher's behavior may be necessary. If teacher behaviors are found to covary with a treatment variable (Mandelker, Brigham, Bushell, 1970), then the effects of teacher behaviors should be tested independently of the reinforcing functions of the tokens. The requirement for more detailed specification of treatment variables leads, in turn, to the requirement for more sophisticated data collection instruments capable of generating the required information.

Application of behavior analysis to education has generated many questions. Ample demonstration of teacher reinforcement control over student deportment behaviors is available in the literature. It is now important to be able to answer the other questions which proliferate with such research. What other behaviors of students are benefitted by "improvements" in their deportment (Ferritor et al., 1972; Harris & Sherman, 1973)? Will the changes in behavior have any generality to other settings or situations (Pinkston et al., 1973; Sajwaj et al., 1972)? Will the behavior of the whole class change as a result of the change in one of its members (Walker & Buckley, 1972)? Tests for generalization across behaviors, across subjects, and across settings require a measurement technology with increased capability.

Many behavior analysts are turning to more sophisticated multiple-baseline designs for evaluation of classroom research. These designs also require sophisticated observation and recording technologies capable of simultaneously recording multiple behaviors. Thus, advancement in observation and recording becomes crucial as researchers attempt a more complete specification of treatment variables; attempt to check for generality of treatment effects across behaviors, subjects, and settings; and attempt to measure multiple behaviors for multiple-baseline designs.

Field Descriptions

"Psychology like the other natural sciences depends for its advancement upon both descriptive accounts and functional analysis of its primary data" (Bijou, Peterson, & Ault, 1968). Descriptive accounts of the sort illustrated by Bijou and his colleagues will do much to stimulate new and better directions in applied educational research. Thought provoking suggestions for new behaviors to study have been criticized in the past for lack of objective description of those behaviors. Likewise, ideas germaine to the improvement of evaluation of educational applications have been rejected by some editors for failure to include specific procedures and tools useful in conducting behavioral research. Field-descriptive studies will develop the needed definitions of new behaviors and stimulus events found in innovative and experimental educational settings. Field studies will also stimulate the development of advanced recording technology for measuring these events. In addition, descriptive field studies will discover new behavioral phenomena, explore the settings in which the phenomena occur, and establish provocative and significant questions for later functional analyses. Finally, the significance of these contributions from descriptive field studies must be recognized and given appropriate status in the scientific literature.

Social Significance

Major contributions of the "behavior analysis group" to education have been summarized by Bijou (1970). These contributions consist of a philosophy of science, some learning concepts and principles, procedures for the application of these concepts and principles to teaching, and a research method for evaluat-- ing those applications. The research to date, said Bijou, (1970) "suggests that behavioral principles can be applied to the teaching situation with gratifying re- sults" [p. 68]. The question now becomes: what must be accomplished in the classroom through the application of behavioral principles? One dimension for improvement of educational application is the social significance of the findings.

Events of considerable significance are occurring on the American educational scene to which behavioral researchers can make important contributions. Phil- osophies and procedures are rapidly emerging which are very different from the nineteenth century traditions which have been dominating the schools. Re- definitions of educational purposes, aims, and responsibilities are generating new curricula, new roles for teachers, students, and community, different materials, architecture, and classroom organization. The educational practices which devel- oped as an emergency response to rapid industrialization are being challenged and the role of the educational process in society questioned. The contributions of this "small minority" identified by Bijou can be of enormous value in the design and development of the new education but only if they listen to other "small minorities" and attend to a broader viewpoint of social need.

Many behaviorists point this out and urge a reevaluation of applied behavior- al science's relationship to education. These statements are frequently misinter- preted. Winett and Winkler (1972), for example, suggest that classroom appli- cations are narrow in scope and that research is needed in many new and, as yet, unstudied behavioral areas and educational settings. Their article elicited a number of defensive reactions (published in the same issue of JABA). One commentator argued that traditional classroom behaviors such as sitting still and attending to a teacher may have later functional value (as though Winett and Winkler had suggested that they should not be taught). Another reviewer suggested that the overemphasis on reduction of inappropriate behavior would disappear before the manuscript reached print. That was in 1972; such does not yet seem to be the case. Yet another reviewer fell back on the rationale that the behaviors which Winett and Winkler suggest need research attention can- not be studied because they cannot be objectively defined. It is difficult to believe that a group of researchers capable of identifying *appropriate* behavior should balk at the prospect of developing behavioral equivalents for *initiative, leadership,* or even that time honored bugaboo, *creativity.* In fact, de Bono (1970) has defined target behaviors for the study of creativity and is well into programmed instruction for children.

There is no basic incompatibility between the new educational directions and applied behavior analysis. The philosophy, concepts, research methods, and procedures of application which the behavioral group has to offer are just as valuable and necessary in the new education as the traditional. As behaviorists acquaint themselves with these new directions through intensified field study and analysis, they will not only develop "better applications: but make significant contributions to the improvement of an obviously critical and important social enterprise.

REFERENCES

Baer, D. M., Wolf, M. M., & Risley, T. R. Some current dimensions of applied behavior analysis. *Journal of Applied Behavior Analysis,* 1968, *1,* 91-97.

Barrish, H. H., Saunders, M., & Wolf, M. M. Good behavior game effects on individual contingencies for group consequences on disruptive behavior in a classroom. *Journal of Applied Behavior Analysis,* 1969, *2,* 119-124.

Bijou, S. W. What psychology has to offer education – now. *Journal of Applied Behavior Analysis,* 1970, *3,* 65-71.

Bijou, S. W., Peterson, R. F., Harris, F. R., Allen, K. F., & Johnston, M. S. Methodology for experimental studies of young children in natural settings. *Psychological Record,* 1969, *19,* 177-210.

Bijou, S. W., Peterson, R. G., & Ault, M. A method to integrate descriptive and experimental field studies at the level of data and empirical concepts. *Journal of Applied Behavior Analysis,* 1968, *2,* 175-191.

*Bolstad, O. D., & Johnson, S. M. Self-regulation in the modification of disruptive classroom behavior. *Journal of Applied Behavior Analysis,* 1972, *5,* 443-454.

Broden, M., Bruce, M., Mitchell, M., Carter, V., & Hall, R. V. Effects of teacher attention on attending behavior of two boys at adjacent desks. *Journal of Applied Behavior Analysis,* 1970, *3,* 199-203.

Buell, J., Stoddard, P., Harris, F., & Baer, D. M. Collateral social development accompanying reinforcement of outdoor play in a preschool child. *Journal of Applied Behavior Analysis,* 1968, *1,* 167-173.

Bushnell, D., Wrobel, P. A., & Michaelis, M. L. Applying "group" contingencies to the classroom study behavior of preschool children. *Journal of Applied Behavior Analysis,* 1968, *1,* 55-61.

Chadwick, B. A., & Day, R. C. Systematic reinforcement: Academic performance and underachieving students. *Journal of Applied Behavior Analysis,* 1971, *4,* 311-319.

Coleman, R. A conditioning technique applicable to elementary school classrooms. *Journal of Applied Behavior Analysis,* 1970, *3,* 293-297.

*Cossairt, A., Hall, R. V., & Hopkins, B. L. The effects of experimenter's instructions, feedback, and praise on teacher praise and student attending behavior. *Journal of Applied Behavior Analysis,* 1973, *6,* 89-100.

*Indicates reference reviewed for Table 1 but not cited in text deBono, E. *Lateral thinking: Creativity step by step.* New York: Harper & Row, 1970.

*Dietz, S. M., & Repp, A. C. Decreasing classroom misbehavior through the use of DRL Schedules of reinforcement. *Journal of Applied Behavior Analysis,* 1973, *6,* 457-463.

Ferritor, D. F., Buckholdt, D., Hamblin, R. L., & Smith, L. The noneffects of contingent reinforcement for attending behavior on work accomplished. *Journal of Applied Behavior Analysis,* 1972, *5,* 7-17.

*Hall, R. V., Fox, R., Willard, D., Goldsmith, L., Emerson, M., Owen, W., Davis, F., & Porcia, E. The teacher as observer and experimenter in the modification of disputing and talking-out behaviors. *Journal of Applied Behavior Analysis,* 1971, *4,* 141-149.

Hall, R. V., Lund, D., & Jackson, D. Effects of teacher attention on study behavior. *Journal of Applied Behavior Analysis,* 1968, *1,* 1-12.

Hall, R., Panyan, M., Rabon, D., & Broden, M. Instructing beginning teachers in reinforcement procedures which improve classroom control. *Journal of Applied Behavior Analysis,* 1968, *1,* 315-322.

Hamblin, R. L., Hathaway, C., & Wodarski, J. Group contingencies, peer tutoring and accelerating academic achievement. In E. A. Ramp, & B. F. Hopkins (Eds.), *A new direction for education: Behavior analysis, 1971.* Lawrence, Kansas: The University of Kansas, 1971.

Harris, V. W., & Sherman, J. A. Use and analysis of the "good behavior game" to reduce disruptive classroom behavior. *Journal of Applied Behavior Analysis,* 1973, *6,* 405-417.

*Hart, B. M., Reynolds, W. J., Baer, D. M., Brawley, E. M., & Harris, F. R. Effect of contingent and non-contingent social reinforcement on the cooperative play of a preschool child. *Journal of Applied Behavior Analysis,* 1968, *1,* 73-76.

*Hart, B. M., & Risley, T. R. Establishing use of descriptive adjectives in the spontaneous speech of disadvantaged preschool children. *Journal of Applied Behavior Analysis,* 1968, *1,* 109-120.

Herman, S., & Tramontana, J. Instructions and group *versus* individual reinforcement in modifying disruptive group behavior. *Journal of Applied Behavior Analysis,* 1971, *4,* 113-119.

*Hopkins, B. L., Schutte, R. C., & Garton, K. L. The effects of access to a playroom on the rate and quality of printing and writing of first and second-grade students. *Journal of Applied Behavior Analysis,* 1971, *4,* 77-87.

Kazdin, A. E. The effect of vicarious reinforcement on attentive behavior in the classroom. *Journal of Applied Behavior Analysis,* 1973, *6,* 71-78. (a)

Kazdin, A. E. Methodological and assessment considerations in evaluating reinforcement programs in applied settings. *Journal of Applied Behavior Analysis,* 1973, *6,* 517-531. (b)

Kazdin, A. E., & Klock, J. The effect of nonverbal teachers approval on student attentive behavior. *Journal of Applied Behavior Analysis,* 1973, *6,* 643-654. (c)

*Kirby, F. D., & Shields, F. Modification of arithmetic response rate and attending behavior in a seventh-grade student. *Journal of Applied Behavior Analysis,* 1972, *5,* 79-84.

Kubany, E. S., & Sloggett, B. B. Coding procedure for teachers. *Journal of Applied Behavior Analysis,* 1973, *6,* 339-344.

Long, J. D., & Williams, R. L. The comparative effectiveness of group and individually contingent free time with inner-city junior high school students. *Journal of Applied Behavior Analysis,* 1973, *6,* 465-474.

Lovaas, O. I., Frietag, G., Gold, V. J., & Kassorla, E. C. Recording apparatus and procedures for observations of behaviors of children in free play settings. *Journal of Experimental Child Psychology,* 1965, *2,* 108-120.

Lovitt, T. C., & Curtiss, K. A. Academic response rate as a function of teacher and self-imposed contingencies. *Journal of Applied Behavior Analysis,* 1969, *2,* 44-53.

*Indicates reference reviewed for Table 1 but not cited in text

Madsen, C. H., Becker, W. C., & Thomas, D. R. Rules, praise and ignoring; elements of elementary classroom control. *Journal of Applied Behavior Analysis*, 1968, *1*, 139-150.

Mandelker, A. V., Brigham, T. A., & Bushell, D. The effects of token procedures on a teacher's social contacts with her students. *Journal of Applied Behavior Analysis*, 1970, *3*, 169-174.

McAllister, L. W., Stachowiak, J. G., Baer, D. M., & Conderman, L. The application of operant conditioning techniques in a secondary school classroom. *Journal of Applied Behavior Analysis*, 1969, *2*, 277-285.

Medland, M. B., & Stachnik, T. J. Good-behavior game: A replication and systematic analysis. *Journal of Applied Behavior Analysis*, 1972, *5*, 45-51.

Miller, L. K. Reviewers comments on Kazdin's methodological and assessment considerations in evaluating reinforcement programs. *Journal of Applied Behavior Analysis*, 1973, *6*, 517-531.

O'Leary, D. K. Behavior modification in the classroom: A rejoinder to Winett and Winkler. *Journal of Applied Behavior Analysis*, 1972, *5*, 505-511.

O'Leary, D. K., Becker, W. C., Evans, M. B., & Sandargas, R. A. A token reinforcement program in a public school: A replication and systematic analysis. *Journal of Applied Behavior Analysis*, 1969, *2*, 3-31.

Packard, R. G. The control of "classroom attention": A group contingency for complex behavior. *Journal of Applied Behavior Analysis*, 1970, *3*, 13-28.

Patterson, J. R., & Wetzel, R. J. Group contingent reinforcement in a special education classroom. Paper presented to the American Psychological Association, New Orleans, September, 1974.

Pinkston, E. M., Reese, N. M., LeBlanc, J. M., & Baer, D. M. Independent control of a preschool child's aggression and peer interactions by contingent teacher attention. *Journal of Applied Behavior Analysis*, 1973, *6*, 115-24.

Ramp, E., Ulrich, R., & Delany, S. Delayed time-out as a procedure for reducing disruptive classroom behavior: a case study. *Journal of Applied Behavior Analysis*, 1971, *4*, 235-239.

Reynolds, N. J., & Risley, T. R. The role of social and material reinforcers in increasing talking of a disadvantaged preschool child. *Journal of Applied Behavior Analysis*, 1968, *1*, 253-262.

Ringer, V. M. J. The use of a "token helper" in the management of classroom behavior problems and in teacher training. *Journal of Applied Behavior Analysis*, 1973, *6*, 671-677.

Sajwaj, T., Twardosz, S., & Burke, M. Side effects of extinction procedures in a remedial preschool. *Journal of Applied Behavior Analysis*, 1972, *5*, 163-175.

Sanders, R. M., & Hanson, P. J. A note on a simple procedure for redistributing a teacher's student contacts. *Journal of Applied Behavior Analysis*, 1971, *4*, 157-161.

Schmidt, G. W., & Ulrich, R. E. Effects of group contingent events on classroom noise. *Journal of Applied Behavior Analysis*, 1969, *2*, 171-179.

Schutte, R. C., & Hopkins, B. L. The effects of teacher attention on following instructions in a kindergarten class. *Journal of Applied Behavior Analysis*, 1970, *3*, 117-122.

Sidman, M. *Tactics of scientific research*. New York: Basic Books, 1960.

Sidman, M. Reviewers comments on Kazdin's methodological and assessment considerations in evaluating reinforcement programs. *Journal of Applied Behavior Analysis*, 1973, *6*, 517-531.

Silberman, C. *Crisis in the classroom*. New York: Random House, 1970.

Solomon, R. W., & Wahler, R. G. Peer reinforcement control of classroom problem behavior. *Journal of Applied Behavior Analysis*, 1973, *6*, 49-56.

Thomas, D. R., Becker, W. C., & Armstrong, M. Production and elimination of disruptive classroom behavior by systematically varying teacher's behavior. *Journal of Applied Behavior Analysis*, 1968, *1*, 35-45.

Walker, H. M., & Buckley, N. K. The use of positive reinforcement in conditioning attending behavior. *Journal of Applied Behavior Analysis,* 1968, *1,* 245-250.

Walker, H. M., & Buckley, N. K. Programming generalization and maintenance of treatment effects across time and across settings. *Journal of Applied Behavior Analysis,* 1972, *5,* 209-224.

Wasik, B. H., Senn, K., Welch, R. H., & Cooper, B. A. Behavior modification with culturally deprived school children: Two case studies. *Journal of Applied Behavior Analysis,* 1969, *2,* 181-194.

Weick, C. Systematic observational methods. In G. Lindzey, & E. Aronson (Eds.), *Handbook of Social Psychology.* Reading, Mass.: Addison-Wesley, 1968. Pp. 357-451.

Winett, R. A., & Winkler, R. C. Current behavior modification in the classroom: Be still, be quiet, be docile. *Journal of Applied Behavior Analysis,* 1972, *5,* 499-504.

Wodarski, J. S., Hamblin, R. L., Buckholdt, D. R., & Ferritor, D. E. The effects of low performance group and individual contingencies on cooperative behaviors exhibited by fifth graders. *Psychological Record,* 1972, *22,* 359-368.

Wolf, M. Reviewers comments on Kazdin's methodological and assessment considerations in evaluating reinforcement programs. *Journal of Applied Behavior Analysis,* 1973, *6,* 517-531.

22

Application of Operant Principles to the Hyperactive Behavior of a Retarded Girl

Kaoru Yamaguchi

Tokyo Gakugei University

The study of brain-injured mentally retarded children was started by Werner and Strauss in 1940, and has been developed by Lehtinen, Kephart, and Cruickshank.

Based on these studies, Cruickshank (1970) cited hyperactivity, distractibility, dissociation, perseveration, and figure-background reversal as the psychological traits of brain-injured children and, as is well known, he took these traits into account in working out special training programs and teaching tools.

The subject in this study was a mentally retarded girl, presumably with a brain injury, as will be described below. No doubt, she had what Cruickshank cited as the psychological traits of the brain-injured child. Then, what is the relation between brain injury and the abovementioned psychological traits?

It seems that the researchers cited see the relation between brain injury and psychological traits as cause and effect. However, in the behavioristic point of view, it is clear that organismic variables stemming from brain injury are no more determinant than other physical, chemical, and social variables related to psychological behavior, even though they play an important role in causing the specified psychological traits.

Cruickshank's special training programs may be said to represent an attempt to change the behavior of brain-injured children by controlling environmental stimuli; similarly, the purpose of our study was to modify the subject's hyperactivity and distractability by applying operant conditioning techniques.

PURPOSE

The purpose of this study was to modify the hyperactive behavior displayed by the subject to the extent that she could carry out a given task as fast as possible, concentrating only on the task.

THE SUBJECT

Tomoko, the subject, was 4 years and 3 months old when this study began. Her mother claimed to have suffered influenza during the fifth and sixth months of pregnancy. After a 10-month pregnancy, the mother gave birth to a 3,100 gm baby at the cost of a rupture of the membranes and inertia uteri.

The baby could lift her head at 5 months, but had difficulty in turning over in bed; started crawling on hands and knees at 11 months; grew teeth at 7 months; began uttering "papa" and "mama" at 12 months; and started walking at 19 months. This information indicates some signs of retardation, in terms of physical and mental development during early infanthood, especially the motor skills.

EEG Reading

An EEG was recorded regularly when the subject was 1 year and 7 months old, 2 years old, 4 years and 9 months, and 6 years and 1 month. The subject showed asymmetry and spike component early. According to the record at the age of 6 years and 1 month, a prominent spike and wave complex appeared frequently when she fell asleep, indicating a case of epilepsy or similar neurological state. She was administered an anticonvulsant by a medical specialist.

Result of IQ Tests

A Tanaka Binet Test (revised, 1954) was conducted at age 4 years and 10 months. The IQ was 64. A Tanaka Binet Test (revised, 1970) was conducted again one year later. The IQ was 63. From the results of the IQ tests and the observation of her daily behavior, it was concluded that she was a mildly retarded child.

Family

The subject came from a middle-class family, consisting of father, mother, and a brother (three years older than the subject).

Problem Behavior

The subject's problem behavior was prominent restlessness and impulsiveness. As shown in Figure 1, she changed the items that she was playing with 15 to 20

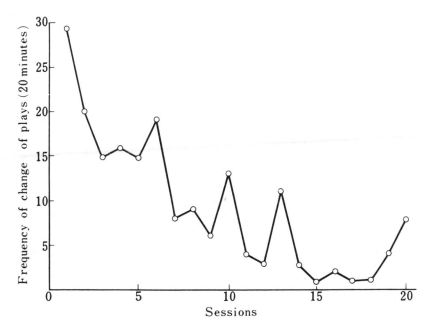

Figure 1   Frequency of change of play activity during 20-min free-play sessions.

times during the 20-min free-play period in a play room in the early stage of the experiment. For example, she stopped at a piano on her way to pick up a ball and tried the piano two or three times, picked up a toy telephone and hardly dialed before she beat the drum, and then started fishing at the next moment.

EXPERIMENT 1

Task

The subject was seated in front of a pegboard containing 100 holes (10 x 10) (see Fig. 2), on which some sheets of drawing paper depicting fish, cars, trains, rabbits, flowers, and crabs (see Fig. 3) were placed, and was asked to put the pegs into the eyes of the fish and the rabbit, the wheels on the car and the train, and so on. The number of the pegs she put into place were counted after a 10-min session. The experimental period lasted approximately four months.

Experimental Setting

Tomoko came to the laboratory twice a week. After playing freely for 20 min in a play room (about 21 m²), she was given a task to do alternately in a play

Figure 2   Peg placement task in Experiment 1.

room (on even-numbered sessions) and in the special training room for brain-injured children (on odd-numbered sessions), with no stimuli other than the task itself.

Reinforcement Procedure

Every time Tomoko finished a task (10 pegs), the teacher put one piece of chewing gum in a transparent container, and after the session was over, she was given the pieces of gum. For further rewards, a plate of chocolate candy and another plate of cookies were also used at a later stage of the experiment.

Observation and Records

The number of pegs put into place and the time required for this task were recorded. The time was 10 min minus the time Tomoko spent on actions other than putting the pegs into place (staying away from the desk or placing her face on the desk).

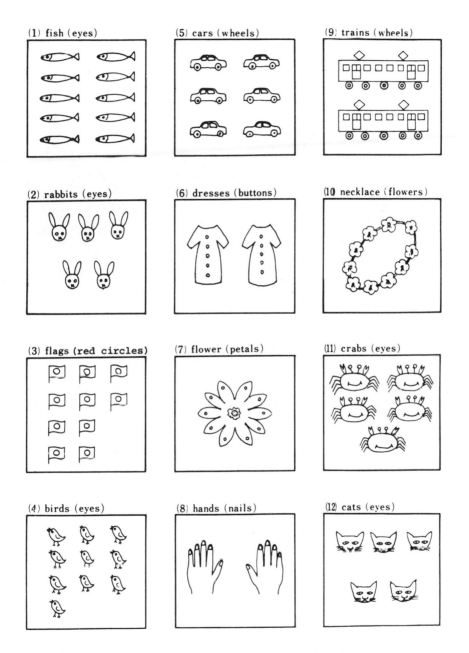

(1) fish (eyes)

(5) cars (wheels)

(9) trains (wheels)

(2) rabbits (eyes)

(6) dresses (buttons)

(10) necklace (flowers)

(3) flags (red circles)

(7) flower (petals)

(11) crabs (eyes)

(4) birds (eyes)

(8) hands (nails)

(12) cats (eyes)

Figure 3   Pictures used in peg placement task in Experiment 1.

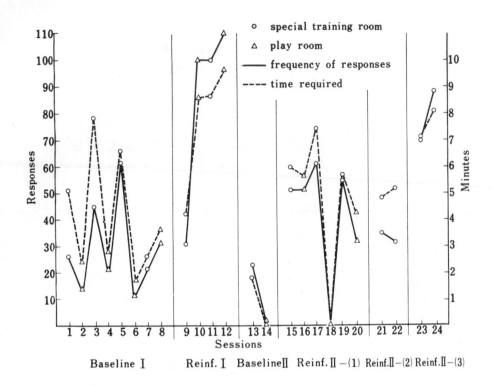

Figure 4   Number of pegs placed and time required for placement as recorded in training room and play room across sessions in Experiment 1.

Results

The results are shown in Figure 4.

In Baseline I, the subject placed 10-30 pegs in the play room, and 20-60 pegs in the special training room.

In Reinforcement I (Sessions 9-12), the score rapidly increased to 100, *100*, and 110. (The italicized numbers indicate the tasks accomplished in the special room).

In Baseline II, the score sharply decreased from *23* to 2. So the Reinforcement II phase was begun.

Reinforcement II was divided into three stages. In Reinforcement II(1) the same procedure was used as in Reinforcement I, and the score changed from *51* to 51, *61*, 0, *55*, and 32. Thus it did not increase as expected. Then a plate of chocolate candy was used as a reinforcer in Reinforcement II(2), and thereafter, the experiment was conducted only in the special room. In Reinforcement II(2), the score remained low at 35 and 32, so the reinforcer was changed again. In

Reinforcement II(3), Tomoko was allowed to choose one of whatever she wanted from chewing gum, chocolate candy, or some other kind of snack, every time she finished a sheet of drawing paper. The scores in Reinforcement II(3) were 70 and 88.

A change was also observed in the time required to accomplish the task. It should be noted that the average time for placing 10 pegs was more than one minute in Baseline I and Reinforcement II(1) and II(2), but was less than one minute in the second and later session of Reinforcement I and in the second session of Reinforcement II(3).

EXPERIMENT 2

Task

The same kind of pegboard was used as in Experiment 1. The subject was asked to fill in the horizontal line of 10 pegs, then move to the second, and so on. The other lines were covered with paper while the first line was being filled, and, after the first line was finished, the second line was revealed.

Experimental Period

The experiment was conducted in the special training room for both the baseline and reinforcement periods, twice a week as a rule (for a total of 29 sessions).

Experimental Setting

During the baseline periods, a 30-min free-play time was followed by a 10-min task in the special training room, whereas during the reinforcement periods, the 30-min free-play time was provided as a reinforcement after the 10-min task.

Reinforcement Procedure

Each time the subject finished a line of 10 pegs, she was given an illustrated card with a verbal "Well done!" (see Fig. 5). The cards depicted in order: (1) a trumpet; (2) a xylophone; (3) a car; (4) a telephone; (5) a box of crayons; (6) playing in the water; (7) a doll; (8) two dolls; (9) doll accessories; and (10) fishing. Judging from observation of free play, these playthings were arranged in reverse order of frequency of use.

The cards were exchanged for the plaything depicted on them during free play after the task. In other words, Tomoko could not use playthings other than those depicted on the cards during free play.

Figure 5   Card depicting playthings to be used during free-play period following task completion in Experiment 2.

Observation and Records

An observer watched through a one-way screen and recorded the number of pegs placed, using specially designed recording paper. The recording was done every ten sec within a 10-min period.

Results

The results are shown in Figure 6. The numbers of the pegs placed in Baseline I decreased from 61 to 52, 12, 25, 5, and 3. In Reinforcement I, the score in the seventh session was 50, but thereafter it stayed high at 92, 92, and 90. In Baseline II, the score sharply dropped to 11 in the second session and thereafter it stayed low at 14 and 2. In Reinforcement II, it rebounded to 80 and 92 and, after declining to 72 and 40, recovered to 92 in the nineteenth session and then stayed high at 90, 86, 92, and 92.

In and after the 24th session, reinforcement with cards was discontinued and only verbal praise was given each time Tomoko finished a line. In these cases, Tomoko was permitted to use any playthings she liked during the free play after the task. The number of pegs placed decreased somewhat from 92 to 86, 62, 82, 59, and 70, but on the whole stayed fairly high.

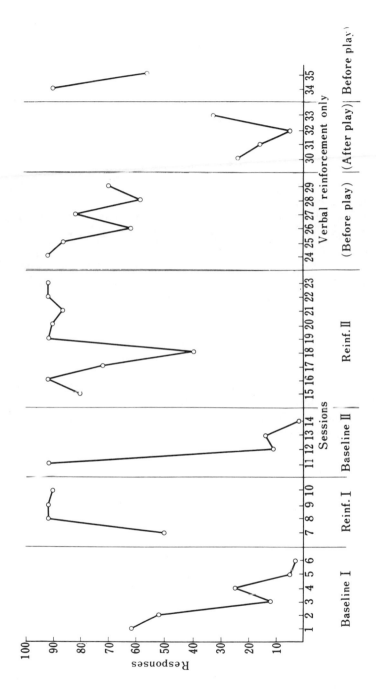

Figure 6   Number of pegs placed across sessions in Experiment 2.

In Sessions 30-33, Tomoko was told to put the pegs into place after a 30-min free-play time, and was given only verbal praise. The number of pegs dropped considerably to 24, 16, 5, and 33. In Sessions 34-35, when free play was provided only after finishing the pegs, the score climbed to 90 and 57.

EXPERIMENT 3

Task

The task of this experiment was a repetition of numbers consisting of three digits. The teacher said three digits at the approximate rate of one per second, and asked Tomoko to repeat them immediately afterward. The teacher picked the three-digit numbers at random from the page numbers of a book with more than 100 pages.

Repetition of three-digit numbers was chosen as the task because it was considered that Tomoko had enough capability to repeat them, and the difficulty of this task always remained at almost the same level (whereas addition and subtraction may change in difficulty as the subject's comprehension advances); thus achievement depended solely on Tomoko's concentration.

Experimental Setting and Conditions

The experimental setting was the same as in Experiment 2. The test was given continuously so long as any part of Tomoko's body touched the chair. When she left the chair, after a 3-min extinction the teacher said, "Sit down and let's try it again, Tomoko." If she refused, the session was discontinued.

The time limit was 30 min. When she finished 100 magnetic buttons within the time limit and had more time to go, she started from the beginning again. In Reinforcement II, however, the session terminated as soon as Tomoko finished 100 buttons.

Any of Tomoko's actions other than the task (opening the curtain or window, or turning off the lamp) were ignored.

Reinforcement Procedure

A paper depicting 10 horizontal rows of 11 squares each was pasted on a steel blackboard. The far left square of each row was painted, the first and second rows were one color, third and fourth another, and so on, with the color changing every 2 rows.

Every time Tomoko repeated a three-digit number (even if it was a wrong number), she was given a button of the same color as the far left square to put it in a square of the same row from right to left. When Tomoko completed one row of ten squares, she could take one of a variety of articles from the corresponding box (a piece of cake, a toy, an illustrated book, etc.) as she pleased. As there were two rows for each color, Tomoko could choose articles twice from the same-colored box.

The first box contained simple articles like seals, and each of the following boxes contained more expensive and attractive articles than the previous box. New articles were replenished for each session. Before each session began, the articles in the box were shown to Tomoko.

Observation and Records

An observer watched and recorded the teacher's stimuli, Tomoko's responses, the teacher's instruction to sit down, and Tomoko's actions in general through a one-way screen, using specially designed recording paper. The recording was done every 10 sec within a 30 min period.

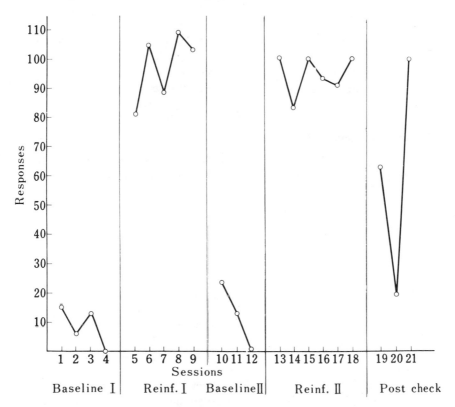

Figure 7   Number of three-digit numbers repeated by subject across sessions in Experiment 3.

Results

Baseline I

Tomoko's responses in Sessions 1-4 in the first baseline were 15, 6, 13, and 0. During this period, she left her chair, leaned on the teacher, picked up the book used for presenting stimuli, and turned off the light. In the fourth session, she refused to enter the learning room.

Reinforcement Period I

Tomoko's responses in Sessions 5 to 9 were 81, 105, 88, 109, and 103. Before Session 5 began, Tomoko was shown what each of the yellow, white, green, red, and blue boxes contained (a seal, some figured paper, a play-doctor kit, plastic dolls, etc.), and was told that she could get any article she liked if she tried hard.

Baseline II

Sessions 10 to 12 in the second baseline were conducted, strictly speaking, under conditions different from the first baseline. Reinforcement by means of toys, etc., was not given in the second baseline, but Tomoko was given a button for each repetition of the number and put it on the blackboard as she did in the first reinforcement period. Tomoko's responses in Sessions 10 to 12 were 24, 13, and 1.

Reinforcement Period II

Each of Sessions 13 to 18 in the second reinforcement period terminated after 100 responses, even if Tomoko still had time left over. Tomoko's responses were 100, 83, 100, 93, and 100.

Generalization

Sessions 19 to 21 were for generalization. There was a rather long interval between Sessions 20 and 21. Tomoko's responses were 62, 20, and 100.

DISCUSSION

In Experiment 1, responses proceeded almost as expected in Baseline I, Reinforcement I, and Baseline II, but did not in Reinforcement II(3), the reinforcer was changed again: this time Tomoko was allowed to choose from a piece of chewing gum, a plate of chocolate candy and a plate of cookies. The result was a substantial increase in rate. The effective functioning of the reinforcer in Reinforcement Periods I and II(3) was also clear from the fact that the average time for putting ten pegs in place was reduced from more than one minute in other sessions to less than one minute. At this point, the school term came to a close, and the teacher had to be replaced; therefore, Experiment 1 had to end.

Tomoko placed more pegs in the special training room than in the play room, showing that she had difficulty with distracting stimuli.

In Experiment 2, rate declined in Baseline I, rapidly rose in Reinforcement I and sharply dropped in Baseline II. Rate peaked at 92 in the first session in Baseline II. The reason may be that the relation between the illustrated cards not being given for peg placing with no free-play period after the task could be "understood" only after the first session.

In Reinforcement II, rate rapidly increased at first, again declined gradually, and then recovered to a high level: in the last two sessions, it reached the peak of 92, indicating effective reinforcement.

In Sessions 24 to 29, reinforcement by means of illustrated cards and playthings was replaced with verbal praise, and rate remained at a fairly high level. This indicates considerable concentration.

The 30-min free play preceded the peg task in the Baseline, whereas it followed the peg placing in the Reinforcement Period (including the verbal praise period). The reason is that the high rate in the praise period may have interacted with the succeeding free play.

To analyze this point, verbal reinforcement was given only after the 30-min free-play period in Sessions 30-33, while in Sessions 34 and 35, free play again preceded the task. The results showed that free play after the task functioned to reinforce the achievement of the task.

The task in Experiment 3 was quite different from that in Experiments 1 and 2. Rate in Baseline I was very low, dropping to zero in Session 4, but it rose sharply in Reinforcement I, dropped rapidly in Baseline II, and increased considerably in Reinforcement II. This shows that the reinforcement was very effective.

In Reinforcement I, repetition started again from the beginning after the first 100 repetitions, but Reinforcement II ended with 100 repetitions. (Perhaps the task should have ended with the first 100 repetitions, for better experimental design.) The use of magnetic buttons in Baseline II constituted a somewhat different condition than Baseline I, and this poses a problem. However, the magnetic buttons probably had little intrinsic reinforcing function, until they were exchanged for playthings. In this sense, the magnetic buttons can be said to have played the role of a token.

In three sessions of generalization, rate reached a higher level than in the baseline, and especially in the last session which was conducted after a long interval, Tomoko accomplished all 100 pegs at the last moment. This indicates that concentration and maintenance of attention to this kind of task had been substantially established.

Throughout the experimental periods, considerable changes in Tomoko's behavior were noted even in free play. In Figure 1, it is seen that Tomoko moved from one type of play to another about 20 times during a 20-min free-play time at an early stage of the experiment, but later she came to be engaged in the same type of play for a longer period. The latter part of the figure shows another increase in the types of play. But it was clear that there was a qualitative change. For example, she caught a fish, washed it in water, roasted and cooked it, and gave it to a bear, which had a stomachache and was rushed to a hospital in an ambulance for an operation. Thus, she began to enjoy consistent, sequenced play, and this trend increased.

Tomoko entered an ordinary day nursery halfway through the experiment period, and later entered a regular class in a primary school.

ACKNOWLEDGMENTS

The author appreciates the help of Mr. Y. Hirai, Ms. K. Abe, Mr. Y. Nitamizu, and Mr. M. Kawamata in this study.

BIBLIOGRAPHY

Bijou, S. W., & Baer, D. M. *Child development I. A systematic and empirical theory.* New York: Appleton-Century-Croft, 1961.

Bijou, S. W., & Baer, D. M. *Child development: readings in experimental analysis.* New York: Appleton-Century-Croft, 1967.

Bijou, S. W., Peterson, R. F., Harris, F. R., Allen, K. E., & Johnson, M. S. Methodology for experimental studies of young children in natural setting. *Psychological Record,* 1969, *19,* 177-210.

Cruickshank, W. M., Bentzen, F. A., Ratzeburg, F. H., & Tannhauser, M. T. *A teaching method for brain-injured and hyperactive children — a demonstration-pilot study.* New York: Syracuse University Press, 1961.

Yamaguchi, K. The application of operant principles to mentally retarded children. In T. Thompson, & W. Dockens (Eds.), *Applications of behavior modification.* New York: Academic Press, 1975.

Part III

NEW ANALYSES OF BEHAVIOR

Setting Events Due to Sidney W. Bijou

A Bibliography of Bijou's Work
in the Area of Analyses of Behavior,
with Self-Evident Function
for the Papers Published Here

Bijou, S. W. Laterality as a clinical problem. *Delaware State Medical Journal*, 1938, *9*, 112-115.

Bijou, S. W. The performance of normal children on the Randall's Island performance series. *Applied Psychology*, 1938, *22*, 186-191.

Bijou, S. W., Stockey, M., & Ainsworth, M. H. The social adjustment of mentally retarded young women paroled from the Wayne County Training School. *American Journal of Mental Deficiency*, 1942, *48*, 442-448.

Bijou, S. W. A study of experimental neurosis in the rat by the conditioned response technique. *Journal of Comparative Psychology*, 1943, *36*, 1-20.

Bijou, S. W. Behavior efficiency as a determining factor in the social adjustment of mentally retarded young men. *Journal of Genetic Psychology*, 1944, *65*, 133-145.

Bijou, S. W., & Kenny, D. T. Ambiguity of pictures and extent of personality factors in fantasy responses. *Journal of Consulting and Clinical Psychology*, 1953, *17*, 283-288.

Bijou, S. W. Patterns of reinforcement and resistance to extinction in young children. *Child Development*, 1957, *28*(1), 47-54.

Bijou, S. W. Operant extinction after fixed-interval schedules with young children. *Journal of Experimental Analysis of Behavior*, 1958, *1*, 25-29.

Orlando, R., & Bijou, S. W. Single and multiple schedules of reinforcement in developmentally retarded children. *Journal of Experimental Analysis of Behavior*, 1960, *4*, 339-348.

Bijou, S. W. Application of operant principles to the teaching of reading, writing and arithmetic to retarded children. *New Frontiers in Special Education*. Council of Exceptional Children, Washington, D.C.: National Education Association, 1965.

Bijou, S. W. Systematic instruction in the attainment of right-left form concepts in young and retarded children. In J. G. Holland & B. F. Skinner (Eds.), *An analysis of the behavioral processes involved in self-instruction with teaching machines* (Research Report, Grant No. 7-31-0370-051, 3). Washington, D.C.: United States Office of Education, Department of Health, Education and Welfare, 1965.

Bijou, S. W., Birnbrauer, J. S., Kidder, J. D., & Tague, C. Programmed instruction as an approach to the teaching of reading, writing, and arithmetic to retarded children. *Psychological Record*, 1966, *16*, 505-522.

Hawkins, R. P., Peterson, R. F., Schweid, E., & Bijou, S. W. Behavior therapy in the home: Amelioration of problem parent-child relations with the parent in a therapeutic role. *Journal of Experimental Child Psychology*, 1966, *4*, 99-107.

Sloane, H. N., Johnston, M. K., & Bijou, S. W. Successive modification of aggressive behavior and aggressive fantasy play by management of contingencies. *Journal of Child Psychology and Psychiatry*, 1967, *8*, 217-226.

Bijou, S. W. Studies in the experimental development of left-right concepts in retarded children using fading techniques. In N. R. Ellis (Ed.), *International review of research in mental retardation* (Vol. 3). New York: Academic Press, 1968. Pp. 66-96.

Peterson, R. F., Cox, M. A., & Bijou, S. W. Training children to work productively in classroom groups. *Exceptional Children*, 1971, *37*, 491-500.

Grimm, J. A., Parsons, J. A., & Bijou, S. W. A technique for minimizing subject-observer looking interactions in field settings. *Journal of Experimental Child Psychology*, 1972, *14*, 500-505.

Grimm, J. A., Bijou, S. W., & Parsons, J. A. A problem-solving model in teaching remedial arithmetic to handicapped young children. *Journal of Abnormal Child Psychology*, 1973, *1*, 26-39.

Bijou, S. W., Morris, E. K., & Parsons, J. A. A PSI course in child development with a procedure for reducing student procrastination. *Journal of Personalized Instruction*, 1976, *1*, 36-40.

23

Teaching Reading Through a Student-Administered Point System[1]

Teodoro Ayllon
Stephen Garber

Georgia State University

In recent years, educators have been faced with the difficult problem of providing individualized instruction for a large number of children performing on different levels within the same classroom. Proposed solutions to this problem have included the use of teaching machines and programmed materials. Such devices are expensive and for the typical teacher whose children do not have access to such resources, other remedies are needed. Alternative solutions to this problem have focused on the use of students to tutor other students and the use of reinforcement procedures.

Of the two alternative solutions, tutoring has had the most widespread application. Numerous "youth tutoring youth" projects have been implemented across the nation, often with encouraging results (Cloward, 1967; Hassinger & Via, 1969). These tutorial programs were designed to remediate individual problems and usually shared three common characterics: (1) a one-to-one ratio of tutors to pupils; (2) use of older students to tutor younger ones; and (3) use of facilities outside of the regular classroom (Hassinger & Via, 1969; Lippitt, 1969; Fox, Lippitt, & Lohman, 1971; Cloward, 1967; Thelen, 1969; Newmark & Melargno, 1971).

The above characteristics limit application of tutorial programs in the classroom. For example, a one-to-one ratio severely limits the number of students who can be helped to the number of available tutors who can be located and trained. Similarly, using older children to teach younger ones presents scheduling

---

[1]A portion of this chapter was presented at the meeting of the Southeastern Psychological Association, New Orleans, 1973.

and management problems for the teachers of both children. Finally, sending students out of their regular classroom to be tutored requires locating, equipping, and financing additional space. In addition, it also creates the problem of generalizing behavior results obtained in these special settings back to the classroom in which the child must ultimately learn to function.

Next to tutoring, token reinforcement procedures have been one of the most widely heralded solutions to classroom problems (Ayllon, Layman & Burke, 1972; O'Leary, Becker, Evans, & Saudargas, 1969; Birnbrauer, Wolf, Kidder, Tague, 1965; Staats & Butterfield, 1965; Wolf, Giles, & Hall, 1968; McLaughlin & Malaby, 1971). Most of these programs have used point systems administered by teachers with the help of aides. The administration of such systems often require the expenditure of considerable time and effort by the teacher. Thus, despite the effectiveness of such systems in increasing academic performance of students, they often take away from teaching time. Also, such systems are most effective in motivating students to perform tasks already within their repertoire. The development of new skills still requires considerable shaping by teachers and when individual instruction is not available, point systems may fail.

The present study represents an attempt to combine tutoring and reinforcement procedures in such a way as to overcome the previously mentioned problems associated with each separately. The disadvantages of teacher-administered reinforcement were minimized by having students administer virtually all aspects of the point system. In an attempt to solve some of the problems connected with tutoring, the tutorial process was brought into the classroom and integrated into the point system. Some aspects of the tutoring such as age of the tutor and number of pupils per tutor were varied to determine the most effective method of improving the academic performance of an entire classroom.

STUDY 1:
GROUP TUTORING ADMINISTERED BY SEVENTH GRADERS

This study was undertaken to determine the feasibility of having students tutor groups of up to five children at one time. The index of tutorial effectiveness used here was the academic performance of the children being tutored.

Setting

The entire study was conducted within a regular second-grade classroom. For several months prior to the present study, children in this class had been earning points for engaging in academically relevant behaviors. These points, which the teacher marked on 3" x 5" cards similar to those developed by Philips (1968), were spent on a number of different items ranging from edibles to special privileges and events.

The regular teacher (who was in her second year of teaching) continued throughout this study to be responsible for teaching the children, and for implementing all additional behavioral procedures.

Subjects

The students to be tutored were 19 second-grade inner city children. The tutors were drawn from a seventh-grade classroom in the same school. These older children were also involved in a point-reinforcement program, in their own classroom.

Procedure

At the beginning of each day, the seventh-grade teacher selected, at random, students to serve as tutors in the second-grade class. Random selection as used here means tutors were chosen on a rotating basis. Both high and low achievers were included in this process. To assure that no seventh graders missed too many of their own classes, students were allowed to tutor only once a week. This was the sole criteria used in the selection of tutors.

On entering the second-grade classroom, the tutors were introduced to the younger children as "assistant teachers" and then were taken to the teacher's desk for at most ten minutes of procedural briefing. During this time, the tutors were assigned tasks and given needed materials. Procedures were explained but no tutor training as such was given.

Previously during reading time, the teacher had worked with one group of students while the rest of the class was allowed to work independently on written or other directed activities. For the purposes of this study, the class was divided into four equal groups of five students each. The desks in each group were arranged in a U-shaped configuration and a chair placed in the mouth of the formation. The teacher then sat with one group while a tutor worked with each of the remaining three groups. (A fourth tutor sat at the teacher's desk and graded papers.) The teacher worked with each child in the group on three dimensions of reading: vocabulary, oral reading, and written work. Each of three tutors was responsible for teaching only one of these dimensions. The teacher set a standard kitchen timer for 20-min periods and at the end of each period, the teacher and tutors rotated one group. There were 4 such periods during the morning, thereby enabling the teacher and the 3 tutors to meet with each of the 4 groups. It usually took the teacher and tutors several minutes to move from one group to the next. During this time the students were allowed to relax. These brief rest periods seemed to be sufficient.

Definition of Academic Performance

Reading was chosen as the subject matter on which the effectiveness of tutoring was measured. The three main dimensions of reading suggested in the teacher's guide of the reading series were selected as the dependent variables. They were defined as:

1. sight vocabulary recognition: the intelligible verbalization of words within 5 sec of the presentation of the stimulus on a 3" x 5" card;
2. oral reading: intelligible reading out loud from the basal reader;
3. written work: filling in the appropriate answers in the workbook accompanying the series.

The first two dimensions were recorded directly by the teacher when she conducted the reading groups. This procedure created little extra work for the teacher even though she was already introducing vocabulary words on cards and having oral reading in these groups. For vocabulary, three new words were introduced each day and two old ones were reviewed, as per the teacher's guide. She recorded on a data pad the number of correct and incorrect responses made by each child to the 5 stimuli. For oral reading, the students read, in turn, an equivalent number of successive pages from the basal reader. When a child could not read a word or completely mispronounced it, the teacher helped the child sound out the word and then marked it as an error on the data pad. This record was kept in such a way that later it was possible to calculate the percent of words each child read correctly on each day. The third dimension, written work, was corrected by another upper-grade student and a percentage of pages correct for each child was computed (percentage of pages correct = number of pages done 70% or more correct/number of pages completed). This 70% criterion was consistent with the level set by the reading series.

Reliability checks were conducted by a research assistant once a week at random on each of the 3 dimensions. On a different day each week the research assistant came without warning into the second-grade class. The assistant sat 5 feet behind the teacher in a position which allowed seeing and hearing the students but not seeing what the teacher marked on the data pad. The assistant and the teacher simultaneously made independent records of the childrens' performance on vocabulary and oral reading. Later the records were compared and the number of agreements was divided by the total number of observations. Reliability averaged 95% for vocabulary and 90% for oral reading. The assistant also randomly selected a page from each child's workbook and checked the correctness of the tutor's grading against the answers in the teacher's guide. Because of the objective nature of these workbook answers, 98% agreement between scoring was obtained.

Tutors' Duties

Tutors were responsible for a wide variety of activities. They handed out and collected all academic materials, kept records of each student's progress, informed students of new assignments, graded all written work, and gave points for academic performance and nondisruptive behavior. Tutors were also in charge of exchanging points for back up reinforcers and running reinforcing activities. In addition to the general duties above, one tutor was assigned to teach each of the three dimensions of reading already defined.

Tutor for vocabulary.   This tutor was given a stack of flash cards containing the three new words for the day plus any previous words given that week by the teacher. These words were taken from the suggested list in the teacher's guide of the series and three new words were added to the cards each day. (This was the prescribed rate of introduction of new words.) The tutor was instructed to flash the cards quickly, giving each child 5 sec to identify the word. Moving clockwise, children were called upon until one responded correctly, and then that child was given one point for the correct answer. All of the children then repeated the answer. They then proceeded to the next word. There was no criticism if a child did not know the answer but rather help was given in sounding out the word.

Tutor for oral reading.   The tutor was given the basal reader for the series and told which pages were to be covered for the day's lesson. Instructions were given to have the students read, in turn, successive pages from the assignment. If a student had trouble with a word, the tutor helped the child sound it out. One point was given for each page read with less than four mistakes.

Tutor for written work.   The second graders received one point for each workbook page done 70% or more correct. Students were allowed to work as many pages or as few pages as they wanted. The tutor helped the children with their workbooks by explaining instructions and teaching principles but not by giving the answers. At the end of each 20-min period the tutor collected the students' work and gave it to the grader. After correcting all student work, the grader went around the room and gave out the points that had been earned.

Experimental Design

Because the students in this study showed extreme deficits in reading skills, a mean of two years below grade level, it seemed superfluous to obtain further data of the children's lack of performance. A baseline, therefore, was obtained with the behavioral procedures in effect. Following the baseline, behavioral procedures were withdrawn and then reinstated thus producing a reversal design. This design resembles the one used by Ayllon and Azrin (1968). In the present study such a design was carried out successively on each of the three dimensions of reading. This meant a reversal was obtained by removing, for a week, and replacing the tutor for a particular dimension. During all phases, points distributed by the teacher, were continued.

Results and Discussion

Group tutoring significantly increased the academic performance of the children being tutored (see Table 1). Whenever group tutoring was used (periods designated as "a"), the children's reading performance was characteristically high. Conversely, when the tutorial method was withdrawn (periods designated as "B"), the children's reading performance dropped significantly.

For example, the average percentage correct for all students on vocabulary decreased from 78.7% to 49.9%. A t-test for repeat measures indicated this difference was highly significant ($p = .01$). A return of tutoring brought the performance back up to 81.2% ($p = .01$). Following week three, there is a downward trend in vocabulary performance, but as can be seen in the table, all

TABLE 1

The Effects of Group Tutoring on the Performance of 19 Children
Across 3 Dimensions of Reading[1] ($N = 19$)

Weeks	1	2	3	4	5	6	7
Vocabulary	a	B	a	a	a	a	a
(%)	78.7	49.9*	81.2	74.2	70.3	71.2	71.5
Oral Reading	a	a	a	B	a	a	a
(%)	73.0	44.7*	71.8	62.6**	73.0	71.5	69.7
Workbooks	a	a	a	a	a	B	a
(%)	77.2	70.7	73.6	89.1	88.0	72.0*	95.0

[1]Group tutoring is designated as "a" and the absence of group tutoring "B"
*p = .01
**p = .05

of the remaining "a" periods are still far above the reversal phase. In addition to these group effects, analysis of individual data indicate 15 students improved more than 20 percentage points (range: 20-65 percentage points). This represents changes of 50 to 100% in performance. Another 3 students showed change in vocabulary scores of 10 to 18 percentage points, or 30%.

In oral reading, the reversal from 71.8% to 62.6% to 73% was less dramatic. Only one student showed a clear reversal of more than 20 points. There was, however, during week two, a most interesting change in this dimension which was reflected in all but one of the students' scores. Apparently the fluctuation in oral reading, from 73% to 44.7% to 71.8% was linked to the reversal in vocabulary and was highly significant (p = .01). Such a relationship between these two dimensions may be explained by the fact that the children's reading passages contained many of the same words taught during vocabulary sessions.

Finally, a clear reversal was obtained in written work. Scores on workbook pages decreased from 88% to 72% (p = .05) and then increased to 95% (p = .01).

In addition to the major findings, the results also indicate group tutoring was more successful on some dimensions than on others. Both vocabulary and written work were improved more than oral reading by tutoring. In fact, the tutoring in vocabulary led to greater increases in oral reading than did tutoring in oral reading itself. This suggests that tutors may be more profitably used in certain simple stimulus-response learning tasks which require presentation of stimulus materials, than in more complex subjects. Concentrating tutors on these simpler tasks can have multiple effects in other areas.

The results of this study also indicate that group tutoring with points can be effective at least in ratios of one tutor to five students. The implications of such a finding are encouraging. First, by using tutoring on a group basis instead of in the usual one-to-one format, the average as well as the poor student can receive help, thus increasing the total number of children helped. Secondly, by including whole classes of children in the tutorial process, the focus of tutoring can include not only simple remediation, but also the maintenance and acceleration of good performance.

While the tutorial system described in this study produced many benefits, at first glance it seems to require a great expenditure of time and effort on the part of the teacher. It is possible that monitoring such a system might distract the teacher from teaching duties and thus prove detrimental.

To determine if such a problem was occurring, a research assistant made daily recordings of the total amount of time the teacher spent in each of three types of activities. Prior to the institution of the tutorial system these recordings revealed the teacher spent 40% of the time grading students papers, 50% managing routine matters of classroom functioning, such as discipline and material disbursement, and only 10% of the time teaching. Once the tutorial program began the proportion of class time the teacher spent teaching increased to 76%. Management time decreased to 25% and grading time, of course, dropped to 0% The interobserver reliability of these observations averaged 93%. These data thus indicate that, rather than detracting from teaching time, the tutorial system actually allowed the teacher to spend more time teaching while releasing her from the responsibilities of more mundane aspects of classroom functioning.

STUDY 2:
GROUP TUTORING ADMINISTERED BY SECOND GRADERS

The results of Study 1 indicated that tutoring may be effective in ratios much larger than one tutor to one tutee. This finding suggests that the efficiency of tutoring must depend on factors other than the nature of the one-to-one relationship. One such factor might be some characteristic of the tutors such as their age. Study 2 therefore undertook to determine if the age of a tutor was related to the academic performance of the students being tutored.

Method

This study was a systematic replication (Sidman, 1960) of Study 1. Briefly, this meant that the children to be tutored, as well as the materials and procedures, were identical to those of the first study. The only change made was the substitution of three second-grade peers for the seventh graders as group tutors. These peer tutors were selected from a number of more advanced second graders in the target class who worked independently and were not part of the regular reading groups.

The design was a simple AB. The A phase consisted of five days during which group tutoring was conducted by seventh graders. In the B phase all tutoring was done by second graders.

Results and Discussion

The results demonstrated that peer tutors were as effective in teaching groups of 5 second-grade students as seventh graders had been in Study 1. The data for each dimension of reading are shown in Table 2. It can be seen that differences in performance under these two types of tutoring range from 1 to 5%. None of these differences are statistically significant and do not indicate the superiority of either group of tutors. The data here were remarkably stable (range: 5-10%) and no trends of either increasing or decreasing performance was noted during this experiment.

The functional equivalency of group tutoring done by students differing in age by five years or more indicates that the efficacy of tutoring may not be dependent upon the age of the tutor. Furthermore, because of the obvious differences in the academic levels of second and seventh graders, it appears that the academic repertoire of the tutor is also not a critical variable in the success of tutoring. Thus, the essence of these procedures seems to be the systematic

TABLE 2

The Effects of Cross-Age Versus Peer Tutors on Reading Performance
of Second Graders (N = 19)

	Seventh-Grade Tutors (in %)	Second-Grade Tutors (in %)	Difference (in %)
Vocabulary	72.2	73.2	+1.0
Oral Reading	76.2	72.2	−4.0
Workbooks	81.8	87.2	+5.4
Mean	76.7	77.5	+1.2

presentation by tutors, of stimulus items and reinforcement for correct responding. Of course the second graders began tutoring only after the seventh graders had been used for some time. It is possible that such initial work by older tutors is necessary for later success of younger tutors. Further research of this question is needed. Still, the results of Study 2 demonstrate that, at least, academically advanced second graders are capable of effectively administering such a point system. Such a finding opens the way for peer tutoring on a group basis by academically advanced students, and thus provides a partial solution to the logistical problems of widespread tutoring in the classroom.

STUDY 3:
INDIVIDUALIZED TUTORING ADMINISTERED
BY SECOND GRADERS

While most students had made good progress in reading during Studies 1 and 2, three students were judged by the teacher to still be deficient in reading. It would appear, then, that while group tutoring may be an effective and inexpensive means of helping the majority of students (85% in this case), there may be some students who will always require other forms of academic assistance. Study 3 was undertaken to explore an intensive means of remediating the academic problems of such students.

In planning such remediation, it was necessary to take into account possible reasons why group tutoring had failed these students. One possibility was that these children possessed low intellectual capabilities such that they could not profit academically. Such labeling of children who do poorly as slow learners is a form of circular reasoning which leads to no constructive alternatives. Another, possibly more constructive, reason for these failures might be that children performing at such low levels of academic performance may not be able to successfully compete for reinforcement in a group situation. Casual observation indicated that tutors confronted with such difficult students often gave up on them and shifted their attention to more promising pupils. In order to rectify this situation and to strengthen the tutors' behavior in dealing with such students, additional procedures were developed in this study, one of which concerned the selection of the peer tutors.

To maximize the motivation of the tutor, a modified form of the one-to-one tutorial method was used. Reinforcement for the tutor was made contingent, not directly on the tutor's activities but rather, on the pupil's success. Only when the pupil met a preestablished criteria of 80% correct, did that tutor receive points. As in Studies 1 and 2, the pupils continued to receive points for their own success. This meant that if a pupil did poorly, neither the pupil nor the tutor received any reinforcement points for their joint efforts.

Subjects

The students to be tutored were three second graders, Stanley, Roderick, and Tanya. While the two boys seemed to be functioning within the normal range of intelligence, Tanya had been near mute all year and psychological testing indicated that she was retarded (IQ = 67). She had never been observed speaking to another child in the class and only occasionally gave even single word answers to the teacher's questions.

In selecting peers as tutors for these children, the question arose as to whether the success of tutoring was limited to the use of tutors who were as academically advanced as in Study 2. In an attempt to explore the feasibility of using peers without restriction to their being advanced students, two second-grade boys were selected, who had been performing in an intermediate range on reading, to tutor Stanley and Roderick. The teacher tutored Tanya.

Definition of Academic Response

In Studies 1 and 2, dependent variables included three dimensions of reading: oral reading, written work, and vocabulary. Because vocabulary recognition was considered by the teacher to be basic to all other reading performance, it was selected as the only dimension to be worked with in Study 3. As in Studies 1 and 2, the teacher continued to record during reading groups both the tutors' and the three subjects' performance in response to the presentation of words on index cards. As in Study 1, a research assistant made weekly reliability checks throughout the study. An average interobserver reliability of 95% was obtained.

Procedure

Each morning before reading period the tutors meet for 20 minutes with their students. During this time they drilled their students on the same words used in reading groups. At the end of this period the teacher tested each student individually on the 5 words for that day. These individual tutorials were provided for each student successively in a multiple baseline fashion.

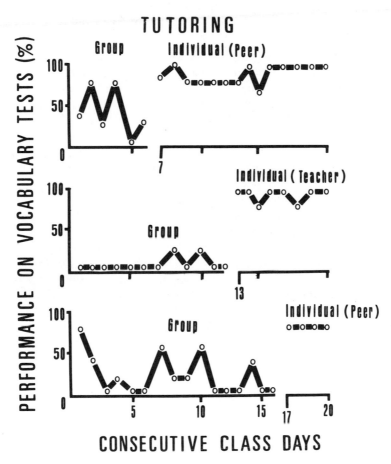

Figure 1   The vocabulary performance (%) of 3 second-grade pupils under 2 types of tutoring procedures (group versus individual). Each point represents both the performance of the pupil in a 20-min session and also the day on which such sessions took place. The gap on each abcissa separates, on a multiple-baseline fashion, periods of group and individual tutoring. The uppermost portion of the figure shows Stanley's performance; the middle segment, Tanya's; and the lower portion, Roderick's.

Results and Discussion

The performance of all three pupils was drastically improved within the first two sessions or 40 minutes of individual tutoring. The vocabulary scores of each tutee before and after receiving special tutoring is shown in Figure 1. Stanley's performance (top graph) increased from an average of 40% correct during baseline to an average of 88.6% during one-to-one tutoring. In systematic replication, Tanya made immediate improvement. under the tutelage of the teacher. Her scores increased from 3% to 95%. Finally, Roderick's performance rose from an average of 21.2% during baseline to a straight 100% as a result of individualized procedures.

Because the tutors and their pupils were working on the same academic materials in the same classroom, it was possible to analyze the effects of this experience on the tutors themselves by comparing their vocabulary scores before and after they became tutors (see Table 3). The vocabulary performance of both peers increased from 20 to 30 percentage points above their initial academic levels.

There are a number of possible explanations for the dramatic improvement made by all three tutees in this study. One possibility is that the additional stimulus presentations provided by the one-to-one tutorial were responsible for the rapid progress made by these children. This contention is supported in that because the pupils in this situation did not have to compete with four other children as in the group tutorial, they received approximately five times as many opportunities to respond. Another explanation for the results of this study is that the tutors were motivated to work more persistently with these problem students. Casual observation indicated that these tutors praised their students more frequently during tutoring and showed greater concern with the results of their pupils' tests. Tutors expressed either great joy or consternation to their students depending on the outcome of these mutually contingent tests.

TABLE 3

Vocabulary Performance of Two Second-Grade Tutors

	Before tutoring another second grader (%)		As a tutor of another second grader (%)		Increase (%)
		Range		Range	
Tutor 1	56.7	(20-100)	85	(80-100)	28.3
Tutor 2	63.7	(5-100)	100	(100)	38.3

In addition to the effectiveness of these procedures in raising the vocabulary performance of the pupils, the data also indicated that the tutors themselves benefited academically from this experience. In fact, one tutor's performance in vocabulary increased 38 percentage points while the other tutor increased 28 points, thereby more than justifying the use of such average students as tutors. These increases in tutor performance are similar to those reported on the high school level by Lippitt (1969). It is worth noting that pairing such children within the same classroom as was done here, has the added advantage of freeing the teacher to concentrate on especially difficult problems such as mute children like Tanya.

SUMMARY AND CONCLUSIONS

Three studies were conducted to examine new ways of solving some of the practical problems which have limited the widespread application of tutoring and reinforcement in the classroom. Study 1 demonstrated that students administering points can effect student performance in ratios of at least one tutor to five pupils. Such a finding extends the range of tutoring beyond the previous limitations of the one-to-one tutorial and makes it feasible to individually reinforce the performance of large numbers of children within the classroom. Study 2 indicated that peer tutors using points can be as academically effective as their cross-age counterparts. The use of peer tutors eliminated the time consuming problems of selecting, training and scheduling cross-age tutors from other classrooms. Finally, in Study 3, contingent peer tutoring on a one-to-one basis was shown to be successful in remediating the problems of severely regressed students who were not helped by group-tutoring procedures. Additionally, this study showed that one-to-one tutoring arrangement benefits the tutors almost as much as their pupils.

Taken together, the results of these three studies suggest a certain sequence of tutorial experiences which the teacher may prescribe to maximize the learning of all students. First, the teacher can use points and tutoring on a group basis to maximize the academic performance of the vast majority of the class. The group procedure is, of course, the most inexpensive form of tutoring in terms of manpower and teacher time and, therefore, should be used first. For those students for whom tutoring on a group basis is not effective, the teacher can then individually prescribe one of several other alternative approaches. For the student who is performing very poorly, the teacher can set up a one-to-one tutorial conducted by a peer. For students doing somewhat better, the teacher can improve their performance by making them tutors, thus helping two children at once as shown in Study 3.

The heavy use of tutors outlined here is in no way intended to suggest that the regular teacher is no longer needed. Rather, this procedure is designed to free the teacher from as many of the routine teaching tasks as is possible, allowing the carrying out of those roles for which only the teacher has the necessary skills. A good example of this is the work done by the teacher in Study 3 with the mute child. Also, it should be noted that all of these procedures added to total teaching time. While such additional instruction might be provided by teaching machines and/or programmed materials, they lack the social fabric within which children experience the joy of learning by helping each other. Thus, the procedures discussed in this chapter might best be viewed as inexpensive means of providing additional instruction for children in a way that enhances both the teacher's and the students' productivity and enjoyment of class time.

ACKNOWLEDGMENTS

This chapter is based on a project supported in part by the Elementary and Secondary Educational Act of 1968 (ESEA) Title 1 and subcontracted by the Atlanta Board of Education to the senior author.

The authors wish to express their deep appreciation to Miss Cindy Kuhlman, the second-grade teacher, who not only effectively carried out all procedures, but also contributed creatively to the design of these studies. Also, a word of thanks is due to Mrs. Libby Skuban, the seventh-grade teacher, for her cooperation in the scheduling of the seventh-grade tutors. Finally, we wish to acknowledge our debts to Dr. Jarvis Barnes, Superintendent, Research and Development for Atlanta Public Schools, and Mr. Milton White, principal of Jesse Mae Jones Elementary School for their cooperation and encouragement throughout this study.

REFERENCES

Ayllon, T., & Azrin, N. *The token economy: A motivational system for therapy and rehabilitation.* New York: Appleton-Century-Crofts, 1968.

Ayllon, T., Layman, P., & Burke, S. Disruptive behavior and reinforcement of academic performance. *Psychological Record,* 1972, *22,* 315-323.

Birnbrauer, J. S., Wolf, M. M., Kidder, J. D., & Tague, C. E. Classroom behavior in retarded pupils with token reinforcement. *Journal of Experimental Child Psychology,* 1965, *2,* 219-235.

Cloward, R. Studies in tutoring. *The Journal of Experimental Education,* 1967, *1,* 14-25.

Fox, R. S., Lippitt, R., & Lohman, J. E. Teaching of social science material in the elementary school. In A. Gartner, M. C. Kohler, & E. Riessman (Eds.), *Children teach children.* New York: Harper & Row, 1971.

Hassinger, J., & Via, M. How much does a tutor learn through teaching reading? *Journal of Secondary Education,* 1969, *44,* 42-44.

Lippitt, P. Children can teach other children. *The Instructor,* 1969, *78,* 41.

McLaughlin, T. F., & Malaby, J. E. Development of procedures for classroom token economies. In E. A. Ramp, & B. L. Hopkins (Eds.), *A new direction for education.* Lawrence, Kansas: University of Kansas, 1971.

Newmark, G., & Melaragno, R. J. Tutorial community project: Report on the first year. In A. Gartner, M. C. Kohler, & E. Riessman (Eds.), *Children teach children.* New York: Harper & Row, 1971.

O'Leary, K. D., Becher, W. C., Evans, M. B., & Saudargas, R. A. A token reinforcement program in a public school: A replication and systematic analysis. *Journal of Applied Behavior Analysis*, 1969, *2*, 3-13.

Phillips, E. L. Achievement place: Token reinforcement procedures in a home-style rehabilitation setting for "pre-delinquent" boys. *Journal of Applied Behavioral Analysis*, 1968, *1*, 213-224.

Sidman, M. *Tactics of scientific research*. New York: Basic Books, 1960.

Staats, A., & Butterfield, W. Treatment of nonreading in a culturally deprived juvenile delinquent: An application of reinforcement principles. *Child Development*, 1965, *36*, 925-942.

Thelen, H. A. Tutoring by students. *The School Review*, 1969, *77*, 229-244.

Wolf, M., Giles, D., & Hall, R. Experiments with token reinforcement in a remedial classroom. *Behavior Research and Therapy*, 1968, *6*, 51-64.

24

State: Effect on Conditioned and Unconditioned Heart Rate Responding in Infants

Yvonne Brackbill

University of Florida

STATE AND UNCONDITIONED RESPONDING

The importance of state in determining unconditioned responding to stimulation is well documented for several response parameters. We know that the organism's state at the time of stimulation influences probability of response evocation (e.g., Wolff, 1966), directionality of response (e.g., Berg, Berg, & Graham, 1971), response latency (e.g., Goff *et al.,* 1966), response magnitude (e.g., Lenard, von Bernuth, & Prechtl, 1968), gradient of generalization of an habituated stimulus (e.g., Apelbaum *et al.,* 1960), and probability of state change in response to stimulation (e.g., Brackbill & Fitzgerald, 1969). The importance of state for response decrement of habituation, however, is one area in which there is more controversy than empirical evidence. ("Habituation" is being used here in the restricted sense of response decrement to an arbitrarily selected, predetermined criterion.) The major question is whether habituation occurs during sleep states or whether, indeed, it occurs at all during any stable state.

Using a variety of psychophysiological measures from adult subjects Johnson and Lubin (1967) concluded that there was no evidence of habituation during any sleep state, although all measures showed habituation when subjects were awake. In later studies, Johnson, Townsend and Wilson (1975) and McDonald and Carpenter (1975) did find some evidence of short-term habituation, though not for all measures or all sleep stages. Using heart rate (HR) and electromyograph (EMG) recordings of limb movements, Hutt *et al.* (1968) found no evidence of habituation in neonates during any of the three states studied: quiet sleep, active sleep, or quiet awake. These authors concluded that habituation is not a real phenomenon but an artifact of state change.

Studying the relation of habituation to state presents many problems not the least of which is that many standard methodological techniques tend to mask habituation. One such technique is to average responses over time as Johnson and Lubin did, or over blocks of trials, as Hutt *et al.* did, rather than analyzing response decrement on a trial-by-trial basis. A second technique masking habituation is that of allowing state to vary in an uncontrolled manner during sessions. As Firth (1973) has pointed out, a sleep state change may in itself precipitate dishabituation, acting as a dishabituating stimulus. Indeed, Johnson and Lubin's own data indicate that this is so. In that study, subjects who habituated while awake showed dishabituation to the same stimulus when asleep. Firth used the alternative strategy of restricting stimulus presentation to one state only during any one session. If the subject's state changed during the session, the session was terminated. Under these conditions in adult subjects Firth found habituation for 14 of his 16 treatment combinations (4 states x 4 psychophysiological variables). A third methodological feature tending to mask habituation is the use of inter-stimulus intervals (ISIs) of constant, unvarying length, as used by Hutt *et al.*, though not by Johnson and Lubin. A constant ISI is by definition the operatioal referent for temporal conditioning — to which infants are for some reason peculiarly prone (Brackbill & Fitzgerald, 1969, p. 205; Fitzgerald & Brackbill, 1976) — a procedure that increases rather than decreases the probability of response evocation.

STATE AND CLASSICALLY CONDITIONED RESPONDING

Whereas the data relating state to unconditioned responding are complicated, those relating state to classically conditioned responding are apparently non-existent[1]. Pavlov noted years ago that somnolence was a predictable side effect of temporal conditioning in dogs. Brackbill, Fitzgerald (1972), and associates observed the same phenomenon recently in temporal conditioning studies with human infants. No systematic studies have followed these casual observations, Neither has the reciprocal problem been studied: the effect of preexisting state on classical conditioning. Indeed, few experimenters have made systematic attempts to control state during classical conditioning, an exception being the recent studies of Porges and associates (Forbes & Porges, 1973; Porges, Stamps, & Walter, 1974).

---

[1]There are two studies of state effects on *operant* conditioning infants (Clifton, Siqueland & Lipsitt, 1972; Papoušek & Bernstein, 1969). There is in addition a study of classical conditioning during sleep in adults (Beh & Barratt, 1965).

PRESENT STUDIES

Present investigations studied the influence of state on conditioned HR-response formation and on response decrement in unconditioned HR responding. Specifically, one study compared rates of conditioned response formation in the same infant subjects under two different states with state controlled during sessions. The second study compared response-decrement rates for unconditioned responding to the same auditory stimuli as used in the first study.

The general expectation was that state would have marked effects on both conditioned and unconditioned responding. Active and quiet sleep states were chosen for study in part because of subject requirements, since neonates spend little time out of these states, and in part because there is more controversy and less empirical evidence about habituation and conditioning during sleep states. The specific expectation was that if active sleep represents a higher level of activation or desynchronization than quiet sleep, it should therefore be less conducive to efficient information processing or simple learning as represented by habituation and conditioning procedures.

EXPERIMENT 1: STATE AND CONDITIONED RESPONDING

Subjects

Subjects were 20 clinically normal, full-term neonates born to mothers whose pregnancies and deliveries had been uncomplicated. All mothers had been delivered under regional or conduction anesthesia; none had received heavy analgesic medication. Ten infants were male and 10 female. No male subject had been circumcised within 24 hours of his first session. Results were not differentially associated with sex of subject or with circumcision status. Median age at time of first testing was 45 hours.

Experimental Procedure

Experimental subjects served as their own control in 2 conditioning sessions separated by a 24-hr interval. During one session the experiment proceeded only when the infant was in quiet sleep (the behavioral equivalent of EEG-referred NREM sleep). Specifically, the procedure began when the infant fell into a quiet sleep state, was interrupted when no longer in that state, and was reinstituted only when returned to a quiet-sleep state. During the other session, the experimental procedure took place only during active sleep (the behavioral equivalent of REM sleep). During sessions conducted in quiet sleep the mean number of interruptions was 1.40; during active sleep sessions, 1.45. State sequence was counterbalanced over subjects and was not differentially associated with conditioning outcome.

The criteria of behavioral state were those developed by Brackbill and Fitzgerald (1969).

[1.] Quiet sleep. The infant's whole body gives the appearance of general muscular relaxation. This is interrupted periodically, however, by brief startles of an apparently spontaneous nature. The infant's eyes are usually closed. Respiration is regular and somewhat slower than in active sleep.

[2.] Active sleep. Characteristic of this state are diffuse movements of relatively frequent occurrence. These movements involve the whole body but are most typically seen in the extremities and in the muscles of the face — in the form of twitches, grimaces, smiling, sucking, and the like. In addition, one can sometimes see conjugate movements of the eyeballs. (As in state 1, the eyelids are usually closed.) Respiration is considerably more irregular and is somewhat faster than in quiet sleep [p. 175].

Judgments of sleep were made concurrently by 2 trained experimenters, who were present at all times. Median interjudge agreement for a pool of 5 such experimenters was .95.

Each session began with a 3-min control period to determine resting heart rate (HR) level. Immediately thereafter, conditioning trials began. Test trials were randomly interspersed among the conditioning trials at a ratio of 1:3. The session ended only when the subject's "cooperation" could no longer be maintained. The number of test trials that could be adminstered ranged from 4 to 13.

Independent and Dependent Variables

The pure tones used to generate stimuli were produced by an EICO Model 377 Audio Generator situated outside the experimental booth in which the infant's crib was placed. The speaker inside the experimental booth was 22 in distant from the subject's head in the horizontal plane. All SPL decibel levels to be reported were measured at the infant's ear by means of a General Radio Company dB meter, scale As.

The CS contained both auditory and temporal components. The temporal component was a fixed-length interstimulus interval of 10 sec between auditory CS offset and UCS onset. The auditory component was a 500 Hz, 75 dB sine wave tone. This frequency and intensity was constant throughout both sessions. The UCS was not constant but changed in accordance with the infant's rate of adaptation to it. Adaptation to the UCS was operationally defined as a change in HR response of less than 10% of resting HR level. Thus, for an infant whose initial resting HR level was 130 bpm, a change of 13 bpm or more was classed as a response, whereas a change of less than 13 bpm was classed as no response, the consequence of which was to use a stronger UCS on the next conditioning trial.

The UCS was always a square-wave tone but differed over trials in other stimulus parameters. Preliminary experimentation had established that unconditioned stimuli could be ranked in terms of their effectiveness for response

TABLE 1

UCS Parameters Ordered by Effectiveness in Response Elicitation

1. 75 dB at 50, 75, 100, 125, 150, 175, or 200 Hz (frequency randomly selected)
2. 80 dB at one of the above Hz values
3. 85 dB at one of the above Hz values
4. 90 dB at one of the above Hz values
5. dB fluctuates between 90 and 75; Hz one of above values
6. At 90 dB, change downward of 50 Hz followed by return to original level; 175, 125, 175 Hz
7. At 90 dB, a change upward of 50 Hz followed by return to original level; 100, 150, 100 Hz
8. At 90 dB, 2 rapid fluctuations in Hz level; 50, 100, 50, 100 Hz

elicitation. This empirically determined rank ordering is shown in Table 1. By way of illustration, the UCS initially used for each subject was a 75 dB tone at 50, 75, 100, 125, 150, 175 or 200 Hz. If the infant responded to this with a 10% or greater change from resting HR level, the second UCS was also a 75 dB tone. However, if the change was less than 10%, the next UCS, 80 dB, was introduced.

During the second session, the UCS parameters of the first day were used unchanged and without regard to response parameters. Thus, each infant received a "customized" set of UCSs on Day 1 and the very same set on Day 2.

The time parameters for stimulus presentation were as follows: duration of CS, 2 sec; CS offset to UCS onset (ISI), 10 sec; duration of UCS, 5 sec; UCS offset to CS onset (ITI), median = 58 sec; range, 46-70 sec. On test trials the UCS was omitted.

Heart rate was recorded by means of miniature Beckman electrodes attached to the top and bottom of the sternum with a ground attached to the left mid-axillary line (V_6 position). Gross motor movement was also measured though not as a true dependent variable since every effort was made to restrict it, as described below. Monitoring was by means of 6 miniature Lafayette Radio VU meters connected in parallel and embedded in the crib mattress. Results were not differentially affected by this variable.

Interbeat interval (IBI), ECG, motor movement, and stimulus events were recorded on a Grass Model 7 Polygraph.

EXPERIMENT 2: STATE AND UNCONDITIONED RESPONDING

Subjects and Experimental Procedure

Subjects were 44 neonates chosen according to the same criteria as used in Experiment 1. Four experimental groups ($N = 11$ in each) were used to assess habituation rate to administration of the CS alone and UCS alone during both sleep states. Specifically, subjects in Group 1 received conditional stimuli during active sleep; subjects in Group 2, conditional stimuli during quiet sleep; subjects in Group 3, unconditioned stimuli during active sleep; and subjects in Group 4, unconditioned stimuli during quiet sleep. Mean numbers of interruptions per session were .50, .60, .54, and .91 for the 4 groups, respectively. All stimulus parameters were the same as those in Experiment 1. (For UCS-only subjects, this required matching on an individual basis for frequency and intensity levels.) The criterion of habituation was a run of 5 consecutive trials on which HR change, regardless of direction, was less than 5% during the 10 poststimulus seconds as compared to the ten prestimulus seconds.

General Procedure

Each session was preceded by feeding, diapering, electrode attachment, and swaddling, in that order. The swaddling material was a 57-g muslin bandage, 10.16cm x 457.30 cm. This was wrapped tightly around the infant's body from neck to toe. Then the infant was placed in a prone position in a crib. The swaddling and prone placement were used to restrict motor movement, to minimize sleep latency, and maximize sleep time (Brackbill, 1971; Brackbill, Douthitt, & West, 1973).

Testing was carried out in a sound-attenuated experimental booth within a private laboratory room in Georgetown University Hospital. Ambient noise level within the booth was 55 dB.

RESULTS

For the data of Experiment 1, heart rate was scored for each second of 2 15-sec periods. One such period, *control,* consisted of the central portion of the ITI, midway between the UCS and the auditory CS that followed it. The other period, *test,* began 5 seconds after auditory CS onset. The central portion of this 15-sec test period consisted of the 5 seconds during which the UCS would have occurred had the test trial been a reinforced trial. The difference between control and test scores is the measure of reference and will be called HR reactivity. It is essentially a refinement of Lang and Hnatiow's (1962) peak-to-valley, or range, measure of HR responding. This measure is useful and appropriate when the focus of interest is responsiveness without regard to directionality (which is generally a problem in infant HR research). Heart rate reactivity was calculated as follows. One standard deviation was calculated for the 15 scores of each control period and another SD calculated for corresponding test period. A median control SD and a median test SD for each subject were submitted to *t*-tests for correlated measures.

There was no significant difference in HR reactivity between control periods for the two sleep states. However, HR reactivity was greater during test periods than during control periods for both sleep states. For quiet sleep this increase was statistically significant. For sessions conducted in quiet sleep, the mean difference in reactivity between test and control periods was .13, SD = .107; $t(19) = 2.97$, $p < .01$. For sessions conducted in active sleep the corresponding difference in reactivity was not significant, $M_D = .080$; SD = .120; $t(19) = .67$. There is evidence, then, that HR conditionability is state dependent.

Scoring and analysis of the data from Experiment 2, which studied unconditioned responding to the auditory stimuli used in Experiment 1 was as follows: the arbitrarily defined criterion of response decrement for the control procedures had been 5 consecutive trials on which HR change, regardless of direction, was less than 5% of prestimulus level. In terms of this criterion, mean number of trials up to and including criterion were 15.09 (to UCS administrations during quiet sleep), 11.36 (to auditory CS during quiet sleep), 28.09 (to UCS during active sleep), 14.27 (to auditory CS during active sleep). By analysis of variance, the main effect of state differences is significant, $F(1, 40) = 6.67$, $p < .05$. These results indicate that unconditioned response decrement is also state dependent.

Directionality of Response

It has recently been found in adult HR conditioning studies that the UCR is predominantly accelerative whereas the CR is predominantly decelerative or multiphasic. The present data were examined to see if the same phenomenon might occur even in infant HR conditioning. Response to the UCS was determined for the conditioning subjects of Experiment 1 by comparing the shortest IBIs and longest IBIs that occurred in the 15-sec control period described above and the 15-sec period following UCS onset. Test trials were scored in the same manner. The definition of an acceleration or deceleration was a change of 5% or more in the appropriate direction from control period to UCS or test period.

The results, as shown in Table 2, indicate that for infants the relative predominance of acceleration as compared to deceleration is greater for unconditioned responding than for conditional responding. An analysis of variance for repeated measures (Dorn, Bartko, & Pettigrew, Noto 1) was performed on the acceleration/deceleration data. (Biphasic data were omitted for statistical reasons.) For the main effect of type of trial (reinforced or test), $F(1, 20) = 55.02$, $p < .001$, indicating that the direction of the HR response is much more frequently accelerative in response to the UCS than in response to the anticipation of it. This is hardly surprising, since an auditory stimulus serving as UCS is chosen for its noxious characteristics, and the response may simply be considered to be a defense reflex. The nonsignificance of state as a main effect,

$F \langle 1.0$, can be interpreted from the same perspective: As the noxious quality of the stimulus increases, the organism's response to it becomes less dependent on state.

In summary, results of the present studies show that under experimental conditions in which state is controlled: (1) response decrement does occur in a stable state; (2) response decrement and simple classical conditioning can and do occur during sleep states; (3) rate of decrement and conditionability are different for active and quiet sleep states; and (4) noxious stimuli, in contrast to neutral stimuli, decrease state differences for response decrement and increase defensive reflexes (HR acceleration) in conditioning.

DISCUSSION

Results of both experiments show that the same stimulus has different effects according to the subject's background level of psychophysiological functioning at the time of stimulus administration. Stated differently, present results demonstrate that state-dependent response differences occur to both unconditioned and conditional stimuli. Specifically, they show that responsiveness to unconditional stimuli. Specifically, they show that responsiveness to unconditioned auditory stimuli, in terms of resistance to habituation, is greater in active sleep than in quiet sleep, whereas responsiveness to conditional stimuli, in terms of probability of CR evocation is greater in quiet sleep than in active sleep. This might seem contradictory, but the apparent discrepancy disappears if one conceives of response decrement/habituation as a simple form of learning or

TABLE 2

Directionality of HR Response on Reinforced and Test Trials

		UCRs* (%)	CRs** (%)
Quiet Sleep	Acceleratory	76.38	56.00
	Deceleratory	16.56	29.60
	Biphasic	7.00	14.40
Active Sleep	Acceleratory	66.96	52.35
	Deceleratory	25.22	38.24
	Biphasic	7.83	9.41

*Reinforced trials.
**Test trials.

information processing. In classical conditioning, experimental operations convey to the organism that the CS must be attended to because something of consequence follows it. In the response decrement/habituation situation, the organism learns that the stimulus must be blocked out of attention because it is functionally inconsequential. The difference in the two situations is that in one the organism learns to respond whereas in the other the organism learns to inhibit responding. Basically, both involve the accurate, orderly processing of information from external stimuli, and both proceed more efficaciously during quiet sleep than during active sleep.

The extent to which this generalization need be limited to the major parameters of this study — response decrement, simple classical conditioning, auditory stimuli, and HR responses — will be indicated by future research. Certainly the literature already extant on state and unconditioned responding suggests that there is no single, overall theoretical statement that will accomodate all empirical results. Rather, results depend on the function measured, on the characteristics of the stimulus, and on the nature of the response. There is, for example, no reason to suppose that other measurable response functions (latency, amplitude, etc.) should be highly predictable from habituation data. Indeed, considering just the single function, response decrement, current generalizations need qualification in terms of both stimulus and response characteristics. For example, with respect to stimulus characteristics, Wolff (1966) has shown that although probability of response to auditory and tactile stimuli is higher in active sleep than in quiet sleep, probability of response to vestibular stimuli is higher in quiet sleep than in active sleep. Further, to the extent that a stimulus loses its neutral characteristics and assumes instead noxious characteristics, so does it lose its dependence on state (Wolff, 1966; this study). The same dissociation holds with respect to the interaction of state and type of response. Johnson and Lubin (1967) found that the magnitude of dishabituation differed for the six psychophysiological measures they used, that magnitude of dishabituation was not predictable from one measure to the next.

The prospect that stimulus specificity and response specificity are more the rule than the exception has already been pointed out by Lacey (1967). Future research in this area may find studies of conditions under which such dissociation increases or decreases the more productive approach than the attempt to formulate unqualified generalizations.

ACKNOWLEDGMENTS

This investigation was supported in part by Research Scientist Award No. MH 5925 from the National Institute of Mental Health and in part by NSF Research Grant No. GB 15155 to the author.

REFERENCES

Apelbaum, J., Silva, E. E., Frick, O., & Segundo, J. P. Specificity and biasing of arousal reaction habituation. *Electroencephalography and Clinical Neurophysiology*, 1960, *12*, 829-839.

Beh, H. C., & Barratt, P. E. H. Discrimination and conditioning during sleep as indicated by the electroencephalogram. *Science*, 1965, *147*, 1470-1471.

Berg, K. M., Berg, W. K., & Graham, F. K. Infant heart rate response as a function of stimulus and state. *Psychophysiology*, 1971, *8*, 30-44.

Brackbill, Y. The cumulative effects of continuous stimulation on arousal level in infants. *Child Development*, 1971, *42*, 17-26.

Brackbill, Y., Douthitt, T. C., & West, H. Psychophysiological effects in the neonate of prone vs. supine placement. *Journal of Pediatrics*, 1973, *82*, 82-84.

Brackbill, Y., & Fitzgerald, H. Development of sensory analyzers during infancy. In L. P. Lipsitt, & H. Reese (Eds.), *Advances in child development and behavior* (Vol. 4). New York: Academic Press, 1969.

Brackbill, Y., & Fitzgerald, H. Stereotype temporal conditioning in infants. *Psychophysiology*, 1972, *9*, 569-577.

Clifton, R., Siqueland, E. R., & Lipsitt, L. P. Conditioned headturning in human newborns as a function of conditoned response requirements and states of wakefulness. *Journal of Experimental Child Psychology*, 1972, *13*, 43-57.

Dorn, K. L., Bartko, J. J., & Pettigrew, K. B. Analysis of variance with repeated measures. Unpublished computer program, Bethesda, Maryland: National Institutes of Health, 1969.

Firth, H. Habituation during sleep. *Psychophysiology*, 1973, *10*, 43-51.

Fitzgerald, H. E., & Brackbill, Y. Classical conditioning in infancy: Development and constraints. *Psychological Bulletin*, 1976, *83*, 353-376.

Forbes, E. J., & Porges, S. W. Heart rate classical conditioning with a noxious auditory stimulus in human newborns. *Psychophysiology*, 1973, *10*, 192-193. (Abstract)

Goff, W. R., Allison, T., Shapiro, A., & Rosner, B. S. Cerebral somatosensory responses evoked during sleep in man. *Electroencephalography and Clinical Neurophysiology*, 1966, *21*, 1-9.

Hutt, C., von Bernuth, H., Lenard, H. G., Hutt, S. J., & Prechtl, H. F. R. Habituation in relation to state in the human neonate. *Nature*, 1968, *220*, 618-620.

Johnson, L. C., & Lubin, A. The orienting reflex during waking and sleeping. *Electroencephalography and Clinical Neurophysiology*, 1967, *22*, 11-21.

Johnson, L. C., Townsend, R. E., & Wilson, M. R. Habituation during sleeping and waking. *Psychophysiology*, 1975, *12*, 574-584.

Lacey, J. I. Somatic response patterning and stress: Some revisions of activation theory. In M. H. Appley & R. Trumbull (Eds.), *Psychological stress: Issues in research*. New York: Appleton-Century-Crofts, 1967.

Lang, P. J., & Hnatiow, M. Stimulus repetition and the heart rate response. *Journal of Comparative and Physiological Psychology*, 1962, *55*, 781-785.

Lenard, H. G., von Bernuth, H., & Prechtl, H. F. R. Reflexes and their relationship to behavioral state in the newborn. *Acta Paediatrica Scandinavica*, 1968, *57*, 177-185.

McDonald, D. G., & Carpenter, F. A. Habituation of the orienting response in sleep. *Psychophysiology*, 1975, *12*, 618-623.

Papoušek, H., & Bernstein, P. The functions of conditioning stimulation in human neonates and infants. In J. A. Ambrose (Ed.), *Stimulation in early infancy*. New York: Academic Press, 1969.

Porges, S. W., Stamps, L. E., & Walter, G. F. Heart rate variability and newborn heart rate responses to illumination change. *Developmental Psychology*, 1974, *10*, 507-513.

Wolff, P. H. The causes, controls, and organization of behavior in the neonate. *Psychological Issues*, 1966, *5*, 1-93.

25

Imitation and Variation in Working Language

Betty Hart

University of Kansas

Almost the only factor in language acquisition upon which both linguists and behaviorists can agree is the human's ability to generalize. Guess and Baer (1973) note that "in view of the size of the behavioral repertoire . . . some such . . . self-generating approach is essential" [p. 8]; McNeill (1970), states that "somehow linguistic abstractions are . . . developed by children" [p. 152]. After this point major differences concerning how language is acquired result from the differing aims and methods of theory construction in the two fields. Behaviorism is potentially committed to an inductive approach to construction of a theory of the development of language performance, while linguistics is concerned with constructing a deductive theory of the development of language competence (Chomsky, 1965). "Theories of performance and competence . . . deal with different topics" [McNeill, 1970, p. 146]. Problems arise, as the linguistic literature makes apparent, because a theory of competence must be based on, and supported by, data from language performance. While explicitly denying the relevance of environmental variables to the development of language competence (McNeill, 1970, p. 46), linguists continually encounter their influence in performance-based data, and attempt to relate such performance variables to the development of competence. This problem does not arise for behaviorists, who are not concerned with what a child "knows" about language, but only with the "production and organization of spoken language" [Guess & Baer, 1973, p. 9], with the development of "working language" (Hart & Risley, 1974). This concern with working language restricts the area of investigation within the topic, performance, to examination of how a child's language production interacts with its environment in ways which lead to increases in the rate and complexity of that production.

Perhaps because of this pragmatic bias, most of the behavioral research on working language has been conducted in a context of remediation, and has emphasized the most essential component of working language, *rate*. Imitation has been shown by this research to be a basic process in the establishment of rate, whether of an initial repertoire (Lovaas, 1966; Sherman, 1965) or of functional rather than deviant speech patterns (Risley & Wolf, 1967). Even after a rate of working language has been established, imitation remains an essential process in the continued development of working language, as the studies cited above and a great many others have shown. Only through their ability to copy the language models presented by their environment can children learn, at the very least, appropriate labels. Children's ability to imitate is essential to the process described by Hart & Risley (1975) as incidental teaching. The incidental teaching process is a child-initiated instructional interaction, initiated by the child with a request which specifies a potential reinforcer, whether a material object, adult assistance, or information. Children employ working language to operate on their environment: "Give me that, " Tell him to stop, " or, "What's that?" The adult responds with language for children to imitate, as "It's an elephant. Can you say that?" or "*You* need to tell him to stop. I'll help you," or with a prompt directed at bringing more working language into use by children as, "What do you think it is?" or "You need to tell me what you want. What is that?" As well as using children's initiations to instruct or to elicit the working use of language, the adult arranges the environment in ways which will prompt children to initiate incidental teaching interactions. Adults arrange the availability of objects and events so that children must work with language in order to obtain them; arranging the availability of their attention as a stimulus for language from the child; and arranging experiences designed to elicit questions and comments. These interactions of mutual prompting and responding by children and adults are cumulative, as children acquire more sophisticated ways of working with language in order to prompt more sophisticated instructional interactions with their environment.

Incidental teaching, then, describes a specific child-initiated instructional interaction in which the adult is deliberately attending to the content or form of a child's language. Like imitation, it is only one among many processes which must contribute to the development of working language. No present-day investigator will disagree with McNeill's (1970) contention that imitation *alone* cannot account for the structural complexity which appears in a child's working language between the ages of 28 and 36 months. All will recognize Brown's (1968) observation that (in nonincidental teaching interactions) parental response is differential to the truth-value of a child's statement rather than its grammatical form. The search for other processes in the development of working language continues because contemporary society is not content with nature but seeks to nurture. For example, Shuy (1970), says, "One of the clear products of almost all research in American urban sociolinguistics is that the major task of the English teacher is not just to teach pupils their own language . . .; (rather), speakers must be helped to use several different social dialects (or parts of these dialects) on different occasions" [p. 346]. When "use" is taken as the key word in this statement, the provision of such help would appear to necessitate a technology for either teaching young children how to discriminate very subtle dimensions of language for imitation (those parts of dialects which are appropriate and those which are not in a specific context), or teaching them how to use working language in order to prompt differential environmental responses, or both. The fact that in the absence of contingencies children do not readily discriminate subtle dimensions of language for imitation, however, has been shown by Cazden (1965) and Feldman and Rodgon (1970; both studies found that no marked changes in children's language resulted from either adult modeling or adult expansion of children's sentences). In McNeill's (1966, p. 69) example of a mother's efforts to correct her child's, "Nobody don't like me," the modeling might have been more effective had it been undertaken in a child-initiated incidental teaching interaction; however, the example is apt of the general imperviousness to adult models of the structures within children's spontaneous speech. Through some process, though, children do acquire in working language sophisticated syntactic and dialectic constructions which are neither explicitly presented for imitation nor differentially responded to by listeners. Compelling evidence that environmental factors are involved in any such process, and that something more than innate ability to discriminate and generalize is at work, may be seen in any preschool class. By the age of four or five, when organization of syntax is largely complete, the individual differences in working language observable within a group homogeneous in terms of age, IQ, and social class, are fully as great or greater than the much-researched differences in language across social classes (Williams, 1970). Below are presented some examples of individual differences in the acquisition of a syntactic structure, and some speculations concerning environmental influences involved.

In the Hart and Risley (1975) study, the incidental teaching process was employed to establish and increase four-and-a-half-year-old black children's use in working language of a specific syntactic structure, a compound sentence consisting of 2 independent clauses coordinated by the conjunction "so." For only 4 of the 11 children had an observer recorded use of "so" as a conjunction during the 2 months of preschool preceeding experimental application of the incidental teaching process. When incidental teaching of compound sentences was begun, the instructional interaction initiated by a child who asked a teacher for a play material was used to prompt a compound sentence. The teacher asked the child to describe why the material was wanted, and presented a sentence for imitation, "Say, 'I want a block so I can play with it' ". At this point, and during the first two weeks of incidental teaching of compound sentences, teachers responded differentially to only 2 components in any child's sentence: the noun in the initial clause which specified the material the child wanted, and the presence of the coordinating conjunction "so." Beginning in the third week of the procedure, however, teachers asked children to state "the real reason" for requesting a play material, a "reason" more descriptive of how the material was to be used than the word "play." Thus teachers began responding differentially to three components in any child's sentence: the noun in the initial clause which specified the material the child wanted, the presence of the conjunction "so," and the fact that the verb in the second clause was other than "play." In the first two weeks of the procedure, then, children could meet all teacher requirements, and obtain any preschool material, with, in their working language, only 2 variations on the specified compound sentence: "I want [new noun never recorded previously in a compound sentence] so I can play with it," and "I want [repeat of a noun previously recorded in a compound sentence] so I can play with it." After the third week, children could meet all teacher requirements and obtain any preschool material with, in their working language, a total of 6 variations on the specified compound sentence: the two variations described above plus, "I want [new noun] so I can [new verb] [with it – optional]," "I want [repeated noun] so I can [repeated verb other than "play"]," "I want [repeated noun] so I can [new verb]," and "I want [new noun] so I can [repeated verb other than "play"]." In fact, however, the children produced 22 additional variations of the specified compound sentence, by producing each of the 6 variations described above in combination with variation of the initial "I want" (as, "Give me," "Can I have," "I need," "Put a") with or without addition of a noun (new or repeated) after the verb in the second, reason, clause. That is, though any child could have obtained a trike throughout the entire incidental teaching procedure by saying, "I want a trike so I can ride it," the children also said, "Can I have a little blue trike so I can ride it on the sidewalk?" Twenty-seven of these 28 possible variations on the specified compound sentence were produced by 1-10 of the children within their first 100 recorded compound sentences.

Figure 1 shows for each child the occurrence of each variation on the specified compound sentence (dotted line) plotted cumulatively against cumulative production of the child's first 100 compound sentences (solid line) after introduction of the incidental teaching of compound sentences in the third month of preschool. The children are numbered according to their ranking in terms of total recorded sentences across the school year (Child 1 produced the most sentences, Child 11 the fewest). The data are from the same source as those shown in Hart and Risley (1975): the observer-recorded 15-min daily samples of each child's spontaneous speech during free play. (In that study, also, the measurement procedures and the experimental manipulations and their effects, are described in detail.) In Figure 1 it may be seen that by the time 100 compound sentences had been recorded for any child in the group, 10 or more (mean, 14) variations of the specified compound sentence structure had also been recorded for that child. Among the first 100 compound sentences, then, each child produced spontaneous structural variations which were neither prompted, nor in all probability even attended to, by teachers. Like the basic compound sentence,

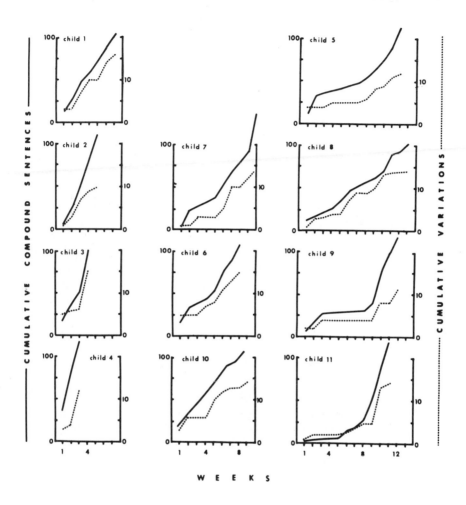

Figure 1   Occurrence of each variation on the specified compound sentence (dotted line) plotted cumulatively against cumulative production of child's first 100 compound sentences (solid line).

though, the variation was reinforced if the language produced the material sought by the child. The production of variation in this aspect of working language is similar across children; its timing, however, is not. The clear correlation seen in Figure 1 between production of syntactic variation and overall rate of sentence production is hardly surprising. What bears accounting for is why the variations appeared at all, especially in the cases of Child 9 and Child 11, children for whom a compound sentence had never been recorded prior to incidental teaching, and who had been present while hundreds of stereotyped compound sentences were modeled by other children and reinforced by teachers.

Why spontaneous syntactic variation occurs has also been questioned by McNeill (1966) in terms of why children abandon the simplicity of holophrastic utterances for the "contraptions of English syntax": "From a strictly functional point of view, there would seem little reason for child language to change" [p. 63]. His explanation is an innate faculté de langage; just as tenable in terms of supporting data is the view that the grammatical play observed by Weir (1962) and others in young children is indication that general stimulus change is a reinforcing event (Bijou & Baer, 1965). The only aspect of the occurrence of spontaneous syntactic variation which may be presently accounted for, then, is that it is somehow correlated with rate in working language. Once syntactic variation has occurred in working language, however, it may be maintained by accidental reinforcement. Instances are numerous, in the observer records from which the present data are drawn, of a child repeating an identical compound sentence several times, and then a single, terminal variation which, one may assume, was followed by delivery of the material requested. Syntactic variation might thus be superstitiously maintained in a child who failed to discriminate the precise dimensions of language necessary to produce a given environmental response: the very fact that language repetitions went unreinforced could become a stimulus for production of a variation. A child who could discriminate the precise dimensions of syntax necessary to reinforcement, then, would be more likely to cease producing variations (Child 2, for instance). In any case, the occurrence of frequent spontaneous variation in children's working language could create those conditions in which environmental response to gross dimensions of that language (as parental response in terms of truth-value alone) would serve to help children discriminate those syntactic features which may vary, and those which may not, in order for communication to be achieved. Children could learn, through prompting environmental response with many variations, the precise combinations and dimensions in language which work, and those which do not. Eventually they might learn which dimensions of language work better than others to produce a specific response in a specific social context. Learning to discriminate those features of working language which are functionally related to production of specific environmental consequences could have a decided influence on how children realize grammar in working language; differences in environmental opportunities to work with language, both in terms of prompting incidental teaching interactions and in terms of displaying language in order to discriminate the relative effectiveness of its structural components, could create large individual differences in children's abilities to use language.

The spontaneous production of language variants as a basis for discriminating those elements of structure which are functional in producing environmental consequences may thus be a naturally occurring child-initiated process similar to incidental teaching. Only further research can confirm it as process and, if so, incorporate it into a technology for the development of working language. Until that time, the implications parallel and support those of the incidental teaching process: rather than an environment in which adults work with language, presenting models, expansions, elaborations and corrections in order that children's language may be worked upon, children need an environment in which they themselves work with language, and above all, an environment in which their language works.

REFERENCES

Bijou, S. W., & Baer, D. M. *Child development* (Vol. 2). New York: Appleton-Century-Crofts, 1965.

Brown, R. Derivational complexity and the order of acquisition in child speech. Carnegie-Mellon Conference on Cognitive Processes, 1968.

Cazden, C. Environmental assistance to the child's acquisition of grammar. Unpublished doctoral dissertation, Harvard University, 1965.

Chomsky, N. A. *Aspects of the theory of syntax.* Cambridge, Mass.: M.I.T. Press, 1965.

Feldman, C. F., & Rodgon, M. The effects of various types of adult responses in the syntactic acquisition of two to three-year-olds. Unpublished paper, University of Chicago, 1970.

Guess, D., & Baer, D. M. Some experimental analyses of linguistic development in institutionalized retarded children. In B. B. Lahey (Ed.), *The modification of language behavior.* Springfield, Ill.: C. C. Thomas, 1973.

Hart, B., & Risley, T. R. Community-based language training. PCMR Conference on Early Intervention with High Risk Infants and Young Children, 1974.

Hart, B., & Risley, T. R. Incidental teaching of language in the preschool. *Journal of Applied Behavior Analysis,* 1975, *8,* 411-420.

Lovaas, O. I. A program for the establishment of speech in psychotic children. In J. K. Wing (Ed.), *Childhood autism.* Oxford: Pergamon Press, 1966.

McNeill, D. Developmental psycholinguistics. In F. Smith & G. A. Miller (Eds.), *The genesis of language.* Cambridge, Mass.: M.I.T. Press, 1966.

McNeill, D. *The acquisition of language.* New York: Harper & Row, 1970.

Risley, T., & Wolf, M. Establishing functional speech in echolalic children, *Behavior Research and Therapy,* 1967, *5,* 73-78.

Sherman, J. A. Use of reinforcement and imitation to reinstate verbal behavior in mute psychotics. *Journal of Abnormal Psychology,* 1965, *70,* 155-164.

Shuy, R. W. The sociolinguists and urban language problems. In F. Williams (Ed.), *Language and poverty.* Chicago: Markham, 1970.

Weir, R. *Language in the crib.* The Hague: Mouton, 1962.

Williams, F. Language, attitude and social change. In F. Williams (Ed.), *Language and poverty.* Chicago: Markham, 1970.

26

The Training of Creativity as an Operant and an Examination of Its Generalization Characteristics

Jacqueline Holman
Elizabeth M. Goetz
Donald M. Baer

University of Kansas

There is quite a reasonable ambivalence toward the experimental study of any highly valued but largely subjective aspect of human behavior: its value dictates a resistance to any analysis which will make the behavior seem ordinary, routine, or within anyone's grasp; its subjectivity allows any tentative analysis to be rejected as having missed the point and/or the "true" behavior. This ambivalence is perhaps nowhere more pronounced than in the case of human creativity (Skinner, 1953, p. 256). Creative experience is often described as personal and private, to the point of becoming avowedly mystical (Moustakas, 1967, p. 27, 32). On the other hand, the fundamental humanistic importance ascribed to creativity implies that any psychology which did not treat its nature would be correspondingly incomplete (Hogg, 1969). This latter consideration seems to be the more compelling one: creativity has steadily attracted psychological analysis and continues to do so. Nevertheless, the need to analyze the concept has not obviated the problems intrinsic in its subjectivity, and in consequence present analyses are diverse, sometimes contradictory, frequently tangential, and always subject to rejection as irrelevant. Even so, an applied analysis may still be worth the effort. There may well be a number of highly desirable behavioral targets to be delineated within the creativity context, even if they are not universally accepted as the true or complete essence of creativity.

In its simplest form, the psychological analysis of creativity consists of testimonials. A person whose creativity is presumably manifest testifies to its nature, function, and etiology (Vernon, 1970, Part 2, pp. 55-88, comments by Mozart,

Tchaikovsky, Spender, and Poincare). If testimonials are not considered convincing evidence (Ghiselin, 1952), the logic and methods of quantitative research can be consulted. In that context, the central problem is the identification of tests, samples, or examples of creative people or creative behavior (Shapiro, 1968). For, once identified, the methods of psychological research will immediately permit the testing of hypotheses concerning the correlates of creativity and any environmental conditions which may control its occurrence[1]. Two basic approaches can be discerned. One is a logical derivative of the testimonial technique: creative individuals are identified, not by themselves, but by disinterested judges; then correlates of these individuals are sought which may discriminate them from other, not so creative individuals (Roe, 1952). Those correlates, it is hoped, may offer the beginnings of an explanation of these individuals' creativity (their distinctive early childhood experiences, or their current philosophical beliefs, or their special methods of viewing the world)[2]. An alternative approach nominates not creative individuals but creative *behaviors*. Having done so, it can proceed similarly to discover correlates of those behaviors which will have explanatory or predictive value (Barron, 1965; Getzels & Jackson, 1963; Stein & Heinze, 1960, pp. 262-341); and, significantly, it can *also* examine environmental conditions which may control the existence, magnitude, or rates of these behaviors.

Of necessity, realization of this potential must proceed first by nomination of some response class as a case in point of creative behavior. An examination of the literature published in this area establishes clearly that no single response class enjoys undoubted agreement as an exemplar of creativity[3] (Stein & Heinze,

[1]But in doing so, as much controversy will be generated as precision gained. Gardner (1973), for example, reviewing the results of this approach, argued: "Research paradigms tend to be artificial, verbal responses are uncritically demanded and accepted, choices are forced, and intricate processes are modeled in tasks lasting but a few moments [p. 18]." A heavily subjective concept reduced to an operational definition will always be vulnerable to attack as artificial, uncritical, forced, and trivial. However, the attack itself may be equally vulnerable to characterization as useless, if it does not pose a better method of study.

[2]For example, Stein (1953) suggested that creative individuals have a special sensitivity for perceiving the gaps existent in their culture, which they respond to with either criticism or attempts at closure.

[3]Taylor (1964) noted that ". . . the problem of the criteria of creativity – perhaps the most crucial problem in this field – has been studied less than any other aspect of our total problem" [p. 9]. But he also stated a behavioral caution: ". . . the criterion problem concerns the evaluation of . . . a product or a performance; it is quite separate from the prediction problem, in which the creative potential of people is estimated" [p. 9]. Shapiro's (1968) discussion of some possibly relevant products (or performances) denoting creative scientific research, cited as examples those that were new, or demonstrated obvious "intellectual activity," or required experimentation after previous failures and in the face of audience scepticism, or were "useful" (McPherson, 1963); those found surprising by their audience (producing a "shock of recognition") (Bruner, 1962, p. 3); those introducing "some new element of meaning or . . . significance" (Ghiselin, 1963, p. 42); those that were diverse (Brogden & Sprecher, 1964); and those that were serendipitous.

1960, for an annotated bibliography of the diverse definitions making up this field). Nevertheless, certain logical themes recur often which seem particularly meaningful (relative to others), and lend themselves to behavioral definition. One such theme is novelty, originality, or uniqueness — the *newness* of a behavior. Such newness is of course relative. Behavior may be considered new because it is the first solution of some problem (Roe's 1952 studies of scientists), or in terms of the culture in which it is displayed (Stein, 1953), or in the terms of the current audience reacting to it (Berlyne, 1960; Freud, 1920, pp. 326-327), or relative to a sample of the individual's peers (Maltzman, 1960), or relative to the behavior previously emitted by the individual (Pryor, Haag, & O'Reilly, 1969; Goetz & Baer, 1973). For an applied analysis, this last approach may well be the most useful. If children can be taught systematically to generate behaviors which have not appeared before in their prior baselines, then a basic skill is established, which subsequently may be discriminated to cultural gaps (as the children learn the culture) and to the various audiences and peer groups that will be encountered. Furthermore, it may be argued that the skill of emitting behaviors which one's culture, audience, or peer group has not seen before may be less demanding (in a literal sense, less creative) than the generation of behaviors which individuals have never previously produced. In the former cases, individuals search their repertoires for behaviors which may not be new to them, but are merely new to the current audience (much as a lecturer may remember which old jokes have been told the current class already, so as to appear always inventive). But when a behavior is new to the individuals' previous repertoires, then it is an example of invention (or at least, imitation), and of inventions, some at least may well be new to the culture or audience of the individuals as well as new to the individuals. The same point may be stated in the opposite direction, for a pragmatic emphasis. How else could one instruct children eventually to generate behaviors which will prove new to their culture, audience, and peers, other than by teaching children to generate behaviors which are new to them?

Several studies have established the possibility of teaching an organism systematically to produce behavior which the organism has not displayed before. The responsible technique so far has been a straightforward application of reinforcement logic. Reinforcement that has been programmed contingent on any response which is different in some identifiable way from any previous responses of the organism. Thus Pryor, *et al.* (1969) reinforced swimming and leaping responses of dolphins which had not been displayed previously. In this procedure, each session required a new response which was then continuously reinforced throughout that session (but would not be reinforced in any future sessions). The dolphins became progressively faster at inventing a new response at the beginning of each session. Goetz and Baer (1973) reinforced any blockbuilding responses of preschool children which had not been displayed before within the *current* blockbuilding session; only the first occurrence of any response within the session would be reinforced. (Thus, unlike the procedures of Pryor *et al.,* each successive reinforced response within a session was new to that session; by contrast, Pryor *et al.* required one new response per session which was new in terms of all previous sessions but could be repeated for reinforcement in the current session.) The children of the Goetz and Baer study responded to the contingency by increasing the number of different blockbuilding responses emitted per session; but they also displayed the pattern of Pryor *et al.*'s dolphins: they invented new blockbuilding responses, different than any displayed in their previous sessions.

The ability to teach an organism to invent new behavior need not be an impressive or socially valuable accomplishment, however, if the inventions are restricted to a very narrow range of behavior. That is, we may doubt the long-term worth of teaching a dolphin to leap in new ways, or a child to stack blocks in new ways, if no other form of increased inventiveness is displayed by these organisms thereafter. In terms of the psychological development of either organism, there would be little evidence of a substantial response class having been organized, or of an extensive concept having been attained, unless some superordinate form of generalization is seen, i.e., the invention of new behaviors outside the range covered by training.

Thus, the studies to be reported below repeated the basic procedures previously found useful in generating new child behaviors (Goetz & Baer, 1973); but these studies also examined the possibility of generalized changes in other baselines of children's behavior. Experiment 1 placed a reinforcement contingency on the form diversity of easel painting, by reinforcing the first appearance of each new form painted by the children within the current experimental session. Meanwhile, ongoing blockbuilding performances by the children were examined for correlated changes. As in the previous study, both the number of different forms produced per session (form diversity) and the number of forms new to that session and all previous sessions (new forms) were considered as pertinent dependent variables. In Experiment 2, four concurrent baselines of child behavior were examined: drawing with felt-tip markers, easel painting, blockbuilding, and Lego-block construction. Training of form diversity was conducted with marker drawing, and generalization was examined in the relatively similar activity of easel painting as well as in the relatively dissimilar activities of blockbuilding and Lego construction. Experiment 2 further analyzed generalization by recording postchecks on all four behaviors several months after training was completed.

EXPERIMENT 1

Subjects

Two preschool boys were selected as subjects, because they consistently used few forms in both their painting and blockbuilding. One subject, Les, was a five-year-old black boy of a low-income family. The other subject, Rick, was a three-year-old white boy of a professional family who had given considerable time and attention to his intellectual upbringing.

Procedure

Each child was invited by the experimenter to a research room, and then asked to paint at an easel. The easel held 3 cups of different colored paint and 3 brushes. The child determined the length of each painting session, usually with a verbal statement of completion, sometimes by removing his painting smock, or by agreeing to the experimenter's query ("Are you done?"), offered when he became inactive for 15 sec while looking steadily at the experimenter. At this time the experimenter thanked the child and gave him a token and a toy of his choice. (The token could be used later as a ticket to gain access to special classroom activities.)

Blockbuilding sessions were held in another, similar research room, usually immediately following an easel-painting session, but sometimes on the following day in place of the easel painting activity, if the child's classroom schedule had not allowed enough time on the preceding day for 2 sessions. (Such days are graphed distinctively in the data figures below.) The procedures used to begin and end blockbuilding sessions were analogous to those used to begin and end easel-painting sessions, and included the use of a terminal toy and token. The blockbuilding room always contained the same collection of 53 blocks. Each subject was requested to use all the blocks in every construction and invariably did.

Conditions

Les's baseline level of easel painting was determined over three sessions during which he recieved no experimental reinforcement while painting. In the following six sessions, the experimenter delivered descriptive reinforcement, a combination of praise and a simple verbal description of the form, contingent on the first appearance of each different form painted on the current sheet of paper. Then, for five further sessions, reinforcement was discontinued, and was resumed again in the final eight sessions. Procedures in Rick's case were similar, except that baseline was five sessions, reinforcement then being programmed for the next eight sessions, followed by a three-session discontinuation of reinforcement and then by six sessions of renewed reinforcement. Thus, in the reinforcement of easel-painting forms, each subject embodies an ABAB reversal design, and the two subjects taken together yielded a multiple-baseline across-subjects design. The blockbuilding activities never received differential reinforcement (other than the terminal toy and token used to maintain attendance).

Definitions of Forms

The basic outcome of the study was seen in changes in the form content of the subjects' blockbuilding and painting activities. The form content of these activities was scored according to a set of defined forms appropriate to each activity. These definitions were developed in part through a survey of the literature describing preschool children's blockbuilding and painting, but in larger part through preliminary surveys of the products of those activities as practiced by the children of this university preschool. In the case of blockbuilding, prior research (Goetz & Baer, 1973) had already established a usable set of form definitions (which nevertheless were added to as a result of experience with the above subjects). In the case of easel painting, prior research (Goetz & Salmonson, 1972) provided a basic set of form definitions from which the felt-pen code in Experiment 2 was later derived.[4] These two sets of forms are listed and defined in Tables 1 and 2, respectively. Forms marked with an asterisk (*) in those tables will be referred to below.

Recording

During each session, both the experimenter and an independent observer tallied the names, number, and sequence of all forms appearing in the current product (block construction or easel painting). From these lists, a *form diversity* score was derived, defined as the number of different forms appearing at least once within the current session. A *new forms* score was also derived, defined as the number of forms appearing for the first time, considering all previous sessions. Both the experimenter and the observer recorded the session duration, defined as the number of minutes and seconds between the experimenter's invitation to begin the session and the child's statement or act of completion. In addition, both the experimenter and the observer recorded whether or not any form was reinforced by the experimenter. Comparison of the experimenter's and observer's records established the reliability of these scores and of the reinforcement procedure. All percentages of agreement on the name, number, and sequencing of all forms, on the occurrence of reinforcement, and on the correctness of the reinforcement contingency exceeded 95%. In addition, the paintings were kept for later checking, and the block constructions were photographed. (Photographs of the blockbuilding products always allowed a precise retrospective analysis of their form content. However, the finished paintings were sometimes ambiguous, in that forms painted early in the session, and reliably recorded at the time, were subsequently painted over by the child, sometimes to such an extent that they could no longer be scored.)

[4]The felt-pen code was developed by Fallon (1975) as an analogue to the easel-painting code; the Lego building code was developed by Beehler (1972) as an analogue to the block-building code.

TABLE 1

Blockbuilding Code

ADJUNCT: two or more forms connected by a fence; at least one of the forms must be an enclosure, subdivision, or a roof.

ARCH: any placement of a block atop two lower blocks not in contiguity.

*ARCH (Storied): an arch built atop another arch.

*ARCH (Variation): a "true" arch made of two arcs leaning together, placed atop two supports.

BALANCE: any story in which the upper block is at least four times as wide as the lower block.

BALANCE (Elaborated): any balance in which both ends of the upper block contain additional blocks.

CIRCLE: an arrangement of four arc-shaped blocks in contiguity to form a circle.

*CIRCLE (Half): two arc-shaped blocks placed end-to-end in contiguity to form a half-circle.

CROSS: any two blocks stacked so that at least one-quarter of the top block extends over each side of the bottom block forming a T or an X.

ENCLOSURE (Complete): any arrangement of fences which encloses an open area, with or without a gate.

*ENCLOSURE (Partial): any arrangement of fences (with at least three sides) which encloses an open area, but leaves an opening equivalent or greater than the largest block used in the arrangement.

FENCE: any two or more blocks placed side by side in contiguity; if not contiguous, then any three blocks placed at regularly spaced intervals in a straight line.

*FENCE (Arched): two V-shaped blocks placed side by side with only the base of the V's touching the floor and the arms in contiguity.

FLOOR: any arrangement of at least two flat blocks serving as a basis for higher building.

INTERFACE: an arrangement of two blocks with curved contours to fit precisely together, as a half circle into an arch-shaped block.

PILLAR: any story in which the lowest block is at least twice as tall as it is wide.

POST: any story in which the lowest block is at least twice as wide, and half as tall, as the upper block.

RAMP: a block leaned against another, or a triangular block placed contiguous to another simulating an inclined plane.

ROOF: two or more slat-shaped blocks placed flat and side-by-side atop at least two supports; or arch-shaped if the sides (not ends) are contiguous.

RECTANGLE FROM TRIANGLE: an arrangement of two equal sized triangles; the hypoteneuses placed in contiguity to form a rectangle or square.

SIMULATION: a construction of blocks which resembles a real-life object and is explicitly labeled by the child as such, as a building, boat, or swimming pool.

S: an arrangement of four arc-shaped blocks in contiguity as two half-circles to simulate an S.

STORY: any two or more blocks placed one atop another, the upper blocks resting solely upon the lower.

SUBDIVISION: two or more enclosures in contiguity with one common block.

TOWER: any story of two or more blocks, each of which is at least twice as tall as it is wide.

TOWER (Alternating): three or more cylindrical blocks stacked atop each other in ascending or descending sizes.

TABLE 1 *(continued)*

WEDGE: two equal sized triangles placed with equal sides of the right angle in contiguity. Triangles rest on one side of the right angle. They may be one-half an inch apart.

X: an arrangement of two V-shaped blocks in contiguity to simulate an X.

*Forms not scored in Experiment 1, but scored in Experiment 2.

TABLE 2

Easel-Painting Code

BLENDED COLOR: any hue formed by mixing two or more pure or available colors onto the paper.

CIRCULAR: any nearly enclosed or enclosed curve including circles, ovals, ellipses, etc., with a diameter of at least 1½" at its widest point. The form may be pointed at one end.

CROSS: two lines which intersect each other, making a crosslike formation and meeting the following requirements.

1. If the lines are of relatively equal length the angle of intersection is arbitrary, but the lines must intersect at relatively the same point on each line.
2. If the lines are not of equal length, the angle of intersection must be relatively close to 90°.

CURVE: a line or any part of a line, at least 3" long continuously bent so that no portion is straight. All circulars get credit for curve.

DIAGONAL LINE: a relatively straight line, at least 3" long, forming a 10° to 80° angle.

DUPLICATE: a relatively exact pair of forms clearly seen as a design, or any of the crossed (+) forms. The size and color may vary but the structure should be essentially the same. Simple forms such as circles require more exactness than more complex forms, such as an irregular enclosure or a simulation. A staccatto grouping itself is not a duplicate; the same grouping must be repeated in another area of the paper.

HORIZONTAL LINE: a relatively straight line, at least 3" long, forming a 0° to 10° angle.

IRREGULAR ENCLOSURE: any enclosed or nearly enclosed unsymmetrical line formation leaving a center area with a a diameter no smaller than 1½" at its widest point.

+LAYER OF COLORS: three or more repeated lines, using two or more different colors, 1" or less in width, which lie side by side. Each line should be a different color than the one directly beside it and separated by no more than half an inch. To be counted as a duplicate, the two groups of layers must contain the same colors, and must be separated by at least 3" of space.

MASS: any combination of strokes in a manner that results in a solid colored area of at least 2" square. No uncolored area may be larger than ½" at its widest point.

+OVERLAPPING SAME FORMS: a duplicate with one form overlapping the other at any point.

+PATTERN: three or more duplicate forms. No member of a pattern may be more than 3" away from another member.

+RECTANGULAR: any nearly enclosed form with 4 relatively straight lines (sides) and 4 90° angles, approximate to within 10°. Two sides must be no smaller than 2" and the other two must be larger or equal.

(continued)

TABLE 2 *(continued)*

+SIMULATION: a configuration which resembles a real life object. Symbols are excluded. To be scored as such, the form must be labeled explicitly by the child and be recognizable to the observer; or two observers must agree.

SPATTER: three or more scattered or dashed small particles or drops resulting from one swing of the brush (usually from flicking the wrist).

+SPIRAL: a winding or coiled line which must include at least two consecutive, complete revolutions. May not be buried when scored as a duplicate, though may be later.

+STACCATTO: three or more quick dabs that are not the result of a spatter, clustered in the same area, within 3" of each other. They may or may not overlap.

+SYMBOL: any configuration which represents anything other than simulation, numbers, letters, signs, etc.

+TINKER TOY LINE: circular forms with one or more straight lines connecting them. The connecting line must be at least 1" long from diameter to diameter. The connecting line may project into but not beyond the circular form unless it is connected to an additional form.

+TRAIN OF COLORS: a series of three or more lines, using two or more colors, forming a line of procession. The colors need not be touching but must be within ¼" of each other. The train need not consist only of lines, but can include areas of color providing they are arranged in train formation.

+TRIANGULAR: any enclosed form with only 3 sides and 3 angles. At least 2 sides must be 1½" long with the third side at least 1" long.

TRICKLE: a flowing or falling drop in a small, broken or gentle stream at least 1" long. (Usually results from allowing paint to drip off the brush.)

UNDULATING LINE: a line with three or more consecutive curves approximately 1" or greater in depth. No part of the undulating line may overlap or touch itself at any point.

VERTICAL LINE: any relatively straight line, at least 3" long and forming an angle between 80° and 100°.

ZIGZAG: a line or any part of a line with three or more consecutive angles formed by turning the brush first one way and then the other. The angle must be fairly sharp. A zigzag cannot overlap itself.

+*See definition of duplicate form.*

Measurement. All angles measured in analyzing the pictures were measured as they lay relative to the bottom of the paper.

Results and Discussion

For both children, the use of descriptive praise for each new painting form resulted in substantial increases in painting form diversity. In Les' case, descriptive reinforcement produced a shift from nonreinforcement levels approximating 7 different forms per painting to an average near 9 the first time reinforcement was applied, and to an average of about 12 the second time. Rick responded more dramatically, departing from his nonreinforcement level of about 5 forms per painting to an average of 8 during the first reinforcement procedure, and to an average near 12 during the second. These changes are shown graphically in Figure 1 as bars.

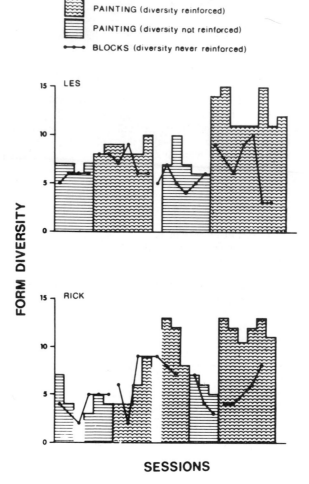

Figure 1   The form diversity exhibited in each painting and block session for both Les and Rick under nonreinforcement and reinforcement conditions.

At the same time that these directly programmed behavior changes were taking place in the form diversity of painting, certain behavior changes were observed in the never-reinforced form diversity of blockbuilding. These changes are presented in Figure 1 as line graphs. Apparently the average levels of change in blockbuilding form diversity were much less pronounced than in painting; however, an approximation to the same basic pattern of increase and decrease appeared as was seen in painting, roughly in conformity with the ABAB design of the study.

In considering the new forms score, a similar pattern of experimental control was apparent in the emergence of new painting forms. In general, new painting forms appeared at twice as high a rate during reinforcement conditions as during nonreinforcement conditions. This pattern is shown graphically in Figure 2.

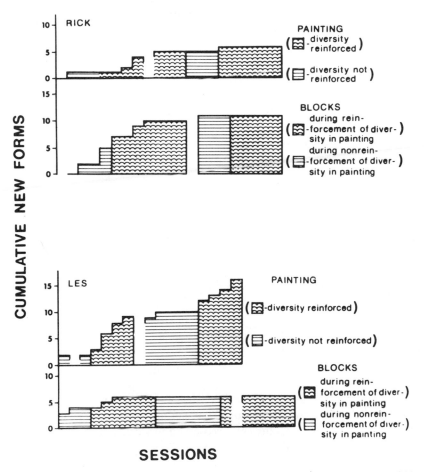

Figure 2   Cumulative new forms as they appeared in each session of painting and block-building for Rick and Less under nonreinforcement and reinforcement conditions.

However, at the same time that this experimental control over the invention of new forms in painting became manifest, no systematic changes in the children's rates of inventing new forms in blockbuilding were seen. In general, new forms appeared in blockbuilding primarily during the early sessions, similarly during nonreinforcement and reinforcement conditions, as shown in Figure 2.

Thus, these results, taken together, constitute a replication of the experimental control demonstrated earlier by Goetz and Baer (1973) with blockbuilding behaviors, now in the case of easel painting. Both form diversity and the rate of inventing new forms responded to the experimental procedures applied to the painting behaviors. However, generalization to concurrent blockbuilding, if credited at all as such, occurred only in the form diversity of blockbuilding, and clearly did not occur in the emergence of new blockbuilding forms. Whether this pattern of behavior in blockbuilding is considered as a weak and incomplete form of generalization, or is more conservatively dismissed as a random pattern of scores deserving no systematic interpretation, the implications are much the same: there is insufficient evidence of a generalized outcome to conclude that reinforcement of form diversity, as practiced in this experiment, is a valuable curriculum method. On the other hand, it might be argued that expecting a generalized outcome in as different a medium as blockbuilding, after instruction only in easel painting, is too severe a test of generalized outcome. Perhaps evidence of generalization should be sought in more closely related behaviors, such as with media which require skills more similar to those used in easel painting. Experiment 2 was performed to examine this possibility.

EXPERIMENT 2

Subjects

Three preschool boys were selected as subjects on the basis of their pattern of initial baseline results, which demonstrated at best only modest levels of form diversity or the invention of new forms among any of the four activities being observed. Two of the boys, Rory and Drew, were from white middle-class, professional families; Rory was four years, six months old, and Drew was three years, ten months old. The third boy, Roger was from a black low-income family; he was four years, seven months old.

Procedure

Each child was invited twice a day by the experimenter to a research room; on the first occasion of the day, the child was asked to work at the 2 building tasks (first blocks, and then Lego), and on the second occasion, at the 2 art tasks (first drawing and then painting). These 2 daily sessions were usually held about 2 hours apart, one in the early morning, the other in the late morning. The blocks and painting materials were identical to those used in Experiment 1. Three felt-tip pens were also provided for drawing, each 13 cm long, colored red, blue, and green, as well as 33 Lego blocks, each the same width (1½ cm) but of 7 different lengths (from .8 cm to 2.5 cm) and colored red, blue, and white. Block-and-Lego sessions ended when the child used the last piece available; painting-and-drawing sessions ended when the child reported being finished (as instructed to do, at the outset of these sessions).

Conditions

Baseline.   Baseline conditions lasted for 3 to 8 sessions, depending on the pattern of the child's 8 daily scores (a form diversity score and a new forms score for each of blocks, Lego, pen drawing, and painting). During Baseline, the experimenter watched the child's activities closely, remaining quiet until the end of the session, thanked the child but offered no other form of reinforcement.

Reinforcement. After the baseline sessions, the experimenter introduced a reinforcement package consisting of descriptive social reinforcement and tokens exchangeable for a preselected toy. For all three subjects, the package was initially applied to diverse pen-drawing forms (chosen because for all subjects its form diversity score seemed lowest and most stable). One subject later received the same reinforcement package for diverse Lego forms.

In reinforcement sessions, a token card was placed on the table in front of the child and a cup of tokens was placed in front of the experimenter. The token card had a moveable arrow to indicate a criterion level. Instructions were then given.

> "Today, [Name], we're going to try something new. First, I want you to pick a toy that you would like to work for. [The experimenter opened a box and allowed the child to make a selection. The box contained a variety of toys, books, etc., of approximately 15-40¢ value, and a food choice, raisins and/or marshmallows]. Fine! You'd like to work for this (name of toy chosen). Now, to earn your (name of toy chosen), you have to earn this many tokens. [The experimenter pointed to the token card and moved a finger slowly to the predetermined criterion number indicated by the moveable arrow]. The way you earn a token is by drawing different things. Each time you draw something different, I will give you a token." The experimenter then drew something on the child's paper with a finger, describing the form made, and supplying a token, e.g., "See, if you drew a straight line up and down [demonstrated with finger] that would be something *different* [token given]; and if you drew a curvy line, [demonstrated] that would be another different thing. Now, to earn your toy, you have to work hard and earn this many tokens [again the experimenter pointed to the arrow]. Remember, you earn a token each time you draw something different. Is that O.K?" The experimenter waited for the child to indicate understanding, and then added, "You can start when you're ready."

Once the child began, the experimenter supplied a token and descriptive social reinforcement, responding with warmth and delight each time the child produced a form which had not appeared previously in the ongoing session. (The form might have appeared in any previous day's session; it would still be reinforced in the current session.) In other words, the experimenter reinforced the first production of any form within each session, but did not subsequently reinforce that form within that session. The experimenter's comments always emphasized the newness of the produced form, and in addition the form was traced over with a finger.

The reinforcement was meant to be continuous, contingent, and immediate. However, this required considerable flexibility on the part of the experimenter, who had to remember which forms had already been produced that day (there was little time for studying the score sheet between form productions). Moreover, an attempt was made to vary the verbalizations, to avoid a stereotyped, repetitive pattern. Thus, occasionally a new form would fail to be reinforced. Furthermore, some forms flowed into others. For example, a circle also implied the form "curve," so the two forms would be reinforced sequentially, if possible:

"Great!, there's two different things. See, this is a curve [the experimenter traced the curve and supplied the token] and you've joined it up to make a circle [the experimenter completed the trace and added another token] — that's good!" Despite these problems, observation of the experimenter's practices showed 98% correct reinforcements, according to a team of reliability observers.

Roger also received reinforcement for Lego forms, as a second condition, following reinforcement of new pen-drawing forms. (At this time, the order of tasks was reversed, from blocks-first-Lego-second to Lego-first-blocks-second, to allow generalization from Lego to the untreated similar baseline of blockbuilding within the same session.) Reinforcement for Lego followed essentially the same pattern as for drawing. The verbal content of the experimenter's praise was now of course descriptive of the Lego task, "Super! look, you made a story — this block fits exactly on top of this block [tracing the edges] — that's a different thing."

Predetermined Daily Criterion

During reinforcement, a subject was required to earn a predetermined number of tokens in order to receive a toy. If the required number was not earned, the toy was not supplied, and the child was told, "Well! you worked hard, but you didn't do quite enough different things [the experimenter pointed to the level on the token card that should have been reached]. Tomorrow you'll have a chance to help me again and try to earn your toy."

The daily criterion for each subject was decided somewhat arbitrarily by the experimenter on the basis of their current form-diversity score. For the initial session, the mean of the baseline form-diversity scores was chosen. Subsequently, the daily criterion was raised by adding one to the previous day's form diversity score until the baseline had approximately doubled. By that stage, it was not reasonable to expect a continuous daily increase, but if a subject maintained a score for two successive days, the criterion would again be raised by one. The new forms score was never used in determining the daily criterion.

Definitions of Forms

As in Experiment 1, the basic outcome of the study was determined according to the form content of each day's activities. The forms defining blockbuilding and painting were identical to those displayed in Tables 1 and 2 of Experiment 1. Forms for the analysis of drawing and Lego construction were developed according to the same logic, after preliminary surveys of the literature and observation of the constructions of several other children with the drawing pens and the Lego blocks. Those forms are listed and defined in Table 3 for pen drawing and in Table 4 for Lego construction. Methods of recording these forms, and assessing the reliability of recording, were identical to those used in Experiment 1. All

TABLE 3

Felt-Pen-Drawing Code

+CIRCULAR ENCLOSURE: any nearly enclosed or enclosed curve, including circles, ovals, ellipses, etc. with a diameter of at least 1½" at its widest point. The form may be point-at one end.

CROSS: two lines which intersect each other, making a cross like formation and meeting the following requirements.

1. If the lines are of relatively equal length the angle of intersection is arbitrary, but the lines must intersect at relatively the same point on each line.
2. If the lines are not of equal length, the angle of intersection must be relatively close to 90°.

CURVE: a line or part of any line, at least 3" long continuously bent so that no portion of it is straight. All circulars get credit for curve.

DIAGONAL LINE: a relatively straight line, at least 3" long, forming a 10° to 80° angle.

DUPLICATE FORM: a relatively exact pair of forms clearly seen as a design, or any of the crossed (+) forms. The size and color may vary but the structure should be essentially the same. Simple forms such as circles require more exactness than more complex forms, such as an irregular enclosure or a simulation. A staccatto grouping itself is not a duplicate: the same grouping must be repeated in another area of the paper.

HORIZONTAL LINE: a relatively straight line, at least 3" long, forming a 0° to 10° angle.

+IRREGULAR ENCLOSURE: any enclosed or nearly closed unsymmetrical line formation leaving a center area with a diameter no smaller than 1½" at its widest point.

+LAYER OF COLORS: three or more repeated lines, using two or more different colors, which lie side by side. Each line should be a different color than the one beside it. To be counted as a duplicate, the two groups of layers must contain the same colors, and must be separated by at least 3" of space.

MASS: any combination of lines in a manner that results in a solid colored area at least 1" square. No uncolored area may be larger than ¼" at its widest point.

+OVERLAPPING SAME FORMS: a Duplicate with one form overlapping the other at any point.

+PATTERN: three or more duplicate forms. No member of a pattern may be over 3" away from another member.

RECTANGULAR: any nearly enclosed form with 4 relatively straight lines (sides) and 4 90° angles, approximate to within 10°. Two sides must be no smaller than 2" and 2 sides must be no smaller than 1½" in length.

+SIMULATION: a configuration which resembles a real-life object. Symbols are excluded. To be scored as such, the form must be labeled explicitly by the child and be recognizable to the observer; or two observers must agree.

SPATTER: using the felt pen by tapping firmly on the paper until the tip is excessively lubricated so that each additional tap spatters tiny dots of ink onto the sheet.

+SPIRAL: a winding or coiled line which must include at least two consecutive, complete revolutions.

+SPIRAL CHAIN: at least two spirals connected by a line which may be straight or curved.

+STACCATTO: three or more dashlike particles, all within a 3" area of each other. They may or may not overlap but must be no larger than ½".

STACCATTO LINE: a line of at least four dashlike particles following each other (not clumped together).

(continued)

TABLE 3 (continued)

+SYMBOL: any configuration which represents anything other than a simulation, numbers, letters, signs, etc.

+TINKER TOY LINE: circular forms with one or more straight lines connecting them. The connecting line must be at least 1" long from diameter to diameter. The connecting line may project into but not beyond the circular form unless it is connected to an additional form.

+TRAIN OF COLORS: a series of 3 or more lines using 2 or more colors forming a line of procession. The colors need not be touching but must be within ¼" of each other. The train need not consist only of lines, but can include areas of color, providing they are arranged in train formation.

+TRIANGULAR: any enclosed form with only 3 sides and 3 angles. At least 2 sides must be 1½" long with the third side at least 1" long.

UNDULATING LINE: a line with 3 or more consecutive curves at least ½" deep. No part of the undulating line may overlap or touch itself at any point.

VERTICAL LINE: any relatively straight line, at least 3" long and forming an angle between 80° and 100°.

ZIGZAG: a line or any part of a line with three or more consecutive angles formed by turning the pen first one way, and then the other. The angle must be fairly sharp. A zigzag cannot overlap itself.

+See definition of duplicate form.

Measurement. All angles measured in analyzing the pictures were measured as they lay relative to the bottom edge (the edge of the picture closest to the child) of the paper.

A template form was made which could be placed over any line, in the event of a question as to whether the line was relatively straight. The template was approximately 4" x 4" square, containing a cut-out portion 3" long with a protractor. If the line deviated from the range of the cut-out line, it was not considered a straight line; the angle of the line could be similarly verified.

TABLE 4

Lego Code

ARCH: any placement of a block atop two lower blocks not touching each other.

ARCH (Storied): an arch built exactly upon another arch.

ARCH (Multiple): any placement of blocks atop three or more lower blocks not touching each other forming at least two arches on the same level.

CORNER: any block stacked on a longer block so that both sides of each block are flush with each other; one end of each block flush with the other.

CORNER (Half): any small block stacked atop a longer block, one end of each block flush and one side of each block flush.

CORNER (Inverted): any corner having the longer block on top.

CROSS: any two blocks stacked so that at least one quarter of the top block extends over each side of the bottom block, forming a *T* or an *X*.

ENCLOSURE (Complete): any arrangement of extensions to enclose an open area. May or may not have a gate.

(continued)

TABLE 4 *(continued)*

ENCLOSURE (Partial): any arrangement of extensions to enclose an open area (with at least three sides) and an opening equivalent to, or larger than, the largest block used.

EXTENSION: any combination of two or more blocks laid end-to-end on the same plane, so the end of one block is butted against the end of the second block, or so the side of one block touches one side of the second block.

EXTENSION (Right Angled): any extension having at least one right angle, where the end of one block is flush with the side of the second block, and both blocks are on the same plane.

EXTENSION (Storied): any extension which is over one level high, and having two or more blocks on the same level.

FLOOR: two or more blocks arranged so the side of te first block touches more than half of the side of the second block.

FLOOR (Double): a floor placed atop another floor.

PROJECTION: any block protruding from either side of a second block, or from an extension, when neither side of the projecting block is flush with the end of the extension block. Also when a corner of the projecting block is touching a side of the extension.

SIMULATION: any construction of blocks which resembles a real-life structure, and is explicitly named by the child.

STEP: two or more blocks stacked one on top of the other both sides flush, but the ends not flush.

STEP (Half Row): two or more blocks stacked one atop the other lengthwise so that one row of one block overlaps the other block. The ends may or may not be flush.

STEP (Inverted): two or more blocks stacked one on top of the other so that the top block overhangs the bottom block on both ends, with the side of both blocks flush.

STEP (Right Angled): any block stacked atop another block with a side and an end flush and forming a right angle.

STORY: two or more blocks of the same size built exactly one on top of the other.

SUBDIVISION: two or more enclosures in contiguity with one or more common blocks.

SYMBOL: any configuration which represents anything other than simulation, as a letter or number.

TREE: any block or extension having two or more projections, the projections being on the same plane.

---

percentages of observer agreement on the name, number, and sequencing of all forms, on the occurrence of reinforcement, and on the correctnesss of the reinforcement contingency, averaged over the experiment, exceeded 97%. Form diversity and new forms scores were derived from these recordings exactly as in Experiment 1.

Results and Discussion

The daily form diversity and new forms scores for each subject, in each of the four activities of blockbuilding, painting, Lego construction, and drawing, are displayed in Figure 3. Clearly the directly treated activity, drawing, was thoroughly responsive to the experimental training applied to it. Each subject showed a reasonably stable baseline of form diversity prior to the application of the

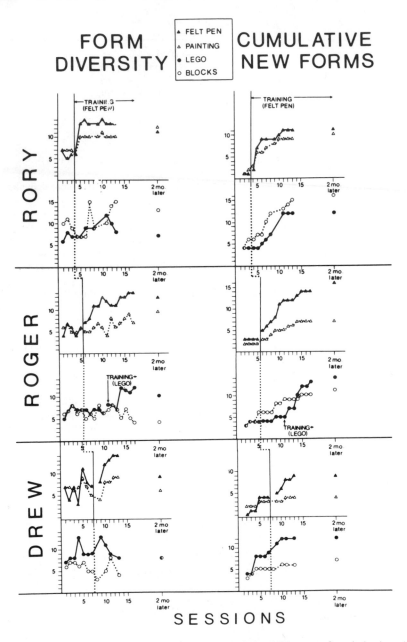

FORM DIVERSITY

CUMULATIVE NEW FORMS

▲ FELT PEN
△ PAINTING
● LEGO
○ BLOCKS

SESSIONS

Figure 3   (a) The form diversity scores of three children on four behaviors (felt-pen drawing, easel painting, blockbuilding and Lego building). (b) The cumulative number of new forms (forms never previously recorded) produced by three children for the four behaviors (felt-pen drawing, easel painting, blockbuilding, and Lego building). All scores represent cumulative increments over the score produced in the first session (not graphed, as every form appearing in that session would have to be considered new).

experimental training, and each showed a prompt increase subsequent to that training, despite varying lengths of baseline preceding the training. In addition, Roger's Lego construction showed a similar, clear increase in form diversity scores when training was applied to it, late in the study.

Accompanying these directly programmed changes in form diversity were similar changes in the rate of producing new forms in the drawing activity. In the cases of Rory and Roger, these allied changes in the cumulative new forms score were quite clear, representing sudden increases from unchanging or nearly un-changing baselines. In Drew's case, the baseline of new forms was variable, and the rate of invention of new forms subsequent to direct training on form diver-sity could be interpreted as an extension of that baseline, rather than a change from it. However, it is also true that Drew had not invented a new form since the fifth session of baseline, yet when training started on Session 8, he promptly be-gan inventing an average of one new form each subsequent session.

Some generalization occurred from pen drawing to painting, the topographi-cally similar task. In terms of daily form diversity scores, this generalization was shown clearly for Rory, reasonably well for Drew, but much less clearly, if at all, for Roger. In terms of cumulative new forms scores, generalization was clear and strong for Roger; it was possible in Rory's case, but arguable due to the brief baseline; and it was nonexistent for Drew. For the one subject who received treatment for a second behavior (Lego building) there was no generalization to its topographically related task, blockbuilding.

By contrast, generalization from drawing to blockbuilding or Lego, the topo-graphically dissimlar tasks, was largely absent. It could be argued for only in Rory's case.

To a sharply limited extent then, the generalization of creative responding was extended more easily, and more reliably, to the similar than to the dissimilar tasks of this study. Nevertheless, with considerable uniformity, the effects of a reinforcement technique applied to daily form diversity produced generalized changes in the rate of inventing new forms, within each directly treated activity, in this study as in Experiment 1 (and as in the (1973) Goetz & Baer study).

The durability of training effects is also important to the question of generality of behavioral change. Durability was assessed in the current study by postchecks conducted two months after the completion of training. Rory and Roger, who had received the greater number of reinforced trials, maintained their high level of form diversity in the directly manipulated activity and in its topographically related behavior. However, the form diversity postcheck declined in Drew's case (he had received fewer reinforced trials).

CONCLUDING DISCUSSION

Creativity has been widely researched because of its fundamental humanistic im-portance. In the past, correlates of creative individuals or creative behaviors have been sought as explanations; more recently, efforts have been made to systematically generate creative behaviors. These studies are of the latter category: the concept of creativity was implemented in two objective behavioral definitions (form diversity and new forms), and was trained as an operant behavior, subject to modification by its consequences and under the discriminative control of task and problem cues. Thus these experiments combined with the Goetz and Baer study (1973), have shown four children's art media susceptible to such analysis: blockbuilding, easel painting, pen drawing, and Lego construction.

In these four cases, a reinforcement training package (of one sort or another) was applied only to daily form diversity; yet with considerable uniformity, a generalized result was seen in the emergence of new forms (new not only to that day's activity but to all prior days' as well). Much more limited, yet undeniable, generalization was seen to untreated tasks, and when this occurred, it was more readily seen in activities topographically similar to the treated task than in topographically dissimilar ones. Finally, a third form of generalization was noted in Experiment 2: durability of the directly produced changes over time, subsequent to termination of the training techniques, was noted in all three subjects.

Nevertheless, generalization across tasks, while observable, was quite variable, somewhat inconsistent, and usually of limited magnitude in these studies. To the extent that generalization across tasks is valued as evidence of a truly valuable behavior change, reasonably interpreted as a concept of creativity usable by the child, the problem of securing such generalization must still be considered unsolved. However, it would be an error to conclude that a behavioral, applied analysis of creativity is impossible because inadequate generalization is seen when a preliminary set of techniques derived from this logic are first evaluated. Instead, the task is to develop new or additional techniques which will not only yield the correlated changes in form diversity and new forms desired, but will also produce the necessary generalization.

In that some generalization across tasks was seen, there is reason to conclude that a generalization-promotion technique can be found: it may be necessary only to capitalize upon a tendency already in existence, within the techniques at hand. Perhaps with the already highly symbolic subjects to which these techniques are meant to be applied, a simple mediation technique may be all that is needed in addition. With these preschool children, what would happen after successful blockbuilding training (say) if the teacher then asked, "You made so many different shapes with the blocks — can you make a lot of different shapes with the [Lego/pens/brush], the same way?"

The need for generalization has been frequently stressed in the literature, and its therapeutic necessity is undisputed, yet generalization has not received from research the attention it deserves. It is important to establish a technology which will specify more precisely conditions that favor the occurrence of generalization. Such a technology may vary across classes of behavior; yet there may be common elements. The development of that technology and the extraction of those common elements in practical forms thus appears to be a major task for the development of this field. This point has not been unrecognized. Baer, Wolf and Risley (1968), admonished their readers, "that generality is a valuable characteristic of applied behavior analysis which should be examined explicitly apparently is not quite obvious and is stated here for emphasis" [p. 96]. Since the need for generalization is widely accepted, the lack of research on its programming seems to have been due to a naive belief in its automatic occurrence, doubtless accompanied by the profound hope that many of the high response cost, intricate follow-up and concurrent measures which have been designed to assess generalization would prove to be unnecessary. However, there has been gradually emerging in the field, a body of studies which have focused on generalization programming. These studies, of which the following are illustrative, herald a more formal approach to the problem, and establish a tentative foundation for a sound technology of generalization.

The development, maintenance, and generalization of social greeting responses of three adult, withdrawn, chronic schizophrenics was examined in an early study by Kale, Kaye, Whelan and Hopkins (1968). Prompts and cigarette reinforcement were employed to produce increases in the rates of greetings, and the prompts were then faded so that the greetings came under the discriminative control of the experimenter's presence. The reinforcement schedule was then decreased so that greetings continued to occur in the absence of cigarette reinforcement. However, low or zero rates of generalization were found to occur in the presence of a second experimenter not previously involved in training. Response generalization to this second experimenter was then deliberately promoted by using five new experimenters in the training procedures. This additional training resulted in all subjects emitting appropriately high rates of greeting to the second experimenter.

Corte, Wolfe and Locke (1971) urged that treatment of self-injurious behavior with punishment must include the active generalization of the effects through a planned program of treating the behavior under as many conditions as are necessary to obtain generalization. This conclusion was based on their finding that response contingent shock effectively eliminated self-destructive behaviors in four profoundly retarded adolescents, but that these punishment effects were specific to the setting in which shock was administered. Generalization of treatment effects occurred only when additional programming was introduced by other shock trainers, or by shocking in different settings.

Stokes, Baer and Jackson (1974) demonstrated the successful acquisition of a social greeting response in 4 institutionalized retarded subjects. Training and maintenance of the greeting response by one experimenter was not usually sufficient for generalization to more than 20 other members of the institution staff who had not particpated in the training of the response. However, generalization was effectively programmed by having a second experimenter train and maintain the response in conjunction with the first experimenter. High levels of generalization were then recorded in a variety of settings, ranging over periods of from 1 to 6 months.

An attempt was made by Garcia (1974) to identify procedures and relationships with respect to the generalization of trained conversational speech form (associated with the display of pictures and questions related to them) in previously nonverbal retardates. Three experimenters measured the use of each sentence in settings different than the one in which training took place, and with different pictures than those used in training. Two types of generalization sessions (during which ten pictures never used during training were displayed to the subject) were conducted.

1. General sessions with noncontingent reinforcement delivery.
2. Intermixed sessions, in which a picture having received training was "also" displayed, and correct responses to this picture were reinforced on a variable schedule.

Both subjects learned the sentences being trained. However, little generalization was evident from this training when all experimenters conducted general probe sessions. Generalization occurred with one experimenter only after that experimenter conducted intermixed probe sessions. Generalization to a third experimenter was then observed (after the first two experimenters had conducted intermixed probe sessions) without the use of intermixed probe sessions by this third experimenter.

Generalization of improved speech-sound articulation in young children was obtained by Johnston and Johnston (1972) only after deliberately programming the nontraining situation. The desired generalization was achieved when each child was provided with a peer, whose presence (the authors suggest) acted as a discriminative stimulus for correct articulation.

The importance of all these studies is their clear demonstration that the problem of achieving generality of behavioral change can be solved, if relevant environmental conditions are programmed so that generalization is facilitated.

The studies so far reviewed, have been concerned with increasing or decreasing behaviors selected as desirable targets for modification primarily from a "clinical" or "social problem" viewpoint. There would seem to be no reason, however, why applied behavior analysis should be limited to these deviant behaviors. Indeed, one might argue that the discipline of behavior modification would benefit from any broadening of perspective which may help to dispel the stereotyped image of operant researchers as isolationist and conceptually blind to the systematic relevance of their work to the general psychological field (Hearst, 1967; Krantz, 1972). A case in point could well be the concept of creativity.

As a focus for psychological investigation, "creativity" or "originality" has had a somewhat erratic history, and though most definitions have elements in common, they also frequently diverge.

"The original must be defined relative to the usual and the degree of originality must be specified statistically in terms of incidence of occurrence" [Barron, 1955, p. 274].

"Creativity occurs best in unpressured, permissive, but task-oriented atmosphere with one-to-one testing ... but ... the burden of proof of possession rests primarily with the individual" [Gross & Marsh, 1970, p. 267].

"Originality refers to behavior which occurs relatively infrequently, is uncommon under given circumstances, and is relevant to those conditions" [Maltzman, 1960, p. 229].

The kind of definition accepted, has naturally guided the type of research being undertaken, and so there has been tremendous variety here also. Some have sought to interrelate creativity and personality (Barron, 1955; Dillehunt, (1973); or to develop tests which assess this behavior (Torrance, 1966; Gross & Marsh, 1970); or to examine family-environmental transactions which facilitate or inhibit creativity (Getzels & Jackson, 1961; Newmeyer, 1973); or to investigate the behavioral principles involved (Maltzman, 1960; Goetz & Baer, 1973).

Since Guilford's (1950) inaugural A.P.A. address in which he urged researchers to pursue the concept of creativity more vigorously, there has been a wealth of studies accumulating in this area, although it is only recently that an experimental approach has begun to replace a descriptive one. The studies below illustrate some recent efforts to assess, train, and facilitate creativity as developed from a more traditional psychological orientation.

ASSESSMENT OF CREATIVITY

One of the most widely used and referenced creative tests is the Torrance Test of Creative Thinking (1966). The Torrance Battery is composed of both verbal and figural tests, each presumably assessing different components of creativity and thereby contributing unique elements to the final score. The tasks are fairly diverse. The verbal part includes "ask-and-guess", product improvement, unusual uses, unusual question, and "just-suppose" activities. The figural part includes picture construction, incomplete figures and parallel line tasks.

Although the basic activities differ, each is scored for fluency, flexibility, originality and elaboration on the assumption that problem solving may be effected either creatively, or uncreatively. Fluency refers to the number of relevant responses produced by a subject, whereas flexibility refers to the number of different categories of questions, causes, consequences, products or uses. The statistical infrequency of the response (based on earlier research) justifies the originality measure, and the number of embellishments on responses provides an elaboration score. Scores for fluency, flexibility, originality, and elaboration are summed separately across all verbal and across all figural subtests.

The Torrance Battery is administered in the format of standardized achievement tests, i.e., there is a definite "examination" atmosphere and each test is timed although the subjects are not told the time limits. They are simply told . . . "you will be timed on each one, so make good use of your time. Work as fast as you can without rushing."

Given that the reliability and validity of such a test is adequate, it may be valuable for use as a predictor of creative potential. The rationale of such use rests on the assumption that creative people should be "selected" out and exposed as early as possible to enriching experiences so that their talents may be further developed. If one rejects this rationale, however, then the value of such tests is somewhat dubious, especially since it seems that creativity assessed in such a structured situation does not generalize even to untimed situations. A study by Torrance (1969) supports this latter statement. Seventy-five sixth-grade children were administered the Torrance tests in a group setting with the standard 5-min test limit. Then the children were asked to work on tests for the next 24 hrs, adding ideas as they occurred. Although a correlation of .23 (p .05) between the two scores was observed, the predictive power of the first set of scores was very slight. Thus, while there was some relationship between the children who produced many or few creative responses in each condition, it was not a sizeable relationship.

Gross and Marsh (1970) evaluated an objective experimental instrument (Gross Geometric Forms) designed to identify what they called "expressive creativity" in three to seven year-old children. Their goal was to develop an instrument with age-appropriate tasks to circumvent the problems of inequality in motor development and conventional verbal learning. The task presented to the child was that of using simple geometric shapes to construct whatever picture concepts the child "was capable of producing." Products were scored for form, name, elaborations (verbal), action, color and communicability. The results indicated age was generally associated with an increase in creativity; there were no sex differences; and a moderate positive correlation with verbal intelligence and perceptual differentiation measures appeared to indicate that creativity and intelligence, as global concepts, were not easily separable operationally. The authors presented their results tentatively. It should be noted, however, that even had their correlations been of greater statistical significance, the conclusions would still be severely limited by the low reliability and subjectivity of the scoring system.

TRAINING OF CREATIVITY

Reese and Parnes (1970) evaluated the effect of programming creative problem solving in high-school students, as measured on certain standard creativity tests (like the Torrance Product Improvement Test). Three groups of subjects were used in a pre- and posttest design. Group 1 was an untreated control; Group 2 worked through programmed booklets of problems; and Group 3 worked through the booklets with an instructor. As compared with the control group, the results clearly indicated that working alone yielded significant gains on the standard measures; working with an instructor yielded even higher gains.

Further research on training techniques was undertaken by Roweton (1972) in a correlational study with college students. Performance on the Hidden Figures Test (a cognitive-style measure of perceptual sensitivity) and grade-point averages were related to several indices of creativity as affected by a checklist procedure and verbal pretraining. The "idea" checklist provided subjects with general or specific lists of ideas suggesting physical improvements; verbal pretraining involved controlled free-association warm-up prior to problem solving. Roweton reported that neither the Hidden Figures test nor grade-point average scores correlated significantly with creativity; the short checklist did not overwhelmingly enhance idea quality; and verbal pretraining facilitated idea fluency but not originality.

Modeling influences on children's creative behavior were examined by Zimmerman and Dialessi (1973), who asked whether the behavior of a human model can vicariously influence an observer's subsequent creative responding. Four groups (120 fifth-grade children) separately observed a model who was either high or low in the fluency (number) and flexibility (quality) dimensions defined by Guilford (1967). Multivariate procedures were used to assess treatment effects on children's fluency and flexibility measures (written responses), collected on parallel and very different types of creative tasks, as assessed by the Torrance Tests of Creative Thinking (1966). The results indicated that high model fluency significantly increased child fluency and flexibility on the parallel task. A marginally significant increase in observer fluency was noted on the different creative task. Contrary to predictions, however, model flexibility produced significant decreases in observer fluency and flexibility measures on both the parallel and dissimilar tasks.

In a fairly unusual study employing 26 mentally retarded children (aged 7 to 16 years), Carter, Richmond and Bundschuh (1973) evaluated the effects of a creativity-training program on the creative development (measured by the Torrance Tests of Creative Thinking) of their subjects. Comparisons were made between three groups:

1. untreated control group;

2. visual-motor treatment group — exposure in group sessions to a variety of artistic experiences such as cutting, pasting, fingerpainting and encouragement from staff to be imaginative; and

3. kinesthetic-motor treatment group — exposure both in group and individual sessions to a variety of exercises, tumbling, games, etc.

Comparisons between the three groups showed that both treatment groups achieved higher creativity scores than the control group, but this finding was not statistically significant. The only significant difference occurred for the factor of flexibility, this difference being primarily due to the visual-motor training.

Overall, it seems fair to conclude that the traditional psychological approach to creativity, as represented in this survey, has not yielded impressive results. The assessment approach has stimulated the development and use of a multitude of creativity measures, which have in turn been correlated with a diverse pattern of variables. Unfortunately, however, the tentativeness of most findings, the failure to replicate other findings, and the seemingly unresolvable creativity-versus-intelligence controversy, severely limits any conclusions which may be drawn. Similarly, the facilitation and training of creativity, has not been shown to be amenable to any one magical technique. By contrast, recent efforts by operant psychologists, though still very limited, have been yielding success in generating creative behaviors.

It is the question of generalization which most needs further analysis, and answers to which would help to dispel the doubts of those authors who see a stimulus-response model as inappropriate for the investigation of creativity (Guilford, 1959). Crockenberg (1972) has specifically suggested that educators shift their emphasis from the selecting of creative persons to studying "the conditions or situations, the practices or experiences, the approaches and attitudes that are conducive to the *production* [our italics] of novel, appropriate, quality ideas" [p. 43] . This suggestion seems to imply that a descriptive correlation and assessment-oriented approach to the area should be abandoned in favor of a more experimental one. The operant model is well able to promote this suggestion.

Stokes and Baer (1977), in their review of generalization research, have recently presented a new analysis and classification, schema for the topic. Research is characterized in terms of directness of applicability to a problem according to the following categories: train and hope for generalization; sequential modification; training sufficient exemplars to yield generalization to the remainder; deliberate use of indiscriminant contingencies; mediated generalization; introduction to natural communities of reinforcement; train loosely; program common stimuli; and training to generalize. It is this final classification, "training to generalize," which is particularly relevant here. The category may be represented by studies by Herbert and Baer (1972), Goetz and Baer (1973), and Parsonson, Baer and Baer (1974). The core concept uniting this category is that generalization is itself conceived of as an operant, i.e. the reinforcement contingency is placed on generalization which is programmed.

Herbert and Baer (1972) and Parsonson, Baer and Baer (1974) used different techniques to effect desired behavioral change, but were essentially concerned with the same problem: how to program the generalization of correct contingencies for all appropriate and inappropriate behaviors. Herbert and Baer (1972) instructed two mothers of deviant young children to count their episodes of attention to all appropriate child behavior in their homes, using wrist counters. The child behaviors were defined as a broad response class so that *every* active behavior could be labeled as appropriate or inappropriate. The parent was given some specific examples of these types of behaviors, but was required to respond in terms of the broad category. Independent observations of parent-child interactions showed that for each mother-child pair, the percentage of maternal attention given following appropriate child behavior increased, as did the child's appropriate behavior. In addition, one mother was instructed to count her attention to inappropriate child behaviors and to "decrease it," but this condition had little effect. Follow-up observations made over the next five months showed the behavioral gains to be durable, suggesting that training "diverse" behaviors in conjunction with self-counting, may be an effective and economical parent-training technique.

Parsonson, Baer and Baer (1974) operating within a kindergarten-style program for institutionalized mental retardates, provided frequent observer feedback to two aides, for their application of generalized correct social contingencies to a wide range of child behaviors, covering ten categories with many possible combinations of appropriate and inappropriate forms. Training successfully increased the proportion of appropriate attention to child behaviors for each aide and follow-up data indicated that the training effects were durable.

What these studies have in common is their concern with training a "generalized" attention skill. The focus was not on programming contingencies for some specifically coded, discrete response such as: shock to decrease head-banging; M & M's to increase color labeling; or attention to increase tricycle riding or decrease shouting. Rather, the focus was to develop a skill of attending to any examples of a broad-response class.

Similarly, in the Goetz and Baer (1973) study cited above, the generalization contingency was placed on movement along the dimension of diversity. Reinforcement was not available simply for any form production; it was available only for "different" form productions, i.e., generalization was programmed by reinforcing only the first appearance of each form per session.

The appeal of studies which fit Stokes and Baer's (1977) "training to generalize" category lies in the essence of their programming a generalized response skill, whose probability of being elicited by, and reinforced within, the natural environment is thereby substantially increased. A technology which can program response diversity rather than response specificity, should be able to effect behavioral change much more efficiently. Experiments 1 and 2 and the Goetz and Baer (1973) study which preceded them fall into this "training to generalize" category. In fact, a major concern in training creativity or originality is the essential fact that variability from what is already trained *must* be induced.

One dimension shown in Experiment 2 to be important in specifying the limits of generalization is that of topographical similarity (cf. also Garcia, Baer, & Firestone, 1971). Thus "training to generalize" programs need specifically to overcome the limitations of topographical similarity, while emphasizing functional similarity: how to invent departures from current productions similarly in different activities despite topographical differences between those activities.

It may be that "training to generalize" is the most active, forceful, and thus productive tactic in the design of research aimed at the improvement of generalization technology. At least, it most clearly emphasizes the conception of generalization as an active behavioral skill, rather than as the passive outcome of operations applied to other behaviors. Whether in fact this is a fruitful conception will presumably depend on the outcome of the research which it generates. Meanwhile, the conception stands as an attractive strategy for furthering generalization methodology, and as a viable one. To the extent that it is chosen by researchers interested in the generalization problem, then creativity programs, defined objectively in terms of the invention of new behaviors, should become a problem of choice in that research. This should be true not because of the social value placed on the label (explored in the beginning of this chapter) but because the essence of creativity (so defined) is the constant generalization from already established behaviors: to be creative (in this definition) is to produce a response related to previous responses but different from them. In this sense, creativity studies may be to the development of a generalization methodology what bar-pressing studies were to the development of operant theory. Thus, whether from the intrinsic value of the concept of creativity for human behavior, or whether from the standpoint of the necessary development of generalization methodology, such creativity studies may well play a central role in the future.

ACKNOWLEDGMENTS

Supported in part by a grant from the University of Kansas Research Fund (Grant number 3336-5038). Additional support was provided by Grant #HD-02528-07 to the Bureau of Child Research, University of Kansas, by the National Institute of Child Health and Human Development.

REFERENCES

Baer, D. M., Wolf, M. M., & Risley, T. R. Some current dimensions of applied behavior analysis. *Journal of Applied Behavior Analysis,* 1968, *1,* 91-97.
Barron, F. The disposition towards originality. *Journal of Abnormal and Social Psychology,* 1955, *51,* 478-485.

Barron, F. The psychology of creativity. In F. Barron (Ed.), *New directions in psychology II.* New York: Holt, Rinehart & Winston, 1965.

Beehler, Kay, A. Effects of social reinforcement on creativity in block constructions. University of Kansas, 1972, unpublished manuscript.

Berlyne, D. E. *Conflict, arousal and curiosity.* New York: McGraw-Hill, 1960.

Brodgen, E. E., & Sprecher, T. B. Criteria of creativity. In C. W. Taylor (Ed.), *Creativity: Progress and potential.* New York: McGraw-Hill, 1964.

Bruner, J. S. The conditions of creativity. In H. E. Gruber, G. Terrell, & M. Wertheimer (Eds.), *Contemporary approaches to creative thinking.* New York: Atherton, 1962.

Carter, K. R., Richmond, B. O., & Bundschuh, E. L. The effect of kinesthetic and visual-motor experiences in the creative development of mentally retarded students. *Education & Training of the Mentally Retarded,* 1973, *8*(1), 24-28.

Corte, H. E., Wolf, M. M., & Locke, B. J. A comparison of procedures for eliminating self-inurious behavior of retarded adolescents. *Journal of Applied Behavior Analysis,* 1971, *4,* 201-213.

Crockenberg, S. B. Creativity tests: A boon or boondoggle for education? *Review of Educational Research,* 1972, *42,* 27-45.

Crutchfield, R. S. Creative thinking in children: its teaching and testing. In O. G. Brim, R. S. Crutchfield, & W. Holtzman (Eds.), *Intelligence: Perspectives, 1965.* New York: Harcourt, Brace & World, 1966.

Dillehunt, H. Q. Creativity in children: A comparison of creativity tests and naturalistic measures of creativity, anxiety and achievement motivation. *Dissertation Abstracts International,* 1973, *33*B, 3282.

Fallon, M. P. The creative teacher: The effects of descriptive social reinforcement upon the drawing behavior of three preschool children. *School Applications of Learning Theory,* 1975, *7,* No. 2, 27-45.

Freud, S. A. *A general introduction to psychoanalysis.* New York: Boni & Liveright, 1920.

Garcia, E. The training and generalization of a conversational speech form in non-verbal retardates. *Journal of Applied Behavior Analysis,* 1974, *7,* 137-149.

Garcia, E., Baer, D. M., & Firestone, I. The development of generalized imitation within topographically determined boundaries. *Journal of Applied Behavior Analysis,* 1971, *4,* 101-112.

Gardner, H. *The arts and human development.* New York: John Wiley, 1973.

Getzels, J. W., & Jackson, P. W. Family environment and cognitive style: A study of the sources of highly intelligent and of highly creative adolescents. *American Sociological Review,* 1961, *26*(3), 351-359.

Getzels, J. W., & Jackson, P. W. The highly intelligent and the highly creative adolescent: A summary of some research findings. In C. W. Taylor & F. Barron (Eds.), *Scientific creativity: Its recognition and development.* New York: Wiley, 1963.

Ghiselin, B. *The Creative Process.* Berkeley, Cal.: University of California Press, 1952.

Ghiselin, B. Ultimate criteria for two levels of creativity. In C. W. Taylor & F. Barron (Eds.), *Scientific creativity: Its recognition and development.* New York: Wiley, 1963.

Goetz, E. M., & Baer, D. M. Social control of form diversity and the emergence of new forms in children's blockbuilding. *Journal of Applied Behavior Analysis,* 1973, *6,* 209-217.

Goetz, E. M., & Salmonson, M. M. The effect of general and descriptive reinforcement on "creativity" in easel painting. In G. B. Semb (Ed.), *Behavior analysis in education, 1972.* Lawrence, Kansas: University of Kansas Printing Service, 1972.

Gross, R. B., & Marsh, M. An instrument for measuring creativity in young children. *Developmental Psychology,* 1970, *3,* 267.

Guess, D., Sailor, W., Rutherford, G., & Baer, D. M. An experimental analysis of linguistic development: The productive use of the plural morpheme. *Journal of Applied Behavior Analysis,* 1970, *3,* 273-287.

Guilford, J. P. Traits of creativity. In P. E. Vernon (Ed.), *Creativity and its cultivation.* New York: Harper, 1959.

Guilford, J. P. Introductory portion of "creativity" presidential address in 1950. In S. J. Parnes & H. F. Harding (Eds.) *A source book for creative thinking.* New York: Charles Scribner's Sons, 1962.

Guilford, J. P. *The nature of human intelligence.* New York: McGraw-Hill, 1967.

Hardiman, S., Goetz, E. M., Reuter, K., & LeBlanc, J. M. Effects of contingent attention, primes and training on a child's motor behavior. Paper presented at the Society for Research in Child Development, Philadelphia, March, 1973.

Hauserman, N., Walen, S. R., & Behling, M. Reinforced racial integration in the first grade: A study in generalization. *Journal of Applied Behavior Analysis,* 1973, *6,* 193-201.

Hearst, E. The behavior of Skinnerians. *Contemporary Psychology,* 1967, *12,* 402-404.

Herbert, E. W., & Baer, D. M. Training parents as behavior modifiers: Self recording of contingent attention. *Journal of Applied Behavior Analysis,* 1972, *5,* 139-149.

Hogg, J. *Psychology and the visual arts.* Harmondsworth, Middlesex, England: Penguin Books, Inc., 1969.

Johnston, J. M., & Johnston, G. T. Modification of consonant speech-sound articulation in young children. *Journal of Applied Behavior Analysis,* 1972, *5,* 233-246.

Kale, R. J., Kaye, J. H., Whelan, P. A., & Hopkins, B. L. The effects of reinforcement on the modification, maintenance, and generalization of social responses of mental patients. *Journal of Applied Behavior Analysis,* 1968, *1,* 307-314.

Krantz, D. L. Schools and systems: The mutual isolation of operant and nonoperant psychology as a case study. *Journal History of the Behavioral Sciences,* 1972, *8,* 86-102.

Maltzman, I. On the training of originality. *Psychological Review,* 1960, *67,* 229-242.

Maltzman, I., Simon, S., Raskin, D., & Licht, L. Experimental studies in the training of originality. *Psychological Monographs,* 1960, *74,* 274-283.

McPherson, J. H. A proposal for establishing ultimate criteria for measuring creative output. In C. W. Taylor & F. Barron (Eds.), *Scientific creativity: Its recognition and development.* New York: Wiley, 1963.

Meadow, A., & Parnes, S. J. Evaluation of training in creative problem solving. *Journal of Applied Psychology,* 1959, *43,* 189-194.

Moustakas, C. E. *Creativity and conformity.* New York: D. VanNostrand Co., 1967.

Newmeyer, J. A. Creativity and non-verbal communication in pre-adolescent white and black children. *Dissertation Abstracts International,* 1973, *33*B, 426.

Parnes, S. J., & Meadow, A. Effects of "brainstorming" instructions on creative problem-solving course, 1960. *Psychological Report, 57,* 357-361.

Parsonson, B. S., Baer, A. M., & Baer, D. M. The application of generalized correct social contingencies: An evaluation of a training program. *Journal of Applied Behavior Analysis,* 1974, *7,* 427-437.

Pryor, K. W., Haag, R., & O'Reilly, J. The creative porpoise: Training for novel behavior. *Journal of the Experimental Analysis of Behavior,* 1969, *12,* 653-661.

Reese, H. W., & Parnes, S. J. Programming creative behavior. *Child Development,* 1970, *41,* 413-423.

Roe, A. *The making of a scientist.* New York: Dodd Mead, 1952.

Roweton, W. E. Creativity: Idea quantity and idea quality. *Child Study Journal,* 1972, *2,* 83-89.

Schumaker, J., & Sherman, J. A. Training generative verb usage by imitation and reinforcement procedures. *Journal of Applied Behavior Analysis,* 1970, *3,* 273-287.

Shapiro, R. J. The criterion problem. Excerpt from R. J. Shapiro, Creative research scientists, *Psychological Africana,* Monograph Supplement, No. 4, 1968, 37-45. In P. E. Vernon (Ed.), *Creativity.* Baltimore: Penguin, 1970, 257-269.

Silberman, C. E. *The open classroom reader.* New York: Random House, 1973.

Skinner, B. F. *Science and human behavior.* New York: Macmillan Free Press, 1953.

Stein, M. I. Creativity and culture. *Journal of Paychology,* 1953, *36,* 311-332.

Stein, M. I., & Heinze, S. J. *Creativity and the individual.* Glencoe, Ill.: The Free Press, 1960.

Stokes, T. F., & Baer, D. M. An implicit technology of generalization. *Journal of Applied Behavior Analysis,* 1977, *10,* (in press).

Stokes, T. F., Baer, D. M., & Jackson, R. L. Programming the generalization of a greeting response in four retarded children. *Journal of Applied Behavior Analysis,* 1974, *7,* 599-610.

Taylor, C. W. *Creativity: Progress and potential.* New York: McGraw-Hill, 1964.

Torrance, E. P. *Torrance tests of creative thinking: Norms-technical manual.* Princeton: Personnel Press, 1966.

Torrance, E. P. Curiosity of gifted children and performance on timed and untimed tests of creativity. *Gifted Child Quarterly,* 1969, *13*(3), 155-158.

Vernon, P. E. *Creativity.* Baltimore: Penguin, 1970.

Zimmerman, B. J., & Dialessi, F. Modeling influences on children's creative behavior. *Journal of Educational Psychology,* 1973, *65*(1), 127-134.

27

Achievement Place: The Modification of Academic Behavior Problems of Delinquent Youths in a Group Home Setting

Kathryn A. Kirigin
Elery L. Phillips
Gary D. Timbers
Dean L. Fixsen
Montrose M. Wolf[1]

University of Kansas

> A small but rapidly growing group of psychologists can now offer educators a set of concepts and principles derived entirely from the experimental analysis of behavior, a methodology for the practical application of these concepts and principles, a research method that deals with changes in individual behavior
>
> · · ·
>
> [Bijou, 1970]

Since the above offer was first extended to educators, their rate of acceptance has been most impressive. In the past five years, the application of the principles and procedures of behavior modification within the classroom has been increasing at an ever accelerating pace. Since that offer was extended, countless teachers at the preschool, elementary, and secondary levels have learned to make effective use of their social attention and a variety of other events available within the classroom setting to reduce disruptive social behaviors, to increase study skills, and to improve the academic performance of their students (O'Leary & O'Leary, 1972; Ramp & Hopkins, 1971).

[1]This research was supported by grants MH 20030 and MH 13664 from the National Institute of Mental Health (Center for Studies of Crime and Delinquency) to the Bureau of Child Research and the Department of Human Development, University of Kansas.

When it has been impossible or impractical to work solely within the classroom setting, behavioral psychologists following the Bijou model have simply sought alternative procedures. With imagination and careful analysis of behavior, several investigators have shown that willing parents can play an active role in improving the school behavior of their children. With a modicum of training in contingency management and sufficiently powerful consequences in the home, parents have been able to work cooperatively with teachers to increase school attendance (MacDonald, Gallimore, & MacDonald, 1970); to reduce disruptive social behaviors (Bailey, Wolf, & Phillips, 1970) and to improve study behavior (McKenzie, Clark, Wolf, Kothera, & Benson, 1968; Bailey, et al., 1970).

The use of consequences in the home to improve a youth's behavior in school has been a particularly important aspect of the Achievement Place treatment program for delinquent and predelinquent youths in Lawrence, Kansas. Operated on a token economy, the program is directed by a professionally trained couple who serve as the teaching-parents for 6 to 8 adjudicated youths from the local community. The teaching-parents are solely responsible, 24 hours a day, for supervising the motivation system and for teaching the youths the requisite behaviors which will enable them to participate effectively in school, family, and community living. Within this setting, youths earn points for learning and displaying appropriate social, self-care, and academic behaviors; they lose points for inappropriate or maladaptive behaviors. For youths just entering the program, points earned each day are exchanged initially on a daily basis, and later on a weekly basis, for privileges available in the home. These privileges include activities such as watching television, bike riding, free time and weekend visits to the natural home. (For a complete description of the Achievement Place program, cf. to Phillips, Phillips, Fixsen, & Wolf, 1974.)

The youths who enter Achievement Place typically have records indicating a variety of school-behavior problems. These problems include irregular attendance, failure of one or more grades, academic deficiencies in reading and math, and other serious misbehaviors. According to Cervantes (1965) these are some of the behaviors common among school dropouts. Consequently, in the Achievement Place program a great deal of emphasis has been placed on school behavior. Because the program is community based, the teaching-parents have been able to work closely with the teachers to remediate many school-behavior problems. The basic procedure used is a daily report card system whereby daily teacher evaluations of the youth's performance in class are backed up by point consequences in the home. This procedure has been extensively evaluated by Bailey, et al., (1970) and been shown to produce dramatic improvements in study behavior (on task) and substantial reductions in disruptive social behavior. In addition to its effectiveness, the system proved to be extremely practical to implement. However, in a number of cases, teacher reports indicated that many youths continued to perform poorly on academic assignments in spite of considerable improvements in their study behavior.

Since success in school is often measured in terms of academic performance, the studies which follow were carried out to explore and evaluate procedures which could be implemented by teaching-parents within Achievement Place to modify specific academic behavior problems.

EXPERIMENT 1

Subjects

The subjects for this study were two boys living at Achievement Place. Both were enrolled in regular math classes at the junior high school. One subject, who will be referred to as Mark, was 15 years old and an eighth-grade student. Before coming to Achievement Place, his school record showed school attendance to be slightly above 50% and failing grades for most classes. In the final eighth-grade semester he failed 5 of 6 classes and was retained in that grade for an additional year. The second subject, who will be referred to as Greg, was 13 years old and in the seventh grade. His school record before coming to Achievement Place showed reports of disruptive social behavior, including assaults against teachers and peers. As a sixth grader, his school behavior was so unacceptable that he had been expelled from 3 elementary schools in one year. As a result he attended classes for approximately 2 months of the school year before he was sent to Achievement Place. No grade records were available for his sixth-grade year. However, he was advanced to the seventh grade in the junior high school.

Recording Procedures

Grades in math were chosen as the dependent measure. Math class was selected because assignments were frequent and the grades were objective measures based on accuracy of problem solving. The grades in math were obtained directly from the teacher's grade book approximately once each week. The grading system also indicated whether or not homework assignments had been handed in.

Experimental Conditions

Baseline

The boys were instructed to report their homework assignments in math upon returning to the home each day. The boys earned 1000 points for filling out a daily homework report indicating whether or not an assignment had been given.

Daily Homework Card 1

The boys were required to carry a daily homework card to school each day. Space was provided for the boy to write in his homework assignment. The math teacher was asked to check the card at the end of class and sign it. At the end of each school day the boys brought the cards home to the teaching-parents.

When the daily card procedure was introduced the boys were told that they could earn 1000-1500 points for completing their homework assignments and that 2000 points would be lost for failure to bring the card or an assignment home. In addition they were told that they would lose 2000 points if they did not complete their assigned work. At the teacher's request, Greg's card included a question concerning his social behavior in class. If the teacher checked that his behavior was inappropriate, he lost 2000 points. Homework time was scheduled each day after school for approximately an hour. During this time, at least one adult (one of the teaching-parents or the first author) was present to help the boys with their assingments, to tutor them on the difficult problems, and to check to see that the assignments were completed with a high level of accuracy. Tutors were instructed to continue to tutor until the assingment was completed as close to 100% as possible (determined by the tutors' ability to detect procedural and computational errors without access to an answer key).

Daily Homework Card 2

To permit the teaching-parents to determine whether the completed homework assignments were returned to class, an additional question was added to the homework card. The boys still wrote in their homework assignments, but the teacher was asked to check *yes* or *no* to indicate whether the previous day's assignment had been returned to class. Under this condition the boys were told that they would continue to earn points for a completed assignment and that an additional 500 points could also be earned for handing in the assignments to the teacher. For not handing in the assignment the boys would lose 2000 points. The points were earned or lost solely on the basis of the teacher's response to the question on the card. Tutoring continued to be available.

During the Card 2 condition the boys were told that they could also earn points for weekly grades of C and above (5000 for C, 7500 for B, and 10,000 for A) and would lose points for D's (−7500) and F's (−10,000). Weekly grade evaluations were obtained from the teachers as a routine part of the Achievement Place program.

No Cards

To determine whether the combined consequences for completed homework, handing in assignments, and weekly grades were necessary to maintain the changes in grade behavior, the cards and all point consequences were removed. The boys no longer were required to carry the daily card. They were instructed to continue to do their homework, but tutoring was no longer available.

Daily Homework Card 2

The Card 2 condition was reinstated. When this condition was reinstated, Mark was no longer on the point system, but had advanced to the merit system. While on the merit system, he no longer earned points for appropriate behavior or lost points for inappropriate behavior and all privileges were free. The consequence for failure to maintain acceptable behavior while on the merit system was a return to the point system thus delaying the opportunity to return to the natural home. While this condition was in effect Mark passed the merit system and advanced to the next phase of the program where he spent less time at Achievement Place and nearly all of his time in his natural home. However, he continued to carry the daily card to school and continued to come to Achievement Place for homework sessions each day after school.

During the Card 2 condition Greg also advanced to the merit system. On his first attempt, Greg failed the merit system because of poor school behavior. In the seond week of the merit system Greg's social behavior in the classroom failed to maintain at an acceptable level and he received a warning to improve it. On the next day he received a *no* on his math card for failing to hand in his homework assignment. This constituted his second warning and he was returned to the point system.

Results

Daily Grades

Figure 1 shows daily math grades for each boy for each of the treatment conditions. The data points represent homework grades, but also include grades for in-class assignments and tests. In Mark's class, accuracy was recorded as a letter grade: 90-100% was an A, 80-89% a B, and so on. A grade of zero (0) indicated that the assignment was not handed in to the teacher. A zero score was equivalent to an F. In Greg's class, accuracy was recorded as a ratio: the number of problems correct over the total problems assigned. These ratios were recorded on the graph as percentages.

Baseline. In the *baseline* condition, Mark's daily grades ranged from A to F and showed no apparent trend. Greg, on the other hand, scored consistently below 50% accuracy on 8 of 11 assignments. During this condition, the boys reported an average of one homework assignment per week. However, an independent check with the teachers revealed that both boys were less than 50% reliable in reporting homework. Mark accurately reported 3 of 7 assignments and Greg reported 4 of 9.

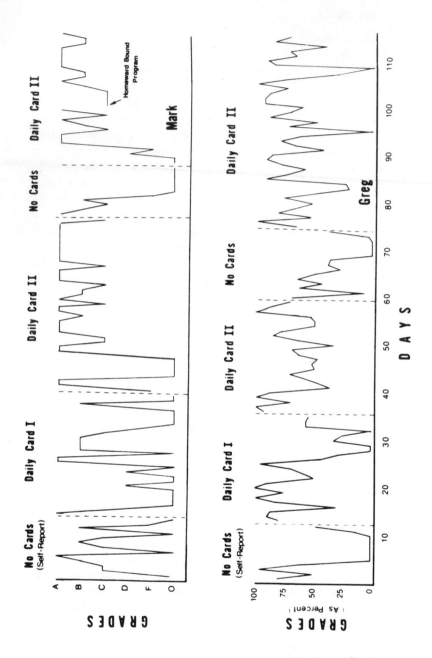

Figure 1   Daily grades in math for all experimental conditions.

Daily Card 1.   When the homework card was introduced to encourage more accurate daily reporting of homework and points were earned for completed homework assignments at home, Mark's grades showed no improvement. If anything, he received a greater proportion of Ds and Fs during this condition. Greg's grades showed an initial improvement but the effect was not maintained and his grades deteriorated. The median grade for this condition was 50% for Greg and zero for Mark (indicating failure to hand in his assignments).

Daily Card 2.   When the boys were able to earn points for completing their assignments at home, for handing in completed assignments at school, and for weekly academic performance, both showed dramatic improvement in daily grades. Mark's grades increased to better than a C average with most grades falling within the A to C range. The median grade for this condition was A. An unscheduled procedural change resulted in the initial cluster of zeros when the Card 2 condition was introduced for Mark. During this time the teacher began to check *yes* that the assignment had been handed in at the beginning of class without asking to see the assignment. This brief period of noncontingent checking was corrected by a visit to the teacher. When the Card 2 condition was in effect for Greg, his median grade was 70%.

No Cards.   When the cards and consequences were removed Mark continued to complete assignments and hand them in for a few days. However, his grades dropped steadily. During the last week of this condition Mark did not hand in any assignments. Greg's grades deteriorated immediately to below the 50% level and continued to decline to near zero for the final days of this condition. During this condition, both teachers reported problems with the boys' classroom behavior, and by the end of the third week of the reversal Greg's teacher requested that the card be reinstated.

Daily Card 2.   When the Daily Card 2 condition was reinstated with point consequences for completed homework, handing in assignments and for weekly grades, both boys showed an immediate improvement in math grades. The grades in the Card 2 condition were consistent with those recorded in the initial Card 2 condition. Although Mark advanced through the merit system to his natural home, his grades were maintained at C or better quality. Greg's grades in this condition were also consistently better than those in the No Card condition His median grade for this condition was 68%.

Figure 2 shows the percentage of weekly homework assignments that were completed and handed in to the teacher for each boy for each treatment condition. When there were no consequences for turning in homework (Baseline and Card 1 conditions) Mark handed in less than 50% of his assignments. Although he earned points for completing assignments in the home when the Card 1 condition was in effect, zero scores indicated that many of the assignments did not get back to class. When the consequences for handing in homework were added,

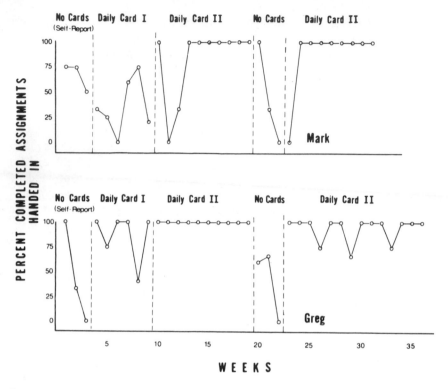

Figure 2   The percentage of completed homework assignments handed in each week for all experimental conditions.

Mark's hand-in rate increased to 100% where it remained until the condition was terminated. When the card and consequences were removed the percentage of assignments handed in decreased. When the treatment condition was reinstated, the hand-in rate returned to the previous 100% level.

Greg's behavior showed similar effects with the changes in procedures with one difference. When he was earning points for completing assignments in the group home the majority of his assignments were getting back to class. When consequences were introduced for handing in assignments, the behavior was maintained consistently at 100%, deteriorated when the cards and consequences were removed and returned to a high level, though not consistently 100%, when the treatment condition was reinstated.

Weekly Grades

Figure 3 shows the weekly-grade evaluations given by the teacher on the basis of the boys' weekly performance. No evaluations were available until the third week of the Baseline condition. Of the three measures perhaps this is the least objective. It is not clear that the teachers made the evaluations solely on the basis of grades recorded in the grade book. However, these grades appeared to correlate with the daily homework scores.

When there were no consequences for weekly grades (Baseline and Card 1 condition) for Mark, he received Cs and Ds for all but one week. When consequences for weekly grades went into the effect in the Card 2 condition his weekly grades were C or better throughout the Card 2 condition. The grades decreased when the cards were removed and returned to a C or better level when the Card 2 condition was reinstated.

Greg's weekly grades showed similar effects. His grades showed a downward trend during the Card 1 condition, increased and maintained at C or above during the Card 2 condition, deteriorated to Ds and Fs during the No Card condition and returned to about a C level during the second Card 2 condition.

EXPERIMENT 2

This second experiment was carried out at Achievement Place for Girls in Lawrence. The program is a replication of the first Achievement Place program. Two questions were asked. Could contingencies be arranged within a replication of

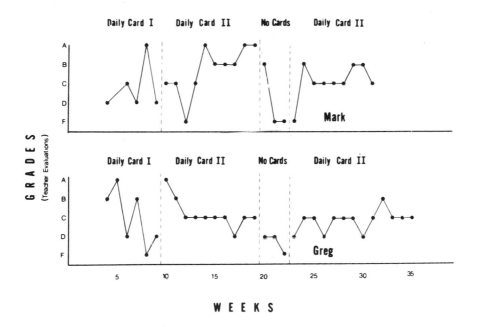

Figure 3   Weekly teacher evaluations of math performance (grades) in all experimental conditions.

the original treatment program to effect the academic performance of the youths? Could grade improvements be obtained in a more practical, efficient manner, that is without the use of a tutor?

Subjects and Setting

The subjects were three adolescent girls living at Achievement Place for Girls. All had school records which indicated below average academic progress: two had failed at least one grade. Mary and Donna were in the seventh grade; Dora was in the eighth grade and they all attended the same junior high school.

The experiment was carried out while the girls were enrolled in regular math classes. Math was chosen as the target class for two reasons: (1) weekly grade reports and several phone calls from the teachers indicated that all the girls were in danger of failing math; and (2) because objective data (daily grades) could be regularly obtained to permit evaluation of the effectiveness of our experimental procedures. Although Mary and Dora were enrolled in regular math class, both were working in lower-level math workbooks because according to teacher reports and standardized test scores, they lacked sufficient skills to work in the regular text. Donna was in seventh grade and worked in the regular textbook.

Recording Procedures

Grade data were collected by contacting the girls' teachers approximately once each week. Grades were obtained directly from the teachers' record books. Two teachers were involved and both used a similar 10-point grading system to record assignment accuracy. The system was based on percentage scores, which were rounded to the nearest 10 for ease of recording. A score of 10 was given for a perfect paper; 9 indicated accuracy 99-85%; 8 represented scores 84-75%; and so on.

Experimental Conditions

Baseline

During baseline and throughout the experiment, the girls earned points for weekly grades in all classes. In math, the girls earned from 1,000 to 10,000 points for grades of D or better and they lost 10,000 points for an F. (These weekly letter grades were assigned by each teacher and were based on the average number of points the youths had earned for the week.) No other systematic point consequences for academic behavior were in effect.

Daily Card

Following several days of consistently low grades, a daily report-card procedure was introduced. The card was designed in cooperation with the math teacher, who specified the problem behaviors and indicated the kind of information

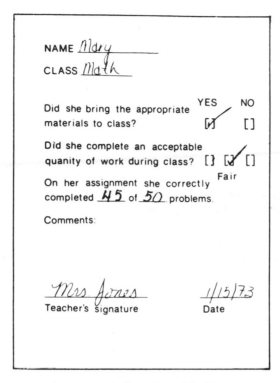

Figure 4   Daily math card for Mary.

that could be conveniently provided on a daily basis. The card is snown in Figure 4. When Mary began taking the card she was told that she could earn 3,000 points for a good report. Three thousand points was equivalent to about an hour of maintenance or about one-half hour of academic work. A good report was defined as a card indicating that she had brought the appropriate materials to class, had completed at least a *fair* quantity of work and achieved an accuracy level of 70% or better. Each question that was marked *no* resulted in the loss of 3,000 points and accuracy falling below 70% was equivalent to a *no*.

Tutoring

When the daily card condition failed to produce any change in Donna's math grades, a tutoring condition was introduced. Under this condition, a tutor was provided to help Donna with her daily assignments. Donna was required to complete each assignment prior to the onset of tutoring. To obtain an estimate of first-time accuracy, the tutor corrected Donna's assignment. The tutor then tutored her over the problems she had missed by providing examples of similar problems and working through the solution with her. Tutoring sessions averaged about an hour. The tutor recorded first-time accuracy on the back of the daily card, using the same grading system used by the teachers. During tutoring, Donna earned 100 points per minute (the rate for academic work) as an incentive to participate in the tutoring sessions. During the tutoring condition the same consequences remained in effect for Donna (3,000 points for a good school report and −3,000 points for each *no* or an accuracy level below 70%).

Untutored Assignments

On five separate occasions during the tutoring condition, the tutor did not work with Donna on her assignments. On two of those days the tutor corrected the assignment but told Donna time couldn't be arranged to work with her that evening and to do the best she could in correcting her mistakes. On the remaining three days the tutor was unavailable.

Reliability.   Reliability of the tutor's grading of the pretutored assignment was assessed in two ways: by comparing the tutor's and the math teacher's grading of the same assignment; and by having a second observer grade the assignment before the tutor graded it. Reliability in both cases was calculated by summing the total number of agreements in scoring and dividing the total by agreements plus disagreements. Reliability between the tutor and the teacher averaged 95%. Reliability between the tutor and the independent grader ranged from 94 to 100% with a mean of 96%. Reliability of the teacher's grading of Mary and Dora's assignments was assessed by having a second scorer re-grade a sample of assignments already graded by the teacher. Agreement averaged 100%.

Results

Mary and Dora

The daily grades for all three girls for all experimental conditions are shown in Figure 5. As the key indicates, a score of 10 was an A, 9 an A−, 8 a B, 7 a C, 6 a D, and 5 or below an F. The results for Mary and Dora are discussed together as both required only the daily report card. Or the first two weeks (approximately 4 data points per week) Mary's performance in math was variable but accuracy was consistently high, ranging from F to A with a median grade of B. For the third and fourth week of Baseline Mary failed to hand in any assignments. The teacher reported that she had stopped working during class. When the daily card was introduced for Mary, her grades showed an immediate improvement and throughout the condition, accuracy never fell below a 6 or D level.

The baseline condition for Dora remained in effect for about 8 weeks. During this time her accuracy ranged from 0 to 9. The median for the final 3 weeks of the condition was a 4 or F. When the daily card and the contingencies were introduced, grades showed an immediate increase to D or better and thereafter stabilized at a 7 or C level.

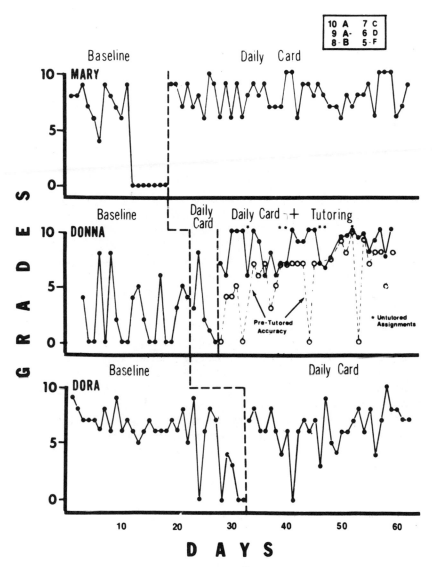

Figure 5   Daily grades in math for all experimental conditions.

Donna

The baseline period for Donna remained in effect for 5 weeks (20 data points). During the baseline, Donna's grades maintained below a level of 6. When the daily card was introduced for Donna, her grades remained unchanged. After a week of consistently failing grades, the tutoring procedure was introduced. Figure 4 shows the pretutored accuracy (open circles) and the final grade achieved on the daily assignments (dark circles) during the daily-card-plus-tutoring condition. When tutoring was added to the daily card procedure, there was an immediate increase in grades but little initial change in first-time accuracy. As first-first-time accuracy data show, there was a gradual improvement in this measure throughout the tutoring condition. For the final 3 weeks of the condition the average first-time accuracy was an 8 or B. During the tutoring condition, daily assignment grades maintained consistently above a D level, with an average grade of 9 (A −). The untutored assignment probes, shown by the starred data points indicated in Figure 5 that when tutoring was not available for assignments, the grades averaged a 7 or C. Although these untutored assignment grades fell below the median, they did not decrease to the untutored Baseline and Daily Card Only levels.

GENERAL DISCUSSION

The results of Experiment 1 indicate that the academic performance of delinquent youths in a group-home treatment program can be modified by applying the appropriate contingencies and a tutoring procedure within the home. When the boys carried the daily homework card and participated in the tutoring program and earned points for completing assignments, handing them in and for weekly grades, all of these measures improved. Because tutoring and the contingencies were always in effect simultaneously a second experiment was carried out to isolate the effect of contingencies alone with tutoring.

The results of Experiment 2 indicate that point consequences may be sufficient to improve the academic performance of some children. However, with one of the three girls (Donna) point consequences alone failed to produce any improvement in her grades. Donna's academic performance improved only after a tutoring condition was introduced. These results suggest that poor academic performance may, in some cases, be more than just a problem of insufficient motivation and that differential consequences for accuracy alone may not be sufficient to improve academic behaviors. When consequences fail to produce the desired improvements, a remedial program may be needed.

Together the experiments support the notion that academic behavior problems can be changed by providing contingencies and remediation procedures outside of the classroom setting without reliance on special materials or direct intervention in the classroom. There are a number of advantages to this remediation approach. The daily-card procedure requires only the cooperation of the teacher (willingness to fill out a daily report card), little or no training since the measures of interest are those which teachers are trained to record (grades), and very little time. Both teachers involved in this study indicated that the benefits of the procedures far outweighed any possible inconvenience to them. The daily-card procedure provides regular feedback to both the youth and the parents or teaching-parents about the youth's performance in the classroom. In this way, academic successes can be reinforced and problems can be dealt with immediately to minimize future error. That is, if a youth fails to grasp an important concept in class, tutoring procedures can be implemented in the home to supplement the learning process.

The results of this study seem to support the findings of several other investigators who have trained parents to provide consequences in the home to improve the classroom behavior of their children (MacDonald *et al.*, 1970; McKenzie *et al.*, 1968; Bailey *et al.*, 1970). Together these studies suggest that in addition to procedures which can be employed by teachers in the classroom, the small but growing group of psychologists can now offer parents, foster parents and guardians a number of procedures which will permit them to enhance the academic achievement of their children.

REFERENCES

Bailey, J. S., Wolf, M. M., & Phillips, E. L. Home-based reinforcement and the modification of pre-delinquents' classroom behavior. *Journal of Applied Behavior Analysis,* 1970, *3,* 223-333.

Bijou, S. W. What psychology has to offer education now. *Journal of Applied Behavior Analysis,* 1970, *1,* 65-72.

Cervantes, L. F. *The dropout.* Ann Arbor: University of Michigan Press, 1965.

MacDonald, W. S., Gallimore, R., & MacDonald, G. Contingency counseling by school personnel: An economical model of intervention. *Journal of Applied Behavior Analysis,* 1970, *3,* 175-184.

McKenzie, H. S., Clark, M., Wolf, M. M., Kothera, R., & Benson, C. Behavior modification of children with learning disabilities using grades as tokens and allowances as back-up reinforcers. *Exceptional Children,* 1968, *38,* 743-752.

O'Leary, K. D., & O'Leary, S. G. *Classroom management: The successful use of behavior modification.* New York: Pergamon Press, 1972.

Phillips, E. L., Phillips, E. A., Fixsen, D. L., & Wolf, M. M. *The teaching-family handbook.* 1974.

Ramp, E. A., & Hopkins, B. L. *A new direction for education: Behavior analysis, 1971.* The University of Kansas, Support and Development Center for Follow Through, Department of Human Development, 1971.

28

Sharing at an Early Age[1]

Harriet L. Rheingold

University of North Carolina at Chapel Hill

Sharing is the commonest of behavior. All of us share with others. As scientists we share our thoughts with each other, as well as the joys and griefs of discovery. Husbands share their thoughts and possessions with wives, wives with husbands, and both share with their children. Children share. And since we know that they do share, we may ask when does sharing start. With whom and what do they share? What is the nature of the first sharing?

I would like to be able to tell you that these questions came to my mind in the order I have set forth, that is, by theorizing that because sharing is a common behavior, when and how it begins would be of interest. The facts, however, are quite different. The interesting varieties of children's behavior occur to me only by watching children. No one sees everything; our prejudices alert us to different facets of the child's behavior. What determines what I see and what guides my observations is, I believe, a predisposition to view the child as the happy experimenter, an explorer eager for new experiences, and at the same time a truly social being almost from birth.

The facts then are these. In a recent study (Rheingold, 1973) we set out to show that some of the infant's behavior heretofore treated in the literature as dependence qualified as the opposite; that is, satisfied the definition of independence. To support the argument, we charted the activities of 12- and 18-month-old children in a free-play situation in the laboratory. We measured the nature, frequency, sequence, and duration of the child's use of space, toys, and the mother, she being instructed to play a passive role. We found that the children promptly entered the rooms adjoining the starting room and in a few seconds

[1]This chapter was originally presented as the Presidential Address, Division 7, American Psychological Association, Montreal, August 30, 1973.

489

were playing with the toys they found there. They spent much more time play-ing with the toys than staying with their mothers. The behavior of most chil-dren was marked by vivacity and gaiety; they ran, smiled, laughed, shrieked — and they talked. One could conclude that the behavior of the children at both ages was "marked by an independent energetic spirit and by a readiness to undertake and experiment." These findings lent credence to the proposal that much of their behavior could be characterized as independent, and suggested that we do young children a disservice by focusing so much attention on their dependence.

In addition to the above measures, I also dictated a narrative account of the child's behavior. To my surprise, the accounts revealed that many of the chil-dren *showed* the toys to their mothers and also *brought* toys to them, deposit-ing them in the mothers' laps. These behaviors added considerable weight to the claim that the children behaved in an independent fashion. Here were little children — 12 and 18 months of age — taking the initiative in making the other person, the mother, a partner in their play. The children were the givers, the mothers were the receivers.

These incidental findings seemed important enough to warrant study in their own right. Sharing is a valued trait in every society, and one many parents are at pains to inculcate in their children. In laboratory settings, sharing has been studied among older children and adults, but sharing in the laboratory or else-where has not been studied among children under 2 years of age. Therefore, if it can be shown that children do share from an early age — long before parents consciously exhort their children to share — we add a new dimension to our view of the very young child.

Sharing, as I shall use the term, conforms exactly to its dictionary definition (Webster's, 1969). It "implies that one as the original holder grants to another the partial use, enjoyment, or possession of a thing though it may merely imply a mutual use or possession" [p. 798].

THE STUDIES

The series of studies had several purposes. The first and most elementary pur-pose was to define sharing more precisely than in the previous (Rheingold, 1973) study; and, instead of using narrative accounts alone we now used the more objective measures of frequency and duration, as well as of the order in which the behaviors occurred. We asked about the characteristics of objects children would share, whether toys or other objects. Would novel objects in-crease sharing? And then, would children share objects with persons other than their mothers?

The data come from two sources; mostly from laboratory studies but also from field observations. I propose that for the behavior of interest, sharing, no real dichotomy exists between these two sources. The laboratory is one in name only. For the average children of the community in which I work, our laboratory environment in many respects resembles environments they have already been exposed to in the normal course of events.

The children were about 18 months of age. They were normal children, reared in the homes of parents who were above average in education. Although in the study of independence we had seen sharing in 12-month-old children, it occurred more frequently among the 18-month-old children. Their more efficient locomotion and larger repertoire of behavior recommended them for the present studies, but I do not at all mean to imply that sharing does not occur earlier — even earlier than 12 months.

All the laboratory studies took place in the same setting, a suite of three adjoining rooms: a fairly large room and two smaller ones. The mother sat in a chair placed against the center of one wall of the large room, called the "starting room." The wall she faced contained doors to the smaller rooms, the "toy rooms." The child always started from the mother's chair. The doors to the smaller rooms were fastened open. Each smaller room contained two toys or other objects as the study demanded, one near the threshold, the other near the rear wall.

In all studies the behavior of the mother was controlled. Generally, she was instructed to remain passive. She was not to direct the child's behavior in any way. If the child showed a toy from a distance, the mother could respond with a nod and a slight smile. If the child brought a toy to her, she could murmur a few words as she accepted it. The experimenter took pains to explain that we wanted to see what the child would do, that we had no firm expectations, and that if the child chose to sit on her lap for the duration of the trial, that too was all right.

Three responses were selected to index sharing: *showing* the mother an object, *giving* her an object, and *playing with* an object that has been brought to the mother and that was still in contact with her, that is, in her lap or hand.

1. Showing included pointing to an object or holding an object up, with some clear indication that the child was directing the mother's attention to the object. The child would usually look toward the mother, often with smiles and pleasant vocalizations.

2. Giving was defined as the child's *bringing* an object from a distance, that is, from one of the rooms to the mother, placing it in the mother's hand or lap, and *releasing* it. It subsequently the child took the toy away, only to return and release it once more, a second give was recorded.

3. Playing with object and mother was defined as the duration of time spent manipulating the object while it was still in contact with the mother.

These three measures were recorded independently by two observers behind one-way windows. Their agreement satisfied fairly acceptable standards (discussed below) and most of the measures I shall report are the averages of their records.

The observers also recorded two other measures, contact of toys and contact of mother, in the absence of any of the sharing behaviors. These two measures only kept track of what else the child was doing, but might eventually help us learn more about the sharing measures.

Supplementary data were obtained by video tapes of the children's behavior, by audio tapes of their and their mothers' vocalizations, and by a running narrative account dictated by another observer.

Effects of Novel Toys

The first study of the series had several purposes. It provided the opportunity to test how reliably the three sharing responses could be recorded. It provided baseline data for subsequent studies. And by changing the toys for one group of subjects in a second trial, we could measure the effect of novelty on sharing. Above all, it would offer corroborating evidence for the by-the-way observations of the independence study.

Twenty-four children, evenly divided by sex, were randomly assigned to experimental or control conditions. In Trial 1 half the children had one set of toys, and half another, to insure that the results would not be specific to only one set of toys. In Trial 2, the control group had the same set as in Trial 1; the experimental group had the other set. Each trial lasted 10 min. As each child entered the environment, two of these toys had been placed in each of the toy rooms.

In Trial 1, all 24 children exhibited some sharing of the toys with their mothers. Twenty-three of 24 children showed the toys a mean of 5 times, 20 of 24 carried toys and placed them in the mothers' laps or hands a mean of 9 times, and then played with the toys in the mothers' possession for a mean of 36 seconds. The one child who did not show a toy, nevertheless gave, while those who did not give, showed. Every child, then, shared by our definition; and most exhibited all 3 of the responses during the first 10 minutes of observation.

Much variability in the frequency of showing and giving occurred, of course. One child showed toys to the mother 18 times and another gave the mother toys 25 times.

In Trial 2, the number of children who shared decreased somewhat. Now only 21 of 24 showed a toy, and only 17 of 24 gave a toy or toys to the mother. The experimental subjects showed and gave the new toys more often than the control subjects showed and gave their familiar toys, but the differences were small and a multivariate analysis of variance of all the measures revealed no significant effect of experimental treatment. That is, sharing was not reliably increased by the introduction of new toys in the second trial. Although I did not expect this finding, I am now impressed by the extent to which the familiar toys were able to maintain sharing at close to the original level of Trial 1.

The children spent more than half the first trial playing with the toys and only 9% of the time contacting the mother. In the second trial they still were spending almost half the trial in play with the toys, while contact of the mother increased but only to 18% of the trial duration.

Some toys were given to the mother more often than others, but all the toys were given at least once. The toy given most often was the "roly-poly ball," heavy and difficult to grasp as it was. The plastic chain and the blocks and dowels were next most popular. Six of 24 children gave all the available toys to their mothers in Trial 1.

Sex Differences

The behavior of boys and girls differed reliably in only two respects. Girls contacted their mothers more in Trial 2 than boys, and boys showed toys to their mothers more often in Trial 2 than in Trial 1.

Summary

In summary, this first study showed that 18-month-old children did in fact share toys with their mothers; the earlier observations were confirmed. The children pointed to toys, held them up for the mothers to see, carried them to their mothers and released them in the mothers' laps or hands. Furthermore, they shared familiar toys at about the same frequency as novel toys.

Effect of Social Reinforcement[2]

The next study asked whether sharing could be increased by varying the mother's response to the child's giving her a toy. Half the mothers were instructed to make only a minimal response — if the child brought them a toy to take it without saying anything; the other mothers were instructed to smile broadly, say thank you, naming the child, to do this as pleasantly and enthusiastically as possible, and also to reach out to take the toy if the child brought it to them, and then to place it in their laps.

The study took place in the same laboratory setting with one of the previous sets of toys. Duration of trial was 10 minutes.

So far, eight pairs of children have been seen. With so few pairs, the effects of the mother's exaggerated response to the child's bringing and giving a toy to her are not conclusive. Although the reinforced children showed and gave toys more often, only showing was reliably greater. They showed an average of nine times versus three for the nonreinforced children.

It would be premature indeed to conclude that only showing and not giving responds to reinforcement. More pairs of children must be studied. The failure to find a reliable difference in giving, if supported by additional data, might suggest that the behavior is already well established. I suspect, however, that more skill is needed in programing the mother's behavior; it has proved difficult to get some mothers to be very minimally responsive and to get others to be exuberantly responsive.

[2]This experiment was primarily the effort of Dale Hay, a graduate student.

Increased Showing

The next study focused on pointing, a component of showing. To increase pointing we added attractive stimuli to the environment.

This study followed the social reinforcement study, after a break of only a few minutes. Now, when the child entered the large room with the mother, three colorful posters hung from the walls, a bright wooden mobile hung in one corner of the room, and a large mobile of black and white circles hung from the center of the ceiling. The toy rooms meanwhile contained the same four toys of the previous trial. And the trial lasted five minutes.

Pointing was defined as extending the arm, usually with extended index finger, accompanied by regard of the mother. To measure the effect of the added stimuli, the posters and the mobiles, the frequency of pointing to these objects was compared with the frequency of their pointing to nontoy objects during the first five minutes of the preceding trial, where the nontoy objects were such things as the TV camera, microphones, door knobs, etc.

The results showed a large and reliable difference. Nineteen of the 21 children in this study pointed to the posters and mobiles, in contrast to only 8 of 21 pointing to nontoy objects in the just preceding trial. The children now pointed an average of 5 times, in contrast to a mean of less than 1; the increase was actually seven-fold, with one child pointing as many as 21 times.

We concluded, therefore, that pointing, by our definition a component of showing, and hence of sharing, could be increased just by adding posters and mobiles to the environment.

I cannot leave the behavior of pointing without comment. Pointing occurs at every age and no doubt in every culture and throughout history. It is a gesture of communication. Its effect on the beholder is immediate and compelling. Words are not needed. One looks where the other person's finger points. The meaning of the gesture is probably learned early by infants, and they learn to use it early. Not only do children look where others point, but we observed that our mothers looked where their children pointed, even at so ordinary an object as the ceiling.

Other Recipients of Sharing: The Father

The purpose of this study was to find out if the children would share toys with fathers as well as with mothers.

Thirteen children, 11 boys and 2 girls, were studied individually with their fathers. All but one had been studied previously with their mothers. The same suite of rooms was used but three new toys replaced three former ones.

The fathers were instructed to behave as were the mothers in the first novel-toy study, neither entirely passively nor especially responsively. They sat in the same chair as had the mothers. Duration of trial was 10 min.

All 13 children seen in this study shared with their fathers. Eleven showed toys, 10 gave toys to their fathers, and 9 subsequently played with the toys now in contact with the fathers. For those who exhibited the behavior, the mean frequency of showing toys was 7. They also gave toys to their fathers a mean of 7 times, and played with the toys in the fathers' possession for a mean duration of 29 seconds.

The results, therefore, showed that fathers too could be the recipients of sharing. Sharing is not confined to mothers alone. Furthermore, when we compared the responses of these 13 children to their fathers with those of the 24 children of the first study to their mothers, we were struck by the similarity of the findings. Not only were the frequencies of showing and giving similar, but the amounts of time spent playing with toys and contacting the parent were practically identical. These results also extend the generality of the original findings in still another dimension, for the responses were similar even with other toys. Up to this point we had observed the behavior of the children with 11 different toys — a truck, a shape-sorting box, a boat train, and so on. All had been shared by one child or another.

Other Recipients and Other Objects of Sharing

The purposes of this study were to see if children would direct sharing behavior toward a less familiar person, the experimenter; and to see if children would share nontoy objects as they had shared toys — nontoy objects that they could pick up and carry.

This study followed the study with fathers after a short break. The experimenter, a female, entered the experimental environment with both father and child. The adults sat in chairs placed at a slight angle to each other, yet facing the two smaller rooms. The experimenter and the father chatted but both behaved toward the child with all the abovementioned constraints. The objects were, in one of the test rooms, a set of realistic looking plastic fruits in the near position and a wastebasket filled with video tape in the far position. The other room contained a plastic tea set in the near position and in the far position a wastebasket filled with wadded paper, some small empty boxes, and some strands of red wool. (Although I label these nontoy objects, to the child they may be as much toys as the conventional toys used earlier.) In all other respects, the same measures and procedures obtained as in the previous studies.

Ten children, 9 boys and 1 girl, were studied. Nine of them gave one or more of the sharing responses to the experimenter. Seven of the 10 showed one or more of these nontoy objects to the experimenter, one child as many as 9 times; 6 gave objects to the experimenter, one as many as 13 times; and 5 of these children played with a toy while it was in contact with the experimenter. Children at this age, then, do share objects with an unfamiliar person.

But note that they did direct more sharing toward the father. All 10 of them gave the father one or more objects, while only 6 gave the experimenter any; and the mean frequency of giving was 7 to the father and 3 to the experimenter, a reliable difference. A familiar person *was* a more frequent recipient than a less familiar one. Yet that the unfamiliar person was a recipient at all seems noteworthy and attests to the generality of the behavior.

The wastebaskets proved less interesting to the children than we had expected. The artificial fruits were far and away the most frequently given objects — to father and experimenter alike. Every child gave one or more of the fruits to the father, and they were the objects given first; for 6 of the 10 children they were the only objects given. Thus, sharing can be influenced by the nature of the objects in the environment.

SUMMARY OF THE STUDIES

The series of laboratory studies showed that children 18 months of age shared what they saw, and what they found, with other persons. They shared with their fathers as well as with their mothers, and even more remarkable they shared with a relatively unfamiliar person. Furthermore, they shared familiar toys at about the same rate as they shared new toys. There was some evidence that sharing could be increased by the adult's response, while pointing was reliably increased by increasing certain kinds of environmental stimuli. Finally, sharing was not restricted to only a few objects but occurred with as many as 11 different toys, and even with such objects as teacups, wads of paper, and strands of wool.

Much work remains. What about sharing with other children? Will just the extended hand of the adult increase sharing, the open extended hand appearing to be a powerful gesture? Some preliminary work showed that we could quite successfully increase sharing by making a game of it. We gave the children a small toy, extended a hand, and responded effusively when they placed the toy in our hands. Three children who had earlier not given a toy to the mother in this pilot attempt gave toys a mean of 6 times.

We need also to learn how to measure such other components of sharing as children's smiling and laughing when they have accomplished a difficult task such as getting a tower of blocks to stand. And we have omitted entirely the children's talking to persons about what they find and are doing.

FIELD OBSERVATIONS

Once we became aware of the children's sharing, we began to see it everywhere. Here I summarize 19 field observations made by members of the laboratory within a week. The ages of the children ranged from 11 months to 3 years. The places of the observations included the campus, streets, stores, restaurants, and airports. The objects shown ranged from wares in store windows to one's own belly button, and the objects given ranged from lollipops to twigs. The recipients included parents, strangers, siblings, and the observers themselves. As for pointing, you can scarcely observe 18-month-old children out of doors for more than 10 sec without seeing them point at something.

Still another class of information bears on the subject. I have yet to tell a parent or child psychologist of our interest who does not nod in assent and supply a corresponding memory. L. J. Stone, for example, replied: "How well I recall all those wet cookies stuffed in my mouth." From informal questioning of parents I gather that an early appearance of giving – if not the first – occurs when children at about 12 months offer parents a bit of their own food. One nice report told of a 9-month-old girl offering zwieback to the family dog.

Similar data come from Anderson (1972), who watched children with their mothers in London parks. The children ranged in age from 15 to 30 months. He reported that half of them brought the mother an object they had picked up from the ground.

I am so confident of the occurrence of the young child's sharing that I predict you will observe it before you reach home, now that I have called it to your attention.

JUSTIFICATION OF THE MEASURES

Let me now take a few minutes to justify the use of the term "sharing" and to consider what recommends the use of the three behaviors as measures of sharing.

First, I believe the response as a whole exactly fits the dictionary (Webster's, 1969) definition of sharing; that sharing "implies that one as the original holder grants to another the partial use, enjoyment, or possession of a thing though it may merely imply a mutual use or possession" [p. 798].

How else might the behavior be labeled? Should it be labeled "dependency"? No, because I do not think the child is seeking attention, approval, or recognition. As I have argued, independence – in the sense of children taking the initiative to include the other person in their discoveries, achievement, and pleasure – is really the more fitting term. Nor do I think children's showing and giving of toys to strangers, as we saw in the field observations, should be regarded as appeasement behavior. Blurton Jones (1967) has reported how often children from three to five years of age, in the nursery schools he visited in England, held out toys to him, a stranger – behavior also seen by Halverson (1973) in Bethesda. Neither observer implied that the children were thereby seeking to appease the stranger.

Altmann (1967) proposed that a classification of behavior is natural to the extent that it fulfills either of two criteria that he calls the logical and the biological. The logical criterion, as defined by Kaplan (1964), demands that the behaviors fall into a classification, as it were, by themselves. Furthermore, to constitute a natural class the concept of sharing should be able to enter into propositions other than those that state the classification itself. The biological criterion, on the other hand, demands that the classification represent behaviors that occur in the species' natural habitat. It seems to me that the three behaviors we used to define sharing satisfy both sets of criteria and qualify as natural, rather than as arbitrary, units.

The three measures may be weighed in still other balances. What are their psychometric properties? For example, how well do the three measures of sharing stand up to the criterion of observer agreement? Giving was recorded the most reliably; the median percentage of agreement calculated over 4 of the studies was 100. Showing was recorded next most reliably; the percentages ranged from 84 to 92. Playing with an object given to the adult and still in contact with the adult (a duration measure) proved the most difficult to measure reliably, percentages here ranging from 81 to 85. These results may suggest that giving should be accorded more weight. These observer-agreement measures, however, were taken on the spot, through one-way windows, and the observers often missed behavior that was clearly visible on the video tapes. When some day we calculate observer agreement from the tapes, showing and playing with a toy given to the adult may prove to meet more acceptable standards.

Second, the degree to which one of the three measures is correlated with the others can provide information on still another of their properties. Showing and giving generally were not correlated within children. But, playing with a toy already given and still in the possession of the recipient tended to be positively related with giving. Still, these correlations were not high enough to suggest that "playing with" is a redundant measure.

We can also learn more about the measures from seeing how they are distributed in time. Did all the showing occur early in the trial? No, for although the rate decreased gradually, children were still showing toys in the last minute of the trial. Did giving develop later in the trial? No, in general it was most frequent at the beginning, then decreased gradually, but it too was still occurring in the last minute of the trial. Unlike these two measures, playing with a toy already given did increase gradually over the trial.

Lastly, we shall know more about the three measures when, as we pursue the studies, we learn the effects of different experimental manipulations on each — the contingencies into which they enter.

THE ORIGINS OF SHARING

Some speculation on the origins of sharing may be appropriate. How in any one child does sharing begin?

In the first instance, because of the human infants' slow motor development, almost everything they need for survival must be brought to them. The simplest example is the mother's sharing her milk. But this is only the first example. The list of things brought to them grows apace as children grow — first things for their survival, then for their comfort, and then for their amusement. Each object brought may be viewed as an example set, a model provided. The examples, perhaps trivial in themselves, abound and multiply. Thus, we can speculate that the children's bringing things to their parents may be accounted for, at least in part, by that easy and flexible mode of learning we label imitation.

Although the first parental sharing is giving — bringing something to infants — showing that something to them before it is given must occur when infants are only a few months old. Thus, the parents hold the bottle, the spoonful of food, the bright object, for the children to see. Before the infants are much older parents accompany the showing with words. They say, "Here's your bottle," "Look at the pretty toy." And, only a little later, before children can understand the words, parents point to objects, saying "See the dog," and so on. Parental showing must be as common as parental giving. So, too, we can speculate that parents engage in some manipulation — play, if you wish — of the objects children already hold.

Thus, each behavior enumerated as a component of sharing by children has often been exhibited toward them by parents, siblings, relatives, baby sitters, and other persons. Long before they are a year old they have boundless opportunities to observe. As soon as they acquire the motor skills, they imitate the showing, giving, and playing with the objects given to other people.

But imitation need not carry the whole burden. In large measure children's first sharing behavior, which I believe to be showing — holding out an object toward someone — often meets with some response from the person toward whom the object is directed. At the least, the person looks, but we may surmise that on many occasions the looking is accompanied by turning the head, and by verbal responses, such as "Yes, I see it," "That's a cookie," and so on. Where children point, we look, as we saw our mothers do. Tiedemann (Murchison & Langer, 1927) in 1787 reported of his son when the child was 8 months and 20 days old: "Whenever he met with anything novel or strange he would point with his finger at it to call other people's attention to it, and employed the sound 'ha! ha!' That the pointing as well as the exclamation were addressed to others was apparent from the fact that he was satisfied as soon as people signified that they also had taken note" [p. 219]. Now, even more of a response is elicited from the recipient when something is given. The earliest account of giving I found was Guillaume's (1926/1971) of his daughter at 9 months and 25 days of age offering to put in other people's mouths the candy she had put in her own. How does one respond? We smile, say thank you, and like as not name the object. Everyday observation thus offers abundant evidence for the child's learning to share by the rich social response of others.

Still another process of learning may be invoked. On several occasions I have seen a game of give-and-take develop between parents and children about 12 months of age. As the children take the object from the parents, the children laugh; they offer it to the parents; as the parents take it, the children laugh again. The sequence is repeated many times, in almost exactly the same way, and always accompanied by glee. The children are controlling the behavior of the other person, as the other person is theirs. But, even more, they seem to enjoy their power to initiate and sustain sensory and motor feedback by their own behavior; it is a kind of self-reinforcement.

However, then, sharing does in fact originate, there has been ample opportunity for children to learn it — first, by observing the behavior of others toward them, and second by the responses of both others and themselves to their own behavior.

But setting forth the opportunities that infants and young children have to learn to share does not prove that they do in fact learn to share; any more than specifying the processes by which they *could* learn the response proves that it is in fact by these processes that they did so learn. I speculate only on possibilities that await experimental evidence.

SHARING AMONG OTHER SPECIES

Another avenue of speculation about origins took me to a survey of sharing among other mammals.

Does man alone share with others? Obviously not. Many mammals share food with their young beyond the characteristic that defines a mammal, that is, that the mother suckles the young. I have seen a domesticated female dog regurgitate part of her meal to be eaten avidly by her pups. A dramatic example, currently to be seen in a Jane Goodall television special on the wild dogs of the Serengeti Plain, is the regurgitation of part of a kill for the pups by adults of both sexes.[3] And cats are reported to bring mice to their kittens.

Now, among the nonhuman primates, sharing of food with the young appears to occur very infrequently, based on reports in the literature and my own observations. That may be easily accounted for — although perhaps not accurately — by the ready availability of food at hand and by the ability of the monkeys or apes to secure food by themselves while still very young. Evidence of sharing among primates does occur in reports of meat sharing. Recently Teleki (1973) detailed the capturing of live prey by male chimpanzees and the sharing of the meat — eventually with all members of the troop, but not directly with the young.

I could find in the literature, however, no evidence that the young of any species, even of the great apes, shared anything with others — no showing, no bringing to, no giving. This does not mean that it does not occur. I may not have read widely enough. Or the investigators may not have paid attention to the behavior when it did occur, an omission that occurs even in the human child literature, as I have been at pains to show.

[3] Also described in van Lawick, H. & Goodall, J. *Innocent killers.* Boston: Houghton Mifflin, 1971.

SIGNIFICANCE OF CHILDREN'S SHARING

I come back now to children's sharing. The advantages of others' sharing with them are clear: their lives depend on it. But their sharing with others possesses many advantages for them, too. They obtain the attention, pleasure, and approval of others. As others respond verbally and name what children show or give them, children also acquire information about their universe. The differences in responses teach them about the differences in the people around them. In a still more important way, they are practicing a behavior of consequence for living with others. They are reciprocating past favors and they are cooperating.

Viewed in this way, young children's sharing with others may be characterized as adaptive. They do not share because their ancestors shared; we have long since discarded the theory that individuals repeat the phylogenetic history of their group. And they do not share because they must share when they grow older. They share because sharing had and has survival value for them as children. As Ghiselin (1973) and Konner (1972) have proposed, we should view children as adapted organisms. Their sharing *now* — as infants and young children — is a pattern of behavior that has been selected for in the evolutionary sense. Children's sharing is a behavior adapted to their social environment; it confers both social and educational advantages. In Ghiselin's (1973) words: "A child, like a caterpillar, is an organism in his own right, adapted to his own ecological niche" [p. 967]. Rather, it is possible, according to Konner (1972), that "the characteristic features of adult human behaviour have evolved . . . because they are the result of an ideal adaptation in infancy" [p. 302].

This interpretation of infants' sharing forces a developmental perspective. We start with young organisms already sharing. What happens to that behavior as children mature? What changes occur that make it necessary for parents, only a few months later, to begin to exhort them to share? Which of life's experiences altered this early flowering of truly social behavior? And what of the form parental tutelage takes? Staub (1971) has suggested that children in our society are more often taught prohibitions, without sufficient emphasis on the norms that *prescribe* prosocial behavior. It is easy to be pessimistic about the outcome, knowing as much as we do about the mean, selfish, and heedless behavior of so many adults. But just as properly we may take comfort from our frequent altruistic behavior and see it as the later development of that early sociability. Fortunately, the altruistic behavior of older children is now commanding increasing interest from developmental psychologists.

I have been at pains in the past to show that infants welcome new objects, people, and experiences, that they venture forth with zest to learn the nature of their world, and that they strive to be independent. Now I see them displaying at a very early age the social behaviors people everywhere value, even when they do not always honor that value. A major task confronting us as psychologists, parents, and citizens is how to build upon that generous nature.

REFERENCES

Altmann, S. A. The structure of primate social communication. In S. A. Altmann (Ed.), *Social communication among primates*. Chicago: University of Chicago Press, 1967.

Anderson, J. W. Attachment behaviour out of doors. In N. Blurton Jones (Ed.), *Ethological studies of child behaviour*. Cambridge: Cambridge University Press, 1972.

Blurton Jones, N. An ethological study of some aspects of social behaviour of children in nursery school. In D. Morris (Ed.), *Primate ethology*. Chicago: Aldine, 1967.

Ghiselin, M. T. Darwin and evolutionary psychology. *Science, 1973, 179,* 964-968.

Guillaume, P. *Imitation in children* (E. P. Halperin, trans.). Chicago: University of Chicago Press, 1971. (Originally published, 1926.)

Halverson, C. F. Personal communication, August, 1973.

Kaplan, A. *The conduct of inquiry: Methodology for behavioral science*. Scranton, Pa.: Chandler, 1964.

Konner, M. J. Aspects of the developmental ethology of a foraging people. In N. Blurton Jones (Ed.), *Ethological studies of child behaviour*. Cambridge: Cambridge University Press, 1972.

Murchison, C., & Langer, S. Tiedemann's observations on the development of the mental faculties of children. *The Pedagogical Seminary and Journal of Genetic Psychology, 1927, 34,* 205-230.

Rheingold, H. L. Independent behavior of the human infant. In A. D. Pick (Ed.), *Minnesota Symposia on Child Psychology* (Vol. 7). Minneapolis: University of Minnesota Press, 1973.

Staub, E. Helping a person in distress: The influence of implicit and explicit "rules" of conduct on children and adults. *Journal of Personality and Social Psychology, 1971, 17,* 137-144.

Teleki, G. The omnivorous chimpanzee. *Scientific American, 1973, 228,* 33-42.

Webster's seventh new collegiate dictionary (17 ed.). Springfield, Mass.: Merriam, 1969.

29

Imitative Behavior of Preschool Children: The Effects of Reinforcement, Instructions, and Response Similarity

James A. Sherman
Hewitt B. Clark
Karen K. Kelly

University of Kansas

The development and analysis of the imitative behavior of children has been the topic of a great deal of research in recent years, primarily because of the pivotal role that imitation plays in theoretical accounts of the behavioral development of children. In several early studies of the development of imitation, training techniques involving reinforcement procedures were used to teach imitative behavior to children who were initially nonimitative (Metz, 1965; Lovaas, Berberich, Perloff, & Schaeffer, 1966; Baer, Peterson, & Sherman, 1967). In these studies it was found that after some imitative behavior had been taught to the children, new imitative responses could be produced and maintained simply by demonstrating those responses without direct training or use of reinforcement. These results, the occurrence and maintenance of unreinforced imitation, have been labeled "generalized" imitation and have occasioned a number of studies designed to investigate the conditions responsible for the phenomena.

Several studies have shown the role that cert in reinforcement operations can play in controlling generalized imitation in both normal children with existing imitative repertoires and children with experimentally developed imitative repertoires (Baer & Sherman, 1964; Baer *et al.,* 1967; Brigham & Sherman, 1968; Peterson, 1968; Risley, 1968; Waxler & Yarrow, 1970). In these studies the maintenance of unreinforced imitations was found to be a function of reinforcement for other imitative responses. When the children were reinforced for imitating some responses, they not only imitated these responses but also displayed other imitative responses for which there were no experimental consequences. However, when the children were no longer reinforced for some imitative responses or when demonstrations of these reinforced responses were no longer exhibited by the model, the children did not imitate the unreinforced responses as consistently or as accurately. Thus, reinforcement for some imitative responses can, at least in part, control the occurrence and accuracy of unreinforced imitations.

However, several recent studies have also clearly shown that the unreinforced imitative behavior of children may be controlled by a number of variables other than reinforcement operations. Two studies by Steinman (1970a, b), as well as the study by Waxler and Yarrow (1970), have indicated that children's likelihood of imitating responses can be affected by various instructions to the children. Studies by Steinman (1970a), Bandura and Barab (1971), and Garcia, Baer and Firestone (1971) have shown that the topographical similarity between reinforced and unreinforced responses can influence the degree to which children imitate unreinforced responses. A study by Peterson and Whitehurst (1971) has shown that the presence or absence of an experimenter can affect the degree to which children imitate responses. Finally, a portion of the results obtained by Burgess, Burgess, and Esveldt (1970) suggests that observation of another child imitating or not imitating certain responses can influence children's unreinforced imitations.

This chapter presents four experiments which examine variables potentially related to the maintenance of unreinforced imitative behavior of normal children. The experiments examined the effects of reinforcement for imitation or non-imitation, the effects of instructions, the effects of topographical similarity between reinforced and unreinforced responses, and the effects of allowing children a choice of demonstrations to imitate.

THE EXPERIMENTS

Seven normal children, four to five years old, from the University of Kansas Child Development Laboratory were employed in this study (two boys and two girls for Experiments 1 and 2, a boy and two girls for Experiments 3 and 4).

Sessions were held in a small room furnished with a table and two chairs, and observed from an adjacent observation booth through a one-way window. Two small cups (one filled with marbles, the other empty) and recording sheets for the experimenter were on the table.

An adult female served as the experimenter and model for each study. Experimental sessions were held four times a week (Monday-Thursday) unless a child was absent. To start sessions, each child was brought to the experimental room and was shown an assortment of toys and the two cups. The experimenter told the child that when all the marbles had been earned (30 in Experiments 1 and 2, 25 in Experiments 3 and 4), the child could choose a toy to take home.

Following each *imitation demonstration,* the child was reinforced only for imitating. Following each *nonimitation demonstration,* the child was reinforced for doing anything except imitating. Following each *probe demonstration,* the child was not reinforced regardless of what was done.

Imitation demonstrations (reinforced demonstrations).   To present imitation demonstrations, the experimenter looked at the child and demonstrated a response for about 1 sec. If the child imitated the response within 5 sec the experimenter praised the child ("Very good" or "Good girl"), transferred a marble into the child's cup, recorded the response on the data sheet, waited 5 sec, and presented the next demonstration. If the child did not imitate within 5 sec, the experimenter recorded this, waited 5 sec, and presented the next demonstration.

During the first session of Experiment 1 and Experiment 3, only imitation demonstrations were presented and these were initially preceded by the experimenter saying, "Can you do this?" This question was no longer used after the first 12 demonstrations because all the children were reliably imitating demonstrations by this trial.

Nonimitation demonstrations.   These demonstrations were presented in the same manner as the imitatve demonstrations except that the consequences were different. If the child imitated within 5 sec then the experimenter recorded this, waited 5 sec, and presented the next demonstration. If the child did not imitate within 5 sec, the experimenter praised the child, dropped a marble in the cup, recorded the response, waited 5 sec, and presented the next demonstration.

Probe demonstrations.   These demonstrations were presented as were the above demonstrations, except that the child was never reinforced. The experimenter simply recorded the response after the child imitated or after 5 sec if the child did not imitate, waited 5 sec, and presented the next demonstration.

Interobserver reliability.   Following each demonstration, the child's response was scored as imitative or nonimitative. Periodically, a second scorer observed sessions through the one-way window and scored the responses to assess the reliability of the experimenter's scoring.

Experiment 1

This experiment investigated whether a history of reinforcement for imitative and nonimitative responses would affect the likelihood that a child would imitate probe demonstrations which were never followed by reinforcement. Imitative responses to imitation demonstrations and nonimitative responses to nonimitation demonstrations were both brought under stimulus control. Probe demonstrations were then displayed in the presence of the two stimuli to determine whether the context of the demonstration controlled the probability of these new probe demonstrations being imitated.

Procedure

The two stimuli used in this experiment were different colored aprons worn by the experimenter. During imitation demonstrations the experimenter always wore a yellow apron; during nonimitation demonstrations she always wore a blue apron. The experimenter always put the apron on in the presence of the child and asked what color it was. She verbally praised correct answers and stated the color if it was named incorrectly by the child.

Imitation demonstrations.   The experimenter wore the yellow apron and presented 4 different motor imitation demonstrations in random order. When the child had earned 30 marbles for imitating the demonstrations the session was terminated and the child chose a toy. This experimental condition was unchanged until the child imitated 90% or more of the total demonstrations within a session.

Nonimitation demonstrations.   After being trained to imitate in the presence of the yellow apron, the child was trained on nonimitation in the presence of the blue apron. The experimenter presented the same 4 motor responses used when wearing the yellow apron, but now presented them as nonimitation demonstrations while wearing the blue apron. Because the children were imitating almost every response they had to be trained to not imitate. The experimenter presented a nonimitative demonstration and immediately held the child's hands for 5 sec. Because the child had not imitated, praise and a marble were given. Gradually over demonstrations the experimenter held the child's hands for shorter and shorter periods until she only presented the nonimitation demonstration, waited 5 sec, and reinforced nonimitation. This condition was continued until a child imitated 15% or less of the demonstrations within a session during which the experimenter had not provided the child with any assistance.

Multiple schedule: imitation and nonimitation demonstrations.   During the multiple schedule, both stimulus colors were presented during each session: The child was reinforced for imitative responses when the experimenter wore the yellow apron (imitation demonstrations) and reinforced for nonimitative responses when the experimenter wore the blue apron (nonimitation demonstrations). A session was terminated only after 15 marbles had been earned for imitation in the yellow condition and 15 for nonimitation in the blue condition.

Probe demonstrations within the multiple schedule. Once a child was reliably imitating demonstrations (in yellow) and reliably not imitating demonstrations (in blue), four probe demonstrations were interspersed among the demonstrations of the two colors. Probe demonstrations were never reinforced regardless of the child's response. Responses to these probe demonstrations were used to determine whether the reinforcement context controlled the likelihood of the probes being imitated. For the first session with two children, two probe demonstrations were presented in yellow and no probe demonstrations were presented in blue. The other two children were shown two probe demonstrations in blue and none in yellow. During the next session the other two probe demonstrations were placed in the alternate color. This two-session sequence was then repeated. Next, two of the probe demonstrations were placed in one color and the other two probe demonstrations were placed in the other color within a session. During the next session this process was repeated except that the probe demonstrations were reversed between the two colors. Finally, one pair of probe demonstrations was shown in the presence of both colors. On the final session the other pair of probe demonstrations was shown in the presence of both colors. Table 1 lists the sequence of conditions for each child and the responses demonstrated.

Results

Altogether, 387 responses were observed by both the experimenter and the second scorer during Experiments 1 and 2. On only 3 trials did these 2 people disagree in scoring imitative and nonimitative responses.

The mean percentages of demonstrations imitated by each child for each condition of this experiment are shown in Figure 1. Solid bars show the percentages of demonstrations imitated in yellow and stippled bars show the percentages of demonstrations imitated in blue. Bars with asterisks (*) over them show the percentages of probe demonstrations imitated in yellow (solid bars) and blue (stippled bars). The sets of graphs shown for each child represent the percentages of demonstrations imitated: (1) before any probes were introduced; (2) when a different pair of probes appeared in yellow and blue during separate sessions; (3) when different pairs of probes appeared in yellow and blue within the same session; and (4) when the same pair of probes appeared in yellow and blue within the same session.

Figure 1 shows that the children imitated a large percentage of demonstrations when imitation was reinforced (solid bars) and imitated a small percentage of the demonstrations when nonimitation was reinforced (stippled bars). In addition, probe demonstrations were imitated when they were in the context of

TABLE 1

Responses and Conditions of Experiment 1

Responses used as Both Imitation and Nonimitation Demonstrations	Responses Used as Probe Demonstrations
1. Clap both hands	1. Hands Circle each other in a rolling motion
2. Both hands held over head	2. Both hands over ears
3. Both arms held out at sides	3. One leg crossed over the other
4. Wave both hands	4. Both feet stamp floor

	Number of Sessions for Each Subject			
Conditions of the Multiple Schedule (in Sequence)	Al	Sally	Jonny	Judi
No probe demonstrations	3	3	3	4
Different probes in the yellow condition and in the blue condition during different sessions	4	4	4	4
Different probes in the yellow condition and in the blue condition during the same session	2	2	2	2
Same probes in the yellow condition and in the blue condition during the same session	4	2	5	2

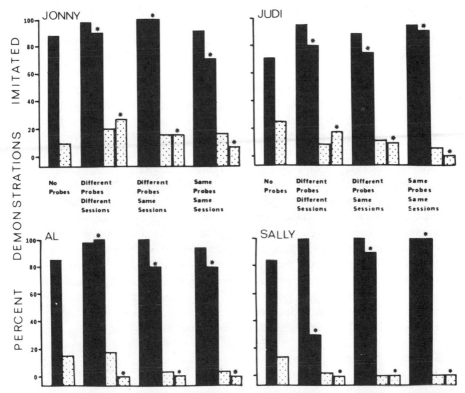

Figure 1   Mean percentage of demonstrations imitated for each condition (Experiment 1). Solid bars show the percentage imitated when the yellow apron was worn (reinforcement of imitation). Open dotted bars show the percentage imitated when the blue apron was worn (reinforcement of nonimitation). Performance on probe demonstrations is noted by an asterisk (*) above the bar.

imitation demonstrations (solid bars with asterisks) and not imitated when they were in the context of nonimitation demonstrations (stippled bars with asterisks). This type of contextual control over responses to probe demonstrations was shown for all four children.

EXPERIMENT 2

The purpose of this study was to determine the relative effect of instructions over reinforcement and stimulus control of imitation.

Procedure

This study was a continuation of Experiment 1, in that the same children and multiple-schedule conditions were employed. The experimenter presented imitation demonstrations when she wore the yellow apron and presented nonimitation demonstrations when she wore the blue apron. In addition, two probe demonstrations were interspersed among the other two types of demonstrations in both yellow and blue. Because it seemed likely that some instructional conditions might make it impossible to deliver 15 marbles in both yellow and blue during a session, yellow and blue were alternated after the experimenter had either delivered 15 marbles in a color, or presented 30 demonstrations in that color.

Prior to this experiment the only instruction the children had received was, "Can you do this?" for the first few responses during training prior to Experiment 1. Now the effects of four instructional conditions were investigated. In one instructional condition the experimenter said, "Do this," before each demonstration in both yellow and blue. In a second instructional condition the experimenter said, "Don't do this," before each demonstration in both yellow and blue. In a third instructional condition the experimenter said, "Do this," only before probe demonstrations in blue. In a fourth instructional condition the experimenter said, "Don't do this," only before probe demonstrations in yellow. For two children (Al and Sally), several sessions without instructions were interspersed among the sessions with the various instructions. These sessions without instructions were presented following sessions in which instructions were shown to be functional in changing the probability of imitation and were used to evaluate whether in the absence of instructions, the probability of imitation would return to its previous level. Table 2 shows the number of sessions for each child under these instructional conditions.

Results

Figure 2 shows the percentages of demonstrations imitated under the various instructional conditions investigated in this study. The solid bars show the percentages of demonstrations imitated in yellow (asterisk above probe responses)

TABLE 2

Number of Sessions for Each Subject under the Various
Instructional Conditions of Experiment 2

Condition	Al	Sally	Jonny	Judi
"Do this" before all demonstrations in both Yellow and Blue	3	3	2	4
"Don't do this" before all demonstrations in both Yellow and Blue	2	3	2	4
"Do this" before all probe demonstrations in Blue	–	–	2	2
"Don't do this" before all probe demonstrations in Yellow	–	–	1	2
Interspersed sessions with no instructions	3	5	–	–

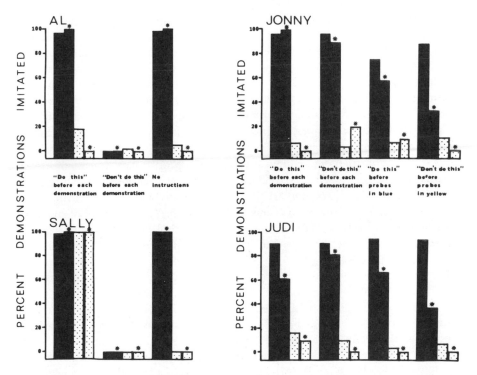

Figure 2   Mean percentage of demonstrations imitated by the subjects under each of the instructional conditions investigated (Experiment 2). Solid bars show the percentage imitated when the yellow apron was worn (reinforcement of imitation). Open dotted bars show the percentage imitated when the blue apron was worn (reinforcement of nonimitation). Performance on probe demonstrations is noted by an asterisk (*) above the bar.

and the stippled bars show the percentages of demonstrations imitated in blue (asterisk above probe responses). The results of the instructional conditions were highly variable across children. For Al, the instruction, "Do this," before each demonstration had little effect on his performance. He imitated almost all demonstrations in yellow and imitated very few of the demonstrations in blue. However, the instruction, "Don't do this," before each demonstration eliminated almost all his imitative responding in yellow. During the sessions with no instructions (which were interspersed among the instructional sessons), Al imitated almost all demonstrations in yellow and almost no demonstrations in blue. Sally followed both the "Do this" and the "Don't do this" instructions. When all demonstrations were preceded by "Do this," Sally imitated almost all of the demonstrations in both yellow and blue. When all demonstrations were preceded by "Don't do this," almost none of the demonstrations were imitated. However, in those interspersed sessions when no instructions were given, Sally imitated demonstrations in yellow and did not imitate them in blue.

The data from Jonny and Judi show somewhat different results. None of the instructional conditions appeared to have a powerful effect upon the percentage of demonstrations imitated in either yellow or blue, with the exception of the instruction, "Don't do this" given before only probe demonstrations in yellow (last set of bars). For both children this last instructional condition seemed to produce a decrease in the percentage of probe demonstrations imitated in yellow (solid bar with asterisk above it). However, the percentage of those probe demonstrations imitated in yellow was still higher than the percentage of probe demonstrations imitated in blue.

Thus, the instructional conditions did not appear to have consistent effects across children. For Sally, instructions appeared to override the reinforcement control of imitation or nonimitation that she had exhibited without instructions. For Al, only one of the instructions ("Don't do this") appeared to override the reinforcement control over imitation that he had displayed without instructions. For Johnny and Judi, the instructions appeared to have minimal effects.

Experiment 3

In most of the studies cited in the introduction, the topography of the unreinforced-probe response has been similar to, or involved the same parts of the body, as the group of reinforced imitative responses. For example, Baer *et al.* (1967) taught retarded children to imitate simple motor responses involving the hands, arms, legs, and feet. After a period of training on these responses, the children would also imitate new probe demonstrations involving these parts of the body even though no direct training and no reinforcement was given for these imitations. In the studies by Lovaas *et al.* (1966), Brigham and Sherman (1968), and Burgess *et al.* (1970), when imitation of certain vocal demonstrations was reinforced, the children also imitated new probe vocal demonstrations even though these imitations were never reinforced.

Although imitation of new probe responses has been shown in a number of studies, one result of the study by Baer *et al.* (1967) suggests that there are limits to the kind of new demonstrations that will be imitated. In this study, after children had displayed both reinforced and probe imitation of simple motor responses, vocal demonstrations were displayed to the children. None of the children initially imitated these vocal demonstrations in spite of their widely generalized motor imitative repertoires. In a more recent study, Garcia, Baer, and Firestone (1971) have shown with retarded children that the kind of new responses which will be imitated can, in part, be controlled by the kind of responses that the children have already been trained to imitate. In addition, Bandura and Barab (1971) found that children showed a greater likelihood of imitating probe responses which were topographically similar to reinforced imitations than probe responses which were topographically dissimilar to reinforced imitations. The purpose of the present study was to further investigate the relationship between the kind (topography) of imitations trained and the kind of unreinforced probe responses that would be imitated.

Procedures

To investigate this relationship, four different kinds of demonstrations were used: demonstrations of responses involving only hands and arms; demonstrations of responses involving only feet and legs; demonstrations of responses involving movement of the entire body; and demonstrations of vocal responses. For each child, three different hand-arm responses were initially trained using the procedures described above. Once a child imitated each of these demonstrations once without instructions, four probe demonstrations (one each of the above four kinds) were displayed to the child. Probe demonstrations were randomly interspersed among reinforced demonstrations at a ratio of one to three,

TABLE 3

Reinforced and Unreinforced Probe Demonstrations
within Each Group of Experiment 3
(Probes are indicated by *)

Hand and Arm
1. Both hands clap.
2. Both arms held out straight out at side.
3. Both arms held over head.
*4. Both hands wave, with elbows bent.

Leg and Foot
1. Both legs held out straight in front of body, feet off the floor.
2. One leg crossed over the other at the knee.
3. One leg held out straight, foot off floor.
*4. Both feet on floor, placed out to the sides.

Vocalizations
1. "a" vowel sound as in "car."
2. "oo" vowel sound as in "hoot."
3. "i" vowel sound as in "bite."
*4. "e" vowel sound as in "even."

Entire Body
1. Stand up, walk to door, touch door knob with either hand, go back and sit down in chair.
2. Stand up, walk to certain corner of room, bow head in corner, go back and sit down in chair.
3. Stand up, walk to certain wall, place both hands on wall about chest high, go back and sit down in chair.
*4. Stand up, go to corner where a chair is placed, sit down in chair, go back and sit in usual chair.

TABLE 4

Sequence of Conditions for Each Subject of Experiment 3

Condition	Clyde	Janet	Peggie
I			
Reinforced demonstrations: three different hand and arm responses			
Probe demonstrations: one hand and arm response one leg and foot response one vocal response one entire body response	two sessions with each type of probe; total of eight sessions	two sessions with each type of probe; total of eight sessions	two sessions with each type of probe; total of eight sessions
II			
Reinforced demonstrations: three different responses involving entire body			
Probe demonstrations: one hand and arm response one leg and foot response one vocal response one entire body response	two sessions with each type of probe; total of eight sessions	two sessions with each type of probe; total of eight sessions	two sessions with each type of probe; total of eight sessions
III			
Reinforced demonstrations: three different vocal responses			
Probe demonstrations: one hand and arm response one leg and foot response one vocal response one entire body response		two sessions with each type of probe; total of eight sessions	two sessions with each type of probe; total of eight sessions

respectively. Responses to probe demonstrations were never followed by reinforcement.

For each child, the probe demonstration of only one kind of response was displayed within any one session. Thus, during a session the experimenter might display three reinforced demonstrations of hand-arm responses and the probe demonstration of a vocal response. During the next session the experimenter might demonstrate the same three hand-arm responses and the probe demonstration of a hand-arm response. The sequence in which each kind of probe was used over sessions was unsystematic.

After a child had been trained (reinforced) to imitate hand-arm responses and the four kinds of probe responses had been displayed in separate sessions, the child was trained to imitate three responses of a second kind (those responses involving the entire body), using the same training procedures. Once the child reliably imitated each of these demonstrations, various probe demonstrations were interspersed among these reinforced demonstrations, one kind of probe response within each session. (Table 3 lists the reinforced responses and probe responses within each group, and Table 4 lists the sequence of training and probe conditions for each child.)

Results

Of a total of 260 responses jointly scored during Experiment 3 by the experimenter and the second scorer, no disagreements in recording imitation or nonimitation occurred.

Figures 3, 4, and 5 show the percentage of demonstrations imitated for reinforced and probe responses for Clyde, Janet, and Peggie respectively. Solid bars show the percentage of reinforced responses imitated and stippled bars show the percentage of probe responses imitated. Each pair of bars represents the data from the two sessions during which a particular kind of probe response was employed. The first set of axes for Clyde (see Fig. 3) shows sessions in which three hand-arm imitations were reinforced. As can be seen, Clyde imitated nearly all of these responses during these sessions. He also imitated all hand-arm and vocal probe demonstrations, and the majority of foot-leg probe demonstrations. Only on entire-body probes did Clyde show a low probability of imitation: approximately one-third of these probes were imitated. When the kind of reinforced imitations was changed to those responses involving the entire body (second set of axes), Clyde imitated all of the entire-body probes. He also imitated most of the other probes as well. For Janet (see Fig. 4), when hand-arm imitations were reinforced, she imitated hand-arm and foot-leg probes, but imitated very few of the entire-body and vocal probes. When imitations involving the entire body were reinforced, Janet imitated hand-arm, foot-leg, and entire-body probes, but did not imitate many of the vocal probes. When vocal imitations were reinforced, Janet imitated a high percentage of all probes. The data for Peggie (see Fig. 5) are very similar to those of Janet.

CLYDE

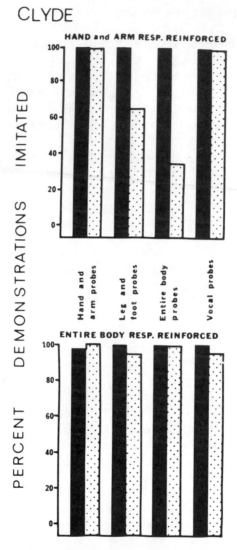

Figure 3   Mean percentage of reinforced demonstrations and probe demonstrations imitated (Experiment 3). The solid bars represent the kind of reinforced demonstration presented (see label across top of each graph). The open dotted bars represent the probe demonstrations. Labels along the abscissa indicate the kind of probes presented.

For each child, there was some indication that the kind of response that was reinforced exerted some control over the kind of probe responses that would be initially imitated. However, this control was not perfect, as exemplified by the fact that all three children imitated some foot-leg probes, even though no foot-leg imitations had ever been reinforced. Clyde also imitated vocal probes even

JANET

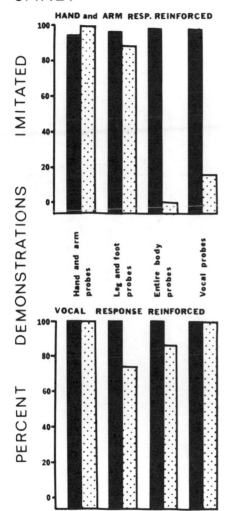
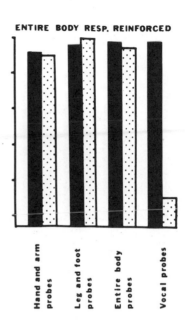

Figure 4   Mean percentage of reinforced demonstrations and probe demonstrations imitated (Experiment 3). The solid bars represent kind of reinforced demonstration presented (see label across top of each graph). The open dotted bars represent the probe demonstrations. Labels along the abscissa indicate the kind of probe presented.

though no vocal imitations had been reinforced. Further, once a child had imitated a probe demonstration, this imitation was maintained despite changes in the kind of imitation that was reinforced. For example, when imitations involving the entire body were reinforced (second set of axes in Figs. 3, 4, and 5), all

PEGGIE

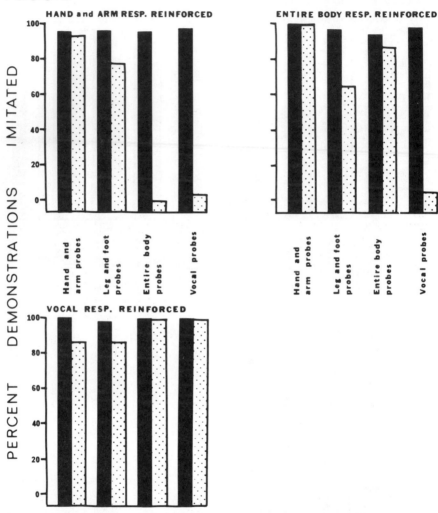

Figure 5   Mean percentage of reinforced demonstrations and probe demonstrations imitated (Experiment 3). The solid bars represent kind of reinforced demonstration presented (see label across top of each graph). The open dotted bars represent the probe demonstrations. Labels along the abscissa indicate the kind of probe presented.

three chidren continued to display a high percentage of imitation to the hand-arm and foot-leg probes. Further for Janet and Peggie, when vocal imitations were reinforced, these two children had not only imitated vocal probes, but also imitated the other three kinds of probes. Thus, the data show some indication that the initial probability of imitating probe demonstrations can be controlled by the topography of responses trained, although the maintenance of imitation to these probes (once imitation had been generated) appeared to be independent of the kind of imitations currently being trained.

Experiment 4

This study was designed to investigate a possible account for the maintenance of unreinforced probe imitations. Several writers (Gewirtz & Stingle, 1968; Bandura, 1969; Bandura & Barab, 1971) have suggested that when demonstrations for both reinforced and probe imitations are interspersed, a child may not discriminate differential consequences for the different responses, and because of this failure to discriminate the differential consequences, the child may continue to exhibit unreinforced probe responses. However, recently Steinman (1970a, b) and Steinman and Boyce (1971) have presented data which are not consistent with this account. In these studies, children who were reinforced for imitating some demonstrations and were never reinforced for imitating probe demonstrations continued to display imitation of all demonstrations. Then the children were shown two demonstrations, one of which would produce reinforcement if imitated (reinforced demonstration) and the other of which never produced reinforcement if imitated (probe demonstration). Steinman found that when both demonstrations were displayed, the children typically emitted the imitation that produced reinforcement. Nevertheless, when each demonstration was presented singly, the children continued to exhibit imitations that never produced reinforcement. The study below was an attempt to replicate these results.

Procedures

When a child completed Experiment III, he was started on the procedures below.

Choice procedure.   A choice procedure was arranged to investigate whether the children could (or could be trained to) discriminate among those demonstrations that, if imitated, produced reinforcement (reinforced demonstrations) and those demonstrations that, if imitated, did not produce reinforcement (probe demonstrations). This procedure involved presenting the child with two demonstrations, one a reinforced demonstration and the other a probe demonstration, and allowing the child to imitate either one. For the first three choice trials the experimenter said, "I am going to do two things. Wait until I do both, then you do either one you want." The experimenter then demonstrated two responses and said, "Now you can do either one." The instructions for all trials after the first three were, "You can do this" (demonstration) "or this" (demonstration). For half of the choice trials a reinforced demonstration was the first one displayed to a child, and for the other half of the trials it was the second demonstration displayed.

For the choice trials, the reinforcement procedures were as follows. If the child imitated the reinforced demonstration within 5 sec of the demonstration, the experimenter praised the child, dropped a marble in the child's cup, recorded the response, and presented the next pair of demonstrations. If the child imitated the probe demonstration or neither demonstration within 5 sec, the experimenter recorded this, and presented the next pair of demonstrations. Finally, if the child imitated both demonstrations or exhibited a response not demonstrated, the experimenter recorded this, waited 5 sec, and then presented the next pair of demonstrations.

For Janet and Peggie, all reinforced demonstrations in the choice procedure involved the 3 reinforced vocal responses. Within each session, the same probe demonstration was presented with the 3 reinforced vocal demonstrations. Thus, in one session the foot-leg probe demonstrations might be presented with each of the 3 reinforced vocal demonstrations. In the next session the vocal probe demonstration might be presented with each of the 3 reinforced vocal demonstrations, and so forth. Each kind of probe demonstration was presented with the vocal demonstrations for 3 sessions (a total of 12 sessions for all probe demonstrations). For Clyde, the reinforced demonstrations in the choice procedure involved the 3 responses of the entire body. Each kind of probe demonstration was presented with the reinforced demonstrations for only one session (a total of 4 sessions for all probe demonstrations).

Demonstrations presented singly.   Following the choice procedure, the children were returned to the procedure employed in Experiment 3 in which demonstrations were presented singly with probe demonstrations interspersed among reinforced demonstrations. As before, only one kind of probe demonstration was used within any session. For Janet and Peggie, all reinforced demonstrations were vocal responses and each of the 4 probe demonstrations was employed within 2 separate sessions (a total of 8 sessions). For Clyde, all reinforced demonstrations involved movements of the entire body, and each of the probe demonstrations was employed within 3 separate sessions (a total of 12 sessions).

Results

During the choice procedure, imitation or nonimitation of each demonstration within 5 sec of the demonstrations was scored. Under the single-trial procedure, responses were scored as they were in Experiment 3. Of the 221 trials observed by both the experimenter and the second scorer during Experiment 4, only one disagreement occurred.

Figure 6 shows the results of the choice procedure for each child. Each set of axes shows the percentage of imitation to reinforced demonstrations and probe demonstrations for each session in which the children were shown two demonstrations on each trial. As can be seen in this figure, Clyde imitated most of the

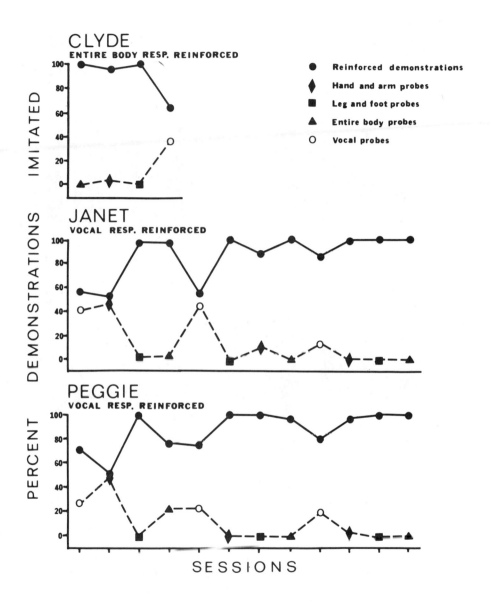

Figure 6   Mean percentage of reinforced and probe demonstrations imitated under the choice procedure during which the reinforced and probe demonstrations were presented in pairs (Experiment 4). The solid line connects percentages for the reinforced demonstrations, and the dashed line, percentages for the probe demonstrations.

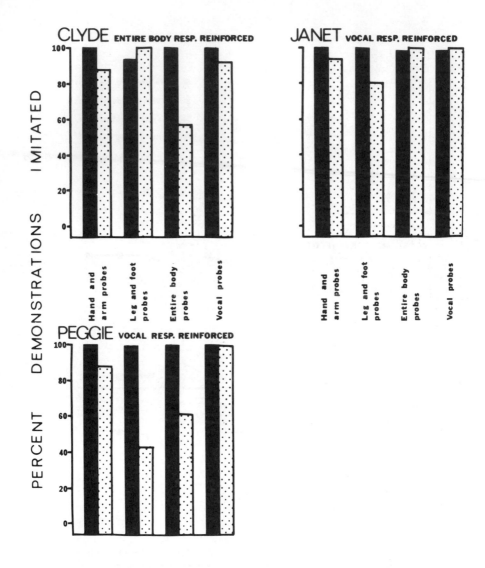

Figure 7   Mean percentage of reinforced demonstrations and probe demonstrations imitated when again presented singly (Experiment 4). The solid bars represent the kind of reinforced demonstration presented (see label across top of each graph). The open dotted bars represent the probe demonstrations. Labels along the absicca indicate the kind of probe presented.

reinforced demonstrations and a few of the probe demonstrations from the very beginning of the choice procedure. Janet and Peggie, on the other hand, initially imitated both reinforced and probe demonstrations about equally during the first two sessions. As the choice procedure was continued, however, both of these children began to imitate most of the reinforced demonstrations and few of the probe demonstrations. Thus, all children eventually displayed a clear discrimination between reinforced and probe demonstrations. Despite this clear discrimination, the children continued to imitate most of the probe demonstrations when they were again presented singly, interspersed among the reinforced demonstrations. These results are shown in Figure 7, which shows the percentage of reinforced demonstrations (solid bars) and the probe demonstrations imitated (stippled bars) over all sessions when the single-trial procedure was reinstated following the choice procedure.

Discussion

The findings of Experiment 1 provide additional evidence that reinforcement is a relevant variable for maintaining reinforced and unreinforced imitative responses. In Experiment 1, discriminatative control was established over imitative and nonimitative responding. Once established, this reinforcement context controlled, to a great extend, the probability of imitating the unreinforced probes. These results are consistent with the conclusions drawn from several earlier studies with retarded and normal children (Baer & Sherman, 1964; Lovaas *et al.*, 1966; Baer *et al.*, 1967; Peterson, 1968; Risley, 1968; Brigham & Sherman, 1968).

The finding concerning contextual control of unreinforced imitation is also consistent with recent findings involving stimulus control of unreinforced match-to-sample behavior in preschool children (Sherman, Saunders, & Brigham, 1970). Children were trained (reinforced) to match sample and choice stimuli under one condition, and mismatch sample and choice stimuli under another condition. After training, unreinforced probe trials with a new sample stimulus were occasionally interspersed among the reinforced trials of these conditions. There was a high probability of matching probes when they were introduced in the context of reinforcement for matching. Similarly, there was a high probability of mismatching probes when they were introduced in the context of reinforcement of mismatching.

The conclusion that imitative behavior (both reinforced and unreinforced) can be controlled by reinforcement operations, however, requires several qualifications. First, not all subjects who have been exposed to conditions in which imitation is no longer reinforced have shown a decline in imitative behavior. Waxler and Yarrow (1970) used instructions and social consequences to produce imitative behavior by normal preschool children. When the children were exposed to conditions in which there were no longer any social consequences for imitation, both previously reinforced and unreinforced imitative behavior of most of the children decreased. However, some of the children showed little or no decrease in imitative behavior. Steinman and Boyce (1971) found that normal children who were allowed to imitate either of two demonstrations reliably displayed imitations which produced reinforcement in contrast to imitations which did not produce reinforcement. However, when single demonstrations were displayed, these same children showed little or no decrease in imitative behavior under either a condition in which reinforcement was delivered before imitations or a condition in which no reinforcement was delivered. Steinman (1970a) had reported similar results with a normal child in an earlier study. Peterson and Whitehurst (1971) found that normal children imitated a variety of responses whether or not there were consequences for any imitative behavior as long as an experimenter remained in the room while the responses were performed by the children. When the experimenter left the room before the children responded, the amount of imitative behavior displayed by the children declined. Thus, although the experimental consequences used by Peterson and Whitehurst were not shown to be reinforcers, the presence or absence of an experimenter seemed to be more important in controlling imitation than the consequences arranged for imitation.

Second, even in several studies where reinforcement has affected imitative behavior, this behavior was only partially eliminated when reinforcement was no longer delivered contingent upon imitation (e.g., Baer & Sherman, 1964; Brigham & Sherman, 1968). Although the failure to eliminate imitative behavior completely may be simply due to the children's not having been exposed to the conditions of nonreinforcement for a long enough period of time, it is also possible that other variables maintained some level of imitation.

Third, some children who have shown a decrease in imitative behavior during one condition of nonreinforcement have not shown such a decrease during other conditions of nonreinforcement. Burgess et al. (1970) found that previously reinforced imitative behavior of normal children decreased when reinforcement was given immediately after a demonstration and before imitation occurred. However, one of the children whose imitative behavior decreased under this condition had previously shown no decrease in imitative behavior when he was exposed to a condition in which reinforcement was no longer delivered immediately following imitations. Similarly, the imitative behavior of one of the retarded children in the study by Baer et al. (1967) showed no decline when reinforcement was no longer delivered immediately following imitative behavior, but did decline when reinforcement was delivered immediately following a demonstration and before imitation occurred. However, for this child, once imitation had decreased, it continued to remain low even when the condition was returned to that which was originally shown ineffective.

Thus, although reinforcement has been shown to be functional in controlling reinforced and unreinforced imitative behavior, apparently immediate reinforcement alone cannot account for the maintenance of all imitative behavior for all children.

Experiment 2 examined the effects of instructions on imitative behavior. Although the instructions used in Experiment 2 did not have consistent effects across all children, for some children, at least, those instructions exerted stronger control over imitation than the reinforcement contingencies for imitation. Steinman (1970a, b) has previously shown that instructions to children affected their likelihood of imitating unreinforced demonstration. Waxler and Yarrow (1970) found that children told that they did not have to imitate if they did not want to, did not continue to imitate reinforced or unreinforced demonstrations as long under.conditions of nonreinforcement as did children who were not given these instructions.

Experiment 3 examined the effects of topographical similarity between reinforced and unreinforced probe demonstrations on children's likelihood of imitating the probe demonstrations. Although there were some indications that the children were intially more likely to imitate probe demonstrations which were topographically similar to reinforced demonstrations, once a child began to imitate probe demonstrations the maintenance of these imitations was not related to the topography of reinforced imitations currently being reinforced. Garcia *et al.* (1971) obtained similar, although clearer, results with retarded children. In that study the children were trained to imitate responses within several topographical boundaries. Initial development of probe demonstrations within these topographical boundaries was clearly related to the kinds of reinforced imitations that were trained. Bandura and Barab (1971) found that the majority of children in their study displayed more imitation of probe responses similar in topography to reinforced responses than of probe responses topographically dissimilar to reinforced responses. Steinman (1970a) employed a choice procedure in which children were shown two demonstrations, either one of which they could imitate. He found that the children consistently exhibited those imitations that produced reinforcement in contrast to those imitations that did not. Nevertheless, the children did imitate some of the unreinforced responses. Of these, the majority were responses which were similar in topography (involved the same parts of the body) to the reinforced imitations in contrast to those involving different parts of the body than the reinforced imitations. Steinman and Boyce (1971), however, used similar procedures and responses in a later study and found little systematic relationship between the topography of reinforced imitations and whether or not probe responses of similar and dissimilar topography would be exhibited.

The results of Experiment 4 and the results of several earlier studies (Steinman, 1970 a, b; Steinman & Boyce, 1971) suggest that the maintenance of unreinforced imitation is not due to the failure or inability of children to discriminate between reinforced and unreinforced responses. In each of these studies, when children were given the opportunity to imitate either of two demonstrations, they displayed those imitations that produced reinforcement in contrast to those imitations that did not. However, when demonstrations were presented singly, the children imitated the great majority of all demonstrations. Thus, on the choice-demonstrations trials the children showed differential performances to reinforced and unreinforced responses but did not do so when these responses were demonstrated to them singly.

Nevertheless, Bandura and Barab (1971) have argued that these kinds of results are not convincing evidence for rejecting the discrimination hypothesis. They suggest that, while children may discriminate between reinforced and unreinforced responses (as on the choice trials), other variables present in most studies of imitation (such as the experimenter's instructions to match the demonstration) may serve to maintain unreinforced imitations when single demonstrations for these responses are interspersed with demonstrations for reinforced responses. Thus, they argue that the results simply show that instructions can override the effects of differential reinforcement.

The results of the study by Bandura and Barab (1971) support their contentions. In this study, both instructions and other cues from the experimenter for the child to imitate (like eye contact between the experimenter and the child) were minimized. In one condition of the study, the children were reinforced for imitating demonstrations by one experimenter but were not reinforced for imitating demonstrations by another experimenter. In this condition, almost all of the children imitated a high percentage of the responses which were reinforced, but showed a markedly lower percentage of imitation of unreinforced responses. In another condition of the study, one experimenter demonstrated both reinforced and unreinforced responses, but some of the unreinforced responses were similar in topography to the reinforced responses and some of the unreinforced responses were dissimilar in topography to the reinforced responses. In this condition the majority of children showed greater imitation of the similar unreinforced responses than of the dissimilar unreinforced responses. Thus, Bandura and Barab concluded that when the unreinforced responses could be easily distinguished from the reinforced responses (e.g., by different models presenting each, or by the topography of the responses themselves), and in the absence of various other conditions which might maintain all imitation (e.g., instructions to the child to imitate), children will imitate reinforced responses but will eventually stop imitating unreinforced responses.

As noted above, the suggestion by Bandura and Barab (1971) that instructions or cues to the child to imitate can play an important role in controlling unreinforced imitation is, in part, supported by the results of Experiment 2 and by the studies by Steinman (1970a, b) and Waxler and Yarrow (1970). Also, the study by Peterson and Whitehurst (1971) which showed that the presence or absence of an experimenter influenced the degree to which children imitated, suggests that the experimenter, or cues provided by him, may serve to control imitative behavior. At this point, it seems clear that a complete analysis of the conditions that can control imitative behavior will require extensive investigation under conditions in which minimal instructions or cues are provided to the children by an experimenter or model, as well as systematic manipulation of these variables. In the present experiments, except when instructions were manipulated, an attempt was made to minimize instructional effects by not employing any instructions regarding imitation after the first session. However, the instructions used at first may still have had an effect on imitation during the later sessions even though they were no longer used. Perhaps a closer approximation to a situation involving minimal social interaction between experimenter and child is exemplified in the study by Sherman *et al.* (1970) which investigated the matching-to-sample behavior of normal preschool children. In this study, both the stimuli and the consequences for behavior were presented automatically by electromechanical equipment. Even though some initial instructions were given to the children, in the absence of the experimenter or instructions the consequences for behavior controlled the matching and mismatching behavior of the children. Further, whether or not children matched or mismatched certain unreinforced sample stimuli was a function of whether reinforcement was delivered for matching or mismatching other sample stimuli. Thus, it would appear that even in a situation which involves minimal social interaction between experimenter and subject, some control over unreinforced responses can be exerted by reinforcement for other responses.

The results of Experiments 1-4 and those of previous research indicate that a number of variables may control imitative behavior of children. The functional variables which have received most research attention, to date, are reinforcement conditions, instructions, and response similarity. The relative contribution of each of these variables to the maintenance of imitation does not appear to be consistent across children, nor do there appear to be strong reasons why this should be the case. Presumably, the degree to which these (and other) variables affect imitative behavior will depend not only on the conditions of the experiment but also on the extent of an individual child's existing or experimentally developed imitative repertoire, the child's past history of reinforcement for imitation, the degree to which the child has been taught to and been reinforced for following instructions, and the like. Because individual children probably will differ greatly on these and other characteristics prior to serving in experiments, a considerable amount of variability should exist in their responses to experimental conditions. For these reasons, it would appear that a precise specification of the conditions controlling the maintenance of imitative behavior requires extensive control over the previous behavioral history of a child. This control has, in part, been realized in those studies in which retarded and autistic children presumably without prior imitative repertoires have been trained to imitate (e.g., Lovaas *et al.,* 1966; Baer *et al.,* 1967; Garcia *et al.,* 1971). However, this type of control over the prior behaviors of normal children has not been attempted and, obviously, would present a number of practical difficulties.

ACKNOWLEDGMENTS

This research was supported by the National Program in Early Childhood Education in association with the Central Midwestern Regional Education Laboratory, Inc., under a grant from the U.S. Office of Education (No. OEC 3-7-070706-3118). The third author, who acted as the experimenter-model for this research, was partially supported by an Undergraduate Research Participation Award, No. 3912-5038 from The University of Kansas General Research Fund. Preparation of this manuscript was partially supported by PHS Training Grant HD 00183 from the National Institute of Child Health and Human Develment to the Kansas Center for Research in Mental Retardation and Human Development.

The authors wish to thank Miss Donna Mae Ida and Mr. John W. Macrae for their assistance in preparation of this manuscript.

REFERENCES

Baer, D. M., & Sherman, J. A. Reinforcement control of generalized imitation in young children. *Journal of Experimental Child Psychology*, 1964, *1*, 37-49.

Baer, D. M., Peterson, R. F., & Sherman, J. A. The development of imitation by reinforcing behavioral similarity to a model. *Journal of the Experimental Analysis of Behavior*, 1967, *10*, 405-416.

Bandura, A. *Principles of behavior modification.* New York: Holt, Rinehart, & Winston, 1969.

Bandura, A., & Barab, P. G. Conditions governing nonreinforced imitation. *Developmental Psychology*, 1971, *5*, 244-255.

Brigham, T. A., & Sherman, J. A. An experimental analysis of verbal imitation in preschool children. *Journal of Applied Behavior Analysis*, 1968, *1*, 151-158.

Burgess, R. L., Burgess, J. M., & Esveldt, K. C. An analysis of generalized imitation. *Journal of Applied Behavior Analysis*, 1970, *3*, 39-46.

Garcia, E., Baer, D. M., & Firestone, I. The development of generalized imitation within topographically determined boundaries. *Journal of Applied Behavior Analysis*, 1971, *4*, 101-112.

Gewirtz, J. L., & Stingle, K. G. Learning of generalized imitation as the basis for identification. *Psyhological Review*, 1968, *75*, 374-397.

Lovaas, O. I., Berberich, J. P., Perloff, B. F., & Schaeffer, B. Acquisition of imitative speech by schizophrenic children. *Science*, 1966, *151*, 705-707.

Metz, J. R. Conditioning generalized imitation in autistic children. *Journal of Experimental Child Psychology*, 1965, *2*, 389-399.

Peterson, R. F. Some experiments on the organization of a class of imitative behaviors. *Journal of Applied Behavior Analysis*, 1968, *1*, 225-235.

Peterson, R. F., & Whitehurst, G. T. A variable influencing the performance of generalized imitative behaviors. *Journal of Applied Behavior Analysis*, 1971, *4*, 1-9.

Risley, T. Learning and lollipops. *Psychology Today*, January, 1968, 25.

Sherman, J. A., Saunders, R. R., & Brigham, T. A. Transfer of matching and mismatching behavior in preschool children. *Journal of Experimental Child Psychology*, 1970, *9*, 489-498.

Steinman, W. M. Generalized imitation and the discrimination hypothesis. *Journal of Experimental Child Psychology,* 1970, *10,* 79-99. (a)

Steinman, W. M. The social control of generalized imitation. *Journal of Applied Behavior Analysis,* 1970, *3,* 159-167.

Steinman, W. M., & Boyce, K. D. Generalized imitation as a function of discrimination difficulty and choice. *Journal of Experimental Child Psychology,* 1971, *11,* 251-265.

Waxler, C. Z., & Yarrow, M. R. Factors influencing imitative learning in preschool children. *Journal of Experimental Child Psychology,* 1970, *9,* 115-130.

30

Response Cost and Human Aggressive Behavior

Howard N. Sloane, Jr.
K. Richard Young
Terri Marcusen

University of Utah
    and
Jordan School District

A variety of laboratory studies have indicated that aggressive behavior can be instigated in animals by pain or other aversive conditions (Johnson, 1972; Knutson, 1973; Maple & Matheson, 1973). Experimental studies indicating a relationship between aversive events and aggressive behavior in humans are less common, with the exception of studies relating to modeling procedures and aggressive behavior (Gelfand *et al.,* 1974). Other effects of punishment on human behavior have been reviewed by Johnston (1972).

Ulrich and Favell (1970) had child subjects stack bottle stoppers into piles. Each subject was told that another child was performing the same task in another room and that this subject had a button which when pressed could vibrate the subject's table and knock over his pile of stoppers. The subject also had a button, and was told if pushed, it would vibrate the table of the hypothetical child. Results showed an increase in button pressing for all four subjects as a function of having their table vibrated. In a somewhat similar study, Frederiksen and Peterson (1973) told subjects that another (nonexistent) subject controlled their rate of reinforcement. Subjects had a switch which they were told could deliver white noise to this other (nonexistent) subject. Subjects pressed the "white noise" switch more often when their frequency of reinforcement was lower than when it was higher. In both studies it was concluded that subjects became more aggressive as a function of a lower rate of reinforcement, or of having their opportunity for reinforcement decreased. However, most people have been reinforced for attack behavior towards others by the termination of similar behavior directed towards them, and this history may have controlled the alleged "aggressive" responses, which can be viewed as simple learned operants with no particular aggressive characteristics.

Several studies have examined extinction as a precursor of aggressive behavior. Rheingold, Gewirtz, and Ross (1959) demonstrated increased "emotional outbursts" in infants as a function of extinction. Sajwaj, Twardosz, and Burke (1972) noted increases in "disruptive behavior" when other behavior was ignored which had previously been reinforced. Kelly and Hake (1970) placed knob pulling, which had formerly been reinforced with money, on extinction. Subjects also could escape from an aversive noise either by button pressing or by punching a cushion. The relative frequency of punching the cushion compared with button pressing increased as a function of the extinction condition for knob pulling. In an extension of this, Harrell (1972), using similar procedures, showed that the magnitude of the punching response increased due to extinction, as well as its relative frequency.

Oliver, West and Sloane (1974) reported on two studies relating aggressive behavior to aversive events. In the first experiment, adults working on a plunger-pulling task received an electric shock unrelated to plunger pulling at 75% probability every 2 min. Subjects could press a toggle switch to deliver electric shock to the experimenter, who was visible to the subjects as an alleged observer. Three sessions in which no shock was delivered alternated with two sessions in which shock was delivered. In shock sessions subjects pressed the toggle switch and shocked the observer at an average rate more than 9 times higher than in the nonshock sessions.

In the second experiment, the effects of noncontingent time-out from positive reinforcement on the aggressive behavior of two child subjects was investigated. Noncontingent time-out appeared to control an above baseline rate of aggressive behavior during segments of a multiple schedule (in a classroom setting) in which the time-outs were programmed. In schedule components in which time-out was contingent upon aggressive behavior, aggressive behavior decreased. Noncontingent time-out also appeared to produce high aggressive rates in segments in which no time-out, contingent or noncontingent, was programmed, but which were adjacent to segments containing noncontingent time-out.

The two current studies further explored the role of aversive events in producing aggressive behavior in humans. In the first, the role of noncontingent response-cost on the aggressive behavior of adolescent boys was examined. The second examined the effects which a response-cost programmed contingent upon a nonaggressive response had on aggressive behavior in adolescent children.

EXPERIMENT 1

Subjects and Setting

Seven teenage boys who were students in a special token-economy classroom served as subjects. The setting was a physical education class in a gymnasium. The first 10-15 min of this class consisted of exercises, and this period was not included in the study. The remainder of the class, which usually was about 30 min, consisted of structured prescribed activities (basketball, volleyball, trampoline, etc.) for all subjects. The experiment took place during this latter period. Subjects could earn up to 120 points for participation, redeemable at a later time for special privileges and free time.

Dependent Variables

Each 30-sec interval was scored for the presence or absence of aggressive behavior for each subject if any one of the four behaviors below occurred.

1. Physical assault. Hitting, kicking, biting, scratching, pulling, grabbing, jumping on, throwing an object at another person, or attempts to do these things.

2. Assault on surroundings. Knocking materials off shelves, overturning furniture, throwing materials or equipment other than at a person, kicking doors, walls or furniture.

3. Verbal assault. Threatening physical assault as defined above; or threatening physically destructive actions (killing, cutting); verbally resisting instructions; stating dislike or other negative feelings about another; threatening or predicting hurt or disaster for another; making derogatory remarks about the looks, competence or ancestry of another (name calling); or making a culturally defined obscene gesture at another.

4. Out-of-the-room. Unauthorized leaving of the room accompanied by muttering, threats, kicks, or other aggressive behavior. This behavior was coded in *each* interval until the subject returned.

Reliability and Conditions of Recording

The observer was equipped with a clipboard and stopwatch. The nature of the students' activities required that the observer move freely about the gymnasium. The observer carried a score sheet marked off in 30-sec squares with a row labeled for each subject. At the end of each 30-sec interval, the observer made a separate mark in each square for each of the four recorded behaviors for each subject. If none of the recorded behaviors occurred, a dot was made. As subjects emitted the defined behaviors in less than one-third of the intervals on the average, one observer was able to record for all subjects.

Eight reliability checks were conducted, one each for the initial and final baseline periods, and one during the experimental period for each subject, with one exception due to observer absence. During a reliability check two observers who could not see what the other was recording, independently recorded all behaviors. One agreement was counted for each score recorded by both observers in an interval. One disagreement was scored for each score recorded in an interval by either observer for which the other observer had no score or a different score. Percentage agreement was computed by dividing 100 times the total agreements by the sum of the agreements plus the disagreements. Data from all subjects in a session were summed in computing this score. Although data analysis did not differentiate between the four types of aggressive acts recorded, an agreement was scored only when the same aggressive behavior was scored in an interval. Reliability ranged from 73% to 92%, with an average of 84%.

Experimental Conditions

Baseline

During baseline conditions no consequences were programmed contingent upon aggressive acts, and no points were removed.

Noncontingent Response-Cost

During this condition, the experimental subject received three "fines" at arbitrary times, while the other subjects remained on baseline. The observer record sheet for the experimental subject had three intervals picked randomly and marked in advance of the session. The observer signaled the teacher just before the start of the interval, and the teacher handed the subject a 3 x 5 card with his name on it and the words "minus 40 points" on it. If a subject had a negative number of points after the day ended it was scored as a zero.

Before the experiment started, subjects were told they might be docked points for arbitrary reasons, but were given no further instructions. When a subject was docked points no comments were made by the teacher, nor were questions from the subject or other students responded to (on this topic). The teacher was given the card a second or two before the interval started; the noncontingent response-cost was always delivered right at the start of the interval. No other response-costs were used, nor were there any consequences programmed for aggressive behavior.

Design and Sessions

After six baseline sessions one student was randomly selected to be Subject 1. Noncontingent response-cost was in effect for this subject for the next three sessions (7, 8, and 9), while other subjects remained on baseline conditions. Before the start of the tenth session, another student was randomly selected to be Subject 2. For the next three sessions, Subject 2 received noncontingent response-cost while all other students (including Subject 1) received baseline conditions. This procedure was continued until all seven subjects had received noncontingent response-cost for three days, in a randomly selected order. Two additional days of baseline completed the experiment.

Results

For each subject, the percentage of intervals in which aggressive behavior occurred is presented in Figure 1. Although there is a great amount of variability in the aggressive behaviors emitted by a subject over the course of the experiment, for most subjects the noncontingent response-cost produced an increase in aggressive behavior over the adjacent sessions, even though rates in more remote sessions were higher due to uncontrolled classroom events.

This effect appears more clearly when short term effects on the aggressive behavior of each subject are examined in the noncontingent response-cost sessions themselves. Nine noncontingent response-costs were delivered to each subject except Subject 7, who inadvertently received 10. Thus 64 intervals started with noncontingent response-cost. Of these 64 noncontingent response-costs, all but five were followed by an aggressive response in the same interval, that is, an aggressive response occurred following a noncontingent response cost 92% of the time. However, only 29% of the total intervals contained aggressive responses, thus aggressive responses were 3.6 times as frequent in intervals starting with a noncontingent response-cost as for intervals in general. For all subjects, and for every noncontingnet response-cost session, this was true. Individual data by sessions describing this are presented in Table 1.

EXPERIMENT 2

Subjects and Setting

Five teenage boys from a group of 12 who were students in a special token-economy classroom served as subjects. The setting was a physical education class in a gymnasium, one hour per day. Members of the group earned points during this time contingent upon dressing, being on time, calisthenics, running laps, and

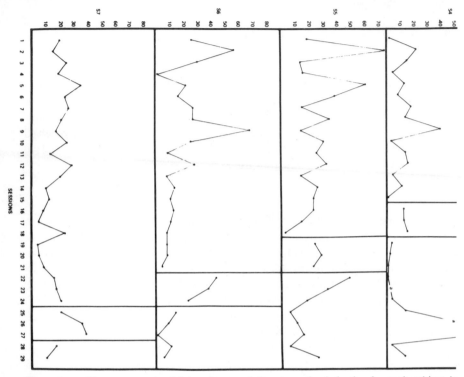

Figure 1   The percentage of intervals scored for aggressive behavior for each subject in

participation in free play. A total of 140 points could be earned per day, and were redeemable at the end of the period for special activites and free time. The setting was the same as for Experiment 1, but took place a year later with different subjects.

Dependent Variables

A trained observer recorded both aggressive and nonaggressive behaviors. Aggressive behaviors were defined essentially as in Experiment 1; except that out-of-the-room behavior was prohibited and not recorded.

Nonaggressive Behavior Recorded

The following nonaggressive behaviors, which were a part of the independent variable, were also recorded: failure to be synchronized in calisthenics; being out-of-step; failure to complete the specified number of calisthenics; being out of line; and not facing forward.

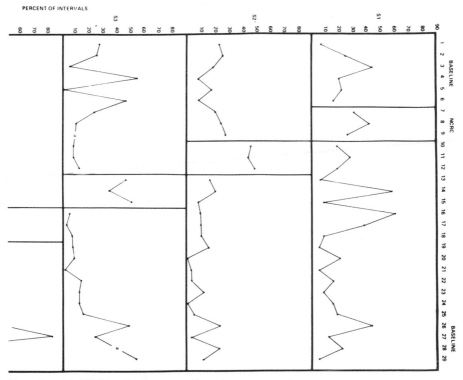

Experiment 1. NRCR refers to noncontingent response-cost.

Reliability and Conditions of Recording

Reliability checks were made during each of the four phases of the experiment. On a designated day, an assistant also recorded the two behaviors in the same manner as the observer. Reliability for the two observers was computed as in Experiment 1.

Separate reliability was computed for each class of behaviors, aggressive and nonaggressive, for each experimental condition. Reliability for aggressive responses ranged from 91% to 100% with a mean of 97%, while reliabilities for nonaggressive responses ranged from 75% to 100% with a mean of 90%.

Experimental Conditions

Baseline

During baseline, both aggressive and nonaggressive behaviors were recorded. No consequences were programmed for either class of behavior. No response-costs were delivered.

TABLE 1

Location of Aggressive Responses in Experimental Sessions

Subject	Session	Response-cost Intervals Coded (in %)	Total Intervals Coded (in %)	Response-cost Total (in %)
1	7	100	23	4.3
	8	100	41	2.4
	9	100	23	4.3
2	10	100	42	2.4
	11	100	44	2.3
	12	100	33	3.0
3	13	100	46	2.2
	14	100	30	3.3
	15	100	47	2.1
4	16	100	12	8.6
	17	67	12	5.6
	18	100	15	6.7
5	19	33	23	1.4
	20	100	32	3.1
	21	100	22	4.5
6	22	100	34	2.9
	23	100	33	3.0
	24	67	22	2.3
7	25	100	20	5.0
	26	100	35	2.6
	27	67	12	4.1
Mean:	All	92	29	3.6

Treatment

During the response-cost condition, both aggressive and nonaggressive behaviors were recorded. However, during this condition, a response-cost was issued to a subject contingent upon the emission of any of the nonaggressive behaviors specified above. The fine was computed by dividing the total possible number of points that could be earned during the baseline period by the average number of times each behavior occurred during baseline per subject per period. Using this formula, the value of the fine was fixed at ten points.

As the observer was busier than in Experiment 1, response-costs were delivered by a teaching assistant, who informed the subject of the fine and explained briefly the behavior for which the subject was being fined each time a response-cost was delivered. On the first day of the experiment, the subjects had also been informed of the response-cost conditions and the behaviors for which they would be fined and how much they would be fined.

There were no other programmed differences in the gym period except for the presence of the observer.

Design and Sessions

A reversal design (ABAB) was used. The first phase (baseline), lasted five days, and was followed by the treatment phase for five days. The third phase of the experiment was a return to baseline, with all the conditions of the first phase resumed. This phase lasted five days. The fourth phase was a replication of the second phase, wherein response-cost conditions were reinstated contingent upon the emission of the nonaggressive behaviors. This phase lasted three days.

During all phases, aggressive behavior and nonaggressive behavior were recorded and no consequences were programmed for the emission of aggressive behaviors.

Results

In general, the response-cost conditions, issued contingently, increased the frequency of aggressive behavior in all five subjects. The fines had little effect on reducing the frequency of the nonaggressive behavior.

Baseline 1

During initial baseline, the mean number of aggressive responses recorded per day was 0.2. Two subjects exhibited no aggressive behavior, and the highest recorded in any one day for one subject was 2. The mean number of nonaggressive responses occurring per day during baseline equaled 2.0 (see Table 2).

Treatment 1

During the initial treatment phase, the mean number of aggressive responses occurring per day rose to 2.0. None of the subjects exhibited an absence of aggression during this 5-day period, and all increased over baseline. The mean number of nonaggressive responses recorded per day remained the same at 2.0.

Baseline 2

During the second baseline, aggressive responses per day decreased to 0.6. Nonaggressive responses per day rose to 3.4.

Treatment 2

The mean number of aggressive responses per day during the final treatment phase jumped to a high of 2.9. Nonaggressive behaviors recorded per day during this period averaged 2.7.

Table 2 shows mean values of aggressive and nonaggressive behaviors per day for each individual subject. As indicated, all subjects increased their aggressive behavior over baseline conditions in both treatment phases. There was some variability in the increase for two subjects.

CONCLUSIONS

The results of Experiments 1 and 2 tend to support prior findings indicating that aversive events increase aggressive behavior in humans. Experiment 1 indicates that noncontingent response-cost may produce aggressive behavior, and thus, extends the findings of Kelly and Hake (1970) who utilized extinction, and of Oliver, West and Sloane (1974) who used time-out from positive reinforcement and electric shock. The results of the individual subject within-session analysis of the temporal relationship between noncontingent response-cost and aggressive behavior is congruent with the assumption that punishment elicits aggressive behavior, but does not exclude other explanations, such as that punishment makes some aspect of aggressive behavior reinforcing and thus may be viewed as a motivating operation or setting event (Bijou & Baer, 1961). Aggressive behavior may, of course, be under multiple control, and a single stimulus event, such as shock or time-out or a response-cost, may have more than one stimulus function with respect to a particular response class. The temporal analysis in Experiment 1 does suggest that the noncontingent response-cost immediately elicited aggressive behaviors; the generally higher rate of aggressive behaviors

TABLE 2

Mean Number of Aggressive and Nonaggressive Behaviors
Recorded Per Day for Each Individual Subject

Subject	Behavior	Baseline 1	Treatment 1	Baseline 2	Treatment 2
1	Aggressive	0.6	1.0	0.0	5.4
	Nonaggressive	3.2	2.8	3.6	4.0
2	Aggressive	0.0	1.2	0.0	0.3
	Nonaggressive	3.0	2.8	3.5	2.6
3	Aggressive	0.0	4.6	1.0	3.7
	Nonaggresive	1.2	1.2	0.5	0.3
4	Aggressive	0.2	1.2	1.4	3.5
	Nonaggressive	1.6	2.6	5.6	4.0
5	Aggressive	0.2	2.0	0.6	2.0
	Nonaggressive	0.8	0.8	3.2	2.7
Average	Aggressive	0.2	2.0	0.6	2.9
	Nonaggressive	2.0	2.0	3.4	2.7

during the noncontingent response-cost condition compared with baseline sessions suggests some more general effect, characteristic of a setting event.

In Experiment 1, and in other studies on "elicited" aggression, it is usually assumed or implied that the noncontingent aspect of the aversive event is a necessary or significant factor. However, this "randomness" is, in most studies, confounded with the fact that the aversive event is not contingent on the aggressive behavior in particular. Thus, it may be the case that aversive events in general increase aggressive behavior, unless the aversive event is directly contingent upon the aggressive behavior and punishes it, or unless it exerts some discriminative control over aggressive behavior. In the Oliver, West and Sloane (1974) study noncontingent time-out from positive reinforcement appeared to increase aggressive behavior both under stimulus conditions directly associated with the noncontingent time-out, and under other stimulus conditions, as long as these stimulus periods were not occasions for the punishment of aggressive behavior.

The effects of contingent punishment (response-cost) of nonaggressive behavior upon the rate of aggressive behavior was examined in Experiment 2, and the results suggest that such contingent response-cost can, indeed, lead to an increase in aggressive behavior. Some confusion in interpreting these results arises due to the fact that the response-costs did not decrease the rate of those behaviors on which they were contingent. However, the experimental periods were brief, and the behaviors were under instructional control due to the subjects' past histories. In addition, the behaviors were occurring at an already low rate. Verbal statements by the subjects characterized the response-costs as extremely aversive.

In both of these experiments, brief periods of exposure to aversive stimuli and stimulus intensities which were within the range of everyday occurrences to the subjects were used, through the use of aversive stimuli which were nonphysical. Permissions were obtained from school authorities and parents. In addition, close monitoring of all subjects assured that no harmful or unwarranted effects occurred, and a committee on research using human subjects was consulted in advance.

Currently, greater attention is being paid to the precursors of aggressive behavior than in the past. A powerful analysis with implications for social change will require an experimental analysis from a natural science point of view.

ACKNOWLEDGMENTS

Experiment 1 was partially supported by Grant 1836-255 from the University Research Committee of the University of Utah, and partially by the Bureau of Educational Research of the University of Utah. Experiment 2 was a master's thesis done by the third author. The cooperation of Jordan School District (Utah) in both studies is gratefully acknowledged.

The extent of the debt owed to Sidney W. Bijou will probably not be fully appreciated for many years. Sid's insistence that human development, typical or atypical, receive an experimental analysis from a natural science point of view marks a renaissance in this field of study. Without such an emphasis, progress in understanding human development is basically stagnant. Although constructs and methods may change, real progress in the field will continue to rest upon the level of analysis quietly promoted by Sid. A second contribution is Sidney Bijou's insistence that service to people and research into human development are complementary, not opposed. While many of us were discussing "research versus service" in graduate school, Sid was showing people how to provide treatment packages that generated basic research as an integral part of the package. A third major contribution is the people that Sidney Bijou has trained, hired, influenced, or otherwise encouraged. Sid's students, formal or informal, comprise a significant proportion of the behavioral therapists and researchers dealing with children. Sid's final contribution is his research, publications, and verbal presentations. The growing body of literature contributed by Sidney Bijou is of incalculable value and assures that his influence will continue to spread.

REFERENCES

Bijou, S. W., & Baer, D. M. *Child development I: A systematic and empirical theory.* New York: Appleton-Century-Crofts, Inc., 1961.

Fredericksen, L., & Petersen, F. Aggression during various fixed-ratio schedules of reinforcement. *Proceedings of the 81st Annual Convention of the American Psychological Association, 1973, 8,* 873-874.

Gelfand, D. M., Hartmann, D. P., Lamb, A. K., Smith, C. L., Mahan, M. L., & Paul, S. C. The effect of adult models and described alternatives on children's choice of behavior modification techniques. *Child Development, 1974, 45,* 585-593.

Harrell, W. A. Effects of extinction on magnitude of aggression in humans. *Psychonomic Science, 1972, 29,* 213-215.

Johnson, R. N. *Aggression in man and animals.* Philadelphia: W. B. Saunders, 1972.

Johnston, J. M. Punishment of human behavior. *American Psychologist, 1972, 27,* 1033-1054.

Kelly, J. F., & Hake, D. F. An extinction induced increase in an aggressive response in humans. *Journal of the Experimental Analysis of Behavior, 1970, 14,* 153-164.

Knutson, J. F. (Ed.). *The control of aggression.* Chicago: Aldine, 1973.

Maple, T., & Matheson, D. W. *Aggression, hostility and violence — Nature or nurture?* New York: Holt, Rinehart, and Winston, 1973.

Oliver, S. D., West, R. C., & Sloane, H. N. Some effects on human behavior of aversive events. *Behavior Therapy, 1974, 5,* 481-493.

Rheingold, H. C., Gewirtz, J., & Ross, H. Social conditioning of vocalization. *Journal of Comparative and Physiological Psychology, 1959, 32,* 68-73.

Sajwaj, T., Twardosz, S., & Burke, M. Side effects of extinction procedures in a remedial preschool. *Journal of Applied Behavior Analysis, 1972, 5,* 163-175.

Ulrich, R. E., & Favell, J. Human aggression. In C. Neuringer & J. L. Micheal (Eds.), *Behavior modification in clinical psychology.* New York: Appleton-Century-Crofts, 1970.

31

Teaching Daily Self-Help Skills for Long-Term Maintenance

Carol M. Thomas
Sally E. Lukeris
Michael Palmer

Mansfield Training School

Beth Sulzer-Azaroff

University of Massachusetts

Bijou (1972) states: "The problem of maintaining and extending learning acquired in the classroom looms up as a far more serious one than the problem of retardation itself" [p. 285], and that "... the problem of maintaining and extending the behavior a child acquires in the special class has not been faced because it demands changing conditions both in the home and in the classes to which he is subsequently assigned" [p. 286]. In a large institution for the retarded, the problem of changing conditions in the residential setting and in other teaching or training programs becomes an even more serious problem. Staff-resident ratios, supervisory training personnel limitations, and limitations in the response repertoires and motivational levels of residential care staff seriously impede attempts to alter conditions to support many types of newly acquired resident behaviors.

An alternative to achieving maintained performance by changing conditions in the "home" is to start by examining home conditions for strengths. Current environmental conditions could be assessed to select initial target behaviors, the acquisition of which would be mutually beneficial to trainees as well as to the persons who play significant roles in their environments. The accomplishment of those initial goals would produce several effects: the trainee would acquire a new, constructive behavior, and the parents or caretakers would be exposed to the application of effective teaching methods while profiting by the trainee's consequent contribution to the group or family. Such mutual reinforcement would enhance the likelihood of staff willingness to accept the gradual introduction of subsequent training programs.

An intial examination of conditions in large state institutions may be discouraging. The residents spend most of their time in large dayhalls where there is little interaction with attendant personnel (Bensberg & Barnett, 1966). The lack of stimulation and other environmental factors appears to generate more stereotypic (Klaber & Butterfield, 1968) and other aimless behaviors. The attention of normal adults can produce more normal behavior (Mosely, Faust, & Reardon, 1970), but such attention tends not to be readily available. Housekeeping and other custodial duties consume much staff time (Bensberg & Barnett, 1966) and even when the staff is present, the employees frequently tend to ignore most resident behaviors (Warren & Mondy, 1971). Furthermore, the higher the resident-aide ratio, the less social and training interaction time available to the residents from each aide (Harris, Veit, Allen, & Chinsky, 1974).

Identification of more constructive activities for institutionalized retarded persons that could be implemented with little demand on aide time would obviously be extremely helpful. Since many effective teaching or training procedures have been developed for moderately and severely retarded persons, a good strategy would be to identify training procedures that would be mutually advantageous to trainees, trainers, and staff.

Many recent studies center on the training of severely retarded persons, and many different training strategies have been employed. Three which hold great promise are instruction, modeling, and graduated guidance. Altman, Talkington, and Cleland (1972) found that neither modeling nor verbal instruction alone were sufficient to produce learning in their severely retarded subjects. However, combining the procedures has been effective in teaching a variety of skills. Severely retarded subjects were taught gross motor responses to verbal instructions, using physical guidance which was faded as the subjects began to respond correctly (Whitman, Zakaras, & Chardos, 1971). Self-feeding has been similarly taught (Berkowitz, Sherry, & Davis, 1971) as well as a variety of other self-help skills (Bensberg, Colwell, & Cassel, 1965).

Token systems have frequently been used for motivation of mentally retarded persons. Even before the token economy (Ayllon & Azrin, 1968) became so widely known, tokens were used to motivate academic behavior in retarded children (Bijou, 1965). Tokens were shown to be more effective than social praise to improve academic performance in mildly to severely retarded children by Dalton, Rubino, and Hislop (1973). There were significant changes demonstrated by their groups which persisted for a year after their program ended. Baker, Stanish, and Fraser (1972) found tokens effective in reducing disruptive behavior in young moderately and severely retarded children, demonstrating that retarded children, four to seven years of age, can respond to tokens. Similar token programs have been used to reduce aggression and increase work output in retarded sheltered workshop clients (Gardner, 1971). Gardner (p. 224) cites a variety of programs in which tokens have successfully been used with retarded persons, involving work, social, and academic behaviors.

Even with effective motivational systems, apparently in accordance with Bijou's statement above, maintenance of trained behaviors has been a perpetual problem once the subject returns to the natural environment. Some studies mention this problem but few present data. Paloutzian, Hassazi, Streifel, and Edgar (1971) were successful in training imitative and interactive behaviors in an experimental setting. They felt that there was some generalization to the ward, but no data were presented. Similarly, Twardosz and Baer (1973) trained two severely retarded adolescents to ask questions of an experimenter while off the ward. They did not collect data on maintenance of this behavior, but suggested that the behavior would quickly reverse due to lack of attention to such behavior by staff. This prediction was supported by the two surveys by Warren and Mondy (1971) in which staff ignored 75.5% and 82.2% of the residents' appropriate behavior.

O'Brien, Bugle, and Azrin (1972) found that a profoundly retarded girl's eating skills did not maintain without specific program intervention, but performance improved very quickly when a modified program was reinstated. Thus, maintenance can be facilitated if provisions are made. A simple maintenance procedure was successful in supporting proper self-feeding of three profoundly retarded children for at least 34 weeks (Song & Gandhi, 1974). In the classroom, successful maintenance of high rates of work output by difficult subjects was demonstrated by Peterson, Cox, & Bijou (1971).

This chapter discusses a study implemented to design a system to both train and maintain daily self-help skills, such as housekeeping, in a natural setting. In the institution in which this study took place, a common experience with training has been that residents were trained away from their wards. Generalization often failed to occur, leaving ward staff with the impression that the training was not a very useful endeavor. If generalization did occur, a swift reversal of performance usually followed.

The authors of this study felt that through the judicious selection of responses to be trained that such reversals would not necessarily have to take place. Since housekeeping tasks took up so much staff time, preventing them from spending more time training residents, it was felt that teaching housekeeping skills to the residents would have a dual advantage: to free aides from tasks they did not particularly enjoy, giving them more time to take over the responsibility for maintenance of the residents; and to teach the residents more adaptive self-care skills that would advance them one step closer to more autonomous behavior. Thus, it was decided to teach residents to acquire such tasks and then to attempt to generate maintained performance of the skills by integrating them into the normal ward routine with the cooperation of the residential care staff.

THE EXPERIMENT

Subjects

Four young women from one ward of a large state institution for the retarded were chosen as subjects. They ranged in age from 15 to 21 and in IQ from 27 to 39. They had all the basic self-help skills but did not attend school nor were they involved in formal programming or on-grounds work assignments at that time. These young women were representative of the residents of this ward. Formal observations in the ward showed that ward residents spent their day, except for meals and toileting, in the dayhall. While there, a large percentage of their time was spent motionless or in aimless or self-stimulating behavior (Amy Sue, 73%; Emily, 49%; and Barbie, 73).

Setting

All training was done within the residence building. The building was comprised of 4 wards with a large eating hall in the center. The ward was made up of a bathroom-shower area which opened on one side into a dormitory room 36 by 56 feet for the ward's 30 residents, and on the other side into a 30 by 45 feet dayhall, containing 30 plastic chairs, two tables, one or two plastic balls, and a television. Normal staffing of this ward on the day shift was from one to two attendants, responsible for all housecleaning of the area, care of the residents' clothes including most of the laundering, ward paperwork, escorting residents to clinic and dental appointments, and administering medication. The observed staff-resident ratio within the dayhall itself averaged 1:24.

Training was conducted in the dormitory and in the dining room. The materials used were those which the staff would use to perform the same tasks: a dishrag, pan of soapy water, and six tables; a dustmop and the floor area under six beds; and the clean nightclothes of the residents and a dormitory bed for a work surface. The trainer had scoring sheets, a stop watch, a supply of 2-inch square pasteboard tokens, and back-up reinforcers including barrettes, candies, cookies, trinkets, small toys, magazines, and packaging materials. Back-up reinforcers were packaged in waxed sandwich bags. The "cost" of each item was shown on a slip of paper attached to each bag: a slip with two empty squares the same size as the tokens would cost two tokens. If the resident had enough tokens to cover all the squares on the slip, she could purchase what was in the bag.

Tasks

The ward staff was asked to choose tasks which the residents could not do at the time, and which would be both helpful to the staff and to the residents. These would be tasks the staff could easily have the residents do, with supervision and reinforcement, as part of the daily ward routine. Thus, the aides would be encouraged to maintain the skills rather than resuming performance of the tasks themselves, and the residents would have constructive activities to replace idle time and to add to their repertoire of functional behaviors. The skills they chose were table washing in the dining hall, dust mopping under the beds in the dormitory, and folding residents' night clothes after they were washed each day.

Each task was divided into units for purposes of training and a criterion assigned for correct performance of each. In table washing, a unit was a single table and the criterion was that it must be wiped over its entire surface with no food particles remaining, the chairs then wiped and placed upside down on the table. The initial response required first two tables, then three, and ultimately four. The unit for dust mopping was the surface under a single bed and the criterion that the entire area had to be wiped, with no feathers or dusty patches remaining. The task required dusting under six beds. The unit for clothes folding was a single article of night clothes, a nightgown or pajama top or bottom. The criterion was that it be folded right side out, with no twisting of arms or legs, so the edges were parallel within two inches. The garment was folded into a rectangle. Each of ten garments had to be sufficiently smooth to be piled eight garments high without falling over. They were then sorted into piles with other garments of the same type.

Training

A trainer from the institution's Title 1 Grant taught the skills. This person had a BA in therapeutic recreation and no formal training in behavior modification. The training and supervision of the trainer were by the other authors.

Training consisted of "tell," "show," and "guide" prompts. First, the trainer verbally instructed the subject in the correct way to do the task (tell). If verbal instructions were insufficient, the trainer modeled the correct response and instructed the subject to imitate (show). If the subject were still unable to perform the correct response, the trainer would use graduated guidance, taking the subject's hands and physically guiding her through the correct movements (guide). An example of guidance was physically moving the subject into a squatting position in order to reach under the bed with the dust mop. Clothes folding proved difficult and the full graduated guidance procedure was needed: the trainer stood behind the subject, placed her hands on top of the subject's hands, and gently assisted the subject to move through the motions necessary to complete the task. In the event that the subject resisted, the trainer was instructed to wait until the subject relaxed and cooperated in the motion. (This occurred rarely during training as the subjects were very cooperative.) The guidance was then faded. As the trainer felt that the subject was beginning to initiate the motion, the trainer moved her hands further up the arms of the subject and played a gradually less and less active role. Finally, all physical contact was removed. This procedure, described and referenced by Panyan (1972), ensures that success and consequent reinforcement is maximized, and failure is avoided. Guidance was faded until modeling or instruction could be followed, and these also were faded until all that was necessary was a single instruction to begin the task ("_____, please wash these two tables and those two on that side.").

Scoring

The dependent variable measure was the number of successfully completed units, in the absence of any prompts. Scoring sheets were organized so that the trainer and reliability observer, when present, could score the type of prompt given for each training trial. Reliability was measured on 32 occasions, with the trainer and observer independently scoring the type of prompt given. Point by point comparisons of trials were assessed.

Experimental Design

The primary purpose of the study was directed toward the development of effective maintenance procedures for tasks in which performance would quickly deteriorate without reinforcement. For this latter purpose, a multiple baseline-type design (Wolf, Baer, & Risley, 1968) was used, but the cessation of reinforcement rather than the onset was employed as the manipulation. The role of the reinforcement would be demonstrated if dropping the reinforcement from one behavior resulted in a drop in performance in that behavior but did not affect the other reinforced behaviors of that subject. The training aspects of the project served primarily as the baseline. Using the design described, the failure of the performance to maintain would be demonstrated, and the later performance during maintenance could be compared with this.

Reinforcement was dropped from only one task for three of the four subjects for a number of reasons. An adequate demonstration of the importance of reinforcement would be provided (and in fact the staff was very impressed). Dropping of reinforcement produced strong emotional reactions in the subjects and we feared disrupting them too much by repeating the manipulation. For example, Paula began deliberately dropping the pan of soapy water on her way to wash tables when she knew she would not be reinforced. Since the trainer was being promoted and would not be replaced, there were time constraints which further hindered replication. The manipulation was replicated in one subject (Emily), and the results were identical to the other reversals, which suggested that further replications would not provide much new information.

Phases of Experiment

Training began with only social reinforcement for correct responses. The second phase began when tokens were introduced. Before tokens were given for the tasks, all subjects took part in a single session to familiarize them with the tokens, in which each was given four tokens to exchange. A token was given after each unit of a task performed correctly. This phase was continued on all tasks for all subjects until the first task reached criterion. The criterion level was the correct performance, with no prompting by the trainer, of over 75% of the units of a task (3 of 4 tables cleaned, 4 of 6 bed areas dusted, or 8 of 10 garments folded), in two consecutive sessions. On the last day reinforcement was given, the subjects were told that they would not be earning tokens on that task for a while.

In the third phase, all reinforcement was withdrawn from the first task to reach criterion, until the performance level dropped sharply or until the seventh session in this phase, whichever came first. (The third phase was used in two of Emily's tasks rather than one as with the other subjects.)

At this point, the fourth phase was begun. Reinforcement was reinstated as in the second phase, and chaining began after the task had been performed at the criterion level for 2 consecutive days. Chaining was accomplished by delivering tokens after every second correct unit (fixed ratio 2) rather than after each correct unit. After 3 days above the 75% criterion level, the ratio was thinned further. Ultimately, all tokens were delivered when the entire task was completed; 1 token for each unit correctly performed (4 tables correctly washed = four tokens). At this point maintenance was begun.

Maintenance

Table cleaning was turned over to the supervision of an aide working in the kitchen area. This aide rated the subject's performance on a good-fair-poor basis for one week. The aide continued the token system, with a modification which allowed the subjects to go to a local restaurant for ice cream occasionally.

Dust mopping and clothes folding were taken over by ward staff, with tokens being used on an irregular basis. Some months after training ended, one subject (Emily) began to receive a special recreation period in return for dust mopping and bed making as part of a new ward program.

Follow-Up

From six to ten months after training ended, follow-up was conducted. Subjects were observed doing table washing under the supervision of staff, when that was naturally occurring at a time that it could be observed. When this was not possible with table washing, and with the other tasks, the tasks were performed under the supervision of experimenter. No reinforcer, other than praise, was delivered during these sessions.

Amy Sue was observed twice washing tables but was then transferred to another facility so that no further data were available. Paula was washing tables a few times a month for the staff on weekends and was involved in a school program during the week. She had been transferred to a new ward and neither dust mopping nor clothes folding were being maintained there. Barbie was working evenings in a central cafeteria at the institution, a job she obtained as a result of her training in this project. She washed tables on weekends in her building from time to time. Weekdays she went to school. The other two tasks were not being maintained. Emily was also in school and washed tables on weekends as the others did. She also did dust mopping on a regular basis, but clothes folding was done only rarely.

Results

Data on the percentage of successful completion of each unit without prompts are presented in Figures 1, 2, 3, and 4. The points in each figure represent training sessions. The beginning of each month is marked on the abscissa for ease of comparison, as the number of sessions varied widely from month to month and from task to task. The ordinate shows the percentage of correct units. A unit was counted as correct only if the subject completely met the criterion for that unit without any prompts whatsoever. Two independent observers took reliability measures on this, scoring on 32 occasions. Reliability averaged 97.6% (agreements over agreements plus disagreements).

For all subjects in all tasks, performance improved substantially after tokens were added. The first task on which Emily reached the criterion level was table washing. She was the only subject who did not show an immediate drop in performance when the tokens and praise were withdrawn. Her performance dropped in the fourth session and varied widely. After tokens and praise were reinstated on the table washing, they were withdrawn from the dust mopping task. (Note that the abscissas are training sessions and not equivalent in time. The number of training sessions possible varied from month to month and from task to task.) Performance dropped immediately in the dust mopping task, but her performance on the clothes folding task was not effected by these reversals.

For both Paula and Amy Sue, table washing was also the first task to reach criterion, and both subjects' performance dropped immediately when reinforcement was withdrawn. The only follow-up data available for Amy Sue, due to her transfer, indicates that her skill in table washing was maintained.

Dust mopping was the first task on which Barbie reached criterion, and her performance also fell immediately upon withdrawal of reinforcement.

During follow-up (see Table 1), the level at which the skill was maintained was clearly related to whether the aides had regularly required the subjects to engage in the task between training and follow-up. Of the tasks which had been performed on a fairly regular basis by the three subjects who remained at the institution, three were found to be at an average accuracy level above 75% during maintenance. The five tasks which had not been performed regularly were all no higher than 50% during maintenance.

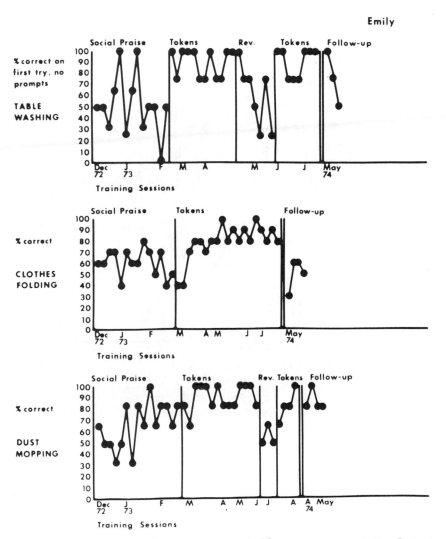

Figure 1   Percentage of correct units completed without any prompts, Emily. Letters on ordinate indicate the months of the year during which the data were collected. D, December; the first J, January; F, February; the first M, March; A, April; the second M, May; the second J, June. Numbers of training sessions varied from month to month, depending upon particular conditions (for example, Clothes folding was only possible when laundry had recently been done). (Names of all subjects are fictitious.)

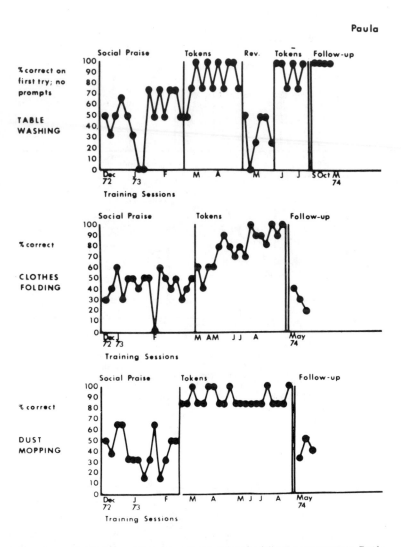

Figure 2   Percentage of correct units completed without any prompts, Paula.

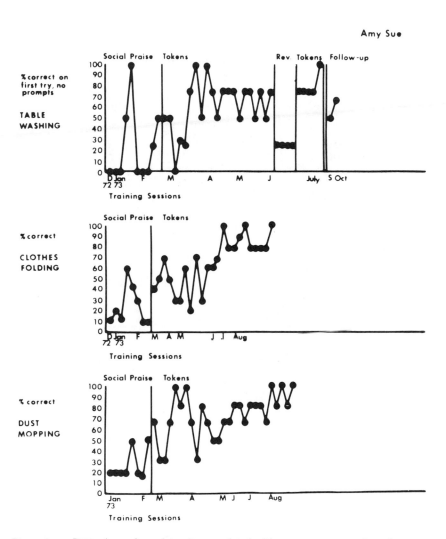

Amy Sue

Figure 3   Percentage of correct units completed without any prompts, Amy Sue.

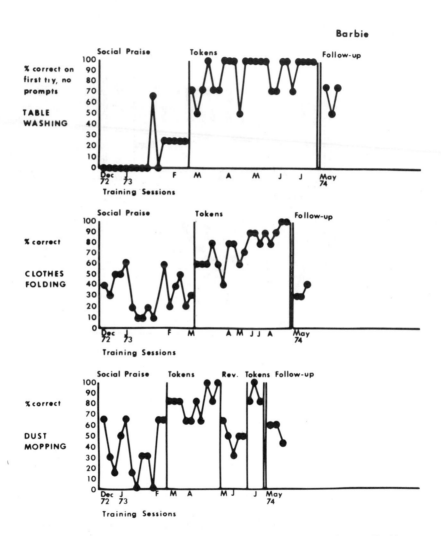

Figure 4   Percentage of correct units completed without any prompts, Barbie.

TABLE 1

	Tasks Performed Regularly for the Aide Staff		Tasks Not Performed Regularly for the Aide Staff	
Maintained at or above an average of 75%	Paula: table washing	100%		
	Emily: table washing	75%		
	Emily: dust mopping	85%		
Maintained below 75% level	Barbie: table washing	67%	Paula: clothes folding	30%
			Paula: dust mopping	40%
			Emily: clothes folding	50%
			Barbie: clothes folding	33%
			Barbie: dust mopping	40%

Discussion

Withdrawal of tokens and praise demonstrated that the newly acquired skills would quickly deteriorate unless they were maintained by the environment. Follow-up data suggest that long term maintenance, over a six to nine month period, was achieved in those skills which the subjects continued to perform regularly for the staff.

In this institution a common sequel to training of residents has been the deterioration of skill due to lack of maintenance by building staff. The data show that this would also have occurred with these skills, but the maintenance can be achieved with skills which are well integrated into the daily ward routine.

Paula, for example, was still occasionally washing tables for the staff at the time of follow-up, but had not dust mopped for some months. This is clearly reflected in her performance level. The aides commented that she usually refused to do tasks such as dust mopping for them, yet she willingly performed for the experimenter Although the experimenter used no reinforcement, doing the task for a relative stranger was novel, which might have been reinforcing. It thus seemed likely that Paula would perform for the staff of her new ward, if they were to introduce reinforcement. Several months after follow-up a token economy was introduced onto her ward, and she was willingly performing a variety of tasks she formerly refused to perform. The staff reports her performance to be good.

CONCLUSIONS

Thus, it appears that the more handicapped residents of institutions for the retarded can perform routine duties with a high degree of accuracy if given proper conditons for training and maintenance. Learning such skills can improve residents' progress toward self-sufficiency while providing an alternative to the inactivity of the dayhall environment. Providing these conditions are an administrative problem in modifying aide behavior, which, in this case, was partially solved by asking aides to choose target behaviors. Helpful target behaviors are reinforcing for the aides to maintain, since supervising the residents' doing the tasks might be easier than to perform them personally.

With proper supervision by the staff, retarded residents can learn to perform useful tasks such as routine ward housekeeping, while freeing aides for other things. Additionally, a program such as this facilitated more positive interaction with the residents by the staff as they carried out the token exchange. In this particular case, staff apparently were reinforced by the program, as they have supported subsequent programs that promise to be almost exclusively beneficial to the residents.

ACKNOWLEDGMENTS

Thanks are due to Building Supervisor Marian Sargent and her staff for their cooperation, to Louis Boly for making a trainer available, and to Andrew Billings for his early morning observations of table washing during follow-up. Special thanks are due Superintendent Francis P. Kelley for his support and encouragement of these training and research activities.

REFERENCES

Ayllon, T., & Azrin, N. H. *The token economy*. New York: Appleton-Century-Crofts, 1968.
Altman, R., Talkington, L. W., & Cleland, C. C. Relative effect of modeling and verbal instruction on severe retardates gross motor performance. *Psychological Reports,* 1972, *31*, 695-698.
Baker, J. G., Stanish, B., & Fraser, B. Comparative effects of a token economy in nursery school. *Mental Retardation,* 1972, *10*(4), 16-19.
Bensberg, G. J., & Barnett, C. D. *Attendant training in southern residential facilities for the mentally retarded: Report of the Southern Regional Education Board attendant training project.* Atlanta: Southern Regional Education Board, 1966.
Bensberg, G. J., Colwell, C. N., & Cassell, R. H. Teaching the profoundly retarded self-help activities by behavior shaping techniques. *American Journal of Mental Deficiency,* 1965, *69*, 674-679.
Berkowitz, S., Sherry, P. J., & Davis, B. A. Teaching self-feeding skills to profound retardates using reinforcement and fading procedures. *Behavior Therapy,* 1971, *2*, 62-67.
Bijou, S. W. Application of experimental analysis of behavior principles in teaching academic tool subjects to retarded children. Paper presented at Kansas Symposium, Lawrence, Kansas, 1965. (U. S. Public Health Service, NIMH, MH01366 and MHO2232).
Bijou, S. W. Teaching the retarded child. In *Behavior modification in education:* National Society for the Study of Education. Chicago: University of Chicago Press, 1972.
Dalton, A. J., Rubino, C. A., & Hislop, M. W. Some effects of token rewards on school achievement of children with Down's syndrome. *Journal of Applied Behavior Analysis,* 1973, *6*, 251-260.
Gardner, W. I. *Behavior modification in mental retardation.* Chicago, Ill.: Aldine Atherton, 1971.

Harris, J. M., Veit, S. W., Allen, G. J., & Chinsky, J. M. Aide-resident ratio and ward population density as mediators of social interaction between retarded children and their aides. *American Journal of Mental Deficiency*, 1974, *79*, 320-326.

Klaber, M. M., & Butterfield, E. C. Stereotyped rocking — A measure of institution and ward effectiveness. *American Journal of Mental Deficiency*, 1968, *73*, 13-20.

Mosely, A., Faust, M., & Reardon, D. Effects of social and nonsocial stimuli on the stereotyped behaviors of retarded children. *American Journal of Mental Deficiency*, 1970, *74*, 809-811.

O'Brien, F., Bugle, C., & Azrin, N. Training and maintaining a retarded child's proper eating. *Journal of Applied Behavior Analysis*, 1972, *5*, 67-72.

Paloutzian, R. F., Hasazi, J., Streifel, J., & Edgar, C. L. Promotion of positive social interaction in severely retarded young children. *American Journal of Mental Deficiency*, 1971, *75*, 519-524.

Panyan, M. C. *Managing behavior 4 behavior modification: new ways to teach new skills.* Lawrence, Kansas: H & H Enterprises, 1972.

Peterson, R. F., Cox, M. A., & Bijou, S. W. Training children to work productively in classroom groups. *Exceptional Children*, 1971, *37*, 491-500.

Song, A. Y., & Gandhi, R. An analysis of behavior during the acquistion and maintenance phases of self-spoon feeding skills of profound retardates. *Mental Retardation*, 1974, *12*, 25-28.

Twardosz, J., & Baer, D. Training two severely retarded adolescents to ask questions. *Journal of Applied Behavior Analysis*, 1973, *6*, 655-661.

Warren, S. A., & Mondy, L. W. To what behaviors do attending adults respond? *American Journal of Mental Deficiency*, 1971, *75*, 445-449.

Whitman, T., Zakaras, M., & Chardos, S. Effects of reinforcement and guidance procedures on instruction-following behavior. *Journal of Applied Behavior Analysis*, 1971, *4*, 283-290.

Wolf, M. M., Baer, D. M., & Risley, T. R. Some current dimensions of applied behavior analysis. *Journal of Applied Behavior Analysis*, 1968, *1*, 91-97.

32

The Effects of Self-Recording on the Study Behavior of Female Juvenile Delinquents[1]

Pauline Young
Jay S. Birnbrauer

University of Western Australia

Robert W. Sanson-Fisher[2]

*Nyandi Treatment and Research Centre for Adolescents,
Bentley, Western Australia*

Self-management techniques have been proposed as an aid to obtaining improvements in behavior and as a means of increasing the likelihood that improved behavior will generalize to other settings and continue when formal programs have been discontinued. Of the several components of self-management — self-assessment, self-recording, self-determination of reinforcement, and self-administration of reinforcement (Glynn, Thomas & Shee, 1973) — self-recording is the aspect of self-management of concern in the studies to be reported in this chapter.

As an intervention procedure, self-recording has been observed to have effects on weight reduction, smoking, face touching, studying and disruptive behavior in a classroom (Broden, Hall & Mitts, 1971; Hall, 1972; Lipinski & Nelson, 1974; Mahoney, Moore, Wade, & Moura, 1973; Mulligan, 1974; Stollack, 1967). The

[1]A dissertation on this research was submitted by the senior author to the University of Western Australia in partial fulfillment of the requirements for the degree of Bachelor of Arts with Honors. An earlier version was presented at the Ninth Annual Conference of the Australian Psychological Society, Perth, Western Australia, August 1974.

[2]Now at the University of Western Australia.

effects appear very similar to those obtained when observers or other novel features are introduced; the results usually are immediate, temporary, in the desired direction (for example, studying increases and number of cigarettes smoked decreases), and as Kazdin (1974) concludes in his review, highly variable. To suggest that self-recording functions similarly to presence of observer and novelty is not meant as an explanation. The pattern of results obtained to date is also consistent with the view that self-recording functions as conditioned reinforcement (Bandura, 1971; Kanfer, 1971).

Either way one views self-recording, the conclusion of Broden *et al.* (1971) appears accurate. They say that "the most promising feature of self-recording will be to use it as a procedure for initiating desirable levels of appropriate behavior to a point where ... [others] ... can more easily reinforce the desired behavior with ... [other reinforcers]" [p. 198]. We would add, however, that the other reinforcers would not have to be social but could consist of intrinsically reinforcing properties of the improved behavior such as might apply with cessation of smoking, weight loss, and more skillful performance of a client-desired behavior.

The two cases presented by Broden *et al.* illustrate nicely the above summary of self-recording as an intervention procedure and the importance of "backup" reinforcement. Both of their eighth-grade pupils showed marked changes in behavior in the teacher-desired direction when self-recording was introduced. Talking-out by the male pupil declined and studying by the female pupil increased. When baseline conditions were reinstated their behavior returned to baseline levels. Introducing self-recording a second time had no effects on the boy's talking-out. He had neither requested assistance nor received reinforcement during self-recording or while behaving more appropriately. The problematic aspect is not the failure to replicate, but the reduced talking-out in the first instance which persisted for 21 sessions.

The girl, on the other hand, increased studying when self-recording was used the second time and continued to study at the improved rate for three weeks of follow-up; She had expressed some interest in improving her study habits, received differential social reinforcement from a counselor, and the teacher had also praised her somewhat more often. Significantly, performance on days in which she "forgot" to record was as high as when she did record, but failing to receive a recording slip from the counselor consistently resulted in low study rates. The act of self-recording may, in itself, have had very little to do with the outcome in this case. The main point, that instruction in self-recording may instate behavior that other reinforcers may maintain nonetheless stands.

The second use of self-recording has been as a transition step from externally controlled reinforcement programs to return to normal conditions. The rationale is essentially that with external regulation such as in token classrooms, behavior will return to baseline levels when tokens are discontinued, as Birnbrauer, Wolf, Kidder and Tague (1965) and others have found, because the subjects have not been taught to evaluate and reinforce their own behavior. Hence, training in self-recording and self-administration of reinforcement have been evaluated with varying results. Bolstad and Johnson (1972) found that self-regulation after external control was more effective than external control alone with disruptive first- and second-grade children. Glynn *et al.* (1973) and Kaufman and O'Leary (1972) reported that self-control programs appeared at least as effective as the externally controlled programs they employed (the latter with emotionally disturbed adolescents). Santogrossi, O'Leary, Romanczyk, and Kaufman (1973), with boys from the same sample as in the Kaufman and O'Leary study, obtained rapid return to baseline rates.

The results of Santogrossi *et al.* (1973) are the more understandable, for it is difficult to see why students who require the attention of behavior analysts will engage in self-management behavior with any greater probability than they will engage in other appropriate behavior. Granted they are certain to have difficulties if they cannot distinguish appropriate and inappropriate responses in their own repertoires and self-recording should train them to make these discriminations. Whether or not they apply these skills still would depend upon externally controlled positive and negative reinforcement contingencies.

A final possibility is that self-recording contributes to behavior change and persistence of behavior because it enlists the student's participation in the rehabilitation, changes social reinforcement contingencies, and adds whatever reinforcement value is inherent in gaining control of oneself. These possibilities, together with the promising results reported in some studies, more than justify continued study of self-management procedures.

The studies below were conducted with adolescent delinquent girls, a group that generally shows very low motivation to change behavior and achieve scholastically. Seymour and Stokes (1976) have demonstrated that when used as a component in a "treatment package", self-recording was effective in modifying the work behavior of female juvenile delinquents, but it was not possible to analyze objectively the separate effects of the various components in the program. Hence, the purposes of the first experiment were:

1. to assess the effectiveness of self-recording as a behavior-change technique when tangible and social reinforcement are controlled;
2. to assess the degree to which effects of self-recording transfer to another learning situation in which self-recording is not required;
3. to compare the effects of different schedules of self-recording; and
4. to examine the relationship between accuracy of self-recording and behavior change.

To accomplish the third objective the subjects were asked to record on the average every 90 sec (VI 1.5) in one phase and every three min (VI 3) in another. If self-recording functions as reinforcement, then behavior should stabilize at a higher level with VI 1.5 than with VI 3. With respect to the final objective, some authors report that accuracy of self-recording is not necessary (Broden *et al.* 1971; Herbert & Baer, 1972), while Bolstad and Johnson (1972) maintain that it is crucial to the effectiveness of the procedure. Typically, however, accuracy of self-recording has not been assessed because of difficulties in obtaining independent records.

EXPERIMENT 1

Subjects and Setting

The experiments were conducted at Nyandi, a state treatment and research center for female adolescent delinquents at Bentley, Western Australia. The center comprised a maximum security unit and an open cottage. Girls were admitted to the center for a variety of reasons, including offences such as robbery, arson, and unlawful use of motor vehicles; others were primarily behavior problems, displaying such behaviors as aggression and noncompliance. Girls admitted to Nyandi had an average of 4.5 court appearances, 6 stays in other centers, and were referred to Nyandi when other treatment units had been unsuccessful.

The center operated a token economy, with the girls earning tokens for a variety of behaviors judged important for successful adjustment in the community. A wide variety of back-up reinforcers was available: cosmetics, clothing, outings, and other special privileges. Typical problems in the classroom included verbal and physical aggression, talking, shouting, giggling, and refusal to work. An extremely variable pattern of classroom behavior was characteristic, with some of the girls fluctuating from almost perfect classroom behavior to entirely disruptive behavior in consecutive class periods.

Four subjects were selected on the basis of their availability for the duration of the study. Since the average treatment period at the center was six weeks, they were either recent admissions or readmissions. Ages ranged from 13 to 17 years; intelligence level ranged from borderline defective to average. Two of the girls were Australian Aborigines and two were of European parentage.

A special experimental classroom was set up to control work materials and the time the girls spent in class. Subjects attended the class for 2 30-min periods before lunch and 2 30-min periods after lunch. The first period in each case was devoted to English assignments, which were English Expression (ERA, Martin, undated) in the morning and SRA (1964) in the afternoons. The second period in both the mornings and the afternoons was devoted to specially prepared materials that included such topics as the use of a telephone directory, use of a street map, sex education, and budgeting (all of which will be referred to as "Skills" hereafter). Assignments were programed and enabled each subject to work at her own pace and level. The same teacher supervised the class for all 4 periods throughout the experiment. Subjects sat at the same desks.

During self-recording phases, tape recorded signals were used to cue the subjects to self-record. These signals ("bleeps") were programed to occur every three min on the average in the first phase and every 90 sec on the average, thereafter. This cueing procedure was similar to that used by Glynn, Thomas, and Shee (1973).

Observation

Two sets of data were recorded by an observer present during every class period throughout the experiment. The primary data were obtained by rating each girl for 5-min periods in each class period, in a random order. Each 10 sec a girl's behavior was coded into one of 6 categories. These categories, which were based on those devised by Seymour and Stokes (1976), covered disruptive behavior, positive and negative interactions with the teacher, and three degrees of study behavior. Only the most demanding of the three study categories, "independent study behavior," was used in this analysis. It was defined as: "Complete attention to task. Head oriented towards task; sitting at desk. Following teacher's instructions, working on the task set by the teacher for all of the 10-sec interval." Independent study behavior was expressed as a percentage of all rating intervals excluding those involving interactions with the teacher.

Teacher behavior was also coded in those instances when the teacher was interacting with the girl currently under observation. Briefly, the four categories were: positive attention, negative attention (interaction relating to work and/or behavior), praise comments, and ignoring.

Reliability of observation was assessed by having a naive observer independently rate the same behavioral sequences. A total of 33 reliability checks were made with at least 5 checks during each phase. Percentage of agreement between observers was obtained by dividing the number of intervals x interval agreements by the total number of observations x 100.

A second set of records assessed accuracy of subjects' self-recording of study behavior. The observers recorded the behavior of all four subjects each time they were cued to self-record. For this rating, the observers used the same behavioral definitions as were given to the subjects on their self-recording slips. These were: (1) sitting at desk, looking at set work, and reading or writing; (2) working quietly without talking, whispering, or mumbling to self or other girls; and (3) following teacher's instructions, that is, working on the task set by the teacher. All that was required of the observers was a simple dichotomous decision, whether or not each subject's behavior satisfied the three criteria when the "bloop" sounded. The teacher also recorded at these times, thus providing an additional measure of reliability.

Design

A multistimulus-baseline design (Birnbrauer, Peterson & Solnick, 1974), employing class periods as stimulus situations, was used. Each of the two baselines consisted of one morning and one afternoon period, one an English period and one a Skills period. The sequence of the experimental class periods was: (1)

first morning period, English E.R.A. assignments (Baseline 1); (2) second morning period, Skills assignments (Baseline 2); lunch break followed by (3) first afternoon period, English S.R.A. assignments (Baseline 2); and (4) second afternoon period, Skills assignments (Baseline 1). The study extended over six weeks. The teacher was instructed to use her normal methods of classroom control and to ignore the observer's presence in the classroom.

Baseline

Before commencement of baseline data collection, the observer and the reliability observer were present for all four periods on two consecutive days. Baseline observations were recorded for the next seven days.

Self-Recording 1 (SR1)

On the eighth and ninth days, self-recording procedures were introduced in Baseline 1 Skills period and English period respectively, while baseline conditions continued in the two Baseline 2 periods. The teacher issued the self-recording slips and demonstrated their use. On each slip were ten boxes arranged horizontally. Subjects were instructed to place a check mark in the first box on the left if they were studying, as defined, when they heard the first "bleep." If they were not studying, they were to place an X in that box. On subsequent "bleeps" they were to fill the boxes from left to right across the self-recording slip. At the beginning of this phase, the teacher explained to the pupils that correct assessment and recording of their own behavior was a valuable skill that could help improve their ability to concentrate. The teacher told the girls that she, too, would record their behavior when the "bleep" sounded, but no consequences were placed on accurate recording. To avoid differential social reinforcement by the teacher, each girl was given an envelope and instructed to place the recording slip in the envelope at the end of the period. When a girl handed in her envelope, she was given tokens. The tokens were therefore contingent only on the subject's handing her envelope to the teacher. Tokens were easily distinguishable from those in the center's token economy and could be exchanged only for sweets or fruit at the end of the morning and afternoon class periods. The teacher never saw the girls' records and was instructed to carry on as usual.

Ten "bleeps" occurred at random intervals throughout each period, averaging one every 3 min. The teacher started the tape recorder which gave the "bleeps," and issued and collected the self-recording slips. During this phase, which continued for 8 days in the English period and 9 days in the Skills period, baseline conditions were maintained in Baseline 2.

Self-Recording 2 (SR2)

While still continuing baseline observations in Baseline 2, the frequency of self-recording signals in Baseline 1 was increased from one every three min on the average, to one every 90 sec on the average, that is, 20 "bleeps" occurred in each 30-min period in Baseline 1. Modified self-recording slips containing 20 boxes were issued to the girls. All other procedures were the same as in the previous phase.

Baseline 2

After 22 days of baseline conditions, self-recording (20 cues) was introduced into Baseline 2. Thus, for the final 8 days of the experiment, subjects were self-recording their study behavior in all four class periods.

Results

Reliability of observations.   Data gathered by the main observer were used for the behavioral analysis; only one category, Independent Study Behavior, was selected for the dependent variable. Percentages of interobserver agreement on this category averaged 90% with a range of 71% to 98%. In only 6 of the 33 re-reliability checks did the agreement percentage fall below 85%.

Frequency.   Figure 1 shows the percentage of study behavior in the 4 class periods, averaged over the 4 subjects. Study behavior in Baseline English period increased slightly in SR1 (average study behavior 56% in Baseline, 66% in SR1) and there was a further slight increase when SR2 was introduced (average study behavior 74%). In Baseline 1 Skills period, study behavior increased from an average of 34% during baseline to 62% during SR1, with a further slight increase to 69% on introduction of SR2, representing an overall increase of 35 percentage points.

Individual results for Baseline 1 class periods indicate that subjects generally showed a greater improvement in study behavior in SR2 (VI 1.5) than in SR1 (VI 3). As can be seen in Figure 1, however, the differences between the 2 self-recording phases were slight (mean increases in English 8%, and in Skills, 7%). Since SR1 was not replicated with Baseline 2, it seemed worthwhile to determine whether the observed differences in Baseline 1 were statistically reliable. Two nonparametric tests were used: the group data were analyzed by the Kruskal-Wallis Analysis of Variance, and each individual separately by the Friedman Two-Way Analysis of Variance (Siegal, 1956). Neither statistic approached significance. Thus, it appears that the different schedules of self-recording did not produce reliably different effects.

The effect of self-recording in Baseline 1 did not generalize to Baseline 2.

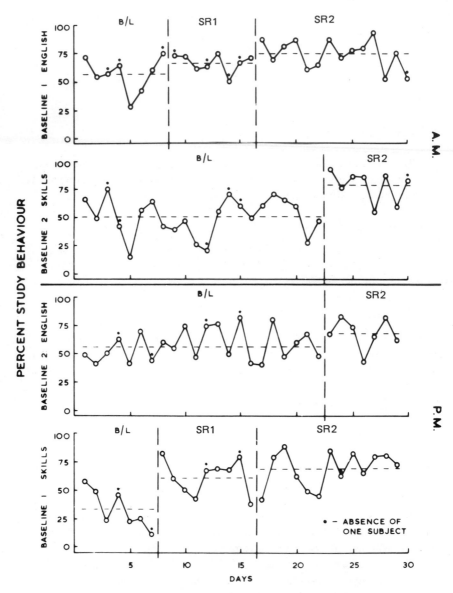

Figure 1   Mean daily percentages of study behavior for four subjects in each class period. Averages for each phase are shown by broken lines.

On the introduction of SR2 into Baseline 2 Skills period, the effect obtained earlier in Baseline 1 Skills period was clearly replicated, average study behavior increasing from 50% to 78%. The effect was also replicated in Baseline 2 English period, although less dramatically (11 percentage points).

The group means in Figure 1 are representative of individual functions. The greatest increase in study behavior occurred during the two Skills periods. Three of the four subjects showed the greatest improvement in the last period of the day. For all three subjects, lower baseline observations were recorded during this period than for the other three periods.

The recordings of teacher behavior yielded fewer praise statements during self-recording periods (Baseline1: 2.85 per 5 min during baseline; 0.6 in SR1; 0.7 in SR2; Baseline 2: 1.9 in baseline; 0.4 in SR2). Although the reliability of these data is suspect, it appeared to the observer that the teacher did more extra jobs, such as preparing materials, during SR periods. However, it was also noted that the teacher gave liberal social reinforcement at the end of the period after formal observation had finished.

On the final day of the study, the girls were asked as a group what they thought had been going on. Pamela and Jennifer suggested that the program was designed to teach them to concentrate. When asked if they felt their behavior had changed, there was general agreement that their manners had improved because the teacher ignored them if they did not address her correctly. Two girls (Erica and Jennifer) said they had studied harder to please the teacher. The consensus was that they would have recorded without tokens.

Subject accuracy.   Table 1 shows the mean percentage of accuracy of the subjects' self-recording of study behavior as compared to the observer's record. The average percentages of accuracy for the entire class are also shown in this table. Subjects were generally highly accurate, but as with study behavior, there was considerable variability. The data indicate that accuracy for the entire class was slightly higher during English periods than during Skills periods. Overall accuracy was slightly lower in SR2 than in SR1 in each period of Baseline 1.

Discussion

The results indicate that self-recording was an effective method of inducing behavior change in desired directions, even though the subjects had not sought change. While the results were consistent with other results in that high day-to-day variation and variability among subjects was evident and accuracy was not correlated with behavior changes, the effects were not as small and temporary as our analysis of self-recording had predicted. In the final period of the day, attention to studies doubled and remained at the higher level for 22 days. Overall, in the final phase the girls were meeting stringent criteria for studying 71% of the time observed. The equivalent figure during baseline was 48%.

TABLE 1

Mean Percentages of Accuracy of Subjects' Self-Recording of Study
Behavior as Compared to Observer's Record
(% Expressed to Nearest Whole Number)

Class period	Esme		Erica		Jennifer		Pamela		Class Mean			
					(Self-recording phases)							
	1*	2**	1*	2**	1*	2**	1*	2**	1*	2**	1 & 2	Baseline
English	87	82	71	64	85	85	78	84	80	79	80	Baseline
Skills	–	72	–	45	–	76	–	76	–	–	67	Baseline
English	–	79	–	64	–	87	–	65	–	–	74	Baseline
Skills	78	63	70	75	85	72	78	65	78	69	73	Baseline

*10 cues per 30-min class period
**20 cues per 30-min class period

Despite measures to prevent social reinforcement from confounding the effects of self-recording (the girls' putting self-recording slips in envelopes) it is not possible to rule out completely an explanation in terms of increased social reinforcement. The data on teacher praise suggest that teacher comments declined during self-recording, yet the observer noted that the teacher gave liberal praise at the end of the period after formal data collecting had ceased. (Teacher praise was for study behavior, not for self-recording; the teacher was trained in operant conditioning techniques and contingent social reinforcement was part of her normal classroom control.) Also, the replies given by two girls at the end of the study are consistent with an interpretation that they worked for delayed social reinforcement in that they maintained that they liked to please the teacher. Hence, a possible explanation is that self-recording induced improved study behavior, maintained by the teacher's increased social reinforcement at the end of each period. A second possibility, the girls' reports notwithstanding, is that the procedure of paying tokens as the girls turned in their records was an important factor, especially at first. Later, teacher reactions and tokens complemented each other in maintaining improved performance.

The greater effect of self-recording seen in Skills relative to English periods may be attributable to the former having more intrinsic reinforcement value, being novel and relevant; or Skills occupying the second period of each session, immediately preceding token exchange and the accompanying social interaction. The first explanation would suggest transfer to the other period in which the materials were used, from Baseline 1 Skills to Baseline 2 Skills. There were no signs of transfer. Secondly, average performance in Baseline 2 Skills and English periods was quite similar, with greater variability during Skills, which does not support the thesis that Skills was more reinforcing, in itself. Choosing between these explanations is thus not possible at this point.

EXPERIMENT 2

The first purpose of Experiment 2 was to replicate the above study with no token reinforcement for self-recording and greater control of teacher social reinforcement at the time of submitting the records. The second objective was to assess the effects of period *versus* nature of assignment. To accomplish this, Skills were omitted; only the two English programs, E.R.A. and S.R.A., were presented. To ensure that the subjects could distinguish appropriate and inappropriate responses, a recognition-training phase was included. The discrimination-training sessions were based on those used by Sanson-Fisher, Seymour, Montgomery, and Stokes (1974), in which a similar group of subjects was taught to discriminate between prosocial and antisocial conversation.

Since self-recording apparently was not going to have an effect under these circumstances, subsequent phases were intended to determine the effects of self-recording and token reinforcement on maintenance of behavior with SR only, and a matching requirement to assess further the relationship between accuracy of SR and behavior change. Matching required that the subject's record closely approximated the observer's record to receive reinforcement. Santogrossi *et al.* (1973), studying subjects similar to the girls at Nyandi in motivation and stability, introduced matching for one day only, because of the extremely negative reactions of the pupils.

Subjects and Setting

The setting and observer were the same as in Experiment 1. A different teacher, however, was used. Two subjects were Australian Aborigines and four were of European parentage. Intelligence level ranged from borderline defective to average, and ages ranged from 13 to 17. Two of the subjects, Erica and Pamela, had participated in Experiment 1.

All classes took place in the afternoon; subjects attended the class for 2 30-min periods before afternoon tea and 2 30-min periods after tea break. During the first period of each class, E.R.A. lessons were assigned; during the second, S.R.A. The study extended over 26 days.

During self-recording phases, subjects were cued to self-record as in Experiment 1 using VI 1.5 schedules. That is, the frequency in all phases was 20 "bleeps" per 30 min.

Observation

The same rating procedure as in Experiment 1 was used. Seventeen reliability checks were carried out, there being at least one check in each phase of the experiment.

Baseline

Baseline observations were recorded in all four class periods for the first six days.

Self-Recording 1 (SR1)

Self-recording was introduced in Baseline 1 class periods, those being the first period before tea and the last period after tea. Instructions to the subjects were given as in Experiment 1, with the exception that no tokens were contingent on the subjects' handing in their self-recording slips. At the end of SR periods, the girls were asked to leave their records on their desks before leaving the room.

During this phase, subjects attended three special training sessions with a counselor, immediately prior to class. These sessions were designed to train the girls to recognize and record study behavior accurately. Subjects were issued with self-recording slips; a videotape of two girls displaying study and nonstudy behavior was shown and subjects were instructed to record whether or not the two girls were studying each time a "bleep" sounded. Each subject was given immediate feedback on her accuracy of recording study behavior. During this phase baseline conditions were maintained in Baseline 2.

Self-Recording + Tokens

In this phase, which lasted for six days, subjects earned points according to *their* records of study behavior. Each day, when the girls first entered the classroom, the counselor asked for their self-recording slips from the previous day. Each girl was allotted points on an individual basis according to her record of study behavior, and a target was set for the current day's class periods by means of competitive contracting. That is, the subject and counselor agreed on the target. The counselor always left the room immediately following the setting of targets. Baseline conditions were maintained in Baseline 2 throughout this phase.

"Crossover" Phase

Self-determination of token earning was introduced into Baseline 2, while the Baseline 1 periods reverted to self-recording only. Subjects were therefore self-recording their study behavior in all 4 30-min class periods. Several tapes of random signals were used in order to control for the possibility of subjects' anticipating cues. The counselor continued to see the girls when they first entered the room for the afternoon classes, but asked for only their self-recording slips for Baseline 2 periods. This phase lasted for 3 days.

Matching Phase (SR + Tokens + Matching)

During the last eight days of the experiment, matching was introduced in Baseline 2, while self-recording only was continued in Baseline 1. Instead of subjects receiving points purely on the basis of their records of study behavior (self-determination of reinforcement), they were instructed that they must now match, within four points, the teacher's record of their study behavior. (In actuality, their records were compared with the observer's record.) In order to earn the maximum number of points, subjects had to meet their targets *and* record accurately. If their records of study behavior matched the observer's record, they received a bonus for accuracy, irrespective of whether they reached their targets.

In all the token phases, subjects were allowed to spend their tokens at the end of the afternoon. Tokens could be exchanged for cigarettes, swimming time, sweets, comics, and cool drinks. As in Experiment 1, these tokens were quite separate from the normal token system of the center in order to avoid any confounding effects.

Results

The percentage of interobserver agreement on independent study (see Fig. 2) averaged 91% (range, 79%-100%); agreement fell below 85% on only one of the 17 reliability checks. The average percentage of agreement on studying/not studying when the "bleeps" sounded (see Fig. 3) between observers was 95% (range, 92%-100%), and between principal observer and teacher was also 95% (range, 86%-100%).

Figure 2 shows the mean daily rates of study behavior for the entire class. Rates during baseline (B/L) were lower than in Experiment 1, except for the first period, and no changes were obtained during SR1. Individual patterns during self-recording can be seen in Figure 3, in which the girls' and observer's records of studying when the "bleep" sounded are displayed. (The two periods of each baseline have been combined as no information was lost in so doing.) Thus, there were 40 opportunities to self-record. Each point is the actual number of times studying was recorded. (These numbers will not add up to those in Figure 2 because the latter is the observer's continuous recordings.) Three of the girls either did not record on some signals or marked Xs across their slips although the observer rated them as studying on some occasions. Two of them (Pamela and Erica) had been in the first experiment, and said they were not going to record "for nothing." Although the other three girls recorded quite accurately, their behavior also did not improve.

During the first token phase (SR+Tokens), the behavior of all of the girls improved considerably, and by and large their records and the observer's were quite similar. Some of the girls, however, did consistently overestimate their performance, but rarely by very much. Behavior when self-recording and tokens did not apply (Baseline 2) remained unchanged.

After the "cross-over," the results for the group (see Fig. 2) suggested return to baseline conditions in self-recording-only periods (SR2) and improved behavior during SR + Tokens condition, which continued through the final stage in which matching was an added requirement. Individual patterns during SR2 in Figure 3, however, were noteworthy for their extreme day-to-day fluctuations and between-subject variation. Jane's behavior remained near perfect in all periods. Linda and Erica often studied much better during SR2 than would have been predicted from their baselines and their "bad" days appeared related to uncontrolled variables and the introduction of the matching requirement in Baseline 2. Marilyn's performance in SR2 also dropped when matching was instated and then returned gradually to the baseline level. The remaining two subjects, Pamela and Connie, promptly performed at baseline and below-baseline levels respectively. Thus, three of the girls (Linda, Jane, and Erica) had not yet returned to baseline levels within 11 days of SR2.

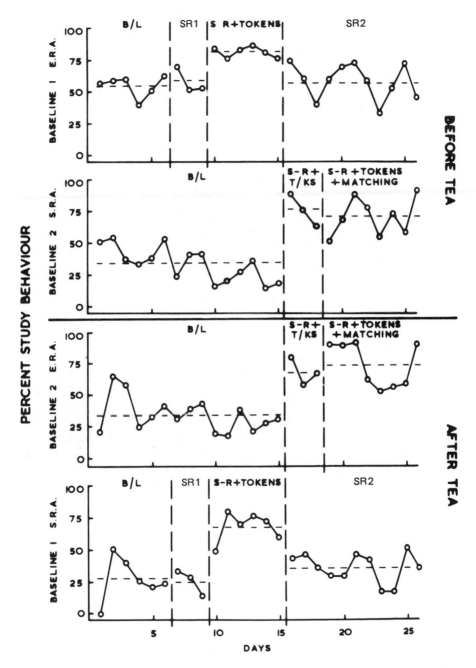

Figure 2   Mean daily percentages of study behavior for entire class. Averages for each phase are shown by broken lines.

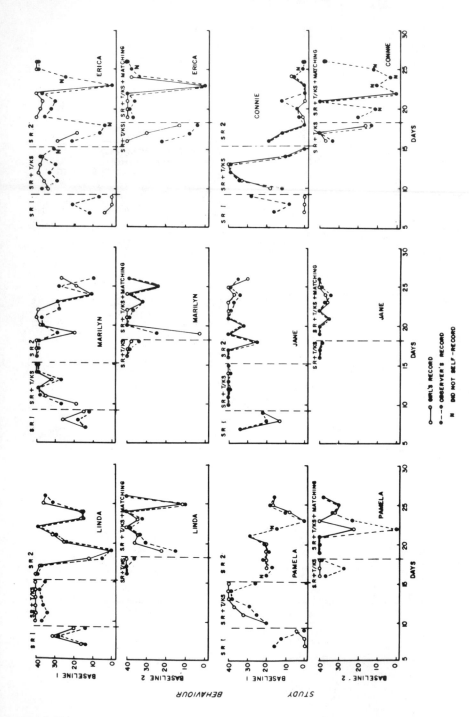

Figure 3   Subjects' and observer's record of study behavior. The ERA and SRA components of each baseline have been combined.

The matching procedure effectively eliminated discrepancies between the girls' and observer's records in most cases. Although the introduction of matching was associated with lower study rates on one or both baselines with five subjects, only Connie refused to cooperate.

The data on teacher behavior revealed few praise comments and little difference between phases (Baseline 1: 0.7 per 5 min during Baseline; 0.7 in SR1; 0.2 in SR+Tokens; and 1.1 in SR2; Baseline 2: 1.3 during Baseline; 1.7 in SR+ Tokens; 1.1 in Matching). Again, the reliability of these data is suspect. However, the observer noted that the teacher (who was inexperienced in the use of operant techniques in classroom control) tended to deliver social reinforcement on a noncontingent basis.

The original intention was to question the girls as a group at the end of the study (as in Experiment 1), in order to obtain their views on the reasons for improved studying. It was not possible, however, to fulfill this plan.

GENERAL DISCUSSION

Self-recording alone did not effect improvements in studying. The girls who cooperated by recording accurately showed as little change as those who did not. Since the effects of self-recording have been quite consistently greatest when first introduced, it is not likely that the results are attributable to the brevity of this phase. Subsequent performance with tokens verified that the subjects were capable of accurate recording and greater attention to studies. Thus, that variable may be ruled out. The remaining differences between experiments: in the teachers' roles, in tokens, in baselines of studying, and the presence of two girls from Experiment 1, all may have added up to stacking the deck against there being a self-recording effect.

The remainder of Experiment 2 was a demonstration of the effects of externally administered reinforcement on self-recording *and* studying. Whether or not self-recording was causative in any way cannot be said on the basis of the data, even though the performance of some subjects during the second presentation of self-recording (SR2) indicated better maintenance than would have been obtained without self-recording. It is plausible to suppose, however, that the similarity of procedure between baselines abolished the discrimination demonstrated earlier between performance relevant to reinforcement (Baseline 1) and that which was not (Baseline 2). The correlation between behavior during SR2 periods and matching periods indicates nonindependence. It is to be noted that Drabman, Spitalnik, and O'Leary (1973) obtained generalization to no-token periods embedded in periods when tokens were dispensed. The children were instructed to self-record in all periods; the no-token period (which varied from day to day) was announced beforehand.

The unexpectedly high rate of accuracy of subjects' self-recording is in contrast to that found by Fixsen, Phillips, and Wolf (1972, Experiment 1), whose predelinquent adolescent boys' records of bedroom cleaning were extremely inaccurate when compared to an independent adult observer's record. They concluded that self-recording had no effect on bedroom cleaning. No consequences for room cleaning or for accuracy were scheduled. Other apparent major differences were that the value of self-recording was emphasized by the teacher, whereas Fixsen *et al.* simply asked the boys to check their rooms before leaving for school, and the girls were told that the teacher was also scoring their behavior when the "bleeps" sounded.

It was expected that especially after points were contingent on the subjects' records, these girls would cheat. Three subjects did cheat, but matching eliminated this. Although matching was introduced without the extremely disruptive behavior that Santogrossi *et al.* (1973) reported, the potential for a similar problem clearly was present. One girl, Connie, whose behavior was poorly controlled before matching, became extremely uncooperative, and other girls studied relatively less on the day of introduction. The recovery of control may have been due to offering a large accuracy bonus. Santogrossi *et al.* promised their boys a small bonus for accuracy and loss of points for discrepancies greater than one point. Drabman *et al.* (1973) made no mention of difficulties when they added a matching requirement.

In sum, these studies have demonstrated that delinquents will accurately record their own study behavior and that, in some conditions, self-recording has potential for both inducing behavior change and contributing to greater maintenance of behavioral gains. In neither study, however, could contaminating token and social reinforcement effects be ruled out. The successful conditions may have been those in which reinforcement contingencies were ambiguous. These are not difficult to arrange in natural environments and may be the reason everyone exhibits self-control when they do.

ACKNOWLEDGMENTS

The authors wish to thank Keith Maine, Director, Department for Community Welfare, for his continued support and encouragement of research; Jeanette Dolman, the reliability observer; and Ruth Jodrell and Dawn Pearce, the teachers in the special classroom. Ruth Jodrell, occupational therapist, Nyandi Treatment and Research Centre, also prepared the "Skills" material used in Experiment 1.

REFERENCES

Bandura, A. Vicarious and self-reinforcement processes. In R. Glaser (Ed.), *The nature of reinforcement.* New York: Academic Press, 1971.

Birnbrauer, J. S., Peterson, C. R., & Solnick, J. V. The design and interpretation of studies of single subjects. *American Journal of Mental Deficiency,* 1974, *79,* 191-203.

Birnbrauer, J. S., Wolf, M. M., Kidder, J., & Tague, C. E. Classroom behavior of retarded pupils with token reinforcement. *Journal of Experimental Child Psychology*, 1965, *2*, 219-235.

Bolstad, O. D., & Johnson, S. M. Self-regulation in the modification of disruptive classroom behavior. *Journal of Applied Behavior Analysis*, 1972, *5*, 443-454.

Broden, M., Hall, R. V., & Mitts, B. The effect of self-recording on the classroom behavior of two eighth-grade students. *Journal of Applied Behavior Analysis*, 1971, *4*, 191-199.

Drabman, R. S., Spitalnik, R., & O'Leary, K. D. Teaching self-control to disruptive children. *Journal of Abnormal Psychology*, 1973, *82*, 10-16.

Fixsen, D. L., Phillips, E. L., & Wolf, M. M. Achievement Place: The reliability of self-reporting and peer-reporting and their effects on behavior. *Journal of Applied Behavior Analysis*, 1972, *5*, 19-30.

Glynn, E. L., Thomas, J. D., & Shee, S. M. Behavioral self-control of on-task behavior in an elementary classroom. *Journal of Applied Behavior Analysis*, 1973, *6*, 105-113.

Hall, S. N. Self-control and therapist control in the behavioral treatment of overweight women. *Behaviour Research and Therapy*, 1972, *10*, 59-68.

Herbert, E. W., & Baer, D. M. Training parents as behavior modifiers: Self-recording of contingent attention. *Journal of Applied Behavior Analysis*, 1972, *5*, 139-149.

Kanfer, R. H. The maintenance of behavior by self-generated stimuli and reinforcement. In A. Jacobs, & L. B. Sachs (Eds.), *The psychology of private events: Perspectives on covert response systems*. New York: Academic Press, 1971.

Kaufman, K. F., & O'Leary, K. D. Reward, cost, and self-evaluation procedures for disruptive adolescents in a psychiatric hospital school. *Journal of Applied Behavior Analysis*, 1972, *5*, 293-309.

Kazdin, A. E. Self-monitoring and behavior change. In M. J. Mahoney & C. E. Thoresen (Eds.), *Self-control: Power to the person*. Monterey: Brooks/Cole, 1974.

Lipinski, D., & Nelson, R. The reactivity and unreliability of self-recording. *Journal of Consulting and Clinical Psychology*, 1974, *42*, 118-123.

Mahoney, M. J. Self-reward and self-monitoring techniques for weight control. *Behavior Therapy*, 1974, *5*, 48-57.

Mahoney, M. J., Moore, B. S., Wade, T. C., & Moura, N. G. M. The effects of continuous and intermittent self-monitoring on academic behavior. *Journal of Consulting and Clinical Psychology*, 1973, *41*, 65-69.

Martin, R. D. *E.R.A. formalities and written expression*. Lockleys, South Australia: E.R.A. Publications, undated.

Mulligan, B. Maladaptive eating patterns of obese and overweight persons: The differential effectiveness of individual control techniques. Unpublished master's dissertation, University of Western Australia, 1974.

Sanson-Fisher, R. W., Seymour, F. W., Montgomery, W. A., & Stokes, T. F. The use of self-recording to increase appropriate conversation by delinquent girls in a corrective institution. Unpublished manuscript, 1974.

Santogrossi, D. A., O'Leary, K. D., Romanczyk, R. G., & Kaufman, K. F. Self-evaluation by adolescents in a psychiatric hospital school token program. *Journal of Applied Behavior Analysis*, 1973, *6*, 277-287.

Seymour, F. W., & Stokes, T. F. Self-management in training delinquent girls to increase work and elicit staff praise. *Journal of Applied Behavior Analysis*, 1976, *9*, 41-54.

Siegel, S. *Nonparametric statistics for the behavioral sciences*. New York: McGraw-Hill, 1956.

S.R.A. Reading Laboratory IIIa. Chicago: Science Research Associates, 1964.

Stollak, G. E. Weight loss obtained under different experimental procedures. *Psychotherapy: Theory, Research and Practice*, 1967, *4*, 61-64.

Part IV

BIJOU AS SUBJECT

Reinforcers Earned

A Listing of Honors, Awards,
and Experiences Reflecting
and in Part Contributing
to Bijou's Work

Professional Appointments:

1936-1937	School Psychologist, Board of Education, New York City
1937-1939	Clinical Psychologist, Delaware State Hospital & Mental Hygiene Clinic, Farnhurst, Del.
1940-1941	Graduate Assistant, University of Iowa, Clinical Psychology and Speech, Iowa City, Iowa
1941-1942, 1946-1947	Research Associate and Staff Consultant, Wayne County Training School, Northville, Mich.
1942-1946	Captain and Director, Convalescent Branch, Psychology Division, Office Air Surgeon, Headquarters, American Air Force
Summer, 1946	Visiting Lecturer, University of Michigan, Graduate School in Special Education, Ipsilanti, Mich.
1946-1948	Assistant Professor of Psychology and Director of Graduate Training in Clinical Psychology, Indiana University, Bloomington, Ind.
Summer, 1948	Visiting Professor, San Diego State College, San Diego, Cal.
Summer, 1960	Visiting Professor, University of California at Los Angeles
Summer, 1963	Visiting Professor, University of Hawaii, Honolulu
1948-1965	Associate Professor and then Professor of Psychology and Director, Gatzert Institute of Child Development (now Developmental Psychology Laboratory), University of Washington, Seattle, Wash.
1961-1962	Postdoctoral Study at Harvard (National Institute of Mental Health Senior Fellowship)
1965-1975	Professor of Psychology, Member of the Institute for Research on Exceptional Children and Director of Child Behavior Laboratory, University of Illinois, Champaign, Ill.

Summer, 1968	Visiting Professor, University of Hawaii, Honolulu
1972	Spring semester, Associate, Center for Advanced Study, University of Illinois, Champaign, Ill.
1975	Professor Emeritus, University of Illinois, Champaign-Urbana
1975	Professor of Special Education and Psychology, University of Arizona, Tucson

Honors and Awards:

1940	Society of the Sigma Xi, Fellow
1948	Psi Chi, Member
1961-1962	National Institute of Mental Health Senior Fellowship to study at Harvard University
1971-1972	Associate, University of Illinois Center for Advanced Study
1974	1974 Research Award, The American Association of Mental Deficiency
1974	Certificate of Merit, University of Veracruz, Mexico
1974	Presentation of Festschrift for S. W. Bijou, American Psychological Association, New Orleans
1976	Fulbright-Hays Fellowship

Editorships:

1955-1957	Associate Editor, *Child Development*
1963-1972	Editor, *Journal of Experimental Child Psychology*
1961-1964	Consulting Editor, *Journal of Experimental Analysis of Behavior*
1966-1970	Editorial Board, *International Review of Research in Mental Retardation*
1969-present	Associate Editor, *Journal of Behavior Therapy & Experimental Psychiatry*
1972-present	Editorial Board, *Journal of Abnormal Child Psychology*
1972-present	Editorial Board, *Journal of Experimental Child Psychology*
1974-present	Editorial Board, *Journal of Applied Behavior Analysis*

Professional Organizations, Committees and Offices:

1938-1945	American Psychological Association, Associate
1938-1945	American Assoication for the Advancement of Science, Associate
1938-1941	Eastern Psychological Association

1941-1949	Midwestern Psychological Assoication
1942-1947	Michigan Psychological Assoication
1942-1947	Michigan Academy of Science, Arts, and Letters, Member
1942-1947	American Association of Mental Deficiency, Associate
1942-1945	American Association for Applied Psychology: Clinical Section, Associate (Organization disbanded in 1945)
1944-1945	American Association for Applied Psychology: Military Section, Associate (as above)
1945	American Psychological Association, Fellow
1945-1951	American Association for the Advancement of Science, Fellow
1947-1948	Indiana Association of Clinical and Applied Psychologists (Secretary-Treasurer 1947), Member
1947-1948	Indiana Academy of Science, Member
1947	American Psychological Association: Clinical and Abnormal Division, Childhood and Adolescence Division, Military Division, Fellow (Resigned Military Division, 1950)
1948-1965	Washington State Mental Hygiene Society, Member
1948-1965	Washington State Psychological Association, Member (Vice President, 1950, President, 1955)
1948-1965	Puget Sound Psychological Association, Member (President, 1949)
1949	American Association of University Professors, Member
1950	Society for Research in Child Development, Member
1949-1965	Western Psychological Association
1960-62	Western Psychological Association, Member of Executive Committee
1964-1968	New York Academy of Science, Fellow
1958-1961	American Psychological Association Evaluation Committee of Education and Training Board
1961-1962	American Psychological Association Committee on Retardation
1958-1960	American Psychological Association Executive Committee, Division 7 (Developmental)
1964-1967	American Psychological Association Convention Committee
1964-1965	Society for Research in Child Development, Nomination Committee
1964	Psychonomic Society, Fellow
1964-1967	American Psychological Association Council of Representatives, Division 7 (Developmental)
1964-1968	American Psychological Association Executive Committee, Division 25 (Experimental Analysis of Behavior)
1965-1966	American Psychological Association President, Division 7 (Developmental)

1965	Midwestern Psychological Association
1966-1967	American Psychological Association Policy and Planning Board, Chairman, Division 7 (Developmental)
1966-1967	American Psychological Association Nomination Committee, Division 7 (Developmental)
1969	Society for Behavior Therapy & Experimental Psychiatry
1970	International Society for the Study of Behavior Development
1970-1971	Society for Research in Child Development: Member of Program Committee
1969-1973	American Psychological Association, Elected to Credential Committee, Division 7 (Developmental)
1971-1974	American Psychological Association, Elected to Council for Division 7 (Developmental)
1972-1973	American Psychological Association Credentials Committee, Chairman, Division 7 (Developmental)
1972-1974	American Psychological Association Finance Committee
1974	American Psychological Association, Chairman, Commission on Behavior Modification
1974	Association for Advancement of Psychology, Member of Board of Trustees
1974	Midwestern Association of Behavior Analysis, Member of Organizing Committee
1974	Chairman, International (South American) Committee on Behavior Modification Symposia
1975	Member of Council, Midwestern Psychological Association

Certification Boards:

1948	Clinical Psychology: American Board of Examiners in Professional Psychology (Diplomate)
1956	Certified psychologist·in the State of Washington, No. 3

Consultantships:

1948-1965	Veterans Administration
1956-1959	United States Army
1959-1963	United States Public Health Service, National Institute of Mental Health (Study Section)

1964-1965	Special Consultant to the Department of Psychology, University of Brasilia
1964-1967	Child Health and Human Development Program Project Committee (Study Section)
1965-1967	Linwood Project on the Treatment of Autistic Children
1968-1973	National Institute of Mental Health Clinical Program Projects Committee (Study Section)
1969-1973	National Science Advisory Board, National Program on Early Childhood Education, Central Midwestern Regional Educational Laboratory
1968-1969	Illinois State Department of Mental Health; Illinois State Psychiatric Research and Training Authority
1972-1974	Consultant to the Champaign School for Autistic Children, Champaign, Ill.
1965-present	National Association for Retarded Citizens, Research Advisory Committee, Chairman, Task Force on Parent Training
1965-present	American Institute of Research
1970-present	Advisory Board, Review of Early Childhood Education (Educational Resources Information Center)
1972-present	National Advisory Board, Illinois State Pediatric Institute
1973-present	Consultant on Research to Portage Project, Portage, Wisc., on Parent Training
1974-present	Professional Advisory Committee, Johnny Cake Child Study Center Foundation
1974-present	Consultant, Department of Psychology, Universidad Nacional Autonoma de Mexico, Mexico City
1974-present	National Research Council, Assembly of Life Sciences, Panel on Behavior Modification
1974	Consultant, Graduate Program in Psychology, Universidad Central de Venezuela, Caracas

Listings:

Blue Book of Great Britain

International Scholars Directory

Contemporary Authors

Men of Achievement

Outstanding Professionals in Human Services

American Men of Science (9th-11th ed.), *American Men and Women of Science* (12th ed.)

The Compendium, Persons of Eminence in the Field of Exceptional Children (1st ed.)

Community Leaders of America (7th ed.)

American Board of Professional Psychology (2nd ed.)

Leaders in Education (4th, 5th ed.)

Dictionary of International Biography (Great Britain, 1971; Vol. 10; Vol. 11, 1st ed.; Vol. 12)

International Who's Who in Community Service

Who's Who: on the Pacific Coast; in the Far West; in the Midwest (13th ed.); *in America* (36th-39th ed.); *in the World* (3rd ed.); *in American Education — Leaders in American Science Education* (2nd ed. VIII).

33

An Interview with
Sidney W. Bijou

Leonard Krasner

State University of New York at Stony Brook

As this chapter is being written in the mid 1970s, the field of behavior modification is in a crisis which involves issues of values, ethics, identification, and broad strategies of research and application. In order to understand where we are and to help make rational decisions as to the directions which the social movement of behavior modification should take, one needs to examine the historical and social context within which this field developed, and particularly the impact and influence of individuals who have been instrumental in the development of this field.

This chapter presents an interview with Sidney W. Bijou which took place on June 17, 1974 at the Hilton Hotel, Tallahassee, Florida. This author believes that Bijou's influence on the work of investigators in this field has been so pervasive that he is among the three or four strongest sources of influence in behavior modification. However, the goal here is not to document this assertion nor to initiate controversies as to who deserves credit as the key influencers. Our interest is in the influences on the influencer. This interview is an element in the psychology of social influence as well as in the history of behavior modification.

LK: Sid, I've been talking to some of the people who were influential in the early days of behavior modification, primarily to get some idea of the influences on them. First, tell me a little about your formal training. By formal training I mean where you got your degrees and who influenced your thinking in psychology. Who would you say?

SB: I took my Ph.D. degree with Kenneth Spence at the University of Iowa where I went after my master's degree in psychology at Columbia University. My M.A. thesis research was on the standardization of an individual performance

587

test for retarded children. The results were published in the *Journal of Applied Psychology,* in 1938, I think. You know who my supervisor was? Henry Garrett.

LK: When was this?

SB: I got my master's degree in 1937. I had planned on continuing graduate work in psychology at Columbia, but the eclectic approach of Garrett, Woodworth, Poffenberger, and Warden didn't particularly appeal to me, so I began to explore courses at Teachers College. One of the courses I took was with George W. Hartmann, a Gestalt psychologist, well-known at that time. I expressed my discontentment to him and he suggested that I transfer to the University of Iowa where I could study child-clinical development with Kurt Lewin, a promising young German Gestalt psychologist. I became enthusiastic about the potentialities of Gestalt psychology after taking Hartmann's course, so I decided to transfer to Iowa, although I postponed going for about two years. In the interval I worked as a clinical psychologist at the Delaware State Hospital and Mental Hygiene Clinic with Joseph Jastak. During my tenure there, Jastak and I developed a clinical school-achievement scale, the Wide Range Achievement Test, which, as you may know, turned out to be a phenomenally popular test.

Well, in 1939, I went to the University of Iowa, hoping to work with Kurt Lewin. When I arrived, I was surprised, having registered in psychology, to find that Lewin wasn't in that department at all, but was in the Child Welfare Station (later called the Institute for Child Development). So there I was, stuck in the wrong department. Kenneth Spence became my advisor and close friend. Although students in psychology didn't ordinarily take courses in the Child Welfare Station, Spence permitted me to take Lewin's two-semester course in personality development. I was grateful for the opportunity to study with Lewin, but I became more and more intrigued with learning theory through courses and frequent contacts with Spence. I was nevertheless still interested in child-clinical psychology, but the best thing the department could do to accommodate me was to let me major in experimental psychopathology. So for my Ph.D. thesis, I studied experimental neurosis in the rat. Spence was interested in this problem because it was based on Pavlov's early work and was related to Neal Miller's concept of conflict with approach and avoidance gradients. I was Spence's second Ph.D. – he had only recently started his career.

During the time I was at Iowa, Hull was preparing his first book on principles of learning. He sent the manuscript to Spence, one of his former students, who organized a seminar to review Hull's manuscript. All of us in that group, which included the late Margaret Kuenne (later to be Mrs. Harry Harlow), Howard and Tracy Kendler, Ben Underwood, Iz Farber, Art Irion, and Bob Grice, memorized the postulates. Consequently, when I left Iowa I was a well-trained Hull-Spence behaviorist. My first post-Ph.D. appointment was as research psychologist at the Wayne County Training School in Michigan.

LK: What year was that?

SB: That was in 1941. The Training School, a residential school for mildly retarded children where research was emphasized by the superintendent, Robert Haskell, had attracted a large group of research psychologists which included Sam Kirk, Alfred Strauss, Boyd McCandless, and Heinz Werner. In a way, this collection of psychologists at the Training School could be attributed to the economic depression of the early 1940s. There were few good academic positions available and most new Ph.D.s were glad to find an opportunity to do research. I was there for only about a year when World War II began and I left to enter the military.

LK: What did you do in the military?

SB: I worked first as a psychologist in an Army Induction Center. Later, I transferred to the Air Force and worked as an aviation psychologist with John Flanagan's outfit in the selection of pilots, navigators, and bombardiers. Then, as the war progressed, I was transfered to the Office of the Air Surgeon to head up the Convalescent Branch, in the Psychological Division of the Personnel Distribution Command. I was the clinical psychologist for all psychological units in the Rest and Rehabilitation Centers in the various resort areas of the country. My commanding officer was Lawrence Shaffer, who later became a dean at Teacher's College, and my close colleague in the Headquarters Office was Merle Roff, now at the University of Minnesota. When the war was over, I returned to the Training School, since I had technically been on military leave.

LK: When did you first come in contact with Skinner?

SB: I had a brief visit with him when I visited Stuart Cook at the University of Minnesota and discussed his study on experimental neurosis in the rat. That was about 1939. But I had no real contact with him until 1946, when as chairman of the department at Indiana, he was looking for a clinical psychologist with an experimental orientation to head up their clinical training program. Cook had apparently recommended me to Skinner. I was invited to come to Indiana for an interview, and I was appointed as an assistant professor. Here, too, I was fortunate to be surrounded by an outstanding group. In addition to Skinner, among the department members were J. R. Kantor, Bill Verplanck, Norm Guttmann, Bill Estes, Doug Ellson, Roland Davis, Winthrop Kellogg, Parker Lichtenstein, and Irv Wolf. This was my first close contact with Skinner. An interesting thing is that neither Kantor nor Skinner, both of whom became strong influences in my life, did anything obvious to change my Spence-Hull point of view. During the year that Skinner was on leave at Harvard, we had a faculty-student seminar on both Hull and Skinner, which gave those in both camps a chance to sound off with emotion.

Skinner frequently kidded me about working with rats when I could be working with people, and when I'd come from my lab disgusted that I hadn't gotten good results that day, he'd slyly remark that the animal is always right. At the time, he was giving a seminar in preparation for his *Science and Human Behavior* book, and he welcomed faculty, so I sat in on it. But mainly our relationship was social. In 1948, Skinner left Indiana to go to Harvard, and I left to go to the University of Washington.

LK: You were at Indiana about how long?

SB: About a year and a half. I thoroughly enjoyed Indiana, but the offer from Washington as associate professor of psychology and Director of the Institute of Child Development, and the opportunity to work with children again was hard to turn down. I inherited Stevenson Smith's job. Remember Smith and Guthrie, authors of the old psychology book with a learning approach to personality and adjustment? When I got to Washington, I found that the Institute was in fact only an outpatient child clinic, so I added a research arm, which was what the department had wanted. Being a Hullian still, I turned to Sears' model for research with children — doll play, in which you give a child some dolls and toys and record his behavior with them. I was terribly disappointed with the results. All you could get were correlations of responses, since there were no controls over the presentation of stimuli. I wanted a method that would do what we had been doing in the animal laboratory, not necessarily point for point, but one that would allow presenting stimuli and recording responses. Obviously I had to review the various possibilities before deciding what to do. At Indiana, I had attended some of Kantor's classes, and he, like Skinner, had also kidded me about the Hullian approach: the notion that Hull thought he was dealing with actual or potential physiological processes. I began to have some doubts about the feasibility and generality of Hull's theory. I found myself thinking of Skinner's work, so, using his newly published *Science and Human Behavior,* I began to reeducate myself. I soon reached the conclusion that the most promising path lay in using Skinner's experimental theory and methodology and Kantor's philosophy of science.

I explored laboratory procedures that would be comparable in methodology to the animal research situation. I started with a ball-drop response, my analogue of a lever press, and the forerunner of the marble-drop response used by many investigators later on. The ball was a handball, which rolled through a series of tubes and switches, finally activating a dispenser delivering trinkets, candy, cookies or tokens. There was a problem with the ball-drop, however. Every once in a while, a kid would miss the hole and the ball would roll to the floor, or he would play with it, and it was soon apparent that more "errors" were made during extinction than during reinforcement. It wasn't a good technique in terms of experimental control of conditions. Nevertheless, I sent some data to Skinner. He was quite excited about them, but said in a note on a postcard that he wondered what results I'd get if I had a situation with continuous responding, as in a free operant. At about that time I was reading very carefully Ferster's paper on the use of the free operant in the analysis of behavior. I replaced the ball-drop with a lever press and embedded the lever in a clown's face so that a child had to push the nose to make a response, and I used an event recorder for stimulus onsets and response occurrences. Lo and behold, I began to get orderly data. The only orderly data then in the literature that even approximated them had been published by Warren and Brown, who had done a study to see whether operant principles would work with kids, and they concluded that indeed the principles did hold. I went on to explore schedules and all the things I was comfortable with. Well, that got me into laboratory studies with children.

LK: When was your first article in this field published?

SB: In 1955. It was on a systematic approach to the study of young children, published in *Child Development,* and described the ball-dropping response, or the discrete-operant method. The next one, which described the free-operant method was published in *Psychological Reports* two years later.

LK: Did you have any difficulty in publishing your kind of articles?

SB: Oh yes. I sent a manuscript of a study with only three children as subjects to *Child Development.* It was rejected out of hand because the N was "too small to generalize." I wrote back a letter of protest, and after reconsideration, they relented and did publish it. It was a hassle, but was worth it because this episode served to open the way for others on the Institute staff to get single-subject articles published. Although, on one occasion, when an article by Florence Harris was rejected on that basis, I found it necessary to write to the editor of the *Journal of Educational Psychology* to explain the difference in objectives in individual and group designs.

LK: Where are we at this point in time?

SB: About 1955. I remember that because of a comment from a Norwegian psychologist, Aase Skard, who came to this country that year to learn about child development programs, and was astonished to find a child laboratory using the Skinnerian approach. While we had no difficulties in introducing behavior principles to the practices in the research laboratory and the child guidance clinic, the nursery school was another matter. The director had a psychoanalytical orientation, and in her opinion, she and her staff knew everything they had to know about children's behavior and the only need was for survey types of research. But gradually, as they interacted more with the lab group, the nursery-school staff began to think in terms of contingencies in natural settings rather than in meeting children's hypothetical needs. There was a real break in the continuity of the work at Washington in 1961-62; I took a leave and went to Harvard on an NIMH senior fellowship to study with Skinner.

LK: What were you doing?

SB: Several things. One, was working on an experimental analysis of complex processes. The specific problem I selected for study was abstracting behavior (concept formation) involving two-dimensional stimuli which varied in their right-left orientation. The subjects were retarded children at the Fernald School and normal children at the Peabody School. The results of that study were published in the *International Review of Research in Mental Retardation.* Another thing I was doing was surveying programs on early and remedial education in schools in the northeastern section of the country: O.K. Moore's responsive-environment program in Hampden, Connecticut, Burt Blatt's program in Boston, and Zeaman's program at Mansfield Training School in Connecticut. My general impression was that very little was being done to help the retarded child learn new social and academic skills. I went back to Washington with the conviction that we could set up a program based on behavior principles that would accomplish a lot more. Fortunately I had a good relationship with Dr. Wesley White, Superintendent of the Rainier School, where we also had a research laboratory, funded by NIMH. White was eager to cooperate with the University of Washington to improve his school's services and promote research. An experimental classroom was established on the basis of a budget pieced together from the school district, the Rainier School, and the NIMH research grant. One of the teachers was Cecilia Tague Harper, who had taken an extension course with me, and the other was John Kidder, who had taken a summer course with Bill Verplanck. Jay Birnbrauer, a member of the Department of Psychology at Washington, had for several years served as coordinator, and Mont Wolf, who was working with Bob Orlando in our Rainier Research Lab, joined Jay.

Jay was added to the Department of Psychology after Don Baer was appointed. Jay, an Indiana Ph.D. in clinical, was appointed in child psychology as assistant professor. Don Baer, appointed assistant professor in child psychology several years before, came from the University of Chicago where he had studied with Jack Gewirtz and Howard Hunt. Mont Wolf, appointed a research associate on the NIMH grant on retardation, came from Arizona State University, highly recommended by Iz Goldiamond. Like Jay and Don, this was Mont's first full-time post-Ph.D. appointment. Incidentally, both Don and Mont did their Ph.D. research in animal laboratories. I might add that Howard Sloane, who replaced Bob Orlando as head of the Rainier Research Laboratory, also came with a background and training in animal research.

The Institute had two other major slots: one, director of the nursery school and the other, director of the child guidance clinic. I used the latter on a one-year rotational basis, mostly as a child-clinical training position for new Washington Ph.D.s. Among those in that position were Ivar Lovaas, Bob Wahler, and Bud Wetzel.

LK: Could you tell me something of the origin of the token economy program in the experimental classroom at Rainier?

SB: Mont and Jay worked that out. My impression is that Mont got the idea from his work as a graduate student assisting Art Staats in his reading experiments. He transformed Staat's marble reinforcement system into a system of marks. While using reading, writing, and arithmetic programs that were being developed, the teachers put marks on slips of graph paper to indicate progress in learning. Point loss wasn't part of the procedure.

LK: This takes us up to the early 1960s, doesn't it? What happened then?

SB: Two things happened that I think are of some significance. I received a phone call from the superintendent of the State Psychiatric Hospital for Children, asking us to train a four-year-old autistic boy named Dicky, to wear his glasses. Mont and I interviewed the parents and observed the boy who was obviously grossly disturbed, since he had a temper tantrum every few minutes. At a conference with the superintendent, we made it clear we couldn't train Dicky to wear glasses unless we eliminated many of his other serious problem behaviors. We specified the conditions under which we could operate with the hospital psychologist, Hayden Mees. Mont would serve as consultant, I would be liaison, and Mees' responsibility would be to see that the program was carried out. The actual work was done by the attendants under Mees' immediate supervision, and it ran the gamut: changing the boy's eating behavior, sleeping behavior, tantrums, and a host of others. When the study was reported by Mont at the Western Psychological Association meeting, the audience rose and applauded. Dicky's progress was followed until the family moved from the area. He was rediscovered recently and we learned that people outside his family didn't know that he had ever been hospitalized. Even his teacher hadn't realized he was a "special" child.

This study, I believe, opened the field for a behavioral approach to child therapy. The new recording techniques, time-out, successive approximations, all were cooked up as treatment progressed. There was only one precedent — the work of Charlie Ferster. If it hadn't been for Charlie's program on autistic children, which I had visited several times, I don't know that we'd have dared to arrange a program with a severely disturbed child like Dicky.

LK: How did you come in contact with Charlie?

SB: I first met Charlie while he was working with Skinner at Harvard on an experimental analysis of schedules of reinforcement. I was visiting Fred to show him some data on children, using a free — operant technique with continuous recording. Later, I visited Charlie at the Indiana University Medical School where he had an animal lab and an autistic child project with Marion DeMyer, a psychiatrist.

LK: That influenced Dicky's program or the token program?

SB: I'm sure it influenced Dicky's treatment, and the token system was part of the treatment program.

Another fortuitous circumstance was that Florence Harris, the newly appointed director of the nursery school, although like her predecessor, psychoanalytically oriented, was nevertheless enthusiastic about introducing behavioral techniques into the nursery school. The first case she brought to the research staff's attention was a girl with "regressive" crawling. Florence told us that the child had once walked, but after the arrival of a new baby in the family, she had reverted to crawling. As one might have expected, the nursery staff had concluded that the child needed lots of attention, so they heaped it on her particularly while she was off her feet or crawling, but they reported that wasn't helping. The staff was asked to give the child attention when she was on her feet and walking and to withhold attention when she was in a crawling position or crawling. The new strategy worked, and the case was published as a study in the *Journal of Educational Psychology.*

LK: Behavior modification, and that's what we're talking about, to a very large extent came out of that laboratory setting, didn't it? As a matter of fact there were more people with you at Washington than I thought.

SB: Besides those I've already mentioned, there were people like Todd Risley, one of Don's graduate students who worked closely with Mont in the clinic and laboratory with extremely retarded and disturbed children, using milk, ice cream, and TV dinners as reinforcers. He also worked with Mont on the Dicky study.

LK: A couple more things about this historical thing. You left Washington in 1965 and Don Baer also left. Why?

SB: I left because a majority of the psychology department were antagonistic toward the program. It seemed that the better known our work became, the more antagonistic they became. Among other things, when members of the child development program received attractive offers from other universities, no attempt was made to keep them at Washington with counter offers. So when Don decided to go to Kansas, Jay to North Carolina, and Mont to Arizona, I decided to make our dissatisfaction known by leaving, too. Interestingly enough, the administration – the LAS dean and the vice-president – urged me to remain because they wanted as much support as they could get for a new child development and mental retardation center in the medical school.

LK: Without mentioning specific names, which people – clinical, experimental – were the antibehavioral groups?

SB: The experimental group, whom I expected would be pleased to see applications of experimental techniques and principles to practical problems, were opposed to our work. And the fact that all the courses in child development were taught from a behavioral point of view didn't sit too well with those in the social and clinical programs, because of their own cognitive and psychoanalytical orientations.

LK: Wasn't that the time that Gene Galanter was chairman?

SB: Yes. Gene supported our work, but he was not effective because he was soon removed from the chairmanship.

LK: Going back for a minute, where did you get your bachelors' degree?

SB: At the University of Florida.

LK: Did you go directly to graduate school?

SB: No, I got my degree in '33 during the economic depression, and went to Columbia a year later.

LK: Were you a teacher in that period?

SB: No, I wasn't. My undergraduate degree was in business administration. In my senior year I found myself more engrossed in psychology than in business administration, so I decided to go to graduate school and study psychology. I went to New York, took some courses at the New School for Social Research, got married, and enrolled in graduate school at Columbia. The fact that my wife had a teaching appointment in the N.Y.C. public school system enabled me to begin my graduate studies.

LK: So you weren't a teacher?

SB: No. My experience with children began at the Wayne County Training School. As a research psychologist, I worked with the staff of the residential school. Although the children were only mildly retarded, their school achievement was practically zero, so the principal and I devised a motivational system of "goal-beaters" and "goal-meeters." Each teacher was instructed how to set goals for each child in her class in reading and arithmetic, and how to keep individual progress charts. At the end of the school year, during a special assembly, the "goal-meeters" and "goal-beaters" were given recognition and awards. That would be considered a kind of token economy now.

LK: Where do you see behavior modification going and where would you like to see it go?

SB: The path and the goal — destination — of behavior modification are hard to separate. Extrapolating from the tremendous gains that have taken place in such a short time, I'm confident that behavior modification will be the accepted approach of the future.

LK: The accepted approach to what?

SB: Education, for sure, to say nothing of clinical. I mentioned earlier that there is a reluctance to use what we know, but that reluctance will erode with continued demonstration that by using all the knowledge we have, we can become more effective. I think it will utlimately be a powerful influence in the educational system, from preschool on up. Before long, I expect we'll be able to show that the behavioral approach is not only a feasible teaching technique but also a feasible method of decision making and problem solving. The main question is, How do you decide on the goals of an educational program?

LK: Who's the "you?"

SB: Behavior analysts. We can begin with objectives for preschool education. This is presumably done by experts, followers of Piaget, Montessori, and the like. The behavior analysts have been slow in specifying objectives. Typically they say, "Tell us what your objectives are and we'll show you an effective way of teaching them." But they too, can contribute to specifying objectives. I don't see why not.

LK: Where will the objectives come from?

SB: From what we know about the behavior analysis of child development, the analysis of society, and a philosophy of the evolution of society. You can't have a viable preschool program without a philosophy of society. There is no such thing as a program that's built solely on the needs of children. You don't have children painting, constructing things, playing, dancing, and singing in a vacuum. They're in a building, and participating in a program that also includes procedures for coming and leaving school, toileting, health hygiene, resting, snacking, and so on — all of which are cultural practices. The objectives of a nursery school should be built around the needs of *both* children and society. With that in mind, we can begin to work out objectives with parents and teachers and with the other people involved. This approach couldn't be construed as superimposing the behavior analysts' values on the school, as some claim.

If you were to ask a parent, "Would you like to see your child more independent, more creative?" most parents would, of course, say "yes." The same would be true of goals that are perfectly compatible with the behavioral approach and perfectly acceptable from the point of view of the needs of society.

I also believe parent training is really the thing of the future. There are several parent-training projects that are gaining attention. For example, the Portage Project, under Dave Shearer. This project shows clearly that teachers can train parents to train their handicapped children. Participating parents in Portage can see what their children are capable of doing. If, when a child is then sent to a regular school, the teacher says he or she doesn't think the child is ready for school, or that he has a learning disability, the parent can show by records what the child has accomplished during the home training. That kind of alert parent attitude is eventually going to have an impact on the entire educational system, because it originates with the consumer.

LK: Do you have any suggestion on the training influence on teachers? I mean regular classroom teachers, not special ed.

SB: Training teachers is no different than training anyone else. At this stage, the problem of teacher training is two-fold: one, how to get colleges of education to introduce behavior methods and principles; the other, how to spot and retain teachers who are discontented with current classroom practices and their own performance, and offer them training in the behavioral approach. My own inclination is to train by means of demonstration projects. Let teachers actually see what can be done with children, normal and handicapped. Such an approach will attract primarily those who aren't being reinforced by the present system. Sure, you'll get changes in educational practices by means of rules and regulations with all of their aversive contingencies, and sure, educators will continue to wait for the next new panacea but, in the long run, demonstrations will do more to change behavior, especially if the training is based on positive reinforcers and the procedures are explicit and self-correcting.

LK: Where do you think token economy in the classroom is going? There have been some criticisms of the goals of such programs, such as those by Winett and Winkler.

SB: It's true that some practictioners of behavior analysis have used token economies in the classroom to establish and maintain behaviors that are more advantageous to them than to the children. Winett and Winkler's criticism should be directed to the poorly trained and ethically questionable appliers, not to the research psychologists who have shown that generalized positive reinforcers can be used in practical situations to establish and maintain academic and social behaviors in the classroom. Initially, researchers on this topic were content to show that positive generalized reinforcers could be conveniently used to establish and maintain an orderly classroom and they went on the assumption that such an accomplishment would enhance learning. Now they are doing studies that relate the use of classroom token economies to the achievement of educational goals. This is as it should be.

I want to make two other points about token economies in the classroom. One is that token economies are often used when they're not needed. A well-trained, student-oriented teacher with a class of normal children has little need to introduce a formal token economy because she should automatically be individualizing instruction and giving functional reinforcers to establish and maintain the goals for her class. The second point is that a token economy need not apply to all the pupils in a class. The selective use of a token economy has been demonstrated many times over to be expedient and effective despite the conviction of many educators that "it won't work."

LK: In terms of your values, what is a good society?

SB: To me, the individual and the environment are a united system, absolutely inseparable. Hence, a good society is one in which its members lead, in the long haul, a satisfying life and at the same time contribute to the maintenance and strength of their society. This requires that we behave appropriately for remote goals, and demands the practice of effective self-management techniques. In other words, society must survive in order for the individuals to survive. People are linked inseparably with their society and they must behave in ways that preserve and extend their society. A so-called strong society with hostile and anxious people is not what we want, nor do we want contented people in a society that is obviously deteriorating. Those are the kinds of social values that I don't perceive as being linked with our current economic system: the concern for the future of mankind.

LK: What do you think of the work of Roger Barker?

SB: I had hoped that Barker would deliver what he promised: a collection of objective information about behavior in relation to the environment. But he didn't. His data are full of preconceptions, interpretations, and inferences about goals. Not only do Barker and his colleagues read intent into the behavior of their subjects, but they rehash their data before they write up the interactional episodes. Barker claimed that his accounts would be as objective and neutral as a collection of rocks in a museum. It didn't turn out that way. You can't use Barker's data unless you accept his theory of human behavior with all of its inner determinants, and his method of observation. They claim that they can't avoid introducing mentalistic terms like intentions and cognitions. We behavior analysts have found that we must repudiate much of the observational method of people such as Barker and the Whitings because of its subjectivity. To be consistent with the behavior analysis' core method, we had to decide to watch the individual and count selected instances of occurrences. It paid off.

LK: Is there anything else about history that I forgot to ask?

SB: Yes. I believe that J. R. Kantor had more of an influence on my thinking than we mentioned up to now. From the time I met him, I was impressed with the man as a philosopher and with his interbehavioral Gestaltlike approach. I believe Kantor supplied the philosophy I needed, and Skinner, the experimental methodology and the behavioral technology. Together they forced me to think of events as they occur naturally in field settings. Just as you can't separate people from society, in the broader sense, you can't separate people from their environment. I think psychology will eventually move to this kind of field-analysis approach wherein you're not thinking of a response and a stimulus, you're talking instead about a setting condition in which an antecedent event changes, behavior changes, and several consequent conditions change — all defined functionally.

LK: You mention the touch of Gestalt. What was its impact on you?

SB: Lewin had quite an influence: the idea of plotting the life space and of interrelating things. But he had a problem that bothered him to the very end of his career: how does one know what the individual's perceptions are. Or in other words, how does one know what the environment means to the person? Lewin said you have to interpret the environment in terms of the eyes of the individual. Well, how does one do that? Lewin's solution was to ask him. But all you can get from that is a correlation between what a person says and what he does, and Lewin really didn't want that. He wanted a functional field system. It's my opinion that one of the reasons Lewin left the personality-developmental field and went into action research was the fact that he couldn't solve that problem.

But Kantor solved Lewin's problem with his concept of stimulus functions. You watch a child going to the door, opening it, seeing someone, and cringing. You observe further to determine whether the removal of that person strengthens the child's preceding behavior. It does, and you conclude that the person is an aversive stimulus for that child. Another child, opening the same door and seeing the same person, might not cringe at all, but might say, "Hi, I'm glad you're here," and you infer that the person is a positive reinforcer for that child. But you observe further to see whether that person's behavior strengthens the child's preceding behavior. You infer the function of a stimulus event from the behavior of the person, and you look for, or create, test situations. You're not in the old box of correlating two sets of responses of the same person.

I went along with Lewin in the early years but I found it to be a blind alley, like Hull's physicalistic learning theory. Then I came across Kantor and Skinner with their philosophical and experimental solutions, and needless to say, I've gone along with them since. But their answers aren't final. We are undoubtedly moving toward a field approach in which one must take into account five or six classes of variables in a contingency field system and relate changes in any part of the field to changes in all parts of the field.

Well, it's been pleasant for me to reminisce about the "influencer" and the "influenced." You're a good listener, Len.

34

The Development of Behavior Analysis in Mexico: Sidney W. Bijou's Contributions

Ely Rayek
Emilio Ribes-Iñesta

National Autonomous University of Mexico

Until 1964 the study of psychology in Mexico was centered mainly in Mexico City. The general orientation was mentalistic, with a great emphasis on psychoanalysis. Nevertheless, for the last two or three years, an increasing interest in experimental psychology, especially learning theory, had developed among a minority of students. As a consequence of this, in 1964 a group of young psychologists from the National University had the opportunity to create a new Department of Psychology at the University of Veracruz, in Xalapa (Diaz-Guerrero, 1966). This new Department mounted an effort to introduce, for the first time, an experimental approach to the teaching and application of psychology.

In 1966, O. Hobart Mowrer was invited to give a series of lectures in Xalapa. While there, he invited some of his Mexican colleagues to visit him at the University of Illinois. Through this association, the members of the Department of Psychology at the University of Veracruz met Sidney W. Bijou.

Bijou visited Xalapa for the first time in January 1967. On that occasion, he conducted a seminar for the staff members of the Department of Psychology. This seminar marked a changing point in the theoretical and practical approach to psychology held by most of the staff members of the department.

Seven months later, Florente López created the first operant center for training and research in special education (Center for Training and Special Education, CTSE). Patterned after Bijou's Child Behavior Laboratory, the CTSE was designed both as a center to serve the community and as human behavior laboratory. We think that this double aim is one of Bijou's outstanding contributions to behavior analysis in general, that is, to combine a technological interest with the search for functional relationships relevant to behavior theory.

In 1968, a master's program in behavior modification was created in the psychology department at the University of Veracruz. The program was based, partially, on the seminars given by visiting professors. Bijou gave the first one in January 1969. During this visit he provided valuable suggestions in regard to the curriculum of the M.A. program and the organization of the CTSE. He came back to Xalapa in 1969 to conduct another seminar, as part of a more extensive training program with a larger number of students, some of them from different Latin American countries.

It was during this visit that the First Symposium on Behavior Modification was planned, to be held in Xalapa in January, 1971. The organization of the symposium was a challenge. It was the first time that outstanding American scientists were going to be grouped in a conference to discuss common problems with Latin American psychologists. Funds had to be gathered and editorial contacts had to be made. Thanks to Bijou's enthusiasm and active help, all these difficulties were overcome, and in January 1971, the symposium was held successfully. Around one thousand people attended it and the basis for the following conferences was laid.

It is needless to say that the master's program in Xalapa and the symposium afterwards, played a decisive role in changing psychology in Mexico. Since 1968, a number of changes began taking place at the National University and some other of the country's universities, with an increasing interest for developing applied programs in behavior analysis. Bijou was able to meet these developments and to advise the newcomers to the field on how to deal successfully with the problems they were facing. Undoubtedly, the atmosphere created during this period helped to set up the conditions for establishing the Department of the Experimental Analysis of Behavior at the National University of Mexico in 1971.

The Second, Third and Fourth Symposia on Behavior Modification were held in Mexico City in 1972, 1973, and 1974, respectively. The organizers always had Bijou's assistance. Since the Symposium had originally been planned as a means of promoting behavior analysis in Latin America, the Latin American Committee for the Organization of the Annual Symposium on Behavior Modification was created in 1973. This Committee included outstanding psychologists of Latin American countries having programs or projects in behavior analysis. Chile, Brazil, Panama, Mexico, Colombia, and Venezuela were represented. As a recognition to his assistance in the development of the Symposium, Bijou was elected Chairman of the Committee. The Symposium in 1975 was held in Caracas, Venezuela.

In April 1974, during the First Mexican Congress of Behavior Analysis, a testimony was planned to acknowledge seven years of rapid progress in the field. Bijou was recognized for his contributions both to behavior analysis in human development and for the first programs in Mexico. An audience of 800 professionals and students of behavior analysis constituted the gathering where the officials of the state government and the presidents of three universities gave him a gold medal and a diploma in recognition. This was only a small tribute to Bijou's generous behavior toward Mexican psychology.

Bijou's involvement with Mexico has not ended. He is assisting in new developments and at present he is serving as a consultant to the National University of Mexico in the design and planning of the Open University System in Psychology. The application of behavior analysis principles to this effort promises to be one of the most important contributions to higher education.

We have tried to describe Bijou's participation in the creation and evolution of behavior analysis in Mexico. But, it is important to stress that his influence has especially been on the scientific behavior of all those who had the good fortune of knowing and interacting with him as both a teacher and as a researcher.

REFERENCES

Diaz-Guerrero, R. Mexico. In S. Ross, I. E. Alexander, H. Basowitz, M. Werber, & P. O. Nicholas (Eds.), *International opportunities for advanced training and research in psychology*. Washington, D.C.: American Psychological Association, 1966.

Author Index
by Chapter

Chapter Descriptors

Chapter 3

MATERNAL RESPONDING AND THE CONDITIONING OF INFANT CRYING: DIRECTIONS OF INFLUENCE WITHIN THE ATTACHMENT-ACQUISITION PROCESS

Jacob L. Gewirtz

Chapter 4

A THREE-STAGE FUNCTIONAL ANALYSIS FOR CHILDREN'S COERCIVE BEHAVIORS: A TACTIC FOR DEVELOPING A PERFORMANCE THEORY

G. R. Patterson

Chapter 5

THE DEVELOPMENT AND MAINTENANCE OF LANGUAGE: AN OPERANT MODEL

Todd R. Risley

Chapter 6

GENERALIZED IMITATION AND THE SETTING EVENT CONCEPT

Warren M. Steinman

Chapter 7

NUTRITION AND HUMAN
DEVELOPMENT

Jack Tizard, Ph.D.

Brain, growth
Caldwell inventory
Ecology
Ethnic differences
Family, stimulation
Language development
Malnutrition
   cognitive effects
   motor defects
Nutrition

Prenatal life
Social environment
Stimulation
   cognitive
   intellectual

Chapter 8

IMITATION, RESPONSE
NOVELTY, AND LANGUAGE
ACQUISITION

Grover J. Whitehurst

Abstraction
Appositive phrases
Communication
   generative
   novel
Comprehension-imitation-production
     hypothesis
Discrimination, observational
Imitation
   selective
   topography
Infinitive phrases
Language
   acquisition
   creativity
   novelty

Linguistics
Modeling
Participial phrases
Place learning
Prepositional phrases
Response
   imitative
   novelty
Syntax, in imitation
Vocabulary acquisition, in imitation

Chapter 9

ARE EXPERIMENTAL
PROCEDURES AND SERVICE
OBLIGATIONS COMPATIBLE IN
A PRESCHOOL PROGRAM FOR
YOUNG HANDICAPPED
CHILDREN?

K. Eileen Allen

Keith D. Turner

Educational philosophy for early childhood
Hyperactivity
Measurement
Precision teaching
Self-management
Staff research

CHANGING-CRITERION
DESIGNS: AN ALTERNATE
APPLIED BEHAVIOR ANALYSIS
PROCEDURE

R. Vance Hall

Richard G. Fox

BEHAVIORAL DEFINITIONS
IN APPLIED BEHAVIOR
ANALYSIS: EXPLICIT OR
IMPLICIT?

Robert P. Hawkins

Robert W. Dobes

LABORATORY INVESTIGATION
OF APPLIED BEHAVIOR
ANALYSIS TECHNIQUES:
PROCEDURES DESIGNED TO
DECREASE OR ELIMINATE
RESPONDING

Judith M. LeBlanc

Katherine E. Reuter

Donald N. Miller

Gary L. Schilmoeller

Maintenance
Natural environment
Recovery, spontaneous
Reinforcement
   continuous
   intermittent
   partial
    variable interval
    variable ratio
Restricted operant response
Schedules

concurrent
continuous
DRO
FDRO
intermittent
reinforcement
uncorrelated
VDRO
  variable interval
  variable ratio
Social repertoire

Chapter 13

Naive observation
Observation
   bias
   drift
   methodology

SOURCES OF BIAS IN
OBSERVATIONAL RECORDING

K. Daniel O'Leary

Ronald N. Kent

Chapter 14

Attention, selective
Cognitive approach
Complex behavior
Covert behavior
Discriminative stimulus
Encoding
Functional analysis of behavior approach
Information processing approach
Interactions
   complex
   simple
Match-to-sample
Mediation, overt response
Moral behavior
Moral conduct
Moral reasoning
Nonprecurrent response
Operant chain
Precurrent behavior, overt
Problem-solving

COMPLEX INTERACTIONS:
A FUNCTIONAL APPROACH

Joseph A. Parsons

Douglas Peter Ferraro

Processing
Reductive approach, hypothetico constructs
Retrieving
Self-control
S-R learning approach
Storing

Chapter 15

Antecedent stimuli
Differential reinforcement
Deviant behaviors
Ethical implications
Headbanging
Hydropsychotherapy
Movement restriction
Problem parent-child relationship
Punishment
Retardate
Slapping
Social implications
Social isolation

HYDROPSYCHOTHERAPY: WATER AS A PUNISHING STIMULUS IN THE TREATMENT OF A PROBLEM PARENT-CHILD RELATIONSHIP

Robert F. Peterson

Linda W. Peterson

Chapter 16

Adult presence
Choice
    measure
    procedure
Compliance
Context
Demand characteristics
Discrete trials
History, pattern
Imitation
    generalized
    nonreinforced
Instruction
Persistence
Preference, response bias
Reinforcement
    negative adult
    noncontingent
    positive adult
    schedule
    social
    token
Research methodology
Response, rate
Satiation
Schedules, of social stimuli
Social behavior, of children
Social control

A METHODOLOGY FOR STUDYING SOCIAL STIMULUS FUNCTIONS IN CHILDREN

William H. Redd

Andrew S. Winston

Edward K. Morris

Social stimulus, adult presence
Strategy
Superstition
Two-choice
    discrimination
    procedure

Chapter 17

BEHAVIORAL PROCEDURES FOR ASSESSING VISUAL CAPACITIES IN NONVERBAL SUBJECTS

Ellen P. Reese

Jane S. Howard

Chapter 18

COMPLEXITIES OF AN "ELEMENTARY" BEHAVIOR MODIFICATION PROCEDURE: DIFFERENTIAL ADULT ATTENTION USED FOR CHILDREN'S BEHAVIOR DISORDERS

Thomas Sajwaj

Anneal Dillon

Chapter 19

AN EXPERIMENTAL ANALYSIS OF CRITERION-RELATED AND NONCRITERION-RELATED CUES IN "ERRORLESS" STIMULUS CONTROL PROCEDURES

Kathryn J. Schilmoeller

Barbara C. Etzel

Stimulus control
  criterion-related cues
  errorless
  fading
  noncriterion-related cues
  shifting

    transfer
Stimulus shaping
Superimposition
Transfer, of stimulus control
Trial-and-error learning
Yoked tasks

Chapter 20

Attitude
Feelings
Home-based reinforcement
Observational procedures
Phenomenological covariates of observable
    events
Prediction
Ratings
Self-report

PHENOMENOLOGICAL REPORTS: AN EMPIRICAL MODEL

Robert G. Wahler

Robert M. Berland

George Leske

Chapter 21

Adaptation level
Anecdotal records
Behavior
  collateral
  continuous
  discrete
  target
Classroom
Coding relativism
Creativity
Cumulative clocks
Empirical theories
Education
Evaluation
Events, time-sampled
Field descriptions
Frequency counts, within interval
Generalization
Graphing
Initiative
Interval sampling
Leadership
Measurement, simultaneous

TECHNICAL DEVELOPMENTS IN CLASSROOM BEHAVIOR ANALYSIS

Ralph H. Wetzel

Joseph R. Patterson

Multiple baselines across subjects
Multiple behaviors
Multiple subjects
New Education
Observation technology
Observation instruments
  complex
  simple
Observer bias
Recording, paper and pencil
Recording technology
Research convenience
Sampling techniques
  fifteen-second interval
  subject

Chapter 22

APPLICATION OF OPERANT PRINCIPLES TO THE HYPERACTIVE BEHAVIOR OF A RETARDED GIRL

Kaoru Yamaguchi

Chapter 23

TEACHING READING THROUGH A STUDENT-ADMINISTERED POINT SYSTEM

Teodoro Ayllon

Stephen Garber

Chapter 24

Auditory stimulus
Classical conditioning
Electromyograph recordings
Habituation
Heart rate
   conditioned
   interbeat interval
   unconditioned
Interstimulus intervals
Neonate
Noxious stimuli
Psychophysiological measures
Reflexes
Response

STATE: EFFECT ON CONDITIONED AND UNCONDITIONED HEART RATE RESPONDING IN INFANTS

Yvonne Brackbill

decrement
directionality
latency
Sleep
   active
   quiet
State change

Chapter 25

Deductive theory
Dialect
Ecology of language
Generative language
Imitation
Incidental teaching
Inductive approach
Language acquisition
Linguistic abstractions
Performance-based data

IMITATION AND VARIATION IN WORKING LANGUAGE

Betty Hart

Reinforcement, accidental
Sociolinguistics
Spoken language
Syntax
Working language

Chapter 26

Conversational speech
Creativity
   assessment
   elaboration
   flexibility
   fluency
   form diversity
   generalization
   "idea" checklist
   kinesthetic-motor treatment
   mediation technique

THE TRAINING OF CREATIVITY AS AN OPERANT AND AN EXAMINATION OF ITS GENERALIZATION CHARACTERISTICS

Jacqueline Holman

Elizabeth M. Goetz

Donald M. Baer

Chapter 27

ACHIEVEMENT PLACE: THE MODIFICATION OF ACADEMIC BEHAVIOR PROBLEMS OF DELINQUENT YOUTHS IN A GROUP HOME SETTING

Kathryn A. Kirigin

Elery L. Phillips

Gary D. Timbers

Dean L. Fixsen

Montrose M. Wolf

Chapter 28

SHARING AT AN EARLY AGE

Harriet L. Rheingold

Chapter 29

Discrimination, of reinforcement
Imitation, generalized
Instruction
Probe
Reinforcement
Response similarity
Schedule, multiple
Stimulus control, of imitation

IMITATIVE BEHAVIOR OF PRESCHOOL CHILDREN: THE EFFECTS OF REINFORCEMENT, INSTRUCTIONS, AND RESPONSE SIMILARITY

James A. Sherman

Hewitt B. Clark

Karen K. Kelly

Chapter 30

Aggressive behavior
Assault
Aversive events
Discriminative control of aggressive behavior
Extinction
Fines
Instructional control
Response cost, noncontingent
Setting event
Time-out, noncontingent

RESPONSE COST AND HUMAN AGGRESSIVE BEHAVIOR

Howard N. Sloane, Jr.

K. Richard Young

Terri Marcusen

Chapter 31

Caretakers
Ecology of maintenance
Generalization
Home conditions
Housekeeping
Institutions
Instruction
Maintenance
Modeling
Motivation
Personnel training
Programming
Retardates
Self-help

TRAINING DAILY SELF-HELP SKILLS FOR LONG-TERM MAINTENANCE

Carol M. Thomas

Beth Sulzer-Azaroff

Sally E. Lukeris

Michael Palmer

Shaping
Token systems

Chapter 32

Juvenile delinquents
Matching procedure
Self-control
Self-management
Self-recording
Study behavior

THE EFFECTS OF SELF-RECORDING ON THE STUDY BEHAVIORS OF FEMALE JUVENILE DELINQUENTS

Pauline Young

Jay S. Birnbrauer

Chapter 33

Autistic child
Baer, D.
Barker, R.
Birnbrauer, J.
Conflict
Cook, S.
Davis, R.
DeMeyer, M.
Ellson, D.
Estes, W.
Experimental neurosis
Farber, I.
Ferster, C.
Flanagan, J.
Free operant
Galanter, E.
Garrett, H.
Gestalt psychology
Gewirtz, J.
Goldiamond, I.
Grice, R.
Guthrie, E. R.
Guttmann, N.
Harper, C.
Harris, F.
Hartman, G. W.
Haskell, R.
Historical context of early behavior
    modification
Hull, C. L.
Irion, A.
Jastak, J.
Kantor, J. R.
Kellogg, W.
Kendler, H.

AN INTERVIEW WITH SIDNEY W. BIJOU

Leonard Krasner

Kendler, T.
Kidder, J.
Kirk, S.
Kuenne, M.
Learning
Lewin, K.
Lichtenstein, P.
Lovaas, I.
McCandless, B.
Mees, H.
Miller, N.
Moore, O.K.
Orlando, R.
Poffenberger, A. T.
Risley, T.
Roff, M.
Science and Human Behavior
Shaffer, L.
Shearer, D.
Skard, A.
Skinner, B. F.
Sloan, H.
Smith, S.
Social context of early behavior
    modification
Spence, K.
Staats, A.
Stimulus functions
Strauss, A.
Successive approximations
Time-out

Chapter 34

THE DEVELOPMENT OF BEHAVIOR ANALYSIS IN MEXICO: SIDNEY W. BIJOU'S CONTRIBUTIONS

Ely Rayek

Emilio Ribes-Inesta

Volume Descriptors